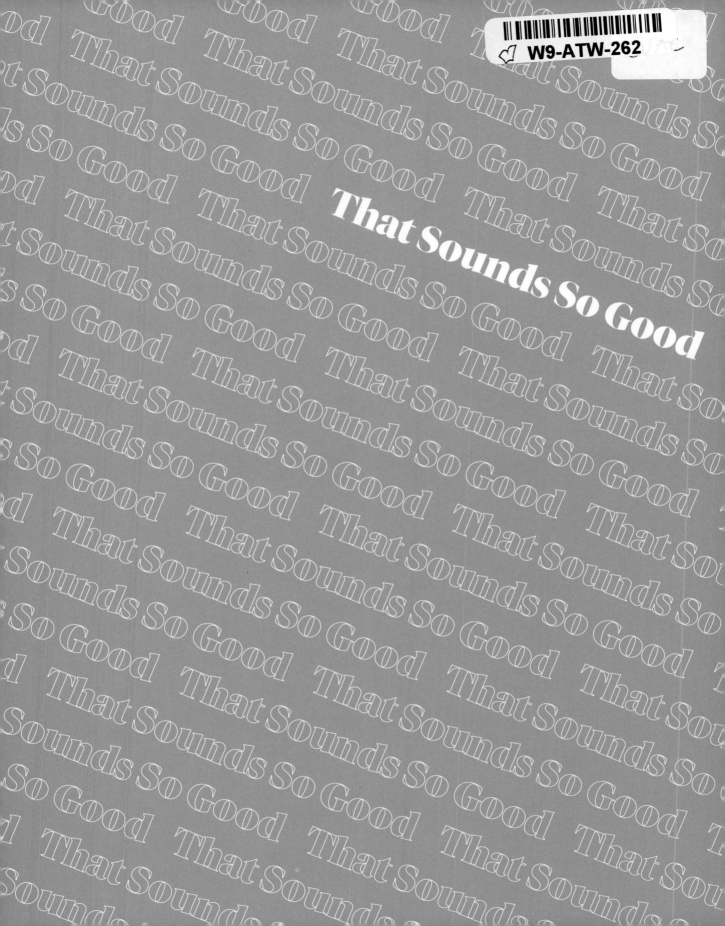

That Sounds So Good

That Sounds So Good

That Sounds So Good

100 REAL-LIFE RECIPES FOR EVERY DAY OF THE WEEK

Carla Lalli Music

Photographs by Gentl and Hyers

Clarkson Potter/Publishers
New York

For Uncle Renato,
who loved food, family,
and red wine

contents

Part III: The Recipes (Friday and the Weekend)

Chapter 6
Day Drinking & Lazy Lunches

Chapter 7
I Love to Grill

Chapter 8
S Is for Sunday Soup, Stew & Sauce

Chapter 9
Give It Up for Vegetables

Introduction
Cooking is a feeling that makes you feel things

Since my first book, *Where Cooking Begins*, was published in 2018, I have been lucky enough to meet, hang out with, get hugged by, and take selfies with hundreds of people who showed up at my signings, Q&As, and other events. I've taken compliments and answered cooking questions all along the way, but there's been a through line of feedback that has meant more to me than any scrap of praise I've received. Over and over, I've been told that my recipes and advice have given my readers a way to connect with the most important people in their lives.

I met a woman in Austin who told me that my videos were the one thing she and her mother could bond over after years of estrangement, and they were setting a date once a week to make and eat dinner together. I talked to a guy in Los Angeles who said my book brought him back into the kitchen after a yearslong hiatus to share meals with his roommates. Another man messaged me to say that my approach helped him heal from an eating disorder, and he was back in the habit of cooking for himself and his husband. A similar story about recovery was told to me by a young woman at a podcast event in Brooklyn, and I heard another at a signing in San Francisco. My pastry dough has spawned many celebratory galettes—for birthdays, graduations, baby showers, and holidays.

Hearing from so many people that eating, making, and sharing food has brought them joy is validation for my entire worldview. I grew up in a close-knit Italian American family; the rhythm of our life was marked by what meal was in front of us. If we were having spaghetti with clams, that meant it was Friday—that plate of pasta has been "the usual" since I was a teenager. (Now I have a teenager, and he, too, knows what Friday night with his grandparents will bring.) Grilled pizza defined summer weekends. Pasta e fagiole was Sunday stuff. Marble cake with fudge frosting is still everybody's birthday cake, and whenever we make plans to see each other as a family, we start talking about the menu. Text threads and email chains run long, usually kicked off by my father,

Frank, asking, "But what will we eat?" A thousand messages later, someone will hit on the winning menu, which my dad will acknowledge by responding, "Oooooooh, *that sounds so good*."

Some people Rollerblade, some people foster puppies, some people live life through their travels, some people make music. And that's all great—I am so happy for those people. But everything in my life comes back to food, and I am inspired by making whatever sounds good in the moment I'm in. The purpose of this book is to provide recipes and kitchen encouragement to go with every hunger. I have a recipe for everything! People are coming over: I'll roast two chickens. It's peak zucchini season: I am going to master the fritter. Let's hang out this weekend: Great, what should we make? I just got dumped: Come over for a long lunch. I'm tired but I'm hungry: Grains and leafy greens, with yogurt on top. We're getting on a plane: I'll pack food. The holidays are coming: I'm grilling a turkey and I can't be stopped. It's another cold, dark winter: Get your braise on. I need a break from eating: How about a big salad?

There are one hundred recipes in this book, and each is designed to help remove any psychic and emotional barriers that get in the way of cooking at home. I will never tell you to do something I'm not willing to do myself, which means there are no desserts with meticulously arranged, color-coded fruit, and no subrecipes that send you hunting for ingredients at three different specialty stores. Every recipe includes multiple suggestions for substitutions under the "Spin It" heading, because having dinner upended by a single missing ingredient is never not annoying.

I make meals for sustenance and for pleasure and because I love the act of cooking. Even a completely ordinary day can accommodate a few tasty pauses. If you can weave a few homemade dishes into your daily life, I think you will be richer for it, and I hope this book gives you even more ways to cook with me. More important, I hope these recipes bring you closer to the people in your life.

My niece, Gia, the only redhead in the family.

there's a food for every feeling

Chapter 1

ABC: Always Be Cooking

*Here's how to celebrate and embrace the act of cooking
and eating in your everyday life, no matter what*

Cook in this moment, whichever moment you're in

This book is organized by situation and occasion, rather than by ingredient or recipe type. I've divided a typical week into two buckets: Monday through Thursday, and Friday and the Weekend. My life looks a lot different on a Tuesday evening—after finishing work and catching up with a family that's been scattered all over the place—than it does on a Saturday afternoon, when I might have enough free time to let one of my cats take a nap on my chest. But no matter what day of the week it is, a girl's gotta eat! Within the weekday and weekend sections of this book, the individual chapters are devoted to the sorts of everyday scenarios you and I might find ourselves in—an effort to capture the types of meals that will fit into your actual life.

In the weekday chapters, you'll find stovetop suppers and dinner salads, and a chapter on the healthyish recipes that I crave after a weekend of eating and drinking and sleeping in. With many of us juggling work, school, housekeeping, caretaking, and commuting, these weekday dishes make the most of short active times. Half an hour of effort can add up to a complete meal if you know how to prioritize your prep and cook times.

By comparison, the weekend section is mostly devoted to recipes with longer cook times and some with larger serving sizes: soups, stews, braises, roasts, and things to grill. That said, even when you do have the downtime to afford to park something on the back of the stove or in a low oven for a couple-few hours, I don't want you to spend more than about half an hour of active cooking time to get that meal going or finish it up. (Grilling is a bit of an exception, since it's one of the few times that cooking overlaps with hanging out. But there are many grilling recipes here that can be made before your friends arrive, if that's how you like to party.) I love having people over, but my overambitious-entertainer phase—when I could be found piping out *gougères* at 2 a.m. the night before a holiday party—is behind me. My kind of weekend food isn't annoying, complicated, or technically challenging. I treasure my time off, and I don't want to spend every minute of it standing in one spot, staring at a cutting board. There are also plenty of weekend recipes here for the kinds of weekends where you are *really* feeling lazy.

By all means, make whatever you want on any day you like! I don't bake during the week, which is why the desserts chapter falls in the weekend section of the book, but if you want a cobbler on a Tuesday, I'm not going to stop you. Some of the big salads found in the weekday section make excellent, uncomplicated additions to a mellow lunch on the weekend, and can also be treated as quick-to-prepare vegetable sides to go with a big braise. There's a set of suggested menus on page 281 that I put together to help you mix and match meals from the recipes throughout the book.

Monday through Thursday:
Your time is precious. How to get big payoff from short active times

The recipe instructions in this book are written chronologically, which means that I will rarely call for things to be already prepped in the ingredient list (i.e., "1 cup chopped onions"). Instead, you'll see whole ingredients listed, and I'll cue the most efficient moment in which to prep them in the recipe method itself. I am all about balancing inactive and active times, and using inactive time to your benefit when cooking. Despite what you might have heard chefs say about their restaurant mise en place, it doesn't always make sense to prep every single thing before you start cooking. I've set up my recipes so you start the longest-cooking item first, and while that is in process, you'll use the downtime (inactive time) to prep the things that go with it. If I'm going to have rice with a meal, I put that on at the top, then use the 18 minutes it takes the rice to cook to make whatever else will be on the table (see the recipe for Gingery Ground Beef with Lime and Herbs on page 60 for an example). Rice can sit after it's done, so if it takes me a little longer to finish the other components of the meal, dinner won't suffer. If something needs to marinate, like the tomatoes on page 217, or soak, like the crunchy vegetables in the salad on page 71, I'll prompt you to get that going, then turn to the other ingredients.

There are absolutely occasions when you should chop and measure everything before anything hits a skillet, such as when you're making a stir-fry, deep-frying something, or making caramel sauce. There's no downtime built into the steps of those types of recipes, because the dish can be ruined if you try to pause in the middle. When that's the case, I make it clear that you need everything ready before you switch on a burner. These choices and approaches are all about time management and informed prioritizing—and they will reduce the overall time you spend on your meals.

When making a quick dinner, the inactive and active times overlap neatly from beginning to end, and you can use every minute to your advantage. Take the pork chops on page 41: They are seasoned in the first step and left to sit for a few minutes while you wash the radicchio and slice the onion that go with the pork. After cooking, the chops rest for 10 minutes—a necessary part of their journey!—while you sauté the vegetables in the pork drippings left in the skillet. Once the veggies are done, the pork will be ready to slice and you can eat. Filling inactive time with active steps that keep you moving toward the finish line means you've used time to your advantage.

Layer short bursts of prep over inactive time to make the most of every minute.

Heading to the backyard with my son, Leo, and my other friends—wine.

Friday and the Weekend:
Your time stretches out.
How to layer prep times over stretches of inactive time

If weeknight cooking is all about stacking active and inactive times, weekend cooking affords you the chance to front-load a meal with a finite amount of busywork, then lean into truly hands-off methods.

In the weekend section, you'll find plenty of cold-weather slow roasts and braises. Ideally, the proteins are seasoned (days) ahead of time, then left to gently cook, unattended, while you do whatever you want in some other room. There are warm-weather vegetable dishes that benefit from long marinating times; set them up when you feel like it and eat hours later. There are bean dishes accompanied by quick-blitzed pestos (see page 138), and an Italian-style steak salad that is best at room temperature (that recipe is on page 122). There are soups that can be reheated gently when it's dinnertime. My grilling recipes are organized around the idea that you can prep your ingredients while the fire heats up, then grill in waves, snacking on things as they are ready, rather than trying to have an entire meal's worth of dishes miraculously char to completion at the same time.

The idea that links the weekend recipes is that you can stretch the inactive time to suit the rhythm of your day, bracketing your active involvement so that your free time stays free. Whenever you find yourself with a free day, you can take advantage of this approach, and these recipes are incredibly adaptable for anyone who works from home. If you have the flexibility to start a dish in the early part of the day and come back to check on it a few hours later, hands-off recipes are your support crew.

When I hear the phrase "project cooking," it makes me think that a lot will be required of me over a long period of time. This is true of cassoulet, Persian rice, shoyu ramen, and orange marmalade. It's fun to cook like that—sometimes. Like when a blizzard is on the way, a major birthday milestone needs celebrating, or you're coming up with distractions so you don't have to finish writing your book. That's not what my style of weekend cooking looks like, though (I *never* procrastinate). In my home, the weekend is for dishes that taste and feel like a lot went into them, only because they rely on hands-off methods and passive time devoted to flavor development (dry brines, marinated veggies, and slow roasts, for example). They are generously portioned for sharing with friends or to ensure a couple of days' worth of leftovers—perfect for meal preppers and lunch packers.

Chapter 2

How to Win in Your Kitchen

Strategic shopping advice, life-changing organizational guidance, multipurpose equipment, and freeing words on improvisation

10 kitchen tools you might not own but could definitely use

In addition to basic cooking equipment such as cast-iron and stainless-steel skillets, a big pot for boiling noodles or making soup, rimmed baking sheets for frying, roasting, and baking, and an enameled Dutch oven for braises and beans, there are a few tools that I rely on daily. I'm not a big fan of tools that do only one thing—such as egg slicers or corncob scrapers. Everything on my top ten list can be deployed to do lots of jobs, and they're worth keeping on your countertop caddy and in your easily accessed cabinets. Having these things makes it easier to cook well, and I think makes the act of cooking more enjoyable.

1. Kunz spoons

The chef Gray Kunz, who passed away in 2020, designed these stainless-steel spoons to his personal specifications, with a wide bowl; an angled tip for precise pouring; and an elegantly proportioned handle. I was introduced to them in the first restaurant kitchens I worked in, where we used them for everything from butter-basting steaks to neatly spooning sauce onto a plate. The original ("regular") size is a stellar stirring, saucing, and everyday serving spoon, but there are also smaller ones, perforated ones, and extra-large ones with handles long enough to reach to the bottom of a stockpot. I have a couple of each, and I use them all.

2. Mesh spider

These open-weave, saucer-shaped skimmers originated in East Asia and are commonly used to skim unwanted bits of things from soups and stocks, to lift fried food out of oil, and to scoop hot food out of boiling or simmering liquid and transfer it somewhere else. The ones with bamboo handles are affordable and come in various sizes; I've had the same one for years! I use it to transfer rice noodles and pasta from their cooking liquid to a pan of sauce, to scoop out edamame or blanched greens from boiling water, to lower several eggs at a time into simmering water, and to move those same eggs to an ice bath when they're done. Despite the fairly open mesh pattern (they're called spiders because the wires look like a spiderweb), you can also use these to remove cooked grains like brown rice or wheat berries from a pot of water.

3. Digital scale

If you never bake anything, you don't need a digital scale. But if you ever bake even one single thing, you should own one. Scooping and leveling is inaccurate— even if you do it the same way every time, you will probably end up with a different amount of flour or other dry ingredient than the recipe developer whose dessert you are trying to make intended. Not only that, but weighing ingredients saves you time and eliminates bowls to clean. Instead of doling out multiple individual ingredients with different cup measures, you can set a bowl on the scale and weigh each item into the bowl (watch any episode of *The Great British Baking Show* to see this in action). All the desserts in this book include weights in grams, which I hope will help you get flawless results in your home.

4. Food mill

People think you don't need a food mill if you have a food processor. But—you do. I am emotionally attached to mine: I bought it on sale over twenty years ago, when I was a line cook in New York City and wanted to own the same heavy-duty stainless-steel model I used at work to make velvety mashed potatoes and puréed taro root. When you turn the hand crank of a food mill, the blade forces the food through a perforated disc, which is designed to uniformly grind whatever you put into it. A food processor, by contrast, may be quick and motorized, but it has a tendency to unevenly and roughly chop, while also aerating. Food mills are best for cooked or naturally soft foods, and most come with fine, medium, and coarse discs. You can put a can of whole peeled tomatoes through to make passata (a simple tomato sauce that is great on pizza or in soups). You can puree a portion of the ingredients in a bean- or other vegetable-based soup, then return the milled mixture to the pot to make the soup creamy while retaining some of its texture. I often cook halved, unpeeled, uncored apples down to mush, then run them through the food mill to make applesauce; it holds back the seeds and skins. A food mill is excellent for making baby food, if you have a young'un in the house, and a generously sized one is really convenient for doing things in larger batches. The stainless-steel models are much more resilient and hardworking than the plastic or hybrid ones. I stretched to make that investment way back when, but it's worth having something that lasts.

5. Mortar and pestle

In the never-ending game of "you can have this or that, but you can't have both" that I've been forced to play in my small home kitchen, I chose my mortar and pestles over a spice mill. Not only can a mortar and pestle grind spices as fine or coarse as you want, it can break nuts into smaller pieces; smash garlic, ginger, and anchovy to a paste; reduce bread and crackers to crumbs; emulsify aïoli and different kinds of pestos; knock out a chile paste; and crush dried herbs to a powder. (If you are in the habit of making and using a sizable volume of spice mixes in your daily cooking, then an electric spice mill absolutely makes sense, too.) I love the act of grinding things in the mortar—it might take a little longer, but the smells and process are really rewarding on a sensory level.

6. Steamer

When it comes to cooking techniques, I came to steaming late in life, and I'm trying to make up for lost time. Steaming is a high-heat and high-moisture method, which means it is a spectacular way to cook foods quickly without drying them out. In fact, it bathes whatever you're steaming in moisture, making it a very forgiving and efficient technique. Bamboo steamers like the one pictured at left are lightweight and inexpensive, and can likely be used in tandem with the pots and pans you already own, since they sit on the pot's rim and come with their own domed lids. I'm also a fan of the folding stainless-steel types that have little legs to perch in the bottom of a pot. Favorite things to steam include all kinds of potatoes (including sweet potatoes); eggs (hard-boiled in 11 minutes!); chicken breast for chicken salad; dumplings; and flaky fish like striped bass and hake. I don't have a microwave, so I use my steamer to gently reheat cooked rice (line the steamer with cabbage leaves or a piece of parchment paper so the grains don't fall through).

7. Chopsticks

Obviously chopsticks are eating utensils. They're also extremely nimble off the table, which I learned while spending time with professional chefs who use them as an extension of their hands. I always choose chopsticks to maneuver individual pieces of food when frying or browning, such as the mushrooms on page 141 and the potatoes on page 234. If you are deep-frying something like doughnuts or battered fish, chopsticks are excellent at turning them over without piercing or puncturing them or displacing a lot of hot oil.

(If you push one side of the food down into the oil with the tip of a chopstick, it will naturally dip and flip over with very little effort.) I use chopsticks to emulsify nut butter and tahini that has separated in the jar, to poke steam holes into batches of rice, and to check tenderness for large pieces of protein that I'm braising or slow-roasting, like pork or lamb shoulder. A pair of chopsticks is an unparalleled way to whip eggs for a stir-fry or omelet. You can also use the wider end to peel ginger; it's especially useful for getting into the little elbows and around the edges of all the nubs.

8. Black carbon-steel pan

All the heat retention of a cast-iron pan at a fraction of the weight—that's what carbon-steel pans deliver. These skillets are virtually indestructible and can move from stovetop to oven, or be used directly on the grill grates over hot coals. I recommend having a 6-inch pan for frying eggs or griddling tortillas, and an 8-inch one for getting a good sear on a piece of protein or making fried rice. They are not expensive!

9 & 10. Masking tape and . . . Sharpies

Picture walking around a grocery store where none of the products had labels. Imagine trying to figure out what was inside a jar or a can if it didn't announce itself—you'd never buy anything! That's an extreme way of me making the argument that you should label all the leftovers in your fridge, any spices or dry goods you decant into a jar, and all the goodies you sock away in your freezer, so that these things will get eaten instead of discarded. Sharpies are my permanent marker of choice, and masking (or "artist") tape is cheap and can be removed from containers without leaving behind sticky residue.

The pantry that will set you free

If you have a diverse, stocked pantry, you will require very small amounts of fresh produce and protein to make a complete and very fulfilling meal. Instead of limiting your pantry to a collection of canned goods and a few spices, redefine it broadly as *anything that isn't going to go bad anytime soon.* That encompasses dried and canned beans, vinegars, and condiments, but also perishables like yogurt and lemons. When I survey my cabinets, my refrigerator, and my freezer, I realize that the majority of the food in my house falls into this category. Here's how to expand your pantry zones, and what you might want to keep there.

Dry dry goods

This is where I keep my beans, grains, and noodles, along with other shelf-stable things that aren't wet (I'll explain). It's smart to have a few types of dried beans around—a large white bean like gigante or butter beans; a fast-cooking type like lentils, mung beans, or moong dal; and something in between both in terms of size and cooking time, such as black-eyed peas. I usually have one short-grain rice and one long-grain rice in the house, along with other whole grains such as farro, cracked wheat, and/or spelt berries, plus a bag of cornmeal, grits, or polenta. The dry dry zone also includes rice noodles, dried udon and soba, and pasta (fresh ramen noodles are stored in the freezer). Most of my meals include one of these carbs, and I like having a choice of noodles at the ready, along with the option to cook a whole grain (recipes for Perfect Pot of Rice and Blank-Slate Whole Grains are on pages 274 and 275, respectively). While weeknights are for canned beans, I rarely go to sleep on a Friday night without soaking some dried beans overnight. I seldom know whether I'll be using them for a soup, a pasta dish, or simply as a side dish, but it's always good to have beans hydrating. The dry dry goods section is also home to nori, kombu, dried anchovy, oats, and nuts.

Baking

Set aside some space for flour, sugar (granulated, confectioners', and light or dark brown), leaveners, vanilla extract, cocoa powder, baking chocolate, cornstarch, and birthday candles.

Spices

I keep my spices together in a lower cabinet drawer. Spices are expensive, and the flavor of pre-ground spices fade quickly, so limit yourself to those that you actually like and use. If you don't add spices to your food very often, you're better off buying whole seeds (i.e., cumin seeds as opposed to ground cumin) and grinding them as needed.

Wet dry goods

If it comes in a can, jar, or bottle, it lives here, along with anything wet, sticky, or semi-liquid. (I know, I sound like a weirdo!) This is home to shelf-stable items that are—well—not totally dry: canned tomatoes and beans; tamarind paste; dried fruit; tuna, anchovies, sardines, and/or other canned fishes; coconut milk; vinegars and oils; ghee; mirin; soy sauce; and backup jars of mayo, mustard, and nut butters. I store Tetra packs of rice milk and/or oat milk (which we use all the time for smoothies) with the wet dry goods as well.

Refrigerator

Yes, the pantry includes plenty of foods that need to be kept cold. That translates to dairy, such as buttermilk, yogurt, Parm, and eggs, and produce like lemons and limes. These foods can be stored for weeks on end without fading, and they can be deployed in myriad ways to enrich or enhance the flavor of a dish. The fridge is condiments HQ: miso, gochujang, harissa, tomato paste, mayonnaise, mustard, pickles, kimchi, sauerkraut, prepared horseradish, chili oil, hot sauce, sesame oil, tahini, capers, jam, and chutney, to name a few.

Not my real pantry, but you get the idea.

My schlep-free, totally liberating, waste-reducing strategy for food shopping

I wrote extensively about grocery strategy in my first book, *Where Cooking Begins*, and the rules I laid out then are still the ones I live by. There are two keys to my approach, and they tie back to both the pantry zones explained earlier and the From the Market/At Home lists that live on the recipe pages. All my recipes also include a "Spin It" category so you can make on-the-fly adjustments based on actual ingredients or availability. If you already have a spice in your cabinet that will work, I don't expect you to go out and buy a brand-new jar of a different one. Same goes for proteins and produce, and I've noted that wherever applicable. Basically, you can make all these recipes even if you don't have the exact ingredients.

Cover home base and know when to go to the market

Divide your ingredient inventory into two parts: those things that you should always have on hand, and those things you should pick up in person right around when you want to use them. My completely obvious naming device for this distinction can be found on every recipe page under the columns called "From the Market" and "At Home." The At Home ingredients correlate to your expanded pantry and include anything that comes in a sealed bag, cardboard box, jar, or can: oil and vinegar, salt and sugar, pasta and grains, condiments and spices, dried and canned beans. Citrus and dairy are in this arena, too. These are things I almost always buy online. They're heavy, they're bulky, and I don't bring any value to the transaction by picking out which box of kosher salt I put in my shopping cart— each one is exactly as the other. Having groceries delivered saves me time, hassle, and, in many cases, money. (As a rule, I avoid vendors or services that rely on labor from undercompensated gig workers, and I tip generously, in cash whenever possible.) You may choose to hand-shop these items, and that's fine. Regardless of how you get them into your house, anything I assume you keep stocked will be under the At Home column.

That leaves the From the Market category. This broadly encompasses produce and proteins, but I put good bread and non-deli cheese in this section, too (they're hard to order online). My core advice for purchasing produce and proteins is to shop first, choose your recipe second. When you're at the store, grab the vegetables that look the best rather than buying something that's on your list regardless of what shape it's in. Talk to the butcher and the fishmonger before you make a selection; they're usually happy to point you to an item they're proud to have in the case.

Most important, shop smaller—studies show that US residents throw out between 15 and 25 percent of the food we buy due to spoilage or misuse, and as a country, we waste up to 40 percent of the food we produce. Not only is that staggering when you consider how many households are food insecure, but it also represents a huge loss of personal income and puts an unnecessary strain on natural resources. If you buy less to start with, you'll have less opportunity to create waste once that food is in your possession. Try purchasing only the perishables you expect to use over the next few days, rather than stocking up for weeks at a time. You may end up shopping more often, but those in-person shopping trips will be less time-consuming; you will get through the store faster and have less to schlep home and unpack. When I stopped shopping for groceries in big, infrequent waves about five years ago, I started throwing way less food away, and it's a habit that has stuck. Additionally, it's easier to track inventory of a leaner, less-crowded fridge or pantry, which means you're less likely to lose things in the nether reaches of the top shelves or the way-backs of the crisper drawers. Once you are comfortable balancing perishable ingredients with your exquisite pantry selections, you'll be able to craft meals that draw seamlessly from both categories.

*Switching up spices is just
one way to personalize and
reimagine any recipe.*

What I mean when I say "Spin It"

All my recipes include a section called "Spin It," where I offer suggestions for ingredients that can pinch-hit if something I've called for isn't available at the store, isn't something you like to eat, or is something you simply don't have on hand. I love Spin Its for a few reasons. I want you to think of recipes the way I do—as living, breathing road maps that you should feel empowered to modify to suit your preferences, cooking style, and inventory. Because I believe you should purchase ingredients that look good, rather than blindly following items on a shopping list, it would be hypocritical of me to enforce rigidity on my recipe pages. The way I arrive at these substitutions isn't scientific, and I freely admit to not having tried each and every option I've offered (far from it). Another way to think about the Spin It column is to pretend you texted me for advice and I thought about it for a minute before giving you my best educated guess.

The key to cooking instinctively, confidently, and with flexibility is recognizing that any dish is a balance of sweet, sour, salty, bitter, and umami flavors, and that texture plays a big role, too. When you can start to see ingredients as representative of a larger umbrella category, you're on your way to making informed, intuitive substitutions.

Other things to consider when making an ingredient swap are flavor, texture, relative cooking time, and what family the ingredient belongs to. For example, cider vinegar is an acidic liquid component, and its function as the sour part of any recipe can, of course, be replicated with a different vinegar or with citrus juice. When I need to find a substitute for a spice, I'll think about the flavor the original spice would have added (bright/citrusy, warm/spicy, herbal/earthy?), then expand that to other spices in the same family. With vegetables, consider at what stage they're added to the recipe to figure out what their texture is meant to be and how much flavor they're adding to the dish. Is the vegetable going to end up being hard and crunchy, sweet and soft, fresh and juicy, or wilted and tender? What other vegetables will behave like the one called for originally? With liquid ingredients and

condiments such as hot sauces and mustards, I try to approximate pucker, spice, and tang when giving a second or third option. This is some of the work I've tried to jump-start for you with Spin It, and the more you experiment with making adjustments, the more you'll get attuned to how to do this on your own.

It's important to note, however, that by giving a swap suggestion, I am in no way saying that two ingredients are the same, or that their flavor is necessarily equivalent, or that I am unaware that there may be cultural implications when you change how a dish is made. For example, Aleppo pepper and gochugaru pack about the same amount of spiciness, teaspoon to teaspoon, so I will swap one for the other if necessary; even though one is from Syria and the other is Korean, and Syrian or Korean recipes will probably not suggest this substitution. Polenta and white corn grits are not the same, but they behave very similarly when being cooked, have a comparable texture, and will take about the same amount of time to get tender; that's a reasonable, resourceful swap. Cooks engage in this kind of experimentation and improvisation all the time; in the comfort of your home, do whatever feels right.

However! There are some dishes that frankly aren't themselves if they are missing a key ingredient. If you leave the ginger out of Hainanese chicken rice, the resulting dish can't fairly be described as Hainanese chicken rice. That's not to say it won't be scrumptious or satisfying, but some diversions take you to a totally different destination. If you set out to make Filipino chicken adobo and use water instead of vinegar, it's no longer adobo. It's something, and it's yours, but don't call it adobo. You can't use sauerkraut instead of kimchi and still call the end result kimchi jjigae. Spin Its are meant to be a constructive way to take liberties with a given recipe, but I don't want to give the impression that I think substituted ingredients are identical to the original, or that it is okay to divorce an ingredient from the cuisine from which it originates without being sensitive to the impact of that change. The goal is to keep cooking and hopefully end up with something you really like—so have fun with your riffs, but be thoughtful!

the recipes

monday through thursday

Chapter 3

Stovetop Suppers

Being able to cook a meal for yourself at the end of a busy day should feel like a joy, not a chore. Big results without a big pile of dishes or a bunch of prep? I got you!

Pasta with Cacio e Walnut

4 servings

Cacio is an Italian word for sheep's-milk cheese, and this is a variation on pasta cacio e pepe (literally "pasta with cheese and pepper"), which was one of the inexpensive but extremely satisfying dinners I made a lot when I was in college. The toasted nuts add some crunch, which will make you appreciate the creaminess of the sauce that much more. If you're hustling, you can definitely chop the parsley and grate the cheeses while the pasta is cooking, but do these bits of prep ahead of time if you're at all hesitant about your kitchen speed. I like to cook the pasta in a big (6-quart) Dutch oven, which is the ideal vessel for finishing the pasta in the sauce, but a large pasta pot will work, too (make sure you're stirring all the way down to the bottom of the pot).

Kosher salt; freshly ground pepper

6 garlic cloves

1 cup walnut halves

⅓ cup extra-virgin olive oil

1 pound paccheri or other large tubular pasta

4 ounces Manchego

2 ounces Parmigiano

1 cup packed parsley leaves and tender stems

Bring a large Dutch oven or other pot of water to a boil and salt it generously.

Meanwhile, smash the garlic; roughly chop the walnuts. Combine the oil and garlic in a small saucepan and place it over medium heat. Cook, pressing down on the garlic with a wooden spoon to help break it into smaller pieces, until oil is sizzling and garlic is very light golden, 1 to 2 minutes. Add the walnuts and stir to coat; season aggressively with pepper (this is the "pepe" part of the cacio e pepe). Cook, stirring and tossing frequently, until garlic and nuts are golden brown, 3 minutes more. Remove from the heat and season with salt.

Boil the pasta, stirring occasionally, until very al dente. In the meantime, grate the cheeses on the large holes of a box grater (you should have about ¾ cup when combined); roughly chop the parsley. Set the cheeses and parsley aside separately.

Scoop out 2 cups pasta cooking liquid, then drain pasta and return it to the pot over medium heat. Scrape in the walnut-garlic mixture and add about 1 cup pasta cooking liquid. Stirring continuously, gradually add about ⅓ cup cheese and cook, still stirring, until cheese melts and liquid thickens. Add another ½ cup pasta liquid and half the remaining cheese and simmer, stirring, until cheese is melted. Add the last bit of cheese and cook, adding big splashes of pasta water as needed until the sauce becomes glossy and emulsified and lightly coats the pasta. Turn off the heat. Add the parsley and stir to combine. Taste and adjust seasoning.

From the Market	Spin It		At Home	Spin It
Parsley	In place of Manchego, try Pecorino Romano or aged Gouda		Olive oil	Almonds or pistachios can stand in for the walnuts
Manchego			Garlic	
			Walnuts	
	Use ¼ cup mint instead of the parsley		Salt and pepper	Use Pecorino Romano instead of Parmigiano
			Parmigiano	
			Paccheri	Rigatoni, fusilli, or spaghetti can replace the paccheri

Salt-and-Sugar Pork Rib Chops

2 servings

A little bit of sugar mixed into the salt helps these chops brown during their relatively short cook time, and while they rest, make the wilted greens (which are actually red) in the pork drippings. It's a dead-simple combination that adds up: salty, savory, meaty, sweet, and a touch bitter. If you wanted to scale this up to make enough for four, there are a couple ways to do it: You could bust out a second skillet and cook your chops in two pans simultaneously, then go down to one when it's time to wilt the radicchio. Or you can wipe out the pan, add another 3 tablespoons oil, and cook the second batch of chops in the same skillet before moving on to the greens.

2 teaspoons kosher salt

1 teaspoon sugar

1 pound (1-inch-thick) bone-in pork rib chops

1 head Treviso or other radicchio (12 to 14 ounces)

1 small yellow onion

1 lemon

4 tablespoons grapeseed or other neutral oil, divided, plus more if needed

Honey, for drizzling

Flaky salt and Dijon mustard, for serving

Mix kosher salt and sugar in a small bowl. Lightly pound the pork chops with a meat mallet, rolling pin, or the heel of your hand until they're about ½ inch thick. Pat dry, then season all over with the salt-sugar mixture. Let chops sit while you prep the radicchio and onion.

Trim the Treviso and separate it into individual leaves. Cut the leaves into irregular 3- to 4-inch pieces. Thinly slice the onion crosswise, then separate into rings. Cut the lemon in half.

Heat a large cast-iron skillet over medium-high for 2 minutes. Pour in 3 tablespoons oil (this should be enough to thoroughly coat the surface, but add more if needed), then carefully slip the pork chops into the pan. Press down to ensure that the center of each chop is making good contact with the hot oil and the pan. Cook, turning every minute, until the chops are very well browned with some charred spots on the fattiest areas, 5 to 6 minutes total. They will still be a little pink—if you like yours well-done, add another 1 or 2 minutes of cooking time. Transfer to a large plate to rest.

Carefully pour off fat from the skillet and wipe out any burned bits. Return pan to medium heat and add remaining 1 tablespoon oil. Add the onion and season with kosher salt. Cook, stirring occasionally, until onion rings are floppy and lightly browned, about 4 minutes. Add the radicchio, tossing and letting the leaves wilt before adding more, until all the radicchio is in the skillet. Season with kosher salt and cook, tossing, just until the leaves are wilted and tender but the thickest part of the rib still has a little bite to it, 3 to 4 minutes. Squeeze in juice of one lemon half, then toss to combine; transfer the radicchio to a platter. Drizzle a little honey over radicchio. Slice chops against the grain and add to platter; drizzle with any accumulated juices. Season with flaky salt. Serve with remaining lemon half and some Dijon for dragging the pork through.

From the Market	Spin It		At Home	Spin It
Pork chops	Use pork shoulder steaks, boneless, skinless chicken thighs, or skirt or flank steak, cut into 4-inch sections		Kosher salt	Any onion will do (as long as it's a small one)
Treviso or other radicchio			Sugar	
			Onion	Prepared horseradish can be used in place of mustard
	Escarole, napa cabbage, or savoy cabbage are good alts for Treviso		Grapeseed oil	
			Lemon	
			Honey	Use kosher salt instead of flaky salt
			Dijon mustard	
			Flaky salt	

Steamed Lemongrass Mussels

2 to 4 servings

Shrimp paste, a salted-and-fermented shrimp-based ingredient, gives this simple mussel dish a rich umami flavor that amplifies the sweet brininess of the mussels. There are Thai, Vietnamese, Cantonese, Malaysian, Filipino, Laotian, and Indonesian versions of shrimp paste: Some are packed in oil; others, like belacan, the Malay type, are dried and crumbly. I used a Thai type called kapi when I developed this recipe because that's what I had in the house. This is a nontraditional use of this condiment, which is used throughout Southeast Asia in many ways, typically to flavor stir-fried vegetable or meat dishes or fried rice, or to give intensity and body to condiments like sambal or nam phrik.

2 pounds mussels

1 lemongrass stalk

2 garlic cloves

1 serrano chile

1 large onion

¼ cup vegetable oil

3 tablespoons shrimp paste

Kosher salt

¼ cup mirin

1 baguette

Unsalted butter, at room temperature, for serving

1 small bunch chives

Pick over the mussels and discard any with cracked or gaping shells. Pull off any beards that are sticking out of the shells. Transfer mussels to a colander and rinse well; scrub with a coarse brush or scrub pad if needed.

Trim off the top third of the lemongrass stalk and peel off the tough outer layers. Using the blunt edge of a chef's knife, smack the lemongrass along the length of the stalk to bruise it (this will help release its essential oils). Use a Microplane to finely grate the lemongrass, garlic, and serrano into a small bowl. Slice the onion into ½-inch-thick rounds.

Heat oil in a 4-quart Dutch oven or other medium heavy pot with a lid over medium-high. Add the lemongrass, garlic, and serrano and cook, stirring, until the mixture starts to stick to the pot and there are some very light golden bits in the mix, 1 minute. Add the shrimp paste and cook, stirring, until very fragrant, 1 minute more. Add the onion, season with salt, and cook, tossing, until it is shiny and coated with shrimp paste, 1 to 2 minutes. Add ¼ cup water, lower the heat to medium, cover, and cook, stirring occasionally, until the onion is floppy and translucent, 5 to 6 minutes.

Add the mirin and mussels to the pot and stir well to combine. Cover and cook until the mussels have opened, 5 to 7 minutes (discard any mussels that refuse to open).

Meanwhile, cut the baguette in half crosswise, then split each half open lengthwise. Toast the baguette and spread a generous amount of butter over the cut sides. Cut the chives into ½-inch-long pieces and toss them into the mussels. Serve with the baguette for dipping.

Buying Bivalves

You're most likely to come across farmed mussels, which tend to be very clean and grit-free, making them super easy to prep. If given a choice, go for rope-grown, which are the most eco-friendly.

From the Market	Spin It		At Home	Spin It
Mussels	Littleneck or manila clams can be swapped for mussels		Garlic	Use 3 shallots to replace the onion
Lemongrass			Onion	Sake can be used in place of mirin
Serrano chile	A 3-inch piece of ginger can replace the lemongrass		Vegetable oil	Ghee can replace butter
Shrimp paste			Kosher salt	
Baguette			Mirin	
Chives	Crab paste or 3 anchovies can be used in place of shrimp paste		Butter	

Herbed Rice with Shrimpy-Kimchi Tomato Sauce

2 to 4 servings

Kimchi and butter complement each other like hot sauce and sour cream. The push-pull of spice, tang, and sweet richness is the foundation of this abundantly umami-ish, saucy, bouncy, and extremely easy 20-minute dinner. The spicier your kimchi, the hotter the sauce will be—and you can add a few dashes of hot sauce if you want to amp it up at the end.

1 cup short-grain white rice

1 cup cabbage kimchi

6 tablespoons (3 ounces) unsalted butter

8 ounces cherry tomatoes, any color

1 pound large shrimp, peeled, deveined, and cut into 2-inch pieces

Kosher salt

½ cup basil leaves

Place the rice in a fine-mesh strainer and rinse under cold running water until the water mostly runs clear, about 1 minute. Drain well, then combine the rice and 1¼ cups water in a small saucepan and place it over medium-high heat. As soon as the liquid is at a simmer, reduce the heat to medium-low, cover, and cook until the rice is tender and the water has been absorbed, 18 minutes.

Meanwhile, roughly chop the kimchi. Melt butter in a medium saucepan over medium heat until it foams, then add the kimchi and any of its juices and cook, stirring occasionally, until the liquid is simmering, 3 minutes. Add the tomatoes and stir to coat. Simmer gently, stirring occasionally, until the tomato skins are wrinkled and tomatoes are starting to collapse, 3 to 4 minutes. Use the back of a wooden spoon to press gently on the tomatoes so they split and release their juices and simmer until the sauce is thickened, 3 minutes more. Add the shrimp to the sauce, lower the heat, and cook very gently, stirring occasionally, until just opaque, 5 minutes. Don't boil the shrimp—cooking them slowly keeps them tender and juicy! Taste the sauce and season with salt if needed (between the kimchi and the naturally salty shrimp, you may not need additional seasoning).

Thinly slice the basil. Fluff the rice with a fork, then gently mix in the herbs. Serve the rice with the shrimp sauce spooned over.

From the Market	Spin It	At Home	Spin It
Cherry tomatoes	A chopped large tomato can replace the cherry tomatoes; the cook time will be 1 or 2 minutes faster	Short-grain white rice	Use any type of whole grain that you like
Shrimp		Kimchi	Ghee can replace butter
Basil	Chives, cilantro, and/or perilla leaves can replace the basil	Butter	Serve over cooked rice noodles instead of rice, or use a wheat noodle (such as ramen or udon)
		Kosher salt	

How-I-Like-It
Tuna Salad

How-I-Like-It Tuna Salad

Makes 4 sandwiches

There are lots of ways to make tuna salad, and I'm sure you already have yours. Is it the way your grandmother did it, or your favorite deli or most treasured diner? Whatever that way is for you, I'm certain it's the best way. Which recipe was that, again? It must have celery. It better not have celery. It needs more mayo. The big mistake is that people use mayo. If it doesn't have dill, you're fired. If it has dill, I won't eat it. Sorry—I was mentally transcribing the torrent of comments you haven't sent me yet. I understand. But I don't care. Tuna salad is ordinary, it's affordable, it's a pantry staple, and it can be deeply personal. This is how I make mine.

Delicious Fishes

When it comes to purchasing tuna, I find the oil-packed varieties to be much better-tasting than the ones packed in water. As I've said a million times before, fat is flavor. While we're being choosy, the sustainability of tuna fishing varies wildly, and some methods can impact other species, which are harvested inadvertently. Seek out albacore and skipjack types that have been caught by pole-and-line or by trolling, if possible.

1 small shallot

1 lemon

Kosher salt; freshly ground pepper

2 (6-ounce) jars tuna fillets packed in oil

2 pickled peperoncini

¼ cup mayonnaise, plus more for the bread

2 teaspoons prepared horseradish

Green hot sauce

8 slices sandwich bread

Iceberg lettuce, for serving

Finely chop the shallot and transfer it to a small bowl. Halve the lemon and squeeze the juice over, then season with salt and pepper and stir to combine. (Letting the shallot macerate in acid for a few minutes tames it.)

Drain the tuna and scoop it into a medium bowl. Finely chop the peperoncini and add them to the bowl, along with a teaspoon or two of brine from the jar. Add the mayonnaise and horseradish and use a fork to mash everything together until combined. Add a few dashes of hot sauce, then stir in the shallot mixture (juice and all). Taste and adjust the seasoning with salt and pepper. If you want more brightness, add more peperoncini brine. If you like your salad very finely textured, keep mashing until you get there.

Lightly toast the bread and spread mayo on one side of each slice. Build sandwiches with thick slabs of iceberg and tuna salad.

From the Market	Spin It	At Home	Spin It
Iceberg lettuce	Any crunchy lettuce will work—romaine hearts, for example	Shallot	A couple tablespoons of diced onion can replace the shallot
Sandwich bread	I like this on whole-wheat, but ciabatta, challah, and Pullman are all fantastic. It's just a sandwich!	Lemon	White wine vinegar or unseasoned rice vinegar can replace the lemon juice
		Salt and pepper	
		Jarred tuna	
		Pickled peperoncini	Pickled banana peppers can be substituted for the peperoncini, or use kimchi or pickled cucumbers
		Mayonnaise	
		Prepared horseradish	A dab of Dijon mustard can replace the horseradish
		Green hot sauce	Use any hot sauce you have on hand

Pork Burgers with Cabbage Slaw

4 servings

I don't know what it is about having a burger for dinner, but it makes me feel like I'm on vacation, especially when eaten during the week. There's lots of creamy, tangy slaw paired with these pork burgers, which are seasoned so they take on a homemade-pork-sausage vibe. A satisfying blend of crunchy, creamy, and chewy awaits you.

1½ pounds ground pork

2 teaspoons kosher salt, plus more as needed

½ teaspoon ground cumin

½ teaspoon cayenne

2 teaspoons fennel seeds

Freshly ground pepper

½ cup plain Greek yogurt

2 tablespoons cider vinegar

2 tablespoons Dijon mustard

1 tablespoon mayonnaise

¼ head savoy cabbage

Vegetable oil, for drizzling

4 sandwich rolls or burger buns

Place the pork, 2 teaspoons salt, cumin, and cayenne in a medium bowl. In a large dry skillet, toast the fennel seeds over medium heat, stirring frequently, until they darken slightly and release aromas, about 2 minutes. Transfer the seeds to a mortar and let cool, then lightly crush (alternatively, scoot them into a pile on your cutting board and use a heavy pot to crack them). Spoon half the fennel seeds into the pork mixture, season with some black pepper, and use your hands to combine until the seasonings are evenly distributed. Form the pork mixture into 4 equal balls (do not pack them tightly).

In a medium bowl, whisk together yogurt, vinegar, mustard, mayonnaise, and remaining fennel seeds. Season dressing with salt and black pepper. Cut the cabbage into roughly 1½-inch pieces; add them to the dressing and use your hands to thoroughly toss. Taste and season with more salt and pepper to your liking.

Heat a large heavy skillet over medium-high for 2 minutes, then drizzle it lightly with oil and swirl to coat. Add the pork to the pan, spacing the balls out, then immediately use a spatula to smash them down into ½-inch-thick patties. Cook, undisturbed, until well seared, crisp, and very brown on the underside, about 4 minutes. Turn and cook until just cooked through, 3 minutes more. Transfer the burgers to a plate and let rest.

Split the rolls and lightly toast them. Build sandwiches by placing the slaw on the bottom halves, then a pork burger, then adding more slaw on top, so every bite will be a bun-slaw-burger-slaw-bun palindrome of delights.

From the Market	Spin It	At Home	Spin It
Ground pork	Use ground turkey, beef, lamb, chicken, or plant-based ground "meat" instead of pork	Salt and pepper	Chili powder can replace the cumin
Savoy cabbage		Cumin	Red pepper flakes can replace the cayenne
Sandwich rolls	Any cabbage (red, green, pointy) will work, as will a resilient lettuce like iceberg	Cayenne	Sour cream can replace the yogurt or mayo, or use a combination
		Fennel seeds	
		Greek yogurt	
		Cider vinegar	
		Dijon mustard	White wine vinegar or malt vinegar would be a good substitute for cider vinegar
		Mayonnaise	
		Vegetable oil	

One-Pot Chicken and Rice with Blender Green Sauce

4 servings

There are many examples of this dish (arroz con pollo, notably), which is seductive because of its promise: perfectly cooked rice and chicken, harmoniously together in one pot. The truth is, though, that sometimes the rice is mushy and the chicken is dry, and sometimes the rice is crunchy and the chicken is . . . still dry. The ratio of rice to water is as important as the heat level and vessel you use; nail those variables and you're on your way to a brag-worthy dish. I cook everything in a 6-quart Dutch oven because it can hold the chicken snugly in a single layer.

4 skin-on chicken leg quarters (thigh and drumstick; about 3 pounds total)

Kosher salt

3 tablespoons vegetable oil, divided

1½ cups jasmine rice

3-inch piece ginger (about 2 ounces)

1 bunch cilantro, divided

1 jalapeño

1 avocado

2 limes

Season chicken legs on both sides with salt. Heat 1 tablespoon oil in a 6-quart Dutch oven over medium-high, then add the chicken, skin side down and not overlapping. Cook, undisturbed, until the skin is golden brown and crisp, 4 to 6 minutes. Transfer to a large plate, skin side up (the chicken will not be cooked through).

Meanwhile, rinse the rice in a fine-mesh strainer under cold running water until the water runs mostly clear, about 1 minute. This will remove surface starch so the grains will be fluffy and individuated when cooked. Let rice drain. Peel and thinly slice the ginger.

Pour off all but 2 tablespoons of fat from the pot, then return it to medium heat. Add the ginger, season with salt, and cook, stirring, until translucent and starting to brown, 2 minutes. Add the rice and stir to coat, then spread it into an even layer. Arrange chicken on top of rice, then pour in any accumulated juices from the plate. Place half the cilantro on top of the chicken. Pour in 2½ cups water and bring it to a simmer. Lower the heat to maintain a very bare simmer, cover the pot, and cook until the rice and chicken are cooked through and the liquid has been absorbed, 26 to 28 minutes.

Meanwhile, roughly chop remaining cilantro and place it in a blender. Halve the jalapeño lengthwise, remove the seeds if you want less spice, then add to the blender. Add avocado flesh, the juice of both limes, and ¼ cup water. Season with salt and blend on high speed until smooth, 30 seconds. Taste and adjust the seasoning as needed. It should have the consistency of soft whipped cream. If it seems very thick, blend in a little more water.

Remove the cilantro from the chicken. Transfer the chicken to four plates. Drizzle the remaining 2 tablespoons oil over the rice and increase the heat to high. Cover and cook, without stirring, until the rice is browned and crisp underneath, 5 to 7 minutes. Let sit, covered, for 3 minutes to steam, then spoon the crispy rice onto the plates alongside the chicken. Top with blender sauce.

From the Market	Spin It	At Home	Spin It
Chicken legs	Bone-in chicken thighs can replace the legs; cook for the same amount of time	Kosher salt	Any long-grain white rice can stand in for the jasmine
Cilantro		Vegetable oil	
Jalapeño		Jasmine rice	
Avocado	Use any spicy fresh chile you like	Ginger	A small onion can replace the ginger
		Limes	
	Replace the avocado with ½ cup Greek yogurt		Use rice vinegar or lemon juice instead of lime juice

Everybody Loves a Chicken Cutlet

2 to 4 servings

When breaded pan-fried chicken cutlets are good, they're good for all the same reasons that any piece of fried chicken is good: crunch followed by juicy followed by crunch. When they're bad, though, there are many missed targets to blame. The breading can come out crumbly and mealy, the chicken might be dry and overcooked, sometimes the coating never really gets crisp and there's a gummy layer where it meets the chicken, or the whole thing can be greasy and underseasoned. I tried to address these pitfalls in simple ways that don't mess with the standard three-step breading method (flour–eggs–bread crumbs). Chicken thighs guarantee flavor and are almost impossible to overcook, potato starch offers unparalleled breading adherence and extends the window for crispiness, and some judicious seasonings banish blandness.

Super Bird

While I find cutlets captivating without embellishment, there are lots of ways to dress them up. Top with chopped arugula and tomatoes drizzled with olive oil for the Milanese treatment, or slice and place them on a rice bowl with some pickled vegetables. They're awesome in a cutlet sandwich, especially with mayonnaise and mustard, or on a soft roll slathered with Spicy Creamy Sauce (page 274). Cutlet dinner is simply the best.

½ cup potato starch

3 large eggs

1½ cups panko bread crumbs

Kosher salt; freshly ground pepper

4 boneless, skinless chicken thighs (about 1 pound)

1 teaspoon garlic powder

½ cup vegetable oil, or more if needed, for frying

Flaky salt, for serving

Place the potato starch, eggs, and panko in three separate dinner plates, pie plates, or small rimmed baking sheets. Season the potato starch and eggs with salt and pepper; whisk the eggs to blend. Fit a rimmed baking sheet with a wire rack or line with paper towels.

Place the chicken thighs on a sheet of waxed paper or plastic wrap. Use your fingers or kitchen shears to remove any larger bits of fat still attached to the thighs. Lay the thighs flat and place a second sheet of waxed paper or plastic wrap on top. Use a meat mallet, rolling pin, or saucepan to lightly pound and flatten the thighs. Season both sides with salt and pepper, then with the garlic powder, dividing it evenly.

Working with one piece of chicken at a time, dip the cutlet into the potato starch, making sure to coat both sides evenly, then pat off excess. Dip into the eggs, then let excess drip back into the plate. Place in the bread crumbs and press to adhere, then turn and press firmly to coat the second side. Place the breaded cutlet on a second rimmed baking sheet and repeat with remaining cutlets.

Pour the oil into a large skillet (I like to use my cast iron) to reach a depth of about ¼ inch; add more oil if needed. Heat over medium-high until very hot, 5 to 6 minutes; when it's ready, a pinch of panko should bubble and float to the surface within a couple seconds of hitting the oil. Carefully lower the cutlets into the pan and cook, gently shaking the skillet back and forth occasionally and rotating the cutlets so they brown evenly, until very dark golden brown and crisp on the underside, 2 to 3 minutes. Turn and cook until evenly browned on the second side, 1 to 2 minutes more. Transfer the cutlets to the prepared baking sheet and season with flaky salt. Serve hot!

From the Market	Spin It		At Home	Spin It
Potato starch	All-purpose flour, cornstarch, or rice flour can be used in place of potato starch		Eggs	Onion powder or dry mustard powder can be used instead of— or in addition to— garlic powder
Chicken thighs			Panko	
	If you prefer skinless chicken breasts, use them (the cook time may be 1 or 2 minutes shorter)		Salt and pepper	
			Garlic powder	Any neutral oil can be used for frying; my favorites are peanut oil and grapeseed oil
	Pork loin medallions can also be used instead of chicken thighs		Vegetable oil	
			Flaky salt	Kosher salt is fine if you don't have flaky salt

Fat Noodles with
Pan-Roasted Mushrooms
and Crushed Herb Sauce

Fat Noodles with Pan-Roasted Mushrooms and Crushed Herb Sauce

4 to 6 servings

This method of cooking mushrooms—by pan-roasting them, then finishing with browned butter—is incredibly effective, whether you're adding them to pasta or not. In the second step, the butter and aromatics wash a ton of flavor over the mushrooms, glossing them up.

Kosher salt; freshly ground pepper

6 garlic cloves, divided

1 lemon

½ cup extra-virgin olive oil, divided

1 teaspoon mild chile flakes, such as Aleppo pepper

1 shallot

1 pound maitake mushrooms

Chunk of Parmigiano, for grating and serving

2 cups lightly packed herbs (leaves and tender stems), such as parsley, mint, and/or arugula

2 tablespoons unsalted butter

1 pound wide pasta noodles, such as lasagnette or pappardelle

Bring a large pot of water to a boil and season it very aggressively with salt (figure ¼ cup salt per 6 quarts water). Pick out the smallest garlic clove and finely grate it into a small bowl. Grate in the zest of the lemon, then stir in 2 tablespoons olive oil and the chile flakes. Season oil mixture with salt and pepper and set aside.

Thinly slice the remaining 5 garlic cloves and the shallot. Trim the mushrooms; tear into bite-size pieces. Juice the zested lemon into a small bowl. Grate enough Parm to yield ¼ cup (save what's left for passing at the table). Set all aside.

Add the herbs to the boiling water and cook until very softened, 2 minutes. (Cooking the herbs both mellows and deepens their flavor; they will have less fresh brightness but take on a richer, more vegetal flavor.) Use a mesh spider or tongs to remove the herbs and hold them under cold running water until cool enough to handle, about 10 seconds. Squeeze out as much excess liquid as possible. Thinly slice the herbs and stir them into the oil mixture. Taste and adjust with more salt and chile flakes, if desired. Set the herb sauce aside.

From the Market	Spin It		At Home	Spin It
Mild chile flakes	Instead of Aleppo pepper, use a smaller quantity of regular red pepper flakes or lots of black		Salt and pepper	A few dashes of sherry vinegar or white wine vinegar can replace the lemon juice and zest
Shallot			Garlic	
Tender herbs			Lemon	
Maitake mushrooms			Olive oil	
Wide pasta noodles	Replace the shallot with ¼ onion		Parmigiano	
			Butter	Grana Padano or pecorino can replace the Parm
	The herbs are truly interchangeable, in any ratio, and can include basil, chives, tarragon, and/or dill			
	Use shiitake, oyster, and/or cremini mushrooms instead of maitake			
	Big tubes like rigatoni or paccheri are good too			

Tall Pot Alt

If you don't have a Dutch oven, use a large heavy skillet to cook the mushrooms and combine with the shallot and garlic. Scoop out 2 cups of pasta cooking liquid, then drain the pasta and return to the pot, and build your sauce from there. If the sauce gets tight or sticky, or the cheese clumps together, lower the heat and add more water than you think you should. Cook over low heat, stirring gently but constantly, until the cheese melts and the sauce is smooth.

Lower heat under the boiling water to maintain a simmer—you want to get your mushrooms going before starting the pasta. Heat a large Dutch oven over medium-high for 1 minute, then add 3 tablespoons olive oil and half the mushrooms. Cook, tossing, until the mushrooms are coated with oil, then cook, undisturbed, until browned on the underside, 2 to 3 minutes. Season with salt and toss, then cook, stirring occasionally, until the mushrooms are browned all over and cooked through, 4 to 5 minutes more. Transfer mushrooms to a large plate and repeat with the remaining 3 tablespoons oil and mushrooms, then add these mushrooms to the first batch. Bring the water back to a boil.

Melt the butter in the Dutch oven over medium heat until it foams, 15 to 30 seconds. Add the sliced garlic and shallot and cook until the garlic and butter are golden brown and the shallot is translucent, about 2 minutes. Return the mushrooms to the pot, along with any accumulated juices, and cook, tossing, until well combined. Lower the heat to keep warm.

Meanwhile, add the pasta to the boiling water and cook, stirring occasionally, until very al dente, 2 to 3 minutes less than the time indicated on the package. Use a mesh spider to transfer pasta to the pot with the mushrooms, then add 1 cup of the pasta cooking liquid. Increase the heat to medium and cook, tossing energetically, until a sauce forms that coats the pasta, 2 minutes. Add the ¼ cup grated cheese, 1 tablespoon lemon juice, and another big splash of pasta water and cook, tossing, until cheese is melted and the sauce is clinging to the noodles, 1 to 2 minutes more. Add a few spoonfuls of herb sauce to the pasta and stir to combine. Serve with remaining herb sauce and more cheese at the table.

Gingery Ground Beef with Lime and Herbs

4 servings

This savory, glazed stir-fry goes quickly once everything hits the pan, so make sure to prep all of your ingredients before the cooking gets underway. If you want to scale up for a bigger crowd or to ensure leftovers, you can double this; cook the meat in two batches so you don't sacrifice browning and crisping. (Combine both batches of beef before adding twice the amount of liquids and building the pan sauce.) This is spicy and a little salty since it's meant to be served with rice and lettuce; you can use low-sodium soy sauce if you like.

Cooked rice (see page 274) and/or lettuce cups, for serving (optional)

3-inch piece ginger

6 garlic cloves

1 shallot

2 limes

¼ cup soy sauce

2 tablespoons sriracha

1 tablespoon fish sauce

1 tablespoon vegetable oil

1½ pounds ground beef chuck (80% lean)

Kosher salt

½ cup thinly sliced cilantro leaves and stems

If you plan on having rice with this, get that going. If you need to wash and dry your lettuce leaves, do that now. Peel the ginger and cut it into thin matchsticks; thinly slice the garlic.

Finely dice the shallot and put it in a small bowl or measuring cup. Finely grate the zest of 1 lime into the bowl, then add the juice of both limes (you should have somewhere between ¼ cup and ⅓ cup, depending on your limes). Add the soy sauce, sriracha, and fish sauce and stir to combine.

Heat a large cast-iron or other heavy-bottomed skillet over high for 2 minutes. Add the oil and tilt to coat. Add the ground beef, season with salt, and immediately use a wooden spoon or metal spatula to smash it against the pan, at once flattening the meat and breaking it into smaller pieces. Cook, undisturbed, until the underside is browned and the beef looks juicy on top, 5 minutes. Add the ginger and garlic, toss to combine, and cook, stirring occasionally, until the ginger and garlic are golden and the beef is starting to crisp, 2 minutes more. Add the lime mixture and cook, stirring, until the sauce has reduced to a light glaze, about 3 minutes. Turn off the heat and toss in the cilantro. Serve with rice and/or lettuce cups for wrapping around the meat, if desired.

From the Market	Spin It		At Home	Spin It
Lettuce (optional)	Use ½ red onion in place of the shallot		Rice (optional)	Use ¼ cup unseasoned rice vinegar to replace the lime juice
Shallot			Ginger	
Ground beef	Ground lamb or dark-meat turkey can be substituted for the beef		Garlic	Sambal oelek can replace the sriracha; add 1 teaspoon sugar to the lime mixture
Cilantro			Limes	
	Use cubed very firm tofu for the beef (and use a nonstick pan)		Soy sauce	
			Sriracha	
			Fish sauce	
	Use ¼ cup mint instead of cilantro		Vegetable oil	Any neutral oil can be used
			Kosher salt	

Skirt Steak with Potatoes and Black Pepper–Horseradish Sauce

4 servings

Skirt steak is an awesome cut—very flavorful, nicely marbled, quick-cooking, and affordable. But it's a funny shape—long, narrow, and flat—and it's often rolled up when displayed in the butcher's case. Make sure to unfurl it before cutting it into portions at home. It also has a noticeable grain that runs across the width, making it easy to see which direction the muscle fibers run. Make certain to slice it on an angle against the grain before serving so that you get tender (not ropy) bites.

1 (1½-pound) skirt steak, cut crosswise into 4 equal pieces

Kosher salt; freshly ground pepper

1½ pounds small Yukon Gold potatoes, scrubbed

1 cup crème fraîche (8 ounces)

2 tablespoons prepared horseradish

Vinegary hot sauce, such as Tabasco or Louisiana

Handful chopped chives

1 lemon

Vegetable or other neutral oil

Season the steak on both sides with salt and pepper. Let it sit at room temperature while you make the potatoes.

Place potatoes in a medium stockpot and cover with cold water. Add a generous amount of salt and place over high heat. Bring to a boil, then lower the heat to maintain a rapid simmer. Cook, stirring occasionally, until the potatoes are tender through and through when pierced with a cake tester or the tip of a paring knife, 18 to 20 minutes.

Meanwhile, make your horseradish sauce: In a medium bowl, combine the crème fraîche, horseradish, a few dashes of hot sauce, and the chives. Squeeze in the juice of one lemon half. Season with salt and very generously with pepper (like, 15 cranks!). Stir to combine, then taste and adjust with more of everything as desired.

When the potatoes have 8 minutes, heat a large (12-inch) cast-iron or other heavy skillet over medium-high for 3 minutes. Drizzle with just enough oil to coat, then add the steak. Press down firmly with a spatula to make sure the meat comes into good contact with the surface, then cook, undisturbed, until dark golden brown underneath, about 3 minutes. Turn and cook until the second side is also very brown and crisp and the interior is medium-rare, 3 to 4 minutes longer. Transfer to a large plate and let rest for at least 5 minutes, or until it's time for the next step.

Drain the potatoes and return them to the pot. Use a wooden spoon or potato masher to crush them into 2 or 3 pieces each. Season with salt, then add two heaping spoonfuls of horseradish sauce and toss gently to coat. Slice steak thinly across the grain and serve with potatoes. Pass extra sauce at the table.

From the Market	Spin It	At Home	Spin It
Skirt steak	Flank or hanger steak will cook in about the same amount of time	Salt and pepper	Replace the horseradish with a couple tablespoons of pickle brine or kimchi brine plus ¼ teaspoon cayenne
Potatoes		Horseradish	
Crème fraîche	Small creamer potatoes can be used in place of Yukon Golds	Hot sauce	
Chives		Lemon	Any hot sauce you like will work
	Use sour cream or Greek yogurt instead of crème fraîche	Vegetable oil	Use unseasoned rice vinegar or cider vinegar instead of lemon juice

Left to right, top to bottom: Fernando and Cosmo in Udaipur, India; with Leo and Cosmo at Franny's in Brooklyn; the whole fam; with my mom and a big turkey; Leo's birthday breakfast in bed; Nina, Gia, and a turkey leg; Cosmo in Rome; King Jeffrey and Peggy; Frank and Nina's joint birthday; Henrietta Music and Fernando; nursing Cosmo and eating cake; my mom and her torta rustica

I Love You, Let's Eat

One of the ways that I can tell if I like you is if you think I'm funny. And one of the ways that you can tell if I like you is how I cook for you.

I'm not the heartsiest person, but I will cook all day, any day to show you that you're important to me. I learned to do this in my childhood home. I grew up in an upwardly mobile Italian American family with two hardworking parents, Frank and Carole, and I knew I was loved because I was extremely well fed. We all eat for survival and pleasure, but my mom's meals ranked very high on the pleasure end of the spectrum. She made exceptional family dinners, and she threw legendary dinner parties. She also made lots of dishes that were for *someone's* personal enjoyment, even when she wasn't sitting down to eat herself.

There was Saturday night fusilli Alfredo that my mom prepared for me and my sister hours before she cooked a second dinner for her and my dad. When I was sick, she brought thick slices of buttered toast to my bedside. Every March, she baked, froze, and shipped a birthday cake to my sister at college, which I envied even though I'm a summer baby and always get a never-frozen cake. Through these self-effacing acts of pure generosity and caretaking, life's biggest lesson was revealed: If you truly care about someone, you will prove that by executing a meal for them and not partaking in it at all. At the end of this journey, you, too, can be a Nonna standing in a spotless kitchen while the rest of your family sits and eats Sunday ragù (see page 188).

I practiced my "let me cook for you" methods here and there until I became a parent, at which point it was Game On. When my first child, Leo, was born, I wanted everything he ate to be unprocessed, unadulterated, and straight from the goddamned source—starting with the best breast milk I could provide. During the first few weeks of new, sleepless parenthood, when my husband, Fernando, and I were very tired and overwhelmed, he would occasionally say things out loud like, "Wow, I'm exhausted," and I would rebound with "I am literally keeping your child alive with food that I am making with my own body."

I wasn't complaining; it was an honor. I had *become the food*. When Leo was old enough for solid food, I did my research. His first real meal was a few spoonfuls of ripe avocado—nutrient-rich and easy to digest. He teethed on cooked chicken drumstick bones that had been picked clean of any bits of cartilage. When I went back to work after maternity leave, I spent my weekends preparing big batches of roasted, steamed, simmered, and pureed foods, which I vacuum sealed in small portions, to be doled out over the coming days. If I couldn't be there with him in person, I would be there in the form of a premade meal. I felt connection through a dinner that he ate when I wasn't there.

Time went on. A second child, Cosmo, arrived, and he got an avocado, too. Eventually, the meal prep became bigger and more elaborate. I realized I was wasting valuable hours shopping and cooking to try to lessen the guilt I felt about having a career and not dining with my kids during the week. The boys had caretakers who liked to cook, and I began the arduous emotional process of being okay with the fact that they could thrive on dinners that someone else made and ate with them. On the weekends, I cooked for pleasure—theirs and mine—and we sat together as a family to eat.

The COVID-19 pandemic was the first time in my adult life that I ate dinner with my children every night of the week, for hundreds of nights in a row. As horrific as this time has been (it is still a crisis as I write this), and as sketchy as some of my "I really don't feel like cooking dinner" dinners were, I was grateful for our end-of-day meals and the captive audience my children had become. They had nowhere else to be, and I was there to look them in the eyes while they ate. The guilt of not being around for all those years morphed into an awareness that, at least for the time being, there is a tremendous amount of pleasure, comfort, and security to be found during mealtime, both in the food and in the time spent together. Our outside world had shrunk down to our little nuclear unit, and there was no part of me that wanted to cook and not eat. The truth is that you can find selflessness in cooking for the people you love, but you'll be much better nourished when you eat together.

Chapter 4

Big Salads

These salads have enough going on to qualify them as actual dinners on nights when you're in the mood for something vibrant and crunchy, or as hefty sides when you want to keep the go-withs simple

Radicchio with Parm Crackers and Dates

4 servings

The first time I made frico, I was a private chef and caterer. I served the lacy, crisp baked rounds of Parmigiano as little hors d'oeuvres, sometimes topped with arugula, sometimes as cheesy crackers on their own. In this salad, they act as salty, shattering croutons that cling to the mix of chicories and sweet dates.

½ cup walnuts

1 cup finely grated Parmigiano, lightly packed (about 1 ounce)

6 tablespoons fresh lemon juice

¼ cup white wine vinegar

3 tablespoons extra-virgin olive oil

1 teaspoon honey

Kosher salt; freshly ground pepper

6 Medjool dates, pitted

1 medium head radicchio (about 12 ounces)

2 Belgian endives (5 to 6 ounces each)

Preheat oven or toaster oven to 350°F. Place the walnuts on a small rimmed baking sheet and roast until they're a couple of shades darker and fragrant, 10 minutes, tossing halfway through. Spread them out on a cutting board and let cool slightly, then crush the walnuts in your fist to roughly break them into smaller pieces.

Place a small or medium nonstick skillet over medium heat, then sprinkle 2 tablespoons of the Parmigiano in an even layer over its surface (if it's not a neat round, it's fine—it's more important that the Parm isn't piled up in one spot). Cook until the cheese melts, is bubbling, and turns light golden brown around the edge, 1 to 2 minutes. Turn off the heat and sprinkle about one-quarter of the walnuts over, then let the frico sit until the sizzling noises stop and the edge is set. Gently slide the frico onto a plate (walnut side up) and repeat with remaining Parm and walnuts to make 3 more frico. Some walnut pieces will fall off in transit; don't worry about it.

In a large serving bowl, whisk together lemon juice, vinegar, oil, and honey. Season the dressing with salt and pepper.

Cut dates crosswise into 3 or 4 pieces each. Trim radicchio and endive; separate into individual leaves. Tear the largest radicchio leaves into smaller pieces (you'll use a knife and fork for this salad, so they don't need to be bite-size). Add dates, radicchio, and endives to the bowl with the dressing and toss with your hands to combine. Add the frico and fold together gently. Some of the frico will break into smaller pieces as you do this. Try not to smash them to smithereens.

From the Market	Spin It		At Home	Spin It
Medjool dates	Barhi, Dayri, or Deglet Noor dates can be used instead of Medjools, or use golden raisins or Turkish apricots		Walnuts	Pecans or almonds can be subbed in for the walnuts
Radicchio			Parmigiano	
Endive			Lemon	Grana Padano can replace the Parm
	Any radicchio, such as Treviso, Castelfranco, or Chioggia, can be used		White wine vinegar	
			Olive oil	Use whatever vinegars you like in place of the white wine vinegar
	Escarole or frisée can replace the endive		Honey	
			Salt and pepper	Sub maple syrup, date syrup, or brown rice syrup for the honey

Crunchy and Juicy Feta Salad

4 servings

You could give me this bowl of snappy vegetables topped with slabs of feta for dinner every night of the week, and I'd be happy. Urfa biber is a Turkish dried chile related to Aleppo pepper; it's mildly spicy and has dark chocolaty-raisiny sweetness along with some smoky notes. You can order it online or find it at specialty stores, especially those with deep Middle Eastern sections.

1 fennel bulb

1 bunch radishes, tops removed

4 Persian (mini) cucumbers

Kosher salt; freshly ground pepper

3 tablespoons extra-virgin olive oil, plus more for drizzling

1 tablespoon fresh lemon juice

1 tablespoon red wine vinegar

1 teaspoon dried oregano, crumbled

1 teaspoon dried mint

1 teaspoon Urfa biber, plus more for serving

6 ounces feta

6 ounces cherry tomatoes (about 1 cup)

2 tablespoons toasted sesame seeds

Thinly slice fennel and radishes. Cut the cucumbers crosswise into ½-inch-thick rounds. Submerge the fennel, radishes, and cucumbers in a large bowl of generously salted ice water. This icy bath will take some of the bite out of the radishes, along with making all the vegetables super crunchy and resilient and seasoning them at the same time.

While the veggies soak, prep the other components: In a small bowl, whisk together 3 tablespoons oil, 1 tablespoon lemon juice, vinegar, oregano, mint, and Urfa biber. Taste dressing and season with salt and pepper. Cut the feta into ¼-inch-thick slabs.

Drain the fennel, radishes, and cucumbers and transfer to a clean kitchen towel; fold the towel over and press and pat vegetables dry. Transfer to a large serving bowl. Halve the tomatoes and add them to the vegetables; add sesame seeds and dressing. Season with salt and pepper and toss with your hands to combine and coat everything with dressing. Divide salad among four shallow bowls and top each with a couple pieces of feta. Sprinkle with more Urfa and drizzle with oil.

From the Market	Spin It	At Home	Spin It
Fennel	Try daikon, black radish, watermelon radish, French, and/or icicle radishes	Salt and pepper	If you don't have a lemon, use 2 tablespoons red wine vinegar
Radishes		Olive oil	
Persian (mini) cucumbers		Lemon	If you can't find dried mint in the spice aisle, cut open a mint tea bag and use that
Urfa biber	Lemon cucumbers or 1 large English cucumber can replace the Persian ones	Red wine vinegar	
Feta		Dried oregano	
Cherry tomatoes		Dried mint	
	A chopped large beefsteak tomato can replace cherry tomatoes	Toasted sesame seeds	
	Ricotta salata or any young sheep's-milk cheese can sub in for the feta		
	Instead of Urfa biber, use Aleppo or Maras pepper		

Avocado and Fresh Chile Caprese

4 servings

Is it still a caprese if you add avocados and spicy chiles? Considering that I kept the holy trinity of mozzarella, tomatoes, and basil intact, I think it's allowed. And while not strictly classic, the extra few dashes of vinegar added right before serving round out the rich fats and sweet summer fruits at play in this dish.

1 fresh long red chile, or
2 or 3 medium chiles,
such as Fresno

Kosher salt

1 small garlic clove

¼ cup extra-virgin olive oil,
plus more as needed

1 pound fresh mozzarella,
preferably salted, at room
temperature

6 ounces cherry tomatoes
(about 1 cup)

1 avocado

Red wine vinegar, for drizzling

Flaky salt

Handful Italian (Genovese)
basil leaves

Thinly slice the chile crosswise into rings and transfer to a small bowl. Season with a large pinch of salt and finely grate the garlic over. Toss until the salt dissolves and the chile rings look shiny and wet. Stir in ¼ cup oil and set aside. (If you have not let your mozzarella come to room temperature yet, let the chile-garlic mixture sit while the cheese warms up.) Halve the tomatoes.

Tear mozzarella into 2-inch pieces; arrange on a serving platter. Scatter tomatoes hither and thither. Halve, pit, and peel the avocado; cut into bite-size pieces; and add to the platter. Spoon the chile-garlic mixture over everything, letting chiles slide off the spoon along with the oil. Season everything with a few dashes of vinegar and some flaky salt. (You can let the salad sit at room temperature at this point—the mozzarella will exude some liquid and so will the tomatoes, which is very nice if that's how your timing works out, but it's not essential.) Tilt the platter and spoon any accumulated juices over. Serve topped with a generous drizzle of oil and the basil.

From the Market	Spin It	At Home	Spin It
Red chile	Burrata is a decadent option if you can get it; low-moisture mozzarella can be substituted for fresh in a pinch (it won't tear as easily)	Kosher salt	Thinly slice a couple of scallions, a small shallot, or a small wedge of red onion instead of the garlic
Fresh mozzarella		Garlic	
Cherry tomatoes		Olive oil	
Avocado		Red wine vinegar	
Basil	Dice a large tomato instead of using cherry tomatoes, or substitute a ripe peach or nectarine	Flaky salt	Try white wine vinegar or sherry vinegar instead of red wine vinegar, or use fresh lemon juice
	Any type of basil, such as Thai or purple (or a combination), can be deployed		

Little Gems with Sugar Snap Peas and a Ranch-y Dressing

4 servings

It hurts my feelings when people say they bought buttermilk for pancakes and don't know how to use up the leftovers. There is always buttermilk in my fridge, and plenty of ways to get your money's worth. For one thing: This salad! Buttermilk has the amazing ability to be creamy and tangy and unexpectedly light (buttermilk is naturally low-fat), qualities that you'd normally have to combine several ingredients to achieve. For this ranch-esque dressing, I added sour cream for heft, lemon juice and mint for levity, and nutritional yeast to evoke cheese without any sharpness or funk. Buttermilk keeps for weeks in the fridge, or maybe less now that you know what to do with it.

3 heads Little Gem lettuce

8 ounces sugar snap peas

¾ cup buttermilk

¼ cup sour cream

1 tablespoon extra-virgin olive oil

1 tablespoon nutritional yeast

1 teaspoon dried mint

1 teaspoon granulated garlic

2 tablespoons fresh lemon juice

1 garlic clove

Kosher salt; freshly ground pepper

Trim the lettuces, then separate the leaves, wash, and dry them. String the peas and thinly slice them crosswise on an angle. Chill the lettuce and the peas while you make the dressing.

In a medium bowl, whisk together the buttermilk, sour cream, and oil to blend. Whisk in the nutritional yeast, mint, and granulated garlic. Add the lemon juice. Finely grate half the garlic clove into the bowl; whisk to combine. Taste and season with salt and pepper—a lot of salt and pepper. Like, *a lot* a lot. You need aggressive seasoning to balance the predominantly sweet and tangy flavors of the dairy. If you want more sharp raw garlic flavor, grate in the remaining half clove. Place the lettuce and peas in a salad bowl and season with salt and pepper. Add the dressing and toss gently with your hands to coat.

From the Market	Spin It	At Home	Spin It
Little Gem lettuce	Romaine, Bibb, or any red-leaf or green-leaf lettuce you like can be used instead of Little Gem; you need about 6 cups leaves	Sour cream	Greek yogurt or crème fraîche can replace the sour cream
Sugar snap peas		Olive oil	Any vegetable oil can be used in place of the olive oil
Buttermilk	Replace the peas with 2 Persian (mini) cucumbers or 1 bunch small radishes, thinly sliced	Nutritional yeast	Grated Parm can replace the nutritional yeast
		Dried mint	
		Granulated garlic	Try onion powder or a finely grated garlic clove in place of the granulated garlic
		Lemon	
		Garlic	
		Salt and pepper	

Roasted Squash aux Lardons

2 servings

Is it still a salad if it's hot? Ponder that existential question as you make your way through a tower of runny egg, salty crackly pancetta, sharp escarole, and sweet-and-substantial roasted squash.

1 medium acorn squash (about 2 pounds)

Extra-virgin olive oil, for drizzling

Kosher salt; freshly ground pepper

1 head escarole

4 ounces pancetta, thinly sliced

1 tablespoon sherry vinegar

1 tablespoon fresh lemon juice

2 large eggs

Preheat the oven to 425°F.

Scrub the squash (sometimes they have a waxy film on them in addition to little patches of dirt), then halve it through the stem and scoop out the seeds (no need to peel). Lay the squash on the cut sides, then cut it into ½-inch-wide wedges. Transfer to a rimmed baking sheet and drizzle with oil. Season with salt and pepper and toss to coat. Roast until the squash is lightly browned on the underside and tender when pierced with a cake tester or paring knife, 20 to 25 minutes.

Meanwhile, trim the escarole and separate it into individual leaves. Wash, drain, and dry. Tear any very large leaves in half.

Put the pancetta in a large nonstick skillet, then place over medium heat and cook, turning every few minutes, until the fat has rendered and the pancetta is shriveled and golden, 8 to 10 minutes. (Starting it in a cold pan will help it release its fat before it starts to brown.) Increase the heat to medium-high and cook until crisp, 2 to 3 minutes more. Transfer to a plate, leaving drippings behind. Add the escarole to the skillet and toss to coat. Season with salt and pepper and cook, tossing, until the leaves are wilted but the ribs still have some crunch, 3 to 4 minutes. Turn off the heat and stir in the vinegar and lemon juice. Transfer the escarole to a bowl.

Wipe out the skillet and return it to medium heat. Add enough oil to generously coat the surface, then fry the eggs until the whites are set and the yolks are still runny, about 4 minutes. Season with salt and pepper. Layer the squash, pancetta, and escarole on plates, and top each with an egg.

From the Market	Spin It		At Home	Spin It
Acorn squash	Butternut, honeynut, or delicata squash, can be used (peel butternut)		Olive oil	If you don't have any lemons, use 2 tablespoons rice vinegar or cider vinegar
Escarole	Instead of escarole, use 2 bunches frisée or ¼ head green cabbage		Salt and pepper	
Pancetta			Lemon	Top with a couple slices of fresh mozzarella instead of the eggs
	Bacon or guanciale can replace the pancetta		Eggs	
			Sherry vinegar	Red wine vinegar can replace sherry vinegar

Wild Rice with Pomelo, Coconut, and Cashews

6 servings

This dish owes everything to yum som-o, an iconic Thai salad featuring pomelo, a sweet, juicy cousin of grapefruit. Along with denuded pieces of bittersweet pomelo that burst when you bite into them, yum som-o usually contains ground toasted coconut and peanuts, Thai chiles, dried shrimp, fresh and/or crispy shallots, herbs, and a dressing made with fish sauce, lime juice, soy sauce, and palm sugar. The result is not just a textural bonanza—it's a deft balance of sweet, sour, spicy, salty, and bitter flavors. Inspired by but clearly diverging from that dish, I've made a wild rice salad that combines chewy with crunchy and a simple, tart dressing.

1¼ cups wild rice (not wild rice blend)

2 teaspoons kosher salt, plus more as needed

1 large shallot, sliced into thin rings

2 tablespoons vegetable oil

Pinch of cayenne, plus more as needed

½ cup unsweetened dried coconut chips

½ cup raw cashews

1 pomelo

¼ cup fresh lime juice

2 teaspoons sugar

Handful cilantro

Soak rice for a couple of hours (or overnight), if possible, which helps it cook more quickly (unsoaked rice may need longer than 45 minutes to cook). Drain, place in a medium stockpot, and cover with 3 cups water. Add 2 teaspoons salt and bring to a simmer over high heat. Adjust heat to maintain a gentle simmer and cook, stirring occasionally, until the rice is tender and most of the grains have split open and started to unfurl, about 45 minutes; top off with water along the way if necessary. (Wild rice isn't really palatable until it gets to this point of doneness.) Drain and spread out on a rimmed baking sheet to cool.

Meanwhile, slice shallot into thin rings. Heat a medium skillet over medium-high. Pour in oil, then add shallot and cook, stirring, until dark golden brown and crisp, 4 minutes. Transfer to a small plate with a slotted spoon and season with salt and a pinch of cayenne. Wipe out the pan and return it to medium-high heat. Cook coconut chips, stirring continuously, until golden brown, 3 to 4 minutes. Transfer to the plate with shallot, season with salt, and let cool (they will darken and crisp as they sit). Cook the cashews, stirring, until golden brown in spots, about 5 minutes. Add them to the plate with coconut and shallot; season with salt.

Cut off the stem and bottom ends of the pomelo, then use a paring knife to score the skin from top to bottom, spacing the cuts about 1½ inches apart. Peel the pomelo, then pull it apart and use your fingers or the knife to peel back the membranes. Dig out the fruit in big pieces, transferring them to a serving bowl as you go. Add the lime juice and sugar and toss gently to combine and dissolve sugar. Add the cooled rice, shallot, cashews, and coconut chips. Roughly chop the cilantro leaves and stems and toss into the salad. Taste for salt and cayenne before serving.

From the Market	Spin It	At Home	Spin It
Wild rice	Replace the coconut chips with ½ cup kettle-cooked potato chips; don't cook them	Kosher salt	Anything spicy, like a dried Thai or chile de árbol, or a pinch of red pepper flakes, can be used instead of the cayenne
Dried coconut chips		Shallot	
Pomelo		Vegetable oil	
Cilantro	In place of the pomelo, use 2 grapefruits; add more sugar if bitter, or more lime juice if sweet	Cayenne	
		Cashews	
		Lime	Rice vinegar can be used instead of lime juice
		Sugar	

Sorry, I Like Celery

4 to 6 servings

All the flavors of a Caesar salad are here: garlic, anchovy, Parm, and olive oil, in quite outgoing proportions. The difference between this and a more textbook Caesar is not only that I've swapped out the romaine for fantastically crunchy celery, but also that this dressing is more of a free-flowing vinaigrette that coats every slice. Instead of croutons, there are tender, salty olives and vinegary peppers.

3 anchovy fillets packed in oil, drained

2 garlic cloves

Kosher salt; freshly ground pepper

¼ cup fresh lemon juice

¼ cup extra-virgin olive oil

½ teaspoon Aleppo pepper

10 Castelvetrano olives

6 piparra peppers

1 bunch celery (1 pound)

2 ounces Parmigiano

½ cup parsley leaves and tender stems

In a mortar and pestle or mini chopper, combine the anchovies and garlic with a big pinch of salt and many grinds of black pepper. Pulverize until a paste forms. (Alternatively, you can finely chop the anchovies and garlic together on a cutting board, then season with salt and black pepper and use the flat edge of the knife blade to smash the ingredients into a paste.) Scrape into a medium bowl and whisk in lemon juice, olive oil, and Aleppo pepper until combined. Taste and season with more salt and black pepper, if needed.

Use the flat side of a chef's knife to smash the olives and loosen the pits, then tear the flesh into 2 or 3 pieces (discard pits). Cut peppers in half lengthwise, then halve crosswise. Place the olives and peppers in a salad bowl. Trim the celery at both ends, then separate the bunch into individual stalks; wash and dry. Snap off the light green leaves from innermost stalks and set those aside. Cut the celery into very thin slices on a dramatic angle, then transfer to the bowl with the olives and peppers. Use a vegetable peeler to shave half the Parmigiano over. Add most of the dressing and toss with your hands to coat. Add the parsley and reserved celery leaves and toss gently to combine. Shave the other half of the Parm over, drizzle with dressing, and top with a few more grinds of black pepper.

From the Market	Spin It		At Home	Spin It
Castelvetrano olives	Another firm green olive, such as Cerignola or Lucques, can replace the Castelvetranos		Anchovies	Replace anchovy with 2 teaspoons Dijon mustard instead
Piparra peppers	Use pickled peperoncini instead of piparra peppers (peperoncini are spicier, though, so adjust as needed)		Garlic	White wine vinegar can replace the lemon juice
Celery			Salt and pepper	
Parsley			Lemon	
	Trade fennel, peeled celery root, kohlrabi, romaine hearts, or Little Gems for the celery		Olive oil	Gochugaru can replace the Aleppo pepper, or use ¼ teaspoon red pepper flakes
			Aleppo pepper	
	If you don't like parsley, leave it out		Parmigiano	Use Grana Padano instead of Parmigiano

Charred Broccoli with Spicy Avocado Sauce

4 servings

I am a huge broccoli fan, and it deserves a flavor profile outside of my usual and obviously Italian garlic–olive oil–chile flake scenario. Cutting it into long spears and searing it keeps the broccoli crunchy while softening its fibers a bit, and the creamy avocado sauce acts as a sort of dip. There's no reason to discard the broccoli stem, which has a radishlike crunch and sweet flavor. You can fork-and-knife this or eat it with your fingers.

2 avocados

Kosher salt; freshly ground pepper

¼ cup sour cream

2 tablespoons buttermilk

1 lime

1 serrano chile

5 tablespoons vegetable oil, divided

1 tablespoon raw hulled sunflower seeds

1 teaspoon coriander seeds

1 bunch broccoli (2 or 3 stalks, about 1¼ pounds)

Green hot sauce, for serving

Halve and pit the avocados, then scoop into a medium bowl and smash with a fork until chunky. Season with salt and pepper, add the sour cream and buttermilk, then use a whisk to beat into a slightly coarse puree. Taste and adjust the seasoning. Squeeze lime juice into a small bowl, then thinly slice the serrano and add it to the juice. Season with salt. Set avocado sauce and chile-lime mixture aside separately.

In a small skillet, combine 2 tablespoons oil, sunflower seeds, and coriander seeds. Cook over medium heat, swirling often, until the seeds are golden brown, 1 to 2 minutes. Use a slotted spoon to transfer seeds to a plate; season with salt and let cool. Save the coriander oil.

Trim the woody end from broccoli stalks, then peel with a vegetable peeler until you get down to the tender light green layer. Cut the stalks lengthwise through the crown into ½-inch-wide spears with florets and stalks attached. Some florets will break off, which is no big deal.

Place a large cast-iron skillet over high heat and add the coriander oil plus remaining 3 tablespoons oil. Working in batches if needed, add the broccoli to the pan, cut side down, and season with salt. Toss to coat, then arrange in a single layer and cook, undisturbed, until golden brown on the underside, 2 minutes. Turn and cook until the second side is browned, 2 minutes more. You want to slightly soften the broccoli and get good color on it.

Spread avocado sauce onto a platter. Spoon chile-lime mixture over, then place broccoli on top. Scatter seeds all over and add some dashes of hot sauce.

From the Market	Spin It		At Home	Spin It
Avocados	Any medium-hot fresh pepper can replace the serrano		Salt and pepper	Cow's milk, nondairy milk, or water can sub in for buttermilk
Serrano chile			Sour cream	
Broccoli			Buttermilk	Rice vinegar or lemon juice can replace the lime juice
	Try cauliflower, romanesco, or peeled carrots instead of broccoli		Lime	
			Vegetable oil	
			Sunflower seeds	Pepitas (pumpkin seeds) or unsalted peanuts are good alts for the sunflower seeds
			Coriander seeds	
			Hot sauce	

Spicy Cucumber and Watermelon with Pan-Fried Peanuts

6 servings

This quenching salad draws on ingredients and inspiration from Southeast Asia and treats watermelon as the key component in a savory dish. I mean it is a gourd! The dressing uses chiles, lime juice, and fish sauce, a combination prevalent throughout Thailand and Vietnam. That mixes with the sweet, crunchy melon and grassy, mild cucumbers to make a very juicy, subtly sour summer refresher. I'd eat this standing up in the kitchen for dinner during a heatwave, or alongside fatty grilled meats at a barbecue.

¼ cup peanut oil

½ cup unsalted peanuts

Kosher salt

Pinch of sugar

2 limes

¼ small red onion

1 small fresh Thai chile

5 Persian (mini) cucumbers, chilled

2 cups cubed seedless watermelon (from about ¼ small melon), chilled

Extra-virgin olive oil, MSG, fish sauce, and flaky salt, for serving

Heat peanut oil in a small skillet over medium, then add the peanuts and cook, shaking the pan often, until dark golden brown, 3 minutes. Use a slotted spoon to transfer them to a plate; season generously with salt and the sugar. Finely grate zest of 1 lime over the nuts while they're still hot; toss to coat, then let cool.

Thinly slice the onion and place in a medium bowl. Finely grate the chile over. Juice both limes directly into the bowl and season with salt. Toss to combine and set aside to marinate.

Place the cucumbers on a cutting board and smash lightly with a rolling pin, meat mallet, or pestle until the skins split and the cucumbers are a little bit flattened. Use your hands to tear cucumbers into fat strips, then transfer to a serving bowl and add the watermelon. Add onion mixture and toss, then add half the peanuts. Season with a drizzle of olive oil, some MSG, a few dashes of fish sauce, and flaky salt, as desired, then top with remaining peanuts.

From the Market	Spin It	At Home	Spin It
Thai chile	A serrano chile, half a small Scotch bonnet pepper, or a small jalapeño can replace the Thai chile, or crumble a couple dried Thai chiles into the mixture	Peanut oil	Use any neutral oil
Persian (mini) cucumbers		Unsalted peanuts	Unsalted cashews can replace the peanuts
Seedless watermelon		Kosher salt	
		Sugar	A large shallot can be used instead of red onion
	An English cucumber or lemon cucumbers can replace the Persian ones	Limes	
		Red onion	
		Olive oil	In a pinch, a dab of anchovy paste or a mashed-up anchovy fillet can be used in place of fish sauce; not the same, but still good
		MSG	
		Fish sauce	
		Flaky salt	

**Watercress with
Dijon Vinaigrette &
Purple Cabbage
and Parm**

Watercress with Dijon Vinaigrette

4 servings

This salad takes a mustardy green and pairs it with a mustardy dressing, for a bracing pepper-on-pepper effect. I love it on its own, but it's also super alongside a rich roast, like the tandem roasted chickens on page 137 or the pork and beans on page 198.

2 bunches watercress

¼ small red onion

1 tablespoon red wine vinegar

1 tablespoon sherry vinegar

Kosher salt; freshly ground pepper

1 tablespoon Dijon mustard

3 tablespoons extra-virgin olive oil

Nutritional yeast, for serving

Trim, wash, and dry the watercress. Keep chilled until ready to eat.

Finely grate onion into a medium bowl. Add both vinegars and season generously with salt and pepper. Let sit for 10 minutes, then add the mustard and whisk in oil.

Place the watercress in a serving bowl. Add the dressing and toss gently with your hands to coat. Top with a liberal sprinkling of nutritional yeast.

Best Cressed

There are a few types of stemmed baby watercress (often sold as "cresson") on the market these days. They're lovely, but too flimsy for this salad. You want the sturdy, stemmy stuff!

From the Market	Spin It	At Home	Spin It
Watercress	Escarole, arugula, baby mustard greens, radicchio, or endive can replace the watercress	Red onion	A shallot can be used instead of the red onion
Nutritional yeast		Red wine vinegar	
	Grated Parmigiano can be substituted for nutritional yeast	Sherry vinegar	Play around with a combination of vinegars, such as cider and white wine
		Salt and pepper	
		Dijon mustard	
		Olive oil	

Purple Cabbage and Parm

4 servings

When I was in my twenties and on a very tight budget (my rent gobbled up most of my take-home pay!), I lived on this salad. It's insanely simple—essentially a cabbage slaw with Parmigiano and a Dijon dressing—but it never let me down. It's filling, healthy, and affordable, with lots of great textures, and I could get everything I needed at the corner bodega. Because it's so crunchy, it takes a while to eat, which, at the time, was a way to trick myself into thinking I had more to eat than I did. I would make myself a huge bowl after getting home from work, sit in front of the TV, and chomp the night away.

2 tablespoons red wine vinegar

1 tablespoon Dijon mustard

1 garlic clove

Kosher salt; freshly ground pepper

1 medium purple (red) cabbage (about 1 pound)

3 tablespoons extra-virgin olive oil

3 ounces Parmigiano

In a small bowl, combine the vinegar and mustard; finely grate garlic into the bowl. Season with salt and pepper and whisk to combine. Let mixture sit while you prep cabbage.

Remove the outermost leaves (anything tough, wilted, or scraggly) from cabbage, then quarter it through the root. Cut quarters crosswise into ⅛- to ¼-inch-thick slices. Transfer to a salad bowl and season with a 4-finger pinch of salt; toss to disperse seasoning.

Whisk oil into vinegar mixture, then drizzle the dressing over the cabbage and toss very well with your hands to coat thoroughly. Use a vegetable peeler or the wide blade on a box grater to shave Parmigiano over salad (eyeball about ½ cup). Toss again to combine; the cheese will break into smaller pieces, which is fine. Taste and adjust the seasoning with salt and pepper, if needed.

From the Market	Spin It		At Home	Spin It
Purple (red) cabbage	Green cabbage, savoy cabbage, or napa cabbage can all be substituted for the red cabbage		Red wine vinegar	Try white wine vinegar, sherry vinegar, cider vinegar, or lemon juice in place of red wine vinegar
			Dijon mustard	
			Garlic	A diced small shallot can replace the garlic
			Salt and pepper	
			Olive oil	Grana Padano, Manchego, pecorino, or aged cheddar can replace the Parm
			Parmigiano	

Radishes and Croutons with Horseradish Dressing

4 servings

If you can't find radishes with greens, no worries. You can substitute 2 cups baby arugula,
baby kale, or radish sprouts for the radish tops.

1 bunch radishes (with greens)

Kosher salt; freshly ground
pepper

2 (½-inch-thick) slices crusty
bread

3 tablespoons extra-virgin olive
oil, plus more for drizzling

½ cup plain yogurt (Greek,
Persian, or regular)

1 tablespoon prepared
horseradish

1 tablespoon white wine
vinegar, plus more for serving

Flaky salt, for serving

Separate the radish greens from the radishes. Wash and dry the radishes and greens separately; set greens aside. Cut radishes into small wedges and soak in a bowl of salted ice water for at least 15 minutes (this will season them, mitigate some of their bite, and make them extra crunchy).

Meanwhile, cut or tear the bread into ½-inch pieces. Place in a large skillet and drizzle 3 tablespoons oil over. Squeeze the bread to help the oil saturate fully; season with kosher salt. Place the skillet over medium heat and cook, tossing frequently and pressing down on the bread with a wooden spoon to help it continue to soak up the oil and make contact with the pan's surface, until the croutons are dark golden brown and crisp, 5 to 7 minutes. Let cool in the pan, tossing occasionally.

Combine yogurt, horseradish, and vinegar in a small bowl and stir to combine. Taste and season with kosher salt and pepper.

Drain radishes and pat dry. Spoon the dressing onto a platter or into a large salad bowl. Arrange the radishes on top. Top with 2 cups of the radish greens (reserve any remaining greens for another use) and season them with a few dashes of vinegar and a drizzle of oil. Season the salad with some flaky salt and scatter the croutons over.

From the Market	Spin It		At Home	Spin It
Radishes	Use any radish you can find: Easter Egg, French, icicle, watermelon, daikon, and black radish are out there for the taking		Salt and pepper	Try sour cream or crème fraîche instead of the yogurt
			Crusty bread	
			Olive oil	A dollop of Dijon mustard can replace the horseradish
			Plain yogurt	
			Prepared horseradish	
			White wine vinegar	Cider vinegar or 2 teaspoons distilled white vinegar can be used instead of white wine vinegar
			Flaky salt	

Grab Some Olive Oil

I keep a large, round, bright pink plastic tray next to my stovetop. It has been there for more than twenty years, and it is filled with all of the things I cook with every day—vinegars, a dish of softened butter, my pepper mill, soy sauce, flaky salt, crushed red pepper flakes. But the thing I touch the most is the glass bottle of extra-virgin olive oil that stands proudly above the crowd. Since almost everything I make starts the same way, my hand and that bottle are comfortably linked through a series of repetitive motions that connects my intent with a reflexive action. A pot or skillet lands on the stovetop; burner clicks on; and my arm reaches instinctively for that bottle. It's topped with a bartender's spout; there's no cap to unscrew or lid to pop off. Even when I'm not sure exactly how the rest of the dish will come together, I upend the bottle and spin my wrist to send thick threads of oil across the surface of my pan. Whatever happens after that, happens. It's almost as if I'm not cooking unless I've doused olive oil all over the place.

Olive oil is both a cooking medium and a seasoning; you can cook vegetables in it and then drizzle more of it over them at the end. You can use it to confit vegetables, or to marinate them (like the tomatoes on page 217). Its flavor is prized on its own or as part of a sauce or dressing. I even rub it into my hands and lips when they're dry, and yes, there was that one summer in my teens when my best girlfriend, Chandra, and I used it as tanning oil (what can I say, we ran out of baby oil—it was the '80s!). I've been fortunate to learn from experts about how olive oil is made and I try to follow their rules: Always buy extra-virgin olive oil, ideally sourced from one country (as opposed to bottles that contain a multinational blend). Because olive oil oxidizes and changes flavor when exposed to air and light, buy it in smallish quantities and re-up often. Stick to a fairly neutral, versatile option for cooking, and something peppery and more vegetal for serving raw.

A couple of years ago, the green glass bottle that housed my olive oil got knocked over and shattered. I felt like I had broken a bone. That bottle was recycled from my mom's kitchen, and I had been filling and refilling it for two decades. I thought of it like a cast-iron skillet or steel blade—indestructible and permanent. When it broke, I felt suspicious about using any other, as though the bottle had mythical powers. Would my food still taste good? Would I lose my EVOO-mojo? I decanted into a new bottle, this one a little smaller than the original one. My hand got used to grabbing it. It's not the vessel, I told myself, it's what's inside and how you use it that counts. Then, while we were shooting the grilling chapter for this book, I knocked *that* bottle onto the pavers in my backyard and it, too, busted into a million pieces. I was able to salvage the bartender's spout, and the next time I saw my mom, I harvested yet another glass bottle from her pantry, closing the loop. I hope this bottle survives the next couple decades, but as long as the oil flows, good things will follow.

Chapter 5

Burning Clean

My husband coined this term before we were parents, when we spent many long, fun weekends eating and drinking and staying out late. On Mondays he would say, "Let's burn clean tonight," which meant we'd still eat (of course!), but healthfully. Years later, I still love to burn

Lentils, Greens, and Marinated Feta

4 servings

This vegetarian bean bowl makes epic leftovers for anyone looking to bring lunch to work the next day. Each element—the dressed lentils, the greens, and the marinated feta—can be stored separately in the refrigerator for at least 3 or 4 days. Lentils don't take that long to cook, but you can also start with canned (drained and rinsed) lentils, black beans, chickpeas, or small white beans.

1 cup black lentils (aka "caviar" or "beluga" lentils)

Kosher salt

2 teaspoons Dijon mustard

1 tablespoon cider vinegar

6 tablespoons extra-virgin olive oil, divided, plus more for drizzling

8 ounces feta

Crushed red pepper flakes, to taste

3 or 4 sprigs thyme and/or rosemary

2 bunches leafy greens, such as collards and/or Swiss chard

1 teaspoon brown or yellow mustard seeds

½ teaspoon ground turmeric

¼ teaspoon cayenne

Rinse lentils, then place in a medium pot and add cold water to cover by 2 or 3 inches. Season generously with salt and bring to a boil over high heat, then lower the heat and simmer gently until the lentils are barely tender, 20 to 30 minutes. In the meantime, whisk together the mustard and vinegar, then gradually whisk in 2 tablespoons oil; set dressing aside.

Marinate the feta: Slice it into ¼-inch-thick slabs, then break into large shards and place in a shallow dish. Season with red pepper flakes. Squeeze the thyme and rosemary to lightly bruise, then add them to the feta. Drizzle enough oil, then turn to coat.

Strip the greens from the stems, then slice leaves crosswise into ¼- to ½-inch-wide ribbons. (If using Swiss chard, reserve the stems for making Spiced and Braised Greens, page 221.) Wash and drain the greens. Don't shake off the excess water, which will help the greens wilt and steam in the next step.

Heat remaining 4 tablespoons oil in a large skillet over medium-high until starting to shimmer. Add the mustard seeds, turmeric, and cayenne and cook until the seeds start to pop, 1 to 2 minutes. Carefully add the greens (the oil will spatter a bit) and cook, tossing, until softened. Season with salt and cook, tossing occasionally, until the liquid has almost completely evaporated and greens are tender, 5 to 6 minutes.

Drain lentils, then transfer to a medium bowl and spoon the dressing over while they're still warm; stir to coat. Serve lentils and greens with a few pieces of marinated feta, drizzling any marinade over the top.

From the Market	Spin It		At Home	Spin It
Feta	Ricotta salata, Halloumi, or farmer's cheese can replace the feta		Black lentils	Use French green lentils or mung beans
Thyme and/or rosemary	Use whatever herbs you have lying around		Kosher salt	Any vinegar works
Leafy greens	Escarole, spinach, or any type of kale can be used for the greens		Dijon mustard	Fennel seeds or coriander seeds can replace the mustard seeds
			Cider vinegar	
			Olive oil	
			Red pepper flakes	Ground cumin can replace the turmeric
			Mustard seeds	
			Ground turmeric	Hot paprika can replace the cayenne
			Cayenne	

Pantry Eggs in Purgatory

4 servings

Typically, eggs in purgatory is eggs poached in a spicy tomato sauce—the red-hot cauldron being punishment for whatever sins the eggs have committed during their time in the carton, I guess. The method, which closely resembles shakshuka, will work with any pan sauce you feel like throwing together, as long as there's enough liquid to make sure things get steamy. For a weeknight dinner, a can of beans adds protein, fiber, and creaminess, and the parsley salad is not only a resourceful way to use up herbs, but also adds some nice cold/hot, fresh/saucy contrast to the dish.

4 garlic cloves

1 small onion

4 tablespoons extra-virgin olive oil, divided

Kosher salt; freshly ground pepper

½ teaspoon crushed red pepper flakes

1 tablespoon tomato paste

1 (15-ounce) can chickpeas

6 large eggs

2 cups parsley leaves and tender stems

1 lemon

3 tablespoons toasted sesame seeds

Slice the garlic cloves and finely chop the onion. Heat 3 tablespoons oil in a large (10-inch) skillet over medium, then add the garlic and onion and stir to combine. Season with salt, black pepper, and red pepper flakes and cook, stirring occasionally, until the onion is translucent and browned around the edges, about 5 minutes. Add the tomato paste and stir to coat, then cook until it has darkened a shade or two, 1 minute. Meanwhile, drain and rinse chickpeas. Add them to the skillet and season with salt. Pour in 1 cup water and bring to a simmer, stirring.

Add the eggs to the pan, one by one, spacing them out around the edge (try to fit 5 eggs around outer edge and put the sixth in the center). Season the eggs with salt. Reduce heat to low, cover the pan, and cook 4 minutes for runny yolks.

While eggs are cooking, roughly chop the parsley and place it in a medium bowl. Halve the lemon and squeeze its juice over the parsley, then season with salt and black pepper and toss to coat. Add the remaining 1 tablespoon oil and sesame seeds; toss gently together.

Spoon the eggs and sauce onto plates and top with parsley salad.

Green Team

A salad with Big-Batch Vinaigrette (page 276) goes nicely on the side, along with some bread for soaking up all the saucy juices.

From the Market	Spin It	At Home	Spin It
Parsley	This would work with basil instead of parsley, or any salad greens you like	Garlic	Harissa can replace the tomato paste (omit the red pepper flakes)
		Onion	
		Olive oil	
		Salt and pepper	
		Red pepper flakes	Cannellini or baby lima beans could replace the chickpeas
		Tomato paste	
		Canned chickpeas	Any crunchy seeds, like sunflower seeds or even poppy seeds, can be substituted for the sesame seeds
		Eggs	
		Lemon	
		Toasted sesame seeds	

Fernando's Famous Burned Broccoli

4 servings

My husband, Fernando, is famous for three dishes: cheesy eggs, something called "Daddy Pasta," and this broccoli, which he has been making for me since forever. I gave it a fancy name because he's fancy, but this is really just roasted broccoli and garlic that's been taken to the very edge of charred. It comes out very tender but crisp at the same time.

1 bunch broccoli (2 or 3 stalks, about 1¼ pounds)

8 garlic cloves, unpeeled

⅓ cup extra-virgin olive oil

Kosher salt; freshly ground pepper

½ teaspoon crushed red pepper flakes

Nutritional yeast, for seasoning

Preheat the oven to 450°F.

Trim the woody ends of the broccoli stems. Peel stems until you get down to the tender light green layer. Working from the bottom toward the crown, cut stems crosswise into ¼-inch-thick coins, stopping 2 to 3 inches from the base of the florets. Cut into florets with a length of stem attached. Transfer sliced stems and florets to a rimmed baking sheet. Smash the garlic cloves to split the skins and add them to the baking sheet with the broccoli. Drizzle oil over and toss to combine. Season with salt, black pepper, and red pepper flakes and toss again to combine. Spread it all out, turning the broccoli pieces onto their cut sides without being maniacal about it.

Roast until the broccoli is starting to get brown on the undersides, 15 minutes. Toss and roast until the broccoli has lots of charred bits around the edges and the garlic cloves are golden brown, 5 to 10 minutes more. Let cool slightly, then season with as much nutritional yeast as you like (I like *a lot*). Peel the garlic and serve the broccoli with grains, eggs, or alongside any type of cooked protein.

Broccoli Bowl

Serve this atop Blank-Slate Whole Grains (page 275), with a lemon or lime wedge for squeezing over.

From the Market	Spin It		At Home	Spin It
Broccoli	Use Broccolini instead of broccoli; trim the ends but leave the pieces otherwise intact		Garlic	A thinly sliced onion can be used instead of (or in addition to) the garlic
	Cauliflower or romanesco can replace the broccoli		Olive oil	Any spicy sprinkle can replace the red pepper flakes
			Salt and pepper	
			Red pepper flakes	Grated Parm can replace the nutritional yeast
			Nutritional yeast	

15-Minute Roasted Squash with Spicy Greens and Yogurt

4 servings

I don't know what it is about green and orange foods together, but it's a combination I always crave when I want to eat well, especially in the colder months. The grounding nature of butternut squash and sturdy greens, along with the crunch of the seeds and belly-warming spices in this dish, never gets old. I usually don't peel the squash, but if the skin feels especially thick or waxy to you, take it off. Placing the baking sheet at the bottom of the oven puts it closest to the heat source, which helps the squash roast super quickly.

1½ pounds butternut squash

⅓ cup extra-virgin olive oil, plus more for drizzling

1 teaspoon kosher salt, plus more for seasoning

1 bunch Tuscan kale

1 tablespoon unseasoned rice vinegar

¼ cup untoasted sesame seeds

¼ cup hulled sunflower seeds

½ teaspoon mustard seeds (any color)

¾ teaspoon crushed red pepper flakes

¾ cup Greek yogurt

Preheat the oven to 500°F with a rack in the lowest position.

Starting at the neck end and continuing to the belly end of the squash, cut squash crosswise into ½-inch-thick rounds, then scoop out the seeds with a spoon. Transfer the squash to a large rimmed baking sheet and drizzle generously with oil, turning to coat. Season both sides with salt, then arrange in a single layer. Roast on the bottom rack until the squash is tender and lightly browned around edges, 15 minutes (I don't even bother turning it, preferring to get one side as dark as possible).

While the squash roasts, use your hands to strip the kale leaves from the stems, then cut leaves crosswise into ¼-inch-wide ribbons. Wash and dry the leaves, then transfer to a large bowl. Drizzle vinegar over, then toss to coat.

Stir together ⅓ cup oil, sesame seeds, sunflower seeds, mustard seeds, and 1 teaspoon salt in a small skillet or saucepan. Place over medium-high heat and cook, swirling the skillet often, until the seeds are golden brown and starting to pop, about 3 minutes. Remove the skillet from the heat, quickly stir in the red pepper flakes, and immediately pour oil mixture over the kale—there will be a bit of spattering as the hot oil hits the moisture on the leaves, so take care with this step. Toss to combine.

Spoon the yogurt onto a platter or divide among four plates. Top with the roasted squash, then pile the sizzled greens on top.

From the Market	Spin It		At Home	Spin It
Butternut squash	Use acorn, koginut, or honeynut squash instead of butternut (no need to peel)		Olive oil	Lemon juice or cider vinegar are good replacements for the rice vinegar
Kale			Kosher salt	
			Unseasoned rice vinegar	
	Any type of kale can be used, but curly kale bunches tend to be larger, so you'll probably only need half a bunch		Untoasted sesame seeds	Try pepitas slivered almonds, and/or chopped hazelnuts, in place of any of the seeds
			Sunflower seeds	
			Mustard seeds	Fennel seeds, cumin seeds, or coriander seeds can replace the mustard seeds
			Red pepper flakes	
			Greek yogurt	

Tomato Soup in the Style of Sauce

2 to 4 servings

You know how sometimes you're eating spaghetti with a delectable fresh tomato sauce, and when you get to the bottom of the bowl, there are no noodles left, but just enough sauce for a last little forkful or swipe of bread? This soup is meant to re-create that perfect bite, but you get a whole bowlful. I wouldn't use canned tomatoes for this; they'll wind up tasting thin and acidic because of the abbreviated simmering time.

3 pounds beefsteak tomatoes

6 garlic cloves

⅓ cup extra-virgin olive oil, plus more for serving

Kosher salt; freshly ground pepper

½ teaspoon crushed red pepper flakes, plus more for serving

Handful basil leaves, stems attached

Flaky salt, for serving

Quarter and core the tomatoes, then transfer them to a food processor. Pulse in short bursts until finely chopped, taking care not to aerate or liquefy them in the process. (Alternatively, pass the tomatoes through the medium disc of a food mill.) Set aside.

Thinly slice the garlic. Combine garlic and ⅓ cup oil in a medium saucepan, then place over medium heat. Season with kosher salt and black pepper and cook, stirring frequently, until the garlic is pale golden and starting to crisp. Use a slotted spoon to transfer the garlic to a small plate. Spread the slices out so they're not overlapping and set aside for topping the soup.

Add the tomatoes to the pan with the garlic oil and season with kosher salt and red pepper flakes. Add the basil and stir to combine. Raise the heat to medium-high and simmer, stirring occasionally, until the mixture is reduced by about half and tomatoes are tender, 16 to 18 minutes. Pluck out the basil. Taste and adjust the seasoning. Ladle the soup into bowls and top with garlic chips and a pinch of flaky salt. Drizzle with more oil and pass more red pepper flakes at the table.

From the Market	Spin It	At Home	Spin It
Beefsteak tomatoes	Peak-season beefsteak tomatoes are excellent, but large heirloom types are a level-up substitute	Garlic	Use any type of crushed red pepper you like: Ordinary red pepper flakes are pretty spicy; Aleppo pepper, Urfa biber, and gochugaru are less so
Basil	Use ripe plum tomatoes instead of beefsteaks	Olive oil	
		Salt and pepper	
	Any type of basil would work— Thai, purple, Italian, etc.	Red pepper flakes	If you don't have flaky salt, finish the soup with a little kosher salt
		Flaky salt	

Chickpea Pancakes with
Shaved Vegetables &
Watermelonade (page 275)

Chickpea Pancakes with Shaved Vegetables

4 servings

The starting point for this recipe is the Mediterranean chickpea pancake called socca, which is delicate enough to feel light, while satisfying enough to be a base for a meal. When made the typical way, using only chickpea flour, they are gluten-free, but they're also so tender that I personally have a hard time turning them over without tearing them. I added a little bit of all-purpose flour to help with structure and some mashed chickpeas for heft. You get a soft but toasty pancake on the bottom, a cold and crisp salad on top, and plenty of dressing to flavor everything on the plate.

FOR THE PANCAKES

1 cup chickpeas (from one 15-ounce can)

½ cup chickpea flour

¼ cup all-purpose flour

¾ teaspoon kosher salt

2 tablespoons extra-virgin olive oil

FOR THE VEGETABLES AND ASSEMBLY

1 medium watermelon radish (4 to 5 ounces)

1 fennel bulb

2 Persian (mini) cucumbers

Kosher salt

2 tablespoons fresh lime juice

1 tablespoon toasted sesame oil

2 teaspoons extra-virgin olive oil, plus more for drizzling

2 avocados

1 ounce sprouts, such as pea or mung bean

2 tablespoons toasted sesame seeds

MAKE THE PANCAKE BATTER: Rinse and drain the chickpeas. Transfer to a medium bowl and roughly smash with a fork or potato masher.

In a medium bowl, whisk together the chickpea flour, all-purpose flour, and salt. Add 2 tablespoons olive oil and 1 cup water and whisk until no lumps remain (batter will seem thin but will thicken up). Let sit for 20 minutes to hydrate the flour. Stir in the smashed chickpeas.

PREP THE VEGETABLES AND ASSEMBLE THE PANCAKES: Meanwhile, scrub the radish. Cut the tops off the fennel bulb; save them for stock or discard. Thinly slice the radish, fennel, and cucumbers (I use a mandoline for this, or cut them as thinly as possible with a knife). Transfer them to a medium bowl and season with salt. Using your hands, toss vegetables, squeezing lightly, until they start to exude some juices and become pliable, about 1 minute. Drizzle the lime juice over and toss to disperse, then add the sesame oil and 2 teaspoons olive oil and toss until the vegetables are evenly coated with dressing.

Halve and pit avocados, then scoop the flesh into a medium bowl and season with salt; smash very lightly with a fork.

Batter Up

The pancake batter should be thin enough to easily spread and coat the skillet; if it's too thick, adjust with a couple tablespoons of water. If it still seizes up, reduce the heat under your pan and let it cool for a minute before trying again.

Place a medium (8-inch) nonstick pan over medium-high heat and drizzle lightly with olive oil. When oil is very hot, about 15 seconds, scoop a scant ⅓ cup batter into the pan, then immediately tilt the skillet in all directions so the batter spreads out into a round. Cook until the underside is deeply browned and many air bubbles have broken across the entire surface, about 2 minutes. Turn and cook until browned on the second side, 1 minute more. Slide pancake onto a plate. Wipe out the skillet and repeat with additional oil and remaining batter to make 4 pancakes total (you won't have to wait for the oil to heat up after the first pancake is done, and subsequent batches might cook a little bit faster than the first).

Add the sprouts to the vegetable salad and toss gently to coat with dressing. Place the pancakes on individual plates and top with avocado, dividing it evenly, then add the salad and sprinkle with sesame seeds.

From the Market	Spin It	At Home	Spin It
Chickpea flour	To make these gluten-free, use ¾ cup chickpea flour and omit the all-purpose flour	Canned chickpeas	Baby lima or cannellini beans can replace the chickpeas
Watermelon radish		All-purpose flour	
Fennel	Instead of chickpea flour, use ¼ cup whole-wheat flour	Kosher salt	A neutral oil like grapeseed can replace the olive oil
Cucumbers		Olive oil	
Avocados	Any crunchy vegetables can be used, including radishes, asparagus, turnips, carrots, and/or cabbage	Limes	Rice vinegar or fresh lemon juice can replace the lime juice
Sprouts		Toasted sesame oil	
		Toasted sesame seeds	A nut oil, such as walnut or hazelnut, can be substituted for the sesame oil, or use extra-virgin olive oil
	A crisp apple can replace the fennel		

Flash-in-the-Pan Chicken with Burst Tomato Sauce

2 servings

Despite their enduring popularity, boneless, skinless chicken breasts can be very disappointing. They're quite lean—which is what some people love about them—and that's exactly what can cause them to be bland and dry. But when they're good, they bring power to the paillard. Cooking them almost all the way through on one side will result in a chewy crust and superlative browning, and prevents the chicken from overcooking. If you go a tiny bit over, the bright and juicy tomato pan sauce will camouflage your mistakes.

2 boneless, skinless chicken breasts (10 to 12 ounces total)

Kosher salt; freshly ground pepper

1 large shallot

3 garlic cloves

Handful chives

5 tablespoons extra-virgin olive oil, divided

Pinch of crushed red pepper flakes

2 cups cherry tomatoes (12 ounces)

2 tablespoons red wine vinegar

Pat the chicken breasts dry and season both sides with salt and black pepper. Place them between two sheets of waxed paper or plastic wrap and, using a rolling pin or meat mallet, pound them out to about ¼ inch. Thinly slice the shallot into rings, thinly slice the garlic cloves, and thinly slice the chives. Set all these things aside separately.

Heat a large skillet over medium-high. Add 3 tablespoons oil, then place the chicken in the skillet. Press down on the cutlets firmly with a spatula to ensure the chicken is making good contact with the surface of the pan, then cook, undisturbed, until the underside is deep golden brown and there is a thick band of cooked flesh around the edge, 4 to 6 minutes. About halfway through, lift up the cutlets from one corner and let oil flow underneath, then place them back down. Turn cutlets and cook until light golden brown on second side and just cooked through, 1 to 2 minutes more. Transfer the chicken to a plate.

Lower the heat to medium and add the remaining 2 tablespoons oil. Add the garlic and shallot and cook, stirring, until the shallot is translucent and garlic is starting to turn light golden brown, 1 to 2 minutes. Season with salt and a pinch of red pepper flakes. Add the tomatoes and cook, stirring occasionally, until their skins start to shrivel, 4 minutes. Using the back of the spoon, gently smash tomatoes until they split open and release their juices (don't flatten them, simply encourage them to burst), then cook until slightly saucy, 2 minutes more. Add the vinegar and stir to combine. Remove from the heat and stir in chives. Spoon burst tomato sauce over chicken cutlets.

From the Market	Spin It	At Home	Spin It
Chicken breasts	This works with 4 boneless, skinless chicken thighs or pork medallions	Salt and pepper	Half a red onion can replace the shallot
Chives		Shallot	
Cherry tomatoes		Garlic	Use sherry vinegar instead of red wine vinegar
	Basil, dill, tarragon, or parsley can replace the chives	Olive oil	
		Red pepper flakes	
	A chopped large tomato or two can replace the cherry tomatoes	Red wine vinegar	

Soft Tofu and Clam Soup

4 servings

I love the contrast of slippery, silky tofu and chewy, briny clams in this soup, a combination I fell in love with when I had haemul sundubu jjigae for the first time at Jenny Kwak's Korean restaurant Dok Suni (sadly now closed) in New York City's East Village. Everyone should keep sheets of kombu in their pantry for making an umami-rich broth anytime, and the method here is as pared-down as it gets (lacking the dried anchovies, onion, and mushrooms that would amplify a proper version).

2 ounces kombu

24 littleneck clams

2 bunches scallions

1 pound soft silken tofu

1 tablespoon vegetable oil

2 anchovy fillets packed in oil, drained

2 tablespoons mirin

1 tablespoon soy sauce

Toasted sesame oil, gochugaru, and toasted sesame seeds, for serving

Place the kombu in a medium stockpot and cover with 8 cups water. Let soak 25 minutes while you prep the rest of the ingredients. Place clams in a colander and scrub with a coarse vegetable brush or scrub pad under cold running water. Be thorough; there's almost nothing worse than biting into a gritty clam. Transfer to a bowl, cover with cold water, and let soak 5 minutes, then lift the clams out of the water so that the grit stays behind, and return the clams to the colander to drain.

Separate white and green parts of scallions. Thinly slice them crosswise and set aside in separate bowls. Drain the tofu; cut into 4 pieces.

Bring the kombu and its soaking water to a boil over high heat, then immediately turn off the heat. Pour the broth through a fine-mesh strainer set over a large bowl; discard kombu. Set the broth aside.

Rinse the pot, dry it, and return it to medium-high heat. Add the oil, then the scallion whites and anchovies. Cook, stirring, until the scallions have softened and anchovies are dissolved, 2 to 3 minutes. Add the mirin and soy sauce and stir to combine. Add the clams and stir to coat, then pour in 6 cups kombu broth. (Store extra broth in the refrigerator for up to 2 days or freeze for up to 3 months.)

Add the tofu to the pot and stir very gently to combine without breaking it up. Bring to a simmer, then cover the pot and cook until the clams open, 6 to 8 minutes; discard any that refuse to unhinge. Taste the soup and season with more soy sauce, if needed. Serve topped with scallion greens, a drizzle of sesame oil, gochugaru, and some sesame seeds.

From the Market	Spin It		At Home	Spin It
Kombu	In a pinch, use instant dashi powder instead of kombu broth		Vegetable oil	If you have dried anchovies, add 10 to the water along with the kombu in the first step
Littleneck clams			Anchovies	
Scallions			Mirin	
Tofu			Soy sauce	
	Mussels or manila clams can be substituted for the clams		Sesame oil	To replace anchovies, add a few dashes of fish sauce in the last step
			Gochugaru	
	1 large shallot can replace scallion whites		Toasted sesame seeds	

Spicy-Tangy Green Beans and Tofu

2 generous servings

My younger son, Cosmo, is an on-again, off-again vegetarian, but even when he's in an omnivore phase, he's always psyched for tofu. (He's proof you can be both a sugar fiend and a tofu enthusiast.) Pressing the liquid out of firm tofu condenses it and helps it get crisp—tearing it creates irregular pieces that get as crunchy as popcorn shrimp. Pressing the tofu only takes about 15 minutes; start your prep with this step and by the time you have the rest of the ingredients measured out, it will be ready to go.

14 ounces firm or extra-firm tofu

1 pound green beans

1 large bunch scallions (12 scallions)

1½-inch piece ginger (about 1 ounce)

¼ cup mirin

2 tablespoons soy sauce

2 tablespoons gochujang

1 tablespoon black vinegar

⅓ cup vegetable oil

Kosher salt

Drain the tofu and cut it lengthwise into 6 planks. Place a clean kitchen towel on a baking sheet, with plenty of overhang. Arrange tofu in a single layer on the towel, then fold the towel over to cover. Place another baking sheet on top, then put a heavy skillet, Dutch oven, or a few big cans of tomatoes on top to weigh it down, for 15 minutes. The towel will absorb the excess liquid.

In the meantime, trim the stem ends of the green beans, then halve the beans on an angle. Trim the scallions, then slice the white and green parts into ¼-inch-thick rounds. Peel and finely grate the ginger. Set beans, scallions, and ginger aside separately.

In a small bowl, whisk together the mirin, soy sauce, gochujang, and vinegar. Go time! Heat the oil in a large high-sided skillet over medium-high until shimmering. Tear tofu into jagged ¾-inch pieces. Working in two batches, add the tofu to the pan in one layer and cook, undisturbed, until dark golden and crisp on the underside, 5 to 6 minutes. Toss tofu to release, then turn onto other side and cook until browned, 4 minutes more. Use a slotted spoon to transfer the tofu to a large plate; season lightly with salt. Repeat with remaining tofu.

Return skillet to medium-high heat and add the green beans, scallions, and ginger. Season with salt and toss to coat. Cook, tossing occasionally, until the vegetables are very well browned and slightly shriveled but still have some juiciness, 4 to 6 minutes. Pour in the mirin mixture and simmer until a little bit thickened, 1 minute. Return tofu to the skillet and stir to coat, 30 seconds.

From the Market	Spin It		At Home	Spin It
Firm tofu	Any other snap bean, such as sugar snaps or snow peas, can replace the green beans; or use thinly sliced carrots, broccoli spears or Broccolini, and/or asparagus		Ginger	In a pinch, combine 1 tablespoon each miso paste and sriracha and use as a stand-in for the gochujang
Green beans			Mirin	
Scallions			Soy sauce	
			Gochujang	
			Black vinegar	Sherry vinegar or malt vinegar can be substituted for the black vinegar
			Vegetable oil	
			Kosher salt	

Seared Sweet Potatoes with Kale and Lime Pickle

2 servings

Sweet potatoes are the foundation for this vegetarian dinner that's both filling and virtuous. I put a hard sear on the sweet potatoes to add another dimension to their, well, sweetness and leaned hard on lime pickle to bring dynamic flavor to the kale. If you haven't had it, lime pickle is a fermented Indian condiment of salted and spiced limes (there's a similar pickle made with lemons, too). The spices vary depending on which region of India the pickle is from, but it often contains ginger, mustard seeds, red chiles, and asafetida. It's pungent and sour, and I salivate just thinking about it.

3 small sweet potatoes (1 pound)

½ cup walnuts

⅔ cup labneh

1 lime

Kosher salt; freshly ground pepper

2 tablespoons Indian lime pickle

2 bunches Tuscan kale

3 tablespoons extra-virgin olive oil, divided

Fill a medium pot with a few inches of water and fit it with a steamer basket. Bring water to a simmer over medium-high heat. Scrub the sweet potatoes, then steam, covered, until they're completely tender when pierced with a cake tester or skewer, 20 to 25 minutes.

Meanwhile, preheat oven or toaster oven to 350°F. Toast the walnuts on a small rimmed baking sheet until they're a couple of shades darker and fragrant, 10 minutes, tossing halfway through. Dump onto a cutting board and let cool. Place labneh in a medium bowl. Cut the lime in half and squeeze its juice into the labneh. Season with salt and pepper and stir to combine. In a small bowl, stir together the lime pickle and a couple splashes of water to loosen.

Using your hands, strip the kale leaves from the stems; tear leaves into 2- to 3-inch pieces. Wash kale; spin dry. Heat a large nonstick skillet over medium-high, then pour in 2 tablespoons oil. Add the kale, season with salt and pepper, and cook, tossing occasionally, until wilted, bright dark green, and browned in spots, 6 to 7 minutes. Stir in the lime pickle mixture and toss to coat. Transfer to a medium bowl; wipe out the skillet.

When potatoes are cool enough to handle, remove their skins and tear flesh into large pieces. Return the skillet to high heat; pour in the remaining 1 tablespoon oil. Add the sweet potatoes, season with salt, and press down to flatten. Cook, undisturbed, until charred in spots on the underside, 3 minutes. Turn and cook until charred on the second side, 2 minutes more.

Spread the lime labneh onto two plates, dividing it evenly. Top with the kale and sweet potatoes. Sprinkle walnuts over, crushing them with your hands to break them into smaller pieces.

From the Market	Spin It	At Home	Spin It
Sweet potatoes	Greek yogurt or skyr can replace the labneh	Walnuts	Almonds or cashews can replace the walnuts
Labneh		Lime	
Indian lime pickle	Indian lemon pickle or spicy mango pickle can be used instead of lime pickle	Salt and pepper	Use lemon juice instead of lime juice
Tuscan kale		Olive oil	
	Any type of kale, such as curly green or red Russian, is fine		Any neutral oil can be substituted for olive oil

the recipes

friday and the weekend

Chapter 6

Day Drinking
& Lazy Lunches

A weekend of kicked-back meals can require as little of you as a quick weeknight dinner, but enjoying them can extend for hours. More time to chill, no reason to stress

Cold Sliced Steak with Arugula and Parm

4 servings

People talk about a "hot juicy steak" as the height of steak enjoyment, but there's something to be said for a cold or room-temperature version. This flavor combo is based on a classic Italian presentation—arugula, Parm, olive oil—and I added a shortcut Caesar sauce to link the pleasantly chewy steak with the sharp and salty toppings. If you want to make the steaks a day ahead, don't slice them; let cool, then wrap and refrigerate. Let them sit at room temperature for a couple of hours before slicing and serving.

2 (1½-inch-thick) boneless New York strip steaks (about 2 pounds total)

Kosher salt; freshly ground pepper

Extra-virgin olive oil, for drizzling

3 anchovy fillets packed in oil, drained

1 garlic clove

1 lemon

½ cup mayonnaise

2 cups baby arugula

4 ounces Parmigiano, for shaving

Flaky salt, for serving

Season steaks generously on both sides with kosher salt and pepper. (You can do this an hour or two in advance and let the steaks sit at room temperature. Or refrigerate them, uncovered, for 2 to 3 days.)

Heat a large heavy skillet over medium-high and drizzle with a thin coating of oil. Place the steaks in the pan on the fatty edge and cook until the fat starts to render, 1 to 2 minutes. Turn steaks onto a flat side, press down, and cook, turning every 2 to 3 minutes, until they are very dark brown and crisp and a thermometer inserted into the center registers 115° to 120°F for medium-rare. On the first or second turn, the steaks won't be that browned, but turning them frequently will help them cook more evenly, and they will eventually pick up fabulous color. Transfer to a small rimmed baking sheet or dinner plate and let steaks rest until they're at room temperature, about 30 minutes.

At any point while the steaks are resting, mince the anchovies, then sprinkle with some kosher salt and pepper and scrape the edge of your blade back and forth against the anchovies to smash them into a paste on your cutting board. Scrape into a medium bowl and finely grate the garlic and zest half the lemon over. Cut the lemon in half and squeeze the juice into the bowl. Add the mayo and stir to combine. Taste sauce and season with kosher salt and pepper.

Thinly slice the steak against the grain and transfer to a platter. Drizzle with sauce. Scatter arugula over, then use a vegetable peeler to shave Parmigiano over. Drizzle with oil and top with a few pinches of flaky salt.

From the Market	Spin It	At Home	Spin It
New York strip steaks	Tender, not-too-fatty cuts of steak, like Denver steak, tri-tip, or top sirloin, can be used in place of New York strip	Salt and pepper	Season the mayo with a little fish sauce instead of the anchovies
Baby arugula		Olive oil	
		Anchovies	Any crumbly salty cheese, such as feta, Halloumi, pecorino, ricotta salata, or even aged cheddar, can replace Parm
	Instead of baby arugula, chop mature arugula, or use endive, mustard greens, or watercress	Garlic	
		Lemon	
		Mayonnaise	
		Parmigiano	
		Flaky salt	

123 Day Drinking & Lazy Lunches

Tomatoes with Thyme and Fried Capers

6 servings

This is a variation on a fail-safe formula: raw tomatoes plus herbs plus salt. Frying the capers (the salt in the equation) causes them to crisp and unfurl like a popcorn kernel. I prefer salted—as opposed to brined—capers for this; their texture is a little meatier and they tend to be bigger and fatter. The hot oil they were cooked in is then added to the thyme leaves in the dressing, which tempers and blooms the herbs.

2½ pounds tomatoes, any types

1 teaspoon flaky salt, plus more for seasoning

2 bushy sprigs thyme, or more as needed

2 tablespoons capers

¼ cup extra-virgin olive oil, plus more for serving

1 lemon

Cut the tomatoes into shapes and sizes that make you happy, such as slicing the big guys crosswise or into wedges if you're feeling that, cutting the little ones in half, or even leaving some of the smallest ones whole. Your salad, your choice! Transfer them to a big platter as you go, then season liberally with flaky salt. Let sit to get the juices going.

Pick the leaves from thyme sprigs (you should have about 2 tablespoons—if not, pick more thyme!). Combine the thyme and 1 teaspoon flaky salt in a mortar and pestle and pound until the leaves look dark and wet, and the mixture resembles a fine, crumbly paste, about 3 minutes. (You can use a mini chopper or a spice grinder for this; if you don't have those, finely chop the thyme and combine it with salt in a small bowl.)

Rinse the capers, if salted, or drain them if they're brined. Heat oil in a small skillet over medium-high, then add the capers. Cook, swirling skillet often, until the capers sizzle, burst open, and turn golden brown inside and out, about 2 minutes. Pour fried capers and their oil over the pounded thyme and stir to combine. Let cool until warm, a few minutes, then spoon thyme mixture over the tomatoes. Cut the lemon in half and squeeze juice over. Drizzle salad with more oil. This is killer straight out of the gate, but also very desirable if it sits for an hour or two at room temperature. Tilt the platter and spoon the accumulated juices over the tomatoes before serving.

From the Market	Spin It	At Home	Spin It
Tomatoes	Use rosemary, lavender leaves, or marjoram instead of the thyme	Flaky salt	Use kosher salt instead of flaky salt
Thyme		Capers	Use 3 chopped anchovies instead of the capers
		Olive oil	
		Lemon	A couple tablespoons of any type of vinegar can be used in place of the lemon juice

Spicy Seafood Stew

4 to 6 servings

Telling you to use homemade fish stock or assuming you can buy a really good-tasting one are two truly unlikely scenarios, let's be real. Instead, the base of this soup rests on shrimp shells, plus coriander, cumin, and some onion. You add layers of compatible flavors on top of those ingredients as the soup cooks: A cilantro puree amplifies the coriander seed; fennel and jalapeño complement the cumin; and shrimp and cod soak it all up as they poach in the broth.

🕐 Get Ahead

I wasn't expecting this to be the case when I was working on this recipe, but because I had leftovers, I discovered that this soup is weirdly enjoyable when it's been chilled—almost like a cold, green, seafood gazpacho. The recipe makes four to six servings, but if you're cooking for only one or two people, make the whole amount for dinner, then have it again—without reheating—the next day.

1 pound shell-on large shrimp

2 teaspoons coriander seeds

1 teaspoon cumin seeds

1 large onion

4 tablespoons extra-virgin olive oil, divided

Kosher salt; freshly ground pepper

1 jalapeño

1 cup cilantro leaves and stems

4 anchovy fillets packed in oil, drained

6 garlic cloves

1 fennel bulb

8 ounces small potatoes

1 pound skinless cod

Lime wedges, for serving

Use a pair of shears to snip down the outer, curved side of the shrimp, then peel off the shell and tail, reserving them. Put the shrimp on a small plate or in a container, cover, and chill until ready to use.

Lightly crush the coriander and cumin seeds. Quarter the onion and cut out the root. Heat a medium (3-quart) saucepan over medium-high. Add 1 tablespoon oil, the shrimp shells and tails, the coriander and cumin, and one-quarter of the onion. (Hang on to the other 3 wedges of onion.) Cook, stirring, until the shells are bright red and the spices are popping, 2 to 3 minutes. Carefully pour in 8 cups water (it will sputter when it hits the pan) and season with salt and pepper. Bring to a simmer, then lower the heat and simmer gently until the stock is lightly flavored, 30 minutes. Strain stock, discarding solids, and set aside.

Meanwhile, roughly chop the jalapeño and place it in a blender with the cilantro, anchovies, 2 garlic cloves, and 1 tablespoon oil. Remove the fennel fronds from the bulb and roughly chop half of them (reserve the remainder for serving); add to the blender. Season with salt and pepper. Pour in 1 cup cold water and blend on high until smooth.

Thinly slice remaining onion quarters. Halve and thinly slice the fennel bulb. Thinly slice remaining 4 garlic cloves. Scrub the potatoes. Heat the remaining 2 tablespoons oil in a medium pot over medium-high. Add the onion, fennel, and garlic, stir, and season with salt and pepper. Lower the heat to medium, partially cover the pot, and cook, stirring occasionally, until the vegetables are very soft and starting to brown, 10 to 12 minutes. Add the stock and bring to a simmer. Add the potatoes; season with salt and pepper. Lower the heat to medium-low, partially cover the pot, and simmer gently until the potatoes are tender, 16 to 18 minutes.

Meanwhile, cut the cod into 2-inch pieces.

Stir the jalapeño-cilantro puree into the stew. Add the cod and shrimp and reduce the heat to low. Cover the pot and cook very gently just until the fish and shrimp are cooked through, 2 to 3 minutes. Serve the stew topped with a squeeze of lime juice and some reserved fennel fronds.

From the Market	Spin It	At Home	Spin It
Shrimp	Smaller shrimp can be used; they cook quickly, so add the cod first	Coriander seeds	Fennel or caraway seeds can replace the cumin seeds
Jalapeño		Cumin seeds	
Cilantro		Onion	
Fennel bulb	Replace jalapeño with ½ serrano	Olive oil	2 or 3 shallots can sub in for the onion
Potatoes		Salt and pepper	
Cod	Swap basil for cilantro	Anchovies	
	Hake, pollack, or sable can be used in place of cod	Garlic	
		Lime	

Zucchini Fritter of My Dreams

Spicy Seafood Stew

Zucchini Fritter of My Dreams

Makes 10 to 12 fritters

Trying to love zucchini is like forcing yourself to finish a very long, boring book that everyone else loved . . . so you keep plodding away, even though you aren't into it. My feelings about zucchini are on public record: They're basically water in vegetable form. Ironically, I love love love *zucchini fritters, but in order for them to get crunchy, you need to coax out as much liquid as possible. That happens in stages here: first by salting and squeezing; then by cooking over moderately high heat to force evaporation; and finally by drying out the fritters in the oven after they're fried. If you want to love zucchini, you have to put in the time.*

4 medium zucchini (1½ pounds total)

1 medium Yukon Gold potato (½ pound)

2 teaspoons kosher salt, plus more for seasoning

¼ cup all-purpose flour

¼ cup potato starch

1 teaspoon baking powder

1 cup lightly packed basil leaves (about ½ ounce)

2 large eggs

1 garlic clove

1 teaspoon cumin seeds

½ cup grated Monterey Jack (about 2 ounces)

½ cup vegetable oil, divided

Flaky salt and lemon wedges, for serving

Cut the zucchini in half crosswise, then into thin planks lengthwise. Stack 3 or 4 planks and cut them into long strips to make thin matchsticks. Scrub and peel the potato, then cut it into thin matchsticks as you did the zucchini. Cutting (rather than shredding) the zucchini will prevent it from becoming a soupy mess, which makes for a crispier fritter. Transfer zucchini and potato to a colander or large sieve and season with 2 teaspoons kosher salt. Toss to coat, squeezing lightly to soften the vegetables and encourage them to start releasing liquid; some of your nice long strips might break in half while you do this, and that's okay. Let sit 15 minutes.

Meanwhile, whisk together the flour, potato starch, and baking powder in a small bowl. Roughly chop the basil and beat it with the eggs in a medium bowl. Finely grate garlic into the eggs, then add the cumin and potato starch mixture; whisk to combine (batter will be thick). Season with kosher salt; set aside.

Squeeze excess liquid from the zucchini-potato mixture. It should release quite a lot. Transfer vegetables to a large clean kitchen towel, then twist the towel over the sink to wring out even more liquid, as much as you possibly can. Open up the towel, fluff the vegetables, and squeeze again. So. Much. Squeezing. The vegetables should be very floppy, matte, and limp. Transfer them to the batter along with the cheese and toss to coat. There will be just enough batter to thickly coat everything.

Preheat the oven to 325°F. Fit a rimmed baking sheet with a wire rack.

I Dip, You Dip

Hot and crispy fritters love cool tangy sauces. Pair these with the Lemony Yogurt on page 276.

Heat ¼ cup oil in a large cast-iron skillet or shallow Dutch oven over medium to medium-high until a pinch of the batter bubbles energetically within a few seconds of being added. Working in three batches, scoop ¼-cupfuls of the batter into the hot oil and press down to flatten fritter to about ¼ inch. Cook until golden brown and crisp on the underside, 3 to 4 minutes, then turn, press down again, and cook until the second side is golden brown, 2 to 3 minutes more. Browning the fritters gradually will help drive off some of the moisture; lower the heat if things are moving too fast. Transfer to the prepared rack to drain; repeat with remaining batter, replenishing oil as needed.

Transfer fritters on rack (atop baking sheet) to the oven and bake until they're a couple of shades darker and crisp around the edges, 30 to 35 minutes. Serve fritters hot, seasoned with flaky salt, with lemon wedges alongside for squeezing over.

From the Market	Spin It	At Home	Spin It
Zucchini	Summer squash can be used instead of zucchini	Kosher salt	A small shallot can replace the garlic
Yukon Gold potato	A russet (aka Idaho) potato can replace the Yukon Gold	All-purpose flour	Try coriander seeds, fennel seeds, red pepper flakes, or ½ teaspoon ground turmeric for the cumin
Potato starch	Make this with 2 pounds potato and omit the zucchini for a potato pancake	Baking powder	
Basil	If you don't have potato starch, use ½ cup all-purpose flour or cornstarch instead	Eggs	Cheddar or feta can replace the Monterey Jack
	Any type of basil can be used, or substitute mint, dill, chives, and/ or fennel fronds	Garlic	Use kosher salt if you don't have flaky salt
		Cumin seeds	
		Monterey Jack	
		Vegetable oil	
		Flaky salt	
		Lemon	

Extremely Green Grain Salad

4 servings

More broccoli content! A hardworking grain salad can be a veg, a side, and a starch all in one. This one combines chewy farro with crunchy bits of raw broccoli and a sassy herb dressing, brightened by fresh ginger juice. Heads up to all you raisin haters (I know you're out there): This dish has secret raisins for sweetness.

1½ cups farro

1 tablespoon kosher salt, plus more for seasoning; freshly ground pepper

⅓ cup extra-virgin olive oil, plus more for drizzling

1 bunch broccoli (2 stalks, about 1 pound)

1 bunch scallions (5½ ounces)

Small bunch basil (about 2 ounces)

Handful flat-leaf parsley

3-inch piece ginger (about 2 ounces)

½ cup unsalted cashews, toasted, divided

1 lime

¼ cup golden raisins

Rinse farro, then place in a medium pot and cover with 6 cups water. Add 1 tablespoon salt and a drizzle of oil and bring to a boil over medium-high. Lower the heat and simmer, stirring occasionally, until the grains are tender but still have a little chew, 35 to 45 minutes. Drain and spread out on a rimmed baking sheet or large plate to cool, tossing occasionally. (Save the grain-cooking liquid! It's very flavorful and can be added to soups or used to cook beans or another batch of grains.)

While farro cooks, trim woody ends of the broccoli stems, then peel the stems. Roughly chop the broccoli stems and florets. Transfer broccoli to a food processor and pulse until finely chopped (or do this by hand). Transfer to a medium bowl. Wipe out the processor bowl.

Bring a small pot of water to a boil; season with salt. Trim scallions, then cut into 3-inch lengths. Boil scallions until softened and tender, 3 minutes. Use a slotted spoon to transfer them to a plate. Roughly chop the basil and parsley, then boil until wilted and tender, 2 minutes. Add herbs to plate with scallions. When cool enough to handle, squeeze excess liquid from scallions and herbs.

Finely grate the ginger, then place it in a small strainer set over a small bowl and press with the back of a spoon to release the ginger juice. You should have a scant 1 tablespoon juice.

Pulse ¼ cup cashews in food processor until finely chopped, then add the scallions and herbs. With motor running, drizzle in ⅓ cup oil. Cut lime in half and squeeze in juice. Add the ginger juice, then process the dressing until emulsified. Taste and season with salt and pepper.

Combine the grains, broccoli, and dressing in a large bowl. Roughly chop raisins and remaining cashews; add to bowl. Toss to combine. Taste salad and adjust the seasoning.

From the Market	Spin It		At Home	Spin It
Broccoli	Use Broccolini, any type of snap bean, or asparagus instead of broccoli		Farro	Use your fave whole grain: Brown rice, bulgur, rye berries, barley, and teff are all good choices
Scallions			Kosher salt	
Basil			Olive oil	
Parsley			Ginger	
Golden raisins	If you hate raisins, use dates, dried apricots, currants, dried gooseberries, or barberries		Cashews	Almonds, pecans, hazelnuts, or walnuts can replace the cashews
			Lime	

Roasted Red Bell Peppers with Garlic Chips and Sumac

8 servings

These peppers are spicy, smoky, garlicky, and slippery. I love spearing a couple strips and then nudging a bite of roast chicken or crispy-skinned fish onto the same forkful. Sweet, soft, and charred, the peppers get better as they sit in their marinade, and you can leave them at room temperature all day on the day you make them, spooning the juices and garlic oil over them every now and again. They also hold for about a week in the fridge—slap them onto a sandwich or chop them up and add to a tomato sauce.

3 large red bell peppers

3 garlic cloves

⅓ cup extra-virgin olive oil

Kosher salt; freshly ground pepper

1 teaspoon Urfa biber

1 teaspoon ground sumac

Leaves from 2 sprigs oregano

Sherry vinegar

Flaky salt, for serving

Place the bell peppers directly on top of stovetop gas burners set to medium-high. Cook, turning with tongs every couple of minutes, until completely carbonized on all sides, 13 to 15 minutes. Initially, the skin will crinkle and char, then it will blacken, then become thick and crusty with a pale, almost iridescent gray sheen to it—that's what you're looking for. (If you don't have a gas stove, broil the peppers on a rimmed baking sheet, turning every few minutes, to the same end point. You can also do this on a charcoal or gas grill.) Transfer peppers to a large bowl and cover; let sit 10 to 15 minutes. They will steam as they cool, which will make them easier to peel.

Meanwhile, thinly slice garlic and combine in a small saucepan with the oil. Season with kosher salt and pepper and place over medium heat, stirring so the garlic slices don't stick to each other. Cook until the garlic is lightly but evenly golden brown, 3 to 5 minutes. Remove from the heat and stir in Urfa biber and sumac. Let cool in pan.

Using your hands and a sheet of paper towel (or a kitchen towel that you don't mind potentially staining), rub off pepper skins. Rip peppers in half and scrape out seeds; discard stems and seeds. Tear or cut peppers into wide strips (I follow the natural pleats in the flesh). Toss in a medium bowl with a spoonful of the garlic-chile oil and half the oregano; season with kosher salt and pepper. Transfer to a large wide bowl or platter and spoon remaining garlic-chile oil over, then season with a few splashes of sherry vinegar. Sprinkle remaining oregano over and top with a little flaky salt.

From the Market	Spin It	At Home	Spin It
Red bell peppers	Any color sweet pepper is fine	Garlic	Use red wine vinegar or cider vinegar instead of sherry vinegar
Urfa biber	Instead of Urfa biber, use Maras or Aleppo pepper, or gochugaru	Olive oil	
Ground sumac		Salt and pepper	
Oregano	Instead of sumac, use the same amount of finely grated lemon zest	Sherry vinegar	
	Basil, tarragon, or chervil can replace the oregano	Flaky salt	

The Tandem-Roasted-Chicken Trick

6 to 8 servings

There are a million roast chicken recipes out there, but what most of them don't tell you is that one chicken isn't enough. A sole bird will feed three, maybe four people, and it is therefore always worth it to roast two at a time. With a hot oven and a basic seasoning mix, you will have juicy, burnished chickens in an hour. You don't need any special equipment, it doesn't take more time, and having leftover chicken is a gift.

2 tablespoons kosher salt

2 tablespoons dried oregano

1 teaspoon cayenne

2 (3½- to 4-pound) whole chickens

Extra-virgin olive oil, for drizzling

Preheat the oven to 425°F.

In a small bowl, mix salt, oregano, and cayenne. Fit a rimmed baking sheet with a wire rack, then place chickens on top. Season all sides and inside the cavities with spice mix, then drizzle with olive oil and rub it in evenly. Place the baking sheet in the oven and carefully pour in enough water to cover entire surface (about 1½ cups should do it; this will prevent drippings from burning during roasting and throws a little bit of steam into the oven). Roast until the skin is browned and crisp and a thermometer inserted into the thickest part of the breast registers 155°F, about 55 minutes. Let sit 20 to 30 minutes before carving.

More Is More

Leftover chicken is the stuff quesadillas, salads, fried rice, and work lunches are made of. Save the carcasses, too, which can be simmered with vegetable scraps to make stock.

From the Market	Spin It	At Home	Spin It
Chickens	Use chicken parts instead of whole chickens; start checking for doneness after 35 minutes	Kosher salt Oregano Cayenne Olive oil	Play around with the spices, combining something earthy or herby with something hot and/or smoky: cumin and paprika; turmeric and Aleppo pepper; dried rosemary and black pepper, etc.

Brothy Basil Beans

6 to 8 servings

One thing I've learned about beans is that some types fall apart when they're cooked no matter what you do. It's not your fault! Some beans have very thin, delicate skins and a fine texture. On the other side of the spectrum are chubby white beans, like gigante, Tarbais, and baby limas. They are naturally predisposed to stay intact on the outside and get super creamy inside, and that's desirable here. As they cook, they'll absorb the flavor of the basil in the cooking liquid. But listen—if your beans fall apart, it won't ruin the dish. The broth might be a little thicker—no big deal!

1 pound dried large white beans, such as gigante, soaked overnight if possible

1 tablespoon kosher salt, plus more for seasoning; freshly ground pepper

6 garlic cloves, unpeeled, divided

1 shallot (skin on), halved

¼ cup extra-virgin olive oil, plus more for drizzling

1 medium bunch basil (4 ounces), divided

¼ cup raw (natural) almonds

1 lemon

Place beans in a medium pot and cover with cold water by several inches (if they're soaked, no need to drain; go ahead and cook the beans in their soaking liquid, adding more water to cover if needed). Add 1 tablespoon salt, 3 garlic cloves, the shallot, a few healthy glugs of oil, and half the basil (including stems). Bring to a boil over high heat, then lower the heat to a very gentle simmer. Cook uncovered, stirring occasionally, until the beans are extremely tender and creamy but not falling to bits, about 1 hour (unsoaked beans will take longer). If the water level gets low, top it off and adjust heat to keep the simmer extremely mellow.

Meanwhile, bring a medium pot of salted water to a boil. Add the remaining 3 garlic cloves and the almonds and cook until slightly softened, 5 minutes. This will diffuse some of the garlic's bite and bring out its sweetness, and blanching softens the almonds so they become smooth in the sauce. Transfer to a small plate with a slotted spoon and let cool. Pluck the leaves from the remaining basil (aim for about 1 cup packed). Stir basil into the boiling water and cook until wilted, 1 minute. Transfer basil to the plate with the garlic and almonds and spread it out to cool. Peel garlic and transfer to a food processor. Pinch almond skins to release nuts (kind of like you're popping an edamame out of the pod); add the almonds to the processor. Finely grate zest of the lemon into processor and pulse until the nuts and garlic are finely chopped, 30 seconds. Squeeze out excess liquid from basil and add it to the processor, along with ¼ cup oil. Blend until the pesto is creamy; taste and season with salt and pepper and blitz again to combine.

Pluck out basil stems and shallot from the beans. Serve beans and their broth topped with spoonfuls of pesto.

From the Market	Spin It		At Home	Spin It
Dried large white beans	Baby lima beans, Tarbais beans, cannellini beans, corona beans, or chickpeas can all replace the gigante beans		Salt and pepper	Use unsalted cashews, peanuts, walnuts, hazelnuts, or shelled pistachios instead of the almonds (blanch any of them, too)
Basil	Cilantro or chives can be used instead of basil		Garlic	
			Shallot	
			Olive oil	
			Almonds	
			Lemon	

Fried Mushrooms with Zesty Chile Salt

6 appetizer servings

Deep-frying can be intimidating—as a method, it's simple enough, but it's a lot of hot oil to cool down and deal with afterward. For this fritto-misto-meets-tempura-ish fried mushroom recipe, I experimented with a shallow fry, which I was pretty sure wouldn't turn out well. Shock and surprise: It worked. The batter crisps and the mushrooms cook through perfectly even though they're not totally submerged.

FOR THE CHILE SALT

1 teaspoon kosher salt

1 teaspoon freshly ground pepper

1 teaspoon MSG

1 teaspoon cayenne

1 lemon

FOR THE MUSHROOMS

1 pound maitake mushrooms

1 to 2 cups peanut oil or other vegetable oil, for frying

½ cup all-purpose flour

½ cup rice flour (not sweet rice flour)

1 teaspoon baking powder

1 teaspoon kosher salt

1¼ to 1½ cups seltzer or club soda (10 to 12 ounces)

MAKE THE CHILE SALT: In a small bowl, combine the salt, pepper, MSG, and cayenne. Finely grate zest of lemon into the bowl, then use your fingertips to mix the spice mixture together thoroughly. Cut lemon into wedges and set aside.

MAKE THE MUSHROOMS: Trim the woody ends of the mushrooms, then tear petals into 2- to 3-inch clusters. Fit a rimmed baking sheet with a wire rack or line it with paper towels. Pour enough oil into an 8-inch cast-iron skillet or other high-sided heavy pan to reach a depth of ¼ inch. Heat over medium-high until the oil reaches 375°F.

Meanwhile, in a medium bowl, whisk together all-purpose flour, rice flour, baking powder, and salt. Gently whisk in 1¼ cups seltzer until the batter is almost homogenous (a few lumps are okay). It should resemble heavy cream; add more seltzer if needed.

Working in three or four batches, add the mushrooms to batter and turn to coat completely. Use chopsticks or a fork to lift them out, letting excess batter drip back into the bowl. Carefully lower battered mushrooms into hot oil, adding only as many mushrooms to the pan as will fit without touching one another (they'll fuse together if given the opportunity). Cook until the batter is very crisp and dark golden and mushrooms are tender, about 4 minutes, turning once halfway through. Use chopsticks, tongs, or a slotted spatula to transfer mushrooms to the prepared baking sheet; season generously with chile salt. Squeeze lemon over. Top off oil in the pan if needed and return it to 375°F. Repeat with the remaining mushrooms and chile salt. These are pretty irresistible right out of the fryer, so make a few, nibble on a few, and make more, until they're gone.

Party Flavor

If the rest of your menu is hands-off, an appetizer like this one is an awesome party starter. I love having people huddled around the end of my kitchen counter waiting for the next batch of mushrooms to be ready, and we eat these with one hand (with a cocktail in the other) as soon as they're cool enough to pick up.

From the Market	Spin It		At Home	Spin It
Maitake mushrooms	Use oyster mushrooms or shiitakes instead of maitakes		Salt and pepper	An equal amount of mushroom powder can replace the MSG, or omit
Rice flour			MSG	
Seltzer	Try this with small pieces of butternut squash, thinly sliced fennel or sweet potato, small peeled shrimp, or zucchini rounds		Cayenne	Use chile powder or hot smoked paprika instead of cayenne
			Lemon	
			Peanut oil	
			All-purpose flour	Lime can replace the lemon
			Baking powder	

Low-and-Slow Spiced Chicken Legs with Garlic Crunch-Crumbs

6 servings

After slow-roasting, this chicken will pull right off the bone and the skin will be paper-thin and crisp, and I love how the super-tender, deeply spiced dark meat contrasts with the aggressively crunchy, garlicky bread crumbs on top. Minced, deep-fried garlic is a common topping in Chinese cuisine and is often paired with delicate or soft foods. My approximation was inspired by the mounds of it that were served with the roast chicken on the bone I used to get at Dim Sum Go Go in New York City. Combining the garlic with panko—though not typical—makes browning it less tricky.

6 chicken leg quarters (thigh and drumstick; about 4½ pounds total)

Kosher salt

2 star anise pods

1 teaspoon fennel seeds

2 teaspoons Sichuan peppercorns

¼ cup vegetable oil, plus more for drizzling

6 garlic cloves

1 cup panko bread crumbs

MSG, for seasoning

Preheat the oven to 300°F. Pat chicken legs dry and arrange in a single layer on a rimmed baking sheet or in a large cast-iron skillet. Season generously on both sides with salt.

Break star anise pods into individual petals. Pulverize star anise, fennel seeds, and peppercorns in a mortar and pestle until a fine powder forms (you should have about 1 tablespoon; alternatively, use a spice grinder). This will take many minutes of smashing and bashing if using a mortar and pestle. Get into it.

Drizzle chicken with oil to coat, then season on both sides with spice mixture, using all of it. Arrange skin side up and roast (without turning it) until skin is golden brown and crisp and the meat is extremely tender, 2½ to 3 hours. Tilt baking sheet and spoon any accumulated juices and rendered fat over chicken, then roast 30 minutes more.

Meanwhile, finely grate or mince the garlic. Heat ¼ cup oil in a large (preferably nonstick) skillet over medium-high until shimmering. Add the panko, season with salt, and stir well to coat panko with oil. Cook, tossing often, until the panko is golden brown and crisp, 4 to 5 minutes. Add the garlic and toss to combine. The garlic is going to want to clump up and stick to itself; smash down on it with a wooden spoon to help break it up and get it to mix into the panko. Cook, tossing, until the garlic is light golden and crumbs are very fragrant, 3 to 4 minutes more. Don't overbrown or burn the garlic, which will make it taste bitter. Season crunch-crumbs with MSG and transfer to a plate to cool.

Cut chicken legs between joint to separate drumsticks from thighs; transfer to a platter. Drizzle any pan juices over, then let it rain crunch-crumbs, piling them high.

Crumb Section

This recipe makes a generous amount of garlic crunch-crumbs. Save extras to sprinkle over any type of noodle dish, a tomato salad, steamed fish or eggplant, a bowl of beans, or roasted cauliflower.

From the Market	Spin It		At Home	Spin It
Chicken legs	Use same weight of any chicken pieces		Kosher salt	Coriander or cumin seeds can replace fennel
Star anise			Fennel seeds	
Sichuan peppercorns	Use 1 cinnamon stick instead of the star anise		Vegetable oil	Fresh bread crumbs can replace panko; crisp them in 300°F oven first
	Use black peppercorns instead of Sichuan peppercorns		Garlic	
			Panko	
			MSG	Substitute mushroom powder for the MSG, or omit

Braised Short Rib Noodle Bowl

Braised Short Rib Noodle Bowl

6 to 8 servings

The marinade for these shreddy ribs has a lot of the ingredients you could expect to find in a Thai curry—ginger, lemongrass, shallots, chiles—but the liquid part of the marinade drifts into a sweet and sour direction with vinegar, mirin, and soy. I definitely recommend marinating overnight since the ribs are cut into such thick pieces; doing so will both flavor and tenderize the beef. Serve them with their sauce over noodles doctored with crunchy radishes, chiles, and chile paste.

FOR THE SHORT RIBS

3 pounds boneless short ribs, cut 1½ to 2 inches thick

1 tablespoon kosher salt, plus more for seasoning

6-inch piece ginger (about 4 ounces)

3 lemongrass stalks

3 shallots

1 large or 2 medium jalapeños

8 garlic cloves

1 tablespoon freshly ground pepper

¼ cup mirin

¼ cup black vinegar

2 tablespoons soy sauce

Vegetable oil, for the pan

TO ASSEMBLE

3 small watermelon radishes (about 1 pound total)

2 jalapeños

½ cup unseasoned rice vinegar

Kosher salt

20 ounces fresh ramen noodles

Vegetable oil, for drizzling

Sambal oelek, for serving

MAKE THE SHORT RIBS: Season meat on all sides with salt. Place on a rimmed baking sheet or in a lasagna pan and set aside.

Peel and roughly chop ginger. Trim off the top third of the lemongrass stalk and peel off the tough outer layers. Using the blunt edge of a chef's knife, smack the lemongrass along the length of the stalk to bruise it (this will help release its essential oils). Thinly slice stalks crosswise. Roughly chop shallots. Stem, seed, and roughly chop jalapeños. Combine ginger, lemongrass, shallots, jalapeño, garlic, and pepper in a food processor and process until finely chopped, 30 seconds. Scrape down bowl and process until mixture is very finely chopped and almost pastelike, 1 minute more, scraping down bowl as needed. Add the mirin, vinegar, and soy sauce and process to combine. Smear marinade all over meat, using all of it (it will seem like a lot).

From the Market	Spin It		At Home	Spin It
Boneless short ribs	Boneless pork shoulder or boneless, skinless chicken thighs can replace the short ribs (the cook time for the chicken will be about 1½ hours)		Salt and pepper	Use sake in place of mirin
Ginger			Garlic	Lime juice can replace the vinegar
Lemongrass			Mirin	
Shallots	Use galangal instead of ginger		Soy sauce	Sriracha or another hot sauce can be used instead of sambal oelek
Jalapeños			Vegetable oil	
Black vinegar	Use a small red onion instead of the shallots		Rice vinegar	
Watermelon radishes			Sambal oelek	
Ramen noodles	A smaller quantity of serranos can replace the jalapeños, or use whatever fresh hot chile you like			

Cover and refrigerate overnight.

Preheat the oven to 325°F.

Scrape any excess marinade from ribs (reserve the marinade). Heat a large Dutch oven over medium and drizzle in enough oil to coat the surface with no bald spots. Working in two batches, brown ribs, turning them every few minutes to get color on all sides, until very well browned all over, 22 to 25 minutes. (Could you crank the heat and go hotter and faster? Sure. Would all the tasty bits from the marinade burn and ruin the braise? Yep. Mirin has sugars that can go quickly from caramelized to scorched, so watch the pan. If your bits start to char, lower the heat.) Transfer ribs to a plate.

Add the reserved marinade to the pot and cook, stirring and scraping continuously with a wooden spoon, until the marinade has darkened and most of the liquid has cooked off, 2 to 3 minutes (again, don't let it burn). Add 3 cups water and bring to a simmer, using the spoon to loosen any browned bits from the surface of the pot, 2 minutes more. Return ribs to the pot, along with any accumulated juices. The liquid should come about three-quarters of the way up the meat; add more water if needed. Cover the pot and transfer to the oven. Cook until the meat shreds easily when you tug at it with a fork or pair of tongs, 2½ to 3 hours.

Remove pot from oven and let ribs sit for 15 to 20 minutes, then use two forks or a pair of tongs to break the meat into smaller pieces. Stir to coat with braising liquid. Taste and season with salt.

ASSEMBLE THE DISH: While the short ribs are cooking, peel the radishes, then cut them into thin matchsticks. Cut the jalapeños into thin rounds. Combine radishes and jalapeños in a small bowl and pour vinegar over. Season with salt and stir to dissolve. Let sit, stirring occasionally.

Bring a large pot of salted water to a boil. Cook noodles according to package instructions. Drain and toss with a little oil to prevent them from sticking.

Gently reheat ribs over medium heat. Serve noodles and ribs with radish-jalapeño mixture and sambal oelek for doctoring each bowl.

Chapter 7

I Love to Grill

I grew up watching my mom grill, and she inspired me to do the same. There's nothing I love more than cooking outside, especially over live fire. Grilling is like any other kind of cooking—a balance between heat and time—and I believe anyone can do it!

Spice-Crusted Pork Spareribs

4 to 6 servings

Grilling over medium heat is the saner, wiser approach to cooking fatty cuts of meat. Rather than jumping all around your backyard like a maniac while flames shoot vertically from your grill grates, a lower temperature lets you savor the outdoor cooking experience without incinerating dinner. As these ribs cook, the spices clinging to their surface will slowly toast and darken while fat from the ribs sizzles around them. The only trick is to make sure you've got a generous bed of coals when you get started, since they become valuable to you only as their heat is waning. As much as I love using 100% lump hardwood, ordinary charcoal briquettes are really useful here—they burn steadily and evenly for a long time. Gas grillers: Dial into medium heat and stay there.

3 tablespoons coriander seeds

2 tablespoons black peppercorns

1 tablespoon crushed red pepper flakes

2 slabs St. Louis–style pork ribs (5 to 6 pounds total)

3 tablespoons kosher salt

Extra-virgin olive oil, for drizzling

Handful cilantro and/or mint, for serving

Lime wedges, for serving

Roughly crush the coriander seeds, peppercorns, and red pepper flakes in a mortar and pestle or in a spice grinder, making sure to preserve some discernible texture.

Cut between the bones to separate the rack into individual ribs. Place them on a large rimmed baking sheet and season all over with the salt (use every bit). Season evenly with the spice mixture, turning to coat. Drizzle ribs with olive oil and turn again to coat. Refrigerate the seasoned ribs, uncovered, for up to 2 days. Alternatively, let sit at room temperature until it's time to grill, up to 2 hours.

Prepare a grill for medium direct heat with a generous amount of coals. I usually fill up a charcoal chimney, light it, and spread out an equivalent amount of coals in the grill kettle. When the coals in the chimney are glowing orange, I pour them over the unlit charcoal and wait until everything has burned down enough that I can hold my hand 6 inches above the grates for a few seconds without recoiling in pain. That's medium hot! (If you use a gas grill, set it to medium heat.) Clean and oil grill grates. Grill the ribs, turning them every 3 to 4 minutes, until evenly and deeply browned, and crisp, 28 to 32 minutes. Regardless of whether you find yourself cooking on a fire escape or perched atop a vast rolling hill, this is enough time to joyously commune with nature while the aromas of smoky pork fat and toasted spices waft through your hair. Enjoy your special moment.

Transfer ribs to a platter and top with herbs. Serve with lime wedges for squeezing over.

Pre-Game

It is worth planning ahead for several of the grilling recipes in this chapter. Seasoning the meats a day or more in advance gives them ample opportunity to absorb the spices and become properly salted. Without giving it that time, the seasoning will sit on the surface. While the exterior crust might have some sass, the interior will be unsalted and spice-free.

From the Market	Spin It		At Home	Spin It
St. Louis–style pork ribs	You can use baby back ribs, spareribs, or country-style ribs for this		Coriander seeds	Sub fennel seeds, anise seeds, cumin seeds, or mustard seeds for the coriander (or combine them!)
	Boneless beef short ribs, cut ½ inch thick, also work		Black peppercorns	
			Red pepper flakes	
			Kosher salt	Use Sichuan peppercorns in place of black peppercorns
			Olive oil	

Crispy Smoky Rice

4 servings

The only thing better than rice is crispy rice, as anyone who has chomped into the socarrat on paella, the tahdig on Persian rice, or the crust on the outside of a yaki onigiri can tell you. I was inspired by all of those rice preparations when I started working on this alfresco side dish. Getting a crackly burnished layer of rice is extremely simple when you start from already-cooked rice. Once you've got your skillet on the grill, all you need to do is sauté some mushrooms, add the rice, press it into the pan, and let it ride. Doing this over live fire should impart some smoky aromas, but you can also make this on a stovetop over medium heat.

8 ounces shiitake mushrooms

7 tablespoons vegetable oil, divided

Kosher salt

2 tablespoons tomato paste

3 cups cooked short-grain rice, cooled (from about 1½ cups uncooked)

Soy sauce, for serving

Prepare a grill for medium-high direct heat.

While the grill comes up to temperature, stem the mushrooms and slice caps crosswise into ¼-inch-wide pieces.

Set a large cast-iron skillet directly on grill grates and heat until very hot, about 4 minutes. Add 3 tablespoons oil and mushrooms and season with salt. Cook, tossing often, until the mushrooms have taken on color similar to the skin of a russet potato and started to soften, 4 to 6 minutes. Add the tomato paste and cook, stirring, until the paste darkens a shade or two, 1 to 2 minutes. Add the rice and remaining 4 tablespoons oil; stir and toss to coat rice with oil and tomato paste and to disperse mushrooms. Position the skillet over even heat and use a spatula to press and compact the rice into an even layer. Cook, shifting skillet often to help rice cook evenly and pressing down every couple of minutes, until the rice is very brown and glassy on the underside, 8 to 10 minutes. (Look for signs of browning on the outside edge of the rice; once it is starting to brown, you should be able to lift it up at the edge to see what's happening underneath.)

Let the rice sit off the heat for a few minutes to help it release, then invert it onto a large plate. Break it into big pieces with a spoon and season with a few dashes of soy sauce.

From the Market	Spin It		At Home	Spin It
Shiitake mushrooms	This would be equally excellent with oyster, maitake, chanterelle, chestnut, and/or morel mushrooms		Vegetable oil Kosher salt Tomato paste Rice Soy sauce	To make this spicy, use harissa in place of the tomato paste, or use 1 tablespoon of each Cooked long-grain white rice can be used instead of short-grain A few dashes of Maggi seasoning sauce can replace the soy sauce

Charred Flatbreads with Whipped Ricotta, Mushrooms, and Scallions

Charred Flatbreads with Whipped Ricotta, Mushrooms, and Scallions

6 to 8 servings

These flatbreads are truly not complicated to make and can be seasoned with whatever spice you like—I've done them up with crushed red pepper flakes, ground turmeric, and paprika. They're grilled in minutes and are a toasty, smoky vehicle for all types of toppings—in this case, mushrooms—held together by seasoned ricotta. To fast-track the process, purchase pocketless pita or lavash, or even use sliced crusty bread instead.

FOR THE FLATBREADS

1 cup (120 g) whole-wheat flour

1 cup (120 g) bread flour, plus more for dusting

1 tablespoon (8 g) kosher salt

2 teaspoons (about 5 g) cumin seeds

1 teaspoon (4 g) baking soda

1 teaspoon (4 g) sugar

½ teaspoon (2 g) baking powder

¾ cup (170 g) Greek yogurt

2 tablespoons (30 ml) extra-virgin olive oil

FOR THE TOPPINGS AND ASSEMBLY

1 cup fresh ricotta

5 tablespoons extra-virgin olive oil, divided, plus more for drizzling

Kosher salt; freshly ground pepper

1 lemon

2 pounds maitake or oyster mushrooms

1 bunch scallions

½ cup finely chopped parsley

MAKE THE FLATBREADS: In a medium bowl, whisk together both types of flour, salt, cumin seeds, baking soda, sugar, and baking powder. Add the yogurt, oil, and ¼ cup (56 ml) water and stir until the dough comes together with some shaggy dry bits in the bottom of the bowl. Turn it out onto a lightly floured work surface, dust with a little flour, and knead until the dough is smooth and feels evenly hydrated, 2 to 3 minutes. Transfer to a clean bowl and cover; let rest at room temperature for at least 20 minutes (and up to several hours).

PREP THE TOPPINGS AND ASSEMBLE: Meanwhile, in a small bowl, whisk together the ricotta and 1 tablespoon oil. Season with salt and pepper and finely grate lemon zest over (reserve remaining lemon). Whisk again to combine. Taste ricotta and season with more salt and pepper, if needed. Chill until ready to serve (or cover and refrigerate for up to several days).

From the Market	Spin It	At Home	Spin It
Whole-wheat flour	You can use only all-purpose flour; the breads will be more fluffy and less chewy	Salt and pepper	You can experiment with any spice in place of the cumin seeds (see recipe headnote)
Bread flour		Cumin seeds	
Greek yogurt	If you have regular (i.e., not Greek) yogurt, decrease the water by half	Baking soda	
Fresh ricotta		Sugar	Neutral oil can replace the olive oil
Maitake or oyster mushrooms	Fresh goat cheese can replace the ricotta	Baking powder	
Scallions		Olive oil	A splash of vinegar can replace the lemon juice (in which case, omit the lemon zest)
Parsley	A couple of Mexican green onions can replace the scallions	Lemon	
	Use mint, basil, and/or cilantro instead of parsley		

Rain Check Method

To make these indoors, sauté the mushrooms in olive oil, or choose a different seasonal vegetable and roast at 450°F—vegetables of most varieties will be suitable, such as cauliflower, broccoli, winter squash, Brussels sprouts, red onions, beets, carrots, or radishes. Leftover cooked vegetables can also be excellent! Instead of grilling the flatbreads, cook them one at a time in a lightly greased cast-iron skillet over medium-high heat, turning them once halfway through.

Prepare a grill for medium-high direct heat. Clean and oil grill grates. Trim the ends off the mushrooms and scallions, place on a rimmed baking sheet, and drizzle generously with oil. Season with salt and pepper and toss to coat. Working in batches if needed, grill the mushrooms and scallions, turning frequently, until tender and dark brown with some charred spots, 10 to 12 minutes for scallions and 14 to 16 for mushrooms. Transfer to a cutting board. Roughly chop the mushrooms and finely chop the scallions. Combine in a medium bowl and season with the juice from half the zested lemon; add the parsley. Taste and season with salt and pepper if needed.

Return grill to medium-high heat, if needed. Divide dough into 4 pieces. Working with one at a time on a lightly floured surface, roll out dough with a lightly floured rolling pin to a 9-inch round. Brush dough round with 1 tablespoon oil and place, oiled side down, on grill grates. Grill until the dough stiffens and is golden brown on underside, and air bubbles appear across the top, 1 to 2 minutes. Turn flatbread with tongs and cook until the second side is also browned, about 1 minute more.

Place one flatbread on a work surface and top with one-quarter of the ricotta mixture and one-quarter of the scallions and mushrooms. Drizzle with oil and cut into wedges to serve. Repeat with the remaining dough, oil, and toppings.

Grilled Squid with Blackened Tomatoes

6 servings

This dish comes together during a series of cumulative, though simple, steps. First, you make a charred tomato base, then add grilled scallions and a spice-infused oil, then finally grill the squid and lay it to rest on the tomato mixture. I personally enjoy hanging at the grill for the time it takes to get from start to finish. I stole the blackened tomato trick from Francis Mallmann's book Seven Fires, *and the method of blooming the spices in oil is an essential Indian cooking technique called tarka or tadka (also known as chhonk or vagar). It's foolish to pick favorite recipes from one's own book, so let's just say I'll never ever get sick of making this one.*

2 pounds squid (bodies and tentacles)

2 teaspoons pimentón de la Vera (smoked Spanish paprika)

6 tablespoons extra-virgin olive oil, divided, plus more for drizzling

2 pounds beefsteak tomatoes

1 bunch scallions

Kosher salt; freshly ground pepper

1 teaspoon cumin seeds

1 teaspoon coriander seeds

Prepare a grill for high direct heat.

While the grill heats, combine the squid, pimentón, and 3 tablespoons oil in a large bowl or rimmed baking sheet and turn to combine.

Clean and oil grill grates. Place a medium cast-iron or other heatproof skillet directly on the grates and let it preheat, 5 minutes. Cut tomatoes in half through the equator and place them in the dry, hot skillet, cut side down. Cook until the cut surface is very charred and the flesh is starting to collapse, 8 to 10 minutes. Use a spatula to scrape the tomatoes off the skillet and transfer them to a cutting board. Let cool.

Meanwhile, drizzle scallions with oil and season with salt and pepper. Grill, turning occasionally, until softened and dark brown, about 4 minutes. Transfer to the cutting board with tomatoes. Tear the tomato flesh into pieces, discarding the cores and skin and transferring to a platter as you go. Season tomatoes with salt and pepper. Roughly chop the scallions and add them to tomatoes; stir to combine. Return the skillet to the grill and scrape up any tomato bits stuck to the pan. Pour the remaining 3 tablespoons oil into the pan, then add the cumin and coriander. Cook, swirling pan frequently, until the spices start to sizzle and pop, about 1 minute. Pour the seed mixture onto the tomato-scallion situation and stir to combine.

Season squid with salt and toss to combine. Working in batches, grill squid, turning occasionally, until golden brown and cooked through, 4 to 6 minutes per batch, using tongs to transfer the grilled squid to the tomato mixture as you go. Drizzle oil over everything and serve the squid with a big spoonful of tomato-scallion sauce.

Serving Strategies

If I'm grilling, I want the rest of the meal to be made ahead and served at room temperature. See the menu section on page 281 for some suggested pairings.

From the Market	Spin It		At Home	Spin It
Squid	Substitute dry sea scallops or large peeled shrimp for the squid		Pimentón de la Vera	Hungarian paprika or ordinary smoked paprika can be subbed in for pimentón de la Vera
Beefsteak tomatoes			Olive oil	
Scallions			Salt and pepper	
			Cumin seeds	Try fennel seeds in place of the cumin or coriander seeds
			Coriander seeds	

**Long Beans with
Vinegar & Basil and
Grilled Chicken Legs
with Warm Spices**

Long Beans with Vinegar and Basil

4 servings

Long beans (aka yard beans, snake beans, bodi beans, asparagus beans, and Chinese long beans, among other names) are legumes that look like super-long green beans, but are actually more closely related to black-eyed peas and cowpeas. They're good lightly pounded and eaten raw, sautéed, stir-fried, or grilled—and they're so long that they won't fall through the grill grates. This dead-simple preparation pairs them with tangy vinegar and summery basil, which complement and brighten the smoky charred flavors of the vegetable, and the recipe is very easy to scale up.

1½ pounds long beans

Extra-virgin olive oil, for drizzling

Kosher salt; freshly ground pepper

Crushed red pepper flakes

5 tablespoons red wine vinegar

1½ cups lightly packed basil leaves

Prepare a grill for medium-high direct heat. Clean and oil grill grates. Trim the stem ends of the beans and place them in a large bowl. Drizzle in enough oil to coat, then season with salt and black pepper and toss, squeezing the beans with your hands to bruise them a bit (this helps tenderize them). Grill the beans, turning with tongs occasionally, until lightly charred and starting to become less rigid, 6 to 7 minutes. Return them to the same bowl and season with a pinch of red pepper flakes. Add the vinegar and toss to combine, then add the basil and toss again. Taste and season with more salt, black pepper, and pepper flakes if desired.

Buying Beans

Young long beans are about 18 inches long, light green, and completely edible, with tender seeds inside. As they mature, the outer hull toughens and is generally discarded in favor of the tender seeds within. When purchasing, look for tender beans without visible bumps, which would indicate that the legume is on the older side. You can find long beans at Asian grocers and at the farmer's market in the summer.

From the Market	Spin It	At Home	Spin It
Long beans	Snap beans, such as green beans, wax beans, haricots verts, Romano beans, and sugar snap peas, can be substituted; use a grill basket or place a wire rack perpendicular to the grill grates so they don't fall through	Olive oil	Neutral oil can be used
Basil leaves	Any type of basil, such as Thai, purple, or Italian (Genovese), can be used	Salt and pepper	Black vinegar, rice vinegar, sherry vinegar, or cider vinegar would all work, or use lime juice instead
	Cilantro, tarragon, or dill can be substituted for the basil	Red pepper flakes	
		Red wine vinegar	

Grilled Chicken Legs with Warm Spices

4 servings

Two things I appreciate about these chicken legs: First off, the mix of warm spices gives them a sweetly fragrant flavor that is deeply harmonious with the wood smoke; the turmeric in particular gives them a beautiful burnished color. Second, this is a textbook example of how grilling something fatty (in this case, skin-on chicken legs) over a moderate fire gives them time to cook through and render their fat without burning the spices or causing insane flare-ups.

2 star anise pods

2 teaspoons cumin seeds

2 teaspoons Aleppo pepper

1 teaspoon ground cinnamon

1 teaspoon ground turmeric

4 chicken leg quarters
(thigh and drumstick;
about 3 pounds total)

Kosher salt

Vegetable oil, for drizzling

Prepare a grill for medium direct heat.

Break star anise pods into smaller pieces, then combine with the cumin seeds in a mortar and pestle and grind until the mixture is sandy (alternately, do this in a spice grinder). Transfer to a small bowl and mix in the Aleppo pepper, cinnamon, and turmeric. Season chicken legs generously with salt, then with spice mix (use all of it). You can season up to 2 days ahead, if desired, and chill, uncovered.

Clean and oil grill grates. Drizzle the chicken on both sides with oil to lightly coat. Place the chicken on the grill, skin side down, and cook, turning every few minutes or whenever there's a flare-up, until the skin is golden and starting to crisp and the chicken is cooked through, 25 to 28 minutes. (To check, cut into the flesh right along the thigh bone and make sure it's opaque. Or, use a digital thermometer, which should register 160°F.) Let the chicken sit for 5 to 10 minutes before serving.

Dreamy Duo

Pair these chicken legs with the grilled long beans on previous page, which can be cooked over high heat while you're waiting for the coals to come down to medium.

From the Market	Spin It	At Home	Spin It
Star anise	Replace star anise with 2 teaspoons fennel seeds or aniseeds	Cumin seeds	2 teaspoons ground cumin can be used instead of cumin seeds
Aleppo pepper	Gochugaru, Urfa biber, or Maras pepper can replace the Aleppo pepper	Ground cinnamon	1 teaspoon grated nutmeg can replace the cinnamon
Chicken leg quarters	The same spices and method would work for pork chops or lamb chops	Ground turmeric	
		Kosher salt	
		Vegetable oil	

Grilled Romaine with Herby Walnut Dressing

4 servings

Lightly grilled lettuces are one of my favorite salad foundations in the summer, because you get a little smokiness and tenderness and, as long as you don't go too far, a little warm-cold contrast, too. I recommend romaine because it is easy to find and has a core that keeps all the leaves together, but sturdy lettuces like Little Gems or chicories such as escarole and radicchio will hold up, too. The jumping-off point for the dressing is Turkish tarator, a garlicky walnut sauce that is often thickened with softened pieces of bread (in other parts of the Middle East, including Lebanon, tarator is a tahini-based dip). Adding buttermilk takes it in another direction. This dressing would be equally awesome spooned over fish or roasted chicken, or used as a dip for pita.

1 cup walnut halves (4 ounces)

1 garlic clove

¾ cup buttermilk, shaken

¼ cup extra-virgin olive oil, plus more for drizzling

Kosher salt; freshly ground pepper

½ lemon

Leaves from 1 small bunch of mint

A few sprigs of dill (leaves and tender stems)

3 romaine hearts

Preheat the oven or a toaster oven to 350°F. Toast the walnuts on a small rimmed baking sheet until very well browned but not burnt, 10 to 12 minutes. (Break one in half to make sure it's golden brown in the center, too.) Let cool completely, then pulse walnuts in a food processor until they're bitsy but not pulverized (about the size of Grape-Nuts), 10 to 12 long pulses.

Transfer the walnuts to a medium bowl; finely grate the garlic over. Stir in the buttermilk and oil and season aggressively with salt and pepper. Squeeze in juice of the lemon half. Taste and adjust the seasoning.

Very thinly slice mint leaves and the dill crosswise; ou should have about ½ cup lightly packed herbs. Add the herbs to the walnut-buttermilk mixture and stir to combine. Chill the dressing while you get the grill going (or cover it and refrigerate for up to 2 days; the garlic flavor will intensify over time).

Prepare a grill for medium-high direct heat: You should have a moderate, even layer of ash-colored charcoal when it's ready. If you can hold your hand 6 inches above the grates for just a couple seconds without recoiling in pain, that's medium-high. Clean and oil grates. Halve the romaine hearts lengthwise and place them on a rimmed baking sheet. Drizzle with oil on both sides and season with salt and pepper. Grill romaine, cut sides down, until the surfaces are lightly caramelized, 4 to 5 minutes. Turn and grill until brown on the second sides, 2 minutes more. Transfer romaine to a platter and let cool slightly, then spoon the dressing over.

From the Market	Spin It	At Home	Spin It
Mint	You can use any tender herbs you have, including chives, basil, marjoram, tarragon, or chervil	Walnuts	Pine nuts, almonds, or hazelnuts can replace the walnuts
Dill		Garlic	
Romaine hearts		Buttermilk	
		Olive oil	A small amount of grated onion or shallot can replace the garlic
	3 Little Gems or a large escarole can replace romaine	Salt and pepper	
		Lemon	Use vinegar instead of lemon juice

Not-Scary Grilled Whole Fish

3 or 4 servings

Even for those who love to grill, a whole fish is treated as one of the high peaks to summit. The perceived challenge comes down to three major issues: The skin will stick; you'll never know when it's done; and without twine or a fish basket, you'll never manage to turn it over. I'm not going to lie—grilling fish can take some finesse, but you can still triumph. May you find reassurance and empowerment with a method that calls for no special equipment or seasonings, that can be adapted for various types of fish, and that results in crisped, smoky skin with tender meat underneath.

1 (2½- to 3½-pound) whole fish, such as red snapper, black bass, or striped bass, scaled and gutted

Kosher salt, for seasoning

Handful tender herbs, such as thyme and/or fennel fronds

¼ cup extra-virgin olive oil, plus more for drizzling

Prepare a grill for medium-high direct heat. Place the fish on a rimmed baking sheet, lasagna pan, or other shallow vessel and season very generously on both sides and inside the cavity with salt. Place the herbs inside the cavity, tucking them under the fish collar to help them stay put. Drizzle the fish with ¼ cup oil, turning to coat both sides. (You will think, "Jeez, this is a lot of oil." You're right. It's a lot of oil, and it's critical insurance against sticking.)

Use a grill brush to scrape grill grates clean of debris (one of the major reasons food adheres to the grill in the first place). Lightly oil grates. Gently place the fish over direct heat. Cover grill and open the vents on the lid (if your lid does not have vents, don't worry about it). Cook until the skin is very dark brown—just this side of charred—and releases easily from the grill, 4 to 5 minutes. Use tongs to grip the tail end of the fish and lift up gently to check: If the skin sticks, don't tug at it. Cook another minute, then check again.

Holding the tail end with tongs, slide a metal spatula under the head end and roll the fish over its spine onto the second side, as though you were rolling a log. This is less risky than picking the fish up completely and flipping it over. Cover the grill and cook until the flesh at the bone looks white—not pink or translucent—and flakes apart, 5 to 6 minutes more. Check for doneness by making a small incision with a paring knife along the spine toward the head, which is the thickest part of the fillet. If the flesh still looks glossy or feels rubbery, cover the grill and cook for 2 minutes more, then check again. (If your fish is closer to 3½ pounds, you will probably need to add a couple minutes more.)

Use tongs and a spatula to transfer fish to a clean rimmed baking sheet or platter. Drizzle with oil and let sit 5 to 10 minutes before filleting.

Saucy Seafood

A batch of Salsa Very Verde (page 277) is just the thing to spoon over the fish when it's done.

From the Market	Spin It		At Home	Spin It
Whole fish	Use any other similarly sized fish, such as porgy or branzino		Kosher salt	Any neutral oil can be used
Tender herbs			Olive oil	
	Stuff with whatever you want, including rosemary, curry leaf, Makrut lime leaf, mint, cilantro, oregano, or scallion greens			

Grill-Roasted Turkey Breast

12 to 14 servings, plus leftovers

I love to grill, and I love turkey; therefore, I love grilled turkey. I know it's usually roasted only once a year and everyone loves to complain about it, but it's not deserved. Turkey is an ingredient native to North America, and preparing it makes me feel a connection to the earliest cooks on this country's land (my own Italian ancestors were definitely not preparing turkey!). I often make it in the summer—it pairs beautifully with corn and tomatoes—and the leftovers will make a sandwich you'll brag about. The dry brine acts as a light cure, and the meat will absorb the flavors of the chili powder, onion, and garlic. The grill time is relatively long; if you're cooking with coals, plan ahead. Conventional charcoal briquettes burn longer and steadier than 100% lump hardwood; I recommend using briquettes here even though they create more ash as they burn. You should also invest in a charcoal chimney starter so you can have lit coals ready to go as the others wane (you'll need to replenish the fire after about 45 minutes).

Indirect Path

Banking the coals on one side of your grill sets you up for indirect-heat, or two-zone, grilling. This means that there's a hot side and a cooler side, which gives you more control inside the kettle. Here, the turkey is positioned over the cooler side and the lid is kept on; the turkey won't burn, and smoke will circulate around the breast the entire time, imparting deep flavor. You can also utilize this method in reverse when cooking fatty steaks, starting them on the hot side for color, then parking them on the cooler side whenever you have flare-ups.

½ cup kosher salt

¼ cup sugar

2 tablespoons chili powder

2 tablespoons garlic powder

2 tablespoons onion powder

2 tablespoons paprika

1 bone-in, skin-on turkey breast (about 10 pounds), fully thawed if frozen

Extra-virgin olive oil or neutral oil, for drizzling

In a medium bowl, stir together the salt, sugar, chili powder, garlic powder, onion powder, and paprika. Place the turkey breast on a rimmed baking sheet and season with dry rub mixture, getting it onto all sides and into the cavity. Refrigerate turkey, uncovered, for at least 24 hours or up to 3 days.

Remove the turkey from the refrigerator a couple of hours before you're planning on grilling; this will take off the chill and help it cook more evenly. Brush off the excess dry rub and return turkey to the baking sheet (do not rinse). Drizzle with oil and use a grill brush or your hands to make sure the seasonings are evenly distributed.

Prepare a grill for medium indirect heat, meaning two-thirds of the kettle should have a pile of lit coals and one-third is left empty. (Or light a gas grill to medium, leaving a zone or two off.) Clean and oil grill grates. Place the turkey, breast side up, on the cooler side of the grill and cover the grill, leaving the vents open (if your lid doesn't have vents, don't worry about it). Cook, rotating the turkey every 20 to 30 minutes for even cooking, but keeping it perched on its backbone, until a thermometer inserted into the thickest part of the breast registers 155°F, about 1 hour 45 minutes. I definitely recommend taking the temperature in more than one spot before pulling it off the grill. Replenish the coals at least once during this time; keep a charcoal chimney full and at the ready, and light the chimney about 20 minutes before you anticipate needing the coals.

Let turkey rest off the heat for at least 30 minutes or up to 1 hour before carving. The internal temperature will continue to climb as it sits, the juices will redistribute, and it will be easier to carve when it's not so hot.

From the Market	Spin It	At Home	Spin It
Turkey breast	This method and the seasonings can be used for leg of lamb or bone-in pork shoulder, but the cook time varies: For lamb, shoot for an internal temperature of 140°F; for pork shoulder, it should hit 190°F and stay there for at least 30 minutes	Kosher salt Sugar Chili powder Garlic powder Onion powder Paprika Olive oil	Try light brown sugar instead of granulated Play around with different spice blends instead of chili powder—garam masala, berbere, and Chinese five-spice powder all typically include warming spices that complement turkey

Cumin-Fennel Lamb Shoulder

8 to 10 servings

My mom always grills a leg of lamb for Easter, and over time I have successfully wrestled that responsibility away from her. This was done under the guise of "helping," but selfishly I'd rather be outside grilling than setting the table or answering the door! This annual experience also taught me how to manage a larger cut of meat on the grill. There are a few different muscles that come together in the leg, some thick and some thin. Turning the lamb frequently during grilling helps cook it evenly. That method applies to this Xinjiang-inspired lamb shoulder here; it's a little smaller and fattier, which makes it extra tasty.

3 tablespoons untoasted sesame seeds

2 tablespoons Sichuan peppercorns

1 tablespoon cumin seeds

2 teaspoons fennel seeds

1 (5½- to 6-pound) boneless lamb shoulder, untied

3 tablespoons kosher salt

Extra-virgin olive oil, for drizzling

Pulverize sesame seeds, peppercorns, cumin seeds, and fennel seeds in a mortar and pestle until coarsely ground (or use a spice grinder). Line a rimmed baking sheet with parchment paper. Place the lamb on the paper and season both sides with salt, then with the spice mix. Drizzle with oil and rub it evenly over. Roll the lamb into a bulky cylinder, then tuck the paper over and around the meat to cover (no need to tie it). Return it to baking sheet and refrigerate for 24 to 48 hours.

Remove the lamb from the refrigerator a couple of hours before you want to start cooking; it will cook more quickly and evenly if it's not fridge-cold. Prepare a grill for medium direct heat: You should have a moderate, even layer of ash-colored charcoal when it's ready. If you can hold your hand 6 inches above the grates for 10 seconds without recoiling in pain, that's medium. Clean and oil grates. Unroll the lamb and grill, turning every 4 to 5 minutes or any time there's a flare-up, until it is mahogany brown all over, the spices are golden and crisp, and a digital thermometer inserted into the center of multiple areas registers 140° to 145°F for medium-rare to medium, 40 to 45 minutes. (A single reading could be inaccurate.)

Let lamb rest off the heat for 20 minutes before carving it into thin slices against the grain. This is also excellent cold or at room temperature. The lamb goes beautifully with garlicky Whipped Aïoli (page 277), which can also be used as a schmear if you want to turn the lamb into a sandwich.

From the Market	Spin It	At Home	Spin It
Boneless lamb shoulder	Boneless leg of lamb can be substituted; ask your butcher to cut it to size	Untoasted sesame seeds	Use pepitas instead of the sesame seeds
		Sichuan peppercorns	Black pepper lacks the numbing properties of Sichuan peppercorns, but it can be used in a pinch
		Cumin seeds	
		Fennel seeds	
		Kosher salt	Use caraway seeds instead of cumin, or use 1 tablespoon ground cumin
		Olive oil	
			1 star anise can replace the fennel seeds

Chapter 8

S Is for Sunday
Soup, Stew
& Sauce

*The biggest effort you should exert on a Sunday
is the occasional shoulder workout from stirring
a pot of soup and swinging the door open to
greet your friends*

Pork and Pozole Stew

8 servings

Mexican pozole is one of my all-time most beloved things to eat and the kind of multi-hour cooking I can really get into. This stew might have pozole, the dish, as muse (and it also contains pozole, the ingredient, aka hominy), but stops short in many respects and is about as pared-down as I could figure out how to make it. It's a good idea to soak the hominy overnight, but aside from some active time spent browning the pork, the self-sufficient simmering all happens in the oven.

1 pound pozole (dried hominy)

2 tablespoons kosher salt, divided, plus more as needed

1 large yellow onion

1 teaspoon cumin seeds

5 garlic cloves

1 bunch oregano

1 dried taviche (tabiche) chile

3½ to 4 pounds boneless pork shoulder, cut into 3-inch pieces

Vegetable oil, for drizzling

2 tablespoons cider vinegar

Sliced avocado, tortilla chips, Mexican dried oregano or regular dried oregano, sliced red onion, hot sauce, and/or cilantro, for serving

Rinse the pozole and soak in water to cover in a large Dutch oven overnight. The next day, make sure pozole is covered by about 4 inches of water (add more if needed). Season with 1 tablespoon salt and bring to a simmer over high heat, skimming off any foam that rises to the surface. Halve the onion (do not peel). Lightly crush cumin seeds. Add the onion, cumin, garlic, oregano, and chile to the pot, then lower the heat to maintain a simmer.

Preheat the oven to 325°F. Season the pork with the remaining 1 tablespoon salt. Heat a large cast-iron skillet over medium to medium-high, then drizzle with enough oil to lightly coat the surface. Working in batches, cook pork, turning occasionally, until very well browned on all sides, 25 to 30 minutes. Use a slotted spoon to transfer batches to a small rimmed baking sheet or large plate as you go. When you have browned all the pork, pour the rendered fat from the pan into a heatproof bowl.

Add the vinegar and ¼ cup water to the skillet and use a wooden spoon to scrape up any browned bits. Pour this liquid into the hominy mixture, then add the pork. Return the mixture to a simmer, cover, and transfer to the oven. Cook until pozole is very tender and most of the kernels have unfurled, pork shreds easily, and liquid has thickened a bit, about 3 hours (stir halfway through, replenishing liquid if needed; if liquid is boiling, lower the oven temperature by 25°F).

Remove the onion halves, chile, and oregano. Taste stew and adjust the seasoning. Serve with avocado, tortilla chips, dried oregano, red onion, hot sauce, and/or cilantro for customizing each bowl.

From the Market	Spin It	At Home	Spin It
Pozole	A small chipotle chile or a pasilla negro chile can replace the taviche	Kosher salt	Any type of onion can be used
Fresh oregano		Yellow onion	
Taviche (tabiche) chile		Cumin seeds	Replace cumin seeds with ground cumin
		Garlic	
Boneless pork shoulder	An equivalent weight of pork stew meat or country-style ribs can be substituted for the shoulder	Vegetable oil	Any vinegar or an equivalent amount of lime juice can replace the cider vinegar
Avocado		Cider vinegar	
Tortilla chips		Red onion	
Mexican oregano		Hot sauce	
Cilantro			

Spaghetti with Melted Cauliflower Sauce

4 servings

In this humble pasta sauce, an extended sauna in olive oil and garlic transforms cauliflower from crisp and peppery to soft and sweet. If the cauliflower you bought is substantially larger than 1 pound, lop off a piece first so the ratio of vegetable to noodle isn't out of whack.

1 small head cauliflower (about 1 pound)

1 large shallot

6 garlic cloves

½ cup extra-virgin olive oil, plus more for drizzling

Kosher salt; freshly ground pepper

4 anchovy fillets packed in oil, drained

1 teaspoon mild chile flakes, such as Aleppo pepper

1 pound spaghetti

½ cup grated Parmigiano, plus more for serving

1 lemon

Trim the base of the cauliflower but don't core it. Snap off the outermost leaves from the base, leaving the pale green inner ones. Roughly chop the cauliflower. Transfer cauliflower to a food processor and pulse into pieces no bigger than ½ inch (some bits will be smaller). Finely chop the shallot. Thinly slice the garlic.

Heat oil in a medium Dutch oven or other heavy-bottomed pot with a lid over medium. Add the shallot and garlic and season with salt and pepper. Cook until the garlic is translucent, about 2 minutes. Add the anchovies and cook, stirring, until they disintegrate, 1 minute more. Add the cauliflower and season with the chile flakes plus more salt and pepper. Cook, stirring, until the cauliflower is coated in oil and starting to sweat, 5 to 7 minutes. Reduce the heat to very low, cover the pot, and cook, stirring occasionally, until the cauliflower is lightly browned and essentially rendered to very tasty mush, 30 to 35 minutes.

Meanwhile, bring a large pot of salted water to a boil over high heat. When cauliflower is almost done, cook the spaghetti, stirring occasionally, until very al dente, 3 to 4 minutes less than the time indicated on the package (it will finish cooking in the sauce). Using tongs or a mesh spider, transfer pasta to the pot with cauliflower sauce, along with about 1 cup pasta cooking liquid (or scoop out about 2 cups of the pasta liquid, then drain pasta in a colander). Bring sauce to a simmer over medium-high heat and cook, stirring and tossing pasta into sauce as you gradually add ½ cup Parm. Cook, tossing and adding more pasta liquid as needed, until the spaghetti is very al dente and sauce has thickened enough to generously coat the pasta, 3 to 4 minutes. Halve lemon and squeeze juice into pot and stir to combine. Serve pasta with more Parm at the table.

From the Market	Spin It		At Home	Spin It
Cauliflower	Romanesco is an excellent sub for cauliflower; or use broccoli		Garlic	Omit the anchovies if you prefer; or season with fish sauce toward the end of cooking
Shallot			Olive oil	
	In summer, try this with zucchini in place of cauliflower; it might take longer to cook because of its water content		Salt and pepper	
			Anchovies	
			Mild chile flakes	Use bucatini instead of spaghetti, or a short tubular pasta, such as mezze rigatoni, or something twisted, like fusilli or gemelli
			Spaghetti	
	Half a small onion can replace the shallot		Parmigiano	
			Lemon	

Greens, Beans, and Sausage Soup

8 servings

This soup sums up my whole soup-making philosophy. It starts with a thoroughly cooked soffritto, which is a pedestrian but powerful mix of vegetables that provide the backbone of the dish. Your soup would be watery and thin-tasting without it. Once that step is done, I add all my other favorite things: a pork product, beans, greens, a couple of Parm rinds that I've been hoarding in my freezer, and plenty of salt. To make this vegetarian, omit the sausage (obviously!) and the Parm (it contains animal rennet), and add an extra 2 tablespoons olive oil when cooking the soffritto.

3 medium carrots

2 celery stalks

1 large onion

6 garlic cloves

1 pound sweet and/or hot Italian sausage

½ cup extra-virgin olive oil, divided

Kosher salt; freshly ground pepper

1 teaspoon cumin seeds

1 cup French green lentils

2 bunches Tuscan kale

1 teaspoon ground turmeric

2 dried bay leaves

2 tablespoons tomato paste

1 or 2 Parmigiano rinds (optional)

Sherry vinegar, for serving

Buttered toasted crusty bread or Carole's Fried Bread (page 278), for serving

Scrub the carrots. Coarsely chop the carrots, celery, onion, and garlic, then process in a food processor until very finely chopped. Remove the casings from the sausages, if using links.

Heat 2 tablespoons oil in a 6-quart stockpot or Dutch oven over medium-high, then add the sausage meat. Cook, using a wooden spoon to break it up into 1-inch pieces, until golden brown on the underside, 3 minutes. Toss and cook until the sausage is just cooked through, 2 minutes more. Use a slotted spoon to transfer it to a plate and set aside (returning the sausage to the soup toward the end of cooking will keep it from getting dry and mealy during a long time spent simmering).

Add the remaining 6 tablespoons oil to the pot, then stir in the chopped vegetables. Season generously with salt and pepper, stirring to coat. Cook, stirring occasionally, until the vegetables start to throw off some of their liquid, 2 to 3 minutes, then partially cover the pot, reduce the heat to medium-low, and continue to sweat the soffritto, stirring occasionally, until the vegetables are completely tender but have not taken on any color, 16 to 18 minutes. The volume of the vegetables should reduce by about half, and the mixture will start to look like a khaki-colored, coarse paste. Don't rush this step. If the pot or vegetables start to brown, lower the heat.

From the Market	Spin It	At Home	Spin It
Carrots	Use half a fennel bulb instead of celery	Onion	Use ground cumin to replace cumin seeds
Celery		Garlic	
Italian sausage	Ground pork can replace the sausage	Olive oil	Other small dried (soaked) beans, can be used instead of lentils; cook time may increase (top off with water as needed).
Tuscan kale		Salt and pepper	
Crusty bread	Any type of kale or escarole can be substituted for Tuscan kale	Cumin seeds	
		Green lentils	
		Ground turmeric	Don't use split lentils, which will disintegrate into the soup
		Bay leaves	
		Tomato paste	A few thyme or rosemary sprigs can replace the bay leaves
		Parmigiano rinds (optional)	
		Sherry vinegar	

While the soffritto is cooking, coarsely crush the cumin seeds. Pick through the lentils, then rinse. Stem the kale, then tear the leaves into 2-inch pieces.

Add the cumin, turmeric, and bay leaves to the soffritto and stir to combine. Cook until the surface of the pot is starting to brown, about 2 minutes. Add the tomato paste and cook, stirring, until the paste darkens, 1 minute. Add 10 cups water and Parmigiano rinds (if using) and bring to a boil over medium-high heat. Season again with salt, then reduce the heat to medium-low to maintain a gentle simmer.

Add the lentils and kale and stir well to combine (kale should be submerged; add another cup of water if needed). Partially cover the pot and cook, stirring occasionally, until the lentils are tender and the kale is very silky, 40 to 45 minutes more. Fish out the bay leaves and Parm rinds. Return sausage to soup, along with any accumulated juices. Simmer until the sausage is hot, 3 to 4 minutes.

Taste soup and season with a few dashes of vinegar. Ladle into bowls. Serve with bread for dunking.

Greens, Beans, and
Sausage Soup

Baked Polenta with Floppy Broccoli

Baked Polenta with Floppy Broccoli

4 servings

Long-cooked broccoli might not retain its vibrant green color, but what it lacks in visual panache, it gains in sweetness, tenderness, and old-school goodness. Once the broccoli is stewing, you can start the polenta and park it in the oven; it will come out as luscious and creamy as it would if you had fussed over it adoringly while it burbled and spat at you on the stovetop.

1 teaspoon kosher salt, plus more as needed

1 bunch broccoli (2 or 3 stalks, about 1½ pounds)

6 garlic cloves

⅓ cup extra-virgin olive oil, plus more for drizzling

½ teaspoon crushed red pepper flakes, plus more for serving

Freshly ground pepper

1 cup polenta (not quick-cooking)

½ cup raw (natural) almonds

4 ounces Parmigiano, plus more for serving

1 lemon

2 tablespoons unsalted butter

Fill a large Dutch oven or other heavy pot with water and bring to a boil over high heat; season it heavily with salt (as you would for pasta—figure ¼ cup salt per 6 quarts water).

While you wait, prep broccoli: Trim off bottom inch of each stem. Peel stems until you get down to the tender light green layer. Cut each broccoli head through the crown into quarters or sixths so you wind up with floret-topped spears with 4-inch-long stems attached. Smash the garlic.

Add the broccoli and garlic to boiling water and return to a boil. Cook for 2 minutes, then drain; return empty pot to medium heat. (Blanching the broccoli and garlic diffuses some of their sharp flavor and plumps them up with moisture so they don't get fibrous and stringy during the long, low cooking that follows. It may feel extraneous, but it's not hard and it doesn't require special equipment, which I hope will justify this extra step.) Pour in ⅓ cup oil and add the red pepper flakes. Add the blanched broccoli and garlic, season with salt and black pepper, and toss to coat. Reduce the heat to very low, cover, and cook, gently tossing every 15 minutes or so, until broccoli is extremely soft, 1 hour. Some of the broccoli will break into smaller pieces, which is fine, but try not to smash it to bits by stirring too energetically.

From the Market	Spin It	At Home	Spin It
Broccoli	The same process (blanching and slow-cooking) can be applied to green beans, long beans, celery, flat beans, cauliflower, kale, fennel, carrots, cabbage wedges, winter squash	Salt and pepper	If you like anchovies, add a few fillets when you add the red pepper flakes
		Garlic	
		Olive oil	
		Red pepper flakes	Use ½ teaspoon cayenne or hot smoked paprika instead of red pepper flakes
		Polenta	
	Use these without blanching first: sweet bell peppers, zucchini, tomatoes	Almonds	Grits can replace the polenta
		Parmigiano	
		Lemon	Try with walnuts, pistachios, or hazelnuts
		Butter	

Polenta Patty

Leftover polenta will solidify when refrigerated. Cut it into slices and cook in a little olive oil in a nonstick skillet until browned on both sides and hot in the middle, then top with a fried egg and some hot sauce.

Meanwhile, preheat oven to 325°F with racks in the upper and lower thirds.

Bring 5 cups water to a simmer in a medium ovenproof saucepan over medium-high heat. Add 1 teaspoon kosher salt and a few cranks of pepper, then gradually add the polenta, whisking nonstop (this is key to preventing clumps). When all the polenta has been added and the mixture is at a boil, cover the pan, transfer to lower oven rack, and bake until the polenta is tender, 35 to 40 minutes.

In a small ovenproof skillet or small rimmed baking sheet, toss the almonds with just enough oil to coat. Season with salt and roast on the top oven rack until deep golden brown and fragrant, 12 minutes. Let cool, then roughly chop. Grate Parmigiano and cut lemon into wedges.

Carefully uncover polenta (the lid and handle will be very hot). Whisk vigorously, scraping bottom and corners of the pan, until the polenta is smooth and thick, 1 to 2 minutes. Whisk in butter, then gradually whisk in the Parm until completely melted and incorporated. Taste polenta and season with more salt and black pepper, if needed.

Serve broccoli over polenta, topped with almonds, an extra drizzle of olive oil, more red pepper flakes, and more Parm, if desired, with lemon wedges alongside for squeezing.

Leo, Ro-Ro the dog, Cosmo, and Gia.

Baby's First Ragù

Gia's Sunday Ragù recipe
See page 188

I love the whole ritual of a Sunday ragù. I love how the extended family gathers early to help with the meatball shaping and the marinara stirring and the braciole tying. I love how the kids run around with their cousins and how the senior men rearrange the furniture to make one big long table for everyone. Don't forget the vine-covered pergola with the dappled light coming through, and Uncle Whoever's house-made hooch that gets passed around. The only problem with this whole fantasy is that I've never spent a day like this in my life. Sunday ragù is not my tradition and never has been, and this whole scene is an extremely hokey version of something out of a Martin Scorsese movie.

But even though my family never *did* Sunday ragù doesn't mean I can never *do* a Sunday ragù. So when my sister, Nina, finally got around to having a baby, it seemed like an irresistible time to start. A big ragù would lure the baby over to my house. I could hold her while her parents ate, and I'd send them home with leftovers. Only one problem: There was no family ragù recipe to wrangle.

I understood the basic premise: braised meats in red sauce, with pasta. But which meats? What kind of sauce? Cook the sauce, then add the meats? I had questions. What is braciole? No, seriously: *What is braciole???* It's a meat cutlet—stuffed (with what?), rolled, tied, and braised. Is it pork or beef? I turned to cookbooks. Braciole is sometimes pork, sometimes beef. Not helpful!

Moving on: Some people put pork chops in their ragù. Some don't. Some claim meatballs are obligatory, but that opens up a whole other can of tomatoes. Pork meatballs? Pork and beef? Pork, beef, *and* veal? You could debate the merits of each decision for the rest of your life, no closer to ragù than when you started.

Fortunately for my open-ended tailspin, I had a hard deadline. The invitation to my inaugural Sunday ragù had been accepted, and the day was fast approaching. I settled on pork spareribs instead of chops, confident they were less likely to dry out, along with pork and beef meatballs, and beef braciole, which I had never made. I knew enough to know that a braise like this one would taste better if I let the meats sit in the "gravy" overnight. I would be organized! I would plan ahead!

I went to the butcher on Friday afternoon and bought everything I needed, but when I finally got around to starting the process late that night, with little piles of parsley and shaved provolone for tucking into my braciole rolls, I realized I had no twine for tying them up, and no toothpicks to hold the rolls together. And that's how I found myself at 12:30 a.m., desperately unweaving lengths of rope that we normally use for bundling our recycling into individual strands that I could use as twine. Were they really hard to tie? Yes. Was I worried the rope might be covered in some weird coating that would melt into the sauce? Yes. Did I keep going? Yes—yes I did.

There were a lot of things wrong with my first ragù. The proportion of meat to sauce to pasta was off. The braciole? A little dry. The middle-of-the-night prep process was not one I care to repeat, which is why my recipe now calls for sausages instead of meatballs (page 188). There was no dappled pergola—in fact, it was already dark out by the time Nina and her husband, Ben, arrived with Gigi. We put candles on the table and made sure the parents got a glass of wine the minute the baby was liberated from her carrier. We all took turns holding Gia while we ate, and no one spilled red sauce on her head. I had a whole quart of leftover sauce when dinner was over—exactly according to plan! It was Gia's first Sunday dinner at our place, and she was the reason any of this was happening, of course. The ragù was a textbook ruse, but an effective one. It's easier to say you're gathering for a meal instead of saying you want to take advantage of every minute you have on earth together, but if the end result is the same, take either path.

Gia's Sunday Ragù

8 servings

Everyone reserves the right to put what they want in their ragù. Mine has pork shoulder, beef braciole, and sausages in a 3-hour tomato sauce. It does not have meatballs, because making them feels like too much work on top of everything else. (If you like meatballs in yours, I'll give you my number and you can have me over sometime.) Most butchers will sell you thin slices of beef top loin for making braciola, the meat rolls that go in the braise; I find it too lean and dry, which is why this recipe calls for short ribs. To spread out the work, season the pork shoulder and roll up your braciole 2 days ahead. Brown the meats and make the sauce 1 to 2 days in advance, then let it cool before covering and refrigerating it. Reheat gently to serve.

2 pounds boneless pork shoulder, cut into ½-inch-thick steaks

Kosher salt; freshly ground pepper

1 (8-ounce) wedge Parmigiano

3 pieces thinly sliced boneless beef short ribs (about 12 ounces total)

¼ cup extra-virgin olive oil

8 garlic cloves

1 yellow onion

2 teaspoons dried oregano

2 bay leaves

¼ cup red wine

3 (28-ounce) cans whole peeled tomatoes

1 pound sweet and/or hot Italian sausage links

2 pounds rigatoni

Crushed red pepper flakes, for serving

Season pork shoulder steaks liberally with salt and black pepper; set aside.

Cut 6 thin slices from the wedge of Parmigiano (reserve remainder for serving). Place the short ribs on a sheet of waxed paper or parchment paper and pound lightly to flatten and spread them out. Cut each in half crosswise to make 6 cutlets. Season on both sides with salt and black pepper. Top each with a slice of Parm, then tuck in the ends and roll each braciola up, turning them seam side down when done. Using butcher's twine, tie each one to secure (not too snugly, since they will bulge a bit when cooked).

Heat oil in a large Dutch oven over medium-high. Add the braciole and cook, turning occasionally, until dark brown on all sides, 8 to 10 minutes. Transfer to a rimmed baking sheet. Working in batches if necessary, add the pork shoulder steaks to the pan and cook, turning occasionally, until very dark brown on both sides and much of the fat has rendered, 14 to 18 minutes (reduce the heat if oil starts to smoke). Transfer pork to the baking sheet.

From the Market	Spin It		At Home	Spin It
Pork shoulder	Use pork shoulder cutlets instead of short ribs		Salt and pepper	Grana Padano or pecorino can replace the Parm
Boneless beef short ribs			Parmigiano	
Red wine			Olive oil	Any large tubular pasta or thick pasta noodles (such as bucatini or fettucine) can be substituted for the rigatoni
Italian sausage			Garlic	
			Onion	
			Dried oregano	
			Bay leaves	
			Canned tomatoes	
			Rigatoni	
			Red pepper flakes	

Me, You, Ragù

To hear about Gia and how
this ragù came about, see
the essay on page 187.

Meanwhile, slice garlic and cut onion into small dice. Add the garlic and onion to the Dutch oven with the drippings; reduce heat to medium. Cook, stirring often and scraping up any browned bits, until the onion is translucent, 2 to 3 minutes. Add the oregano and bay leaves and cook, stirring often, until the vegetables are golden brown at the edges, about 4 minutes. Add the wine and simmer until the liquid is almost completely reduced and the vegetables are again sizzling in oil, about 5 minutes.

While vegetables are cooking, use a hand blender to puree the canned tomatoes, then add them to the vegetable mixture. Rinse out each can by filling it halfway with water and swirling it around; add this water to the pot and bring to a simmer. Cut the rind off your wedge of Parm and add the rind to the pot. Season with salt and black pepper and cook until the sauce is slightly reduced, 25 to 30 minutes. Return braciole and pork shoulder to the pot, along with any accumulated juices. Add the sausages. Stir to submerge. Place a lid slightly ajar on the pot and cook at an unbearably low simmer, stirring every half hour, until the meats are soft enough to feed to a toothless baby, 2½ to 3 hours.

Bring a large pot of generously salted water to a boil (figure ¼ cup salt per 6 quarts water). Cook rigatoni until very al dente, about 3 minutes less than time indicated on the package.

Make sure ragù is a gentle simmer. Discard Parm rind. Carefully transfer pork, sausages, and braciole to a platter; snip off the twine on braciole. Taste sauce and adjust the seasoning.

Use a slotted spoon or spider to transfer rigatoni directly into sauce. Stir to combine and finish cooking the pasta, adding ladlefuls of pasta cooking liquid as needed to adjust consistency of sauce.

Serve pasta with meats on the side, passing Parmigiano and red pepper flakes at the table.

Roasted Poultry and Garlic Stock

Makes about 3 quarts

Stock with a light, clean flavor is versatile enough to fortify braises, sauces, and soups without overwhelming the other ingredients in the dish. This one is rich and robust from deeply roasted poultry bones and caramelized garlic. It's an end point in and of itself, not a bit player in some other main event. Once you have it on hand, a soulful dinner (or breakfast!) is not far behind.

3½ to 4 pounds chicken wings, turkey wings, and/or turkey legs

2 heads garlic (whole, unpeeled)

Extra-virgin olive oil, for drizzling

Kosher salt

1 tablespoon black peppercorns

Handful parsley

2 bay leaves

Preheat the oven to 425°F.

Place the wings and garlic in a very large cast-iron skillet, on a rimmed baking sheet, or in a roasting pan; drizzle all over with oil. Season lightly with salt, then toss to coat. Arrange in a single layer and roast until the skin on wings is very well browned and garlic cloves are soft when heads are squeezed, 1 to 1½ hours, turning once halfway through.

Transfer wings to a tall stockpot and cover with 4 quarts water. Use your hands to pry the heads of garlic open as though you're cracking open a paperback at the spine (no need to separate cloves) and add garlic to the pot. Add the peppercorns, parsley, and bay leaves. Bring to a simmer over high heat, skimming off any foam that rises, then lower the heat to maintain a very (very!) gentle simmer. Cook until the stock is dark, richly flavored, and a little bit reduced, 2½ to 3 hours.

Set a colander over a very large bowl or clean pot. Use tongs or a mesh spider to transfer garlic and wings to colander; let drain without pushing down on bones or garlic. (I like to use a colander for this step since the bones can get unwieldy when using a strainer.) Discard solids. Return any liquid in the bowl to pot with the rest of the stock. Rinse bowl, then pour stock through a fine-mesh strainer into bowl. Let stock cool, then cover and refrigerate for up to 5 days, or freeze for up to 6 months.

Suggestion Box

Slip a poached egg into this broth (see page 194), or wilt a very large handful of sliced hearty greens (such as collards) at a simmer and top with hot sauce. It's also pretty irresistible as a shallow bath for thin noodles or tortellini, topped with lots of grated Parm.

From the Market	Spin It		At Home	Spin It
Chicken or turkey wings, and/or turkey legs	Use an equivalent weight of pork or beef shank bones if desired		Garlic	A large onion, halved, can replace the garlic
Parsley	Fennel fronds or a celery stalk can replace the parsley		Olive oil	Use vegetable oil instead of olive oil
			Kosher salt	
			Black peppercorns	Use 1 whole star anise or 2 teaspoons fennel seeds for black peppercorns
			Bay leaves	Omit the bay leaves if you don't have any

Poached Egg on Toast in Soup

2 servings

Putting a very toasted piece of bread in hot broth sets you on the path of "crispy gone soggy," an end goal that my friend Amiel Stanek argues is one of the most desirable culinary scenarios known to humankind.

2 cups Roasted Poultry and Garlic Stock (page 193)

2 large eggs

2 thick slices bread (or Carole's Fried Bread, page 278)

1 garlic clove

Unsalted butter, at room temperature

Flaky salt; freshly ground pepper

Bring stock to a simmer in a small pot over medium-high; keep it hot (do not reduce).

Bring a small pot of water to a simmer over medium-high, then lower the heat to maintain an almost imperceptible simmer. One at a time, crack eggs into a small fine-mesh strainer and let the thin, watery part of the whites drain off, then transfer eggs to a small bowl. (This will get rid of those long, thin strands of egg white that bedevil any well-intentioned egg poacher.) Tilt bowl to slip one egg into barely simmering water, then add the second egg a little distance away from the first. Cook, gently stirring water so the eggs are coaxed away from the bottom and encouraged to rotate and spin around, until the whites are just set and the yolks are still runny, 2½ minutes.

Meanwhile, toast bread until very dark brown and crisp, then rub with garlic and schmear with butter. Place a piece of toast in each of two soup bowls. Divide stock between bowls, then top each toast with a poached egg. Season with flaky salt and pepper.

Egg Options

To scale up, it would be easier to make jammy eggs than more batches of poached. Lower the whole eggs (not cracked!) into simmering water and cook for 6 minutes. Plunge them right away into an ice bath to cool, then carefully peel. Reheat in hot stock for 30 seconds before serving.

From the Market	At Home	Spin It
Zip, zilch, nada	Eggs	You could warm up any leftover protein or cooked vegetables you have on hand in the stock in place of the eggs
	Bread	
	Garlic	
	Butter	
	Flaky salt	
	Freshly ground black pepper	Leftover cooked rice or grains can be reheated in the stock instead of the bread

Sheet Pan Chicken with Tomatoes and Chickpeas

8 servings

This isn't a true confit because the chicken isn't fully submerged in fat, but there's a very generous amount
to caramelize the tomatoes and chickpeas and create a concentrated pan sauce while the chicken slow-roasts up top.

2 tablespoons paprika

1 tablespoon dried oregano

8 chicken leg quarters (thigh and drumstick; about 6 pounds total)

2 tablespoons kosher salt, plus more as needed

2 (28-ounce) cans whole peeled tomatoes

2 (15-ounce) cans chickpeas

6 sprigs thyme

4 bay leaves

3 chiles de árbol

Freshly ground pepper

1¼ cups extra-virgin olive oil, divided

1 large red onion

12 garlic cloves, unpeeled

Sherry vinegar, for serving

Stir together paprika and oregano. Arrange chicken on a large rimmed baking sheet and season with 2 tablespoons salt, then the spice mixture (use all of it). Set aside at room temperature (or refrigerate chicken, uncovered, overnight).

Preheat the oven to 325°F. Drain tomatoes and tear them into 4 or 6 strips each, transferring to another large rimmed baking sheet as you go. Drain and rinse chickpeas; add to baking sheet. Add the thyme, bay leaves, and chiles, scattering them about. Season with salt and pepper, then pour over ½ cup oil and stir to coat. Bake until tomatoes are shrunken and look a bit dried out, and chickpeas are starting to turn golden brown, 1 hour, stirring once halfway through (this cooks off some moisture in the tomatoes so they'll get nice and jammy by the end).

Meanwhile, peel the onion and cut into ¼-inch wedges. Lightly crush the garlic cloves. Add the onion and garlic to tomato-chickpea mixture. Nestle in chicken, skin side up, then pour over the remaining ¾ cup oil. Bake until the skin is browned and the meat is tender enough to shred with a fork, 1½ hours. If chicken isn't done, bake for 15 minutes more, then check again. Go longer if needed.

Transfer chicken to a large platter. Pluck out bay leaves and thyme sprigs. Using a slotted spoon, spoon tomatoes and chickpeas around chicken. Pour cooking liquid from baking sheet into a glass measuring cup; let settle for a few minutes. Pour most of the oil that rises to the top of the liquid into a clean jar or bowl, then spoon remaining chicken-y juices over the platter. (Cover and refrigerate the extra confit oil; use it the next time you make beans, soup, or roast vegetables.) Season the chicken with a few dashes of vinegar before serving.

From the Market	Spin It		At Home	Spin It
Chicken leg quarters	Use 2 butterflied chickens or 4 half chickens; cook time may be 30 minutes longer		Paprika	In summer, substitute 20 plum tomatoes, quartered, for the canned tomatoes
Thyme	Replace thyme with 2 rosemary sprigs, or season the tomatoes and chickpeas with 2 teaspoons dried oregano		Dried oregano	Omit the bay leaves if you don't have them
			Salt and pepper	
			Canned tomatoes	
			Canned chickpeas	Use Thai chiles or 1 teaspoon crushed red pepper flakes instead of the chiles de árbol
			Bay leaves	
			Chiles de árbol	
			Olive oil	
			Garlic	
			Red onion	
			Sherry vinegar	

Hands-Off Pork and Beans

6 generous servings

This pork roast method falls somewhere between a slow roast and a braise, and I am always astounded that the meat and the beans get done at almost the same time (you do need to soak the beans overnight and season the pork at least 12 hours ahead, however!). As it cooks, the spice mixture on the pork mingles with the melting fat and juices and runs down into the beans, spicing them as they slowly simmer alongside the roast. Almost nothing is required of you at the very beginning and the very end of the cooking process, making this a major-no-brainer meal for entertaining.

1 tablespoon piment d'Espelette

1 tablespoon hot smoked paprika

1 teaspoon cayenne

1 3-pound bone-in pork shoulder (butt)

2 tablespoons kosher salt, divided, plus more for seasoning

Freshly ground pepper

1 pound dried black-eyed peas

1 carrot

1 medium onion

6 garlic cloves

Small handful thyme sprigs

Extra-virgin olive oil, for drizzling

2 tablespoons sherry vinegar, plus more as needed

Stir together piment d'Espelette, paprika, and cayenne in a small bowl. Season pork all over with 1 tablespoon salt, then with spice mixture, patting it on. Wrap pork (I use the butcher paper it came in) and refrigerate for at least 12 hours and up to 2 days.

Pick through the beans for any debris, then rinse. Place the beans in a very large bowl or pot. Cover with 12 cups water; let sit overnight (coordinate your timing with the pork so the beans are done soaking when your pork has been seasoned and chilled for the right amount of time).

From the Market	Spin It		At Home	Spin It
Piment d'Espelette	Replace piment d'Espelette with ½ teaspoon cayenne or 2 teaspoons chili powder		Hot smoked paprika	If you don't have hot paprika, increase the cayenne by ½ teaspoon
Pork shoulder			Cayenne	
Black-eyed peas			Kosher salt	If you don't have cayenne, substitute ½ teaspoon crushed red pepper flakes
Thyme	This would work with the same amount of boneless lamb shoulder or boneless beef shank		Carrot	
			Onion	
			Garlic	
	Another small white bean, such as flageolets or cannellinis, can replace the black-eyed peas		Olive oil	Instead of carrot and onion, substitute 2 celery stalks and 4 shallots
			Sherry vinegar	Replace carrot with 1 small fennel bulb
				Use red wine vinegar or white wine vinegar instead of sherry vinegar

Get Ahead

To make this a day or two before you want to serve it, pause at the step before the pork is reheated in the oven. Let beans and pork cool, then cover and refrigerate. Reheat the bean mixture before pureeing half, and use water instead of the bean liquid on the baking sheet when the pork goes back into the oven.

Preheat the oven to 325°F. Transfer soaked beans, with their liquid, to a large Dutch oven or roasting pan. Scrub carrot; roughly chop. Peel and halve the onion through the root; smash the garlic. Add the vegetables to the beans along with the thyme. Stir in 1 tablespoon salt. Nestle pork on top of beans, fatty side up, and drizzle with oil. Bring liquid to a simmer over medium-high heat, stirring beans around pork and skimming off any foam that rises to the surface, then cover and transfer to the oven. (If using a roasting pan, cover with parchment paper and then foil, crimping edges to seal.) Cook until the beans are cooked through and very tender and you can pull off a bit of pork with tongs and it's not tough or chewy when you eat it, 2 to 2½ hours (or longer, if needed).

Remove the pot from the oven; increase oven temperature to 375°F. Carefully transfer pork, still fatty side up, to a rimmed baking sheet and ladle enough cooking liquid around it to come ½ inch up the sides. Return pork to oven (uncovered this time) and roast until the fat is brown and crisp, 45 to 55 minutes (check it every 15 minutes or so and replenish liquid if it has evaporated).

Meanwhile, remove thyme sprigs from bean mixture. Transfer half the beans, with liquid, to a blender and carefully blend on high speed until thick and creamy, 1 minute. Pour puree back into Dutch oven and stir in vinegar; taste beans and liquid. Season with salt, pepper, and more vinegar as desired. Keep warm.

When pork is ready, transfer it to a cutting board and let sit until no longer screaming hot. Pour any liquid from baking sheet back into bean mixture. Cut pork away from the bone, then slice into ½-inch-thick pieces against the grain (because the pork is so tender, it may shred into smaller pieces as you slice—no stress!). Spoon beans onto a deep platter, then top with pork, or pass pork and beans at the table separately.

Hands-Off
Pork and
Beans

Aromatic Chicken and Ginger Soup

Aromatic Chicken and Ginger Soup

8 servings

You don't have to make stock before you make soup if you make a soup that yields its own stock. That truth is illustrated in chicken-broth-based recipes as disparate as Hainanese chicken and matzo ball soup. By poaching a whole chicken along with lots of spices and aromatics, you create a liquid base that just keeps on giving as the simmering continues in subsequent steps. The ingredient list here may look long, but most of these things are hucked into the stockpot at the beginning, and I tried to keep any slicing and dicing to a minimum.

1 large shallot

1 small head garlic

6-inch piece ginger

2-inch piece fresh turmeric

3 dried pasilla chiles

3 star anise pods

2 lemongrass stalks

2 bunches scallions, divided

1 (3½- to 4-pound) whole chicken

½ bunch cilantro, divided

1 tablespoon kosher salt, plus more for seasoning

Freshly ground pepper

¼ purple (red) or green cabbage

8 ounces fresh or dried wide rice noodles

1 (13.5-ounce) can full-fat unsweetened coconut milk

Chives, lime wedges, hot sauce, fish sauce, soy sauce, toasted sesame oil, Thai basil, and/or bean sprouts, for serving

Have the shallot (leave skin on). Halve the garlic head crosswise (leave skin on). Scrub the ginger and turmeric and halve them both lengthwise. In a large stockpot, combine the shallot, garlic, ginger, turmeric, chiles, and star anise. Trim off the top third of the lemongrass stalk and peel off the tough outer layers. Using the blunt edge of a chef's knife, smack the lemongrass along the length of the stalk to bruise it (this will help release its essential oils). Cut the lemongrass stalks crosswise into 3-inch lengths and add to the pot. Trim one bunch scallions and cut into 2-inch lengths (using light and dark green parts); add them to the pot (set remaining scallions aside). Add the chicken and half the cilantro (set remaining cilantro aside). Pour in 4 quarts water; season with 1 tablespoon salt and about 10 cranks of pepper. Bring to a simmer over high heat, skimming any foam that rises to the surface. Lower the heat to maintain a gentle simmer until the chicken is cooked through, stirring and skimming occasionally, 35 minutes.

Use tongs to transfer the chicken to a large bowl or a rimmed baking sheet. Let sit until cool enough to handle. Continue to simmer the liquid, stirring occasionally, until the broth is reduced by about a quarter and tastes flavorful, 45 to 60 minutes.

Use your fingers to remove chicken meat from bones; discard skin and bones (or freeze them for making stock). Tear meat into bite-size pieces; set aside. Trim and thinly slice remaining scallions and cilantro. Cut cabbage into thin strips; transfer all of these things to separate small bowls or plates for passing at the table. Soften or cook noodles according to package instructions.

Great Base

This soup is flavored in part by star anise and black pepper and served with rice noodles, all of which are commonly found in Vietnamese pho recipes, along with coconut milk and turmeric, which are not. If you want to play around with the aromatic base, try browning the shallot, garlic, ginger, turmeric, dried chiles, star anise, and lemongrass in a little bit of oil before adding water to the stockpot, which will lend the broth a sweeter, deeper taste and dark golden color.

Pour chicken broth through a fine-mesh strainer into a clean pot and return to a simmer over medium-high heat (or, strain it into a large bowl, rinse out the pot, and pour the broth back into the pot). Add the coconut milk and simmer until the flavors have melded, about 5 minutes. Return chicken to soup to heat through. Taste soup and season with more salt and pepper.

To serve, divide noodles among eight bowls and top with soup. Serve with scallions, cilantro, and cabbage. Pass chives, lime wedges, hot sauce, fish sauce, soy sauce, toasted sesame oil, Thai basil, and/or bean sprouts at the table for fixing up each bowl.

From the Market	Spin It	At Home	Spin It
Fresh turmeric	Use 1 teaspoon ground turmeric instead of fresh turmeric	Shallot	Replace shallot with 1 small onion
Pasilla chiles		Garlic	
Star anise	Use medium-hot dried chiles, such as ancho or guajillo	Ginger	Soba, ramen, or other wheat noodles can replace the rice noodles
Lemongrass		Salt and pepper	
Scallions		Rice noodles	
Whole chicken	Use 1 teaspoon lightly crushed fennel seeds in place of star anise	Unsweetened coconut milk	A splash of unseasoned rice vinegar can replace the lime juice
Cilantro		Limes	
Cabbage		Hot sauce	
Thai basil	Substitute 1 teaspoon lightly crushed coriander seeds for lemongrass	Fish sauce	All the go-withs are optional; omit any as you please
Bean sprouts		Soy sauce	
	Use 8 bone-in, skin-on chicken thighs in place of whole chicken; reduce cook time to 20 minutes	Toasted sesame oil	

Pork and Beef Stew with Ginger, Tomato, and Kimchi

4 to 6 servings

If I'm going to eat a rich, meaty stew, I'm always going to go for something with spice and tang over a sticky red wine braise. I definitely had the classic Korean dish kimchi jjigae, a pork and tofu kimchi stew, on my brain when working on this. In all its funky, spicy, rich glory, kimchi jjigae was the only dish that cured my morning sickness when I was pregnant with my second child. For that alone, I'll love it forever. This stew isn't traditional in any sense, but it leans heavily on the spice and fermented flavors of kimchi and amps that up with anchovy, sour-sweet tomatoes, and the brightness of ginger to make a very belly-warming meal.

1 pound pork stew meat
(preferably shoulder)

1 pound beef stew meat
(preferably chuck)

Kosher salt

3 tablespoons vegetable oil

2 bunches scallions

2-inch piece ginger
(about 2 ounces)

1 (14-ounce) jar cabbage kimchi

1 (15-ounce) can whole peeled
tomatoes

1 tablespoon gochugaru

3 anchovy fillets packed in oil,
drained

Cooked rice (see page 274),
for serving

Preheat the oven to 325°F. Pat meat dry and season on all sides with salt. Heat a large Dutch oven over medium-high. Add the oil. Working in batches if necessary, cook pork and beef until well browned all over, 16 to 18 minutes per batch. Lower the heat if the pan looks like it is scorching or the oil starts smoking.

Meanwhile, thinly slice the scallions crosswise; set aside. Peel the ginger and slice it ¼ inch thick. Pour liquid from kimchi into a measuring cup; roughly chop kimchi and place in a medium bowl. Pour liquid from the can of tomatoes into kimchi juice; tear tomatoes into ½-inch pieces and add to bowl with kimchi.

Transfer browned meat to a large plate (reserve the rendered fat in the pot). Add the scallions and ginger to the pot and cook over medium heat, stirring, until the scallions are very soft and browned and ginger is starting to soften, 6 to 8 minutes (lower the heat and cover the pot if vegetables are browning too quickly). Add the gochugaru, anchovies, and kimchi-tomato mixture and bring to a simmer, stirring and scraping up any browned bits. When liquid is slightly reduced, about 3 minutes, return meat to pan and add chopped kimchi and tomato pieces. Stir to combine. Add enough water to come three-quarters of the way up the meat and vegetables. Increase the heat if needed to bring the liquid to a simmer.

Cover the pot and transfer to the oven. Cook until the meat is totally shreddable, 90 to 110 minutes. Serve with rice.

From the Market	Spin It		At Home	Spin It
Pork stew meat	You can use 2 pounds of either pork or beef instead of a mix		Kosher salt	1 teaspoon crushed red pepper flakes can replace the gochugaru
Beef stew meat			Vegetable oil	
Scallions			Kimchi	
Ginger	Replace scallions with 1 small onion or 2 shallots		Canned tomatoes	2 tablespoons fish sauce can replace the anchovies
			Gochugaru	
			Anchovies	
			Rice	Cooked wheat noodles, such as ramen, can replace the rice

Split Pea Soup and Mustard-Chile Sizzle

6 servings

There are vibrant, bright, colorful foods … and then there's split pea soup. She might not be postcard-worthy, but she's a keeper. (If you make this with orange split peas instead of green, it will be less khaki-colored.) This version includes a fragrant spiced oil on top—it's an example of an Indian technique called tarka (aka tadka; see page 158).

3 garlic cloves

2 celery stalks

1 carrot

1 red onion

⅓ cup plus 3 tablespoons extra-virgin olive oil, divided

Kosher salt; freshly ground pepper

2 teaspoons fennel seeds

1 teaspoon ground turmeric

1 teaspoon ground cumin

1 ham hock

1 pound split peas or red split lentils (2 heaping cups)

12 ounces pale lager-style beer, such as Tecate

2 teaspoons yellow or brown mustard seeds

1 teaspoon crushed red pepper flakes

Roughly chop garlic, celery, carrot, and onion, then transfer to a food processor and pulse until finely chopped, scraping down the sides of bowl as needed. Heat ⅓ cup oil in a large Dutch oven over medium. Add the chopped vegetables, stir to coat, and season with salt and black pepper. Cover and cook, stirring occasionally, until the soffritto has cooked down to coarse paste, the individual vegetables are completely tender, and the surface of the pot is starting to brown, 14 to 16 minutes. Lightly crush the fennel seeds and add them to pot, then add turmeric and cumin and stir to combine. Cook until the spices are bloomed, 1 minute.

Meanwhile, use shears to make 2 vertical cuts through the skin on opposite sides of the ham hock, which will help the fat render. Add to the soffritto and cook, turning hock occasionally, until some fat is released, 3 to 4 minutes. Add the lentils; stir to coat. Pour in beer and simmer until the liquid is reduced by half, 4 minutes. Add 10 cups water and return to a simmer. Partially cover the pot and simmer gently over medium-low heat, stirring occasionally, until the peas have more or less disintegrated and meat shreds when you pull at it with tongs, 1½ to 2 hours.

Transfer ham hock to a cutting board. When cool enough to handle, remove the thick band of skin and fat, then pull meaty parts off the bone; very finely dice fat and cartilage and add to soup, if desired, (freeze the bone for making stock). Cut meat into bite-size pieces and return it to the soup. Taste and adjust the seasonings; keep hot.

Heat remaining 3 tablespoons oil in a small skillet over medium. Add the mustard seeds and cook, swirling pan frequently, until some of them begin to pop, about 2 minutes. Remove from the heat and stir in red pepper flakes. Serve soup with a spoonful of the mustard–red pepper sizzle on top.

From the Market	Spin It	At Home	Spin It
Ham hock	4 ounces slab bacon can sub for ham hock; cut into 1-inch pieces	Garlic	Replace celery with ¼ fennel bulb
Split peas		Celery	
Beer	In place of beer, use 12 ounces dry cider, or omit beer and use 11 cups water in the next step	Carrot	Try smoked paprika instead of turmeric
		Red onion	
		Olive oil	Replace ground cumin with ½ teaspoon cumin seeds, lightly crushed
		Salt and pepper	
		Fennel seeds	
		Ground turmeric	
		Ground cumin	
		Mustard seeds	
		Red pepper flakes	

Black Bean Soup with Topper Whoppers

8 servings

Unlike many other bean recipes in this book, there is no need to soak the black beans; the fact that they take a while to go from dried to creamy is part of their impact. The flavor the beans contribute as they simmer is a major element of the soup, and while they cook, you'll have time to pull together the "topper whoppers"—chips, avocado, sour cream, and other finishers.

2 dried costeño chiles

2 dried taviche (tabiche) chiles

2 canned chipotle chiles in adobo

1 pound dried black beans

1 tablespoon kosher salt, plus more for seasoning

Freshly ground pepper

2 large yellow onions

1 serrano chile

¼ cup neutral oil, such as sunflower

1 tablespoon coriander seeds

2 tablespoons Mexican oregano, plus more for serving

1 tablespoon ground cumin

2 bay leaves

1 cinnamon stick

Corn chips, sour cream, avocado, lime wedges, crumbled queso fresco, and/or cilantro, for serving (optional)

Discard the stems from the dried chiles and drop the costeño, taviche, and chipotle chiles into a blender jar. Add 2 cups hot water; let soak 25 minutes.

Meanwhile, pick over beans, then rinse. Put the beans in a large (6- to 8-quart) pot and cover with 4 quarts cold water. Bring to a simmer over high heat, skimming any foam that rises to surface. Season with 1 tablespoon salt and some pepper. Lower the heat to a simmer.

Finely chop onions and serrano (remove serrano ribs and seeds to reduce spiciness, if desired). In a medium cast-iron or other heavy skillet, heat oil over medium-high until shimmering. Add the onions and serrano and season generously with salt. Cook, stirring occasionally, until the onions go from being translucent and juicy to very soft and richly browned, 12 to 14 minutes. Lightly crush the coriander seeds. Add the coriander, oregano, and cumin to the onions. Cook, stirring, for 1 minute more to bloom the spices. Add a couple ladlefuls of bean liquid to the onions and cook, stirring and scraping with a wooden spoon to loosen up any bits, then pour onion mixture into the beans.

Puree chile mixture until smooth. Pour puree into bean mixture, then add the bay leaves and cinnamon. Partially cover the pot and simmer, stirring occasionally, until the beans are very tender but not quite cooked through, 2 to 2½ hours (or longer, depending on beans). Taste and season with salt, if needed. Simmer gently until the beans are completely soft, 15 to 30 minutes more. Remove the bay and cinnamon.

Puree the soup with a handheld or regular blender, or with a food mill, if desired. Serve topped with corn chips, sour cream, avocado, lime wedges, queso fresco, and/or cilantro, along with oregano, if desired.

From the Market	Spin It	At Home	Spin It
Dried costeño chiles	Guajillo or ancho chiles can replace costeño, and chiles de árbol or chipotles can replace taviches	Dried black beans	Pinto beans, ayocote negro beans, or scarlet runners can replace the black beans
Dried taviche (tabiche) chiles		Salt and pepper	
Serrano chile		Yellow onions	
Canned chipotle chiles in adobo	Jalapeño (less spicy) or habanero (more spicy) could replace the serrano	Neutral oil	Ordinary oregano can be used
Avocado		Coriander seeds	
Queso fresco		Mexican oregano	2 teaspoons ground cinnamon can replace the cinnamon stick
Cilantro		Ground cumin	
		Bay leaves	
		Cinnamon stick	
		Corn chips	
		Sour cream	
		Lime	

The Lalli Family's Spaghetti and Clams

4 servings

Friday night is pasta with vongole since forever, and we have come up with lots of variations as the years have gone by. This combination, with chewy pieces of pancetta and some greens, might be the family favorite, but by no means is this canon. Throw some cherry tomatoes in with the garlic and omit the greens, or use both. Leave out the pork product if you want. You can double or triple the recipe as long as you divide the pasta between two big pots. The only real rule is to make sure the table is set and everyone is within earshot when the clams start to open; hot pasta waits for no one.

Kosher salt; freshly ground pepper

36 littleneck clams

6 garlic cloves

1 bunch Swiss chard

4 ounces pancetta (ask for it in one thick piece, not thinly sliced)

⅓ cup extra-virgin olive oil

¼ cup white wine

1 pound spaghetti or thick spaghetti

Crushed red pepper flakes, for serving (optional)

Bring a large pot of water to boil and season it aggressively with salt (figure ¼ cup salt per 6 quarts water). Place clams in a colander and scrub under cold running water. Be thorough. Transfer to a bowl, cover with cold water, and let soak 5 minutes, then lift the clams out of the water so that the grit stays behind, and return them to the colander.

Thinly slice the garlic; set aside. Cut the chard leaves from the stems, then tear leaves into 2-inch pieces; wash, spin dry, and set aside. Thinly slice the chard stems crosswise and set those aside, too.

Cut the pancetta into ½-inch pieces. Place a Dutch oven or other heavy pot with a lid over medium heat and pour in oil. Cook the pancetta, stirring frequently, until golden brown and starting to crisp, 3 to 5 minutes. Remove with a slotted spoon. Add the garlic and chard stems and cook, stirring frequently, until the garlic is pale golden and stems are translucent, 3 to 4 minutes. Add the wine and simmer until reduced by half, 1 minute. Add clams to the pot and stir to coat. Cover the pot and cook, stirring occasionally, until the clams open, 8 to 12 minutes, checking every couple of minutes and using a slotted spoon to transfer any open clams to a large bowl. Discard any clams that refuse to open at all. Turn off the heat under the Dutch oven.

Add the spaghetti to boiling water and cook, stirring occasionally, until very al dente, 3 minutes less than the time indicated on the package. Use a mesh spider or tongs to transfer spaghetti to the Dutch oven, then add the chard leaves and pancetta (or, reserve 2 cups pasta cooking liquid and drain pasta in a colander). Cook over medium-high heat, tossing pasta in the clam juices and adding pasta water by the ½ cupful, until a glossy sauce forms 3 to 4 minutes. Return clams to the pot, along with any accumulated liquid, and toss to combine. Season with black pepper, then taste for salt. Serve pasta and clams with red pepper flakes for sprinkling over, if desired.

The Usual

My son Cosmo's account of what "clam night" with his grandparents is like can be found on page 213.

From the Market	Spin It	At Home	Spin It
Littleneck clams	Manila clams can be used in place of littlenecks	Salt and pepper	Slice 1 shallot or a small onion and add along with the garlic
Pancetta	Use mussels instead of clams	Garlic	A squeeze of lemon juice and ¼ cup water can replace the wine
Swiss chard	Guanciale or slab bacon can replace the pancetta	Olive oil	Any long pasta can be used; this is also exceptional with fregola
	Mature spinach, arugula, or escarole can be used instead of Swiss chard	White wine	
		Spaghetti	
		Red pepper flakes (optional)	

*Carole and Frank
with the Friday usual
(see page 210).*

Clams
by *Cosmo Music*

Any Friday that our family drives up to my grandparents' house in Connecticut for the weekend, we know that we will have linguine and clams that night. When we get there, we wait for my aunt Nina and uncle Ben. But now we have another family member, my little cousin Gia. But this essay isn't about my family. It's about clams and my family. Now let's not get off topic. When you get to the house and throw open the door, you will feel the cold air of the AC, which my grandpa blasts no matter the weather. When you walk into the house, it is the law to yell, "HELLOOOOOO," and you will be greeted by the sweetest, most caring, cheerful grandma ever, Coppa. Her real name is actually Carole, but when my big brother, Leo, was a baby he couldn't say "Carole," so Coppa became her family name. So as Coppa comes in and hugs you, you hug her back. After that comes in your average baseball-, wine-, and reading-loving grandpa, Frankie. As Frankie hugs you and you hug him, he pats you on the back and says, "Haaaaa, I missed you, little guy." After that, you walk in, and you hear the TV blaring, Coppa goes back to slicing garlic and Frankie sits down in a chair to go back to watching basketball or baseball (depends on the season). Seeing this, you're torn between helping Coppa and sitting down and watching TV with Frankie. Naturally, you would go to the TV and watch for a bit and then go to help Coppa, and if you do that, good.

After about 30 minutes to 4 hours, Neenie and Ben show up. As with Coppa, Neenie's birth name is not what we call her. But Neenie and Ben have their own nicknames for each other: THEY ARE BOTH BOBBY, which makes no sense, to me at least.

Once Ben and Neenie come, the dinner really gets rolling. My mom and Neenie help Coppa. And me and Frankie have to go down to the basement and pick a wine, and there are a lot to choose from. Through the course of COVID, we drank a lot of wine—don't get me wrong, Frankie had had a lot of wine before, but he thought we needed more, so he had gotten more (but we're getting off topic, well, not a lot but I'm driving here, so it's off topic). When we pick the wine we'll have with dinner, dinner is probably really close to being done and Frankie will "make" me open the wine. After *that*, there's still more to do, but once we set the table, it's dinnertime. I don't really think that I need to explain how to set a table, so I'm going to skip that part. And finally, it's time to eat! After all that work, it's done—so what are you eating? Clams, dripping with juice; pasta, warm and al dente between your teeth; and the occasional piece of bacon—basically, all you could ask for in a pasta dinner. And before you know it, you're reaching back into the hot steaming bowl for seconds. This has been a family tradition for twenty-plus years, and I hope it doesn't end anytime soon.

Chapter 9

Give It Up for Vegetables

Textured salads, braised greens, roasted roots,
herby grain salads, and cheesy bakes—fresh,
vibrant, and raw, they're all here, and vegetables
are the stars

Tomato Confit Bruschetta

6 servings

Whenever peak tomato season hits in your part of the world, make this. Sometimes I splurge on pretty heirlooms, but almost nothing beats a ripe beefsteak. When you're done enjoying this recipe, strain and refrigerate the marinating liquid, which can be used in vinaigrettes, to lubricate a pot of beans, or for another batch of tomatoes.

3 large beefsteak tomatoes

Kosher salt; freshly ground pepper

3 garlic cloves, divided

3 sprigs marjoram

1 chile de árbol

1 cup extra-virgin olive oil, or as needed

6 thick slices of crusty bread

Red wine vinegar, for serving

Flaky salt, for serving

Core the tomatoes, then slice crosswise into ½-inch-thick rounds. Layer them in a shallow dish, overlapping a bit and not stacking them right on top of each other; season each layer with kosher salt and pepper as you go. Smash 2 garlic cloves and add them to the dish, along with the marjoram and chile. Slowly pour olive oil over so that it barely kisses the top of the tomatoes (you might not need all of it, or you might need a little more, depending on the dimensions of your dish). Let tomatoes marinate at room temperature for up to 24 hours.

To serve, toast the bread and rub the slices with the remaining garlic clove while still warm. Use a slotted spatula or spoon to lift the tomatoes out of the marinade and onto the toasts. Season with a few dashes of vinegar and top with flaky salt and pepper.

From the Market	Spin It		At Home	Spin It
Tomatoes	Oregano, thyme, or any type of basil can be used		Salt and pepper	Almost any dried chile can be used
Marjoram			Garlic	Lemon juice or sherry vinegar can replace the red wine vinegar
Crusty bread	Instead of making bruschetta, chop the marinated tomatoes and use them as an uncooked pasta sauce		Chile de árbol	
			Olive oil	Use kosher salt if you don't have flaky salt
			Red wine vinegar	
			Flaky salt	

Fresh Peas and Snap Beans with Bread Crumb Dressing

6 servings

This is a mash-up of a spring pea salad and an Italian chopped salad—with a hat tip to a three-bean salad—and is bedecked with lots of chewy, crunchy, creamy, salty, and juicy things to bite into. If you can get a variety of beans and peas, terrific. If you can only find one or two, that's fine—aim for a total weight of 2 pounds and it will all work out.

3 (½-inch-thick) slices white or whole-wheat sandwich bread

Kosher salt; freshly ground pepper

1 pound fresh English peas

8 ounces sugar snap peas

8 ounces thin green beans or wax beans

4 ounces young sheep's-milk cheese

2 ounces hard salami

½ cup Cerignola or Castelvetrano olives (about 12)

2 tablespoons distilled white vinegar

2 tablespoons white wine vinegar

5 tablespoons extra-virgin olive oil

Pinch of sugar

1 sprig oregano

Toast the bread until crisp and golden brown, about 4 minutes, depending on your toaster. Let cool, then break into pieces; blitz in a food processor until finely ground. Don't fully pulverize the bread, but don't leave it chunky, either. (If you have a mortar and pestle, you can do the crushing very easily in that, with less cleanup.)

Bring a medium pot of well-salted water to a boil and set a big bowl of ice water near the stovetop. Line a rimmed baking sheet with a clean kitchen towel. Shell the English peas (you should have about 1 cup). Pull the strings off the sugar snap peas, then halve them crosswise. Trim the ends off the green beans. Boil the beans and peas until bright green but still very snappy, 2 minutes, then drain and submerge in the ice bath to stop the cooking. Let cool. Drain, then spread over the prepared baking sheet and pat dry.

Cut cheese and salami into ¼-inch pieces (you should have about ⅔ cup cheese and ⅓ cup salami, give or take). Pit the olives, then tear the flesh into ¼-inch pieces. Combine peas and beans in a large serving bowl, season with salt and pepper, then add the cheese, salami, and olives. In a small bowl, whisk together both vinegars and the oil; season with salt, pepper, and sugar. Pour the dressing over the salad and toss to coat. Strip the oregano leaves right into the bowl. Add most of the bread crumbs and toss to combine. Let sit for a few minutes so crumbs can absorb some of the dressing, then toss the salad again and top with the remaining crumbs.

From the Market	Spin It		At Home	Spin It
Sandwich bread	Panko can be substituted for fresh bread crumbs; toast before using		Salt and pepper	Red wine vinegar can replace either type of vinegar
English peas			Distilled white vinegar	
Sugar snap peas				A drizzle of honey can be substituted for sugar
Green beans	Fava beans can be used instead of English peas; peel shelled favas after removing from ice bath		White wine vinegar	
Young sheep's-milk cheese			Olive oil	
Hard salami			Sugar	
Cerignola olives	Spanish chorizo can replace salami			
Oregano				

Spiced and Braised Greens

4 to 6 servings

The first time I ever cooked greens this low or slow was when I was making my way through Suzanne Goin's cookbook Sunday Suppers at Lucques. *She has a recipe for Tuscan kale with rosemary that uses so much olive oil I thought it was a mistake. Now I know better. As the greens shrivel down to a more concentrated union, they become rich and almost chewy. I like using the Swiss chard stems as part of the aromatic base for this braise, and the mix of spices seems to season the leaves down to the cellular level.*

3 bunches Swiss chard

⅔ cup extra-virgin olive oil

2 teaspoons kosher salt, plus more as needed

1 head garlic

1½ teaspoons coriander seeds

1 teaspoon fennel seeds

1 teaspoon ground turmeric

½ teaspoon crushed red pepper flakes

Trim the woody ends of the chard stems, then cut the leaves from the stems. Cut leaves crosswise into ½-inch-wide ribbons, then wash and drain (some water clinging to the leaves is okay, but chard can be sandy, so be thorough). Very thinly slice stems crosswise; rinse if necessary.

Heat oil in a medium pot over medium; add the chard stems and season with 2 teaspoons salt. (It will look like a lot of oil, and it is, but it's a vital part of the braising liquid.) Stir to combine, then reduce the heat to medium-low, partially cover the pot, and cook, stirring occasionally, until the stems are softened, shriveled, and light golden brown, 12 to 16 minutes. The shriveling and shrinking won't happen until the moisture in the stems is cooked off; give it time.

Meanwhile, smash the garlic. Crush coriander and fennel seeds in a mortar and pestle or in a spice grinder until coarsely ground (alternatively, roughly chop them). Add the garlic, coriander, fennel, turmeric, and red pepper flakes to the chard stems and cook, stirring occasionally and pressing down on the garlic to break it into smaller pieces, until the garlic is soft and the spices are fragrant, 6 to 8 minutes. Gradually add the greens, tossing with tongs as you help get them all in there and coated with oil. Season with salt, cover the pot, and reduce the heat to low. Cook, stirring every 20 minutes or so and lowering the heat if there's any sign of scorching on the surface of the pan, until the greens are extremely tender, wrinkly, and very dark green in color, 1 hour. There will be a point when the liquid from the greens evaporates and the mixture will start to fry a bit in the cooking liquid, which is how you'll know you're at the end of the process.

Serve hot, warm, or at room temperature. Leftovers will keep, covered, in the refrigerator for about a week (see note at left).

Use Me Up!

Add leftover greens to the egg mixture for a frittata, then top with grated cheddar before broiling. Try adding a few spoonfuls to a pot of beans toward the end of their cooking time. For a dead-simple weeknight dinner, reheat leftover greens, then toss with cooked pasta and a few splashes of pasta cooking liquid; season with lemon juice and top with fresh ricotta.

From the Market	Spin It	At Home	Spin It
Swiss chard	Mature spinach, any type of kale, or escarole can replace the chard (in which case, use a couple celery stalks or half a fennel bulb in place of chard stems)	Olive oil	Try caraway seeds instead of coriander
		Kosher salt	Sweet paprika can replace the turmeric
		Garlic	¼ teaspoon cayenne can replace the red pepper
		Coriander seeds	
		Fennel seeds	
		Ground turmeric	
		Red pepper flakes	

Asparagus with Jammy Egg and Pickle Dressing

8 servings

This dressing is based on the classic French sauce called gribiche, a textured vinaigrette made with hard-boiled eggs, capers, and cornichons. It can accompany vegetables as it does here, and it's also pretty terrific spooned over crispy-skinned fish or roasted salmon. One note about the asparagus: I prefer a medium- or thick-stalked asparagus for heft. Pencil-thin asparagus would get upstaged for sure.

1 shallot

Kosher salt; freshly ground pepper

1 lemon

1 to 2 tablespoons sherry vinegar

8 cornichons

6 Castelvetrano olives

Handful flat-leaf parsley

2 eggs

2 pounds medium or large asparagus

1 teaspoon Dijon mustard

½ cup extra-virgin olive oil

Peel and mince shallot; transfer to a medium bowl and season with salt. Juice lemon into a small liquid measuring cup, then add enough vinegar to measure ⅓ cup total. Pour lemon-vinegar mixture over shallot. Let sit while you prep the remaining ingredients.

Thinly slice the cornichons into rounds and place in a small bowl. Smash and pit the olives, then tear the flesh into small pieces; add to the bowl. Pluck the parsley leaves with some tender stem attached, then gather them up on your cutting board and thinly slice into ribbons (save the remaining parsley stems for making stock). Set caper-olive mixture and parsley aside separately.

Bring a medium pot of water to a boil over high heat; fill a medium bowl with ice and water. Lower eggs into boiling water and cook 7 minutes for jammy yolks. Use a slotted spoon or mesh spider to transfer eggs to ice water and let cool; reserve both ice water and boiling water.

Snap off woody ends of the asparagus, then peel bottom two-thirds of stalks. Season boiling water very generously with salt. Add the asparagus and cook until bright green and crisp-tender, 3 minutes. Transfer to ice bath to cool, then pat dry with a clean kitchen towel and arrange on a platter.

Peel and quarter eggs. Arrange them on and around asparagus. Whisk mustard into shallot mixture, then slowly whisk in olive oil (it won't completely emulsify, but the mixture should thicken). Stir in cornichons, olives, and parsley. Taste dressing and adjust with salt and pepper; spoon over eggs and asparagus.

🕐 Get Ahead

The eggs and asparagus can be cooked several hours in advance; cover and refrigerate. The dressing (without parsley) can be made up to a day in advance; cover and refrigerate. Stir in parsley right before serving.

From the Market	Spin It		At Home	Spin It
Sherry vinegar	Unseasoned rice vinegar, white wine vinegar, and/or coconut vinegar can replace the sherry vinegar		Shallot	Replace shallot with ¼ red onion
Cornichons			Salt and pepper	Add a couple of minced anchovies to the dressing, if desired
Castelvetrano olives			Lemon	
Parsley	Any sour pickled cucumber can replace the cornichons; use about a quarter of one		Eggs	
Asparagus			Dijon mustard	
			Olive oil	

Confit Potatoes with Garlic

2 or 3 servings

This is a very gentle and decadent method to cook potatoes. On their way to tender-town, they will absorb the flavor of the olive oil, garlic, and chiles, and any seasonings you add to the pot. Improvise like crazy when it comes to additions: Herbs, halved shallots, whole spices, and coins of ginger can all go into the oil. To store, transfer the potatoes to a clean jar and strain the oil over. Cover and refrigerate; they'll keep indefinitely. Return them to a pot over medium to reheat the potatoes in oil, or scrape off the fat and cook them over high until brown and crisp.

1 pound waxy potatoes, such as fingerlings

6 garlic cloves, unpeeled

Kosher salt; freshly ground pepper

1 or 2 dried chiles, such as guajillo or chile de árbol

Extra-virgin olive oil, to cover (about 1½ cups)

Preheat the oven to 300°F.

Scrub the potatoes and halve them lengthwise. Combine potatoes and garlic in a medium ovenproof pot and season with salt and pepper. Crumble chiles into the pot, then add enough oil to barely cover the potatoes. Cover and transfer to the oven. Cook until the potatoes and garlic are meltingly tender, about 1½ hours. Let cool in oil.

Smoky Destiny

These potatoes are incredible grilled. Remove them from their cooking fat and scrape off excess. Grill them over direct heat until hot and charred in spots, then season with flaky salt and squeeze lemon juice over.

From the Market	Spin It		At Home	Spin It
Waxy potatoes	Try this with scrubbed carrots, parsnips, or acorn squash wedges		Garlic	Instead of olive oil, use schmaltz, rendered duck or pork fat, or a combination of fats
			Salt and pepper	
			Dried chiles	
			Olive oil	

Broccoli Rabe with
Cheese and Chiles
& Sautéed Brussels
with Sesame

Broccoli Rabe with Cheese and Chiles

4 servings

This is a no-brainer side dish that I will make when I have completely forgotten about making a no-brainer side dish and we're 10 minutes away from eating dinner. You can also turn this broccoli rabe into a main dish by tossing it through pasta (with some pasta liquid to make it saucy) or spooning it onto some of Carole's Fried Bread (page 278). Alternatively, put an egg on it, or use it as a pizza topping or calzone filling.

Kosher salt; freshly ground pepper

2 bunches broccoli rabe

6 garlic cloves

⅓ cup extra-virgin olive oil

½ teaspoon crushed red pepper flakes

2 ounces young Pecorino Toscano, crumbled (about ½ cup)

1 lemon

Bring a medium pot of water to a boil; salt generously. Trim and discard woody ends of broccoli rabe stems, then cut crosswise into 3-inch lengths (the stems, leaves, and florets are all edible). Boil broccoli rabe until bright green and very tender, 5 minutes. This mellows some of the broccoli rabe's natural bitterness, and also keeps it juicy when sautéed (instead of becoming tough and fibrous).

While the broccoli rabe is cooking, thinly slice the garlic.

Drain broccoli rabe and set aside. Return the pot to medium-high heat. Add the oil, garlic, and red pepper flakes and stir to combine. Season with salt and black pepper and cook, stirring, just until the garlic is turning pale golden, 1 to 2 minutes. Return the broccoli rabe to the pot and cook, stirring occasionally, until the garlic is golden brown and the broccoli rabe is starting to brown around edges, 3 to 4 minutes. Spoon onto a platter and sprinkle cheese over right away so it starts to melt. Cut lemon in half and squeeze juice over broccoli rabe.

From the Market	Spin It	At Home	Spin It
Broccoli rabe	Regular broccoli or Broccolini can replace the broccoli rabe, or use a head of escarole, leaves torn	Salt and pepper	A thinly sliced red onion or shallot can be added along with the garlic
Young Pecorino Toscano	Any salty, slightly melty cheese can take the place of the pecorino; try ricotta salata, Monterey Jack, aged cheddar, or even salted mozzarella	Garlic	Use 1 teaspoon milder chile flakes, such as gochugaru, Aleppo pepper, or Urfa biber, in place of the red pepper flakes
		Olive oil	
		Red pepper flakes	
		Lemon	Use a few dashes of red wine vinegar instead of lemon juice

Sautéed Brussels with Sesame

4 servings

I don't know what year we started including these on our Thanksgiving menu, but I do know they never left. The Brussels stay crunchy, fresh-tasting, and sweet because they're barely cooked. They are, however, slightly annoying to prep, especially when scaled up for the holidays. We usually give my dad the entire batch, along with a cutting board, a paring knife, and a football game to watch while he works. You can refrigerate the prepped leaves in an airtight container for up to 2 days.

½ cup walnuts

1 pound Brussels sprouts

6 tablespoons extra-virgin olive oil, divided

Kosher salt; freshly ground pepper

Toasted sesame oil, for drizzling

Preheat the oven or toaster oven to 350°F. Place the walnuts on a small rimmed baking sheet and roast until they're a couple of shades darker and fragrant, 10 minutes, tossing halfway through. Spread them over a cutting board and let cool slightly.

Meanwhile, use a paring knife to trim bottom of the sprouts, then cut out the cores. Peel back and pry off the leaves, working your way to the center and dropping the leaves into a large bowl as you go. Set aside.

Heat a large (10-inch) cast-iron or other heavy skillet over high. Pour in 3 tablespoons olive oil, and when it's shimmering, add half the Brussels sprout leaves. Season with salt and pepper and cook, tossing often, until the leaves are wilted and dark brown in spots but still crunchy, 3 to 4 minutes. Transfer to a large plate and repeat with remaining olive oil and Brussels sprout leaves. When second batch is cooked, return the first batch to the pan and toss to heat through. Add the walnuts and a drizzle of sesame oil and toss to combine.

From the Market	Spin It		At Home	Spin It
Brussels sprouts	Chopped savoy or napa cabbage can be used instead of Brussels sprouts		Walnuts	Toasted pine nuts or hazelnuts could replace walnuts
			Olive oil	
			Salt and pepper	
			Toasted sesame oil	Walnut oil, hazelnut oil, or plain olive oil can replace sesame oil

Double-Roasted Winter Squash with Ginger-Chile Brown Butter

6 to 8 servings

The simplest way to deal with a large, tough-skinned winter squash: Put it in the oven and slow-roast it until it is completely soft from base to stem. Because the flesh is sealed inside that thick skin, it stays completely moist; once the squash is done roasting, you can cut it open easily and claim your treasure. The second roasting called for in this preparation concentrates the flesh, and the spicy-sour sauce complements and balances the sweet vegetal flavors of the squash.

4½ pounds whole winter squash, such as kabocha

3 or 4 fresh hot chiles, such as habanero and/or Fresno

3 limes

3-inch piece ginger

Kosher salt

¼ cup extra-virgin olive oil, plus more for drizzling

6 tablespoons (3 ounces) unsalted butter, cut into a few pieces

Handful cilantro leaves and stems, thinly sliced

Flaky salt

Preheat the oven to 300°F. Line a rimmed baking sheet with foil or parchment paper.

Scrub the squash and prick the skin all over with the tip of a paring knife, then place it on the prepared baking sheet. Roast until the squash is extremely tender when pierced with a cake tester or paring knife, 2½ hours.

Meanwhile, stem chiles; remove seeds for less heat, then mince. Place in a small bowl and finely grate the zest of all 3 limes over. Squeeze lime juice into the same bowl. Finely grate half the ginger into the mixture. Add 1½ teaspoons kosher salt and stir to combine. Let chile-lime mixture sit.

Remove the squash from the oven and increase oven temperature to 425°F. When squash is cool enough to handle, cut it open into a few large sections and scoop flesh into a medium bowl, discarding seeds and stringy bits. Grate in the remaining ginger. Add ¼ cup oil, season with salt, and mash well until thoroughly combined but still chunky in places. (Cover and refrigerate squash mixture for up to 4 days before proceeding, if desired.)

Drizzle a large (10-inch) cast-iron skillet or 2-quart baking dish with oil to coat. Spoon squash into the skillet, then use the back of a spoon to spread it out and create swooshes and divots in the surface. Drizzle with a little more oil, then roast until the squash is dark golden brown on peaks, underneath, and around the edges, 50 to 60 minutes (use a thin metal spatula to lift up the edge and peek underneath to check its progress).

About 10 minutes before the squash is done, melt butter in a small saucepan over medium heat until it foams, then cook, swirling pan frequently, until butter is brown, 4 to 6 minutes. Remove from the heat and stir in 2 tablespoons chile-lime mixture. Spoon ginger-chile butter over the squash and top with cilantro and some flaky salt. Serve with the remaining chile-lime mixture alongside.

From the Market	Spin It	At Home	Spin It
Winter squash	Use butternut, acorn, red kuri, delicata, or calabaza squash in place of kabocha; cook times will vary based on size	Limes	Replace lime juice with juice of 1½ lemons or about ¼ cup grapefruit juice
Fresh hot chiles		Ginger	
Cilantro		Kosher salt	
	If you don't like spicy stuff, omit the chiles	Olive oil	Use 2 garlic cloves instead of ginger
		Butter	
	Mint, basil, chives, and/or chervil can replace the cilantro	Flaky salt	

Pan-Roasted Carrots with Chorizo Nubbins

4 servings

If carrots can be famous for anything, they'd be famous for being everyone's favorite root vegetable. Considering your opinion of the competition (rutabaga, celeriac), that might not be saying much. Their prevailing flavor is sweet, which is why I paired them with lots of bright spices, slightly bitter toasted nuts, and smoky-salty-fatty chorizo.

2 ounces Spanish chorizo

1 pound medium carrots

1 tablespoon extra-virgin olive oil

Kosher salt

½ cup walnut halves

2 sprigs mint

1 teaspoon coriander seeds

2 teaspoons sherry vinegar, plus more as needed

Preheat the oven or a toaster oven to 350°F. Cut chorizo into ¼-inch-thick pieces. Scrub the carrots and halve them crosswise.

Place a 10-inch skillet over medium heat, then add the chorizo and cook, turning occasionally, until some of the fat renders and surface of chorizo looks blistered, 1 to 2 minutes (don't overdo it or chorizo will get tough). Transfer chorizo to a small plate, reserving drippings in the pan. Add the oil to pan, then carrots, and season with salt. Cook, tossing intermittently, until the carrots are dark brown on most surfaces, 12 to 14 minutes. The carrots are going to want to roll onto the same spot and stay there, so be deliberate about turning them onto their non-browned sides so the results are somewhat even.

Meanwhile, toast the walnuts in the oven on a small rimmed baking sheet until they're a couple of shades darker and fragrant, 10 minutes, tossing once halfway through. Spread them out on a cutting board and let cool slightly, then roughly chop. Roughly chop the mint (you should have about ¼ cup loosely packed). Set nuts and mint aside separately.

Lightly crush the coriander, then add it to the skillet with carrots and cook until fragrant, which will be pretty much immediately. Pour in 1 cup water and simmer, turning carrots occasionally, until the liquid is reduced by half, 5 minutes. Return chorizo to pan and simmer until the liquid forms a thin glaze and carrots are tender (not soft) at the center, 5 minutes more. Stick them with a cake tester or cut into one to check.

Add the vinegar and toss to coat, then taste and season with more salt and/or vinegar. Toss in mint and walnuts.

From the Market	Spin It	At Home	Spin It
Spanish chorizo	Diced pancetta or slab bacon can be swapped in for chorizo	Olive oil	Pistachios or almonds can replace walnuts
Carrots	Brussels sprouts can replace the carrots; trim them before adding to pan	Kosher salt	Use fennel or cumin seeds in place of coriander (or omit)
Mint	Instead of mint, use cilantro or fennel fronds	Walnuts	Red or white wine vinegar can stand in for sherry vinegar
		Coriander seeds	
		Sherry vinegar	

Potato Insanity

3 or 4 servings

I love a steamed potato, especially when eaten hot, broken open, and glossed up with some softened butter and salt. And that's the primary reason I found myself with cold leftover steamed potatoes one day; I cut them in half, then reheated them in olive oil until they were robustly browned on the flat side. The two-step cooking process is a little involved, but the results are crazy-good and absolutely foolproof.

1½ pounds small waxy potatoes, such as German Butterballs or fingerlings

Extra-virgin olive oil

Flaky salt

Fill a pot with a few inches of water, then set a steamer basket in the pot. Bring water to a simmer over medium-high heat. Scrub potatoes, then place in steamer basket. Cover and cook until the potatoes are completely tender when pierced with a cake tester (or cut one of the larger ones in half to check), 15 to 20 minutes. Drain potatoes and let cool completely, then halve them lengthwise. (To do ahead, let the uncut potatoes cool, then refrigerate in an airtight container for up to 2 days.)

Heat a large (10-inch) heavy skillet over medium-high. Add enough oil to generously coat the bottom (about 3 tablespoons). Working in batches if necessary, place potatoes in pan, cut side down, and cook, undisturbed, until the surfaces are crisp and very dark mahogany in color, 7 to 10 minutes. Rotate pan occasionally to help them cook evenly, but keep them cut side down.

Transfer to a serving platter, cut side up, and season with salt. Serve immediately, or transfer to a rimmed baking sheet and keep warm in a 350°F oven for up to 30 minutes before serving.

Patience, Darling

If the potatoes stick and don't want to release from the pan, let them keep cooking for a minute or two more before trying again. They will eventually form a nice sturdy crust as they brown.

From the Market	Spin It		At Home	Spin It
Waxy potatoes	This will work with any type of potato except sweet potatoes, which have too much moisture		Olive oil	You can use neutral oil or ghee instead of olive oil
			Flaky salt	Use kosher salt in place of flaky salt

Fried Farro with Grated Cauliflower and Shallots

4 servings

With all due respect to those on grain-free diets, the phrase "cauliflower rice" is rude to rice, and also to cauliflower. Where grains are bouncy and nutty, cauliflower bits are steamy and bland. But I do love cauliflower, so instead of treating it like a grain, I combined it with one. Toasting the cooked farro gives it extra bite (especially if it still has the hull), and cooking the cauliflower until brown and crisp eliminates any sog factor. This is somewhere between a stir-fry and a grain salad, and is equally good hot, warm, or as leftovers the next day.

1½ cups farro (wheat berries), preferably unpearled

1 tablespoon kosher salt, plus more for seasoning; freshly ground pepper

½ cup extra-virgin olive oil, divided, plus more for drizzling

1 medium head cauliflower

3 shallots

½ teaspoon crushed red pepper flakes

1 teaspoon cumin seeds

1 lemon

3 anchovy fillets packed in oil, drained, optional

1 cup loosely packed finely chopped tender herbs, such as cilantro, parsley, and/or mint

Rinse farro, then place it in a medium stockpot and cover with cold water by several inches. Season water with 1 tablespoon salt and several turns of black pepper and bring to a boil over high heat. Lower the heat to maintain a simmer and skim off any foam that rises to the surface, then add a few twirls of olive oil. Cook until the grains are truly al dente—tender but with a little chew and no trace of graininess or chalkiness at the center, 35 to 40 minutes (25 minutes if using pearled farro). Drain and spread over a rimmed baking sheet to cool. (Save the cooking liquid to use in braises and soups.)

Meanwhile, trim stem and outer dark green leaves from the base of the cauliflower, then cut it in half through the crown, core and light green inner leaves included. Roughly chop one half, place pieces in a food processor, and pulse into small bits, 20 to 25 pulses (you should have about 2½ cups chopped cauliflower; save remaining cauliflower half for another use, such as the pasta on page 179).

Thinly slice shallots. Heat a large (12-inch) skillet over medium-high and pour in ¼ cup oil. Add the shallots and season with salt. Cook, stirring frequently, until translucent and tender, about 4 minutes. Add the red pepper flakes and cook, stirring frequently, until the shallots are golden brown all over and starting to crisp, 4 to 6 minutes more (don't take them too far; they'll darken further as they cool). Use a slotted spoon to transfer shallots to a plate and season with salt. Wipe out pan.

Return pan to medium-high heat and pour in 2 tablespoons oil. Add the cauliflower and season with salt and black pepper. Toss to coat, then cook, undisturbed, until the cauliflower is sizzling and starting to sweat on the surface, 3 to 4 minutes. Lightly crush cumin and add it to cauliflower, then toss again. Cook, stirring infrequently, until the cauliflower is tender and dark golden brown on the edges, 3 to 5 minutes more. Transfer to a medium bowl. Finely grate half the zest from the lemon directly onto cauliflower; stir to combine. Set aside.

Return pan to medium-high heat and pour in remaining 2 tablespoons oil. Add the anchovies and break them up with a spoon. Cook until the anchovies disintegrate and oil is sizzling, 1 to 2 minutes. Add the farro, season with salt, and toss to coat. Press farro into the pan with the back of the spoon and cook, undisturbed, until starting to brown, 3 minutes. Toss the farro, stirring, then press it back against surface of pan and cook, undisturbed, until hot and crisp, 3 minutes more. Add the cauliflower and herbs to the farro and toss. Cook until the cauliflower is heated through, about 2 minutes.

Transfer the fried farro to a platter and scatter shallots over. Cut the zested lemon in half and squeeze juice over everything.

From the Market	Spin It	At Home	Spin It
Cauliflower	Broccoli or romanesco can replace the cauliflower; choose one that weighs about 1¾ pounds	Farro	Any whole grain, such as brown rice, spelt, or rye berries, can replace the farro
Tender herbs	All tender herbs are fair game, either alone or in combination, including basil, chives, tarragon, and chervil	Salt and pepper	Use 1 red onion instead of the shallots
		Olive oil	
		Shallots	
		Red pepper flakes	Fennel or coriander seeds can be used in place of cumin
		Cumin seeds	
		Lemon	Lime juice, cider vinegar, or unseasoned rice vinegar can replace the lemon juice (omit zest if using vinegar)
		Anchovies	

Fried Farro with Grated
Cauliflower and Shallots

Eggplant
Parmigiana

Eggplant Parmigiana

8 servings

Making eggplant Parmigiana is a colossal, tremendous time suck. It takes hours and involves salting, pressing, breading, frying, layering, baking, and—finally—broiling. A recipe for eggplant Parm that includes all of those steps and leads to subpar results should inspire unmitigated fear and dread in any recipe developer. I sat with these feelings as I was working on my version, and it wouldn't be here if I didn't think it was worth it. I like to cut the eggplant into relatively thick slices so you can actually enjoy its texture when cooked (as opposed to going super-thin and having eggplant that flattens down to nothingness). I also believe that cold leftover Parm is one of the great gifts to humankind. Put it on a seeded hero roll!

Kosher salt; freshly ground pepper

3 pounds Italian eggplants (about 3 medium)

1 pound fresh mozzarella

6 ounces Parmigiano

3 cups panko bread crumbs

1 cup all-purpose flour

4 large eggs

1½ cups extra-virgin olive oil, divided, plus more for foil

1 cup fresh ricotta (8 ounces)

½ cup finely chopped basil

32 ounces prepared marinara (store-bought or homemade)

Line a large rimmed baking sheet with clean kitchen towels or paper towels and coat with a thin, even layer of salt. Peel eggplants and slice crosswise into ½-inch-thick rounds, transferring to prepared baking sheet as you go. When pan is full, season top sides of eggplant slices with salt. Repeat with another layer of kitchen towels, salt, and remaining eggplant. Top with another layer of towels, then a second rimmed baking sheet; weigh it down with a heavy pot or cast-iron skillet. Let sit until eggplant has released excess liquid, 1 hour. Salting and pressing both seasons the eggplant and helps it achieve a custardy texture when baked. Grate the mozzarella and finely grate the Parm (you should have 1½ cups Parm). Measure out the other ingredients and get organized. You're in for a ride.

Place flour in a shallow bowl, pie plate, or small rimmed baking sheet. Beat the eggs in another shallow bowl. Place the panko in a third shallow bowl.

Working one at a time, dredge eggplant slices in flour, patting off excess, then dip in the eggs, allowing excess to drip off. Coat in the panko, turning and packing panko onto the eggplant so both sides are uniformly covered. Transfer breaded pieces to a rimmed baking sheet as you go.

From the Market	Spin It	At Home	Spin It
Italian eggplant	Other varieties of eggplant, such as Japanese or white, would be excellent; use the same weight. They're smaller, so press for 30 minutes; cook time will be closer to 45 minutes	Salt and pepper	Coarse fresh bread crumbs can replace panko (don't use fine bread crumbs, though)
Fresh mozzarella		Panko	
Fresh ricotta		All-purpose flour	
Basil			Vegetable oil can replace the olive oil, or combine them in any ratio
Marinara		Eggs	
	I've omitted the basil before and no one noticed	Olive oil	
		Parmigiano	Pecorino or Grana Padano can replace the Parm
	Regular mozzarella can replace the fresh variety		

Get Ahead

Eggplant Parmigiana can
be made 2 days ahead; do
everything short of broiling.
Let cool, cover with foil,
and refrigerate. Reheat in a
preheated 350°F oven until
bubbling gently at edges, then
broil as directed.

Fit a wire rack into a rimmed baking sheet. Heat ½ cup oil in a large (preferably cast-iron) skillet over medium-high. When a pinch of panko sizzles as soon as it hits the oil, the pan is hot enough. Cook as many eggplant slices as will comfortably fit in pan, turning once, until the crumbs are deep golden, 5 to 7 minutes total. Transfer to prepared rack to drain. Repeat with remaining slices, adding remaining oil to skillet in ½-cup increments and wiping out skillet as needed between batches.

Moving on: Preheat the oven to 350°F with racks in upper and lower thirds.

Combine ricotta, mozzarella, and basil in a medium bowl, season with salt and pepper, and stir to combine. Spread 1 cup marinara over the bottom of a large cast-iron skillet or shallow Dutch oven. Top with a layer of eggplant slices (there will be some gaps between slices; don't worry about filling them in). Spoon 1 cup marinara over and sprinkle with one-third of Parm. Top with one-third of mozzarella mixture. Top with another layer of eggplant, staggering slices so they are not aligned directly on top of the ones below. Top with another 1 cup marinara, half the remaining Parm, and half the remaining mozzarella mixture. Repeat to make a third layer with remaining eggplant, sauce, Parm, and mozzarella mixture. Cover skillet with lightly greased foil and place on a rimmed baking sheet. Bake on lower rack until the eggplant is custardy, 45 to 60 minutes (peel back foil and poke with a cake tester or chopstick).

Remove the eggplant Parm from the oven and uncover the skillet; heat broiler. Broil eggplant Parm on the upper rack until the cheese is bubbling and browned in spots, 3 to 5 minutes (broilers vary wildly, so start checking after 1 minute to be safe). Let rest 30 minutes before serving.

It's always a good day for Carole's Fried Bread (page 278).

In Bread Together

There are nearly as many phases to a loaf of bread as there are days of the week. There's your just-baked bread, day-old bread, slightly stale bread, pretty hard bread, best-for-bread-crumbs bread, and just-trim-that-part-off bread. I cannot recall a day growing up when there was no bread in the house, but I have plenty of memories of cutting off a discreet patch of mold from the bread we did have and making myself some toast. (Please do not send me food safety missives in response to this. I have gotten this far.) I accepted the bread at each stage for two very simple reasons: My mother, Carole, knew from good bread; and she hated to waste food. Before sourdough starters and "high-hydration baking" had the nerve to become trendy in the modern food world, she brought home dark brown hearty boules and other crusty country loaves to complete their life cycle in our city apartment.

Depending on the day, that loaf had a peak purpose. On the first day, there was nothing better than a fat slice spackled wall to wall with room-temperature butter and topped with kosher salt. On the second day, toast—which my father enjoyed practically blackened, his knife noisy as an ice scraper on a frosty windshield as he spread jam over the craggy surface. On the third day, ideally Sunday, slabs of bread fried in olive oil, rubbed with garlic, again sprinkled with salt, and served alongside the beans-and-greens soups my mom made on the weekends. After that, a crouton or bread crumb could be salvaged, and you cannot imagine the amount of glee that I felt the first time I had a bowl of pasta with toasty bread crumbs showered on top. Carbs on top of carbs! Who knew?!

Eventually all that was left of the ordinary weekly loaf was a heel of bread in the bottom of a well-crumpled brown paper bag. The origins of our family's bread-endy appreciation goes back to an earlier era. My parents, both the grandchildren of immigrants, grew up with enough, but they didn't have a lot, certainly not enough to throw away. By the time I was in grade school, they earned enough together to give me and my sister far more than they had as kids, but that didn't mean they all of a sudden would be okay with trashing bread heels! (Come to think of it, we had Parm rinds in the freezer and Swiss chard stems in the crisper drawer, and my dad's one specialty was pasta topped with all the random scraps of vegetables he could find in the fridge, sautéed together and finished with a little cream.)

Good bread—naturally leavened and devoid of stabilizers and preservatives—has more character than its mass-produced supermarket counterparts. It also requires a lot of labor to make. Once you have good bread in the house, treat it like a basket of berries that will turn to mush if you don't get to them, or a heavy tomato with skin about to split. Prioritize it; remember you have it; enjoy it. Find a way to eat the bread, at its prime the day you bring it home, and still exercising its full potential as a crouton a few days later. Sure, it's resourceful, but it's also a way to prolong the pleasure. When you're down to the nub, sprinkle both sides with some water from the tap, then pop it in the toaster. It will absorb that added moisture as it heats, toasting and rehydrating at the same time. My mom likes an endy spread generously with sweet butter and topped—diagonally—with a lone anchovy, like the snack her grandfather Remo Casini used to make for himself. It's just bread. But we're lucky to have it, the bakers who baked it, and the people who taught us to enjoy it, little moldy bits and all.

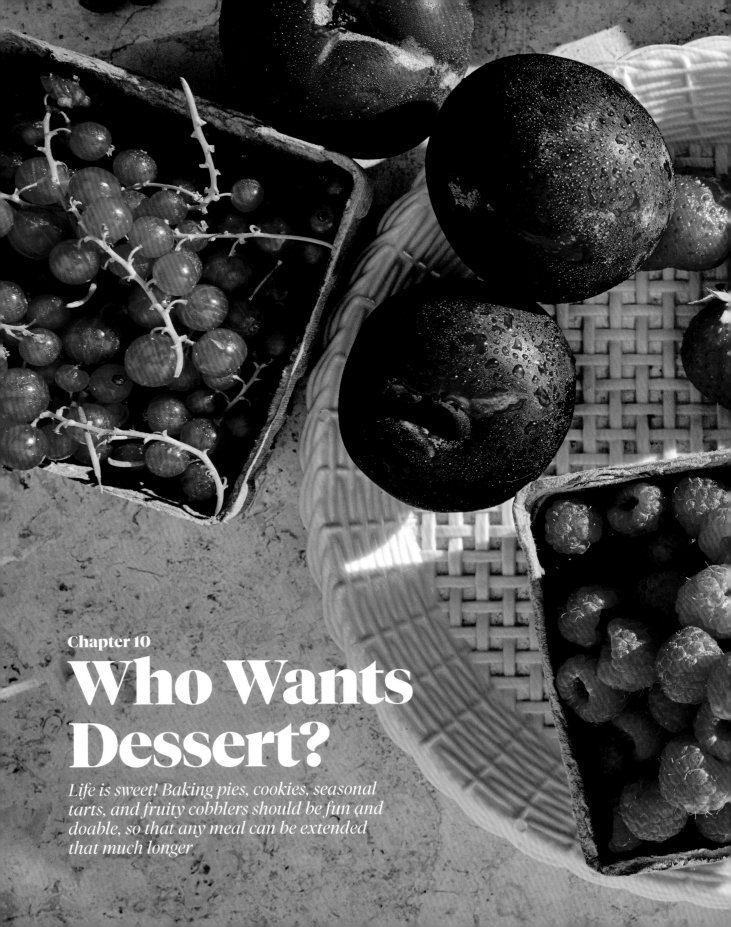

Chapter 10
Who Wants Dessert?

Life is sweet! Baking pies, cookies, seasonal tarts, and fruity cobblers should be fun and doable, so that any meal can be extended that much longer

FRIDAY
and the
WEEKEND

Strawberry-Rhubarb Biscuit Cobbler

8 servings

Adding hard-boiled egg yolks to biscuit dough is not a new thing; I learned it several years ago from making one of legendary pastry chef Claudia Fleming's recipes, but the technique goes back way further than that. The cooked yolk adds richness and heft to the flour mixture, without contributing to gluten formation. The result is a very tender but crumbly, moist biscuit that shape-shifts to cloak a deep bed of red fruit below.

2¼ cups (270 g) all-purpose flour

⅓ cup (64 g) plus 2 tablespoons (24 g) sugar, divided, plus more for sprinkling

1 teaspoon (3 g) kosher salt, plus more for seasoning

2 teaspoons (10 g) baking powder

½ teaspoon (2 g) baking soda

2 hard-boiled large egg yolks

10 tablespoons (5 ounces/140 g) cold unsalted butter, cut into tablespoon-size pieces

1 cup (240 ml) cold heavy cream

2 pounds (896 g) strawberries, hulled, halved if large

1 pound (448 g) rhubarb (about 10 medium stalks), trimmed and cut crosswise into 1-inch lengths

2 tablespoons (16 g) cornstarch

2 tablespoons (30 ml) fresh lemon juice

1 vanilla bean

Whipped cream and/or vanilla ice cream, for serving

Combine flour, 2 tablespoons (24 g) sugar, salt, baking powder, baking soda, and egg yolks in a food processor. Pulse until the yolks are broken into small pieces, about 12 pulses. Add the butter and pulse until the butter is in very small beads and the mixture resembles cornmeal, 35 to 40 pulses. This is not a flaky pastry dough, where you would want to leave rather large pieces of butter visible; taking it further so that the flour is encased in butter and the yolks are interspersed throughout will create a water-resistant barrier around the flour that impedes gluten development. Add all but about 2 tablespoons (30 ml) cream and pulse just to bring dough together, about 5 pulses (don't overdo it).

Turn out dough onto a lightly floured work surface and, with floured hands, pat and press it out to a 10 by 6-inch rectangle, ½ inch thick. Cut in half lengthwise, then make 4 cuts crosswise to yield 8 rectangular biscuits total. Transfer biscuits to a small rimmed baking sheet and chill while you make the fruit mixture.

Preheat the oven to 350°F. Line a rimmed baking sheet with parchment paper or foil.

Gently toss strawberries and rhubarb in a large bowl with remaining ⅓ cup (64 g) sugar, cornstarch, and lemon juice. Split vanilla bean lengthwise; scrape seeds into the bowl. Season with a pinch of salt and toss again to combine. Let sit until juicy, 15 minutes, then transfer to a 2-quart baking dish and place the dish on the prepared baking sheet (this is to catch any juices that bubble over). Remove the biscuits from the refrigerator, brush with remaining cream, then sprinkle liberally with sugar. Place the biscuits on top of fruit, spacing them evenly. Bake until the biscuits are dark golden brown and juices are bubbling around edges, 1 hour. Let cool 20 minutes before serving with whipped cream, ice cream, or both!

From the Market	Spin It		At Home	Spin It
Heavy cream	Raspberries or blackberries can replace the strawberries		Flour	Replace vanilla bean with 1 tablespoon pure vanilla extract, vanilla paste, or almond extract
Strawberries			Sugar	
Rhubarb			Kosher salt	
Vanilla ice cream			Baking powder	
			Baking soda	
			Eggs	
			Butter	
			Cornstarch	
			Lemon	
			Vanilla bean	

Pink Party Cookies

Makes about 24 sandwich cookies

These celebration cookies, referred to as "PPCs," belong to my husband's family. His late maternal grandmother, the famous Grandma Margaret, was an exceptional baker, and Pink Party Cookies were one of her most coveted treats—an impossibly short, blond cookie sandwiching a pastel-pink cream filling. The cookie has no leavener, and there should be almost no discernable color on them when baked. I hope this recipe does right by Margaret, who left behind recipe notecards and lots of oral instructions. If the dough feels too soft or smushy when you are rolling it into balls, chill it for 10 minutes to firm it back up.

FOR THE COOKIES

2¼ cups (270 g) all-purpose flour, plus more for dusting

½ cup (60 g) confectioners' sugar

½ teaspoon (2 g) kosher salt

12 tablespoons (6 ounces/168 g) unsalted butter, at room temperature

¼ cup (56 g) vegetable shortening

1 teaspoon (5 ml) pure vanilla extract

FOR THE FILLING

6 tablespoons (3 ounces/84 g) unsalted butter, melted and cooled slightly

2 cups (240 g) confectioners' sugar

1 tablespoon (15 ml) maraschino cherry liquid, plus more if desired

1 to 2 tablespoons heavy cream (15 to 30 ml)

MAKE THE COOKIES: Preheat the oven to 350°F.

In a medium bowl, whisk together flour, confectioners' sugar, and salt. In a large bowl or the bowl of a stand mixer fitted with the paddle attachment, cream together butter and shortening on medium speed until smooth, 1 minute. Scrape down bowl, then add the vanilla and beat to combine. Add the flour mixture and beat on low until the dough comes together, 1 minute more. Portion dough into about 1½-teaspoon (10 g) pieces, then roll them between your palms to form balls, setting them 2 inches apart on a baking sheet as you go. Use a lightly floured fork to slightly flatten the balls and create a crosshatch pattern, rocking the fork from one side to the other rather than pressing straight down into the dough. Bake until there's a barely perceptible tint of light golden around edge, 8 minutes. Do not overbake. Let cookies cool completely on the pan before filling.

MAKE THE FILLING: In a medium bowl, whisk together melted butter, confectioners' sugar, and cherry liquid to combine. The mixture may look stiff to begin with, and might appear shiny, greasy, or broken once the sugar dissolves. Add 1 tablespoon (15 ml) cream and whisk to combine and re-emulsify. The filling should be spreadable but not too liquidy; add the remaining 1 tablespoon (15 ml) cream if needed (or if the filling stiffens while you're working with it). You can make it more pink, if desired, by adding more cherry liquid ½ teaspoon at a time.

Spoon about 2 teaspoons filling onto the flat side of a cookie, then sandwich with a second cookie, flat side down, and press lightly to adhere. Repeat with remaining cookies and filling (you may have some extra filling). Let filling set before serving or storing cookies.

🕐 Get Ahead

The unfilled baked cookies can be stored in an airtight container in the refrigerator for several days or frozen for up to 2 months. Filled cookies can be stored in the freezer for up to 2 months. Let them come to room temperature before eating (or enjoy them cold).

From the Market	Spin It		At Home	Spin It
Vegetable shortening	I suppose you could use red food coloring instead of cherry liquid, but Grandma Margaret might not approve		Flour	You can use salted butter and omit the kosher salt
Maraschino cherries			Confectioners' sugar	
Heavy cream			Kosher salt	Almond extract can replace the vanilla
	Half-and-half or milk can be used instead of cream		Butter	
			Vanilla extract	

Warm Barley with Berries

6 servings

I have a very distinct and dreamy memory of being served a bowl of warm barley with honey and milk at a friend's house when I was a little kid, and the comfort of having porridge for dessert has stayed with me. I don't remember the mom who made it for us, but I remember so clearly how it tasted, how amazing I thought it was, and how I had never had anything like it. This recipe is a distorted re-creation of that taste memory. I know that as an adult, through decades of foggy memories, I couldn't experience that flavor again, or the way it affected me, so I came at it a different way. It's not the same, but how could it be?

1 cup (216 g) hulled barley (groats)

1 cup (240 ml) buttermilk

¼ cup lightly packed (48 g) plus 1 tablespoon (12 g) light or dark brown sugar

½ teaspoon (2 g) kosher salt, plus more as needed

1 orange

1 lemon

1½ pounds (672 g) raspberries (2 pints)

Combine barley, buttermilk, ¼ cup (48 g) brown sugar, 2 cups (480 ml) water, and salt in a medium saucepan. Use a vegetable peeler to remove wide strips of zest from half the orange and half the lemon; add the zest to the pot. Bring the mixture to a simmer over high heat, stirring to dissolve sugar. Lower the heat to maintain a gentle simmer, partially cover the pot, and cook, stirring occasionally, until the barley is tender, 36 to 40 minutes. Some foam may rise to the surface during cooking and the liquid may look curdled, but go ahead and stir it back in and it will all work out in the end. Pluck out the strips of zest and let mixture sit, covered, while you prepare the berries. (Alternatively, let cool completely, then reheat gently with an additional ½ cup (120 ml) water, stirring occasionally, until warm.)

Place the berries in a medium bowl and finely grate remaining zest from orange and lemon over. Cut citrus in half and squeeze in their juice. Add the remaining 1 tablespoon (12 g) brown sugar. Stir well, breaking up some berries with the edge of the spoon, until mixture is juicy and sugar has dissolved.

Serve barley in shallow bowls, topped with berries and their juices.

From the Market	Spin It		At Home	Spin It
Raspberries	Any berry can replace or be combined with the raspberries		Barley	Make this with any whole grain, such as brown rice, wheat berries, or spelt
			Buttermilk	
			Brown sugar	Use milk instead of buttermilk, or omit the buttermilk and use 3 cups water total
			Kosher salt	
			Orange	
			Lemon	Replace brown sugar with 3 tablespoons maple syrup or honey

Mocha Hazelnut Biscotti

Makes about 24 biscotti

I grew up in the '80s. We had a curved glass-brick wall in the living room, I had unironic Jordache jeans and an asymmetrical bob, and it was cool to order biscotti for dessert. That hairdo is a pretty hard sell today, but these firm but tender cookies deliver. Dunk them in rum, amaro, cold milk, or espresso and, if you're like me, be thankful you went through your awkward phases in an era before digital photography.

½ cup (67 g) hazelnuts

3 large eggs

2 tablespoons (16 g) instant coffee or espresso

2 cups (240 g) all-purpose flour

¼ cup (20 g) unsweetened Dutch-process cocoa powder

2 teaspoons (10 g) baking powder

1 teaspoon (3 g) kosher salt

8 tablespoons (4 ounces/ 112 g) unsalted butter, at room temperature

1 cup (192 g) sugar, plus more for sprinkling

2 teaspoons (10 ml) pure vanilla extract

½ cup (90 g) semisweet chocolate chips

Preheat the oven to 350°F. Line two rimmed baking sheets with parchment paper. Place hazelnuts on a small rimmed baking sheet and toast until darkened and fragrant, 10 to 12 minutes. Wrap in a clean kitchen towel to trap steam and let cool, 10 minutes. Using towel, vigorously rub hazelnuts to remove skins (it's okay if not all of them release); roughly chop nuts and set aside. Reduce oven temperature to 325°F.

Separate 1 egg, placing white and yolk in separate small bowls. Cover egg white; set aside. Crack remaining 2 eggs into the bowl with egg yolk. Add the instant coffee to the whole egg mixture and beat to combine. In a medium bowl, whisk together the flour, cocoa powder, baking powder, and salt.

In the bowl of a stand mixer fitted with the paddle attachment, beat butter and sugar on medium speed until creamy, 2 minutes. Scrape down the bowl, then add the egg mixture and vanilla and beat on medium until combined, 1 minute. Scrape again and beat until creamy. Add the flour mixture and mix on low until combined, 20 seconds; scrape the bowl. Add the nuts and chocolate chips; mix on low to combine.

Scrape dough out onto one prepared baking sheet. With damp hands, press dough into a loaf about 14 inches long, 4 inches across, and 1 inch thick. Beat egg white until foamy, then brush it over the top and sides of the dough. Sprinkle an even, generous layer of sugar over top.

Bake until the loaf is firm in the center when pressed and starting to crisp around the edges, 35 to 40 minutes, rotating pan halfway through (it will spread as it bakes). Remove from the oven; let cool 15 minutes (longer is okay, but it needs at least this much time to firm up a bit). Carefully transfer loaf to a cutting board, then use a serrated knife to cut it crosswise into ½-inch-thick pieces. Using both prepared baking sheets this time, lay slices on a cut side and bake until the surfaces feel dry and crisp, 35 minutes. Let biscotti cool completely before eating. Store airtight at room temperature for up to 1 week.

From the Market	Spin It		At Home	Spin It
Cocoa powder	You can omit the cocoa powder; everything else stays the same		Hazelnuts	Almonds or walnuts can replace the hazelnuts
Semisweet chocolate chips			Eggs	
			Instant coffee	
	The same weight of chopped chocolate or milk chocolate can be substituted for chocolate chips		Flour	You can omit the coffee, but these won't be mocha anymore
			Baking powder	
			Kosher salt	
			Butter	Almond or coffee extract can be used in place of vanilla
			Sugar	
			Vanilla extract	

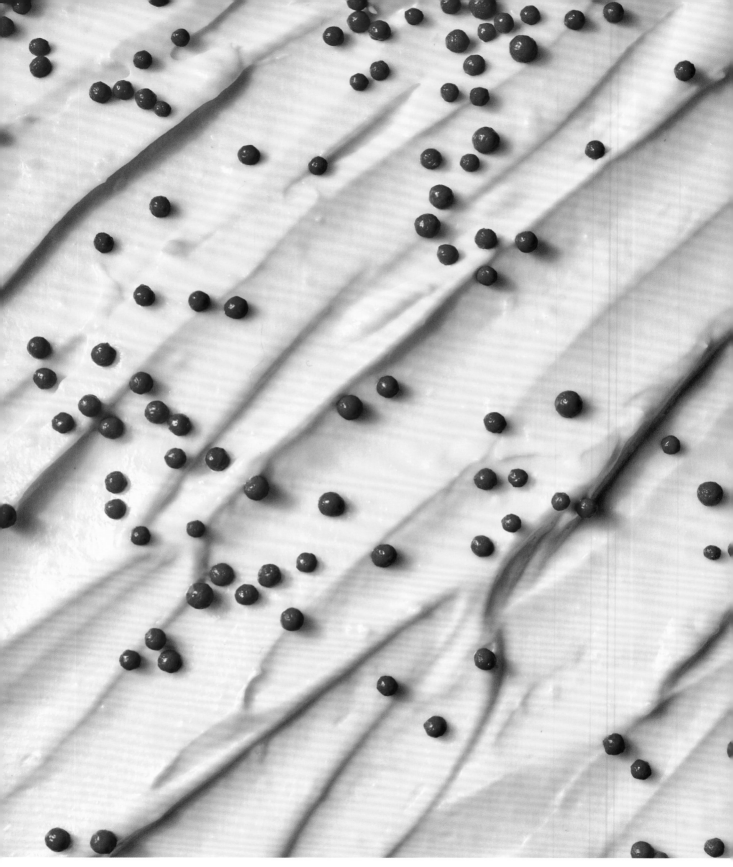

**Lemon Polenta
Sheet Cake with
Cream Cheese
Frosting**

Lemon Polenta Sheet Cake with Cream Cheese Frosting

16 servings

I've never had a particularly deep love for classic yellow cake, but this sheet cake is an exception. The combination of polenta and lots of egg yolks makes it deep canary yellow and more savory than the ordinary birthday cake, and the texture is both tender and rich. (Everyone knows that cream cheese frosting is the best, so there's really nothing to say on that matter!) This is an ideal celebration cake, and it actually gets better on day two, giving you extra incentive to get your baking out of the way early. My friend Sohla El-Waylly helped me workshop the crumb (via text messages, no less!) while I was developing this; I'm grateful for her expertise.

FOR THE CAKE

1 cup (8 ounces/224 g) unsalted butter, cut into tablespoon-size pieces, at room temperature, plus more for the pan

3 cups (360 g) all-purpose flour, plus more for the pan

1¾ cups (420 ml) buttermilk, at room temperature

2 tablespoons (30 ml) extra-virgin olive oil

1 tablespoon (15 ml) pure vanilla extract

1 teaspoon (5 ml) almond extract

½ cup (70 g) medium- or fine-ground polenta

2 cups (384 g) granulated sugar

1 lemon

2 teaspoons (10 g) baking powder

1 teaspoon (4 g) baking soda

1 teaspoon (3 g) kosher salt

3 large eggs

3 large egg yolks

FOR THE FROSTING

8 ounces (224 g) cream cheese

8 tablespoons (4 ounces/ 112 g) unsalted butter, at room temperature

1 teaspoon (5 ml) pure vanilla extract

1½ cups (180 g) confectioners' sugar

1½ teaspoons (4 g) kosher salt

Sprinkles, for decorating (optional)

MAKE THE CAKE: Preheat the oven to 350°F. Grease a 9 by 13-inch pan with butter, then dust with flour, tapping out excess.

In a medium measuring cup, whisk together the buttermilk, oil, vanilla and almond extracts to combine. Whisk in polenta; set aside to let polenta hydrate while you prepare batter.

Place the granulated sugar in the bowl of a stand mixer or a large bowl and finely grate lemon zest over (set zested lemon aside). Use your fingertips to work zest into sugar until the sugar is fragrant and the zest is evenly dispersed (sugar will look a little fluffy), 2 to 3 minutes. Add flour, baking powder, baking soda, and salt and whisk well to thoroughly combine. Add the butter to dry ingredients, then fit mixer with the whisk attachment (or use a handheld mixer) and whisk on low to combine. Increase speed to medium and beat until the butter is in very fine beads and the mixture is pale yellow with a texture that resembles finely grated cheese, 4 to 5 minutes, scraping bowl down halfway through.

Whisk eggs and egg yolks into buttermilk mixture just until combined.

From the Market	Spin It		At Home	Spin It
Almond extract	Omit the almond extract, if you wish		Butter	In place of buttermilk, whisk together 1¼ cups whole milk and ½ cup plain yogurt (not Greek)
Polenta			Flour	
Cream cheese	Stone-ground grits (not quick-cooking) can be used instead of polenta		Buttermilk	
Sprinkles (optional)			Olive oil	Neutral oil can replace the olive oil
			Vanilla extract	
			Granulated sugar	Use 2 teaspoons lime, orange, or grapefruit zest to replace the lemon zest, along with 2 tablespoons of the juice of whichever one you choose
			Lemon	
			Baking powder	
			Baking soda	
			Kosher salt	
			Eggs	
			Confectioners' sugar	

Flip It and Reverse It

This recipe is an example of the "reverse creaming" method, which is not nearly as technical as it sounds but has a big impact on the final texture and shape of the cake. Instead of beating together butter and sugar in the first step, which aerates the butter and leads to a domed cake with larger air bubbles in the crumb, you start this batter by mixing butter and flour until very crumbly. Coating the flour in butter creates a water-resistant barrier, which will help prevent gluten from forming when the liquids are added. The cake will be more tender as a result, with a denser crumb, and the top will rise evenly, without doming.

With mixer on low, gradually whisk half the buttermilk mixture into batter until incorporated, 30 seconds, scraping down bowl as needed. Add the remaining buttermilk mixture and whisk on medium until the batter is smooth, 1 minute. Scrape down bowl, making sure to get all the way to the very bottom. Increase speed to medium-high and whisk until the batter is pale, fluffy, and smooth, 2 minutes, scraping down bowl halfway through. (All this scraping sounds repetitive, I know, but there's a lot of batter in the bowl and making sure it's thoroughly and evenly mixed will prevent the cake from forming a dense, gluey bottom layer when baked.) Scrape batter into prepared pan and smooth top. Bake until cake is dark golden brown and springs back when pressed, 50 to 55 minutes. Run a knife around the edge, then let cake cool in pan on a wire rack for 1 hour. Turn out cake onto wire rack and let cool completely. (At this point, you can wrap cake airtight and store at room temperature for up to 2 days.)

MAKE THE FROSTING: Juice zested lemon and measure 2 tablespoons (30 ml); reserve the rest for another use. In the bowl of a stand mixer, beat together cream cheese, butter, lemon juice, and vanilla on medium-high speed until combined, 1 minute (or use a large bowl and an electric mixer). Scrape down bowl. Add the confectioners' sugar and salt and beat on low until the dry ingredients are incorporated, then increase speed to medium-high and beat until the frosting is pale and fluffy, 3 to 4 minutes more, scraping down bowl halfway through.

Return cake to baking pan or place on a cutting board or rimmed baking sheet. Scrape frosting onto center of cake, then use a spatula, large spoon, or offset spatula to spread frosting over entire surface, creating fun swoops and swirls as desired. Decorate with sprinkles, if desired, before cutting into 16 rectangles. You can serve it from the baking pan (which has the advantage of being portable!), or transfer the cake pieces to individual plates or a serving platter.

Grapefruit-Rosemary Shortbread Cookies

Makes 16 cookies

This cookie was in regular rotation in my house growing up, especially around the holidays, and is probably one of the first savory-salty desserts I fell in love with. The original recipe that my mom used was published in a book called Farmhouse Cookbook *by Susan Herrmann Loomis; I added the zest and messed with some of the proportions, and changed the method to use a food processor. The texture of these is crumbly from the rice flour, but as long as you don't overbake them, they'll stay tender and buttery.*

1½ cups (180 g) all-purpose flour

⅓ cup (53 g) rice flour (not sweet rice flour)

½ teaspoon (2 g) kosher salt, plus more as needed

2 tablespoons finely chopped rosemary leaves

1 cup (8 ounces/224 g) unsalted butter, at room temperature

½ cup (96 g) plus 1 tablespoon (12 g) sugar, divided

2 teaspoons (10 ml) finely grated grapefruit zest

Flaky salt, for topping

Line an 8-inch square baking dish with parchment paper, leaving a few inches of overhang on two sides (for lifting the bars out later). In a medium bowl, whisk together all-purpose flour, rice flour, salt, and rosemary.

In a food processor, combine the butter, ½ cup (96 g) sugar, and grapefruit zest and process until homogenous, 30 seconds. Scrape down bowl and add the flour mixture. Using short pulses, process mixture until crumbly, about 15 pulses, then use long pulses until the dough starts to ball up around blade, scraping down bowl as needed. Transfer dough to the prepared pan, then use an offset spatula to press it firmly and evenly into the pan, smoothing the top. Chill until firm, 1 hour.

Preheat the oven to 350°F. Prick shortbread with a fork in about 10 places, then sprinkle remaining 1 tablespoon (12 g) sugar and some flaky salt over the top. Bake until slightly brown around edges and evenly golden on surface, 30 to 35 minutes, rotating pan halfway through.

Remove from the oven and use a paring knife to cut the shortbread (still in the pan) in half crosswise, so you end up with 2 rectangles, each 4 inches high and 8 inches across. Make 7 vertical cuts, each spaced 1 inch apart, to make 16 bar-shaped cookies, 4 inches high and 1 inch across. Let cool in pan. Using overhanging parchment, lift cookies out of pan and retrace cut marks if necessary to separate the bars.

🕐 Get Ahead

The dough can be wrapped airtight and frozen for up to 3 months; thaw overnight in the refrigerator before baking. The baked cookies can be stored in an airtight container at room temperature for up to 1 week or frozen for up to 3 months.

From the Market	Spin It	At Home	Spin It
Rice flour	Use only all-purpose flour if you don't have rice flour; the shortbreads won't be quite as crumbly, but still good	All-purpose flour	All these basic baking ingredients are nonnegotiable!
Rosemary	Thyme or lavender can be used in place of rosemary	Kosher salt	
Grapefruit	Orange or lemon zest can replace the grapefruit zest	Butter	
		Sugar	
		Flaky salt	

Vanilla–Brown Butter Pear Tart

8 servings

This fruity tart has a buttery, flaky tart shell, and the filling is a mix of pears and a browned-butter batter that feels like a cross between a custard and an airy cake. There are lots of strategies for breaking up the process of making this: The disc of dough can chill for a couple of days, and the unbaked tart shell can be wrapped and refrigerated for up to 2 days. Once the dough is blind-baked, you can let it sit for several hours before filling and baking it.

FOR THE DOUGH

1¼ cups (150 g) all-purpose flour

1 teaspoon (4 g) sugar

½ teaspoon (2 g) kosher salt

8 tablespoons (4 ounces/ 112 g) unsalted butter, cut into 8 pieces and chilled

FOR THE FILLING

8 tablespoons (4 ounces/ 112 g) unsalted butter, cut into 8 pieces and chilled

½ vanilla bean, halved lengthwise

2 pounds (896 g) firm but ripe pears, such as Comice (about 3 large or 4 medium)

1 lemon

3 large eggs

½ cup (96 g) sugar

⅓ cup (40 g) all-purpose flour

1 teaspoon (3 g) kosher salt

MAKE THE DOUGH: In a small measuring cup, combine a few ice cubes with ¼ cup (60 ml) cold water; set aside. Dump the flour onto a clean work surface and toss in sugar and salt with your fingers to distribute. Add butter and toss to coat, then use a rolling pin to roll the butter into the flour until the butter is flattened into long, thin pieces. This will take a few passes to achieve. Pause after every few rolls and use a bench scraper to scrape the work surface and rolling pin clean if butter and flour stick to it, which they definitely will. Flour the pin as needed, and work quickly so the butter stays cold. When the butter pieces are flattened and flexible (not soft and mushy), you've arrived.

Use bench scraper to corral the mixture into a tidy mound, then drizzle ¼ cup (60 ml) ice water over. Using the bench scraper and your free hand, toss until the water is evenly distributed, then gather into a 6-inch-wide rectangle with a short end toward you. Lightly flour rolling pin and roll dough out to a long rectangle about ¼ inch thick, dusting dough, work surface, and pin with flour if needed to prevent any sticking. You'll need to periodically scrape rolling pin clean, letting scraps fall onto dough as you go. The dough will be very crumbly.

Once dough is in a long rectangle, use bench scraper to fold top third over the center, then fold bottom third up and over, as you would fold a letter. Rotate dough 90 degrees and roll out to a rectangle again (flouring and scraping as before). Fold dough into thirds again, rotate 90 degrees, and roll out a third time. At this point, dough should be somewhat homogenous and creamy looking with some dry bits around edges. Squeeze a bit in your palm; it should loosely hold together. If not, repeat rolling and folding a fourth time, then check again. Fold dough in thirds and press it into a disc about 1 inch thick and 9 inches across. *(recipe continues)*

From the Market	Spin It		At Home	Spin It
Vanilla bean	Use 2 teaspoons vanilla extract instead of vanilla bean		Flour	Use 6 table-spoons extra-virgin olive oil instead of the butter; warm it with the vanilla to infuse
Pears			Sugar	
	Use Pink Lady or Granny Smith apples instead of pears		Kosher salt	
			Butter	
	Use peaches, nectarines, or plums; add 1 tablespoon cornstarch when combining with lemon juice		Lemon	Lime juice or 2 teaspoons rice vinegar can replace the lemon juice
			Eggs	

Wrap dough tightly; chill for 30 minutes (or up to 24 hours).

Roll out dough on a lightly floured surface to a round about ⅛ inch thick and 14 inches across. If dough sticks to surface, lift on one side and scatter flour underneath, then make sure the dough moves freely before continuing. Don't stress about cracks around the edge; dust work surface and rolling pin with flour as needed and rotate dough often to prevent wider cracks. Roll dough onto your pin, then unfurl it over a 10-inch tart pan with a removable bottom, letting excess dough hang over the rim. Working your way around edge, lift up the dough at the outside edge and let it slump down into the pan so that it lies against the bottom without being stretched. Use shears or a paring knife to trim overhang to 1 inch, then use the backs of your fingers to press dough flat against the bottom of the pan, making sure it's flush with corners. Fold overhang into tart shell rim so the crust is double thick at edge, then press the edge firmly against rim of the pan. Refrigerate for 30 minutes (or wrap and chill for up to 24 hours).

When ready to bake, preheat oven to 350°F. Line a rimmed baking sheet with parchment paper or aluminum foil.

Prick the surface of the dough with a fork in 6 places, evenly spaced. Line tart shell with parchment or foil, then fill with pie weights, dried beans, uncooked rice, or the quarters and nickels from the jar of change you keep on your dresser. Place the tart pan on prepared baking sheet and bake until the edges are light golden and the surface feels matte and firm, 35 to 40 minutes (carefully lift up the weights and parchment to check). Gently lift out weights and parchment, then bake tart shell until firm and very golden, 20 to 25 minutes more. Let cool at least 10 minutes before filling.

MEANWHILE, MAKE THE FILLING: Place the butter in a small saucepan or skillet; scrape in seeds from the vanilla bean and add the pod. Cook over medium heat until the butter melts, then foams, 1 to 2 minutes. Reduce the heat to medium-low and cook, swirling pan frequently, until the foaming subsides and milk solids at bottom of the pan turn dark golden brown, 2 to 4 minutes more. Scrape any brown butter into a medium bowl; remove vanilla pod. Set aside to cool.

Halve the pears lengthwise (no need to peel them), then use a teaspoon or small melon baller to scoop out the cores. Cut each half lengthwise into thin slices (less than ¼ inch thick). Transfer to a medium bowl and squeeze in juice from lemon; toss very gently to coat.

Add the eggs and sugar to cooled brown butter and whisk to combine. Add the flour and salt and whisk until the batter is thick and smooth, 1 minute.

Arrange pears in tart shell in whatever pattern you like, overlapping them and fanning them out a bit to fit, making sure to cover entire surface of crust. Whisk batter to recombine, then pour it over pears, tapping pan gently against counter to help the batter settle and spread. Bake until the filling is browned, puffed, and set and the pears are tender, 50 to 55 minutes. Let cool at least 30 minutes before serving.

Nectarine and Brown Sugar Streusel Crisp

6 servings

Toasting the oats before combining with the rest of the streusel ingredients helps the topping get truly crunchy and crisp when baked, despite being perched atop a steamy bed of juicy stone fruit.

FOR THE FRUIT

3 pounds (1344 g) nectarines, pitted and cut into ½-inch-wide wedges (unpeeled)

¼ cup lightly packed (48 g) dark brown sugar

¼ cup (48 g) granulated sugar

2 tablespoons (16 g) cornstarch

2 tablespoons (30 ml) cider vinegar

½ teaspoon (2 g) kosher salt

FOR THE TOPPING

½ cup (48 g) rolled oats (not quick-cooking)

½ teaspoon (1 g) ground cardamom

1 cup (120 g) all-purpose flour

⅓ cup lightly packed (64 g) dark brown sugar

⅓ cup (64 g) granulated sugar

½ teaspoon (2 g) kosher salt

8 tablespoons (4 ounces/112 g) cold unsalted butter, cut into tablespoon-size pieces

Soft-peak whipped cream, for serving (optional; see page 278)

Preheat the oven to 375°F. Line a rimmed baking sheet with foil.

PREPARE THE FRUIT: Gently toss the fruit, brown sugar, granulated sugar, cornstarch, vinegar, and salt in a 2-quart baking dish to coat. Let sit while you prepare the topping.

MAKE THE TOPPING: On a small rimmed baking sheet or in an ovenproof skillet, toss oats and cardamom together. Bake until the oats are light golden brown and fragrant, 10 to 12 minutes. Let cool. Transfer to a food processor and add flour, brown sugar, granulated sugar, and salt. Pulse to combine. Add the butter and pulse just until the mixture starts to clump and butter is in pea-size pieces, 30 to 35 short pulses.

Gently toss fruit to redistribute juices. Squeeze handfuls of the topping together to form clumps, then arrange it over the fruit (there will be some bigger pieces of streusel and some floury bits, and that's fine). Place the baking dish on the prepared baking sheet (to catch any drips) and bake until streusel is dark golden brown and juices are bubbling around the edge, 55 to 65 minutes. Serve warm, topped with whipped cream, if desired.

From the Market	Spin It		At Home	Spin It
Nectarines	Peaches, apricots, plums, cherries, berries, apples, pears, or a combination can replace the nectarines		Dark brown sugar	Use light brown sugar instead of dark
Rolled oats			Granulated sugar	All-purpose flour can replace the cornstarch in a pinch (it may make the juices a little cloudy but will thicken them effectively)
Cardamom	Cinnamon, nutmeg, black pepper, or star anise can replace the cardamom		Cornstarch	
			Cider vinegar	
			Kosher salt	Lemon or lime juice can replace the vinegar
			Flour	
			Butter	Ice cream, crème fraîche, or sour cream can be used instead of whipped cream
			Whipped cream (optional)	

Banana Galette with Cashew Frangipane

8 servings

As if to prove that you can make a galette with any fruit, I tried it one time with bananas, which aren't juicy like those beloved berries and stone fruit, nor tart like citrus or tropical fruits. Joy of joys—it worked. The creamy frangipane spread over the surface of the dough is a combination of sweet cashews and rich, slightly bitter tahini, complemented with more than a dash of salt. While you could bake the galette without it, the frangipane ups the ante in a big way and makes this super special.

FOR THE DOUGH

1⅓ cups (160 g) all-purpose flour, plus more for dusting

1½ teaspoons (6 g) sugar

¾ teaspoon (2 g) kosher salt

12 tablespoons (6 ounces/168 g) unsalted butter, cut into ½-inch pieces and chilled

FOR THE FRANGIPANE AND ASSEMBLY

1 cup (5 ounces/140 g) cashews, toasted

1 cup (192 g) sugar, plus more for sprinkling

12 tablespoons (6 ounces/ 168 g) unsalted butter, at room temperature

2 large eggs

½ cup (120 g) tahini, well stirred

¼ cup (30 g) all-purpose flour

1 teaspoon (3 g) kosher salt

1½ pounds (672 g) bananas (about 4), for topping

Heavy cream, for brushing

Toasted sesame seeds, for serving (optional)

MAKE THE DOUGH: In a small bowl, put some ice cubes in about ¼ cup (60 ml) water. In a medium bowl, toss together flour, sugar, and salt to combine. Add the butter and toss to coat, then dump the mixture onto a clean work surface. Use a rolling pin to roll butter into flour until butter is flattened and slightly softened, and has formed long, flexible pieces. This will take a little doing. Use a bench scraper or metal spatula to loosen flour from the surface and to clean off rolling pin as needed.

Use bench scraper to corral mixture into a loose pile, then drizzle 3 tablespoons (45 ml) ice water over. Using the bench scraper and your free hand, toss mixture until the water is evenly distributed. The mixture will resemble dampened clumps of flour with lots of loose bits still in the mix, and this is exactly as it should be. Gather mixture into a 6-inch-wide rectangle with one short end toward you, then dust with flour. Lightly flour a rolling pin and roll out dough to about ¼ inch thick. You'll need to periodically scrape the rolling pin clean, letting scraps fall onto the dough as you go. The middle will be loosely holding together but the edges will look very dry and shaggy. Using the bench scraper, fold the top third over the center, then fold the bottom third up and over, as you would fold a letter. Rotate dough 90 degrees and roll out again (flouring and scraping as before). Fold dough into thirds again, rotate 90 degrees, and roll out a third time. At this point, dough should be somewhat homogenous and creamy looking with some dry bits around edges. Squeeze a bit in your palm; it should loosely hold together. If not, repeat the rolling and folding a fourth time, then check again. Fold dough in thirds and press it into a disc about 1 inch thick and 9 inches across. Wrap tightly; chill 30 minutes.

From the Market	Spin It		At Home	Spin It
Cashews	Blanched almonds or blanched hazelnuts can replace the cashews		Flour	All these baking ingredients are essential!
Tahini			Sugar	
Bananas			Kosher salt	
Heavy cream			Butter	
	Apples, pears, peaches, or nectarines can replace bananas		Eggs	
			Toasted sesame seeds (optional)	
	A lightly beaten egg can be used to brush the dough instead of the cream			

Fun with Frangipane

This recipe makes about twice as much frangipane as you need. You can halve it if you don't want leftovers, but it's really nice to have around! Refrigerate it in an airtight container and use it as you would Nutella or until you feel like making another galette (within a week, ideally). It can be frozen for up to 2 months (thaw overnight in refrigerator before using).

Preheat oven to 350°F. Line a rimmed baking sheet with parchment paper.

Lightly coat work surface with flour, then place dough on the surface and dust with a little more flour. Roll out dough to a round about ⅛ inch thick and 12 to 14 inches across. Gently transfer dough to the prepared baking sheet. Chill dough while you make frangipane.

MAKE THE FRANGIPANE: Place the cashews on a rimmed baking sheet and toast until golden brown and fragrant, 10 to 12 minutes. Let cool. Increase oven temperature to 375°F.

Combine cashews and sugar in a food processor; process until finely ground, 30 seconds. Add the butter, eggs, tahini, flour, and salt; process until smooth, 30 seconds more. Scrape down bowl and all around the blade; process for another 30 seconds to combine. (The frangipane can be stored in an airtight container in refrigerator for up to 1 week; return it to room temperature before using.)

ASSEMBLE THE GALETTE: Peel bananas and cut on an angle into ½-inch-thick slices. Scrape 1 cup frangipane onto center of dough, then use a spatula to spread it out, leaving a 2-inch border (there will be extra frangipane; see note). Shingle the bananas on top of the frangipane, lightly nestling them into it, then fold and pleat the exposed dough over the filling, working your way around the edge and leaving center exposed. Brush dough with cream, then sprinkle exposed surfaces with sugar and sesame seeds (if using) to coat.

Bake the galette until the frangipane has puffed up and become very toasty brown and the crust is walnut brown, 50 to 60 minutes. Let cool slightly before cutting into wedges.

Nuts on the
Bottom
Caramel Tart

Banana Galette
with Cashew
Frangipane

Nuts on the Bottom Caramel Tart

8 servings

I know this recipe looks intimidating, but it comprises three distinct steps that all come together at the end—and it's a showstopper. First you make the dough and prebake it. Then you toast and chop some nuts—no big deal. Then you make a caramel, which I promise is essentially foolproof thanks to the little bit of lemon juice that's added to the sugar mixture at the beginning. Finally, the nuts go into the tart shell and you pour the caramel over. This eats like the best part of a nut-and-caramel candy bar and feels special enough for a holiday or birthday party. Tackle it one step at a time, and you're golden.

FOR THE DOUGH

1½ cups (180 g) all-purpose flour, plus more for dusting

¾ teaspoon (3 g) sugar

½ teaspoon (3 g) baking powder

½ teaspoon (2 g) kosher salt

12 tablespoons (6 ounces/168 g) cold unsalted butter, cut into ½-inch pieces

FOR THE NUTS AND CARAMEL

5 ounces (140 g) pecans

2 cups (384 g) plus 1 tablespoon (12 g) sugar, divided

1½ teaspoons (4 g) kosher salt, divided

1 tablespoon (15 ml) fresh lemon juice

4 tablespoons (56 g) unsalted butter, at room temperature

⅓ cup (80 ml) heavy cream

2 teaspoons (10 ml) pure vanilla extract

MAKE THE DOUGH: In a small measuring cup, combine a few ice cubes with ¼ cup (60 ml) cold water; set aside. In a medium bowl, toss together flour, sugar, baking powder, and salt to combine. Add cold butter pieces and toss to coat, then dump mixture onto a clean work surface. Use a rolling pin to roll butter into flour until butter is flattened, slightly softened, and pliable. Use a bench scraper or metal spatula to loosen flour from the surface and to clean off the rolling pin as needed.

Use bench scraper to corral mixture into a loose pile, then drizzle ¼ cup (60 ml) ice water over. Using the bench scraper and your free hand, toss mixture until the water is evenly distributed. The mixture will resemble dampened clumps of flour with lots of loose bits still in the mix. Gather mixture into a 6-inch-wide rectangle with one short end toward you. Lightly flour a rolling pin and roll out the dough to about ¼ inch thick, dusting the dough, work surface, and pin with flour if needed to prevent any sticking. You'll need to periodically scrape rolling pin clean, letting scraps fall onto dough as you go. The middle will be loosely holding together but the edges will look very dry and shaggy. Using the bench scraper, fold the top third over the center, then fold the bottom third up and over, as you would fold a letter. Rotate dough 90 degrees and roll out again (flouring and scraping as before). Fold dough into thirds again, rotate 90 degrees, and roll out a third time. At this point, dough should be somewhat homogenous and creamy looking with some dry bits around the edges. Squeeze a bit in your palm; it should loosely hold together. If not, repeat the rolling and folding a fourth time. Fold dough in thirds and press it into a disc about 1 inch thick and 9 inches across. Wrap tightly; chill 30 minutes.

Lightly coat work surface with flour, then place dough on surface and dust with flour. Roll out dough to a round about ⅛ inch thick and approximately 14 inches across, rotating it frequently and dusting dough,

From the Market	Spin It		At Home	Spin It
Pecans	Walnuts, pine		Flour	Adding a pinch of
Heavy cream	nuts, almonds,		Sugar	cream of tartar,
	hazelnuts, or		Baking	1 teaspoon light
	cashews can		powder	corn syrup, or
	replace the			1 teaspoon honey
	pecans		Kosher salt	to the sugar
			Butter	instead of the
			Lemon	lemon juice will
				also prevent the
			Vanilla	caramel from
			extract	seizing

the surface, and the rolling pin to prevent sticking. Roll dough onto your pin, then unfurl it over a 10-inch tart pan with a removable bottom and unfurl, letting excess dough hang over the rim. Working your way around edge, lift up the dough at the outside edge and let it slump down into the pan so that it is flush against the bottom. Trim overhanging dough to 1 inch, then use the backs of your fingers to press dough into pan, making sure it's flush with the corners. Fold overhang into tart pan so the crust is double thick at the edge, then press the edge firmly against the rim of the pan. Prick surface of dough in a few places with a fork, spacing evenly, then chill dough in freezer for 20 minutes.

Preheat the oven to 350°F. Line a rimmed baking sheet with parchment paper, aluminum foil, or a silicone baking mat.

Place the freezer-cold tart shell on prepared baking sheet, then line tart shell with parchment or foil. Fill with pie weights, pressing them firmly against dough, including sides. Bake until the surface of tart shell is matte and top edge feels dry and firm, 25 to 30 minutes (carefully peel back parchment to check). Gently lift out weights and parchment, then bake until the surface is dark golden brown, 30 to 35 minutes more. Let cool 20 to 25 minutes (keep the oven on).

PREPARE THE NUTS AND CARAMEL: Toast pecans in the oven on a small rimmed baking sheet until several shades darker and fragrant, 18 to 20 minutes, tossing halfway through. Transfer hot pecans to a food processor and add 1 tablespoon (12 g) sugar and ½ teaspoon (2 g) salt. Pulse until the nuts are roughly chopped (about the size of Grape-Nuts), 20 to 30 pulses.

Combine remaining 2 cups (384 g) sugar, lemon juice, and ⅓ cup (80 ml) water in a heavy-bottomed high-sided saucepan; stir thoroughly with a heatproof spatula to fully saturate sugar. Place over medium-low heat and cook, stirring frequently, until the sugar is completely dissolved and syrup is clear and approaching a simmer, 5 to 6 minutes. Do not rush this step! If the sugar has not dissolved completely before you continue, your caramel may crystallize and seize up, and you'll have to start over.

Once syrup is simmering, increase heat to medium and cook, swirling pan infrequently but no longer stirring, until the syrup turns the color of hay, 7 minutes more. Cook, watching carefully, as caramel quickly becomes auburn and a couple wisps of smoke appear, 2 to 3 minutes more. Cook until caramel is deep mahogany and smells faintly of molasses, 2 minutes more, then remove from the heat and very carefully add the butter, stirring with a heatproof spatula to combine. Carefully stir in the cream. Let sit 5 minutes, then stir in vanilla and remaining 1 teaspoon (2 g) salt.

Sprinkle toasted pecans into shell, then slowly pour in hot caramel. Let sit until the caramel is firm, about 1 hour, depending on temperature in your kitchen, then chill for up to 2 hours, uncovered, or cover loosely and chill overnight. Cut into wedges to serve.

Get Ahead

The dough can be wrapped airtight and refrigerated up to 3 days. Once dough has been rolled and fitted into tart pan, you can wrap it airtight and freeze it for up to 1 week (bake from frozen). The baked tart shell can be wrapped and held at room temperature for up to 1 day before filling.

Chapter 11

Also on the Table

All the little things that help round out a meal, from my favorite creamy dips to foolproof stovetop rice and crunchy toast for dipping

ANY
time
AT ALL

Perfect Pot of Rice

Makes 4 cups

Having leftover rice in the fridge is basically a nonnegotiable in my household; it's what my older son, Leo, is looking for when he opens up the fridge at lunchtime so he can make an egg-and-rice stir-fry, and for our family of four, that means we need to cook 2 cups at a time to guarantee there's some to put away for the next day. I don't own a rice cooker (not enough counter space!), so I use a pot on the stovetop. This method will work with any white rice—whether short- or long-grain. If you're making a larger quantity, scale up proportionally (2 cups rice and 2½ cups water, and so on).

Seen on page 204

Set a medium pot (the one you're going to cook the rice in) in your sink and dump 1 CUP SHORT- OR LONG-GRAIN WHITE RICE into the pot. Run cold water over the rice until it's submerged by a couple of inches. Use your fingertips to comb through the rice and swish it around until the water is cloudy. Drain the rice in a colander and return it to the now-empty pot. Repeat until the water is mostly clear, usually 4 or 5 changes of water. This removes any rice dust (a by-product of processing and packing) from the surface of the rice, and prevents the rice from becoming gummy when cooked. Pour 1¼ CUPS WATER over the rice rinsed, drained and place the pot over medium-high heat (do not stir). As soon as the water is at a simmer, reduce the heat to very, very low and cover the pot. Set a timer for 18 minutes. Keep an eye on the pot; if it bubbles too ferociously, foam will start escaping from under the lid, which is a mess, and you'll need to lower the heat. If you let the water boil off before covering it, there won't be enough liquid in the pot to cook the rice through. Remove from heat. Fluff with a rubber spatula or wooden spoon before serving. Or don't—it doesn't really matter.

Spicy Creamy Sauce

Makes ²/₃ cup

The first recipe I ever made for spicy creamy sauce was out of Japanese chef Nobuyuki Matsuhisa's namesake cookbook, Nobu. A spoonful of this sauce is a winning addition to any fried food or fritter, rice bowl, sandwich or burger, impromptu taco, rotisserie chicken snack, or platter of raw vegetables.

Seen on page 56

In a small bowl, stir together ½ CUP GREEK YOGURT or sour cream, 1 TABLESPOON SAMBAL OELEK (or more, if desired), 1 TEASPOON UNSEASONED RICE VINEGAR or fresh lime juice, 2 TABLESPOONS KEWPIE or other mayonnaise, and 1 TEASPOON SOY SAUCE, liquid aminos, or Maggi seasoning sauce. Season with KOSHER SALT and a PINCH OF SUGAR. Stir in 1 TEASPOON TOASTED SESAME OIL to combine.

Blank-Slate Whole Grains

Makes 4 cups

If you're making a grain bowl, or a grain salad, or you want to add grains to a soup or stir-fry, this is a basic way to cook any type. Different grains cook at different rates, so the key is to use a voluminous amount of water (as if you were cooking pasta) and to taste the grains to check for doneness as they cook. Soaking the grains overnight is any easy way to shorten the cooking time and is said to make them more digestible; I do it when I think of it, but it's not a requirement. While this will definitely work with pearled grains (which cook more quickly), I prefer grains with the hull intact; they are more nutritious and I like the chewy outer husk.

Seen on page 101

Place 1 CUP WHOLE GRAINS (such as barley, farro, wheat berries, spelt, rye berries, or short- or long-grain brown rice; about 6½ ounces) in a medium pot and cover with 6 CUPS WATER. Season with 1 TABLESPOON KOSHER SALT and A FEW GRINDS OF BLACK PEPPER; add a generous guzzle of EXTRA-VIRGIN OLIVE OIL. Bring to a boil over high heat. Lower heat to maintain a very gentle simmer and cook, stirring occasionally, until the grains are tender but still have some bite (add water if needed to cover generously). This will take about 20 minutes for pearled grains; 35 minutes for semi-pearled grains or brown rice; and up to an hour for whole grains such as spelt, farro, or rye berries. Your best bet is to taste them every 5 minutes or so after 20 minutes. Drain grains, then toss with more olive oil to coat.

Watermelonade

Makes about 2 quarts

The thing about watermelon is that when you cut up even a medium-size one, you will get more pieces of fruit than you have containers or room in the fridge for. That's when you make Watermelonade— watermelon juice with lime juice mixed in. This is the most refreshing beverage on the planet, hands-down, and I love bringing it to the beach.

Seen on page 106

Cut a SMALL SEEDLESS WATERMELON into 1½-inch pieces (you'll have about 10 cups). Transfer to a blender and add ¼ CUP FRESH LIME JUICE (from 2 or 3 limes) and a big pinch of KOSHER SALT. Blend on high speed until liquefied, about 1 minute. Pour through a fine-mesh strainer into a pitcher or other container. Serve over ice, with LIME OR LEMON WEDGES for squeezing over.

Use this as a mixer for WATERMELON MARGARITAS if you want to get all adult about it: Combine 2 OUNCES SILVER TEQUILA, 2 OUNCES WATERMELONADE, and 1 OUNCE COINTREAU in a cocktail shaker with ice. Shake until frosty, then pour into a salt-rimmed rocks glass filled with ice.

Cynar Spritz

Makes 1 drink

Always be spritzing! This is my go-to low-ABV (alcohol by volume) cocktail for the pre-dinner hour. It's less sweet than an Aperol spritz, but anyone who likes drinking those will also enjoy this. I put tons of olives in mine.

Seen on page 140

In a highball glass, rocks glass, or wineglass, combine 2 OUNCES CYNAR and 1 OUNCE RED VERMOUTH. Fill glass with ice cubes, then top off with PROSECCO or club soda. Garnish with an ORANGE OR LEMON TWIST or a few BRINY GREEN OLIVES—or both! Or don't garnish at all. Stir together and slurp it down.

Big-Batch Vinaigrette

Makes about 2 cups

Growing up, there was a large glass bottle of this vinaigrette on the counter at all times. There still is. My mom, Carole, makes it by the big-batch in her food processor and it's what we use on our almost-nightly after-dinner salads. As far as I can tell, it does not go bad, but if you don't make salads very often, divide this in half and keep one on the counter and the other in the fridge.

Seen on page 136

Spoon a "hefty blob" (Carole's words) of DIJON MUSTARD (about 2 tablespoons) into a food processor and add a CHOPPED MEDIUM SHALLOT. Season aggressively with KOSHER SALT and FRESHLY GROUND PEPPER. Pulse until the shallot is finely chopped, then add 1½ CUPS EXTRA-VIRGIN OLIVE OIL, ½ CUP RED WINE VINEGAR, and 2 TABLESPOONS BALSAMIC OR CIDER VINEGAR. Blend until the dressing is emulsified. Taste and adjust with more vinegar and salt.

Lemony Yogurt

Makes about 1 cup

If you don't want spicy dip, you probably want lemony dip! I put this out with crudités and swipe it onto toast before topping with canned sardines or leftover roasted vegetables. It's delectable with any kind of fish—roasted, grilled, seared—and terrific with a fritter or spooned onto cooked beans or lentils. You could also swoosh it onto a platter and pile salad greens on top.

Seen on page 128

Place 1 CUP WHOLE-MILK GREEK YOGURT or labneh in a medium bowl and finely grate 1 GARLIC CLOVE and ZEST OF 1 LEMON over. Halve the lemon and squeeze in the JUICE. Stir in 2 TABLESPOONS WATER until combined. Taste and season generously with KOSHER SALT and FRESHLY GROUND PEPPER; drizzle with 1 TABLESPOON EXTRA-VIRGIN OLIVE OIL.

Salsa Very Verde

Makes about 1¼ cups

The little green sauce that goes with every grilled or roasted protein in your repertoire. I like to add this to tuna salad, vegetable-based soups, and brothy beans, and spoon it over fried or hard-boiled eggs, too. You could also use it as the dressing for a grain salad or put it out with roasted, boiled, or steamed potatoes (any type, including sweet potatoes).

Seen on page 166

Place 2 OIL-PACKED ANCHOVY FILLETS on a cutting board and sprinkle with KOSHER SALT. Finely chop the anchovies, then use the edge of your knife blade to smash them against the cutting board until they become a paste. Scrape into a medium bowl and add ½ TEASPOON CRUSHED RED PEPPER FLAKES, 1 FINELY GRATED GARLIC CLOVE, 1 MINCED SHALLOT, 2 TABLESPOONS CAPERS (drained and finely chopped), and a FINELY CHOPPED 1-INCH PIECE SPICY GREEN CHILE, such as jalapeño or serrano. Thinly slice 2 CUPS LOOSELY PACKED TENDER HERBS, such as basil, parsley, tarragon, chervil, chives, cilantro, and/or mint, and add to the bowl. Pour 1 CUP EXTRA-VIRGIN OLIVE OIL over and stir to combine, then stir in 1 TABLESPOON CIDER VINEGAR or distilled white vinegar. Taste and adjust the seasoning with salt and FRESHLY GROUND BLACK PEPPER.

Whipped Aïoli

Makes 1¾ cups

Another creamy dip! I guess I love creamy dips? Anyhoo. Homemade aïoli (aka garlic mayonnaise) is lighter and not as tight as regular mayo, and I like being in control of the flavor of the mustard and garlic. Serve this with grilled or roasted lamb, any type of fish, fried squid—fried anything—raw or blanched vegetables, tuna salad, cold poached or grilled shrimp, steamed mussels, or lobster salad, or spoon it on top of ratatouille or a bouillabaisse-style fish stew.

Seen on page 173

Combine 1 CUP GRAPESEED OIL and ¼ CUP EXTRA-VIRGIN OLIVE OIL in a measuring cup with a spout. In a medium bowl, whisk together 1 LARGE EGG, 1 LARGE EGG YOLK, 1 TABLESPOON DIJON MUSTARD, 2 TABLESPOONS FRESH LEMON JUICE, and a PINCH OF SUGAR. Finely grate 1 SMALL GARLIC CLOVE into the bowl; season with KOSHER SALT and FRESHLY GROUND BLACK PEPPER. Whisk well to homogenize. While whisking continuously, very slowly drizzle the oil mixture into the eggs, drop by drop at first, then in a steady stream once the mixture looks pale, yellow, and opaque. Continue whisking until all of the oil mixture has been incorporated and the aïoli is thick and emulsified. Taste and add a little more salt, lemon juice, or a DASH OF VINEGAR if needed.

Carole's Fried Bread

Makes as many pieces as you want

The answer to "Do we need fried bread on the table?" is always YES. At least it has been for my whole life, especially if my mom is cooking. Frying bread, as opposed to toasting it, is magical. The finished texture is crispy and shattery on the surface, crunchy-chewy in the center. Use a rustic loaf—sourdough, miche, boule, something like that. If it's day-old, all the better. Fried bread is made for dunking in soup or building bruschetta. It wants to absorb an egg yolk. You can tear it into pieces and use them as croutons for salad or to toss onto any pasta. It is good to eat when you're feeling a little meh about things and want to again feel happy and thankful for being alive.

Seen on page 242

Cut BREAD into ¾- to 1-inch-thick slices. (Cut at least 1 slice for every person you're feeding.) Pour EXTRA-VIRGIN OLIVE OIL into a heavy skillet to a depth of about ⅛ inch. That might seem like a lot, but in order to truly fry the bread, you need enough oil to saturate the crumb. It's fried bread, not toast. Place the skillet over medium to medium-high heat until the oil is hot, about 1 minute. Add as many slices of the bread as will fit comfortably in skillet and fry, occasionally pressing down with a spatula, until the underside is dark amber and very crisp, 2 minutes. Turn and cook until the second side is nicely browned, 1 minute more. Place the bread on a wire rack or a paper towel–lined plate and rub a GARLIC CLOVE all over surface while hot (the bread will sort of act as a grater). Sprinkle with FLAKY SALT (or kosher salt). Repeat if you have more bread to fry, adjusting the heat and replenishing the oil as needed.

Soft-Peak Whipped Cream

Makes 2 cups

I like my whipped cream not-too-sweet and "floofy" in texture. It should slump and bulge, barely holding its shape, when you spoon it onto a dessert plate. It's best to do this by hand in a big bowl, which will give you the visual feedback you need to not go too far, and is entertaining to anyone standing in your kitchen with you at the time. It's not really a party until there's whipped cream in your hair, right?!?

Seen on page 265

In a large bowl, combine 1 CUP CHILLED HEAVY CREAM, 2 TABLESPOONS CONFECTIONERS' SUGAR, 1 TEASPOON PURE VANILLA EXTRACT, and a PINCH OF KOSHER SALT. With your largest whisk, whip cream until gentle soft peaks form, about 3 minutes. If your arm gets tired halfway through, dramatically hand the bowl and whisk off to an underling (I use my children) until you regain your strength.

Menu Ideas

Mostly Make-Ahead

Vegetarian

Picnic Party

Outdoor Main, Indoor Sides

Fall Holiday

Best Friend's Birthday

Thank You

I wrote and produced this book in 2020. It was a tumultuous, difficult, humbling time. Thank you to the first responders who kept my city alive, and to the protesters everywhere for fighting for justice. Their respective work gave me hope for the future.

Thank you to the friends who keep me whole. Colu Henry, for our regular "meeting" and a lifeline to sanity. Leslie Robarge, for relentless compassion and acceptance. Vanessa Holden, for resilience. Chandra Kelemen and Delia Kelemen, for sisterhood. Ross Twanmoh, for strength. To my treasured collaborator Molly Baz, for love and confidence. To the brave and powerful Rachel Karten and Emily Schultz, Maaaa girlzzzz forever. Thank you to Rick Martinez, for your moral compass, and to Amiel Stanek, for comrade-erie. To my paisan Scott DeSimon, for always sending texts at the right time.

Thank you to everyone who tested recipes for me: Alex Beggs, Sohla El-Waylly, Jen Fiore, Sarah Jampel, Christina Gregory Jones, Rachel Karten, Carole and Nina Lalli, Kaitlyn Murphy, and Luke Sand. Your notes and feedback were invaluable! To Courtney Harrell and Sam Polito, for happily accepting early drafts of my recipe attempts and keeping the lights on for Peggy and King Jeffrey. Thank you to Michael and Jaclyn Varland, for a kitchen I'll love for the next 20 years.

Thank you to my friends at D'Artagnan, California Olive Oil, Lucini, Rancho Meladuco, and Vermont Creamery for sending me ingredients to create recipes with. I am very grateful for all the purveyors who kept their wheels turning during uncharted times: The employees at Baldor Foods, Fresh Direct, Hayden Flour Mills, Kalustyan's, King Arthur Flour, FedEx, UPS, and the USPS made it possible for me to carry on my work and life from home. In Brooklyn, Bravo Supermarket, Greeneville Garden, Mr. Coco, Mr. Mango, the Meat Hook, Marlow and Daughters, Provisions, Foragers, Wegman's, Leon and Sons, Gnarly Vines, and the producers and workers at New York City Greenmarket adapted so that shoppers like me could get what we needed.

Creative projects are not solo ventures, and I am lucky to be surrounded by people who elevate my ideas. Thank you to Zan Goodman, for funning it up big time. To Andrea Gentl and Martin Hyers, for love and the best light. To Frankie Crichton, for holding it down. To the extraordinary and unflappable Susie Theodorou, the most exceptional food stylist I know. To Cybelle Tondu, for bottomless amounts of skill, care, and attention. Thank you to the crew at Lost & Found prop house, for inspiring all of us on set.

To Doris Cooper, for bringing this book into the Clarkson Potter family, and to Francis Lam, for your exceptional edits and guidance. Thank you also to Aaron Wehner, for investing in me. I am honored to work with Katherine Cowles, who is forever ten steps ahead of me. Your loyalty and professionalism are unmatched.

This book would be impossible without my family. My parents, Frank and Carole, raised me in a household of abundance, where delicious-tasting food and long-running jokes are the magnets that hold us together to this day. For Cosmo and Leo, my hungry bunnies; I love feeding you. My sister, Nina, is funnier than I am, has a better eye, and is the sole reason I haven't gone off the deep end. I love you! Thank you for bringing Ben into this family. I not only got a partner in puns, but more important, we all got the joy of Gia.

Finally, to Fernando—my heart and my partner. There were many days when tea in bed was the only reason I could get out of bed at all. Your unconditional love gives me the strength to take risks in this life. Thank you for being my person.

Index

Published in the United States by Clarkson Potter/
Publishers, an imprint of Random House, a division
of Penguin Random House LLC, New York.
clarksonpotter.com

CLARKSON POTTER is a trademark and POTTER
with colophon is a registered trademark of
Penguin Random House LLC.

Library of Congress Cataloging-in-Publication Data
Names: Music, Carla Lalli, author.
Title: That sounds so good / Carla Lalli Music.
Description: New York : Clarkson Potter/Publishers,
   [2021] | Includes index.
Identifiers: LCCN 2020050815 (print) | LCCN 2020050816
   (ebook) | ISBN 9780593138250 (hardcover) | ISBN
   9780593138267 (ebook)
Subjects: LCSH: Cooking. | LCGFT: Cookbooks.
   Classification: LCC TX714 .M87278 2021 (print) | LCC
   TX714 (ebook) | DDC 641.5—dc23
LC record available at https://lccn.loc.gov/2020050815
LC ebook record available at https://lccn.loc
   .gov/2020050816

ISBN 978-0-593-13825-0
Ebook ISBN 978-0-593-13826-7

Printed in China

Book and cover designer: Zan Goodman
Photographers: Gentl and Hyers
Digital technician: Frankie Crichton
Food stylist: Susie Theodorou
Food styling assistant: Cybelle Tondu
Prop stylist: Nina Lalli
Prop styling assistant: Leo Music
Editor: Francis Lam
Editorial assistant: Lydia O'Brien
Production editor: Joyce Wong
Production manager: Kim Tyner
Composition: Merri Ann Morrell and Hannah Hunt
Copy editor: Ivy McFadden
Indexer: Elizabeth T. Parson

10 9 8 7 6 5 4 3 2 1

First Edition

setting captives free
The Way of Purity

Enjoy Lasting Freedom in Christ
Mike Cleveland

FOCUS
PUBLISHING

Setting Captives Free: **The Way of Purity**
by Mike Cleveland

Copyright © 2007 Focus Publishing

ISBN: 1-885904-62-2

Cover design by Melanie Schmidt
Printed in the United States of America

Dedication

I lovingly dedicate this book to my wife,

Jody

who, after discovering my involvement with
pornography, took it upon herself to become
my teammate in fighting against impurity.
Without your help, Jody, I would be another
statistic of men who ruin their lives.
I love you.

Dedication

I lovingly dedicate this book to my wife,

Jody

who, after discovering my involvement with
pornography, took it upon herself to become
my teammate in fighting against impurity.
Without your help, Jody, I would be another
statistic of men who ruin their lives.
I love you.

Acknowledgments

This course book is evidence of the transforming power of God in my life and in the lives of thousands of men and women who have experienced the same power and have contributed to this work. I wish to take this opportunity to thank some of them here. Although too numerous to mention all of you by name, I do love and appreciate each of you and I thank God for you.

Shon Bruellman, as the executive director for the purity courses at Setting Captives Free, works tirelessly for the cause of gospel freedom in our ministry. Rob Robertson heads our Setting Captives Free—Australia division, and has dedicated his life to helping men to find Jesus and freedom in Him. Brian Hogan, a man of grace and wisdom, truth and humility, provides much needed input and direction as he serves on our board of directors. Pastor Kraig Bowen and Mike Askins also serve on our board, and are both faithful to the Word of God and to ministering grace to people. They have all helped me to think through many of the theological issues in this book, and I am grateful for them. Finally, Karen Wilkinson, my assistant and editor, works with the joy of the Lord in her heart and is faithful in serving her Lord through this ministry every day.

My wife Jody has been my suitable helpmeet in overcoming 15 years of bondage to impurity. She worked with me as a teammate when I was hopelessly enslaved, and next to the sovereign grace of God in releasing me from my chains of sin, Jody gets the credit. As we sensed God's calling to help others, she has provided much godly wisdom and feedback to me through the long hours of writing new course material, even while rearing and homeschooling our four children, mentoring female course members and spouses, and being much in demand as a phone counselor to the wives of those enslaved to impurity. Jody, my "rib," this world has been graced with your presence. I love you dearly and am eternally grateful to you.

Finally, to Jan Haley and all our friends at Focus Publishing, we are grateful to God for giving you such a love of His Word and a desire to publish it for the benefit of many. Thank you for the many hours you have put into **The Way of Purity** project. May God richly bless your kindness to us. We love you!

We are grateful to those who granted us permission to share their testimonies. Although the names have been changed, the personal testimonies included in this book demonstrate how Satan's wiles lead men and women into the pit of impurity, but also the victory that may be found through Jesus Christ and the grace and truth that come from Him.

Mike Cleveland

Table of Contents

Table of Contents

Introduction

Setting Captives Free: The Way of Purity is a study course of 60 lessons designed for men and women who seek to be free from impurity. Many who have taken this course are walking in freedom today because they have implemented the biblical principles found here. As you step out of the darkness and secrecy of impurity, you will find the refreshing cleansing of the gospel, which will impact your relationship with Jesus Christ and with others.

> Repent, then, and turn to God, so that your sins may be wiped out, that times of refreshing may come from the Lord (Acts 3:19).

The Way of Purity course may be studied individually or in a small group setting.

Small Group Setting:

There should be an appointed leader/teacher to head the group, which will meet weekly. The first meeting of the group should be for the purpose of becoming acquainted. The leader will make introductions and explain the method for completing the study. Each group member will work individually through one lesson each day, recording their answers to discuss with the class the following week. At the close of this first meeting, the leader will explain from Hebrews 3:13 the importance of daily accountability and he/she will pair up the students as each reports daily to the other of their freedom from sin. The brief reports may be given on the phone, fax, email, or in person, but they should be given daily. At the second meeting, the discussion leader will take time to review/expound upon the previous week's material, soliciting the members to share their answers for the material they have studied. The leader will also ask if the members have been providing daily accountability reports to their assigned partner. A Leader's/Mentor's Guide is available.

Individual Study

When using this course individually, it is highly recommended that you find a trusted Christian friend with whom you may discuss what you are learning from the course material, and who will also be available to you for accountability. This accountability partner should be someone of the same sex who is walking in victory over habitual sin. Possible options include your pastor, an elder in your church, or a fellow Christian. You may also use your spouse for your accountability partner if he or she is willing. Students need to initiate daily reports to their accountability partner, providing the status of his/her purity.

The genesis of **The Way of Purity** course began on the Internet website, www.settingcaptivesfree.com and the ministry continues to operate successfully. Should you desire to work with an available mentor in the ministry, you may contact us at feedback@settingcaptivesfree.com.

To the extent that his schedule allows, Mike Cleveland is available for conferences and speaking engagements. You may contact him via postal mail at the following address:
Setting Captives Free
P O Box 1527
Medina, OH 44258-1527

DAY 1 - MOTIVATION

Hello Friend, and welcome to The Way of Purity. My name is Mike Cleveland, and I am the author of this course. I will be walking you through the next 60 days as you seek to be free from pornography, adultery, prostitution, homosexuality, sex chatting on the Internet, or any other form of sexual impurity.

First, before I explain how the course works, let me share with you a bit of my own story. I was involved with pornography and many other forms of impurity for 15 years of my life, and my problems got worse as time went by. Through my teen years, I was involved with pornographic magazines such as Playboy, Hustler, Oui...etc., but at 22 years old I was hired as a pilot with Continental Airlines, and began laying over in hotels around the world. This is where pornography really got a hold of me, for I discovered pornographic movies were available at nearly every hotel. Then came the Internet, and sex chatting became a part of my daily life. All of this led to a life of enslavement to impurity where I had no hope of ever being free.

As you continue on in the course, you will read the rest of my story, or at least bits and pieces of it. I've interspersed my story in the lessons so you will know that the teaching in the course comes from one who has "been there, done that" and is now free from pornography and all forms of impurity. My desire in sharing my story with you is not to boast in myself. I am ashamed of what I had become, how my sinful life detracted from the glory of God, and the pain I caused so many people. Rather, it is to boast in the grace of God, as He has eradicated pornography from my life, and to give you hope that He is able do the same for you. I have now been totally free from all forms of impurity (pornography, adultery, masturbation, fantasy, etc.) since January of 1999.

Now, here is a real word of hope for you: I can guarantee to you on the authority of God's Word, you can be completely free from sexual impurity, regardless of your particular struggle, if you will implement the biblical principles in this course. I trust this gives you hope that, no matter how long you have battled this secret killer called sexual sin, you can now be successful over it, by applying the principles taught here. Literally thousands of people, who have gone through this course, are now walking in freedom. You will read some of their testimonies as you continue on in the lessons.

That's it! Enjoy your studies, and seek to apply each biblical principle you learn. Now, here is the first lesson.

Right from the start, we must understand the following foundational truth, or we will not be successful in finding freedom from impurity. The truth is that, in order to be successful in breaking free from impurity, our motives must be right. And what is the "proper motive," you ask? The proper biblical motive for gaining victory over impurity must be the glory of God.

The first teaching we present in The Way of Purity course is that we must have God's glory as our motive for finding freedom from impurity. Most people have their own glory as the motive for finding freedom; they want to get free in order to feel better about themselves, to save their marriage, or to be more productive at work. This, in reality, is self-worship, which should have no place in the heart of the Christian who professes to worship God. God does all things for His own glory (Psalm 21:5; Psalm 63.2; Psalm 79:9; Proverbs 25:27; John 7:18) and, as we also begin to work for the glory of God instead of our own glory, we become people of truth and we inevitably find freedom from habitual sin.

I know that during my years of slavery to pornography, I would try one method after another, one book or support group after another, always seeking that knowledge which would free me so that I would feel better, so that others would see that I was some spiritual giant, or that I would have a better self-image. But, looking back, I see that these motives were all wrong; it was all about me. It was for my own glory, and that's why it never lasted.

Questions

Question 1. Have you discovered that, in the past, you may have desired freedom for the wrong reasons? If so, what motivations have you had for wanting to find victory up to this point?

From here on, we will intersperse some answers from other course members and leaders at Setting Captives Free, as you may possibly identify with their thoughts and answers, as well. All answers are used by permission.

One of our students at Setting Captives Free wrote, "My desire for freedom was mostly the result of PMI (pornography, self-gratification, immorality) not doing for me what I wanted it to do. It wasn't satisfying me and, in fact, was only leaving me more guilt-ridden than ever. I wanted

something that would fill the emptiness inside; something that was lasting, and wouldn't leave me feeling guilty and shameful. My focus for wanting freedom was all about me. I knew my life needed to be rid of this sin but, what I didn't know, was that my eventual freedom would be an incredible opportunity for me to glorify Christ. Today, when I talk about the power of life-dominating sin being broken in my life, the only One Who gets the glory is God. He met the need of my heart, and now I can glorify Him, rather than self with my life!"

The Way of Purity Executive Director, Shon Bruellman, wrote this answer the first time he came across this teaching, "This is an interesting point you bring up here. At first when I read it, I was offended. I thought 'WHAT?!? The first lesson, and you tell me that my motives are wrong for finding freedom?' But then, as I sat here and went through the list of reasons why I want to have freedom, I can see that it is for my own benefit and my own glory. I want to be able to appear as a godly man who has no sin in his life. I want to be free so that my life would be easier and without hindrances anymore. As much as I want to say that my motives are to glorify Christ by my freedom, I have to admit that my motives are purely for myself and how freedom would benefit me. Hmmm...maybe that's why the chains have continued to hold me fast for over 20 years of my life! This question is basically saying that I am to get my eyes off of what this course will do for ME, and instead focus on how God can be glorified through me."

Friend, if we set out on this course to quit pornography, adultery, or any other form of sexual impurity for our own glory, we can not expect God's assistance. Since God is the greatest good, He sets out to work all things for His own glory and, if we seek to find freedom for our own glory, we are at cross-purposes with God. He will not share His glory with another (Isaiah 48:11).

This concept is very important to understand, so let's look at an illustration of this in Judges 7:2,

> "And the LORD said to Gideon, 'The people who are with you are too many for Me to give the Midianites into their hands, lest Israel claim glory for itself against Me, saying, 'My own hand has saved me.'"

Do you see it? God had to REDUCE the size of Gideon's army so that, when they won the battle, Israel would not claim glory for themselves. This could be the very reason why we have not been successful in finding permanent freedom from impurity in the past, because God has not wanted us to boast in ourselves, or in a certain method or program, or in following the advice of some guru. God desires His glory to be great in our salvation. (Psalm 21:5) God works for His own glory! And this is why we must settle this issue of motivation right here in the beginning. Is our motive in desiring to break free to honor Him, or ourselves? Are we working with Him, or are we at cross-purposes with Him?

Now that we understand our purpose, let me tell you that there is great hope in having the glory of God as our motivation! If we have a purpose in our hearts to glorify God, then we are working in concert with God, and He will enable us to do what we seek to do. Please don't miss this. Proper motive in becoming free (the glory of God) will ensure our success, as God Himself comes to our aid, so that He will be glorified. Do you see it?

> "Therefore, whether you eat or drink, or whatever you do, do all to the glory of God" (1 Corinthians 10:31).

Question 2. What should be the Christian's motive for finding freedom from bondage to impurity? Circle one.
   A. To have others admire us
   B. To be more spiritual
   C. To feel better about ourselves
   D. To have a happy marriage
   E. The Glory of God

I believe we must fully understand that breaking free from impurity is honoring to the Lord. Indeed, He is glorified in the daily choice we make to turn away from gratifying our flesh. Now, this is not to say that all who are not involved in pornography, and all who abstain from masturbation (self-gratification) and adultery are glorifying God. Obviously, such is not the case, as there are many people who aren't involved in the things with which you and I have struggled, but who are living their lives for their own glory. However, it is to say that the motivation for the Christian must be to honor the Lord in everything, including our freedom from impurity.

Some time ago, I recognized that I had been trying to break free from impurity for the wrong motives. God convicted my heart, that I needed to have proper motives. I remember when I first confessed to Him that I had been seeking freedom for my own selfish reasons, to draw attention to myself and to feel good about myself. It was a time of deep sorrow in my heart, for I saw that I was attempting to rob God of some of His glory. I remember kneeling by my hotel room bed and praying, "Father I have gone about seeking freedom all wrong. In the past, I've been promoting my own glory, but now I see that I am to do everything for Your glory. No wonder I've not been successful. Would you please forgive me for these wrong motives? Would you please change my heart and help me to desire your glory above all else?"

That prayer was a turning point for me. It was really the start of a new life, as I began to seek the glory of the Lord ahead of everything else. To be honest, at times the flesh still gets in the way and I become distracted again but, overall, I believe the primary purpose of my heart is to honor the Lord now. I want to be able to say with the psalmist in Psalm 115:1:

> Not unto us, O LORD, not unto us,
> But to Your name give glory,
> Because of Your mercy,
> Because of Your truth.

Question 3. Possibly you will want to confess something to God similar to my prayer above. Have you been seeking your own glory, or attempting freedom for the wrong reasons? If so, here is a place where you may write out a prayer of repentance to God.

Now, as I have said, there is real hope for permanent freedom when our motive is the glory of God. If we begin to focus on the glory of God, we will inevitably change. Let's look at the Scriptures that teach this very principle. Please consider the following passages of Scripture, and answer the questions below:

> "[16] Nevertheless when one turns to the Lord, the veil is taken away. [17] Now the Lord is the Spirit; and where the Spirit of the Lord is, there is liberty. [18] But we all, with

unveiled face, beholding as in a mirror the glory of the Lord, are being transformed into the same image from glory to glory, just as by the Spirit of the Lord" (2 Corinthians 3:16-18).

Question 4. According to verse 18 above, what is it that enables us to be transformed?

This is starting to get good, isn't it? Look at the HOPE we should have for real change, as we focus on the glory of God. According to the above passage, as we behold the glory of the Lord, we are being transformed into the same image; that is, into Christ-likeness. As our motives become the glory of God, and as we begin to focus on the glory of God, we become transformed!

One of our Setting Captives Free mentors, Bill Stroud writes, "It is when we change from looking at ourselves with our imperfections, sinfulness, and helplessness and turn to the Lord Jesus and see and depend on His power and perfection, that we can expect a transformation to begin."

Question 5. If you have tried finding freedom before, but have failed, according to the teaching so far, why did you fail?

Robert writes "Because it was all about me; my sin, my guilt, my discomfort, my darkness – instead of beholding Jesus and His glory, His purpose for my life, and His grace."

Question 6. Are you now sensing a hope that you can truly change? If so, upon what is that hope based?

Finally, let us notice what the glory of God really is. The glory of God is multi-faceted, and difficult to reduce to words. I feel inadequate to even try. And yet, God has not left us in the dark as to what His glory is. Notice this passage of Scripture:

"[1] God, who at various times and in various ways spoke in time past to the fathers by the prophets, [2] has in these last days spoken to us by His Son, whom He has appointed heir of all things, through whom also He made the worlds; [3] who being the brightness of His glory and the express image of His person, and upholding all things by the word of His power, when He had by Himself purged our sins, sat down at the right hand of the Majesty on high, [4] having become so much better than the angels, as He has by inheritance obtained a more excellent name than they" (Hebrews 1:1-4).

The following testimony is from Keith:

I grew up in a Christian home and made a profession of faith at age 13, while at a revival where my dad, a pastor, was leading the worship. Satan knew how to hook me, and what bait to use, from an early age to keep me from an intimate walk with God. That bait was pornography.

While visiting my grandparents' home one summer when I was 11 or 12 years old, one of the neighborhood boys had a magazine he'd stolen from his father. We sneaked into the woods and were mesmerized by the women we saw there, baring all.

Even though I lived in a pastor's home, I would get my hands on pornography from time to time, and eventually I was engulfed in a habit of lustful thoughts and self-gratification. I believed myself to be called by God into full-time ministry at age 17. I had all the "head knowledge," knowing what God's Word said, but I was not living a pure life sexually. I attempted at times to be pure, but always in my own strength, and the purity never lasted.

In my second year of college, at age 19, God gave me what I say was my wake-up call. My girlfriend (now my wife) became pregnant and we decided to drop out of school and get married. We had to admit we didn't love each other and ask God to give us that love. He did, but I still held on to the secret sin, the hook having already been set deeply for many years. My wife discovered this and there was much damage done. My sin put a major strain on our marriage. Even seeing the hurt I had caused my wife and knowing that I nearly lost her, I still was gripped so tightly by this sin that I continued to view pornography and give pleasure to myself.

I had given up hope that I would ever be free until I stumbled onto the Setting Captives Free website and The Way of Purity course. I started the study with little expectation of change, but the course pushed me to a point where I had to choose whether I wanted porn and lust to rule my life or I wanted God to rule my life. I chose God, and He removed the hook pornography had in my life and has given me a stronger desire for Him than for my lustful pleasure. He has changed my wicked heart into a heart that seeks Him completely, and I never again want to fill my mind with images or fantasies that will never satisfy. I now have a peace I've not had before and I know what my full identity is in Christ.

God has given me a heart to reach others held in the grasp of porn. He has opened my eyes to see the many who are trapped in this lie and I have had many opportunities in my ministry to encourage others to find The Way of Purity from porn.

Notice that verse 3, above, calls "the Son," Who is Jesus Christ, "the brightness of His glory." This is important. When the above Scriptures direct us to focus on the glory of the Lord, what they are really saying is to see this glory in Jesus Christ, God's Son. So let us make the connection here. If we desire to be transformed, we must focus on God's glory, and God's glory is wrapped up in the Person of Jesus Christ. The Way of Purity course seeks to focus our attention on Christ, and to have us contemplate His glory so that, in fixing our eyes on Him, we will become transformed into His image.

Question 7. Where is the glory of God seen most clearly?

  A. In the Heavens, as they declare the glory of God

  A. On Mt. Sinai, as God descended in all His glory

  B. In the Person of Jesus Christ, the radiance of God's glory

In closing, we must have proper motives to live our lives correctly, including finding freedom from pornography and sexual impurity of all kinds. This course will test our motives as we are confronted with scriptural truth, and we will seek to focus our attention on Jesus Christ for, in doing so, we will inevitably become transformed. And this is our goal, isn't it?

Question 8. Please summarize the teaching of this first day. Include what you have learned, any changes being made in you, and how you will apply what you have studied today.

Robert writes, "I have learned that the answer is not found in me, so that is not the place to look; I know that the problem is within me, so no use going there. The answer is found in Jesus and beholding Him."

Shon writes, "I came to Setting Captives Free doubtful of what I would find since I had been to psychiatrists, therapists and hypnotists and assumed that I would receive similar counsel here. However, this teaching is all new. The advice I had received from secular counselors has been to focus on me and my needs, but when I started to see how it was for the glory of God that He frees the captives, my whole life changed. I understood how it was for HIM I am to seek freedom and now, several years later, I still walk in victory over porn and sexual impurity!"

Mentor Craig wrote this when he first read the truths of this day: "Today's teaching was very insightful. I've realized right off the bat that the reason I've failed up until now is because my motives have been all wrong. Indeed, my wrong focus is the problem at hand, and it needs to change to the right focus, the Person of Jesus Christ, who is the Radiance of God's Glory. I pray the Lord will hear my cries and prayers of desperation and deliver me from pornography and masturbation, as I repent of this horrible sexual sin and, for the first time, attempt to glorify God. This first lesson has also convicted me that, while I may have knowledge of Scripture, for I've read many of these same verses prior to today, that knowledge without application is useless. It is not how much of God's Word I know, it is how much of God's Word I live every moment of every day."

Question 9. Friend, please share with us any final thoughts you may have, and how we may pray for you. Your mentor will read everything you write and is committed to praying for you.

Friend, as you contemplate continuing on in this course, there is something that must be done, without which there is no hope of real or permanent freedom. You must rid yourself of any and all sources of pornography, or anything else that causes you to stumble. Many of us have become so accustomed to pornography that, unless we cut it off, we will, out of habit, return to it. Throw away the magazines, cut off the cable, erase all history of pornography sites on the Internet, cut off access to pornography newsgroups, destroy phone numbers of adulterous or other sinful relationships, do whatever it takes to rid your house, car, and life of pornography and all impurity. Enjoy this "cutting off," have fun with it, stomp on it, burn it, drown it in a lake and laugh as it sinks. This is the first step to freedom.

"And I said to them, 'Each of you, get rid of the vile images you have set your eyes on, and do not defile yourselves with the idols of Egypt. I am the LORD your God'" (Ezekiel 20:7).

Question 10. Will you trash all access to pornography, etc., right now?

  Yes No

Question 11. Please take a moment and write your thoughts about this lesson:

Scripture to Consider

Jesus said: "The Spirit of the Lord is on me, because he has anointed me to preach good news to the poor. He has sent me to proclaim release to the captives and recovery of sight for the blind, to release the oppressed, to proclaim the year of the Lord's favor" (Luke 4:18-19).

Do this, knowing the time, that it is already the hour for you to awaken from sleep; for now salvation is nearer to us than when we believed (Romans 13:11).

Nothing in all creation is hidden from Gods sight. Everything is uncovered and laid bare before the eyes of him to whom we must give account (Hebrews 4:13).

From here on you will be asked accountability questions at the bottom of each lesson. We are doing this to help keep you accountable for purity. Please do only one lesson a day, by answering the accountability questions based on the previous 24-hour period.

The accountability question, "Were you free from sexual immorality since you did the last lesson?" may be confusing, so I will explain what we are asking here. Sexual immorality is anything impure, but it involves physical acts rather than thoughts. The thinking of pornographic thoughts is typical for those who are new to this course, and they usually begin to go away in the next several months if the biblical principles in this course are followed. So, we are not talking about thoughts in this question. Rather, we are asking you about any specific acts of immorality committed, such as prostitution, homosexuality, any inappropriate physical touching...etc. We are also asking about

giving in to lust, and doing things such as staring inappropriately, or doing any physical act that stirs up lust.

We would like to encourage you in your walk with Christ and will now be asking the following questions daily. First, an explanation about "feasting" and what it means.

"Feasting" is a biblical principle, without which there is no hope of freedom from sin's grip! Feasting is reading our Bibles, but it is more than that; it is a term to express the nourishing of our souls in Jesus Christ. It means that we are sitting at the feet of Jesus, hearing His Word and believing, for the purpose of implementing the truths into our lives. It means we are receiving spiritual nourishment and that we are delighting our souls in His grace and truth. This can be done by reading our Bibles, hearing God's Word preached, interacting with others, studying through this course...etc. Feasting is important because if we merely turn away from sin, we will be empty and open to either returning to our sin or experiencing sinful bondage in other areas (see Luke 11:24-26). Feasting is that which makes us full and overflowing with God's grace and truth. See Jeremiah 15:16 and John 6:50-58 for more information.

Did you feast on God's Word in the last 24 hours?

    Yes   No

If so, how did you feast? In other words, how did you enjoy God today? Reading? Prayer? Worship? Fellowship? Witnessing?

Were you free from pornography since you did the last lesson?

    Yes   No

Were you free from self-gratification since you did the last lesson?

    Yes   No

Were you free from sexual immorality since you did the last lesson?

    Yes   No

If you answered "no" to any of the above questions, indicate what led to your fall. If you answered "yes" to the above questions, you may use this area for additional comments.

DAY 2 – LIVING WATER

John Piper of *Desiring God Ministries* once asked, "How do you magnify a fountain? You drink of it, and you drink *only* of it. This shows that the fountain is enjoyable and satisfying" (excerpt from audio tape "Preaching as Worship" from Desiring God.) In the first lesson, we studied and thought through the subject of motivation and how honoring the Lord must be our motive in order to gain freedom from impurity. Today, we will study how God is a "fountain of living waters" and we magnify and glorify Him when we learn to drink exclusively from Him.

Please read through the following biblical account and answer the study questions below. You are about to learn how to be free from sexual enslavement.

When a Samaritan woman came to draw water, Jesus said to her, "Will you give me a drink?" (His disciples had gone into the town to buy food.)

The Samaritan woman said to him, "You are a Jew and I am a Samaritan woman. How can you ask me for a drink?" (For Jews do not associate with Samaritans.)

Jesus answered her, "If you knew the gift of God and who it is that asks you for a drink, you would have asked him and he would have given you Living Water."

"Sir," the woman said, "you have nothing to draw with and the well is deep. Where can you get this Living Water? Are you greater than our father Jacob, who gave us the well and drank from it himself, as did also his sons and his flocks and herds?"

Jesus answered, "Everyone who drinks this water will be thirsty again, but whoever drinks the water I give him will never thirst. Indeed, the water I give him will become in him a spring of water welling up to eternal life."

The woman said to him, "Sir, give me this water so that I won't get thirsty and have to keep coming here to draw water."

He told her, "Go, call your husband and come back."

"I have no husband," she replied. Jesus said to her, "You are right when you say you have no husband.

The fact is, you have had five husbands, and the man you now have is not your husband. What you have just said is quite true."

"Sir," the woman said, "I can see that you are a prophet. Our fathers worshiped on this mountain, but you Jews claim that the place where we must worship is in Jerusalem."

Jesus declared, "Believe me, woman, a time is coming when you will worship the Father neither on this mountain nor in Jerusalem. You Samaritans worship what you do not know; we worship what we do know, for salvation is from the Jews. Yet a time is coming and has now come when the true worshipers will worship the Father in spirit and truth, for they are the kind of worshipers the Father seeks. God is spirit, and his worshipers must worship in spirit and in truth."

The woman said, "I know that Messiah" (called Christ) "is coming. When he comes, he will explain everything to us."

Then Jesus declared, "I who speak to you am he"

Just then his disciples returned and were surprised to find him talking with a woman. But no one asked, "What do you want?" or "Why are you talking with her?"

Then, leaving her water jar, the woman went back to the town and said to the people, "Come, see a man who told me everything I ever did. Could this be the Christ?"

They came out of the town and made their way toward him (John 4:7-30).

Observation: In the above story, Jesus Christ spoke to a woman about two kinds of water:

1. "This water," which would not satisfy and would not quench spiritual thirst. The woman would have to keep coming back again and again to get more of "this water."

2. "The water I give" which would quench thirst eternally.

Then Jesus brought up the fact that the woman had had multiple relationships (five husbands and a current live-in, for a total of six relationships). Obviously, she was finding no permanent satisfaction in these relationships, so she had to keep going back to find a new love, each time hoping that this time would be the last. In bringing up her "unquenchable thirst" for different relationships, Jesus revealed to her that she would never be truly satisfied until she began "drinking" from the water He would give her.

Question 1. List the "water" from which you've been drinking, and how it has left you "thirsty."

Question 2. How many relationships did Jesus say the woman at the well had?
   A. 4   B. 5   C. 6

Question 3: To what did Jesus compare these multiple relationships?
   A. Eating fruit from a rotten tree
   B. Drinking water from a well that does not satisfy

Question 4: What did Jesus mean when He said, "Everyone who drinks this water will be thirsty again?"
   A. The water in that well contained a high amount of salt.
   B. Ongoing relationships (or pornography) will not ultimately satisfy, and will have to be repeated over and over.

Course member Mary writes: "Pornography truly is a ball and chain! I have been drinking from the water of lust and relationship. I have fallen short in each relationship, and continually thirst for true love; now I know that only Christ can satisfy."

Question 5. What kind of water did Jesus offer the woman at the well?

A. Living Water

B. Well water

C. Tonic water

Question 6. What did Jesus say was the difference between the water she had been drinking and the Living Water He offered her?

A. The Living Water was salt-free.

A. The Living Water would satisfy.

B. The Living Water had more nutrients.

Question 7. What did Jesus say the effects of drinking this water would be?

A. More energy and stamina

B. Lower cholesterol

C. Eternal life

Note: Jesus offered this woman Living Water. He said that if she drank it she would not be thirsty anymore; in other words, she would be satisfied, and not desire one relationship after another. Here is hope for you and me! Here is the solution to enjoying freedom from pornography, adultery, or any sexual sin. If you discover how to receive this "Living Water," and how to drink it, you will not be thirsty any more; instead, you will be free from the craving of and slavery to the flesh. The remainder of The Way of Purity course is designed to help you to receive and to drink the Living Water.

Question 8. Please describe how this teaching is giving you hope. How is drinking this water going to satisfy you, and change the way you live? Be specific.

By admitting that gratifying the flesh does not permanently satisfy you, that you have to "drink" of it again and again, you are ready to discover what will satisfy, permanently!*

* From this lesson on, instead of using the term "masturbation," we will use the biblical term "gratifying the lusts of the flesh," "self-gratification," or similar terms. This helps to keep the language biblical, and also removes an oft-used excuse "the word 'masturbation' is not in the Bible, therefore it must be acceptable." For a fuller treatment and explanation of this subject, please send a blank email to masturbation@settingcaptivesfree.com and also to mstrbtn@settingcaptivesfree.com to read two excellent articles on this subject.

Question 9. Have you attempted to stop viewing pornography and/or reading inappropriate literature in the past, but failed?

A. Yes   B. No

Question 10: According to the teaching you've learned today, why did you fail last time, and what will be different now?

Course member Simon writes: "Before, I was trying to quit mainly on my own strength, without replacing my thirst with the Living Water Christ supplies. Now, I believe I can leave it all behind, because Jesus is really helping me. By drinking the Living Water Jesus gives, a satisfying, fulfilling Living Water. Without that, I couldn't quit. With it, I can't but help quitting."

Next, please read through the following passage and provide your comments below:

"Come, all you who are thirsty,
come to the waters;
and you who have no money,
come, buy and eat!
Come, buy wine and milk
without money and without cost.
² Why spend money on what is not bread,
and your labor on what does not satisfy?
Listen, listen to me, and eat what is good,
and your soul will delight in the richest of fare.
³ Give ear and come to me;
hear me, that your soul may live.
I will make an everlasting covenant with you,
my faithful love promised to David (Isaiah 55:1-3).

Pornography, in its essential allurement, promises to quench our thirst. In other words, it promises satisfaction. And honestly, it does satisfy - but only for a short time. Pretty soon, we discover that we are "thirsty" again, and as the years go by, we find that we are really never genuinely satisfied. That is because sin never purely satisfies! It depletes us, not fulfills us. I can recall going from soft-core pornography magazines to X-rated videos, to cyber sex with video cams...etc. I thought if I could just see that perfect picture, or have that perfect sexual experience, that my life would be full and satisfied. This is the nature of sin. It takes us farther and farther, and though it promises to satisfy, it never does satisfy eternally. This is why we keep coming back to it over and over again.

Question 11: Verse 2 of Isaiah 55 above asks an important question: "Why spend money on what does not satisfy?" Have you spent money (or time) on that which does not satisfy? How does this relate to our involvement with pornography, adultery, or other forms of impurity? Write your answer here:

The verses above in Isaiah 55 are an invitation to the thirsty. Play along with me as we question the author of these verses. He says, "Come, all you who are thirsty."

"Alright, I am thirsty, I will come. But where do I come to quench my thirst?"

"Come to the waters."

"Yes, that makes sense; if I am thirsty I should come to the waters, but where are the waters?"

"Ah, excellent question. 'Listen, listen to me, and eat what is good, and your soul will delight in the richest of fare. Give ear and come to me; hear me, that your soul may live.'"

Friend, do you see it now? The water is in the Word of God. Drinking comes by listening. The Bible is our source of true refreshment and quenching of our thirst.

Question 12. According to verse 2 above, what is the result of drinking in the Word of God?

   A. Your H2O makeup increases.

   A. You need to use the restroom more often.

   B. Your soul delights in what you are taking in.

Question 13. According to verse 3 above, what is the result of listening to God's Word?

Question 14. Next, please provide your thoughts on this quote: **"None but God can satisfy the longings of an immortal soul; that as the heart was made for Him, so He only can fill it."** Richard Chenevix Trench: Notes on the Parables. Prodigal Son Osbeck, Kenneth W., 101 More Hymn Stories, (Grand Rapids, MI: Kregel Publications) 1997.

Earlier, we read the Scripture about the woman at the well, who had been "drinking" from the wrong water. She was filling herself with one relationship after another (six total), and she was obviously not satisfied. She was spending herself on what did not satisfy. But Jesus offered her Living Water, which she could receive as a free gift and would satisfy her thirst forever. In the passage above, we are admonished to stop spending our time, energy and money on what will never satisfy us, and to drink the water that brings delight, joy and life to our souls. Do you see what we have been missing while involved in pornography and sexual impurity?

Question 15. How does this verse relate to what we are studying? "Death and destruction are never satisfied, and neither are the eyes of man" (Proverbs 27:20).

The following testimony is from Kenneth:

I hail from a Hindu family in India. My childhood days were like that of an ordinary Indian boy with a strong desire and inclination toward girls. I went away from home for my studies and, while there, was exposed to and indulged in pornographic magazines and videos.

I received the Lord Jesus as my Saviour in 1998. I had some really great times of fellowship with other believers, started praying and reading the Bible, and even saw some answers to prayer, but due to my lack of belief that I could completely overcome the sin of impurity, I ignored this aspect.

In the years to follow, my struggle with pornography became stronger. I viewed pornography and indulged in gratifying the lusts of my flesh almost daily. I was discouraged at my failures, angry with God, and had developed a firm belief that I would have to live with this secret part of my life forever.

A new youth leader in my church spoke to us again and again on the issue of porn addiction, how he himself found freedom in Jesus Christ, and of the Setting Captives Free ministries. I enrolled in The Way of Purity course at www.settingcaptivesfree.com. I took some time to totally implement the truths and had to re-do the course. There was something new to learn and practice in each lesson.

By God's grace, I confessed my sin to my accountability partner (a youth leader in my local church) and my wife. There was no TV or computer at home, but I had to watch myself closely and ensure that I did not keep enough money with me to indulge in the lusts of flesh. Encouraged by the testimonies at Setting Captives Free, I came to believe that God could give me total victory over the sin of impurity. I was encouraged to continue with the course and to seek God even when I had fallen and not to give up. Once I learned to feast in God's presence on a daily basis, I got victory over my thirst for pornography and gratifying the desires of flesh. I have begun to walk in total victory.

I now understand that this Jesus, is the source of Living Water, is the only One who can keep me satisfied.

I want to thank the Setting Captives Free ministries for The Way of Purity course and the prayer support of the mentors.

Friend, I was trapped in pornography for 15 long years as my "eyes were never satisfied." I continued to want excitement, love, acceptance, beauty, and all the other things that pornography offers. But, at the end of those 15 years, I found out that I had been drinking from a putrid, impure source of water, and it defiled me and made me unclean. But, since January of 1999, I have been drinking the clean, refreshing, satisfying, life-giving, thirst-quenching water of Jesus Christ. The teaching of today is foundational to overcoming impurity. Switch water sources! Pornography, gratifying the flesh, adultery, homosexuality, etc. never will satisfy us, ever. The pornography industry makes its billions on customer dissatisfaction, and if we stay in it we will always have a continual lust for more. It is like salt water, giving more thirst than satisfaction.

Question 16. How does this verse go with today's teaching? "Having lost all sensitivity, they have given themselves over to sensuality so as to indulge in every kind of impurity, with a continual lust for more" (Ephesians 4:19).

Questions

Question 17. Write your thoughts on this verse: "My people have committed two sins: They have forsaken me, the spring of Living Water, and have dug their own cisterns, broken cisterns [wells] that cannot hold water" (Jeremiah. 2:13).
Note: God describes Himself as the "Spring of Living Water." He alone is the Source of life, refreshment, joy and nourishment for us. He is ever fresh and new, like a spring, and to "drink" of God is to receive life and be satisfied! Turning to pornography or sinful relationships is like trying to get water from a jar with holes in it.

Question 18. Please read this quote from a famous preacher, Charles Spurgeon, and record your comments about it: **"Men are in a restless pursuit after satisfaction in earthly things. They will exhaust themselves in the deceitful delights of sin, and, finding them all to be vanity and emptiness, they will become very perplexed and disappointed. But they will continue their fruitless search. Though wearied, they still stagger forward under the influence of spiritual madness, and though there is no result to be reached except that of everlasting disappointment, yet they press forward. They have no forethought for their eternal state; the present hour absorbs them. They turn to another and another of earth's broken cisterns, hoping to find water where not a drop was ever yet discovered."** Write your thoughts here:

Course member Paul writes: "Madness! What a perfect description of my relentless pursuit of the next sexual image that will be the one that will satisfy. As the hours slip away and my eyes grow heavy with sleep, I cannot stop. Yet moments, even seconds, after climax it starts again. What madness, indeed!"

We noticed that the woman at the well had been "drinking" of the "water" of multiple relationships (six total) and yet she was still "thirsty." Jesus offered her "Living Water" that would quench her thirst eternally. Now, I want to add one final thought about this story, and show how it relates to our involvement with pornography, self-gratification, and all forms of sexual impurity. Please read the following verses in John 4, the passage we studied earlier:

> [28] Then, leaving her water jar, the woman went back to the town and said to the people, [29] "Come, see a man who told me everything I ever did. Could this be the Christ?" [30] They came out of the town and made their way toward him (John 4:28-30).

Question 19. After speaking with Jesus, the woman at the well went back into town. What did she do with her water jar?
  A. She took it with her
  B. She left it with Jesus
  C. She dropped it

Question 20. Earlier, we saw that Jesus Christ compared the water in that well to what?
  A. Bad habits that will not truly satisfy
  B. Ongoing relationships that leave us thirsty
  C. Unsatisfied cravings
  D. All of the above

Scripture does not specifically say why the woman left her water jar with Jesus, so we cannot know for certain why she left it. Obviously, she did, indeed, need to continue to drink physical water, even after her encounter with Christ. However, the following truths are seen in the passage: first, Jesus compared the physical thirst of the woman with her attempts to quench the thirst of her soul by having multiple and sinful relationships; and secondly, Jesus offered her "Living Water," which would quench the thirst of her soul once and for all. Oh, dear friend, here is good news for us! As we learn how to the drink Living Water that only Jesus can give, we can leave our old "water jar" behind.

Question 22. Please read this quote from Arthur Pink and give your comments:

"She left her water pot because she had now found a well of 'Living Water.' She had come to the well for literal water and that was what her mind was set on. But now that she had obtained salvation, she did not think any more about her water pot. It is always this way. Once our souls truly perceive Christ, once we know Him and receive Him as our personal Savior, we turn away from what we used to think about. Her mind was now fixed on Christ, and she had no thought of well, water, or water pot." Granted, even after we come to Christ and learn to drink of His Living Water, there can be a time when we must learn how to leave the other **"water behind"** and it is certainly not always an instantaneous exchange of water, like the woman at the well did. We are not saying that it always has to happen in this manner, but what we are saying is that as we drink of Christ's Living Water we are able to leave behind the sinful water.

Oh, how I remember the day in my pastor's office when I was challenged to leave behind the filthy waters of pornography and to begin drinking of the Living Water. I'll tell you more about this experience as we progress in the course, but I can tell you that I never want to go back to drinking that "sewer water" again. My heart's desire now is to see you drinking in the Living Water, the water that delights the soul and gives it life, and the water that satisfies forever.

The following testimony is from Rich:

I was about twelve years old when I went into my brother's room and saw a porn magazine on his bed. It started as extreme curiosity and became a thrilling encounter each time I opened my brother's bottom drawer and saw a new magazine. Self-gratification and pornography became prominent all through my high school years.

My parents had brought me up in a good home and we went to church where I learned about Jesus. I prayed for Christ to come into my life when I was about fourteen. As a young Christian, I knew what was right and wrong and felt convicted when I sinned. After praying to God to forgive me, I would feel some peace, but my brother's room was next door, and I would eventually give in for a quick look.

The next few years I began dating and became sexually active. After college I moved to a big city on my own where along with one-night stands I dated a couple of women for a while; but it was all about sexual lust. I remember the first time I got the nerve to go buy an X-rated video. I felt so cheap and dirty, until I got in my car and headed home where I couldn't wait to indulge in it.

Afterwards I would feel like a cheap nothing. I would turn to God and make commitment after commitment. I went to youth groups and had fellowship, but the need for women and the nightlife won out. Yet I could never accept the lifestyle because I knew in my heart that it was wrong.

I thought everything would die down once I was married, but it didn't, and I continued to purchase porn. Eventually I was employed at a company that gave me a laptop computer and I was introduced to Internet porn. I couldn't believe the convenience and privacy I could have with no one knowing what I was doing. Being a salesman with a home office I had flexible time to access the Internet. Naturally, I went deeper into porn.

Even though I had a wife and two little boys who I would take to church almost every Sunday, I was still involved in porn after all those years. I installed porn blockers, only to uninstall them the next day. I ordered satellite porn, just to cancel the subscription after viewing a movie. I bought videos only to watch them once and throw them away. Another $30 down the drain, each time thinking I would stop.

Finally, I went to a search engine and instead of typing some porn star's name, I typed in "pornography addiction." There I saw the Setting Captives Free site and enrolled in this course. I desired so much to get out of this junk. My email accountability friend encouraged me and showed me truth from God's Word that I had never really applied to my life. I learned that asking for forgiveness is only one part. The other is repentance. This is the part I was blinded from over the years.

I had been around this stuff so much and I wanted to dabble in it, but I could not experience any freedom or God's power until I truly ran from it and literally got all sources out of my life. It was then that I began feeling freed from it and knew that Jesus does love me and wants me to experience victory over sin.

I still get tempted and am still a sexual being, but this is now only for my wife. Also, I have the encouragement of a Christian friend to make it through, which I didn't have before. I've exposed the darkness of this terrible sin to my wife and she has helped me eliminate all sources and made me accountable.

God is real in my life and he has given me more assurance each day as I grow with Him. I now believe I am truly on the right track, and through daily prayer, devotion, and humble communion with Jesus, I know my God will prevail over sin. May all glory be to God. Amen.

Question 23. Please provide your closing thoughts on this day of teaching, and summarize the main thought of the lesson. Have you learned anything new, or relearned something you had forgotten? Will anything change in your life as a result of this teaching?

Scripture to Consider

"You have set our iniquities before you, our secret sins in the light of your presence" (Psalm 90:8).

"Whether you turn to the right or to the left, your ears will hear a voice behind you, saying, 'This is the way; walk in it.' Then you will defile your idols overlaid with silver and your images covered with gold; you will throw them away like a menstrual cloth and say to them, 'Away with you!'" (Isaiah 30:21, 22).

"...being confident of this, that he who began a good work in you will carry it on to completion until the day of Christ Jesus" (Phil. 1:6)

Were you free from pornography since you did the last lesson?

    Yes   No

Were you free from self-gratification since you did the last lesson?

    Yes   No

Were you free from sexual immorality since you did the last lesson?

    Yes   No

DAY 3 – INTO THE LIGHT

Dear Friend,

So far, we have discussed the necessity of drinking Living Water from Jesus in order to quench our thirst. We've seen that God is a "Spring of Living Water," and that turning to anything other than God for satisfaction is like spending our lives on something that will not satisfy. We have seen that pornography, adultery, and sexual impurity are "broken cisterns" that will not hold water, and will not quench our thirst (Jeremiah 2:13). Today, we will discuss another principle, that if understood and acted upon, will set us free from all forms of sexual impurity.

Have you ever noticed that most fungi grow best in the dark? If you were to turn the light on the fungus, it would be sapped of strength, whither, and eventually die. Sexual impurity is the same; it, too, thrives in the darkness. Typically, pornography is done in secret, where nobody knows, and as long as the sinning remains in the dark, it will no doubt continue.

During my years of slavery to pornography, I appeared to be a respectable man. I was an airline captain, had been to seminary, taught Sunday School at our church, and was outwardly successful with a good family. But in secret, I was a different man. As a pilot, I would layover in hotels and had much private time. The pornographic channels in the hotel room would draw me powerfully, and I would give in repeatedly, year after year after year. I would pray against it, read my Bible, plan not to fall, but as soon as I would get to the privacy of my hotel room, lust would take over, and I would plunge into pornography.

I was living two different lives. Those who are living in deceit like this will do everything they can to protect the sinful secret life from being exposed. They become very angry and defensive if questioned about any wrongdoing. I remember one time preaching very passionately about the evils of pornography and sexual sins; it truly was a great sermon. Only problem was, I had just stayed up most of the night before indulging in pornography. What horrible hypocrisy! And so, I know first hand that people involved with pornography have a hidden secret life, and they will do all in their power to keep it from becoming exposed. And yet, this exposure is the very thing necessary to eradicating it from the life.

What was happening to me during those years, that I had no power to overcome sin? Why did I give in time and time again, especially when I had prayed so much not to? The answer is that this sinning was all done in the darkness, in secret, where sin thrives. My secret life illustrated the truth of John 3:19-20: "This is the verdict: Light has come into the world, but men loved darkness instead of light because their deeds were evil. Everyone who does evil hates the light, and will not come into the light for fear that his deeds will be exposed."

Question 1. Does this "darkness" scenario fit your situation? Write your answer here:

Here is what eventually happened with me. I met a woman on the Internet six months after my first wife left, and we began corresponding. My sins were still in secret and I convinced this woman, who was a Christian, that I was a fine, upstanding Christian man, quoting many Bible verses to prove my point. We were married in February of 1998, nearly a year and a half after we met the first time. But, I continued with pornography, self-gratification, and sex chatting on the Internet, and my wife soon discovered my sin. She was extremely afraid that I would leave our relationship, so she began seeking help from a counselor. Because of her belief in biblical counseling, rather than the psychological approach, she searched for a counselor through NANC (National Association Of Nouthetic Counselors), who directed us to a pastor in Medina, Ohio, where we began weekly counseling.

One day, during counseling, the subject of pornography came up. I found myself confessing to my pastor about my years in pornography, and I asked for his help to stop my habitual sinning in this area. Friend, this was extremely difficult to do! As you can imagine, it was embarrassing and demeaning to my wife and to me, and it truly broke me to have to admit that I was not, on the inside, who I was claiming to be on the outside. But that very act of humbling myself in front of my pastor was the start of my coming out of the darkness, the sapping of the strength of pornography in my life, and the victory that I am now experiencing on a daily basis since January of 1999.

Now, you may not feel able to confess to your spouse or your pastor right now as this is only the third day in The Way of Purity course and you no doubt still have "shaky knees" in your newfound walk of freedom. But you have already begun to drag this sin into the light. You have started this study and completed your first two lessons. You have just described your own secret sins, and you are making progress, by God's grace!

Please read the following passage:

⁵ This is the message we have heard from him and declare to you: God is light; in him there is no darkness at all. ⁶ If we claim to have fellowship with him yet walk in the darkness, we lie and do not live by the truth. ⁷ But if we walk in the light, as he is in the light, we have fellowship with one another, and the blood of Jesus, his Son, purifies us from all sin.

⁸ If we claim to be without sin, we deceive ourselves and the truth is not in us. ⁹ If we confess our sins, he is faithful and just and will forgive us our sins and purify us from all unrighteousness. ¹⁰ If we claim we have not sinned, we make him out to be a liar and his word has no place in our lives" (1 John 1:5-10).

Verse 6, above, shows that, while I was involved in pornography, I was deceived. I was claiming to have fellowship with God, yet I was walking in the darkness. So in reality, my life was a lie and I was not living by the truth. I'm not saying that I wasn't a Christian while involved in pornography, but that, at the time, I was not walking in truth. This is a very sad scenario, but one that we, here in The Way of Purity course, see quite often. People come here who are hiding a vast majority of their lives from their loved ones, co-workers and friends. They may present the appearance of being spiritual people who are knowledgeable about the Bible. And yet we all know that information is not the same thing as transformation. What these people need to do is to begin to slowly, carefully, expose this hidden life to someone else, using discernment as to "who and when" to approach.

Question 2. How about you? Can you relate to the deception of hiding in the dark? Have you been living in secrecy? Write your thoughts here:

Question 3. According to verse 7 above, there are two results of walking in the light. Please write what each one is:

Did you catch that? Here is truth that packs a punch and can change our lives forever! If we begin walking in the light, not only are we able to fellowship with others who are walking in the light, but also Jesus Himself purifies our lives! Purity will be the thoroughly enjoyable result of coming into the light, as you have already begun doing!

Course member Ted writes: "Pornography and self-gratification are very private activities. Part of the reason we want to be rid of this sin is because of the shame and self-loathing that it creates in our hearts. I thought exposing this sin to another would cause me to feel the shame and loathing more intensely. The opposite was true. What came to me after exposing it was the pure freedom of not having to live the lie. It was not what I expected, but it was a most wonderful gift God gave me."

Question 4. Verse 9, above, tells us how to begin "walking in the light." What is it?
   A. Turn all the lights on in the house
   A. Confess our sins
   B. Always carry a flashlight with us

Question 5: Friends, we know that we are to first and foremost confess our sins to God. Here is a safe environment for you to write out a prayer of confession to Him. This is the first step toward walking in the light that brings purity. Feel free to drag your sin into the light right here, and write a prayer of confession to God.

Question 6: Can you see how putting this Scripture into practice will result in purity? What ways can you think of to begin walking in the light? Keep in mind that you do not have to do each one of these right now, today, but just write out a list of different things you may eventually want to do, in order to sap sin of its strength. List your thoughts here:

For now, just begin asking God to show you ways to begin coming into the light so as to sap the fungus of sexual sin of its strength. It is scary to confess, yes, and it can be humbling to ask for help. I understand that. But, ongoing victory and purity is worth it. I would not trade these past 5 years of purity for the 15 I was walking in darkness for anything. Things are too good now.

Question 7. Please provide your thoughts on this passage of Scripture; specifically list how you will apply this to your life:

"For you were once darkness, but now you are light in the Lord. Live as children of light (for the fruit of the light consists in all goodness, righteousness and truth) and find out what pleases the Lord. Have nothing to do with the fruitless deeds of darkness, but rather expose them. For it is shameful even to mention what the disobedient do in secret. But everything exposed by the light becomes visible, for it is light that makes everything visible" (Ephesians 5:8 - 14).

Some people, in their zeal to confess all, have blurted out their sins to their spouse (or others) in a way that increases the hurt and pain the spouse feels. Please use wisdom and discernment as to the timing and details of the confession. It is not advisable to give details regarding your sin. You may want to ask your mentor for help in planning your confession.

When considering confessing sin to your spouse, please consider the following five points:

Get a second and third opinion about whether confession is necessary and, if so, what should be shared. Obviously, physical adultery should be confessed, as well as sin that is habitual. But, beyond that, there is room for discussion, and it is best to get input from others in the body of Christ.

If confession needs to happen, request assistance from the body of Christ. Ask a pastor, elder, or small group leader to be with you during the confession to help ensure a godly response on all sides.

Use biblical terms, and ask for forgiveness. Don't minimize the sin, call it what the Bible calls it, and then ask forgiveness. If you need to confess physical adultery, say, "I confess that I have committed adultery, and I am very sorry. Will you please forgive me?" Do not say, "I had a small affair..."

Present your plan for leaving sin behind, such as how you have radically amputated the source of the sin, that you are taking the Setting Captives Free 60-day course, and that you have found an accountability partner (if that is not your spouse), and that you are checking in with the pastor or elders once a week to ensure them of your ongoing progress, etc. In other words, don't merely confess sin, but share your plan to be free from it, and what you are doing right now.

Never share details. The confession should be straightforward and honest, without minimizing whatsoever, and yet not include any of the details of the sin. The sharing of details may plant thoughts in the minds of others which make it difficult to forgive. Be firm - no sharing of details.

Scripture to Consider

"Here is a trustworthy saying that deserves full acceptance: Christ Jesus came into the world to save sinners - of whom I am the worst" (1 Timothy 1:15).

"How can a young man keep his way pure? By living according to your word" (Psalm 119:9).

"I will repay you for the years the locusts have eaten the great locust and the young locust, the other locusts and the locust swarm my great army that I sent among you" (Joel 2:25).

Were you free from pornography since you did the last lesson?

    Yes   No

Were you free from self-gratification since you did the last lesson?

    Yes   No

Were you free from sexual immorality since you did the last lesson?

    Yes   No

The following testimony is from Joe:

Somewhere around the age of six or seven, I discovered how to gratify myself sexually and began what would be an ongoing habit for many years. My parents told me I shouldn't do it, but never punished me when I did it (looking back I wish they had). I could choose to blame them for not training me enough in that area, but I know that I alone am ultimately responsible for giving into these temptations and making this a habit.

As I approached my teenage years, I was convicted by my conscience and felt shame, but I was too trapped in the habit to stop. As the years went by, I started to view images and watch TV programs that, though not pornographic, were not good for my spirit.

In my mid-teens, I asked God to tell me whether this practice was wrong. When I prayerfully went to His Word, I concluded that it was, indeed, wrong but that was not the answer I wanted to hear. I wanted God to tell me it was okay. God brought me to Romans 6:21, which says, "What benefit did you reap at that time from the things you are now ashamed of? Those things result in death!"

That same night after midnight, I again fell into sin. I continued to let porn and gratifying myself sexually master me for a few more years, during which I discovered the Spice and Playboy channels on cable. I came to those stations and even without paying for the movies all that time, was able to hear and see quite a bit of the material, which pulled me further under.

One summer I declared a personal war on this after one of my falls and made a vow to God that I would never again satisfy myself in this manner or go to these stations. I ended up in the next couple of years falling time and time again. I was trying to win the war on my own. It wasn't an everyday struggle, but with each return, the sights and sounds of pornography would make me thirstier. I turned it into a creative game, my own war game, which wasn't necessarily wrong except that I was trying to do it on my own, not God's way or with His help. That was wrong. I had determination, motivation and persistence in fighting the battle, but I didn't have one key weapon - humility! I was full of pride and, though I won some battles, I was losing the war badly. I thought I could stand face to face with temptation and just say no. It didn't work that way.

After I viewed hardcore pornography for the first time, I got on my knees and in desperation, cried out to God for deliverance. I said in tears, "I can't do it! It's all hopeless! This is where God wanted me to be. He then delivered me and set me free. Complete amputation from these sins that had ruled me for so long! I have had my ups and downs with lust, but God is working tremendously in that area, cleaning up the leftover garbage.

Developing a habit of drinking those Living Waters of His Word daily does it. It was interesting to me that about a month before He delivered me, He brought me to Psalm 50:14-15, " Sacrifice thank offerings to God, fulfill your vows to the Most High, and call upon me in the day of trouble; I will deliver you, and you will honor me.

This is God's grace to me because I not only wanted and accepted it; I cried out for it in humility. I think that is the key word in this whole testimony. It says in the Psalms that the Lord is close to the brokenhearted and He won't despise a broken heart. God is good!

DAY 4 - THE CROSS

In this lesson, we will examine the gospel to see how it relates to bondage to and freedom from adultery, pornography, and impurity. Let's examine the following passages of Scripture:

> "But your iniquities have separated you from your God; your sins have hidden his face from you, so that he will not hear" (Isaiah 59:2).

My friend, when I was involved in pornography and self-gratification, I was separated from God, and He did not hear my prayers. In fact, my constant sinning caused Him to hide His face from me because He cannot look on sin. I felt as if my prayers stopped at the ceiling, and then fell to the floor. Even though I professed to be a Christian, I was "darkened in my understanding and separated from the life of God..." (Ephesians 4:18). Indeed, this was a very dark time in my life.

Question 1. Can you identify with the feelings of separation from God while involved in immorality? Write your answer here:

Please read the following passage:

> [21] Once you were alienated from God and were enemies in your minds because of your evil behavior. [22] But now he has reconciled you by Christ's physical body through death to present you holy in his sight, without blemish and free from accusation - [23] if you continue in your faith, established and firm, not moved from the hope held out in the gospel. This is the gospel that you heard and that has been proclaimed to every creature under heaven, and of which I, Paul, have become a servant" (Colossians 1:21 - 23).

As I came out of pornography, the above verses showed my past, my present, and my future. I had been "alienated from God" and was His "enemy" because of my "evil behavior." This was my past as I lived in the darkness of secret sins. Though I claimed to be a Christian, and basically told everyone how spiritual I was, the reality is that I was alienated from God, and was His enemy because of my habitual sinning in the area of pornography and self-gratification. I was not genuinely converted until January of 1999 when I turned from habitual sin and became captive to Jesus Christ.

But God took action on my behalf. He "reconciled me by Christ's physical body through death." I am no longer His enemy; I am reconciled to God through the death of Jesus Christ. This is the work that He did; it is nothing that I have done.

Now, please understand that not everyone who has been involved in immorality is an enemy of God. You may be a Christian who has fallen into this trap, and are eager to be released. Personally, I have concluded that although I had claimed to know Christ, I did not truly know Him in a saving way. I knew about Him, but did not truly know Him through genuine repentance, until January of 1999.

These verses in Colossians 1 describe not only how we are saved, but how we come to leave sexual sin behind, as well. So, let us look at the above verses from the perspective of how to be free from all forms of sexual impurity. These verses present three things:

1. The Problem
2. The Solution
3. The Results

1. **The Problem.** Sin, in our case sexual impurity, separates and alienates us from God. We can become so distanced from God that we feel our prayers are not heard, and they may not be. Sexual sin, because it causes us to love the world, eventually leads us to hate God. The following is from an ex-minister of the gospel, after he fell into pornography and sexual impurity. Note how he is now an enemy of God in his mind, because of his evil behavior:

> "Inside of me rages such a depth of anger, so deep it interacts with the depths of hell. It rages and fires against God, all revolving around the loss of the position I cherished so much in ministry. My flesh tells me that God was wrong, unfaithful, incorrect, cruel, and erroneous, and that I should not serve Him who did not keep his word to me. The devil tells me the same. 'He has not met your needs. He has failed you, led you to a position, and then did not rescue you when He could have. Is this the kind of God you want to serve? The God who 'screws' you and leaves you defenseless? He has let you go mad. Is this the faithful deity you want to serve?"

Friend, I was nearly at this point, too. Sin had so hardened my heart, and deceived my very soul, that I was becoming a very hateful and angry person.

Have you experienced this hatred for God? Some may say yes, others no. Let me assure you that if you continue in the path of sin you will eventually get to the place where you do, indeed, hate God. "No man can serve two masters: Either he will love the one and hate the other, or he will be devoted to the one and despise the other" (Matthew 6:24).

2. **The Solution.** God has reconciled us by putting Jesus to death. Because sexual sin causes us to eventually hate God, God took the initiative to reconcile us. He took all our sins off us and put them onto Jesus, who died to pay for them. On the cross, Jesus was treated as a pornographer, a God-hater, and an enemy of God, in order to bring us back to God. On the cross, Jesus removed our sin that prevented us from having a relationship with God. **The solution to the problem is Jesus Christ.**

Question 2. Please write out verse 22 from the Colossians 1 passage above:

Question 3. Where are you with Jesus Christ right now? Can you see that He has dealt with our sin problem?

Dear friend, beware of any teaching, program, or method of finding freedom from sin that does not have Jesus Christ at the center; for there is no other way to solve the sin/problem than through Jesus. There is no other way to be reconciled to God, to be changed from His enemy to His friend, or to cease the evil behavior, than through Jesus.

I remember that I had tried many different avenues to find freedom from pornography. I went to counseling, read numerous books, sought out the help of a famous evangelist, went to meetings with pastors who had fallen, etc. Now that I have been working with course members, I have found that there are literally hundreds of programs, methods, books, etc., being offered to help people become free from this addiction. A simple search on the Internet on "Sexual Addiction" will result in literally thousands of websites.

Question 4. Have you tried other methods to be free from pornography or other sexual sin? If so, what were they?

3. The Results. The death of Jesus Christ tells us that God has done something about our sin problem. It tells us that He is committed to eradicating sin and has taken radical action to dispose of it, by putting His Son to death in our place.

Notice the results of what Jesus did for us on the cross. "But now he has reconciled you by Christ's physical body through death to present you holy in his sight, without blemish and free from accusation." Oh friends, this is a marvelous truth with practical results. Because of Jesus' death on the cross, we who have been reconciled to God are holy, without blemish, and free from accusation.

Question 5. By way of reflection, please list (1) what you used to be, (2) what God has done, and (3) what you are now, according to today's teaching. Please be thorough.

1.

2.

3.

Question 6. Please provide your comments on 2 Corinthians 5:21 below:

"God made him who had no sin to be sin for us, so that in him we might become the righteousness of God" (2 Corinthians 5:21). **Write your comments here:**

Question 7. Please provide your comments on John 3:16-17 and John 1:12-13 below:

"For God so loved the world that he gave his one and only Son, that whoever believes in him shall not perish but have eternal life. For God did not send his Son into the world to condemn the world, but to save the world through him" (John 3:16 - 17). Yet to all who received him, to those who believed in his name, he gave the right to become children of God, children born not of natural descent, nor of human decision or a husbands will, but born of God" (John 1:12, 13). **Write your comments here:**

Question 8. Please provide your comments on 1 Corinthians 15:3-6 below:

"For what I received I passed on to you as of first importance: that Christ died for our sins according to the Scriptures, that he was buried, that he was raised on the third day according to the Scriptures, and that he appeared to Peter, and then to the Twelve. After that, he appeared to more than five hundred of the brothers at the same time, most of whom are still living, though some have fallen asleep" (1 Corinthians 15:3 - 6).

Write your comments here:

Question 9. Friend, possibly you are still an enemy of God in your mind because of your evil behavior. Maybe it is time to put up the white flag of surrender and ask God to reconcile you to Himself. If you know that you need to be holy, without blemish and free from accusation, why not ask God right now for help. Here is a place to put your thoughts and prayers to Him in writing:

I remember that, after the meeting with my pastor where I confessed my involvement with pornography, I began seeking the Lord earnestly. Up to that point, I thought possibly that I had committed the unpardonable sin, and that God was probably finished with me and I was now useless for the rest of my life. But soon afterward, I found Deuteronomy, chapter 4, verses 25-31. This passage states that the children of God would become corrupt, make themselves idols to worship, assimilate into the practices of the surrounding nations, and do evil against the Lord for many years. But then my eyes fell upon verse 29, which states, "But if from there, you seek the LORD your God, you will find him if you look for him with all your heart and with all your soul. When you are in distress and all these things have happened to you, then in later days you will return to the LORD your God and obey him. For the LORD your God is a merciful God; he will not abandon or destroy you or forget the covenant with your forefathers, which he confirmed to them by oath."

Those words penetrated to my soul: "But if from there...." But if from there, you seek the Lord with all your heart, you will find Him. Wherever your "there" is, if you will seek the Lord from "there," you will find Him. And He will make you holy, without blemish, and free from accusation.

"Ask and it will be given to you; seek and you will find; knock and the door will be opened to you. For everyone who asks receives, he who seeks finds, and to him who knocks, the door will be opened (Matthew 7:7).

Question 10. Please summarize the teaching of today. I'm specifically looking for your understanding of any changes that will be made in your life because of the Scripture that you have read today.

The following testimony is from Jim:

I know God sent this Way of Purity Course to me because one day it just showed up in my email box. As I look back, my addiction to porn started when I was a teenager and I found a porn magazine in my dad's room. After starting college I didn't have much to do with porn, just a few magazines every now and then. But after college I moved to a big city where there was much pornography available and I found myself starting to get deeper into it.

For over twenty years I was addicted to porn, movies, magazines, and Internet and visited topless clubs. I even dated topless dancers and was involved in a lot of sexual sin. But as time went on I became so tired of it all.

About a year after moving to a new town and job, I had the urge to go to church. I can remember the sermon even today and feeling as though I was the only one in the sanctuary.

As in the past, I tried to blow off that feeling but couldn't do so that time. That summer I went back to church and they were having a revival, and I had this strong need to go. So I went three nights in a row and on the third night the Lord really began working on me. There was a call to come to the altar and accept Jesus and my feet would not move but as the evangelist called I accepted Jesus that night.

Now Satan was not a happy camper and he tempted me. But this course, which I know was sent by God, has allowed me to finish the job God started over 4 years ago. So to any one who may have just come to Christ, do not become discouraged when Satan keeps coming back over and over. I have become so much stronger in my walk with God because of this course. I know I am unworthy of anything He has to offer but through the shedding of the blood of Jesus I am washed clean of my pornography addiction.

But I also know Satan is still around and I must always put on the full armor of God and fight Satan each day. I love drinking this wonderful water of Jesus and knowing I am loved. And I know now that God will provide me a family one day and I have this course to thank. Thank you, Mike Cleveland, for your help but, most of all, I thank my heavenly Father for never giving up on me.

Scripture to Consider

"Now, brothers, I want to remind you of the gospel I preached to you, which you received and on which you have taken your stand.² By this gospel you are saved, if you hold firmly to the word I preached to you. Otherwise, you have believed in vain.³ For what I received I passed on to you as of first importance: that Christ died for our sins according to the Scriptures,⁴ that he was buried, that he was raised on the third day according to the Scriptures" (1 Corinthians 15: 1-4).

Were you free from pornography since you did the last lesson?

    Yes   No

Were you free from self-gratification since you did the last lesson?

    Yes   No

Were you free from sexual immorality since you did the last lesson?

    Yes   No

DAY 5 - RUNNING LIGHT

"Therefore, since we are surrounded by such a great cloud of witnesses, let us throw off everything that hinders and the sin that so easily entangles, and let us run with perseverance the race marked out for us" (Hebrews 12:1).

This passage of Scripture describes the Christian life as a foot race and the author tells us that, in order to run fast, we must run light. We are instructed to "throw off everything that hinders and the sin that so easily entangles." Here, temptation and sin are described as those things that hinder and entangle, and they must be thrown off.

For me, this meant I had to "throw off" the TV in my hotel room, give away my notebook computer (I was using it to do sex-chatting on the Internet), get rid of my TV at home, and avoid certain situations that tempted me. I had also progressed into actual physical relationships that were sexually impure, and had to sever those as well.

For some, running light may mean not being alone with certain people and, in some cases, ending a relationship entirely. We know this is not an easy thing to do, but purity is worth it whatever the cost.

Question 1. Please describe what things have hindered you from running this race to win.

Question 2. What are we commanded to do with these things that hinder us?

When I first confessed to my pastor that I had been viewing pornography while on the road in hotels, he told me about this principle of throwing off the sin and everything that entangles us. Since one thing which was entangling me was the TV in my hotel room, he suggested I "throw it off" by removing it when I got to my room for the evening. I was desperate to be free of pornography and self-gratification since, by now, I had pretty much stopped running the race and was entangled in the thorns of sin. So, I followed my pastor's advice and began physically taking the TV out of my hotel room (which made for some very interesting discussions the next day.)

Now, let us review what had transpired up to this point. I was now learning to **quench my thirst in Jesus**, so I was running to the Bible every time I felt the burning of lust rise within me. I was **dragging my sin into the light**, and exposing my former deeds done in darkness by talking with my wife and my pastor. I was **asking God to reconcile me**, help me stop the evil deeds that made me an enemy of God in my mind, and now I was beginning to **throw off the sin that was entangling me** so that I

could get back in the race. Do you see all the principles of truth that were being employed? Guess what? Since that meeting with my pastor in January of 1999, where he explained the necessity to throw off anything that hinders and entangles, I have not fallen even one time to pornography or impurity. My decade-long horrible bondage to this terribly destructive sin was over.

Do you see the importance of applying this principle to your own life? As we have been working with people in The Way of Purity course, we have discovered that those who apply this teaching to their lives begin to walk in victory over sin. We have also noticed, unfortunately, that those who will not rid their lives of that which is causing them to stumble, just never seem to get free. They confess to falling, get back up and tell us they are sorry and won't be doing that again. We instruct them that they need to remove that which caused them to fall. They make excuses and say that they have learned their lesson and, because temptations are lessened right after a fall, they think they "have a handle on it" now. We know it is just a matter of time before they fall again and, sure enough, usually within two weeks, down they go. This will continue unless and until they throw off that which causes them to stumble.

Question 3. What things will you throw off so you can run light? Please only list those things that you will get rid of RIGHT NOW. You will be held accountable by your mentor for the things you list here.

"But put ye on the Lord Jesus Christ, and make no provision for the flesh, to fulfill the lusts thereof" (Romans 13:14).

Notice the above verse tells us to "make no provision for the flesh?" You see, when I had access to pornography I could pray about not falling all day long, but as soon as I got to my hotel room, down I would go. Why? I fell because the provision was made for me to gratify the lusts of my flesh through the TV that was sitting there in front of me. Pornography was right there beckoning me, and for years and years I could not resist its drawing power. But when I removed the TV from my room, I was not allowing any provision for my flesh to be gratified.

This is such a key principle to freedom, because if we allow ourselves access to that which causes us to sin, we will inevitably find ourselves giving in during a weak moment.

Question 4. Please list any area(s) in which provision is still made for your flesh to be gratified.

Friend, if you listed any areas above, that is where your next fall to sexual sin will be. It is just a matter of time. You can be drinking the Living Water, exposing your sin and asking for help, and praying to be reconciled to God, but in a weak moment, you WILL fall because there is provision made to fulfill your lusts. So, it is imperative that right now you eradicate that from your life. It has got to go. If you keep it around, you are trying to run a race with a huge burden on your back, and every time you fall in that area, you add weight to the burden. Eventually you will not be able to run the race, but will be fallen down off to the side of the road in the thorns and weeds.

Question 5. Are you willing to part with that which will make you fall? Will you get rid of it right now?

Just about now is when we start getting objections. They usually go something like this, "But it is not the Internet that is the problem, it is my heart. Jesus says that out of the heart come the things that defile us, so I don't want to just deal with the symptom, which is viewing pornography, I need to get my relationship right with Jesus so I can be strong enough to say "No" to pornography, no matter where I might be tempted with it."

This is true! We have no quarrel with the above statements. However, what we are talking about in this lesson is the manner in which we get our hearts right with God, so that we can say "No" to sexual sin when we are tempted by it. And there is only one scriptural way to do this - the total removal of anything that causes us to stumble. We will talk more about this subject within the next week, but for right now, just know that it is a principle of truth that in order to run this race, we must remove anything that entangles us. Our hearts will continue to be defiled if we continue to intoxicate ourselves at the devil's bar of pornography and sexual sin, and the way to be free is to remove the temptation.

You see, I wanted to be able to look temptation in the face and say "No." I thought that I would know myself to be a strong Christian when I could have the temptation and be able to stand up against it. In reality, I wanted to be strong rather than pure. This is not the way to victory over sin.

Notice this next passage:

> "If your right eye causes you to sin, gouge it out and throw it away. It is better for you to lose one part of your body than for your whole body to be thrown into hell. And if your right hand causes you to sin, cut it off and throw it away. It is better for you to lose one part of your body than for your whole body to go into hell" (Matthew 5:29-30).

Friend, the above verses could be summarized by the words "radical amputation." Now, Jesus was not referring to a physical cutting off of our hands or an actual plucking out of the eyeball. Handicapped and blind men still lust. What He was saying is to deal radically with whatever causes us to sin: cut it off, pluck it out, hack it off. Some have stated a desire to be "reasonable" and "balanced" in the approach to overcoming sin. We agree. It is only reasonable to destroy those things in our lives that seek to destroy us. Radically amputating the TV from my hotel room was the most reasonable way to fight this sin. Jesus' method of dealing with sin is radical amputation.

Question 6. Will you, right now, cut off and pluck out anything that is causing you to stumble? Describe your plan:

If the problem is the Internet, there are probably three options, if not more, to handle this:

1. Set your web browser to the highest level of filtering possible.
2. Install the SCF Filter. This filter prevents all access to pornographic sites, and is customizable so that you may choose other categories to block, as well.

   The filter we recommend has a feature to log every website visited, instantly notify (through email or phone) whomever you choose if any "off-limit" sites are visited, and many other features. For more information on this filter, please contact Safe Browse at info@safebrowse.com.
3. Only use the Internet while your spouse, friend or other person is around to monitor the activity.

Dear friends, run the race to win. Remove that which hinders you, and anything that entangles you. It's worth it to be running light! I am no longer encumbered with the heavy and growing burden of habitual sin. I can actually run the race marked out for me, and know that I am running to win, because God has enabled me to throw off the sin that so easily besets me.

Please take this teaching of Scripture seriously. We have seen some students who delay in removing that which trips them up and some who only remove it part-way, and in every instance of a half-done job, there is a fall that is soon to come. Don't hesitate to be radical in dealing with this. After all, God was radical in dealing with sin. He gave His one and only Son to suffer and die on the cross. That's radical! Be willing to part with that which you have loved in the past. Be willing to sacrifice it to be free from it.

Question 7. Record how things are going for you today:

In his book, *The Great Divorce*, C.S. Lewis gives us a good picture of the deception of sin and the need to be radical about amputating it. In his story, he and some others were on a bus trip that took them to the outskirts of heaven. There they are able to get a glimpse of true reality - about heaven and themselves. In this story, the people from the bus trip are "ghosts" for they are not fully human as they will be when they enter heaven for all eternity. Each "Ghost" has something he must give up.

Read this excerpt and see the "radicalness" of the amputation needed:

I saw coming towards us a Ghost who carried something on his shoulder. Like all the Ghosts, he was unsubstantial, but they differed from one another as smokes differ. Some had been whitish; this one was dark and oily. What sat on his shoulder was a little red lizard, and it was twitching its tail like a whip and whispering things in his ear. As we caught sight of him he turned his head to the reptile with a snarl of impatience. "Shut up, I tell you!" he said. It wagged its tail and continued to whisper to him. He ceased snarling, and presently began to smile. Then he turned and started to limp westward, away from the mountains.

"Off so soon?" said a voice. The speaker was more or less human in shape but larger than a man, and so bright that I could hardly look at him. His presence smote on my eyes and on my body too (for there was heat coming from him as well as light) like the morning sun at the beginning of a tyrannous summer day. "Yes, I'm off," said the Ghost. "Thanks for all your hospitality. But it's no good, you see. I told this little chap," (here he indicated the lizard), "that he'd have to be quiet if he came - which he insisted on doing. Of course his stuff won't do here: I realize that. But he won't stop. I shall just have to go home

"Would you like me to make him quiet?" said the flaming Spirit - an angel, as I now understood.

"Of course I would," said the Ghost.

"Then I will kill him," said the Angel, taking a step forward.

"Oh - ah - look out! You're burning me. Keep away," said the

The following testimony is from Tony:

My earliest recollection of pornography was when I was riding my bike through town one day and a pile of magazines under a parked truck caught my eye. My heart leapt as I discovered they were porn magazines. I took them home and hid them in my wardrobe. Now hooked, I continued my fascination with porn and even resorted to buying pictures at school. When I entered my teens, I found TV provided more opportunity to indulge my mind and would search out films likely to have some pornographic content. Later I began attending "X" rated movies (even though I was under age) and watched hardcore videos at home. Although secret about my addiction, I never saw it for what it was.

At age 25, I had an encounter with God, leaving me "born again." Aware of all my sin I burned and destroyed anything that God showed me. I also married my wife and life seemed to have changed for the better. Although I never told her of my addiction, she had been aware of my "movies" that I had gotten rid of.

For many years, I lived "free" on the outside, but always within me was a desire for those old things. One day, at a hotel, a movie came on that I should have turned off, but didn't. I sat there watching it, absolutely transfixed. Although vowing to never again to do that, I did and became increasingly hooked as my life in God became increasingly difficult to live. On the outside, I was a pillar of the church, a youth pastor; and many people came to me for advice. I seemed able to handle all that until one day a man came to see me about his struggle with porn. I was unable to help him and couldn't even tell him why. I believe I could have helped him if I had not been addicted myself.

Rather than admit the seriousness of my plight, I sank further, staying up late flicking channels to find something on which to feast my eyes. My addiction became stronger, and my secrecy more intense. With the advent of the Internet I delved into pornographic web sites, then chat sites. This was all leading me away from God to the extent that I thought of leaving my family, friends and church.

Then one day, I clicked onto a site that asked the question; "Addicted to Pornography?" I followed the link to SettingCaptivesFree.com and enrolled under a false name. I held out little hope but was willing to try anything. What I found was The Way of Purity course that addressed my problems, filled with testimonies of people just like me. Now I found myself accountable to someone on a daily basis. But although I was becoming free, I had also become very secretive about the course.

Eventually, with Gods help, I confessed all of this to my wife. She was shocked and confused, but the change in me was apparent and she became very supportive. I have since told my best friend, who likewise has been an encouragement. This accountability, and openness to my past addiction, has allowed me to live free. Further, my life has taken on new depths in God, and He is bringing to me people who are addicted to this same sin.

I can only encourage anyone reading this testimony, to try this course. Take it a day at a time; God will help you, as he helped me. It's definitely worth it.

Ghost retreating.

"Don't you want him killed?" said the Angel.

"You didn't say anything about killing him at first. I hardly meant to bother you with something so drastic as that."

"It's the only way," said the Angel, whose burning hands were now very close to the lizard. "Shall I kill it?"

"Well, that's a further question. I'm quite open to consider it, but it's a new point, isn't it? I mean, for the moment I was only thinking about silencing it..." said the Ghost.

"May I kill it?" asked the Angel.

"Well, there's time to discuss that later" said the Ghost.

"There is no time. May I kill it?"

"Please, I never meant to be such a nuisance. Please - really - don't bother. Look! It's gone to sleep of its own accord. I'm sure it will be all right now. Thanks ever so much."

"May I kill it?"

"Honestly, I don't think there's the slightest necessity for that. I'm sure I shall be able to keep it in order now. I think the gradual process would be far better than killing it." said the Ghost.

"The gradual process is of no use at all."

"Don't you think so? Well, I'll think over what you've said very carefully. I honestly will. In fact, I'd let you kill it now, but as a matter of fact I'm not feeling frightfully well today. It would be silly to do it now. I'd need to be in good health for the operation. Some other day, perhaps."

"There is no other day. All days are present now."

"Get back! You're burning me. How can I tell you to kill it? You'd kill me if you did."

"It is not so."

"Why, you're hurting me now."

"I never said it wouldn't hurt you. I said it wouldn't kill you"...

The Angel's hands were almost closed on the Lizard, but not quite. Then the Lizard began chattering to the Ghost so loud that even I could hear what it was saying.

"Be careful," it said. "He can do what he says. He can kill me. One fatal word from you and he will! Then you'll be without me forever and ever. It's not natural. How could you live? You'd only be a sort of ghost, not a real man as you are now. He doesn't understand. He's only a cold, bloodless abstract thing. It may be natural for him, but it isn't for us. Yes, yes. I know there are no real pleasures now, only dreams. But aren't they better than nothing? And I'll be so good. I admit I've sometimes gone too far in the past, but I promise I won't do it again. I'll give you nothing but really nice dreams - all sweet and fresh and almost innocent. You might say, quite innocent..."

"Have I your permission?" asked the Angel to the Ghost.

"I know it will kill me."

"It won't. But supposing it did?" asked the Angel

"You're right. It would be better to be dead than to live with this creature."

"Then I may?"

"...Go on, can't you! Get it over. Do what you like," bellowed the Ghost: but ended, whimpering, "God help me. God help me."

Next moment the Ghost gave a scream of agony such as I never heard on Earth. The Burning One closed his crimson grip on the reptile: twisted it, while it bit and writhed, and then flung it, broken backed on the turf.

Some people, rather than cut off the causes of sin, want to stare it in the face and just say "no" or tell it to "be quiet" as C.S. Lewis described. They think that would be true victory. However, this desire to try to be strong rather than pure will not result in victory.

Question 8. Use this space to describe your reaction to the scene in this book by C.S. Lewis:

Scripture to Consider

"I made a covenant with my eyes not to look lustfully at a girl" (Job 31:1).

"Therefore, if anyone is in Christ, he is a new creation; the old has gone, the new has come!" (2 Corinthians 5:17).

"For what I received I passed on to you as of first importance: that Christ died for our sins according to the Scriptures, that he was buried, that he was raised on the third day according to the Scriptures" (1 Corinthians 15:3 - 4).

"The thief comes only to steal and kill and destroy; I have come that they may have life, and have it to the full." (John 10:10).

Were you free from pornography since you did the last lesson?

    Yes   No

Were you free from self-gratification since you did the last lesson?

    Yes   No

Were you free from sexual immorality since you did the last lesson?

    Yes   No

DAY 6 - TURNING

In this lesson, we will discuss the subject of repentance, and see from Scripture exactly what repentance is.

> ⁴For we know, brothers loved by God, that he has chosen you, ⁵because our gospel came to you not simply with words, but also with power, with the Holy Spirit and with deep conviction. You know how we lived among you for your sake. ⁶You became imitators of us and of the Lord; in spite of severe suffering, you welcomed the message with the joy given by the Holy Spirit. ⁷And so you became a model to all the believers in Macedonia and Achaia. ⁸The Lord's message rang out from you not only in Macedonia and Achaia - your faith in God has become known everywhere. Therefore we do not need to say anything about it, ⁹for they themselves report what kind of reception you gave us. They tell how you turned to God from idols to serve the living and true God, ¹⁰and to wait for his Son from heaven, whom he raised from the dead - Jesus, who rescues us from the coming wrath" (1 Thessalonians 1:4).

Please answer the following questions as we think through this most important issue of repentance together.

I was involved in pornography for 15 years, and went through many years of repentance, followed by sin, followed by repentance again. But when God granted me genuine repentance, I turned away completely and have not ever returned. I'm not saying that my repentance before wasn't genuine, but at the very least, I did not learn how to walk away from the sin from which I had turned.

> ¹⁰For, He that would love life, And see good days, Let him refrain his tongue from evil, And his lips that they speak no guile: ¹¹And let him turn away from evil, and do good; Let him seek peace, and pursue it" (1 Peter 3:10-11).

Question 4. How do the above verses define repentance? What are the aspects of true repentance, as shown from these verses?"

Question 1. According to verse 5, in what manner did the gospel come to the Thessalonians?

Question 2. According to verses 8 and 9, what things were being reported about these Thessalonian believers?

Friend, here is a summary of true repentance: "They tell how you turned to God from idols to serve the living and true God." Repentance has often been described as "doing a 180," meaning we turn away from sin and turn to God. This is the very reason that psychology and humanistic programs fall short of truly assisting people who are trapped in sin. They attempt to get the person to turn away from sin, but cannot instruct them to turn to God. So they are, in essence, instructing us to do a 90-degree turn. This half-turning is never sufficient to truly eradicate sin from our lives. True repentance is not only turning from sin, it is turning to God and serving Him.

Question 3. Write the words from verse 9 that define true repentance:

We can see from Scripture that genuine repentance is a complete turn-around from our previous course. For me, that meant totally turning away from the sins of pornography and self-gratification, and turning to God. The turn must be complete! We must put our backs to the sin and walk away from it, never to return again. And we must face Christ and walk towards Him. No half-hearted turning will free us from the power of sin; no partial turning will enable us to escape the trap of the devil in sexual sin.

Oh, the pain in my heart during those long years where I would sin and confess, sin and confess, while not truly turning away from the sin. I was like Lot's wife, who did, indeed, leave the burning city, but longed for it in her heart and turned back just to have a look. Her turning away from the sin of that city was not complete, and she perished in her sin, turning into a pillar of salt. We should remember Lot's wife, for she is a monument to all who will not fully turn away from sin. God has now granted me the repentance that makes me hate my previous way of life and, therefore, turn completely away from it.

This is my hope and prayer for you, too. May God enable you to truly turn away from sin for good, and to begin to walk away from it as fast as you can, and to get as far away from it as possible.

Now, here is another excellent passage that describes the attitude of genuine repentance:

> [8] Come near to God and he will come near to you. Wash your hands, you sinners, and purify your hearts, you double-minded. [9] Grieve, mourn and wail. Change your laughter to mourning and your joy to gloom. [10] Humble yourselves before the Lord, and he will lift you up" (James 4:8-10).

Here is how we can tell when God is granting somebody repentance. They not only make a 180-degree turn, but they also lose their silliness, their hollow laughter, their joking, and their pride. They become earnest in being rid of their sin. They feel sorrow over their sins, and even become somewhat gloomy, as the above verses mention. This does not mean that they live like this the rest of their lives, because joy comes into the life that is committed to purity. But there is a time where all the levity is gone, and there comes a need to be done with sin for good.

As I first came out of pornography, I was a very gloomy and mournful man, because God had made me earnest in repenting. I listened carefully to what others who were walking in purity told me, and I begged God for real repentance. In January of 1999, I made a full turn away from pornography and sexual impurity, and began running as fast as I could away from it. My heart ached because of the offenses I had committed against God and others, and I was very sad. That was several years ago, but I still remember the sorrow that I felt and the gloom that I experienced, and recall it was good and healthy for the soul.

Question 5. Please read the following quote and give your comments below:

"Conviction of sin is one of the rarest things that ever strikes a man. It is the threshold of an understanding of God. Jesus Christ said that when the Holy Spirit came He would convict of sin, and when the Holy Spirit rouses a mans conscience and brings him into the presence of God, it is not his relationship with men that bothers him, but his relationship with God - against Thee, Thee only, have I sinned, and done this evil in Thy sight. Conviction of sin, the marvel of forgiveness, and holiness are so interwoven that it is only the forgiven man who is the holy man, he proves he is forgiven by being the opposite to what he was, by God's grace. Repentance always brings a man to this point: I have sinned. The surest sign that God is at work is when a man says that and means it. Anything less than this is remorse for having made blunders, the reflex action of disgust at himself.

"The entrance into the Kingdom is through the panging pains of repentance crashing into a man's respectable goodness; then the Holy Ghost, Who produces these agonies, begins the formation of the Son of God in the life. The new life will manifest itself in conscious repentance and unconscious holiness, never the other way about. The bedrock of Christianity is repentance. Strictly speaking, a man cannot repent when he chooses; repentance is a gift of God. The old Puritans used to pray for the gift of tears. If ever you cease to know the virtue of repentance, you are in darkness. Examine yourself and see if you have forgotten how to be sorry." (Oswald Chambers, My Utmost For His Highest, December 7th Devotional).

Did you catch that "repentance is a gift from God?" This comes from 2 Timothy 2: 25: "Those who oppose him (the servant of God) he must gently instruct, in the hope that God will grant them repentance leading them to a knowledge of the truth, and that they will come to their senses and escape from the trap of the devil, who has taken them captive to do his will." Notice that repentance is the only way to escape from the devil's trap.

Question 6. Are you escaping the trap? If so, can you see how God has granted you repentance? Explain a little about this repentance. Do you have it? If so, are you enjoying it? If not, will you seek God for it?

Next, let us examine one final passage of Scripture and note the elements of repentance contained in it:

> [6] Seek the LORD while he may be found; call on him while he is near. [7] Let the wicked forsake his way and the evil man his thoughts. Let him turn to the LORD, and he will have mercy on him, and to our God, for he will freely pardon" (Isaiah 55:6-7).

Question 7. Please list the four defining elements of repentance as stated in Isaiah 55:6-7, above. The first one is "Seek the Lord"

1.

2.

3.

4.

Question 8. Please make an honest assessment of your life right now. Are you seeking the Lord, calling on Him, forsaking your sin, and turning to the Lord? If you wish, you may write out your prayer of repentance to God here.

Course member Neptali writes, "I am finding joy seeking the Lord and calling upon him. I have forsaken pornography and self-gratification, and I have turned to the Lord. I am so glad to receive his mercy and forgiveness. I now recognize that gratifying my flesh is a sin. There were struggles in the past as to whether it is a sin or not. A book written by a famous evangelist only confused the issue. However, when I came to this course and recognized it as sin, then I got free. There are no struggles anymore. My daily drink of Jesus' water and my accountability to my mentor through this course are such a big help."

My friend, there is much good news to be found in repentance. It is not as if we were merely turning away from sin only to be left empty and with no excitement in life. You see, as you both turn from immorality and turn to God, there is a blessed life of satisfaction and joy to be found in Jesus Christ. In reality, we are leaving the lesser and temporary pleasures for the greater and eternal ones. Yes, we are giving up the very temporary pleasures of sin, but we are gaining the lasting pleasures of Christ. Indeed, Psalm 16:11 describes the pleasures of Christ as "eternal."

Course member Joe wrote, "My sorrow was in that I was offending God and was not getting close to Him at all. When I confessed in this area, I fell with a broken heart to my knees wanting to be delivered and desiring a closer relationship with God. Repentance is a by-product of God's grace. He is the one who breaks hearts. I believe a broken heart before God over any sin, and a turning from it, is repentance."

Scripture to Consider

"Or do you show contempt for the riches of his kindness, tolerance and patience, not realizing that God's kindness leads you toward repentance?" (Romans 2:4).

⁶ Seek the LORD while he may be found; call on him while he is near. ⁷ Let the wicked forsake his way and the evil man his thoughts. Let him turn to the LORD, and he will have mercy on him, and to our God, for he will freely pardon" (Isaiah 55:6-7).

Were you free from pornography since you did the last lesson?

    Yes   No

Were you free from self-gratification since you did the last lesson?

    Yes   No

Were you free from sexual immorality since you did the last lesson?

    Yes   No

The following testimony is from Ed:

My sins against God were many, and affected different areas of my life. I started sexual exploration at around age nine. It seemed like harmless experimentation at the time but, as I grew older, it led to more and greater sins in my life. This spirit of lust that held me led to Internet porn sites, strip bars, and prostitution. In biblical terms, I was an adulterer and fornicator at least four times a week for twenty-nine years. It corrupted my heart and mind as well.

Four years ago, I heard a preacher on the radio while driving home from work. When he spoke of the judgment of God, it sent shock waves into my life. I listened to him for three nights and one thing he always said was, "Look, don't take my word for it. Go out and get a Bible and read it for yourself."

I was not a Christian by any sense. As I look back and see how blind I was, I am amazed, but this is what Satan does. He is a master of deception and lies, and I was under his command without even knowing it!

As I read the Bible, the Holy Spirit spoke to me Scripture by Scripture. I repented of my wickedness before the Lord and asked him to lead and guide my life because I knew that I had made a rotten mess of it. As each day went on I learned something new; first about the false religion that I was born, raised and baptized into, then my language and the drunkenness.

I was led by the Lord to a Bible-believing church. But there continued to be one problem in my life, and that was the lust that would overcome me. One day, a Christian friend sent me an e-card from crossdaily.com. At the top of the card was this flashing banner that spoke of freedom from pornography and self-gratification. I went to the site, and the more I read about the Way of Purity course, the more I liked it. I signed up for the course that night and started applying the principals of freedom through Jesus Christ into my life. I have now been free for over six years.

The Lord pulled me out of the pit of pornography and self-gratification. I thank the Lord Jesus Christ for His perfect, pure, and holy sacrifice that has redeemed me from my past life of sin and destruction.

DAY 7 - NEW DIRECTION

Please read the following Scripture and provide your thoughts and insight:

⁸ "Even if I caused you sorrow by my letter, I do not regret it. Though I did regret it I see that my letter hurt you, but only for a little while ⁹ yet now I am happy, not because you were made sorry, but because your sorrow led you to repentance. For you became sorrowful as God intended and so were not harmed in any way by us. ¹⁰ Godly sorrow brings repentance that leads to salvation and leaves no regret, but worldly sorrow brings death. ¹¹ See what this godly sorrow has produced in you: what earnestness, what eagerness to clear yourselves, what indignation, what alarm, what longing, what concern, what readiness to see justice done. At every point you have proved yourselves to be innocent in this matter. ¹² So even though I wrote to you, it was not on account of the one who did the wrong or of the injured party, but rather that before God you could see for yourselves how devoted to us you are. ¹³ By all this we are encouraged" (2 Corinthians 7:8-13).

Question 1. From verse 11, write out the seven ways that godly sorrow showed itself in the life of the Corinthians.

1.

2.

3.

4.

5.

6.

7.

Question 2. Go through this portion of Scripture and count the number of times Paul uses the words "sorry," "sorrow" or "sorrowful."

Question 3. According to verses 9 and 10, what does godly sorrow over sin bring about?

Note this well: True sorrowing over sin brings about real repentance. So this being true, we need to pray for sorrow in our hearts that it might lead us to repentance.

The first time my sins were exposed to my pastor, and I was driving away from his office, I began weeping and sobbing uncontrollably. My heart was breaking at the shame I had cast on the name of Christ (as I was a professing Christian during those

years of sin). I was also hurting about what I had made of my life, and all the pain I had caused others. My sorrow was so great that I felt the need to pull the car over and park so I could sit and weep over my sin. This sorrow began working within me a resolve to never return to pornography, sex chatting on the Internet, or illicit sexual relationships again and, to this day, I have not. Godly sorrow brings about repentance, and so this sorrow is our friend. Pray for it, seek after it, and pray to God for it.

Question 4. According to the above passage, what does worldly sorrow bring about?

Question 5. Godly sorrow is the mourning one goes through when he has grieved the Holy Spirit of God with sin. When you are only sorry about your sin because you got caught or because of its consequences, what kind of sorrow would you call that?

Question 6. According to verse 10, what is the ultimate end of only having worldly sorrow?

Note: We can see from this study on repentance that godly sorrow leads to and is a part of repentance that leads to life, whereas worldly sorrow leads to death.

Question 7. Please take a moment and honestly assess your heart right now. Ask the Holy Spirit to illuminate your understanding to know whether you have been granted godly sorrow and genuine repentance unto life, or if you only have worldly sorrow. What are your thoughts?

So, we have seen that part of repentance is experiencing a godly sorrow over sins committed against God.

Question 8. How do the following verses define repentance?

¹⁴ And it will be said: "Build up, build up, prepare the road! Remove the obstacles out of the way of my people."

¹⁵ For this is what the high and lofty One says - he who lives forever, whose name is holy: "I live in a high and holy place, but also with him who is contrite and lowly in spirit, to revive the spirit of the lowly and to revive the heart of the contrite" (Isaiah 57:14-15).

Friend, the habitual viewing of pornography, and ongoing sexual impurity hardened my heart and puffed me up with pride. Sin, pride and hardness of heart always go together (Hebrews 3:13). Genuine repentance brings with it lowliness and contriteness. I remember when I first came out of pornography, although I had some biblical knowledge, I kept quiet and asked for help from others who were free. I asked questions, asked for input, and asked for accountability. I realized all my head knowledge had not benefited me. Information is not the same thing as transformation.

We can recognize this humility in people as they begin to ask questions and to ask for help, instead of presenting all their biblical knowledge and their viewpoints on everything. They become humble and teachable, lowly and contrite.

This repentance is the key to lasting victory over sin. Anything short of true repentance will leave one open to return to the sin. This is why real repentance is a must. Only God can grant repentance, so, please seek the Lord and ask Him for the gift of repentance, and then repent with horror and disgust at past sins.

> **Course member Joe wrote,** "My sorrow was in that I was offending God and was not getting close to Him at all. When I confessed in this area, I fell to my knees with a broken heart, wanting to be delivered and desiring a closer relationship with God. Repentance is a by-product of God's grace. He is the one who breaks hearts. I believe a broken heart before God over any sin is equivalent to repentance."

Friend, the teachings of both yesterday and today define true repentance. It is a turning completely away from sin, doing an about-face, and then pursuing God with reckless abandon. And, it is also sorrowing over sin to such an extent that the heart begins to hate the sin and turns from it in disgust. This is repentance, and if either element is missing, the "freedom" from sin will not be lasting. If one merely feels sorrow over the sin but does not turn from it, he is not free. Or, if one merely turns from the sin but does not develop a heart-sorrow over it, he is not free, either. Both a heart sorrow over sin and a turning away from it must be present.

The following testimony is from Robert:

I was exposed to pornography when I was about seven years old. Self-gratification began when I was about twelve and it was then that my passion for pornography increased and I actively began looking for porn magazines. When I was 18 years old, I committed my life to Jesus and stopped looking at such magazines, but continued to gratify my flesh often.

I completed Bible School and married a beautiful woman who is still my very awesome wife. But when I entered into ministry, things took a turn for the worse and I began to look at magazines again and continued, on and off, for 22 years. I began to believe that I had to live with pornography for the rest of my life. A few times I confessed my sins to other pastors, but they couldn't help me. Later, I found out that they were also bound with similar sexual addictions.

Several years ago, I resigned from my senior pastor position because I basically "hit a wall;" my life caved in. I moved with my wife and four children to another nation. I felt like Israel did when they were deported to Babylon. But after a year we came back, and it was during that time that I really began to cry out to God. I was sick and tired of my pornographic addiction and I knew that God wanted it out of my life.

One day, instead of typing free porn on my computer, I typed pornographic addiction and that is how God led me to Setting Captives Free and The Way of Purity Course. I began to see through the teaching of the course how depraved and destructive sexual sin really was. During that time I was afraid to confess (again) to my wife, and freaked out at the thought of being accountable to another pastor, because I thought I would be rejected. But the opposite actually happened. My wife stood by me, as she has done in the past, and my fellow pastors accepted and encouraged me. (I would like to strongly encourage fellow ministers to be accountable it has personally given me much freedom).

Let me tell you about the greatest thing that has happened. The deception is gone. For 26 years I have been bound and was convinced by the lie that pornography was something that was too strong to break. But the moment I brought my sin into the light, the power it had over me was shattered and my eyes were opened. My thirst for pornography disappeared completely and my intimacy with the Lord and my wife increased dramatically, and continues to do so.

My life will never be the same again; I have been unalterably changed forever. This freedom I am now experiencing is beyond my wildest dreams. Because of Gods wonderful, awesome grace, I have a heartfelt hate for pornography. I am crying as I write this, because I was so hopelessly and completely bound, but I can now say, after 26 years of bondage and darkness: free at last, free at last! Praise God! I am free at last!

Question 9. Are both of these qualities of repentance becoming evident in your life? Are you turning away from sin toward God, and are you sorrowing in your heart over sin?

Next, notice how repentance works itself out in worship. These next few verses show what true worship looks like, and admonishes us to conform:

"Guard your steps when you go to the house of God. Go near to listen, rather than to offer the sacrifice of fools, who do not know that they do wrong. Do not be quick with your mouth, do not be hasty in your heart to utter anything before God. God is in heaven, and you are on earth, so let your words be few. Much dreaming, and many words are meaningless. Therefore stand in awe of God!" (Ecclesiastes 5:1-2, 7).

This passage of Scripture shows that worship of God from a repentant soul brings quietness and an awe of God. I think back on my years in sexual sin, and they were loud years, with much talking and teaching and making myself out to be somebody. All my many words were evidence that I was not in awe of God, but was instead taken with myself. But when God brought me low, and caused my heart to fear Him, I immediately shut up, and began being in awe of God. He was in heaven and I was on earth. I began seeing Him for Who He is, and myself for the loud-mouthed, irreverent man that I was.

Now I don't believe this Scripture is saying that because we are in awe of God we cannot talk. Some people are naturally more talkative than others, and do not necessarily sin when they do so. What these verses refer to is the loud and obnoxious man who feels that what he has to say is so important, and who does not revere the Lord.

So, true repentance evidences itself in the worship of God. It shows us the majestic deity of God, His holiness and power, grace and love, and His awesome character. When we begin to develop awe for Him, we listen more than we talk.

Question 10. What is your life currently like in relationship to this truth? Are you discovering awe of God and becoming quiet before Him?

Please notice the definition of repentance from this verse: "Therefore say to the house of Israel, 'This is what the Sovereign Lord says: Repent! Turn from your idols and renounce all your detestable practices" (Ezekiel 14:6). This applies to those of us who have been involved with sexual sin. Pornography is an "idol," and we are to turn away from it. Self-gratification is a "detestable practice," and we are to renounce it.

Question 11. What are your current struggles and/or victories?

Scripture to Consider

"If at any time I announce that a nation or kingdom is to be uprooted, torn down and destroyed, and if that nation I warned repents of its evil, then I will relent and not inflict on it the disaster I had planne." (Jeremiah 18:7-8).

"I tell you that in the same way there will be more rejoicing in heaven over one sinner who repents than over ninety-nine righteous persons who do not need to repent" (Luke 15:7)

[46] "When they sin against you - for there is no one who does not sin - and you become angry with them and give them over to the enemy, who takes them captive to his own land, far away or near; [47] and if they have a change of heart in the land where they are held captive, and repent and plead with you in the land of their conquerors and say, 'We have sinned, we have done wrong, we have acted wickedly'; [48] and if they turn back to you with all their heart and soul in the land of their enemies who took them captive, and pray to you toward the land you gave their fathers, toward the city you have chosen and the temple I have built for your Name; [49] then from heaven, your dwelling place, hear their prayer and their plea, and uphold their cause. [50] And forgive your people, who have sinned against you; forgive all the offenses they have committed against you, and cause their conquerors to show them mercy; [51] for they are your people and your inheritance, whom you brought out of Egypt, out of that iron-smelting furnace" (1 Kings 8:46-51).

Were you free from pornography since you did the last lesson?

    Yes   No

Were you free from self-gratification since you did the last lesson?

    Yes   No

Were you free from sexual immorality since you did the last lesson?

    Yes   No

DAY 8 - ACCOUNTABILITY

A study was done with horses to determine the true value of team effort. The study revealed that one horse pulling alone was able to pull 2,500 pounds. The test was then repeated with two horses pulling together; it was found that the two horses were able to pull 12,500 pounds! The two horses together were able to pull 5 times the amount of weight that the one horse alone could pull!

There is an aspect to overcoming sexual sin - or any sin, that is extremely important: one alone may be overcome; two can be victorious.

Let's read and observe the following passage from Ecclesiastes 4:

> [9] Two are better than one, because they have a good return for their work: [10] If one falls down, his friend can help him up. But pity the man who falls and has no one to help him up! [11] Also, if two lie down together, they will keep warm. But how can one keep warm alone? [12] Though one may be overpowered, two can defend themselves. A cord of three strands is not quickly broken (Ecclesiastes 4:9-12).

Today we will see the value and necessity of finding and maintaining an accountability partner.

Friend, an accountability partner should, by love of the Scriptures and care for your soul, be able to detect when you are about to "sleep" in the "land of enchantment," which, in our case, is the fantasy life of pornography or the impurity of adultery. "Hope" is restored when another "Christian" helps to wake us up. That accountability partner is indispensable.

> "If one falls down, his friend can help him up. But pity the man who falls and has no one to help him up!" (Ecclesiastes 4:10)

Question 2. Can you recall a time when you've "fallen" into sexual sin and had no strength to "get up?" What were the results? What happened? What did you do?

Question 1. According to verse 9, above, why are two better than one?

> Brothers, if someone is caught in a sin, you who are spiritual should restore him gently. But watch yourself, or you also may be tempted (Galatians 6:1).

Question 3. We all need an accountability partner. From Galatians 6:1, above, what qualifications does your future partner need to possess in order to help you?

Ecclesiastes 4:9 is about spiritual fruit. Teamwork is critical in overcoming pornography and sexual sin. As I have told you, I was in bondage to pornography for 15 years, the last 10 as a professing Christian. I kept my sins a secret because I was too proud to tell anyone else. But God brought me very low, and then began teaching me the necessity of accountability. My wife and my pastor became my accountability partners. Since that time, I've been totally free from all forms of pornography and sexual impurity. Two really are better than one. My freedom and victory are closely related to the accountability that has come into my life.

"Two are better than one, and more happy jointly than either of them could be separately, more pleased in one another than they could be in themselves only, mutually serviceable to each other's welfare, and by a united strength more likely to do good to others" Matthew Henry

Have you ever read Pilgrim's Progress? It is a wonderful allegory of the Christian life. In the ninth scene, a man by the name of "Hope" finds himself desiring to take a nap in the land of Enchantment. But Christian reminds him of 1 Thessalonians 5:6 that states, "let us not sleep, as do others; but let us watch and be sober." Hope, being reminded of the truth of Scripture, becomes very thankful for Christian. He said these words: "I acknowledge that I was wrong; and if I would have been here alone, by my sleeping I would have been in danger of death. I see it is true what that wise man said, 'Two are better than one.' Therefore you being here has been a mercy to me; and you will have a good reward for your labor."

Question 4. What about you? Have you had anyone to come alongside and "help you pull more?" Have you had anyone to "help you up" when you fell into pornography or sexual impurity?

> But encourage one another, as long as it is called Today, so that none of you may be hardened by sin's deceitfulness (Hebrews 3:13).

Question 5. Notice how "daily encouragement" is an antidote to sin. According to this verse, how often should you and your accountability partner communicate?

If we are serious about overcoming sin, we must utilize an accountability partner. Here's how:

Church is important. If you are involved in church, speak with your pastor or other church leader. Simply ask his help in overcoming sexual sin, and ask if he will be an accountability partner for you.

Your spouse, if you are married, should eventually become your number one accountability partner. Have you shared your struggles with him or her and asked for help? If not, possibly this may be the time to do so. Please see an article about this subject, written by Shon Bruellman (Executive Director of Setting Captives Free), on page 32.

Finally, your mentor in this course may double as your accountability partner at your request.

Here are some guidelines to follow when you initiate accountability with your partner:

1. You agree to openness and honesty. Bondage to sexual impurity brings deception with it, and some of us have been deceptive for years. If we want to lose the slavery to sin, we start with honesty, even if it is humbling. If your accountability partner asks how you are doing, and you have just fallen into pornography or other sexual sin, you must honestly admit it.

2. You agree to prepare and share with your accountability partner your "break the chain" plan as taught in this course. Ask your accountability partner to help you by making suggestions to your plan and holding you accountable to it.

3. You agree to give your partner freedom to ask the hard questions, without taking offense. For instance, "Have you seen any pornography today?" Or, "Did you break off that sinful relationship completely, as you said you would?"

4. You agree to initiate communication daily for the first 30 days, as far as is possible.

"It is good for two to travel together, for if one happens to fall, he may be lost for want of a little help. If a man falls into sin, his friend will help to restore him with the spirit of meekness; if he falls into trouble, his friend will help to comfort him and assuage his grief." Matthew Henry

Course member John wrote, "Have you had anyone to help you up? Since I had hidden it so well (even from myself, to a point) no, I did not have someone to pull me up until recently. Oh, I would pick my head up from the muck every once in a while by myself - usually after a good sermon - or some devotional reading struck too close to home, but I never stayed above water too long. That is, until I once again was picked up by God, shook off and placed in front of a mirror to see the filth I was in (that was about 18 days ago now). He lead me to Setting Captives Free—The Way of Purity course, and God is using the Scriptures in the course to give me inner strength to fight the demon of lust in my life and the courage to go to my accountability partner (who

I never truly let in to this secret - though I had hinted of a potential problem) and confessed my need for his help here, as well."

Also, if two lie down together, they will keep warm. But how can one keep warm alone? (Ecclesiastes 4:11).

Ecclesiastes 4:11 refers to spiritual warmth or Christian zeal. It asks the question, "How can one keep warm alone?" The question is rhetorical, and is designed to teach that it is easy to become lukewarm toward Jesus if "alone," but together people can spur one another on toward loving Him more. We can help each other "stay warm" together.

Question 6. Using your own words now, how does this statement "Also, if two lie down together they can keep warm" apply to our topic of study?

Note: In Revelation 3, Jesus tells the church of Laodicea that it had grown "lukewarm." They needed to repent of their sin and open the door to Jesus Christ to restore fellowship.

Question 7. How is your spiritual zeal?

"If two lie together, they have heat. So virtuous and gracious affections are excited by good society, and Christians warm one another by provoking one another to love and to good works." Matthew Henry

And now, we will examine the final verse in this important "accountability" section. Ecclesiastes 4:12 says, *"Though one may be overpowered, two can defend themselves."*

We have discovered that two working together can produce spiritual fruit (vs. 9), that two together can provide spiritual restoration (vs. 10), that togetherness can prompt spiritual zeal (vs. 11), and now we will see that two working together can provide spiritual protection.

Question 8. What does verse 12, above, teach that "two together" can provide?

Question 9. Has this spiritual protection been missing in your life in the past?   Yes   No

Question 10. Have you contacted someone yet to be an accountability partner with you?   Yes   No

To be upfront with you, if you are unwilling to maintain an accountability relationship, then most likely you will not win the battle against sexual sin for any length of time. Remember, "One can be overpowered." (I proved the truth of this fact in my life for 15 years. I did not have accountability, and I was overpowered again and again.) However, if you will contact your pastor, spouse, or others, then "Two can defend themselves" and you can experience victory too! (Man is it ever good to be done with pornography and self-gratification!) We are in a battle, dear friend. We can either be "overpowered" or we can "defend ourselves," depending on our willingness to find a partner.

"United strength. If an enemy find a man alone, he is likely to prevail against him; with his own single strength he cannot win, but if he have a second, he may do well enough: two shall withstand him." Matthew Henry

Notice this biblical story which reinforces the truth we have been studying:

> Joab saw that there were battle lines in front of him and behind him; so he selected some of the best troops in Israel and deployed them against the Arameans. [10] He put the rest of the men under the command of Abishai his brother and deployed them against the Ammonites. [11] Joab said, 'If the Arameans are too strong for me, then you are to come to my rescue; but if the Ammonites are too strong for you, then I will come to rescue you.' [12] Be strong and let us fight bravely for our people and the cities of our God. The LORD will do what is good in his sight" (2 Samuel 10:9-12).

The end result of this battle was victory for the Israelites. Joab, in essence, said, "You help me with my enemy, and I'll help you with yours." And so together they were victorious, whereas separately they would have been conquered. This is an important aspect of an accountability relationship. We should provide one another with spiritual protection from our mutual enemy. The way we do this is to pray for each other; share "battle tips" that helped us, take each other to the Word of God, and help each other radically amputate the causes of sin. This is a winnable war. But it takes two!

"We Christians need each other. There is strength in numbers. When isolated and separated from our brothers, we are easy pickings for the Enemy of our souls." (Robert Daniels *The War Within*)

Question 11. Please provide your comments on the following passages of Scripture:

> Let us hold unswervingly to the hope we profess, for he who promised is faithful. And let us consider how we may spur one another on toward love and good deeds. Let us not give up meeting together, as some are in the habit of doing, but let us encourage one another - and all the more as you see the Day approaching" (Hebrews 10:23-25).

> As iron sharpens iron, so one man sharpens another (Proverbs 27:17).

Scripture to Consider

"Do this, knowing the time, that it is already the hour for you to awaken from sleep; for now salvation is nearer to us than when we believed" (Romans 13:11).

"A person standing alone can be attacked and defeated, but two can stand back-to-back and conquer. Three are even better, for a triple-braided cord is not easily broken" (Ecclesiastes 4:12, NLT).

Were you free from pornography since you did the last lesson?

    Yes   No

Were you free from self-gratification since you did the last lesson?

    Yes   No

Were you free from sexual immorality since you did the last lesson?

    Yes   No

The following testimony is from Marc:

I only had a 'little' problem with porn, not like the rest of the world. I didn't buy as many tapes or books as others or go to strip bars, but it doesn't matter. There is no such thing as a little problem with porn. Like gangrene, the poison destroys your entire body, and will kill you unless you cut it off!

Thanks to Christ working through this course, I have been able to cut it off. The poison is out of my body and I am clean. That does not mean that my flesh has so soon forgotten the poison it relished - thus the need for continued vigilance.

So I prescribe these words to anyone (mostly myself) in dealing with porn: Cut it off, run away, feed on the Word daily and attack the enemy, using God's weapons. And, in the words of Sir Winston Churchill, Never give in! Never give in! Never, never, never.

DAY 9 - PURE GRACE

For the next few lessons, we will examine a pivotal teaching of the Scriptures. The necessity of understanding this principle cannot be overstated. Simply put, grace is what saves us, sanctifies us and will ultimately glorify us. The grace of God is responsible for rescuing us from pornography and all sexual sin and for keeping us out of it until the end.

The value of this truth is that grace can do what the law cannot do. In other words, if I am caught in the trap of pornography, I cannot escape through obeying the law. The law condemns my behavior as sinful, but provides no power to help me stop. On the other hand, the grace of God actually rescues us from the kingdom of the devil, redeems us from slavery to the devil, and releases us from the trap of the devil.

"To run and work the law commands, but gives us neither feet nor hands. But better news the gospel brings, it bids us fly and gives us wings."

John Bunyan

I wonder if you are familiar with the strangle-knot. It is an excellent knot which is used as a running-knot for a snare because the more force that is applied from inside the loop, the more firmly the running-knot prevents the opening of the loop. In short, the harder you pull against the knot, the tighter the knot becomes! The only way to break free of this snare is by cutting the rope with a knife.

Pornography, adultery, and all sexual sin is a strangle-knot for us. All of our own efforts to break free from sin only serve to increase its death-grip on us. The truth is that it is the grace of God alone that can break our bondage and free us from certain death. God's grace is like the knife that will free us from the strangle-knot.

Please read the following example from Scripture of "Pure Grace," and answer the questions below.

> [1] But Jesus went to the Mount of Olives. [2] At dawn he appeared again in the temple courts, where all the people gathered around him, and he sat down to teach them. [3] The teachers of the law and the Pharisees brought in a woman caught in adultery. They made her stand before the group [4] and said to Jesus, Teacher, this woman was caught in the act of adultery. [5] In the Law Moses commanded us to stone such women. Now what do you say? [6] They were using this question as a trap, in order to have a basis for accusing him.
>
> But Jesus bent down and started to write on the ground with his finger. [7] When they kept on questioning him, he straightened up and said to them, If any one of you is without sin, let him be the first to throw a stone at her. [8] Again he stooped down and wrote on the ground.
>
> [9] At this, those who heard began to go away one at a time, the older ones first, until only Jesus was left, with the woman still standing there. [10] Jesus straightened up and asked her, Woman, where are they? Has no one condemned you?
>
> [11] No one, sir, she said.
>
> Then neither do I condemn you, Jesus declared. Go now and leave your life of sin (John 8:1-11).

Nothing is more humiliating than being caught in an act of disobedience! Whether it's a child with his hand in the cookie jar or an adult driving over the speed limit, we all know the sinking feeling of being caught. In John 8, a woman is caught in the act of adultery. Let us study her story and learn. (Some of the following questions are taken from Lesson Builder by Logos.)

Questions

Question 1. From the early verses of the above passage, what do we know about the character and motive of those who bring this woman to Jesus?

Question 2. How do you think the woman felt when the men made her "stand before the group" and publicly expose her sin?

Question 3. While it is obvious that this woman is guilty, what elements of injustice can you find in this situation?

Note: The Pharisees and scribes continued to press their point. They were not after this woman as much as they were after Jesus. They were saying this to "test" Jesus (v. 6). They wanted grounds for "accusing" Jesus. He is the one they are really after here.

This self-righteous, self-appointed group of Pharisees was acting as judge and jury and wanted to stone this woman; but don't mistake it, their ultimate goal was the death of Jesus. They were filled with self-righteous hatred toward Jesus. They kept stressing their point. "They persisted in asking Him." (v. 7a) They kept the pressure on Jesus. "Come on, tell us, teacher, what do You say? Will you kill the woman or kill the Law?"

Scripture makes no definitive statement as to what Jesus wrote in the dirt. However, here is a thought: there are only two other times in Scripture where God is shown to write something with His hand or finger, and both times what was written condemned those to whom He wrote. The first time was when God wrote the Law on tablets of stone, the second time was when He wrote on King Belshazzar's wall. One writer said, "An ancient opinion is that he wrote the sins of the accusers." Note Job 13:26 - "For you write down bitter things against me and make me inherit the sins of my youth."

Question 4. The Pharisees and teachers were often very self-righteous. Why did they go away instead of stoning the woman?

Question 5. Was Jesus condoning the woman's sin by not condemning her? Please explain.

Thoughts: as these religious leaders persisted in questioning him, Jesus stood up and invited any one among them who was sinless to throw the first stone. By this statement they could not possibly say Jesus rejected the law. Jesus specifically told them to throw the first stone. Go ahead, you are right, the Law says stone her. She is guilty. Now, you, who among you is sinless?

Question 6. Why are we tempted to condemn other people's sins, rather than our own?

David wrote: "Amazingly, when I was so deep in sexual sin, I would condemn a man for sexual sin, yet I would have no problem lusting over girls at the swimming pool. Apparently it was easier for me to throw stones at others than to consider my own sins."

Question 7. How would you describe Jesus' attitude toward the woman? (Notice Jesus was the only one who talked to her; the others only talked about her.)

Please notice the last statement of Jesus: "Neither do I condemn you..." This is pure grace. The law required punishment and death of the woman caught in the act of adultery, but Jesus forgave her and gave her life. The woman did not make any excuses (v. 11). She was guilty. She knew it. She stood condemned. She didn't have to be convinced of that fact. She needed grace, but she did not deserve it. "The wages of sin is death." "The soul that sins will surely die." She couldn't earn it. She was a spiritual pauper in need of the riches of God's marvelous grace.

Jesus said to her, "Neither do I condemn you; go your way; from now on sin no more" (v. 11). Let those words soak in. "Neither do I..." "Neither do I condemn you."

The following testimony is from Shon:

My testimony is one of deliverance from a life-dominating sin that threatened to destroy my family, my marriage and my very soul. It is a "secret sin;" one that lurks in the deepest corners of men's heart, and I am speaking of the sin of lust and sexual immorality.

So often it seems that the evil one sinks his claws into people in their youth and I was no exception. I was introduced to the pleasures of the flesh at about five years old and from then on I was drawn to girls and the enjoyment that came from being near them emotionally or physically. I had feelings of attraction and desire from the moment I was exposed to that first fleshly act. I still remember the first time I stole a kiss from a classmate while we were Trick or Treating together one Halloween during third grade. Oh; how my heart beat loudly as I mustered up the courage to show my "true love," just how much she meant to me! So sad to ponder the deception I was swallowing, even as a child.

There wasn't any sexual activity at that time, but there was a continuous history of lust that escalated as I grew older. I tore pictures out of National Geographic, looked in Bible story books around the home of loosely-clothed women and feasted on the Sears catalogs in the lingerie section. My parents found literally hundreds of pictures I tore out of magazines that I had hidden under my mattress, but because they didn't know what to do, they chose to do what so many other parents do.... they did nothing. The hooks sunk deeper....

To make things even worse, in grade school a friend and I found a pornographic magazine that was filled with many vile things (including images of murder and torture) that twisted my impressionable mind even more than what "normal" pornography would do. The hooks sunk deeper....

I was drawn to pornography like a bee to honey, and the enemy was sure to place someone in my life to feed my lusts in school. My adopted "big brother" in high school provided me with stacks of porn to look at and encouraged me to drink often of them and I did. From the age of 12 on through high school I fell to sexual impurity at least once a day. The chains grew tighter as my mind grew darker and more evil.

"Whatever my eyes desired I did not keep from them. I did not withhold my heart from any pleasure, For my heart rejoiced in all my labor; And this was my reward from all my labor" (Ecclesiastes 2:10).

What was my reward? I was miserable, lost, bitter, angry, and had a twisted view of who women were and how they were to be treated. Then I crossed paths with a 17-year-old girl named Julie and, after a year of dating and many sinful decisions, we found ourselves facing the reality that, as 18-year-olds, we were about to become parents. Julie was a bit worried about marrying me because she had seen my wandering eye more than once and, although she didn't know it at the time, there was more than once that I was unfaithful to her - even though she was pregnant and we were engaged. As her pregnancy continued, I insulted her appearance and flirted with other girls in front of her to make her jealous. She got concerned about what type of guy I was and wanted to call off the wedding (rightfully so, huh?) However, I turned on my charm and convinced her I was madly in love with her and even threatened to kill myself if she broke off the engagement.

I knew I was headed for hell and that gave me much concern, so one night soon after we were married I started repenting and wanted to turn from my sin, but I put my trust in the wrong thing. I was taught from my youth that the church would save you; that all you had to do was repent, stop sinning, and join the church and everything would be alright. Everything was OK for a while, but without a relationship with Christ, I inevitably started to fall again; whether it was committing sexual sin in the middle of the night, getting a porn magazine, viewing it and subsequently destroying it, or watching a pornographic movie.

Then the Internet came into our home, and I was totally snowed under by all the porn that was freely available. Many a night I went to check out a few pictures on the way to bed, only to find that the next thing I knew the sun was shining through the windows because I was in a fantasy world where time stopped. I sat there hour after hour seeking THE perfect picture, only to find that it didn't exist....

"Then I looked on all the works that my hands had done And on the labor in which I had toiled; And indeed all was vanity and grasping for the wind. There was no profit under the sun" (Ecclesiastes 2:11).

I wanted to break free but I didn't know where to turn! I went to the church leaders and their advice was to "stop doing it and pray more." When that didn't work they referred me to a psychiatrist. I went to see doctors, counselors and therapists, and their answer was that I was depressed and needed drugs. I took anti-depressants for nearly a decade of my life with little help or improvement. It was like putting a band-aid over a gaping chest wound; the core of the problem was never addressed, which was my sinful heart.

I can say with certainty I was destined for hell even though I was a church person who was a member of a very legalistic, conservative church. I was living the outward life of a Christian, but my private and personal life was a lie and an abomination to God. On October 7, 2000, the very day of my wife's birthday after yet another night of sin on the Internet, I was compelled by the Spirit of God to type in the words "sex addiction" and it was then that my journey to freedom began. I was eventually led to a site called Setting Captives Free, where I was introduced to the Son of God, Jesus Christ.....

"And you He made alive, who were dead in trespasses and sins, in which you once walked according to the course of this world, according to the prince of the power of the air, the spirit who now works in the sons of disobedience, among whom also we all once conducted ourselves in the lusts of our flesh, fulfilling the desires of the flesh and of the mind, and were by nature children of wrath, just as the others. But God, who is rich in mercy, because of His great love with which He loved us, even when we were dead in trespasses, made us alive together with Christ (by grace you have been saved), and raised us up together, and made us sit together in the heavenly places in Christ Jesus, that in the ages to come He might show the exceeding riches of His grace in His kindness toward us in Christ Jesus" (Ephesians 2:1-7).

God is so rich in mercy and loved me so much that even though I was a dirty rotten sinner, He sent His Son to die for me anyway. Fathers; you think about sacrificing one of your own children for the sake of your best friend. Could you do it? Now think about what God did; He sacrificed His Son for the sake of His enemies and those who hated Him. Incomprehensible, isn't it?

"And you, being dead in your trespasses and the uncircumcision of your flesh, He has made alive together with Him, having forgiven you all trespasses, having wiped out the handwriting of requirements that was against us, which was contrary to us. And He has taken it out of the way, having nailed it to the cross" (Colossians 2:13-14).

He wiped out the debt I owed, took it out of the way and nailed it to the cross and said "You are freed; the price is paid. I forgive you; go and sin no more." Before that could take place, though, I had to be broken and admit that there was nothing I could do to earn my freedom or salvation. I had to confess my sins before God and ask Him to forgive me, save me and give me grace to place my faith in the shed blood of His perfect Son, Jesus Christ, on the Cross. He became not only my Savior and Lord, but also my Protector from the darts of the evil one.

By His mercy and grace alone, I have been freed from pornography and sexual impurity since then (freed from all anti-depressants, too) and it is according to that same mercy and grace that I will be able to continue down this same road of freedom from now until the end of eternity.

I am currently the executive director and SCF conference representative for Setting Captives Free. Since I graduated from the course, I have been free from porn and self-gratification.

I have a passionate hatred for the bonds that had a hold on me at one time, and I want to help others learn and have the faith that they can break free from sin's trap, too. I served the devil well for years; it is my prayer I can serve the Lord ten times better in my few moments on this soil before the glories of heaven. It is such a blessing to be able to see God's grace traveling the face of the earth, calling lost, hurting, souls back home while the door of grace is yet open!

By the way, my wife, Julie, is the apple of my eye and she gave her heart and life to Christ on my one-year anniversary of freedom from sexual sin. She said "God is, indeed, a powerful God and He gave me a gift by freeing my husband and I want to make Him my Lord and Savior, too!" Today as a family (along with our three sons), we serve the Lord God Almighty.

How could Jesus offer such a sinner "no condemnation?" He did it the same way He does for us. He knew He was going to the cross to die for her sins. "For while we were still helpless" sinners. That is the way all sinners are - helpless. A helpless sinner doesn't merit forgiveness. A helpless sinner doesn't earn forgiveness. "For while we were still helpless [sinners], at the right time Christ died for the ungodly" (Romans 5:6).

Moreover, "God demonstrates His own love toward us, in that while we were yet sinners, Christ died for us" (v. 8).

To every guilt-ridden sinner who puts his trust in Jesus Christ as their Savior, the LORD God comes today and whispers in his ear, "Neither do I condemn you." "There is therefore now no condemnation for those who are in Christ Jesus" (Romans 8:1).

But Jesus' statement of grace is immediately followed up by an admonition to "Go and sin no more." Theologians have made terms that describe what Jesus did here, and they are "justification" and "sanctification." Justification is: "Neither do I condemn you." Sanctification is: "Go and sin no more." And it is critical to see the order of Jesus' statements, for He did not say, "Go and sin no more, neither do I condemn you." Or, "Clean up your act and then I will forgive you." Jesus Christ here uses grace as the motive for pure living.

Question 8. If you were the woman, how would you feel as you left Jesus' presence?

Course member Mary writes: "I have been like that woman, and have experienced Him saying to me, 'Neither do I condemn you, go and sin no more.' It is such a wonderful experience to simply admit my sin, accept His love and forgiveness, and walk away knowing that He loves me and is helping me to stop sin."

Friend, let us bring this teaching home. Viewing pornography is heart adultery. Jesus said, "Anyone who looks at a woman lustfully has already committed adultery with her in his heart" (Matthew 5:28). Let us call it what it is - it is not just "stumbling" or "slipping up" it is spiritual adultery of the heart. We are adulterers - guilty before God, condemned before men, caught in the act - adulterers. If we are married and viewing pornography, we are committing the sin of heart adultery against our spouse as well.

And yet, there is a place where adulterers can go to find pardon and forgiveness. It is in Jesus, who "justifies the wicked" (Romans 4:5). It is in Jesus, who was "pierced for our transgressions, and crushed for our iniquities." And it is also in Jesus where we find grace to live differently, for it is the grace of God (not the law of God) that teaches us to say "No" to ungodliness (Titus 2:12). Pure grace; we need it; He has it.

In summary, a snare was set for this woman; she was in a strangle-knot with no way to break free. But Jesus cut the knot, by the knife of pure grace. He can do the same for us!

Have you ever heard this song?

> Every promise we can make,
> Every prayer and step of faith,
> Every difference we will make, is only by His grace.
> Every mountain we will climb,
> Every ray of hope we shine,
> Every blessing left behind, is only by His grace.
> Grace alone which God supplies,
> Strength unknown He will provide,
> Christ in us our Cornerstone,
> We will go forth in grace alone.
> Every soul we long to reach,
> Every heart we have to teach,
> Everywhere we share His peace, is only by His grace.
> Every loving word we say,
> Every tear we wipe away,
> Every sorrow turned to praise, is only by His grace.
> ("Grace Alone" Words and Music by Scott Wesley Brown
> and Jeff Nelson, Maranatha! Music, 1998).

Question 9. Do you know the life-transforming power of the grace of God? Do you know the joy of having an Advocate like Jesus Christ? Record your progress and what you are learning here:

Scripture to Consider

I, even I, am he who blots out your transgressions, for my own sake, and remembers your sins no more (Isaiah 43:25).

John testifies concerning him. He cries out, saying, "This was he of whom I said, 'He who comes after me has surpassed me because he was before me.'" [16] From the fullness of his grace we have all received one blessing after another. [17] For the law was given through Moses; grace and truth came through Jesus Christ" (John 1:15 - 17).

If we confess our sins, he is faithful and just and will forgive us our sins and purify us from all unrighteousness (1 John 1:9).

Were you free from pornography since you did the last lesson?

    Yes   No

Were you free from self-gratification since you did the last lesson?

    Yes   No

Were you free from sexual immorality since you did the last lesson?

    Yes   No

Now, as a special bonus, we have secured permission from Chuck Colson's Prison Fellowship Ministries to reprint one of their articles on accountability. This is an excellent article; please take the time to read through it.

By Charles W. Colson: I urge all Christians not only to attend church services regularly but also to establish small groups of other Christians to whom they are accountable. I've seen this simple practice work wonders in my own life. In fact, I would never have developed real Christian maturity merely by staying home, reading religious books and attending church once a week—no more than an athlete can develop by shooting baskets alone in the driveway. We're all parts of a larger Body, and as parts we can't operate alone. Nor is the Body fully formed when some of its parts are not fully integrated.

After I became a Christian, I was surrounded by some loving Christian brothers. I credit my early spiritual growth to that prayer group. They made it clear from the beginning that they would meet with me regularly, and we agreed that I wouldn't make decisions without them.

Why is this necessary? Even if Christ lives in you, and even if you're a committed disciple, there will be times when temptation will be nearly overpowering. We need to remember that we're self-deluding creatures who are fully capable of rationalizing the worst sins, even as Christians. Remember the story of David and Nathan? David, a man after God's own heart, couldn't see his own considerable sin, so Nathan told him the story of a man's obvious sin. David was enraged and told Nathan the man should be punished. Only then could Nathan say, "You are the man!"

A group can tell us when we're off base. A group has the wonderful ability to get us to focus on God rather than on ourselves. We may resist this, but without a group we will likely never recognize how out of focus we're becoming.

Let me be the first to admit that over the years I've been tempted to sin, and I've done things wrong without even knowing it. Because the human heart is deceitful, the accountability of a small group is indispensable.

Reprinted with permission of: Prison Fellowship, P.O. Box 17500, Washington, DC 20041-7500

DAY 10 –
SUPRISING GRACE

There was once a great and noble King whose land was terrorized by a crafty dragon. Like a massive bird of prey, the scaly beast delighted in ravaging villages with his fiery breath. Hapless victims ran from their burning homes, only to be snatched into the dragon's jaws or talons. Those devoured instantly were deemed more fortunate than those carried back to the dragon's lair to be devoured at his leisure. The King led his sons and knights in many valiant battles against the dragon.

Riding alone in the forest, one of the King's sons heard his name purred low and soft. In the shadows of the ferns and trees, curled among the boulders, lay the dragon. The creature's heavy-lidded eyes fastened on the prince, and the reptilian mouth stretched into a friendly smile.

"Don't be alarmed," said the dragon, as gray wisps of smoke rose lazily from his nostrils.

"I am not what your father thinks."

"What are you, then?" asked the prince, warily drawing his sword as he pulled in the reins to keep his fearful horse from bolting.

"I am pleasure," said the dragon. "Ride on my back and you will experience more than you ever imagined. Come now. I have no harmful intentions. I seek a friend, someone to share flights with me. Have you never dreamed of flying? Never longed to soar in the clouds?"

Visions of soaring high above the forested hills drew the prince hesitantly from his horse. The dragon unfurled one great webbed wing to serve as a ramp to his ridged back. Between the spiny projections, the prince found a secure seat. Then the creature snapped his powerful wings twice and launched them into the sky. The prince's apprehension melted into awe and exhilaration.

From then on, he met the dragon often, but secretly, for how could he tell his father, brothers or the knights that he had befriended the enemy? The prince felt separate from them all. Their concerns were no longer his concerns. Even when he wasn't with the dragon, he spent less time with those he loved and more time alone.

The skin on the prince's legs became calloused from gripping the ridged back of the dragon, and his hands grew rough and hardened. He began wearing gloves to hide the malady. After many nights of riding, he discovered scales growing on the backs of his hands as well. With dread he realized his fate were he to continue, and so he resolved to return no more to the dragon.

But, after a fortnight, he again sought out the dragon, having been tormented with desire. And so it transpired many times over. No matter what his determination, the prince eventually found himself pulled back, as if by the cords of an invisible web. Silently, patiently, the dragon always waited.

One cold, moonless night their excursion became a foray against a sleeping village. Torching the thatched roofs with fiery blasts from his nostrils, the dragon roared with delight when the terrified victims fled from their burning homes. Swooping in, the serpent belched again and flames engulfed a cluster of screaming villages. The prince closed his eyes tightly in an attempt to shut out the carnage.

In the pre dawn hours, when the prince crept back from his dragon trysts, the road outside his father's castle usually remained empty. But not tonight. Terrified refugees streamed into the protective walls of the castle. The prince attempted to slip through the crowd to close himself in his chambers, but some of the survivors stared and pointed toward him.

"He was there," one woman cried out, "I saw him on the back of the dragon." Others nodded their heads in angry agreement. Horrified, the prince saw that his father, the King, was in the courtyard holding a bleeding child in his arms. The King's face mirrored the agony of his people as his eyes found the prince's. The son fled, hoping to escape into the night, but the guards apprehended him as if he were a common thief. They brought him to the great hall where his father sat solemnly on the throne. The people on every side railed against the prince.

"Banish him!" he heard one of his own brothers angrily cry out.

"Burn him alive!" other voices shouted.

As the king rose from his throne, bloodstains from the wounded shone darkly on his royal robes. The crowd fell silent in expectation of his decree. The prince, who could not bear to look into his father's face, stared at the flagstones of the floor.

"Take off your gloves and your tunic," the King commanded. The prince obeyed slowly, dreading to have his metamorphosis uncovered before the kingdom. Was his shame not already enough? He had hoped for a quick death without further humiliation. Sounds of revulsion rippled through the crowd at the sight of the prince's thick, scaled skin and the ridge growing along his spine.

The king strode toward his son, and the prince steeled himself, fully expecting a back handed blow even though he had never been struck so by his father.

Instead, his father embraced him and wept as he held him tightly. In shocked disbelief, the prince buried his face against his father's shoulder.

"Do you wish to be freed from the dragon, my son?"

The prince answered in despair, "I wished it many times, but there is no hope for me."

"Not alone," said the King. "You cannot win against the dragon alone."

"Father, I am no longer your son. I am half beast," sobbed the prince.

But his father replied, "My blood runs in your veins. My nobility has always been stamped deep within your soul."

With his face still hidden tearfully in his father's embrace, the prince heard the King instruct the crowd, "The dragon is crafty. Some fall victim to his wiles and some to his violence. There will be mercy for all who wish to be freed. Who else among you has ridden the dragon?"

The prince lifted his head to see someone emerge from the crowd. To his amazement, he recognized an older brother, one who had been lauded throughout the kingdom for his onslaughts against the dragon in battle and for his many good deeds. Others came, some weeping, others hanging their heads in shame.

The King embraced them all.

"This is our most powerful weapon against the dragon," he announced. "Truth. No more hidden flights. Alone we cannot resist him."

Melinda Reinicke, Parables for Personal Growth (San Diego, CA: Recovery Publications, Inc., 1993), pp. 5-9.

Question 1. What are your thoughts on this story? Do you see parallels with your own life? What are your comments?

Have you been so disgusted and shame-filled over your pornography or sexual slavery that you resolved to never do it again, only to find yourself pulled back, as if by the cords of an invisible web? I have. I resolved over and over to stop, to never do that again, and yet all my resolve melted in the heat of the temptation. I was receiving God's grace in vain.

Friend, it is possible to "receive the grace of God in vain" (2 Corinthians 6:1); that is, with no associated heart and life change. Let us examine Scripture and see that the grace and love of God is the cure for any bondage. Sin is a spiritual problem, and requires a spiritual solution. God's grace, given to us at the cross of Jesus Christ, is the solution.

> For if, by the trespass of the one man, death reigned through that one man, how much more will those who receive God's abundant provision of grace and of the gift of righteousness reign in life through the one man, Jesus Christ (Romans 5:17).

Question 2. According to this passage, what will those who receive grace do?

> 9 For I am the least of the apostles and do not even deserve to be called an apostle, because I persecuted the church of God. 10 But by the grace of God I am what I am, and his grace to me was not without effect. No, I worked harder than all of them - yet not I, but the grace of God that was with me (1 Corinthians 15:9-10).

Question 3. Paul said that the grace God gave to Paul was not without effect. What was the effect of God's grace to Paul?

> Now this is our boast: Our conscience testifies that we have conducted ourselves in the world, and especially in our relations with you, in the holiness and sincerity that are from God. We have done so not according to worldly wisdom but according to God's grace (2 Corinthians 1:12).

Question 4. How did Paul conduct himself while among the Corinthians?

Question 5. What was the source of Paul's ability to conduct himself in "holiness and sincerity?"

Question 6. They acted in holiness, according to what?

> And God is able to make all grace abound to you, so that in all things at all times, having all that you need, you will abound in every good work" (2 Corinthians 9:8).

Question 7. What does it take in order to "abound in every good work?"

> 11 For the grace of God that brings salvation has appeared to all men. 12 It teaches us to say "No" to ungodliness and worldly passions, and to live self-controlled, upright and godly lives in this present age (Titus 2:11-12).

Question 8. If we are ever to learn to say "No" to ungodliness, if we are ever to deny worldly passions, if we are ever to live a self-controlled life, what will it take?

Hopefully these verses have taught us one very basic, but essential truth: the grace of God alone will enable us to conquer any sin habit. While we acknowledge that grace is a sovereign gift of God which cannot be earned, Scripture does instruct us on how we can put ourselves into a position to enjoy grace from Him. Let's look at four actions which promote the grace of God in our lives.

1. **Humble ourselves:** God opposes the proud but gives grace to the humble. Submit yourselves, then, to God. Resist the devil, and he will flee from you. Come near to God and he will come near to you. Wash your hands, you sinners, and purify your hearts, you double-minded. Grieve, mourn and wail. Change your laughter to mourning and your joy to gloom. Humble yourselves before the Lord, and he will lift you up (James 4:6-10).

2. **Rid our lives of idols:** Those who cling to worthless idols forfeit the grace that could be theirs (Jonah 2:8). Whatever is between God and us must be given up in order to experience grace. Either forfeit the idols, or forfeit grace.

Course member Eric wrote, "This is a revelation to me. 'Either forfeit the idols, or forfeit grace.' I never knew this and had been deceived about the true meaning of grace. As in the story above, the father could have done nothing for the son unless the son was in the kingdom. He could not receive his father's grace if he could not hear his voice. And, as in the story, I'm grateful The Way of Purity course has aggressively brought me into the kingdom to face my wrongdoings and find grace to cover them."

3. **Seek after it:** Ask and it will be given to you; seek and you will find; knock and the door will be opened to you. For everyone who asks receives; he who seeks finds; and to him who knocks, the door will be opened (Matthew 7:7-8).

4. **Don't miss it:** See to it that no one misses the grace of God and that no bitter root grows up to cause trouble and defile many (Hebrews 12:15). See to it. Make it your primary objective. Do not miss the grace of God. Humble yourself, rid your life of any idol, seek after it, and don't miss it. What is the result? God gives grace; grace makes us more than conquerors through Him who loves us; we reign in life; and we overcome pornography, adultery and all sexual sin.

Often recall the proverb: The eye is not satisfied with seeing nor the ear filled with hearing (Ecclesiastes 1:8b). Try, moreover, to turn your heart from the love of things visible and bring yourself to things invisible. For they who follow their own evil passions stain their consciences and lose the grace of God.

A point of clarification may be warranted here. I am not saying that by doing these things you can earn God's grace, for grace is undeserved. What I am saying is that these actions put you in a place to receive grace. All that is good or ever will be good in us is preceded by the grace of God. While one might claim to have humbled himself, it is God's grace which enables him to do so. It is God who grants grace so that we may turn in repentance away from idols. Men do not seek God first; He seeks them for Jesus tells us, "You did not choose me, but I chose you and appointed you to go and bear fruit" (John 15:16). Ours is the response to His initial work. It is our duty to humble ourselves, repent and seek Him. And He gives us grace upon grace.

Question 9. Are you truly committed to receiving God's grace? Will you employ the above four principles? Please list the four principles, and tell how you will practically apply them:

Principle #1-

Principle #2-

Principle #3-

Principle #4-

Question 10. Write out anything you have learned in this lesson, or any new thoughts or ideas you have had today.

Scripture to Consider

The following testimony is from Harley:

Glory to God. If you wonder why the first three words of my testimony are these, it is because I have learned, in sixty days, that they should be a part of my life, now and forever.

I was thirteen years old when I first discovered pornographic magazines in an old abandoned chest of drawers under an oak tree. I stuffed as many magazines as I could into my coveralls and fled to the nearby woods to view them. As a result, I plunged deeply into self-gratification and sexual deviation. The chaos lasted fifteen years, until I found The Way of Purity course.

Before I fell in love with my wife to be, I had no desire to be with other women, because I was in love with myself and I knew that no woman could accept the types of activities I was involved in on a regular basis. I am a writer, and have recently committed myself to writing suspense. Since then, I got involved with a publishing house that publishes pornographic novels. I was being consumed. Even after being married for ten years, my wife had no idea of any of this until the last year.

Upon my salvation, I knew instantly that I could no longer write what I had been writing and walk with the Lord. I was terrified and remember thinking, "Lord, if I can't write, what will I do?" And the Lord revealed to me that I would write, but I would write for Him.

My addiction to porn and sexual sin was secretly birthed in the woods, but it died in my living room fifteen long years later. It took Jesus Christ to put it to death, because I could not do it on my own. Glory to God!

[8] For it is by grace you have been saved, through faith - and this not from yourselves, it is the gift of God - [9] not by works, so that no one can boast (Ephesians 2:8-9).

Were you free from pornography since you did the last lesson?

    Yes   No

Were you free from self-gratification since you did the last lesson?

    Yes   No

Were you free from sexual immorality since you did the last lesson?

    Yes   No

DAY 11 – ONGOING FREEDOM

"Therefore, I urge you, brothers, in view of God's mercy, to offer your bodies as living sacrifices, holy and pleasing to God - this is your spiritual act of worship. 2 Do not conform any longer to the pattern of this world, but be transformed by the renewing of your mind. Then you will be able to test and approve what God's will is - his good, pleasing and perfect will." Romans 12:1-2

In the above passage, the apostle Paul teaches us that the receiving of God's grace should prompt us to offer our bodies up to the Lord as a living sacrifice. He shows us that God's grace motivates us to offer ourselves to the Lord, which is why we placed this lesson after the two days of teaching on grace. Grace leads us to holiness, to pleasing the Lord with our bodies, and to true worship.

The language of Paul in these verses reminds us of animal sacrifices that God's people in the Old Testament would offer unto the Lord. If a member of God's family sinned, they were required to bring a lamb and present it to the priest as an offering. The priest would sacrifice the animal, which pointed forward to the death of Jesus Christ to pay for our sins, and the person presenting the sacrifice would be released from guilt. In presenting this sacrifice, he was supposed to be worshiping God.

In the same manner, we are to present to God, not an animal sacrifice, but the sacrifice of our own body. And just as the member of God's family in the Old Testament would present the entire animal as a sacrifice, holding no part back, so we are to offer God our entire being: heart, mind, hands, feet, and sexual organs; indeed, every part is to be presented to God.

In light of God's grace, we need to begin offering up our bodies as living sacrifices to God. He gave His all for us; now we are to give our all to Him. I remember learning this truth just a few years back, and I was so eager to give all of myself to God that I burst out into prayer. I remember I prayed something like this, "Oh God, how I have abused this body you gave me. I have used it for wickedness and pleasing my flesh, and for carnal purposes. I have given my eyes over to viewing pornography, my mind over to sex-chatting, my heart to lusting after impurity of all sorts, and my body to adultery. Oh God, I now present me, all of me, to You, and ask You to receive me as a living sacrifice. May my body now be dead to those things that dishonor You so much, and may Your Holy Spirit live in me. I worship You as I present this offering to you."

Questions

Question 1. You may want to take a moment and write out a prayer to God and present Him with your body. If so, here is a place for you to do this.

Right here, let's bring some clarity to what it means to worship God. Is worshiping God going to church and singing songs? Is it hearing a sermon and receiving the Word planted in our hearts? Is it singing in the choir, or participating in prayer? It certainly can be. But the above verses tell us that presenting our bodies as living sacrifices to God is our "spiritual act of worship." If you want to experience worship in the most powerful way, just offer up your body to God for Him to live in, work through, and use to draw others to Himself.

Friend, right now it will be wise for you to develop a daily habit of presenting your body to the Lord as soon as you awake. First thing each morning, let us present our bodies to the Lord to as a living sacrifice. This takes the grace of God to accomplish, as we have already discussed.

Question 2. Will you seek God for grace to offer yourself to Him daily?
    Yes   No

Next, the above verses describe precisely how we may overcome the ongoing habit of becoming involved with sexual sin. Notice verse 2: "Do not conform any longer to the pattern of this world, but be transformed by the renewing of your mind." We are not to be conformed, but transformed. And this is accomplished by renewing our minds. What does this look like in the life of one who has been enslaved to pornography and impurity?

Well, viewing pornography or dwelling on real-life sexual images is like pouring gas on the fire of lust. It makes us walk around all day long with lust in our hearts because of the pornographic images in our minds, and those images may drag us into self-gratification or immorality. This is a very frustrating thing for people who wish to be free from this habitual sin, as the images torment our minds. It is as if the devil is mocking us, or worse yet, it is as if he is raping our souls.

I remember that a pornographic image would get lodged in my brain from something I had viewed even several years back. It would stick with me all day and stir up such lust that self-gratification was inevitable when I got to the hotel room that night. So, how do we combat this?

Well, first we "radically amputate" (more on this tomorrow) by "cutting off" and "plucking out" the source of those images, and second we "radically transform" our minds by renewing them.

The following testimony is from Rob:

"Wow, what a great God we have! That I am alive and telling this story is evidence of His power. Mine is an ordinary story in a way, but to me it is a story of extraordinary life.

As a boy, I was an introvert, and being shy with girls, I gravitated to 'girly magazines' to satisfy my curiosity during my early teens. It became a habit very quickly and I soon had a stash of magazines hidden away. What frightened me was the powerful lust I had for those two- dimensional pictures. And at the same time, I was beginning to come into a primitive relationship with the Lord; quite a contradiction, I know.

At the age of nineteen I met Cheryl, fell in love, and married her ten months later. All sexual thoughts and desires for pornography evaporated, Over the next twenty years the battles with porn were few and far between as a result of having a wife and children and seeking a relationship with the Lord.

But then, during a time of great personal stress for both my wife and me, we succumbed to the temptation of looking at porn together, rationalizing that a little bit of voyeurism would spice up our sex life. For Cheryl, there was no great moral problem as she was not a Christian. But the turmoil for me was horrendous.

I can remember falling to such depths that on a trip to a church convention I took a detour of several hours specifically to pick up some pornographic videos. I spent half the time at the convention praising God and the other half shaming Him and His beloved Son.

I felt condemnation both at my weakness and my hypocrisy of going to church and even preaching in a minor capacity, and yet diving headlong back into sin. It was becoming too much. I wanted to die, and got to the place where thoughts of suicide consumed my mind, when it wasn't consumed by pornography.

Thankfully, our little church was going through a mighty change, from old covenant legalism into the new covenant of grace. I think this was what saved me, as in my few rational moments I was studying those issues with our Bible study group and gradually absorbing some new knowledge. Still, my misery was deepening and I was feeling incredibly shattered at my total inability to control myself.

One evening, I told my wife I was going back to work for a few hours to catch up. However, my intention was to hang myself with a rope that was in my car; and I had picked a place to carry out the act at work. But when I got there I stood outside and just cried. After a bit I looked up into the clear sky and cried out, "Lord, I can't overcome this. And then I heard, so gentle, so still and so small, His voice, "Yes, Rob, but I can."

That was a revelation. It was like a divine awareness flooded through me, that of course I couldn't overcome this by myself. I looked up and said "OK, Lord, you do it." The most powerful thing was the realization that He really loved me; even right there in the midst of my putrid sin. He loved me, tenderly, affectionately. Those five words were full of love. I had been struggling so much because I had always thought God hated and detested me, and that had locked me into the cycle of sin and self-condemnation.

I went home and rid myself of the disgusting material I had just bought a few weeks earlier. I had done that many times before, but always with a feeling of regret at losing the objects of my lust. This time, it was out of desire and thirst for more of this divine awareness and joy - for Him alone. I began to focus on Him, His glory, His holiness, His purity. What a joy. What freedom - freedom from evil desires, because He had given me a desire for Him.

Every now and then the images flash back into my mind, but less frequently. The chains are broken, I flee to Him, to thoughts of my Savior, who saved my physical life that starry night, and who has saved me for eternity. And in Him I am now growing in grace and knowledge and strength. Praise our tender and merciful God! May He be your salvation and freedom too; this is my prayer for all who struggle as I did."

Here is how:

The first thing I do in the morning is present my body to the Lord as a living sacrifice. Then I sit down with my Bible and I read it. As I meditate over the truths, I undergo a change in my thinking. I begin dwelling on Jesus Christ and His perfect sacrifice on the cross, and how I am to die to my flesh. I then begin planning out the day from a spiritual perspective. What will I do to avoid temptation completely? What will I do if I have a "surprise attack?" How will I handle this situation, or that scenario, etc.?

This "renewing my mind" is really just "thinking differently" and thinking differently leads to acting differently.

Question 3. What are some ways you will begin to "renew your mind," by the grace of God? Please be specific.

> Do not conform any longer to the pattern of this world, but be transformed by the renewing of your mind (Romans 12:2).

Notice here that renewing our minds leads to a transformation. The Greek word for this is "metamorphoo" which is where we get our word "metamorphosis." This metamorphosis, which comes by renewing our minds, makes a total change in our nature, and is what enables us to be free on a daily basis. Therefore, it is critical to renew our minds. We do this by reading the Bible, and earnestly seeking the Lord in prayer. This gives us "the mind of Christ" (1 Corinthians 2:16) and enables us to think differently, which produces a real change in our character. Metamorphosis is the same word we use to describe what happens to a caterpillar that changes into a butterfly. What previously inched along the ground in the mud and dirt, can now soar heavenward in perfect freedom of flight. It may take hours of reading the Bible in order to experience the renewing of our minds. After awhile, this habit becomes so very enjoyable!

My friend, I was crawling in the dirt and mud of pornography, self-gratification and immorality for 15 long years, inching my way along the road that goes nowhere. But, in January of 1999, a metamorphosis began to take place in my heart and life, by the grace of God. I began to actually apply biblical principles to my life, instead of just reading about them and spouting them off to others. God made me serious about eradicating pornography, sex-chatting, adultery, and all sexual impurity from my life. As I began offering my body as a living sacrifice every morning, and renewing my mind in His Word, I have been experiencing changes in my thoughts, my desires, and my goals in life! Everything is changing, and I feel as though I have been given wings of grace to soar to the presence of God.

I love this metamorphosis, and don't ever want to go back to crawling in the mud. How about you? This is day 11 for you, and most people begin to see real and ongoing victory just up ahead. But also about this time period, the devil begins stomping his feet and throwing a temper tantrum over his captives leaving. The hardest part for most people is from about the 14th day up to and including the 30th day. I'm telling you this as a warning that things may get harder before they get easier, and to be fore-warned is to be fore-armed.

Question 4. Are you sensing a "metamorphosis" in your life? What are some of the changes taking place in the following areas: heart, life, marriage (if married), work environment, home environment, etc. Write your answer here.

To review, we learned or reviewed two key principles to overcoming sexual sin today.

1 - Offer up our bodies as living sacrifices

2 - Renew our minds, and be metamorphosed as a result

We can only do these things "in view of God's mercy." In other words, Jesus Christ offered up His body as a sacrifice to the Father, to satisfy God's hatred toward sin, and to forgive us our sins. He held nothing back, but presented all of Who He is to God. His back was whipped, His beard was plucked. His hands and feet were nailed to the cross, His head was crowned with thorns, His heart imploded, and then He died. All so that we could live, and be free from slavery to sin! Jesus death on the cross was the demonstration of God's mercy, and in light of that mercy, we, too, should offer our own bodies as living sacrifices, and our minds to be renewed and transformed.

Question 5. What are your final thoughts on this teaching today? Did you learn anything new, or were you reminded of any truths that may have been neglected before? Please answer here.

Scripture to Consider

For you were once darkness, but now you are light in the Lord. Live as children of light (for the fruit of the light consists in all goodness, righteousness and truth) and find out what pleases the Lord (Ephesians 5:8-10).

The LORD is near to all who call on him, to all who call on him in truth (Psalm 145:18).

Were you free from pornography since you did the last lesson?

Yes   No

Were you free from self-gratification since you did the last lesson?

Yes   No

Were you free from sexual immorality since you did the last lesson?

Yes   No

DAY 12 - RADICAL AMPUTATION

If your hand causes you to sin, cut it off. It is better for you to enter life maimed than with two hands to go into hell, where the fire never goes out. And if your foot causes you to sin, cut it off. It is better for you to enter life crippled than to have two feet and be thrown into hell. And if your eye causes you to sin, pluck it out. It is better for you to enter the kingdom of God with one eye than to have two eyes and be thrown into hell (Mark 9:43-47).

My friend, we need to separate ourselves completely from whatever has fueled our pornographic addiction, and from whatever situations might tempt us into sexual sin. This may not seem reasonable, but in dealing with sin, being radical is only reasonable.

After 15 years of pornographic addiction, I desperately needed and wanted to be free. With the assistance of my pastor and my wife, I began to cut off every source of pornography and sexual impurity in my life.

For instance, when I would go to the hotel, I could resolve all day long not to watch pornography, and then find myself suddenly turning on the TV and giving in to lust. (You've been hit with this sudden "surprise attack" right?) My pastor helped me understand the need to amputate porn from my life. He suggested I begin unplugging and unhooking the TV and carrying it into one of my co-workers rooms to leave it overnight. That way, I had no access to pornography. Also, because I was doing "romantic chatting" on the Internet, I gave my notebook computer away. Everything was cut off. What may seem "radical" to others, who do not struggle with this sin problem, is reasonable and right for us to do.

Jesus said that we should "cut off" and "pluck out" whatever causes us to sin, and He warned us that if we don't radically amputate the cause of our sin, we could end up in hell. Friend, do not take this lightly. We are talking about life and death here; heaven and hell. If you thought you were "just playing" with pornography or immorality, please know this: sexual sin will take you farther than you want to go, keep you longer than you want to stay, and cost you more than you want to pay.

Jesus is not referring to a physical cutting off of your foot or a plucking out of your eyeball. Blind men still lust. He's referring to the complete removal of the causes of your sin. He's saying if we want to be free from this sin, some things in our lives have to go, and we must do whatever it takes. For me, this meant getting rid of the TV in my hotel room and my home, and giving away my notebook computer. Please list what "complete removal" means to you.

Questions

Question 1. Please list what "complete removal" means to you.

Karen wrote, "To me, complete removal meant totally severing the adulterous relationship. It was very difficult to do, but has brought much freedom to my life. As painful as the process was, the benefits are well worth it. What a joy it is now to honor Christ in all areas of my life."

Question 2. Please list here what things have encouraged you to sin in the area of sexual impurity.

Question 3. Above, we looked at Mark 9:43-47: What did Jesus say to do with things that cause us to sin?

Question 4. Truth time: Have you totally "amputated" everything that has caused you to sin?

Dear friend, this teaching may seem less than reasonable, indeed it may come across as quite radical. Some people, rather than cut off the causes of sin, want to stare it in the face and say "No." (We will read more about this on Day 19.) They think that would be true victory for them. However, this desire to be strong, rather than pure, will not result in victory. Notice the "radical amputation" principle in the following story:

The following is taken from Sixty Days to Freedom, a Biblical Guide to Freedom from Sexual Addictions, by Timothy R. Salzman. Legacy Press, P.O. Box 7814 Colorado Springs, CO 80933

"When I was 14 years old I was riding my bicycle across an open field on my way home from school and found a copy of a pornographic magazine. That discovery introduced me to masturbation and eventually fornication. The addiction has followed me, even into my marriage. In fact, marriage has

amplified the problem many-fold. I am beginning to get the problem under control by using very extreme measures. For example, I voluntarily gave up my access to our bank account. I have no way to withdraw or spend money at all. That is extremely drastic, but it has worked: no money, no ability to participate in the 'action.' Surprisingly, when I know I can't go to the girly bars, or other places because of a lack of money, the desire is slowly diminishing."

Okay, today is the day to clean house! Are you hiding anything anywhere that may cause you to sin? If so, go throw it away. Get rid of it. Have a "burn party" (Acts 19:19) where you permanently destroy all pornography and all access to anything that may tempt you to sexual sin. View it as the fire of God's love consuming your old life. Or, are you in a sinful relationship of some kind? Cut it off. Destroy all means of contact. Severe it entirely, and burn all bridges to ever returning to it.

Question 5. Please comment on Hebrews 12:1 as it relates to our study today: "Therefore, since we are surrounded by such a great cloud of witnesses, let us throw off everything that hinders and the sin that so easily entangles, and let us run with perseverance the race marked out for us."

Luke wrote, "We must rid ourselves of the things that bind us. If it is our minds, then we must renew them with God! If it is material, then get rid of it. If it is a job that stands in your way, get rid of it! Whatever it is, isn't worth gambling your soul!"

Karen wrote, "This verse tells me that I must not only eliminate everything that might encourage me to sin, but also 'everything that hinders.' There are many things in my life that are not necessarily sinful, but they need to go as well, if they slow me down in the race of life."

Steve wrote, "Not only are you free to run as light as possible, but you are also being surrounded by others who are helping, encouraging, supporting and showing you the track to race upon. It's the opposite of the world around me, that puts more things on my back, makes the path unclear, and puts obstacles in front of me to trip me up or delay my race."

So what do we do if the use of the Internet is tripping us up, yet for some reason we need to have Internet access? There is a solution, and a very thorough one at that. There is a filter and monitoring software called "Safe Eyes." This service monitors every website you visit, generates a report on your activity, and emails your accountability partner so he/she can view this report to see exactly which sites you have visited. It provides not only the best filter available, but also keyword filtering, instant notification feature (email and cell phone), time blocking, and many more features.

This program provides "radical accountability" where radical amputation is impossible. Many of the mentors who are on staff at Setting Captives Free use this product and all highly recommend it.

The following testimony is from Chris:

I have been an overcomer most of my life. Born with cerebral palsy, a crippling muscle disease, I had to work hard to get what came naturally for everyone else - from walking to talking to driving a car.

From an early age, I knew that I was different from other children. I grew up in a loving Christian home, and my parents taught me that God had made me this way for a reason. I believed at an early age that God had a purpose for me and I gave my life to the Lord when I was twelve. Growing up was not easy for me. Doctors, therapists and specialists in my native Texas doubted that I would ever live or work on my own. My parents doubted it, too. Even I sometimes wondered what kind of life I could make for myself. Knowing that I could do nothing on my own, I turned my eyes to God and trusted in Him.

God blessed my life richly, allowing me to attend regular schools and even to excel. Because of my disability, I did not have much social interaction with other young people. It was during this time as a lonely teenager that I felt myself beginning to drift away from God and from the godly principles that had been so firmly instilled in me. I continued to go to church and tried to serve the Lord, but I was starting down a path that would take me far away from the presence of God.

I was about fifteen when I began experimenting with self-gratification. I knew it was wrong the first time I did it. Yet, it offered me something that I had never had before. With my disability, I doubted that I would ever be with a woman romantically so I turned to self-gratification as a way of finding "a satisfaction" that I thought I would never receive from a woman.

At first, I wasn't too worried about it. I knew that a lot of boys tried it, and I assured myself that it was just a phase, and I would soon grow out of it. Instead, it became an addiction that would affect my life and my relationship with God for nearly 15 years. I tried to stop many times. I prayed for deliverance on many occasions but never was able to go more than a week without relapsing.

I was involved in my church; I prayed and read the Bible, but the sin in my life was keeping me from growing in the Lord. Yet I knew that God still had His hand on my life even when I wasn't living for Him. The Lord blessed me with the ability to become a writer for my high school newspaper, and I went on to college where I received a degree in journalism.

Finding a job after college was difficult with numerous rejections from one newspaper after another. Finally I saw my dream of achieving independence become a reality when I was hired as a copy editor at an area newspaper and moved into my own apartment. My life seemed to be on track. However, I continued to struggle with self-gratification. Being on my own allowed me to do as I wanted and no one ever knew about the secret life that I lived. I invested in a computer for my work, which led me even farther down the path of destruction. I became involved in pornography and began spending hours on pornographic sites.

I still believed God had a purpose for my life and that He would use me through my writing. I even began writing a book about how my faith helped me to overcome the obstacles of living with a disability. The Lord granted me favor, and the book was published in 1998.

For two more years, however, I continued to explore pornography on the Internet and became more and more addicted to it as my relationship with God became non-existent. I knew that God would never be able to fully use me for His service until I turned back to Him. It was only when I realized that I couldn't do it on my own that I began to see God move in my life.

Out of desperation, I prayed that God would show me a way out. I asked Him to forgive me and gave "my burden" over to Him. One night while surfing the Internet, God led me to the Setting Captives Free web site, and I immediately knew that this was my way out.

God set me completely free. Since starting the course nearly two months ago, I have seen God move in my life in a new way. The growth that had been halted by the sin in my life was now beginning again. I have truly experienced new life in Christ.

When I look back on my life, and the bad choices I made, I regret all the time I wasted. However, I believe it must be in God's timing and that He will somehow use this experience to encourage others. That is my prayer. I thank God for His wonderful grace.

Read what Matthew Henry states about Radical Amputation:

1. The case supposed: That our own hand, or eye, or foot, offend us; that the impure corruption we indulge is as dear to us as an eye or a hand, or that that which is to us as an eye or a hand, is become an invisible temptation to sin, or occasion of it. Suppose the beloved is become a sin, or the sin a beloved. Suppose we cannot keep that which is dear to us, but it will be a snare and a stumbling-block; suppose we must part with it, or part with Christ and a good conscience.

2. The duty prescribed in that case: Pluck out the eye, cut off the hand and foot, mortify the darling lust, kill it, crucify it, starve it, make no provision for it. Let the idols that have been delectable things, be cast away as detestable things; keep at a distance from that which is a temptation, though ever so pleasing. It is necessary that the part which is gangrened, should be taken off for the preservation of the whole… The part that is incurably wounded must be cut off, lest the parts that are sound be corrupted. We must put ourselves to pain, that we may not bring ourselves to ruin; self must be denied, that it may not be destroyed.

3. The necessity of doing this: The flesh must be mortified, that we may enter into life (Mark 9:43,45), into the kingdom of God (v. 47). Though, by abandoning sin, we may, for the present, feel ourselves as if we were halt and maimed (it may seem to be a force put upon ourselves, and may create us some uneasiness), yet it is for life; and all that men have, they will give for their lives: it is for a kingdom, the kingdom of God, which we cannot otherwise obtain; these halts and maims will be the marks of the Lord Jesus, will be in that kingdom scars of honour.

4. The danger of not doing this: The matter is brought to this issue, that either sin must die, or we must die. If we will lay this Delilah in our bosom, it will betray us; if we be ruled by sin, we shall inevitably be ruined by it; if we must keep our two hands, and two eyes, and two feet, we must with them be cast into hell. Our Saviour often pressed our duty upon us, from the consideration of the torments of hell, which we run ourselves into if we continue in sin. With what an emphasis of terror are those words repeated three times here, where their worm dieth not, and the fire is not quenched! The words are quoted from Isaiah 66:24. The reflections and reproaches of the sinner's own conscience are the worm that dieth not; which will cleave to the damned soul as the worms do to the dead body, and prey upon it, and never leave it till it is quite devoured. Son, remember, will set this worm gnawing; and how terrible will it bite that word (Prov. v. 12, 23), How have I hated instruction! The soul that is food to this worm, dies not; and the worm is bred in it, and one with it, and therefore neither doth that die. Damned sinners will be to eternity accusing, condemning, and upbraiding themselves with their own follies, which, how much soever they are now in love with them, will at the last bite like a serpent, and sting like an adder. Matthew Henry*

*http:// www.ccel.org/h/henry/mhc2/MHC41009.HTM

Course member Tom wrote: Comments on Hebrews 12:1: "I knew when I started this course that if I kept any hidden books or magazines, I would simply fail to get free. So I got rid of everything. And now I am running the race set for me, unhindered by any hidden source of temptation."

C.S. Lewis wrote an article that illustrates, in a very clear manner, the principle we have been talking about today. To receive this illustration, simply send a blank email to purityprinciple@settingcaptivesfree.com. We think you'll be amazed at this story, and it will really help you.

Scripture to Consider

Therefore do not be foolish, but understand what the Lord's will is. [18] Do not get drunk on wine, which leads to debauchery. Instead, be filled with the Spirit. [19] Speak to one another with psalms, hymns and spiritual songs. Sing and make music in your heart to the Lord, [20] always giving thanks to God the Father for everything, in the name of our Lord Jesus Christ (Ephesians 5:17-20).

The thief comes only to steal and kill and destroy; I have come that they may have life, and have it to the full (John 10:10).

Were you free from pornography since you did the last lesson?

    Yes   No

Were you free from self-gratification since you did the last lesson?

    Yes   No

Were you free from sexual immorality since you did the last lesson?

    Yes   No

DAY 13 - SETTING CAPTIVES FREE I

Today we will see a very important reason for Bible study. How can we know the truth if we do not study the Scriptures? And, if we do not know the truth, we will not be set free. But it is not only Bible study that is important. I studied the Bible all throughout the years that I was a captive to pornography and adultery. Many people come to The Way of Purity course knowing much Scripture because of having studied much. No, it is not just studying the Bible that frees us from sin's captivity. Jesus said "If you hold to my teaching..." indicating that it is not merely studying the Scriptures, but embracing them that brings freedom. "Holding Jesus' teaching" has to do with keeping it ever before us, so that when we are tempted, we recognize the lie in the temptation, and flee from it so as to not indulge in it. This is holding onto Jesus' teaching, and is the truth that sets us free.

> [31] To the Jews who had believed him, Jesus said, "If you hold to my teaching, you are really my disciples. [32] Then you will know the truth, and the truth will set you free."
>
> [33] They answered him, "We are Abraham's descendants and have never been slaves of anyone. How can you say that we shall be set free?"
>
> [34] Jesus replied, "I tell you the truth, everyone who sins is a slave to sin. [35] Now a slave has no permanent place in the family, but a son belongs to it forever. [36] So if the Son sets you free, you will be free indeed (John 8:31-36).

This passage contains amazing truth for us who have been involved with pornography and other sexual sin. Let's examine it by answering some questions.

Questions

Question 1. According to verses 31 and 32, what will be the result of holding to Jesus' teachings?

Question 2. What did Jesus say would happen when we know the truth?

According to verses 34-36, Jesus stated that the truth sets us free from sin's slavery. Slaves are not free people; they have a master and must do his bidding. I remember how a pornographic image would lodge in my brain, and even though I could try to pray it away and read the Bible, it kept after me until I would eventually give in and obey the demand to gratify the flesh. I would ask for God's forgiveness, but soon after, I would gratify the lusts of my flesh over a different image, repeating the process over and over. This is slavery to sin. One young teen seeking purity said, "I can't forget the pictures I saw. They are burned into my mind".

Question 3. Have you had this type of "slavery" experience?

Karen wrote, "Yes, I sure have. It was so easy to get involved in the adulterous relationship, but it soon became impossible to extricate myself from it, due to my emotional involvement. Only Christ was able to set me free."

But notice it is the truth that sets us free. You see, if we are slaves to sin, we are deceived; we believe a lie. The lie may be that pornography will satisfy us, or that self-gratification will relieve the stress (when we all know the stress will be back later, and to give in to it only makes it easier to give in the next time), or that giving in to lust will make us happier. For instance, when I was tempted in the hotel rooms to view pornographic movies, the main lie I believed was that I would not be lonely. Here in these movies I had people who wanted to be with me, who would love and accept me, who would make my evening go better. But was that the truth? I think we all know the answer to that. And what is adultery, but believing the lie that this other person has what will make me happy? It is a lie! True happiness comes from being right with God, from cultivating a relationship with Jesus, from walking in the light and living in purity.

Question 4. What are some lies you have believed about pornography, self-gratification, or sexual impurity?

Karen wrote, "While involved in adultery, I not only believed the lies of the enemy, but also the many lies my partner in sin told me. I thought all of our problems were a result of our situation. In reality, the problems were the result of sin. I know now that any relationship based on a lie is doomed to failure from the start."

So, part of our leaving all sexual sin behind is to embrace truth. Examine every temptation and ask, "Is this true?" Will indulging in this sin bring the satisfaction it promises? Will it satisfy me eternally, or will it leave me with guilt and regret?

Question 5. Compare verses 32 and 36 above. What do they have in common?

Friend, Jesus Christ is the Truth that sets us free. When we embrace HIM, we know the truth that sets us free. Jesus says in John 14:6, "I am the Way, the Truth, and the Life. No man comes to the Father but through Me." And in Proverbs 8, Jesus Christ is portrayed as "wisdom", and is shown to be the "way" (verse 1-2), the "truth" (verse 7) and the "life" (verse 35).

Question 6. How does John 14:6 compare with the above verses in Proverbs? "Jesus said, I am the Way, the Truth, and the Life. No man comes to the Father but through Me."

It is clear that Jesus Christ is the Truth that sets us free! He declares: "So if the Son sets you free, you will be free indeed" (John 8:36).

Let's be clear about this. There is no program, system, or coun-seling technique, that can set us free from the slavery to sin. This course will not set you free, apart from Christ. Only Jesus, the Truth, can release us. "Salvation is found in no one else, for there is no other name under heaven given to men by which we must be saved" (Acts 4:12). And the way He sets us free is by enabling us to embrace the Truth, rather than believe the decep-tion and lies of the evil one.

Involving ourselves in pornography is the same as believing lies, and living in a world of deception. Pornography does not satisfy, as it promises to do. It is like drinking from a stream of polluted water, which leaves one "thirstier" than before. In order to over-come this sin, we must drink the Living Water, which quenches our thirst eternally, and we must begin to embrace the truth as it is in Jesus.

Begin to speak the truth, to forsake lies, to refuse to live in any form of deception. Drag your sin into the light, and begin to be honest in all your dealings with others. You see, it is because of our sins that we are taken captive and are made slaves. Notice the following verses from the New Living Translation: "The LORD asks, 'Did I sell you as slaves to my creditors? Is that why you are not here? Is your mother gone because I divorced her and sent her away? No, you went away as captives because of your sins. And your mother, too, was taken because of your sins'" (Isaiah 50:1).

It is the main mission of the Messiah to release men and women from their chains of captivity. Jesus declares His mission in Luke 4:18-19: "The Spirit of the Lord is on me, because he has anoint-ed me to preach good news to the poor. He has sent me to pro-claim freedom for the prisoners and recovery of sight for the blind, to release the oppressed, to proclaim the year of the Lord's favor." He came to release us from captivity to our sins, and to bring freedom from bondage and slavery. His freedom is real. He breaks the power of sin, and releases us from the prison of sin. I testify that I have been free from pornography, self-gratification and adultery since January of 1999 - not to brag about my own strength to overcome, for I have none, but rather to glorify Jesus, who came to earth for this very purpose.

Question 7. Please provide your thoughts on the following verses:

"Then you will call upon me and come and pray to me, and I will listen to you. You will seek me and find me when you seek me with all your heart. I will be found by you," declares the LORD, "and will bring you back from captivity" (Jeremiah 29:12-14).

Yet even now, be free from your captivity! Leave Babylon and the Babylonians, singing as you go! Shout to the ends of the earth that the LORD has redeemed his servants, the people of Israel (Isaiah 48:20).

So now the Sovereign LORD says: "I will end the cap-tivity of my people; I will have mercy on Israel, for I am jealous for my holy reputation" (Ezekiel 39:25).

Graham wrote, "God's great plan is freedom from captivi-ty in all its forms. Jesus' statements are clearly consistent with those of the prophets above. As this has been God's promise from the beginning of his journey with the nation of Israel to today, then it must be true for me and my com-munity, that God desires and will bring us to freedom. Interestingly, we have to leave captivity. God may throw open the gates, but we still have to walk out the gates. I am walking away from captivity, yet I am aware that it is as difficult to overcome the slave mentality as it is to leave exile. I am seeking freedom from each one."

So, to summarize: sexual sin, indeed all sin, makes us slaves. It deceives us, so that as we partake of it, we believe a lie. But Jesus came to break the power of sin, to release us from slavery to sin, to set the captives free! This is why Jesus came to earth.

Question 8. Finally, it is reflection time. Where are you with the above teaching? Is Jesus releasing you from sin's captivity? Do you see how you've believed lies while in pornography and sexual sin? Are you seeking to embrace truth now? Write your thoughts here.

My friend, I can recall my captivity very clearly even today, several years later. If my "master," lust, told me to go and view pornography, I would have to obey. If he told me to get involved with sin on the Internet, then I followed his orders. I was a slave to my lusts, and captive to evil desires. But now Jesus Christ has freed me, by causing me to embrace the truth. And freedom is very precious to me; I never want to return to my slavery again. Jesus made me His prisoner now: "But thanks be to God, who made us his captives and leads us along in Christ's triumphal procession. Now wherever we go he uses us to tell others about the Lord and to spread the Good News like a sweet perfume. Our lives are a fragrance presented by Christ to God" (2 Corinthians 2:14). And when God makes us captives of Christ, we also become prisoners of hope: "Come back to the place of safety, all you prisoners of hope, for there is yet hope" (Zecharaiah 9:12).

So, let us be clear; with Jesus Christ, freedom is not only possible, it is inevitable. We must ask Christ to do His work in our hearts for, when He does, we will be free. No more slavery to sin, no more giving in just because the impulse comes to do so, no more gratifying the flesh several times a day, only to relive the guilt and stress each time. Freedom from habitual sin is real. My prayer is that you will experience and enjoy it!

The following testimony is from Andrew:

"Jesus is releasing me from the captivity of sexual impurity, and its the greatest feeling in the world to feel the weight of that sin lifted off my shoulder and to feel the warm embrace of Jesus welcoming me back to the family of God which I so long ago disowned by continually indulging myself in self-gratification and sin. Believing in all the lies of pornography only led me further into the rabbit hole, making it harder to get out. Embracing the truth now by reading and understanding the word, prayer, and just being accountable is setting me free from my sin, so that I may walk with God again. Diving into the word and doing this lesson daily is a fresh drink of the Living Water. I find it so easy to resist temptation after I've had my drink. If you go for days without a drink, and find a puddle of mud you will drink from it. So doing the lessons and reading the Bible not only help me in other ways, but it also keeps me from being thirsty for that crappy water, praise God."

Scripture to Consider

[1]"When the LORD brought back the captives to Zion, we were like men who dreamed. [2]Our mouths were filled with laughter, our tongues with songs of joy. Then it was said among the nations, "The LORD has done great things for them." [3]The LORD has done great things for us, and we are filled with joy" (Psalm 126:1-3).

"The Spirit of the Sovereign LORD is upon me, because the LORD has appointed me to bring good news to the poor. He has sent me to comfort the brokenhearted and to announce that captives will be released and prisoners will be freed" (Isaiah 61:1).

[5]"God, the LORD, created the heavens and stretched them out. He created the earth and everything in it. He gives breath and life to everyone in all the world. And it is he who says, [6]"I, the LORD, have called you to demonstrate my righteousness. I will guard and support you, for I have given you to my people as the personal confirmation of my covenant with them. And you will be a light to guide all nations to me. [7]You will open the eyes of the blind and free the captives from prison. You will release those who sit in dark dungeons" (Isaiah 42:5-7).

Were you free from pornography since you did the last lesson?

    Yes   No

Were you free from self-gratification since you did the last lesson?

    Yes   No

Were you free from sexual immorality since you did the last lesson?

    Yes   No

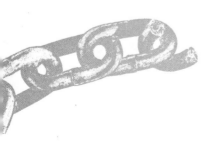

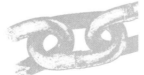
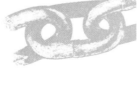

    Yes   No

DAY 14 - SETTING CAPTIVES FREE II

Precisely how does salvation work? Who is it for? What does it look like in the every day life of someone who was previously in bondage to pornography or immorality?

These are the questions we will seek to answer today. And there will be much encouragement from the Scriptures, as we dig into God's Word.

We are about to embark on a fascinating study! You will discover that God had a purpose in your slavery to sin.

vs. 10—Some sat in darkness and the deepest gloom, prisoners suffering in iron chains, vs. 11—for they had rebelled against the words of God and despised the counsel of the Most High. vs. 12—So He subjected them to bitter labor; they stumbled, and there was no one to help. vs. 13—Then they cried to the Lord in their trouble, and He saved them from their distress. vs. 14—He brought them out of darkness and the deepest gloom and broke away their chains. vs. 15—Let them give thanks to the Lord for his unfailing love and his wonderful deeds for men, vs. 16—for he breaks down gates of bronze and cuts through bars of iron (Psalm 107: 10-16).

Today, let us do a verse-by-verse study, and notice together the spiritual condition of the above people. We will also note the reason why things were so bad for them.

"vs. 10—Some sat in darkness and the deepest gloom, prisoners suffering in iron chains,"

This verse states five things about the condition of these people. They were:

1. in darkness
2. in deepest gloom
3. prisoners
4. suffering
5. in iron chains

There may not be a better description of the spiritual condition of a pornography slave, as I was, or anyone enslaved to sexual sin in all of Scripture. Note:

1-**They are in darkness.** It is spiritually pitch black in the life of a person caught in the trap of immorality. His or her lusts are continually stirred up by visual images that have been burned into his mind and the memories of past experiences; his or her mind is dark because of the sin that dominates him; he or she lacks genuine spiritual light, which is wisdom and understanding. Life is dark for the one involved in sexual sin.

2-**They are in deepest gloom.** Oh, not at the beginning, when a new relationship develops, or the middle, when the excitement of a new image floods their hearts and minds but, as the bondage continues, the gloom increases. And this is not just "ordinary" gloom, this is "deepest gloom" -spiritual gloom, dread, fear, pessimism, hopelessness.

3-**They are prisoners.** They are captivated to the "rush" of pornography, imprisoned by the next impulse to look at porn, which they are unable to fight off. Or they are always looking for the next opportunity to engage in illicit sex. They are not free to simply choose to stop, or to "just say no," anymore than a prisoner is free to leave his prison any time he wants.

4-**They are suffering.** Sexual sin causes suffering. Examine the end of anyone who has been enslaved to pornography or to a wrong relationship, and you will see suffering in their lives. I personally suffer for my years of involvement with pornography and adultery.

5-**They are in iron chains.** This is a reference to the strength of the sinful habit patterns. Sexual sin is an "iron chain" - too strong for man to break.

Question 1. As you read through the previous description of someone enslaved to sin, which number(s) described your past prison the most?

Karen wrote, "I can relate to all of them. My years of living in adultery blinded me to the truth about my situation, and left me depressed much of the time. My life revolved around waiting for the phone to ring and arranging my schedule in order to have even a few minutes with that person. Even after I saw that the relationship was sinful and needed to end, I did not know how to get out of it, and my sin caused me a good deal of emotional suffering."

And now, let us notice the reason why these people were in such bad shape:

vs. 11—for they had rebelled against the words of God and despised the counsel of the Most High.

And look what God did next:

vs. 12—So He subjected them to bitter labor; they stumbled, and there was no one to help.

Notice 3 things that happened to these people because of their rebellion:

God subjected them to bitter labor. Were your pornography or other immoral habits ever "bitter labor" to you? Mine sure were. The words "bitter labor" are the same words used in Exodus 1 referring to the slavery of the Israelites. Sexual sin can reduce us to "slave labor."

They stumbled. Friends, please do not miss this: Sexual sin will be your downfall, if you do not totally forsake it. They stumbled and fell. So did I.

There was no one to help them up. You probably know this already, but it is possible to go so far into pornography that nobody can help you.

Question 2. Are you identifying with all this? Have you ever felt that you were in this very predicament? Explain please:

Question 3. From verses 13-16 above, notice the 5 things that God does in response to people crying out to Him. Please write all five here.

Course member Paul wrote, "This Psalm's description is right on target. I rebelled against God, and my reward was bitter addiction to the next image, the next sensuous picture or imagination. It would pull me in, even when I didn't want it. I would ignore my family for my lust. I would go out in cold bitter rain to satisfy my wicked desires. Then I would suffer horrible guilt and shame and feel so trapped so alone."

Concentrate for just a moment on the words in v. 12, "And there was no one to help them up." This is the condition to which God takes all whom he will eventually save. He brings them to the point that they must cast themselves totally on His mercy. They cannot help themselves. Nobody else can help them. They are helpless and hopeless. And yet, what is impossible with man is possible with God!

If the Son sets you free, you will be free indeed (John 8:36).

vs. 13—Then they cried to the Lord in their trouble, and He saved them from their distress. vs. 14—He brought them out of darkness and the deepest gloom and broke away their chains. vs. 15—Let them give thanks to the Lord for His unfailing love and His wonderful deeds for men, vs. 16—for He breaks down the gates of bronze and cuts through bars of iron (Psalm 107:13-16).

Oh friend, here is a prescription for freedom from pornography and immorality. Cry to the Lord. But you say, "I HAVE called to Him, and I'm still falling." Keep crying out to Him! Have you ever noticed that when the Israelites first began calling to the Lord for help, their slavery increased?

God eventually delivered the Israelites by the blood of the lamb, and He can deliver you, too. It is the godless that won't cry to God, and keep crying until He answers: The godless in heart harbor resentment; even when he fetters them, they do not cry for help (Job 36:13).

Be like Jacob, and wrestle with God in prayer until He blesses you with salvation from sexual sin. God purposely takes us to the place where we cannot help ourselves, and there is no one else to help us. In fact, in this same chapter that we are studying (Psalm 107), it says that certain people were "at their wits' end." (vs. 27) They were at the end of their rope, at the end of their resources. No motivational books or self-help guru could help them now. But they cried to the Lord, and He saved them! Friends, when you are at the end of your rope, you are at the beginning of hope, real hope. Call, call, call, and keep calling. He will answer, in His time.

The above verses tell us that, when God saves someone, He destroys the work of the devil in their lives. He frees them from the grip of the devil, removes oppression (though not all temptation), rescues from slavery to sin, and sets us free. We must ever pray for ongoing help and be on guard against backsliding, but the work of salvation is a thorough and ongoing deliverance from sin.

So, to answer the questions we asked at the beginning of this lesson:

1. How does salvation work? People rebel against God, God hands them over to slavery, they come to the end of their rope with nobody to help them, they cry to the Lord, and He saves them.

2. Who is it for? Salvation is for those who have rebelled, those who have gone against the teaching of God's Word, and those who have been in prison to sin.

3. What does it look like in the every day life of someone who was previously trapped in pornography and/or other sexual sin? We come to know that we are powerless to stop using pornography or to stay away from that illicit relationship. We see very clearly that we are enslaved and imprisoned by it. We hear that salvation is available through the cross, and we begin to cry out. Often, God waits. We cry more, and louder. God hears, rescues, redeems, saves. We are no longer in bondage to sexual sin. The Son of God has set us free, and we are free indeed.

Question 4. Honesty time. Where are you in the above scenario? Enslaved? In prison? Calling? Or free indeed?

Course member Dennis writes: "Regarding pornography - calling and free. I really believe God has given me insight and freedom in this. Calling from prison, I know of His deliverance. I believe He has shown me mercy. What a special thing to just know Him, and to receive from Him - to be filled and remain in Him, to have Him in all His fullness in all areas of my heart, mostly the ones of hurt, emptiness and discouragement. It is a joy to truly know and experience and receive His forgiveness and completeness in full measure."

Course member Christoph writes: "I always knew that there was help, if I only could drop my pride and be accountable to a brother. So I continued suffering from the remorse of self-gratification until I found this website. I was given a good kick in the rear to confess to someone, which is all I needed. I always knew God would help me when I let go of my pride in this area."

Question 5. Do you have any comments?

The following testimony is from Dave:

I was exposed to pornography when I was nine years old and came across a porn magazine. And I continued looking and lusting after every vile image I could get hold of. It was an endless effort of trying to fill the void in me with more and more pornography. When I think of all the wasted years of my life, it was like being a prisoner serving a life sentence without hope of parole. The cycle of searching, gratifying my flesh and then depression was never ending. I longed for freedom but it only came in short bursts and then I would fall deeper than before.

I went to counseling and read lots of psychology books but nothing seemed to work. Then I found Setting Captives Free and began to see and feel something different in me that I had not known before, peace in the battle. I realized that it was not by behavior modification or by my own will that I would set me free. It was not my mind that was my problem, but my heart. I learned how to fight the evil desires and win. Having a daily mentor and learning the biblical principals taught in the lessons armed me with the weapons I needed to stand strong against the enemy. The freedom is in and through Jesus and His sacrifice. When I learned who I was in Christ's kingdom and how to operate in that position it really set me free.

If you are searching for freedom, then you have come to the right place. You may have tried everything as I had and you are thinking "Yeah right, you don't know how deep into this sin I am." I have seen all kinds of perverted images and they burned a hole in my mind. But there is One who has given His all for me so that I would not have to bear those images any longer. That person is Jesus and he took every evil deed and thought of mine with Him to the cross on Calvary.

Jesus is our Savior not only from the pit of hell but from the torments of our own past sins. Jesus accepts us just the way we are no matter how perverted we have become. He loves us and wants us to have His peace that passes all understanding. He will help you to become the person He designed you to be; pure and holy.

I know you may be thinking that you can't live without pornography. But God will replace that "need" with His Holy Spirit and you will know the joy of the Lord and it will be more fulfilling than anything you could imagine.

Scripture to Consider

[12] For there is no distinction between Jew and Greek, for the same Lord over all is rich to all who call upon Him. [13] For "whoever calls on the name of the LORD shall be saved (Romans 10:12-13).

Were you free from pornography since you did the last lesson?

Yes   No

Were you free from self-gratification since you did the last lesson?

Yes   No

Were you free from sexual immorality since you did the last lesson?

Yes   No

DAY 15 - SETTING CAPTIVES FREE III

In the book of Exodus in the Bible, God's people were in slavery to the Egyptians. They had been in slavery for 400 years, and theirs was a very hard and bitter slavery. The Egyptians were "ruthless" and "harsh" taskmasters. Notice the wording in Exodus 1:11-14:

"So they put slave masters over them to oppress them with forced labor...and worked them ruthlessly. They made their lives bitter with hard labor, in brick and mortar, and with all kinds of work in the fields; in all their hard labor the Egyptians used them ruthlessly."

My friend this is a picture of our condition in the grips of pornography and sexual impurity. We become "slaves" to that all-exciting image on the TV or to the illicit relationship. Romans 6:20 illustrates this truth: "When you were slaves to sin, you were free from the control of righteousness." Pornography made me a slave. If I had a thought that told me to watch a pornographic movie, I would obey it and watch. If my heart told me to do some "romantic" chatting on the Internet or my body craved visual stimulation from pornography, I obeyed. My impulses controlled my actions for years. I was a slave. My master was pornography. And it was a harsh master. Can you relate to this?

But the Israelites began to cry out to God in their slavery. **Oh friend, God will not turn a deaf ear to "Help me, Oh God. Please. I beg you."** And so He said to His people, ". . .I have indeed seen the misery of my people in Egypt. I have heard them crying out because of their slave drivers, and I am concerned about their suffering. So I have come down to rescue them from the hand of the Egyptians and to bring them up out of that land into a good and spacious land..." (Exodus 3:7-8)

God "came down" to "bring them up." God never changes. The cross of Jesus Christ, where He died, was God "coming down" to "bring us up." He is now coming down to you...in the midst of your slavery. He has seen your misery, He's heard your cries for help, and He's concerned about your suffering. His purpose in coming to you is to "rescue" you and "bring you up." Do you see that? We will soon see how He does that, and it will be an exciting discovery. But for now, please answer the following questions.

Questions

Question 1. How is being enslaved to immorality like being a slave? Write in your answer here:

Pastor Dave wrote, "Addiction to pornography takes away all your personal rights and freedoms. You feel as if someone else owns you. In this state, you come to understand that they will use you whenever they want, and they do not care if you are tired, hurt, injured, or just can't go on. Each day, after being beat up by those who own you, you go back to your slave hut and try to lick your wounds like an animal would lick a cut on its paw. Each and every step is painful, and the worst is that you know you will not have time to heal, before being dragged out and forced to dig in and injure yourself again and again. It breaks your spirit; it makes you bitter; it makes you angry; it makes you want to lash out at those around you - even those who are trying to help you with your

Questions

wounds. You do not want anyone to come near you. In fact, there is a certain satisfaction of being more comfortable in your misery than you are of venturing into the new world of freedom."

Randy wrote, "Once subdued, it pushes you more and more to isolate yourself from anything that might free you or conflict with its power over you. It lets you live only enough to barely survive and have the strength to serve it eventually, at the same time putting you through whatever it takes to numb your brain to its cruel control."

Question 2. Have you, yourself, gotten to the "slavery" part of sexual sin yet?

Question 3. When the Israelites were slaves, what did they do to get help?

Question 4. Did God hear their cry for help?

Question 5. Read the above verses. What words does the Bible use to describe how God felt about His people while they were in slavery?

Question 6. How has pornography or sexual sin enslaved you in the past?

Now, for the life-changing part of this biblical story! The Israelites cried out to God, and He came down to rescue the slaves. First, He sent an assortment of plagues (frogs, hail, locusts...etc.) on the Egyptians to display His power. Finally, because Pharaoh's heart was hard and he would not let God's people go, God sent word that He would destroy the firstborn son of every Egyptian household. But, in order to protect His own people, He instructed them to kill a lamb and put its blood on the doorposts. When the destroying Angel "saw the blood" he would "pass over" that house and not destroy the firstborn.

The Bible says that Jesus Christ is our "Passover Lamb" (1 Corinthians 5:7). He was sacrificed on the cross 2000 years ago, and His blood protects us from death. Oh friend, ask that God would place the blood of His Son, Jesus, on the doorposts of your heart. LOVE the blood of Jesus, as your only protecting agent to save you from death. He died so we can live!

But now, watch this! Not only were the Israelites told to put the blood of the lamb on their doorposts, they were also instructed to eat the lamb. Now, here are some of the most instructive words in Scripture regarding freedom: "This is how you are to eat it: with your cloak tucked into your belt, your sandals on your feet and your staff in your hand. Eat it in haste; it is the Lord's Passover."

Question 7. Consider this for a moment, and please record your thoughts on why they were to eat the Passover lamb with their cloaks tucked into their belts, their sandals on their feet, and their staffs in their hands. Write your thoughts here:

The Israelites were to eat the lamb with their cloak tucked in, their sandals on, and their staff in their hands. In other words, they were to be ready to go. God was saying to them: "Be ready to go, because as soon as you eat the lamb you will leave Egypt." Please don't miss this teaching, for here is real and lasting help for us: The Israelites literally ate their way out of slavery, and so can we! This is the message that is taught to us today: When we feed on the Passover Lamb, we will leave slavery.

So, how do I "eat my way out of slavery?" Answer: feed on the Word of God! Let's talk about that, and then we will have some questions for you.

The way that you and I, today, "eat the Lamb," is to take Scripture and chew on it. We take a small passage and eat it up, so to speak. Eating involves taking in food for nourishment, and that is what Jesus Christ is: Food for the soul! Jesus Christ came, not only to die for our sins and give us eternal life by His death, but He also came to be eaten, and to provide nourishment for our hungry souls. Now, let's get to some questions.

Question 8. How is meditating through a passage of Scripture like "eating the Lamb?"

   A.   Both are nourishing
   B.   It provides freedom
   C.   It gives life
   D.   Both of the above

There is a way out of slavery to pornography, adultery, indeed, all sexual sin! It is through feeding on Jesus Christ. As we become full of Him, through meditating on the Bible, we will discover our freedom. Freedom follows fullness.

Now, to be very practical with this teaching, we're going to ask you to "feed" on the following Scriptures. Write down your thoughts as you consider these Scriptures. As you "feed" and get "full," you will leave the Egypt of pornography and sexual impurity behind. Always remember that sexual purity and freedom from pornography is a by-product of "feeding" on Jesus Christ through thinking and meditating on Scripture. We can't "try" our hardest not to do pornography and be successful; we will always fail. But we can "eat" our way out of slavery. Now, do what Paul told Timothy to do: Reflect on these things, and the Lord will give you insight (2 Timothy 2:7).

Question 9. Please write your thoughts about Psalm 1:2,3: "His delight is in the law of the Lord, and on His law He meditates day and night. He is like a tree planted by streams of water, which yields its fruit in season and whose leaf does not wither."

Question 10. Please write your thoughts about Deuteronomy 8:3: "Man does not live by bread alone, but by every word that comes from the mouth of God."

Question 11. Please write your thoughts about John 6:48-51: "I am the bread of life. Your forefathers ate the manna in the desert, yet they died. But here is the bread that comes down from heaven, which a man may eat and not die. I am the living bread that came down from heaven. If anyone eats of this bread, he will live forever. This bread is my flesh, which I will give for the life of the world.

Question 12. Please write your thoughts about Jeremiah 15:16: "When your words came, I ate them. They were my joy and my heart's delight."

Question 13. Please write your thoughts about John 17:17: "Sanctify them (set them apart from sin) by the truth: your Word is truth."

Question 14. Please write your thoughts about Joshua 1:8: "Do not let this book of the Law depart from your mouth. Meditate on it day and night, so that you may be careful to do everything written in it. Then you will be prosperous and successful."

Question 15. Have you learned something today? Does this teaching give you hope? How will you implement the teaching in your own life?

Course member Mike wrote, "I have never seen how this passage applies to me before, and I have never understood why the Israelites had to eat the lamb all prepared to go. Now it makes perfect sense. The light dawned on me today, while reading this lesson, and I believe I will be free from pornography from now on, as before I had tried to leave slavery without being full of Christ. Now I get it! Now I see! Eat and leave, eat and leave."

Course member Tom responded, "Yes, I can see how I have been empty and attempting to fill my soul with pornography because of its emptiness. Now, I know that I must fill it with Christ in order to not give in to sin. I must feed on God's Word. I must appropriate Christ in order to be free. This has been the missing ingredient from my struggles in the past."

Scripture to Consider

Captives also enjoy their ease; they no longer hear the slave driver's shout. The small and the great are there, and the slave is freed from his master (Job 3:18-19).

When the LORD brought back the captives to Zion, we were like men who dreamed. Our mouths were filled with laughter, our tongues with songs of joy. Then it was said among the nations, "The LORD has done great things for them." The LORD has done great things for us, and we are filled with joy (Psalm 126:1-3).

Were you free from pornography since you did the last lesson?

    Yes   No

Were you free from self-gratification since you did the last lesson?

    Yes   No

Were you free from sexual immorality since you did the last lesson?

    Yes   No

The following testimony is from Kevin:

As humans, it is our propensity to compare ourselves to others by saying, I was never that bad, or I could never be that good. Thankfully, God does not use a sliding scale to determine our worth. Over many years, I have struggled with the fight over pornography.

My first exposure to pornography was in a mall with my brother and his best friend. In one of the bookstores, the friend pulled down a Playboy and showed me the centerfold. I was not even a teenager yet. While I was not sexually excited by what I saw, I was very curious and interested. But I knew it was wrong and so acted as if I didn't want to see it. A few years later, I was house sitting for a neighbor while they were out of town. In the process of bringing in the mail, I was again exposed to the same magazine, but this time, I could peruse it without anyone seeing me. I would not be exposed to porn again until I was in my fourth year of college.

Meanwhile, as a sophomore in college, I heard a friend talk about how he was getting the victory over self-gratification, and since I had honestly never done it to that point, I was curious how he could be entrapped and so I tried it myself. (Looking back, that sounds stupid, and it was.) Soon I was gratifying myself several times a week. I didn't think it was all that wrong. After all, I wasn't viewing porn; I was only responding physically to the thoughts that "God had placed in my mind." It was not God that placed them there.

A couple of years later when I was re-exposed to porn, I still acted as if I disdained what my co-workers were doing, but would secretly view the porn when they were not around. Now there was the additional addictive component of self-gratification. During this whole time, I thought myself better than others because I had not lost my virginity. (I still count this as a gift from God, but no longer a source of pride.) What I didn't realize is that I was going further into the trap of porn. I never bought a movie, and only once bought a magazine, because I couldnt keep them from being seen by others. Instead, I was getting it from the Internet where I could get them free and anonymously. I was no longer just viewing women, but I was now viewing couples (heterosexual and lesbian) and being titillated by the interaction I was seeing. I am sure that if God had allowed me to continue, I would have turned to physical expression with others to try some of what I was seeing.

Many times I tried to quit and not view porn again. It was only when I began (through the Way of Purity course) to study Scripture with the intent of finding escape that I was set free from the chains that the enemy kept using to pull me back to porn.

It has now been over 60 days that I have been porn-free. Some of those times I have had stronger temptations than others, but I am glad to say that God has rescued me from temptation. I am learning more every day about how to fight by running away. I know that God has rescued me from a pit that I could never climb out of by myself, and I am grateful for that. I know that He is willing to rescue you, as well. In fact, the rope is there for you to climb out, but until you grasp hold of it, you will continue to slip further into the trap you have chosen for yourself. If you are into porn, it is an addiction, but it is also SIN. You (as I) chose to allow yourself into it; but God will help you out. Please make this change today.

DAY 16 - TEMPTATION

Today we will study the subject of temptation. We want to discover the nature of temptation, as well as how to combat it. Please read the following passage:

> [1] Jesus, full of the Holy Spirit, returned from the Jordan and was led by the Spirit in the desert, [2] where for forty days he was tempted by the devil. He ate nothing during those days, and at the end of them he was hungry.
>
> [3] The devil said to him, "If you are the Son of God, tell this stone to become bread."
>
> [4] Jesus answered, "It is written: 'Man does not live on bread alone.'"
>
> [5] The devil led him up to a high place and showed him in an instant all the kingdoms of the world. [6] And he said to him, "I will give you all their authority and splendor, for it has been given to me, and I can give it to anyone I want to. [7] So if you worship me, it will all be yours."
>
> [8] Jesus answered, "It is written: 'Worship the Lord your God and serve him only.'"
>
> [9] The devil led him to Jerusalem and had him stand on the highest point of the temple. "If you are the Son of God," he said, "throw yourself down from here.
>
> [10] For it is written: "'He will command his angels concerning youto guard you carefully;
>
> [11] they will lift you up in their hands, so that you will not strike your foot against a stone.'"
>
> [12] Jesus answered, "It says: 'Do not put the Lord your God to the test.'"
>
> [13] When the devil had finished all this tempting, he left him until an opportune time (Luke 4:1-13).

The parallel passage in Matthew 4:1-11 records that this temptation of Jesus happened directly after he was baptized in the Jordan, where heaven was opened to Him, and the Holy Spirit descended upon Him. He received the approval of His Father in heaven who said, "This is my beloved Son in Whom I am well pleased." So the first thing we learn about temptation is that it often happens directly after a high spiritual experience.

I have a friend who preaches weekly, and he said that Sunday afternoon is usually a difficult time for him. Remember Paul who, after He experienced wonderful revelations from God, was given a "thorn in the flesh," a messenger of Satan for his humbling.

Question 1. Have you been tempted after a special time of closeness with God, or after a high spiritual experience at a retreat, conference, or church meeting?

Next, let us notice this temptation took place during a time of physical weakness. Since Jesus did not eat during those 40 days, there must have been a huge physical strain on His body. Temptations often transpire during a time of physical sickness, when the body is in a weak state, hungry, or tired.

Question 2. Have you had an experience where you were hit with temptations during a time of physical weakness?

Then, let us note Jesus was alone when tempted. He was not hit with these fierce onslaughts while in company with His disciples, but only as He was alone in the desert.

Question 3. Have you ever noticed that you can be with people all day long and be fine but, when you get alone, you are beset by intense temptation?

Scripture warns us to expect it, and helps to remove our isolation with this admonishment and reminder: "Be self-controlled and alert. Your enemy the devil prowls around like a roaring lion looking for someone to devour. Resist him, standing firm in the faith, because you know that your brothers throughout the world are undergoing the same kind of sufferings" (1 Peter 5:8-9).

Question 4. What "alone time" is a temptation for you?

Next, let us notice the design of the temptations. The design of the temptations was to get Jesus to sin against God, and to disqualify Him for being the ultimate Sacrifice for the sins of others. All through this temptation, Satan attempts to get Jesus to bypass the cross by which He would save all believing mankind. Satan knew that if He could get Jesus to short-circuit the cross, all mankind would be lost, and must suffer in eternal hell to pay the price for their sins.

Learn this lesson well, for every temptation is designed by the enemy of our souls to cause us to disobey God, and to bypass our own cross. Satan's design is for us to give in and disobey, rather than to resist and offer our bodies a living sacrifice; to indulge our flesh, rather than crucify it.

Next, let us note another design by Satan in tempting us. He wants us to doubt our relationship with God, and to become independent of Him in meeting our own needs.

Notice the first temptation: ³ The devil said to him, "If you are the Son of God, tell this stone to become bread." ⁴ Jesus answered, "It is written: 'Man does not live on bread alone.'" The devil said, "If You are the Son of God." See how he attempts to cast doubt upon Jesus' identity and relationship with His Father? Notice again, that the devil said, "Tell these stones to become bread." He did not say, "Pray to your Father in heaven and ask for bread," but rather "Take matters into your own hands and provide for your own needs." The devil hates anything requiring humility and dependence upon God, and loves to tell us of our own self-sufficiency. Satan's aim is to tempt a Christian to overthrow his relationship to God as a Father, so as to cut off his dependence on Him.

To apply this teaching, you and I have a need for intimacy, (most importantly, with God Himself), and God promises to supply our every need. Will you believe Him, and ask Him to meet your need? Or, will you believe the lie that viewing pornography or having sex outside of marriage will meet your need for intimacy?

Question 5. If you are a Christian, do you see how the devil may use pornography and sexual sin to get you to break your relationship with God and to declare your independence from God? Please explain here.

Next, notice how the temptation was resisted and overcome:

1. Christ refused to comply. In this one aspect, the teaching of the world to "Just say no" is correct, but it falls short, because it does not teach the next point, which is:

2. He was ready to reply to it. He quoted from Scripture, saying, "It is written." Isn't it amazing that Christ answered and baffled all the temptations of Satan with "It is written." Not only was He the Living Word of God, but also God's Word lived in Him, and He was strong and overcame the evil one by the Word of God.

Question 6. How does the following verse apply to our subject of study today?

"I write to you, young men, because you are strong, and the word of God lives in you, and you have overcome the evil one" (1 John 2:14).

Friend, it is not so much our knowing Scripture that gives us the victory, it is the Word of God living in us that enables us to "overcome the evil one." We see many people come to this course with much knowledge of Scripture, yet they are habitually defeated by pornography and/or sexual sin. When I was living in bondage to immorality, I could quote Scripture left and right, but I was not living Scripture. Scripture takes up residence in the heart only through obedience (Psalm 111:10).

Notice the second temptation:

⁵ The devil led him up to a high place and showed him in an instant all the kingdoms of the world. ⁶ And he said to him, "I will give you all their authority and splendor, for it has been given to me, and I can give it to anyone I want to. ⁷ So if you worship me, it will all be yours.

In this temptation, the devil showed Jesus all the splendor of the world. All the beauty, the glory, the power, the magnificence, the grandeur and the luxury of the world was shown to him. Friends, we don't have to be involved with pornography long to see this same offer displayed on our computer screens or TV monitors. The models shimmer with beauty and magnificence, and they are luxurious and glamorous. They "offer us the world" of excitement and pleasure and heart-pounding fun!

The problem is that immorality is demonic (1 Corinthians 10:20), and there is worship involved with it. Just as Jesus had to "worship" the devil if he was to enjoy the splendor and power of the world, so the devil is after our worship and offers us pornography and sexual sin as the enticement.

No, I imply that what pagans sacrifice they offer to demons and not to God. I do not want you to be participants with demons (1 Corinthians 10:20 ESV).

Even though I was a professing Christian for 10 of the 15 years I was involved with pornography and adultery, I was unknowingly worshipping at a demonic altar. The truth is clear from this passage that the devil is after our worship, just as He was with Jesus.

Question 7. Please provide your thoughts on the following commentary by Matthew Henry:

"All this will I give thee." And what was all that? It was but a map, a picture, a mere phantasm, that had nothing in it real or solid, and this he would give him; a goodly prize! Yet such are Satan's proffers. Note, multitudes lose the sight of that which is, by setting their eyes on that which is not. The devil's baits are all a sham; they are shows and shadows with which he deceives them, or rather they deceive themselves.

Notice how Jesus warded off this assault and conquered the enemy:

1. With abhorrence and detestation. A parallel passage states, "Get away from me Satan" (Matthew 4:10). If we are ever going to win this battle against impurity, we must ask God to give us a holy detestation of it, as if we cannot bear the thought of it.

2. With Scripture. "It is written: 'Worship the Lord your God and serve him only.'" When dealing with fierce and intense temptations, answer from Scripture, and answer in brief.

Finally, the third temptation:

> [9] The devil led him to Jerusalem and had him stand on the highest point of the temple. "If you are the Son of God," he said, "throw yourself down from here. [10] For it is written: "'He will command his angels concerning you to guard you carefully; [11] they will lift you up in their hands, so that you will not strike your foot against a stone.'" [12] Jesus answered, "It says: 'Do not put the Lord your God to the test.'"

Here, the devil tempts Jesus to presume upon the promises of God. We presume upon the promises of God when we purposely sin, while clinging to a promise of God. If Jesus had purposely sinned by throwing Himself down from the temple, He would have been testing God to try to rely on God's promise to not let Him fall.

The following testimony is from Phil:

In this short space, I cannot begin to tell you the grievous nature of my sins against God and society. I have hurt many good, caring, and loving people through my addiction to pornography, self-gratification, and other sexual sins that I was involved in for over fifty years. And sadly, for the last twelve of those years, I served as a minister of God's Word.

It started at about age ten when I was introduced to sex by some adults. It was only a short time before I learned about self-gratification, pornography, and alcohol. Over the years I fought an increasingly difficult battle against those sins. I knew that this disgusting stuff was wrong, but everything I tried to do to quit failed, and the sin grew worse. I eventually lost my wife and the love and support of family and friends. It was a helpless downward spiral to ultimate destruction. I had no god but addiction.

I accepted Jesus into my life in 1983 and was delivered from alcoholism. But my struggles in the other areas continued. I was convicted of my sin and helplessness; succeeding for a season now and then but always going back to it. And the Internet accessibility to porn hit me with a destructive vengeance that nearly destroyed me. I would prepare a Bible study or sermon in a hurry so I would have time to surf and gratify myself.

One Sunday late in January, I was physically nauseated by what I was doing. I thought it was over for me. Out of desperation I typed "sexual addiction" into the search box on Yahoo and it took me straight to Setting Captives Free. I found others like me who understood! I also found the road to victory and freedom.

As of this writing I have been free for over 74 days and I am walking in righteousness with Jesus. I am restored through His grace and love. Oh, I still have problems, I must walk carefully, and take care not to place myself in the way of temptation, but I am free. I have been able to put things right with my new wife of eighteen years and with the ministry God gave me. I have a new love and understanding of God's Holy Word. My life has been restored. I praise God for his tender mercies. Many thanks and blessings to my Way of Purity course mentor, Don.

This has direct application to us who have been involved in pornography or any other form of impurity. If I purposely view pornography while claiming God's promise to forgive sin, I am testing God. It's the same as praying, "God please forgive me for this sin I am about to commit" which presumes upon God's grace. The same would be true of asking God to forgive me while making any provision for my flesh. I would be presuming upon His grace.

Please get this principle. The devil will throw all kinds of Scripture our way to get us to sin against God by viewing pornography or being involved in a sinful relationship. Here are some examples of Scripture he might use against us - "I will forgive your sins, and remember your wickedness no more," "All manner of sin and blasphemy will be forgiven among men," "Nothing can separate us from the love of God," "The evil I do not want to do, this I keep on doing," "If we confess our sins, He is faithful and just to forgive us our sins..." and so on. How do we know it is the devil using Scripture and not our own minds? If that Scripture is being used to lure us into sin, it is coming from the evil one.

Question 8. What did you learn today, and how are you doing?

Scripture to Consider

No temptation has seized you except what is common to man. And God is faithful; he will not let you be tempted beyond what you can bear. But when you are tempted, he will also provide a way out so that you can stand up under it (1 Corinthians 10:13).

Were you free from pornography since you did the last lesson?

    Yes   No

Were you free from self-gratification since you did the last lesson?

    Yes   No

Were you free from sexual immorality since you did the last lesson?

    Yes   No

DAY 17 - RETURN TO THE LORD

Scripture records that Solomon's Temple was radiant in its splendor, and brilliant with the Shekinah glory of the Lord. "...the cloud filled the temple of the LORD. [11] And the priests could not perform their service because of the cloud, for the glory of the LORD filled his temple" (1 Kings 8:10b-11). **This Temple was the house of God,** "I have indeed built a magnificent temple for You, a place for you to dwell forever" (1 Kings 8:13) **and was meant to be a "light for all nations."** It was imposing; a holy and glorious dwelling place for God.

It served several purposes: it was a place of worship, a place to find forgiveness of sins, a place where the presence of God was seen, and a place where unbelievers could find God and learn how to worship Him. God's presence made it glorious, pure, holy, radiant with splendor and majestic in beauty.

But the book of Ezekiel, in the Old Testament, records the slow departure of the glory of the Lord from the nation of Israel. The Shekina glory cloud (which symbolized the presence of God) left the Most Holy Place of the Temple, then left the Temple itself, and then the entire land of Israel. The departing of God and His glory brought about monumental changes to the nation of Israel. They no longer had the presence of the Lord; their enemies ransacked their nation, taking captive men, women and children, and they were left without a witness to the nations. They became "Ichabod" which means, "The glory of the Lord has departed." Why did God depart and leave Israel as Ichabod?

Question 3. Please provide your thoughts about this verse: "I said to them, each of you, get rid of the vile images you have set your eyes on, and do not defile yourselves with the idols of Egypt. I am the LORD your God. But they rebelled against me and would not listen to me; they did not get rid of the vile images they had set their eyes on, nor did they forsake the idols of Egypt" (Ezekiel 20:7).

Question 4. Please provide your thoughts about this verse: "This is what the Sovereign LORD says: Will you defile yourselves the way your fathers did and lust after their vile images?" (Ezekiel 20:30).

Questions

To answer our questions, let us take a tour of the book of Ezekiel and we will discover what it was that drove the presence of God from the Temple and the nation. Please note what these verses say about why He withdrew from the Temple.

Question 1. Please provide your thoughts on this verse: "As surely as I live, declares the Sovereign LORD, because you have defiled my sanctuary with all your vile images and detestable practices, I myself will withdraw my favor; I will not look on you with pity or spare you" (Ezekiel 5:11).

Question 2. Please provide your thoughts about this verse: "But as for those whose hearts are devoted to their vile images and detestable idols, I will bring down on their own heads what they have done, declares the Sovereign LORD" (Ezekiel 11:21).

It becomes obvious, from reading these verses, that the people of God were "setting their eyes on vile images" and "defiling themselves with vile images" and with "detestable practices." They were idolatrous, and this is why God withdrew His presence. Sin that is tolerated in the nation, or the home, or the individual, always drives the Holy Spirit of God away.

Course member Jeremy wrote, "Before, I knew what I believed, or at least what I professed to believe. I attended church, paid my tithe, and tried to show outward signs of Christianity, but it was all tainted by my repugnant sin toward God and myself. I was damaging His temple, the dwelling place of God. He couldn't live with that unrighteousness, so I was pushing Him out. I cried out, and He heard me through that nightmare and answered me and drew me out of that pit. I am on my way, and ever growing in His light and love."

So what does this teaching on the Temple have to do with pornography or sexual impurity and us? Again, please record your thoughts on the following verses, writing your comments immediately below the verse. The following verses are from 1 Corinthians, chapter 6:

> The body is not meant for sexual immorality, but for the Lord, and the Lord for the body" (1 Corinthians 6:13).

Question 5. According to verse 13 above, for what is your body meant?

Question 6. In your own words, please tell what you think the statement "Our bodies are meant for the Lord" actually means.

> "By his power God raised the Lord from the dead, and he will raise us also" (1 Corinthians 6:14)

Question 7. Verse 13 states that our bodies are not meant for sexual immorality, but they are meant for the Lord. The very next verse speaks about the resurrection of Jesus Christ, and states that we will be raised as well. What connection do you see between these two verses?

> [15] Do you not know that your bodies are members of Christ himself? Shall I then take the members of Christ and unite them with a prostitute? Never! [16] Do you not know that he who unites himself with a prostitute is one with her in body? For it is said, The two will become one flesh. [17] But he who unites himself with the Lord is one with him in spirit (1 Corinthians 6:15-17).

Question 8. What are your thoughts on verses 15-17 above?

> "Flee from sexual immorality. All other sins a man commits are outside his body, but he who sins sexually sins against his own body" (1 Corinthians 6:18).

Question 9. Dear friend, it is clear from the above verse that we are to flee from sexual immorality. Like Joseph, who ran from Potiphar's wife, we are to flee. Please think through times when you are specifically hit with heavy temptations, and write out how you will "flee." Write your thoughts here.

Question 10. Verse 18 contains an admonishment regarding sexual immorality. What are we to do to overcome it?

> "Do you not know that your body is a temple of the Holy Spirit, who is in you, whom you have received from God? You are not your own" (1 Corinthians 6:19).

Question 11. Verse 19 describes the body as what?

Question 12. According to the same verse, who owns the Temple of my body?

> "You were bought at a price. Therefore honor God with your body" (1 Corinthians 6:20).

Question 13. Verse 20 tells us "we were bought at a price." What was the purchase price?

Friend, these verses tell us that our bodies are temples belonging to the Lord. The Temple of the Old Testament became "Ichabod," because the people of God were "lusting after idolatrous images" in their hearts and committing "detestable practices." God slowly left them, and they were dispersed into foreign lands where they became "captives."

We, too, have spent time lusting after idolatrous images (pornography) and have been involved in detestable practices (self-gratification, adultery, immorality). And depending on how long we were involved, we may have lost the presence and power of God. Our lives may have become "Ichabod." It may

Questions

have happened slowly, over time, but now we are destitute of power, spiritual weaklings trying to fight "principalities and powers of darkness" without Christ. We have been handed over to the enemy, and are now "captives" in exile. But there is hope.

Question 14. Please read and comment on our final portion of Scripture today:

> [17] Therefore say: This is what the Sovereign LORD says: I will gather you from the nations and bring you back from the countries where you have been scattered, and I will give you back the land of Israel again.

> [18] They will return to it and remove all its vile images and detestable idols. [19] I will give them an undivided heart and put a new spirit in them; I will remove from them their heart of stone and give them a heart of flesh. [20] Then they will follow my decrees and be careful to keep my laws. They will be my people, and I will be their God. [21] But as for those whose hearts are devoted to their vile images and detestable idols, I will bring down on their own heads what they have done, declares the Sovereign LORD.

> [22] Then the cherubim, with the wheels beside them, spread their wings, and the glory of the God of Israel was above them" (Ezekiel 11:17-22).

Notice the "removal of the detestable images" brought the captives back to the land and the glory of God returned to the people. Ichabod no more! The glory returned. Friend, are you wondering if, since you have devoted yourself to detestable pornographic images and immoral practices, you will ever enjoy the presence of God again? Remove those vile images and the detestable practices, and the presence and power and purity of God will return. Your body is a Temple.

One of the objections we hear from course members quite often is that they feel that God will not return to them; that they will not experience his presence again. This passage of Scripture should confirm to the questioning soul that God does return to those who repent and return to Him.

Question 15. What are your thoughts and insights on today's teaching? Specifically, how will you apply what you are learning?

I lost the presence and power of God through my involvement in pornography, self-gratification, and adultery, and I didn't even know it. Samson lost the presence of God through his lust, but was not aware of it: Then she called, "Samson, the Philistines are upon you!" He awoke from his sleep and thought, "I'll go out as before and shake myself free." But he did not know that the LORD had left him (Judges 16:20). But, since God has granted me repentance, and I've been away from pornography and all forms of impurity since January of 1999, I can attest to the pres-

The following testimony is from Skip:

I was involved in the sin of pornography, gratifying the flesh, and sexual immorality, since my early teens. I don't recall exactly when it began or what started it. I do know it began with the discovery of how good gratifying the flesh made me feel. It didn't seem wrong, but of course I told no one about this habit. As time went on, I discovered Playboy magazines. I turned 50 years old this past January, so its been at least 35 years since I began. It did not change when I got married. I thought it would, but it didn't. My wife didn't know. With the advent of the Internet, I discovered the online world of pornography. As time went on, it got worse. I never went beyond the world of the Internet and the fantasies in my mind. I tried to stop many times in the past and would succeed for a few weeks at a time. I even confessed my sin of self-gratification to one of my pastors over 20 years ago. I left his office the same as I went in; in fact I cannot recall anything he did. I don't even think he responded to my confession except with silence. A few years ago, my wife caught me and confronted me. I told her I would stop. I couldn't. I would even lock my office door at work and surf the Internet for the usual sites I visited. I was so afraid of being caught, but this did not stop me. This past fall, God led me to two scriptures over a period of a few weeks. I dont remember them except that they seemed to give me some temporary power over my sin, and I stopped it for a few days each time. He was working in my life then in some way, seeking to bring me back to Him I believe, drawing me to Him. Or it may have been a warning I did not heed. I don't really know for sure.

One day my wife dropped me off at work. About the middle of the day, a courier brought me a letter from her. She had taken my son and left home. Somehow, she had discovered I was still involved in viewing pornography and it scared and hurt her. That morning at work before the letter arrived, I was again seeking an opportunity to view pornography on the Internet. But the letter hit me hard. I didn't know where they were. I remember looking almost immediately for help on the Internet for pornography addiction. I found several places, one being the Setting Captives Free site. Another was a link to the local SAA (Sexual Addicts Anonymous) chapter. I called and left a message with a contact from the local SAA chapter who go back to me within a day. One of the members lived close by and gave me a ride to my first and only meeting. I remember this about that meeting and at supper with some of the members afterwards: First, everyone that spoke about their addiction was continuing to fall into their sin; and, two, they seemed to be fascinated about the details of each others addiction. By this time, I had started the Way of Purity course at Setting Captives Free. I began it on Tuesday morning, the "day after." I felt uncomfortable going to any more SAA meetings. God was never mentioned in those meetings; only "my higher power" was mentioned. It seemed that they were trying to escape their addiction by their own power. Although their "higher power" was mentioned, it was never used as a source to escape their addiction, at least among those persons I heard speak. I asked, and my mentor recommended I not go back to any more SAA meetings. The next time the man who had taken me to my first meeting called, I told him I was not going back and that I would like to tell him why, but he cut the conversation with me short as if he did not want to know why or because he was afraid to hear. I had briefly told him why, mentioning God, but not in detail. He seemed afraid to hear anymore and quickly hung up. This approach with going to SAA meetings may work for some people, but it was not going to work for me. I continued to take the Way of Purity course daily. I would arise at 3:30 am to 4 am each day to do my lesson. I even managed to continue my lessons when traveling away on business.

Why did it take my wife leaving to make me finally go beyond asking for forgiveness to repenting? I don't know. Always before, I had asked for forgiveness, but I had never repented. I cant explain what was different this time. It doesn't really matter. What matters is that God heard my cry, my plea for help. This sin is a problem of the heart. My heart cried out to God. I guess He knew my heart and knew it was ready for Him finally. I wish it had not taken so long, but I am glad He finally set me free - truly free from my bondage.

Today, I have been free from pornography, self-gratification, and sexual immorality since November 3, 2003. My wife and son have returned (two weeks before Christmas, 2003). I have confessed my sin to God, to my pastor, to an elder at our church, to a co-worker (not until I had been free of bondage for several months), and to my wife and children. I have changed my Internet service provider to a filtered service and demonstrated to my wife how it works effectively. I have destroyed any pornography I had saved on any computer. I read and study my Bible almost daily. God is revealing His truth to me as I study His Word. I have insights as to the meaning of the scriptures I never had before. I have found a wonderful church. I remember it was so painful at first dealing with my sin. I would cry out to God often. Always He would answer. Ever so quietly He would consistently say the same thing, "Be patient and have faith." My sin caused other problems for my family and me, also. It destroyed all the intimacy with my wife and my family; it has caused us financial problems and some legal problems. One by one, God is dealing with those issues. Is He actually fixing those problems? No and yes. Our marriage is stronger and better in many ways. There is an intimacy there now that was never there before. I have no desire to view pornography. I don't look at women the same way as before. We are only able to deal with the financial problems as our money allows; He didn't make them go away. If I dwell on my problems too much, I worry about what will happen. But when that happens, I remember again Philippians 4:6-7, "Be anxious for nothing, but in everything, by prayer and supplication with thanksgiving, let your requests be made known unto God. And the peace of God, which passeth all understanding, shall keep your hearts and minds through Christ Jesus." He is faithful and has shown me many times and in miraculous ways that He is right there with me, caring for and leading me. He has given me His peace. I am learning how to trust and have faith in Him. When I am tempted, I remember the following scripture: 2 Corinthians 12:9 KJV And he said unto me, My grace is sufficient for thee: for my strength is made perfect in weakness. Most gladly therefore will I rather glory in my infirmities, that the power of Christ may rest upon me.

I have begun mentoring other men who are taking the Way of Purity course from Setting Captives Free. It has been very rewarding. I have had students as young as 16-20 and as old as 56-60. I have mentored single and married men, a former pastor, and a man who is his churchs youth minister. Is God involved in this ministry of Setting Captives Free? I can most certainly and emphatically tell you, YES! There is no way I could have responded to some of these students without the Holy Spirits help. Gods hand is all over this ministry. The other point just hit me this last week, and it was that God knows what I tell my students. He KNOWS! Brother, you didn't come to this course by yourself. Yes, you had a choice, and you chose to take this course. You could have said "No." But know this - God led you there. God is like the father of the prodigal son in the Bible. He is waiting with open arms to welcome you back. I encourage you to be patient and have faith - to continue seeking freedom.

I leave you with the following three scriptures:
Romans 8:5-13
Matthew 6:19-21
Matthew 7:7-8

ence of God returning to me. I sense closeness with Him, unity with Him, and love from and to Him. But this has been a slow process.

Please note: We want to make sure the teaching about grieving the Spirit of God away, that is, having God's presence leave, is not the same as losing one's salvation. Losing God's presence does not mean I am condemned to hell. After all, is Jesus condemned to hell? No! Yet God's presence left him on the cross. Mark 15:34 says:

> And at the ninth hour Jesus cried out in a loud voice, "Eloi, Eloi, lama sabachthani?"-which means, "My God, my God, why have you forsaken me?"

God's presence left Jesus for the same reason his presence leaves us: sin. God is holy! When we are covered with sin, it is our own sin that covers us. When Jesus was covered with sin, it was not His sin that covered him - it was ours.

So, we want to be clear that we are not talking about a Christian losing his salvation.

Scripture to Consider

Ever since the time of your forefathers you have turned away from my decrees and have not kept them. Return to me, and I will return to you," says the LORD Almighty (Malachi 3:7).

"And call upon me in the day of trouble; I will deliver you, and you will honor me" (Psalm 50:15).

[1] Arise, shine, for your light has come, and the glory of the LORD rises upon you. [2] See, darkness covers the earth and thick darkness is over the peoples, but the LORD rises upon you and his glory appears over you. [3] Nations will come to your light, and kings to the brightness of your dawn (Isaiah 60:1-3).

[3] This is what the LORD Almighty says: 'Return to me,' declares the LORD Almighty, 'and I will return to you,' says the LORD Almighty. [4] Do not be like your forefathers, to whom the earlier prophets proclaimed: This is what the LORD Almighty says: 'Turn from your evil ways and your evil practices.' But they would not listen or pay attention to me, declares the LORD (Zechariah 1:3-4).

"[28] Come to me, all you who are weary and burdened, and I will give you rest. [29] Take my yoke upon you and learn from me, for I am gentle and humble in heart, and you will find rest for your souls. [30] For my yoke is easy and my burden is light (Matthew 11:28-30).

Were you free from pornography since you did the last lesson?

    Yes   No

Were you free from self-gratification since you did the last lesson?

    Yes   No

Were you free from sexual immorality since you did the last lesson?

    Yes   No

DAY 18 - EXCLUSIVE DRINKING

The first few days of this course were about satisfying ourselves in the Living Water of Jesus Christ. Today, we want to be very practical in providing help in overcoming pornography and sexual impurity. What does it mean to "drink the Living Water?" What does it look like in daily living to be satisfied in Christ? And how does drinking Living Water, actually enable us to leave our water pots of sin behind? These are the questions we will seek to answer today.

Let us begin with the first question: "What does it mean to drink the Living Water?" At the risk of sounding simplistic, it is as basic as reading the Bible. However, it is possible to read the Bible, but not drink of the Living Water. So what is the difference?

Drinking implies taking something into your system, and receiving nourishment and sustenance from it. I can read that Jesus is Living Water all day long, but not drink of Him. Drinking is directly related to the application of Scripture in my life, and obedience to it; it is much more than mere reading. When you read Scripture, ask God to apply it to your heart, and to change your life by the reading of it. This is what it means to drink the Living Water.

The next question is, "What does it look like in daily living to be satisfied in Christ?" It means rejoicing in the love, forgiveness and grace of God on a daily basis. It is discovering Christ afresh every day, and being irresistibly drawn to him by what we discover. When we become happy in Him, we need not look for happiness in pornography, food, or other sins. So then, as one of the Puritans of long ago said, "Our first duty as Christians is to get ourselves happy in God." This is the only sure means of avoiding pornography and impurity. This is what Jesus taught the Samaritan woman in John, chapter 4, in the earlier lesson.

And how does this drinking actually enable us to leave pornography and immorality behind? Simply put, if we are full and satisfied in Jesus Christ, we don't need anything else. Our hearts have found complete satisfaction, and are in need of nothing.

The problem is, today's society offers so many other "water fountains" from which to drink; each one promising joyful satisfaction and delight. Pornography, in its basic intent, promises to satisfy. It is an invitation to drink of happiness. These same promises are subtly conveyed through the allurement of alcohol, smoking, TV, card playing, money chasing, relationships, gambling, drugs, etc. Even seemingly innocent fun may be an attempt to satisfy the heart; such as family, religion, sports, theme parks, the Internet, vacations, newspaper reading, work, etc. How do we live in today's society that offers so many fountains from which to drink? The answer is to be "exclusive drinkers." What do we mean by that? Notice the following verse:

As they make music they will say, 'All my fountains are in you" (Psalm 87:7).

The context of this passage is that God is gracious to outsiders. He brings pagan gentiles into his family, and calls them his own. And it is those heathen outsiders who, by the grace of God have been brought into God's family, who sing of their enjoyment of God: "All my fountains are in you." This is an affirmation of the truth we have been studying from the beginning of the course; **Jesus alone can satisfy**. And it is a commitment to have no other source of life, refreshment or satisfaction than can be found in Jesus. It is a statement of fact, that they would be "exclusive drinkers."

Now we will examine some very practical ways to ensure that all our fountains are only in Jesus Christ. Please read the following passage and answer the questions below.

[1] The whole Israelite community set out from the Desert of Sin, traveling from place to place as the LORD commanded. They camped at Rephidim, but there was no water for the people to drink. [2] So they quarreled with Moses and said, "Give us water to drink."

Moses replied, "Why do you quarrel with me? Why do you put the LORD to the test?"

[3] But the people were thirsty for water there, and they grumbled against Moses. They said, "Why did you bring us up out of Egypt to make us and our children and livestock die of thirst?"

[4] Then Moses cried out to the LORD, "What am I to do with these people? They are almost ready to stone me."

[5] "The LORD answered Moses, "Walk on ahead of the people. Take with you some of the elders of Israel and take in your hand the staff with which you struck the Nile, and go. [6] I will stand there before you by the rock at Horeb. Strike the rock, and water will come out of it for the people to drink." So Moses did this in the sight of the elders of Israel (Exodus 17:1-6).

Question 1. Where were these people during this event?
  A. At the Taj Mahal
  A. In Egypt
  B. In the desert

Question 2. Why were they complaining?
  A. They missed the soft drink machines of Egypt.
  B. They were thirsty.
  C. They did not like living in tents.

Question 3. What did God tell them to do about their thirst?

Consider the following passage: They all ate the same spiritual food and drank the same spiritual drink; for they drank from the spiritual rock that accompanied them, and that rock was Christ (1 Corinthians 10:3-4).

Question 4. According to the above verses, whom did the rock represent?
  A. Moses
  B. Jesus Christ
  C. Muhammad

Question 5. What did Moses need to do to the rock before the people could drink from it?
  A. Speak to it
  B. Drill a hole in it
  C. Strike it

Notice the teaching from this passage of Scripture. The rock that was struck poured forth water for the people to drink. This rock represents Jesus Christ. Oh friend, here is lasting satisfaction; Jesus Christ, on the cross, was "struck," and he poured out his life that we may drink and live. But the rock that was struck in the wilderness was God's only provision to quench their thirst. They had to drink from that rock.

Are you still thirsting? Are you looking at pornography for your thirst to be quenched? Do you think that relationship will quench your thirst? Your thirst will never be quenched in any temporary pleasure. But come to the cross of Jesus Christ! He was pierced by a Roman soldier, and his life gushed out. It is the cross of Jesus Christ where the "Rock" was struck.

But we must drink only from the Rock. We must say, "All my fountains are in You." We must be exclusive drinkers.

Time for reflection...

Question 6. Are there other "fountains" in your life from which you have been drinking? If so, what are they? List them here.

Question 7. Will you now make a conscious effort to rid your life of all other "drinking" sources? Will you, by the grace of God, say from now on, "All my fountains are in You?"
  A. Yes, by God's grace I will now be an exclusive drinker.
  B. No, I am not ready to give up all other sources of satisfaction.

Please comment on this quote from Matthew Henry:

"Nothing will supply the needs, and satisfy the desires of a soul, but water out of this rock, Jesus Christ, this fountain opened. The pleasures of sense are puddle-water; spiritual delights are rock water, so pure, so clear, and so refreshing — rivers of pleasure." Matthew Henry

Question 8. According to Matthew Henry's quote above, what would you say is a major difference between "drinking" from pornography and impurity and drinking from Jesus? Write your answer here:

Course member Mike wrote, "Porn is like the puddle. The water is shallow, stagnant and full of impurities. It might satisfy for a moment, but it cannot last, and it contains elements that do me lasting harm. Drinking from Jesus, however, is like drinking from the rock. The water is cool, clear and flowing. It contains no impurities, and does me lasting good. And the supply is renewing and lasting, unlike the puddle, which disappears and goes away, forcing me to seek after another puddle. In porn, that relates to the constant quest for new pictures and thrills. It is also like seeking new experiences in entertainment, or never being satisfied with my job. Only in drinking the water of Christ, can I be satisfied and find true contentment. When that contentment is found, however, it has a profound effect on my life."

Course member Dave wrote, "It is amazing that something you know causes such anguish is at the same time so alluring. It's like being addicted to an electric fence."

Course member Larry wrote, "Selfish, indulgent, sinful water is like puddle water. It is contaminated with the poison of pornography, muddied by chaos, stagnant of spirit, small in volume, and quick to dry up, leaving a cracked and broken crust of a soul. The Living Water from Jesus is like the streams of fresh mountain water, which melt from the pure white snow and runs quickly down the mountain over clean rocks — refreshing and satisfying. In another way, one can think of the Living Water being pure and clean, washing away all of the contamination, and replacing it with pure, fresh life-giving water, which satisfies the thirst."

¹ Then the angel showed me the river of the water of life, as clear as crystal, flowing from the throne of God and of the Lamb ² down the middle of the great street of the city. On each side of the river stood the tree of life, bearing twelve crops of fruit, yielding its fruit every month. And the leaves of the tree are for the healing of the nations. ³ No longer will there be any curse (Revelation 22:1-3).

Question 9. How do the above verses in Revelation coincide with the teaching in today's lesson?

Question 10. Please write out a paragraph that summarizes the teaching of today.

Question 11. How is your life going right now? Are you beginning to walk in victory by God's grace?

The following testimony is from Joe:

I was raised in a broken home, and my father rarely came to visit. My older brother sexually abused me when I was 10, and then I discovered pornography in my early teens. This began a 22-year addiction, which I tried literally hundreds of times to break. Though I appeared to be a professional, respectable, businessman, and was well-liked by my peers, yet inside me there was this horrible secret bondage to pornography. Looking back on it now, I can see that I was an idolater. I drank from numerous fountains such as work, religion, sports, and entertainment.

As I mentioned earlier, I had tried numerous things to cease the addiction to pornography. I attended S.A. meetings, went to support groups, read books, and talked with psychiatrists. None of these helped. Then I did a search on the Internet and found the Setting Captives Free course and enrolled in The Way of Purity. In that course, I discovered that I had been looking for Jesus Christ, and soon thereafter began earnestly seeking for him. I radically amputated all access to pornography, took up my Bible and began seeking God with a passion. I found him. And now, Lord willing, I will never return to the sewer water of pornography again. My heart and my life are now satisfied in Jesus Christ. I am so thankful for those who put together this course and that it has pointed me to Christ and taught me how to drink the Living Water, and to quench my thirst in Jesus. Thank you!

Scripture to Consider

[37] On the last and greatest day of the Feast, Jesus stood and said in a loud voice, "If anyone is thirsty, let him come to me and drink. [38] Whoever believes in me, as the Scripture has said, streams of Living Water will flow from within him." [39] By this he meant the Spirit, whom those who believed in him were later to receive (John 7:37-39).

[15] They are before the throne of God and serve him day and night in his temple; and he who sits on the throne will spread his tent over them. [16] Never again will they hunger; never again will they thirst. The sun will not beat upon them, nor any scorching heat. [17] For the Lamb at the center of the throne will be their shepherd; he will lead them to springs of Living Water. And God will wipe away every tear from their eyes (Revelation 7:15-17).

Were you free from pornography since you did the last lesson?

    Yes   No

Were you free from self-gratification since you did the last lesson?

    Yes   No

Were you free from sexual immorality since you did the last lesson?

    Yes   No

DAY 19 - PURITY PRECEDES POWER

Read the following scriptural account and notice how serious these people were about radical amputation.

Many of those who believed now came and openly confessed their evil deeds. A number who had practiced sorcery brought their scrolls together and burned them publicly. When they calculated the value of the scrolls, the total came to fifty thousand drachmas. In this way the word of the Lord spread widely and grew in power (Acts 19:18-20).

There! Did you notice it? Immediately after Scripture records the people "radically amputating" their books of sorcery, it records the power that came with it. Read it again: "In this way the word of the Lord spread widely and grew in power!" Here is the principle: Purity precedes power.

But now, let us examine one of the ways the devil keeps people enslaved to pornography. He tries to turn things upside down and make us think that power precedes purity. Look at this email we received from an anonymous writer:

"I have not continued on in the course because I have been doing pornography. In response to your advice that I 'cut off and throw away the CD ROM' that has the porn on it, I respond that it is not the CDROM that causes me to sin, it is my own heart. It would not be reasonable to cut off the CD ROM and throw it away, as I would just find something else to view. My idea of victory is to be able to have the CD ROM nearby and say "No" to it. I will continue looking for another method of freedom."

This man will not find power to say "No" until he radically amputates his sin.

Here is another response to the "radical amputation" principle:

"The TV and computer haven't 'caused' me to sin; it has been my own sinful desires. As the Bible tells us, we are drawn away by our own sinful desires. I can see this might apply if I were going to a strip bar or porn shop. But, to get rid of TV and a computer altogether because I can't trust myself around them doesn't really get rid of the problem. Yes, I may be great when not being faced with the temptation, but do I really have victory? Is an alcoholic reformed and walking in victory because he is never around alcohol and doesn't drink? I say, he is wise to stay out of the bars, but if he is around alcohol in daily life and still doesn't drink, he is truly reformed. To me, this parallels porn addiction or food addiction or whatever addictions one may have. I am not going into clubs [like an alcoholic to bars] but I do have TV and computers in my daily life. I think it too radical to say I will get rid of both because I can't trust myself. If a dieter is around sweets in his daily life, but does not eat them, that is victory. I find more strength in having tons of junk food around and STILL not eating it. I agree we have to remove temptations or stay away from them as much is

reasonable, but that is the key–reasonable–and I don't feel getting rid of TV and computers [both have been a source of Bible teaching, as well as porn] is the answer."

Notice the references to being "reasonable," and the negative use of the word "radical."

Jodi wrote, "I've been meditating on this whole issue of amputation, and thinking about how some consider that their strength against sin wasn't really being put to the test unless they stood strong when being faced with it. That is so unbiblical. God NEVER tells us to do that. He says to flee—get out of there! Don't stick around! I believe that this is yet another tactic of Satan to cause us to fall flat. It is only tempting/testing the goodness of God in His grace to be dumb enough to put myself back in the path of sin."

Now, read the battle plan that one man devised, and see how he was willing to be radical to halt the sin. He did the following things:

1. He locked up the VCR and gave his wife the key.

2. He locked up the TV and gave his wife the combination to the lock on the TV cabinet.

3. He carried no money or credit cards. He knew that to rent impure videos takes money, so he carried no money with him.

4. He told several men and his wife about his struggles, and asked them to hold him accountable. These accountability partners would regularly ask him questions about whether he was following his plan or not. They were also available to him for confession if he stumbled and prayer support if he was tempted." (Robert Daniels, The War Within)

Warning: those who trifle with the clear teaching of God's Word that we are to deal radically with sin will not achieve lasting purity, will not perceive spiritual matters correctly, and will not receive God's power in their lives.

"There must be a divorce! Within the egg of sin there sleeps the seed of damnation! Man, there must be a divorce between you and your sins. Not a mere separation for a season, but a clear divorce. Cut off the right arm; pluck out the right eye, and cast them from you, or else you cannot enter into eternal life" (Charles Spurgeon, The Chief of Sinners).

Course member Ed wrote, "I just want to respond to the teaching in lesson 19. I truly believe that all forms of ungodliness in our lives must be amputated. If it takes turning off the computer, getting rid of the VCR or cable, then so be it! I only desire purity in life, for only the PURE in heart will see the kingdom of God! I cannot imagine keeping the CD ROM or what have you as a temptation. It is clear in God's example what happens when there are even images that are within the abode. Can God put up with that? God forbid!"

...Why ask for trouble and cause your own downfall...? (2 Chronicles 25:19).

Question 1. What is the title of this lesson?

Now, let us see a powerful demonstration of this truth taught in story form. Here is the background: The Israelites had just won a great victory over the very fortified city of Jericho and were preparing for battle against the small town of Ai. They were not too concerned about the outcome of this battle, due to how small Ai was, but they lost! And they were humiliated. Notice why they lost:

> Israel has sinned; they have violated my covenant, which I commanded them to keep. They have taken some of the devoted things; they have stolen, they have lied, they have put them with their own possessions. That is why the Israelites cannot stand against their enemies...You can not stand against your enemies until you remove it (Joshua 7:11-13).

As it turned out, a man by the name of Achan took a "beautiful robe, two hundred shekels of silver and a wedge of gold..." (verse 21) from the victory at Jericho, and was cherishing and hiding them. But notice the words that God used to show why the Israelites lost the battle: "You cannot stand against your enemies until you remove it."

This is highly instructive for us today. Until we remove that which has caused us to sin, we cannot expect power over the enemy. Purity precedes power. Notice what happened next:

> Then Joshua, together with all Israel, took Achan son of Zerah, the silver, the robe, the gold wedge, his sons and daughters, his cattle, donkeys and sheep, his tent and all that he had, to the Valley of Achor. Then all Israel stoned him, and after they had stoned the rest, they burned them (Joshua 7:24).

Now that is radical amputation. It is removing that which has caused sin. Notice what happened next:

> Twelve thousand men and women fell that day—all the people of Ai. . . So Joshua burned Ai and made it a permanent heap of ruins, a desolate place to this day (Joshua 8:25, 28).

If we want to make pornography and immorality "a permanent heap of ruins - a desolate place" then we must cut off that which causes us to sin. Purity precedes power.

Question 2. Why did Israel lose the battle with Ai?

A. They were outnumbered.

B. They were unskilled in battle.

C. Achan was hiding items devoted to destruction.

Question 3. What words did God use to tell the Israelites why they were defeated by Ai?

The following testimony is from Terrill:

My first exposure to pornography was when I was very young and my friends showed me a porn magazine. From that time until I started college, my years were filled with purchasing and viewing pornography. I accumulated a large collection of porn magazines that I was very proud of and gladly shared them with my college friends. We also started watching porn movies and visiting strip bars. The desires for more excitement continued to grow.

I joined the military a short time later and found that pornography was in abundance along with every other temptation. I traveled to Germany and visited the "red light district." There was a small community in Frankfurt filled with every imaginable sin of the flesh, with blocks of strip clubs, prostitute houses and video stores. There was no limit to what a person could get into there if he had the money.

Many years passed, and I married my wonderful wife. We started to attend church and became Christians. But my sinful habits didn't stop. I found ways to hide them and continue doing what I wanted even while going to church. I eventually became a deacon, treasurer, Sunday school teacher and witness for Christ. During that time I fought my desires as much as possible. I was able to keep up that outward appearance, but inside I was dead. I knew what I was, but for the sake of my kids, wife, and those around me, I had to continue the show that I was a respectable and upstanding Christian.

I finally hit bottom and went through a period determined to stop looking at pornography, but the Internet made it too easy, and the temptations were too great. I was ashamed, embarrassed and hated myself for what I did. If I could make it two days without viewing pornography, I felt pretty good about myself. But I always came back for more.

I finally had enough of the roller coaster ride that Satan had me on, and I was determined to get out. I searched for help and God brought me to Setting Captives Free. I was so ashamed of my behavior that I lied about my name, just in case they wanted to find out who I really was. My embarrassment was at an all-time high.

But when I started the course I found an immediate release from pornography. I really felt like I was going to make it. I found others going though the same thing I was and our stories paralleled. With God's help, I got the porn out and put God in its place. That is the only way I can explain it. He brought me out of the nightmare I had been in for many years. I owe all to the Lord for allowing me to find this website that has been a valuable tool in overcoming my pornography addiction.

While this course was the tool, there is no doubt that God was and is my strength and power to continue to resist temptation and use the tools that these lessons have given me to continue to be free from pornography. I thank God daily for His guidance in bringing me to this course and for His strength. Only God could overcome something with such a grasp on me as porn once had.

Question 4. What did the Israelites do to the man who was cherishing and hiding items of destruction?

A. They learned how to fight while he was still with them.

B. They ignored him and kept fighting battles.

C. They amputated him.

Note: They not only eradicated Achan, but his entire family, cattle, donkey, sheep and "all that he had." They stoned him, stoned the rest, and then burned them all. Here is truth for us. To become pure and powerful in battle, we need to thoroughly destroy everything remotely connected to our previous bondage to pornography and sexual sin. Stone it, burn it, and bury all of its "relatives." Then watch God's power at work in us.

Question 5. What did it take for the Israelites to have power in battle?

A. It took learning battle strategy

B. Purity

Friend, there is a spiritual principle taught in the above passage that has everything to do with our fight against the sin of pornography and sexual impurity. If we will radically amputate anything that can trip us up, God will fight for us. We will have power that results from purity. We cannot expect victory over sin while keeping an "Achan" in the camp. Get rid of it. Cut it off, and experience true power over temptation. Remember, **"You can not stand against your enemy until you remove it!"**

Question 6. Where are you right now with your level of understanding and commitment?

Course member Christian wrote, "Radical amputation seems obvious; I got rid of everything when I started this course. This lesson reminds me to take care and not to approach any source of sin. It is tempting to test yourself and see how strong you are against sin. It is a trick of the devil. I am not strong, I am weak. I am glad I have been 19 days free, but I am not proud of it. I am just doing what I always should have done."

Course member Marc wrote, "Yes! This was a great lesson. I am committed to purity. Purity is so wonderful, so clean, so pure, so healthy, so invigorating. It gives us strength to fight off death and the devil: uncleanness, pornography, smut, dirt, and nakedness. Jesus said to clothe the naked, not unclothe the clothed, right? So let's give thanks for purity - purity of mind, purity of heart, purity of body, purity of emotions, sexual purity."

Throw out your calf-idol, O Samaria! My anger burns against them. How long will they be incapable of purity? (Hosea 8:5)

Question 7. How are you doing? Did you learn anything new in this lesson today, and what will you put into practice?

Scripture to Consider

Blessed are the pure in heart, for they will see God (Matthew 5:8).

Were you free from pornography since you did the last lesson?

Yes   No

Were you free from self-gratification since you did the last lesson?

Yes   No

Were you free from sexual immorality since you did the last lesson?

Yes   No

DAY 20 - IDOLATRY

Friend, viewing pornography and gratifying the flesh is deceitful, self-pleasing, rebellious idolatry and heart adultery. At times in the history of the nation of Israel, they were given over to sins of the same nature. Let's read the following passage, and then answer the questions below:

> [9] These are rebellious people, deceitful children, children unwilling to listen to the LORD's instruction. [10] They say to the seers, "See no more visions!" and to the prophets, "Give us no more visions of what is right! Tell us pleasant things, prophesy illusions. [11] Leave this way, get off this path, and stop confronting us with the Holy One of Israel (Isaiah 30:9-11).

The above Scripture describes the life of one who habitually views pornography. It mentions 4 specific things about them:

1. They are rebellious people.
2. They are deceitful.
3. They are unwilling to listen to godly instruction.
4. They do not wish to be confronted about their sin.

I remember how rebellious my heart was during my 15 years of enslavement to pornography and sexual sin. I would read Scripture that taught me not to look lustfully at a woman, for to do so was committing adultery in my heart (Matthew 5:27-28) and yet I loved my sin, and willfully chose to rebel. I was deceitful, as I would pretend to others that I was some great Bible student, and zealous for Christ, when in reality I was hopelessly trapped in sin. I lied about being involved in pornography, deceived those who wanted to help me, and lived a life that was a total lie. Toward the end of those 15 years of sinful living, many Christians tried to reach me, but I would not listen. I stopped going to church because I did not want to hear "the Lord's instruction," and I avoided godly men and women. One time, a group of five Christians confronted me with my sin, and I was angry over their confrontation. See how my life was evidencing the truth of the above Scripture?

All who continue in pornography, self-gratification, and sexual impurity will find that their lives will come crashing down to the ground and be smashed to pieces. After my first wife left me and moved across the country, I ended up in a tiny hotel room, without family and without friends, nearly losing my job over my emotional distress and turmoil. Soon after I found myself in this situation, I needed to have major surgery. As I was lying on the hospital table waiting to be put to sleep, I secretly wished I would not awake. I was as hopeless as any man has ever been. I was "broken to pieces like pottery, and shattered mercilessly." (verse 14)

And now that The Way of Purity course has been around for several years, we have seen numerous stories of great devastation. Families split apart, jobs lost, pastors asked to resign, and criminals taken in to custody, etc. Possibly your life has come crashing down around you because of your sin. Or, maybe you are not at that stage yet, but are just "having fun" with pornography or immorality and have not experienced this "crash." Possibly you even have gone for several years with seemingly no, or minimal adverse side effects. But, like the giant tree that finally topples after years of internal decay, if you continue on in impurity, your life will fall to pieces, because God cannot be mocked.

Question 2. Please explain where you are with this teaching. Have you crashed yet?

Questions

Question 1. In the past, how has your life resembled these four truths? Which one described you best? Rebellious, deceitful, unwilling to listen, or not wanting to be confronted? Write out an explanation of your life here.

> [12] Therefore, this is what the Holy One of Israel says: "Because you have rejected this message, relied on oppression and depended on deceit, [13] this sin will become for you like a high wall, cracked and bulging, that collapses suddenly, in an instant. [14] It will break in pieces like pottery, shattered so mercilessly that among its pieces not a fragment will be found for taking coals from a hearth or scooping water out of a cistern (Isaiah 30:12-14).

> [15] This is what the Sovereign LORD, the Holy One of Israel, says: "In repentance and rest is your salvation, in quietness and trust is your strength, but you would have none of it.

> [16] You said, 'No, we will flee on horses.' Therefore you will flee! You said, 'We will ride off on swift horses.' Therefore your pursuers will be swift! [17] A thousand will flee at the threat of one; at the threat of five you will all flee away, till you are left like a flagstaff on a mountaintop, like a banner on a hill (Isaiah 30:15-17).

Two things caused by habitual sin are known as escapism and paranoia.

> Escapism is where a person knows he is guilty. His conscience troubles him, and he seeks to escape his trouble by running away. This escapism is described above as "fleeing away on swift horses" and shows the desire of these people to get away from it all.

> Paranoia is where a person exhibits irrational fear of people, places or things, and any of these may literally terrify them. When a person is in habitual sin, there is a fear of getting caught, and they always wonder if they've covered their tracks sufficiently. They can become paranoid that someone will find out, or that God will strike them dead.

Jodi wrote the following, as she describes what life was like while she was in open sin: "I became extremely paranoid during this period of time. I became a faithful seat belt wearer, because I was convinced that the Lord was going to take my life; that He wouldn't let me get by with this." This paranoia is described above as "a thousand will flee at the threat of one; at the threat of five you will all flee away."

Question 3. Have you ever experienced this type of escapism or paranoia?

you will rid your life of them: "Then (after God gives His grace) you will defile your idols….and images…you will throw them away like a menstrual cloth and say to them, 'Away with you!'" We can always tell when God is granting grace to someone, because they willingly rid their lives of their former idols, and it is not uncommon to hear them use strong language of hatred for their former idols such as "menstrual cloth."

Sexual impurity is idolatry: Put to death, therefore, whatever belongs to your earthly nature: sexual immorality, impurity, lust, evil desires and greed, which is idolatry (Colossians 3:5). When God grants us grace, we can't get rid of the idol fast enough!

Question 4. Time for personal reflection. Where are you in the above passage of Scripture? Are you yet rebellious, deceitful, unwilling to listen, and trying to avoid confrontation? Or are you crying out to God for grace? Are you ridding your life of idols and calling them names?

Yet the LORD longs to be gracious to you; he rises to show you compassion. For the LORD is a God of justice. Blessed are all who wait for him (Isaiah 30:18).

Friend, if you find yourself described in the above scenario, there is one thing that will fix it all: the grace of God! The solution to sin is the grace of God. And it is not as though God doesn't want to be gracious, for He "longs to be gracious to you." Another version of the above verse reads that God "waits to be gracious to you." The answer to a life reduced to rubble by the power of sin is the grace of God. It is not to turn to the psychologists and psychiatrists, for they cannot go to the root of the problem. It is not to learn behavior modification, for that does not reach the heart of the problem. Only God's grace changes the heart and goes to the root.

> ¹⁹ O people of Zion, who live in Jerusalem, you will weep no more. How gracious he will be when you cry for help! As soon as he hears, he will answer you. ²⁰ Although the Lord gives you the bread of adversity and the water of affliction, your teachers will be hidden no more; with your own eyes you will see them. ²¹ Whether you turn to the right or to the left, your ears will hear a voice behind you, saying, "This is the way; walk in it." ²² Then you will defile your idols overlaid with silver and your images covered with gold; you will throw them away like a menstrual cloth and say to them, "Away with you" (Isaiah 30:19-22).

The answer to a pornography addiction and immorality is to cry out to God for help. When He hears, He will be gracious to you and answer you. He will send you "teachers" to help you learn and grow, and His Holy Spirit will help you to walk in purity, and provide you direction in life.

And the result of God showing you His grace will be that you begin to detest pornography and all forms of sexual impurity, and

> "²³ He will also send you rain for the seed you sow in the ground, and the food that comes from the land will be rich and plentiful. In that day your cattle will graze in broad meadows. ²⁴ The oxen and donkeys that work the soil will eat fodder and mash, spread out with fork and shovel. ²⁵ In the day of great slaughter, when the towers fall, streams of water will flow on every high mountain and every lofty hill. ²⁶ The moon will shine like the sun, and the sunlight will be seven times brighter, like the light of seven full days, when the LORD binds up the bruises of his people and heals the wounds he inflicted (Isaiah 30:23-26).

When God gives His grace of forgiveness, He also restores fully. Sometimes sin causes such ruin that some relationships cannot be restored (divorce and remarriage), or victims brought back (murder) but, even so, God gives grace to endure these difficulties. God's restoration can even make things "better" than before. Notice the above passage "the moon will shine like the sun," the sunlight will be seven times brighter…when the Lord binds up the bruises of His people and heals the wounds he inflicted.

It has been many years since my sin was found out and my first wife left me, taking our two children with her. I eventually remarried. My wife, Jody, is a loving and God-fearing woman and is a great help to me. We have two sons and twin daughters, a wonderful church with good friends, and are active in ministry. Our ministry together is more effective than anything I have done before, and God is blessing our hearts and lives together with much grace. No, it is not the ideal situation to be divorced and remarried; yet God's grace is plentiful and has made our lives so much better than before. I have been free pornography and all forms of sexual impurity since January of 1999. I am content with Christ and my wife and our home of love. That's not bad for a man who did not want to awake from the operating table. Thank you, God, for the grace of forgiveness and restoration.

Question 5. How are you doing today?

Scripture to Consider

"How great is the love the Father has lavished on us, that we should be called children of God! And that is what we are! The reason the world does not know us is that it did not know him. 2 Dear friends, now we are children of God, and what we will be has not yet been made known. But we know that when he appears, we shall be like him, for we shall see him as he is. 3 Everyone who has this hope in him purifies himself, just as he is pure" (1 John 3:1-3).

Were you free from pornography since you did the last lesson?

    Yes   No

Were you free from self-gratification since you did the last lesson?

    Yes   No

Were you free from sexual immorality since you did the last lesson?

    Yes   No

The following testimony is from Paul:

When I was a young boy around 10, I became involved in the sin of pornography and gratifying the lust of the flesh. The problem got worse as I grew older. When I was 27, I became a Christian. I knew that what I had been involved in was wrong, and God gave me several years of freedom from habitual sin. I'm not sure when or how it happened, but I found myself dabbling in the same sins once again. I got married at 31, hoping that marriage would cure my problem, but it didn't. A couple of years later we got the Internet and it went downhill from there. I became completely enslaved to pornography and lust on the Internet. I asked God to deliver me over and over again. I was sorry for my sin, but what I thought was repentance was really only worldly sorrow, which eventually would have resulted in physical death. It had already resulted in spiritual death, and I was as dry spiritually as a man could be. I was faking a Christian life and I felt terrible. I was very angry inside because of my guilt before God, and it got so bad that I just gave up trying to change. I could not read my Bible or pray because of the grip sin had on me. I thought I would never get free from this bondage because I was in slavery to sin and in an unimaginable state of despair. Pornography is a cruel, ruthless taskmaster, and when my taskmaster said to go on the Internet, I obeyed. I did not have a choice. Over and over again, the pattern continued - until I found the Way of Purity Course, which taught me a few very important principles from God's word.

Recently in church on a communion Sunday, as I had done a thousand times before, I prayed to God for forgiveness and deliverance. I had always felt that God was going to take my life, especially after a communion service. I had been outwardly disobeying God, but His grace endured even while I was in sin. This particular Sunday, there was a short paragraph in the church bulletin recommending a website to help with my problem.

That night, I followed the advice and I went to the SCF site instead of searching the Internet for porn. I secretly signed up so my wife wouldn't find out what I was doing. At first, I did my lessons secretly in the darkness while she was sleeping, but my mentor told me about the need for me to confess to my pastor, or another trusted man, and also to my wife. This was a very difficult thing for me because I had a lot of pride. But I did it anyway, and I made an appointment with my pastor and told him everything. It was truly amazing what God did then. When we obey God's word, something wonderful happens. James 5 says to confess your sins, one to another. Doing so brings them into the light. 1 John 1:7 says, "But if we walk in the light as He Himself is in the light, we have fellowship with one another, and the blood of Jesus His Son cleanses us from all sin". It is remarkable what it was like to confess to another man. As I was leaving my pastor's office that day, he said to me, "Now go and stick another knife into Satan and tell your wife!"

The next day, after much prayer, I confessed to my wife. Her reaction initially was compassion on me. She was shocked and had no idea because I had been so good at my sinful deceit for 12 long years of marriage. But instead of condemning me, she cried with me, and her godly reaction broke my heart. I told her how sorry I was and pleaded with her for forgiveness. As I reflect back on that evening, I realize that God had given me a true godly sorrow over my sin, which led me to true repentance. She did forgive me, and now besides the Lord, she is my greatest help in staying pure. This was a major turning point in my battle for purity.

It has now been almost two years since I have been set free and restored by the Lord Jesus Christ, and my life and my family's lives are dramatically different. I read the Bible and pray every day, and my relationship with my wife is so much better. I see her in a new and wonderful light. God has given me a clean conscience, and for the first time in many, many years, I have NO SECRETS!

When I truly repented over my sin, God forgave me and restored my relationships. My wife and I have fallen in love all over again, and God has filled us with an indescribable joy! In all of this, we are praising God for His grace and mercy toward us, seeing that He truly does work all things together for good, to those who love God and are the called according to his purpose.

DAY 21 - STRENGTH THROUGH CONFESSION

This aspect to fighting pornography and immorality is very important: confession of sins. We'll examine this today, and you will discover that spiritual strength to overcome sin is directly tied to confession of sins. Read the following verses and answer the questions about this passage.

> [3] When I kept silent, my bones wasted away through my groaning all day long. [4] For day and night your hand was heavy upon me; my strength was sapped as in the heat of summer (Psalm 32:3-4).

Question 1. The above verses describe someone in a lethargic condition. His bones were "wasting away," and his strength was "sapped" as in the heat of summer, and God's hand was against him. What was the reason for his affliction?

Question 2. The context of this passage makes it clear that David was keeping silent about a sin he had committed. So what happens when people hide their sin? And do you now, or have you ever felt like the person above?

Note: Sin is debilitating, exhausting, and paralyzing. This "sapping of strength" keeps us powerless to fight the enemy, and ineffective in serving God. It is the opposite of "I can do all things through Christ who strengthens me," and it leaves us spent, tired, and emotionally drained. But there is a way out!

> Then I acknowledged my sin to you and did not cover up my iniquity. I said, 'I will confess my transgressions to the Lord—and you forgave the guilt of my sin.' Therefore let everyone who is godly pray to you while you may be found; surely when the mighty waters rise, they will not reach him. You are my hiding place; you will protect me from trouble and surround me with songs of deliverance (Psalm 32:3-7).

Notice that when David "kept silent" his bones wasted away and his strength was "sapped" as in the heat of summer. But we will see that there were four specific benefits when David "acknowledged" his sin and "did not cover up" his iniquity and "confessed" his transgressions to the Lord. They are:

1. **Forgiveness** (vs. 5). God "forgave the guilt of my sin." Before David "confessed his sin" God did not forgive him; indeed God's hand was "heavy upon him."
2. **Discovering God** (vs. 6). "Let everyone who is godly pray to you while you may be found." This verse teaches that the only way to "find God" is through forgiveness of sins. And forgiveness of sins comes only through acknowledgment and confession of sin.
3. **Spiritual Strength** (vs. 6). "...surely when the mighty waters rise, they will not reach him." You know what this is like: at times, sin comes rushing in like a flood. It overwhelms us and we sink. But notice that confession of sin is immediately followed by this promise of victory. In owning up to our sins we will find that God will protect us from being overcome by the floods of sin.
4. **Spiritual Protection** (vs. 7). "You are my hiding place; you will protect me from trouble and surround me with songs of deliverance."

So, to summarize: hiding our sins (we actually cannot hide them from God, He knows) and refusing to confess them brings about spiritual sickness, loss of strength against further sin attacks, and the anger of God. Confession of sin brings forgiveness, knowing God, spiritual strength and protection. "He who conceals his sins does not prosper, but whoever confesses and renounces them finds mercy" (Proverbs 28:13).

Dear Friend,

Even though this may be difficult, it is important that you make a full confession and disclosure of your sins. This must first be to God, as all sins are against God. But it also must be to the person, or people whom you have sinned against. If you are married and have been viewing pornography, you have been sinning against your spouse. Adultery, of course, is also sinning against the spouse. Both need to be confessed before you can expect real and lasting victory. However, while confessing it to God must be total, complete and immediate, confessing it to others requires wisdom and discernment as to timing and detail. If you are now contemplating making a confession to someone, you might be apprehensive. Most times confession is not an easy thing to do. I understand. If you have felt the consequences of hiding sin, and now see the value of fully confessing, but are just a bit scared and need someone to talk to, please speak to your mentor and ask for help. We want your victory in the Lord, and we pray for it. Confession is a necessary part of that victory. Don't put it off. Next, we will look at how confession brings strength and victory.

> [2] It was a long time, twenty years in all, that the ark remained at Kiriath Jearim, and all the people of Israel mourned and sought after the LORD. [3] And Samuel said to the whole house of Israel, 'If you are returning to the LORD with all your hearts, then rid yourselves of the foreign gods and the Ashtoreths and commit yourselves to the LORD and serve him only, and he will deliver you out of the hand of the Philistines.' [4] So the Israelites put away their Baals and Ashtoreths, and served the LORD only.
>
> [5] Then Samuel said, 'Assemble all Israel at Mizpah and I will intercede with the LORD for you.' [6] When they had assembled

at Mizpah, they drew water and poured it out before the LORD. On that day they fasted and there they confessed, 'We have sinned against the LORD.' And Samuel was leader of Israel at Mizpah.

"⁷ When the Philistines heard that Israel had assembled at Mizpah, the rulers of the Philistines came up to attack them. And when the Israelites heard of it, they were afraid because of the Philistines. ⁸ They said to Samuel, 'Do not stop crying out to the LORD our God for us, that he may rescue us from the hand of the Philistines.' ⁹ Then Samuel took a suckling lamb and offered it up as a whole burnt offering to the LORD. He cried out to the LORD on Israel's behalf, and the LORD answered him.

"¹⁰ While Samuel was sacrificing the burnt offering, the Philistines drew near to engage Israel in battle. But that day the LORD thundered with loud thunder against the Philistines and threw them into such a panic that they were routed before the Israelites. ¹¹ The men of Israel rushed out of Mizpah and pursued the Philistines, slaughtering them along the way to a point below Beth Car" (1 Samuel 7:2-11).

Question 3. We want to discover how the Israelites were victorious over their enemies from this passage. The Israelites employed several of the teachings we have been studying through this course in the past few days. Can you find and name them? Write your findings in the space below.

Question 4. Write out what the Israelites said in verse 6 above:

Notice how "radical amputation" in verses 3 and 4 is followed by "confession" in verses 5 and 6, and "victory" in verse 11. Now, let us note the keys to victory. Write them next to each verse. We will do the first one for you.

Question 5. 1 Samuel 7:2-First key: Seek the Lord

Question 6. 1 Samuel 7:3,4-Second key:

Question 7. 1 Samuel 7:5-Third key:

Question 8. 1 Samuel 7:6-Fourth key:

The following testimony is from Dennis:

I was introduced to pornography at an early age. I'm not sure how old I was, but it was in my early teen years, probably around the age of thirteen. I discovered a pornography magazine that was hidden, so I began my journey down the long dark road of pornography. I was a fish in the water and the worm was the pornography magazine. I bit into the bait of the devil and the hook was set in me. Through many, many years to follow I tried to get free of my addiction to this sexual sin with no luck.

After graduation from school, my pornography hunger grew, and I was soon into self-gratification, as well. I wasn't aware, but the devil was slowly moving me deeper into this sexual bondage and slowly tightening his grip on me. I lived in sin with a girl and got to experience things only married couples should. Even though we were having intimate relations, I still felt deep down inside a thirst for pornography and self-gratification. We lived together two years and then were married. A couple years later, we were having marriage problems, and I was still into pornography and self-gratification. After six years my marriage ended. I was saved in 1983, the same year my marriage ended.

I was now alone again, and I slid still deeper into pornography and self-gratification as the devil continued to tighten his grip on me. My addiction became worse after becoming a child of God. I served God in bus ministries and as a Sunday school teacher for many years.

I met a very godly woman who was much younger than I, and we were married. My loneliness of fourteen years ended, but my addiction to sexual sins still remained. I fought off and on throughout the years, trying to get free of the addiction to pornography and self-gratification, but never had any lasting success. The hook the devil put in me still remained.

We started having marriage problems, and my wife wasn't fulfilling my sexual needs. I know now looking back that I wasn't fulfilling her needs, either. I was searching online at different Christian websites for information that would help to enhance our sex life, and my pride wouldn't let me admit that most of the problems with needs not being met were a direct result of my ongoing addiction to sexual sins. My attitude was bad and my anger problem increased. I wasn't a happy or pleasant person to be near, and I wasn't happy with my actions or life, either.

I was really disgusted one day and went online searching Christian websites again for help, and I found a Christian forum where I read a letter of a wife who was struggling with her husband's addiction to pornography and self-gratification. The reply to her letter was from a gentleman who typed in the Setting Captives Free website. It had to be God who led me there, and I felt I needed to check it out. Two days later, I signed up, not really thinking this would work because of all my past attempted failures.

But praise God, I was FOCUSED and had my mind made up that I wanted to be set free once and for all. I asked God and pleaded with him, and He broke me and then he healed and restored me. And now I have been totally and completely set free by the grace and power of God, and it has been 262 days. During The Way of Purity course, God removed the sexual desires and lust from my heart and replaced it with a holy anger to help destroy the grips of pornography and other sexual sins of others. I feel God wants me to take the mentorship course to mentor others and help them to cut the head off the giant of sexual sin, and to be able to experience true freedom that only comes from Jesus Christ.

After nearly forty years of trying to stop my addiction to pornography and self-gratification on my own, God gave me the instrument and, through His saving grace and power, delivered me completely.

Question 9. Where are you in the above scenario? Have you radically amputated? Or are you rationalizing and excusing? Have you made all necessary confessions (or at least planning to as the Lord opens doors for you)? If you have done these things, please share the victories the Lord is giving you.

Finally, note this very well-worded and impassioned commitment to confession:

"I have been reflecting on God's wonderful grace and the sin from which He has lovingly delivered me. I had tried so many times to stop myself from my sin, and I thought I had failed too many times and God had given me up to my lusts.

'If we confess our sins, he is faithful and just to forgive us our sins, and to cleanse us from all unrighteousness.' I desperately hoped I would never have to confess this sin, except to God Himself. But that is pride. I was not broken enough, not contrite enough, not desirous of Him enough to confess my sin to others. And it defeated me. My unwillingness to do everything, to completely submit, undid me.

"I now want God and His forgiveness, His love, His grace and His mercy more than anything else. I know now that I can't hide. I need Him. I am willing to do anything and everything to secure my portion of Him. I will risk all and forsake all that I previously held too dear to endanger by my confession.

"God gave Himself for me. I am nothing, but I willingly give myself to Him. Not in return for what He did, because that would be futile and ridiculous. I can't ever repay or compensate Him. Just because He loves me and paid the price for me, I am His without reservation or condition."

Friends, words are not enough, for "the kingdom of God is not a matter of talk but of power" (for action)—1 Corinthians 4:20. Unfortunately, the man who wrote that beautifully articulated letter above failed to confess his sin to his wife as he knew he should, and has now returned to the slavery of pornography "as a dog returns to it's vomit" (2 Peter 2:22). Please pray that God would genuinely recover him and grant him true repentance.

Jim wrote: "Hiding sin eats you alive. I have felt like this, but I do not now because I am confessing sin to others. But I remember all too well the bearing sin in silence, not so much because I wasn't confessing it before God, which is the context here, but because I was afraid to confess it to others. The Christian circles I grew up in didn't lend themselves to admitting sin to each other. We know we're sinners, God knows we're sinners, but we have a hard time admitting to one another that we're sinners."

Jim wrote: "This guy (in Psalm 32) had not confessed his sins, and God's hand was against him. That is a horrible place to be. Sometimes in the past, after giving in to lust, I was a wreck the next day. I would feel weak, tired, sick, probably more spiritually than physically. Which is worse? I would rather be sick physically than spiritually. I am familiar with confession, all too well. Today I experienced the refreshment that comes after confession. Although I wish I didn't have to."

"Beside that, dear friends, although we have confessed to ignorance, in many sins we did not know a great deal. Come, let me quicken your memories. There were times when you knew that such an action was wrong, when you started back from it. You looked at the gain it would bring you, and you sold your soul for that price and deliberately did what you were well aware was wrong. Are there not some here, saved by Christ, who must confess that, at times, they did violence to their conscience? They did despite to the Spirit of God, quenched the light of heaven, drove the Spirit away from them, distinctly knowing what they were doing. Let us bow before God in the silence of our hearts and own to all of this. We hear the Master say, Father, forgive them; for they know not what they do. Let us add our own tears as we say, And forgive us, also, because in some things we did know;" (Charles Spurgeon: Jesus The Pleading Savior_).

Scripture to Consider

"When anyone is guilty in any of these ways, he must confess in what way he has sinned…" (Leviticus 5:5).

Were you free from pornography since you did the last lesson?

    Yes   No

Were you free from self-gratification since you did the last lesson?

    Yes   No

Were you free from sexual immorality since you did the last lesson?

    Yes   No

DAY 22 - VIGILANCE

Today we will discuss vigilance, but first we will see what can happen if we neglect to be vigilant. Please note the following correspondence received from a student:

"I am returning to these lessons. I stopped taking the course because I believed the lie that I was completely delivered and totally healed from the sin. After completing 21 days of this course I stopped, because I thought I was free. I should have learned to stay vigilant, because I plummeted right back into pornography, worse than ever, for approximately two weeks. Now, I am making a fresh commitment to the Lord and to this course."

This is just one of numerous emails we receive from students who stop the course before completion. Today we will teach on a subject Scripture speaks much about: the necessity to be vigilant against sin creeping back in to our lives after a period of victory. Let's notice several passages:

> "⁷Do not be idolaters, as some of them were; as it is written: "The people sat down to eat and drink and got up to indulge in pagan revelry." ⁸We should not commit sexual immorality, as some of them did–and in one day twenty-three thousand of them died. ⁹We should not test the Lord, as some of them did–and were killed by snakes. ¹⁰And do not grumble, as some of them did–and were killed by the destroying angel. ¹¹These things happened to them as examples and were written down as warnings for us, on whom the fulfillment of the ages has come. ¹²So, if you think you are standing firm, be careful that you don't fall! (1 Corinthians 10:7-12)

This passage traces the history of the people of Israel after they had been released from their slavery in Egypt. They had come to the desert, where they were involved in the idolatry of sexual immorality. God's wrath broke out against them, and He killed 23,000 of them by snakes. The Apostle Paul tells us that the experiences of the nation of Israel were given as examples and warnings for us. What are we to learn from the experience recorded above? To be vigilant! "So, if you think you are standing firm, be careful that you don't fall."

Question 1. Can you think of a time when you thought you had mastered sin, and were "standing" only to fall?

We have seen course members begin walking in victory over their past sins, and truly be overcomers for many days in a row. Then we may notice some pride creeping in and their answers and emails become quite instructive as if they were becoming an authority. When this happens, it isn't long before they fall, and we often never see these people again. Their fall came because of pride, and pride keeps them in their fallen condition. There is much caution needed, especially when we begin to experience victory.

> ⁴⁰Then he returned to his disciples and found them sleeping. "Could you men not keep watch with me for one hour?" he asked Peter. ⁴¹"Watch and pray so that you will not fall into temptation. The spirit is willing, but the body is weak (Matthew 26:40-41).

The above verses describe the scenario leading up to Judas' betrayal of Jesus. Jesus knew He would be betrayed, and knew He needed strength from above to endure the coming events, so He was seeking His Father in prayer. And it is right here that Jesus instructs His disciples, and us, on how not to fall: "Watch and pray so that you will not fall into temptation." Be vigilant. Watch against a developing chain of events that lead to a fall into sin, and remove a link in the chain. Watch for familiar areas in which you are tempted; watch for the uprising of the flesh; watch out for times you are tired; watch out following a high spiritual experience; WATCH. But don't watch only. Watch and pray. Pray that God will keep you from falling. Pray that He would give you grace to endure temptation without giving in. Pray for power from above to extinguish the fiery darts of the devil.

Question 2. What are some specific areas of temptation in which you need to be watchful and in prayer?

Friend, no matter how many victories we have had, or how long we have been walking in freedom, we always have a need to be vigilant. The reason for this is because "the flesh is weak." The flesh is always weak, no matter how long we've been pure or how strong we are in faith. There is no saint alive who does not have weak flesh, hence the need to watch and pray against falling. Many a Christian has fallen to the lies of the devil late in life, and we must pray to guard against this.

> "⁸Be self-controlled and alert. Your enemy the devil prowls around like a roaring lion looking for someone to devour. ⁹Resist him, standing firm in the faith, because you know that your brothers throughout the world are undergoing the same kind of sufferings (1 Peter 5:8-9).

The above passage instructs us to "be self-controlled and alert" which is translated in the KJV as "be vigilant." We not only must be vigilant because our flesh is weak, but also because our enemy is strong – like a lion. He prowls around looking to devour us. Should he find us not watching and not praying, we are easy prey.

Question 3. Are you aware of the strength of your enemy? What experiences have you with the enemy where you've felt his strength?

Christian, the main character in Pilgrim's Progress, is assaulted by numerous enemies and, in time, comes to watch for them and pray against them. He writes this poem based upon his experiences of surprise attacks from his enemies:

> **"The trials that those men do meet withal,**
> **That are obedient to the heavenly call,**
> **Are manifold, and suited to the flesh,**
> **And come, and come, and come again afresh;**
> **That now, or some time else, we by them may**
> **Be taken, overcome, and cast away.**
> **O let the pilgrims, let the pilgrims then,**
> **Be vigilant, and quit themselves like men."**

Notice that the purposes of the trials, temptations, and assaults of the enemy are that we might be "taken, overcome, and cast away." This is what our prowling enemy seeks to do to us - cast us away from the faith. We must be watchful unto prayer, being ever vigilant.

> ⁵ You are all sons of the light and sons of the day. We do not belong to the night or to the darkness. ⁶ So then, let us not be like others, who are asleep, but let us be alert and self-controlled. ⁷ For those who sleep, sleep at night, and those who get drunk, get drunk at night. ⁸ But since we belong to the day, let us be self-controlled, putting on faith and love as a breastplate, and the hope of salvation as a helmet (1 Thessalonians 5:5-8).

In the above passage, we are admonished not to "sleep," which obviously does not refer to refusing the nightly rest that the body needs, but rather to being vigilant against temptation. The disciples in the garden were sleeping when they should have been watching and praying. Likewise, we sleep when we go about our day ignorant of the power of our enemy, and ignorant of the weakness of our flesh, which work together to cast us down and destroy our faith and make us reprobates.

Question 4. Please state what circumstances in the future may cause you to "sleep" when you should be watching and praying.

Course member Mike wrote, "I tend to 'sleep' spiritually when I am sleepy physically. I'm just not alert enough to watch and pray, and often fall into sin when I'm tired. This lesson helped me to know I need to go to bed at a decent hour and get enough sleep so as to not 'sleep' spiritually, and be overtaken by sin. Thank you!"

Finally, notice these words of Jesus that illustrate the need to be vigilant and not sleep:
³² "But concerning that day or that hour, no one knows, not even the angels in heaven, nor the Son, but only the Father.
³³ Be on guard, keep awake. For you do not know when the time will come.
³⁴ It is like a man going on a journey, when he leaves home and puts his servants in charge, each with his work, and commands the doorkeeper to stay awake.
³⁵ Therefore stay awake—for you do not know when the master of the house will come, in the evening, or at midnight, or when the cock crows, or in the morning—
³⁶ lest he come suddenly and find you asleep.
³⁷ And what I say to you I say to all: Stay awake (Mark 13:32-37 ESV).

Question 5. How does this parable illustrate the truth in today's lesson? Write your thoughts here.

Jesus Christ declared that He whom the Son sets free will be free indeed (John 8:36). And part of His work of making us free is to help us be vigilant. May we not be like those who walk many years in victory, only to fall through lack of vigilance. Watch and pray. Here are some specific ways you may do this:

1. Make sure to attend a Bible Believing church (Hebrews 10:25). The importance of this cannot be overemphasized.
2. Have daily accountability (Ecclesiastes 4:9-12; Hebrews 3:13).
3. Seek the Lord daily (Proverb 2:1-5; Hebrews 11:6).
4. Drag every known sin, and even temptation, into the light. If you struggle with something, humble yourself and talk to someone about it (John 3:19-21).

Question 6. What are some other things you might do to be vigilant against sin? Write them here.

Question 7. Record here an experience of victory when you have remained vigilant in the night time hours.

I was saved at an early age, and I have been struggling with pornography since I was fourteen, which was approximately since the time the Internet first came into widespread use. I tried to quit under my own power and failed hundreds of times. Many times I would resolve not to look and then go look and afterward wonder if God had forsaken me. But He never let me go. He brought people into my life who had had the same struggles, and gradually drew me into relationships with some accountability, but still I continued to fall.

Then one night in frustration, fear, and despair, I typed "pornography addiction" into Google, and God led me to this course. I took it once, and was pornography free for over 100 days. I was overjoyed, but I became overconfident, made opportunity for the flesh, and stopped my accountability. This was a BIG mistake, and I soon fell again, worse than before. But God STILL did not give up on me, and after a year in the desert, brought me back to this course, and gave me ongoing radical amputation and accountability that I have never experienced before. I would not have believed it possible; it has been 59 days of purity. The credit and glory belong to God. The joy of the Lord is incomparably better than the temporary, destructive pleasures of pornography, and I thank him for his grace and unlimited forgiveness.

Scripture to Consider

"³ I will set before my eyes no vile thing (Psalm 101:3).

"¹³ Therefore, prepare your minds for action; be self-controlled; set your hope fully on the grace to be given you when Jesus Christ is revealed (1 Peter 1:13).

³⁴ You will be like one sleeping on the high seas, lying on top of the rigging.³⁵ "They hit me," you will say, "but I'm not hurt! They beat me, but I don't feel it! When will I wake up so I can find another drink? (Proverbs 23: 34-35).

But you, brothers, are not in darkness so that this day should surprise you like a thief. ⁵ You are all sons of the light and sons of the day. We do not belong to the night or to the darkness. ⁶ So then, let us not be like others, who are asleep, but let us be alert and self-controlled. ⁷ For those who sleep, sleep at night, and those who get drunk, get drunk at night. ⁸ But since we belong to the day, let us be self-controlled, putting on faith and love as a breastplate, and the hope of salvation as a helmet. ⁹ For God did not appoint us to suffer wrath but to receive salvation through our Lord Jesus Christ (1 Thessalonians 5:4-9).

Were you free from pornography since you did the last lesson?

    Yes   No

Were you free from self-gratification since you did the last lesson?

    Yes   No

Were you free from sexual immorality since you did the last lesson?

    Yes   No

DAY 23 - ENJOYING THE LIGHT

Earlier in this course, we briefly touched on a subject we would like to dwell on more thoroughly at this point. When I was enslaved to pornography and immorality, I had a secret and hidden sin. There was an area of my life that nobody knew about, that was off-limits even to my wife, and that was protected carefully so as not to be exposed. Sin thrives in hidden areas because the darkness conceals the deeds done.

> *Course member Jeff wrote,* "I can remember closing all the doors, pulling down the shades on the windows, drawing the curtains, turning off all lights in the house, and then, only after everything was dark, did I sit down at the computer for my time of sinning in pornography and self-gratification." Like some mutant, cancerous rat, sin loves to hide in the darkness.

You see, part of gaining the victory over sin is to drag this secret life into the light, and expose it. This is always a scary prospect, but in this lesson I hope to give you helps to exposing the sin in the least painful way, and to assure you that God is always with the one who will begin this task. Please examine the following Scripture and answer the questions below…

> The night is nearly over; the day is almost here. So let us put aside the deeds of darkness and put on the armor of light. [13] Let us behave decently, as in the daytime, not in orgies and drunkenness, not in sexual immorality and debauchery, not in dissension and jealousy. [14] Rather, clothe yourselves with the Lord Jesus Christ, and do not think about how to gratify the desires of the sinful nature (Romans 13:12-14).

Questions

Question 1. What are the "deeds of darkness" listed in verse 13 above? Write them here.

Question 2. What are the "deeds of darkness" that you have been doing in the past?

Question 3. What are we instructed to do with these deeds of darkness?

Question 4. Getting specific now, in what exact way can you "lay aside" those deeds of darkness?

Question 5. With what is light compared?
  A. Heat
  B. Armor

Friend, the above verses tell us that the light is armor, and armor protects a soldier from the attacks of the enemy. This is an important understanding to have: light, in the spiritual realm, is armor. The enemy always shoots at us in the darkness and, if we expose our sin to the light, we have protection from his assaults. I can tell you, based on the authority of Scripture, if you will expose your sin to the light, you will have protection from ongoing attacks of the devil.

After we "lay aside" the deeds of darkness, we are to clothe ourselves with the Lord Jesus Christ. We are to put Him on, to wear Him as our protection against the enemy, and to find our life in Him. I remember that after I came to my pastor and exposed my sin to the light, not only did I have the protection that the light offers, but I also began to find my life in Christ. I loved studying God's Word, singing songs to Jesus in private, praying often and long, going to church to receive God's Word and fellowship with other believers, etc. Though I didn't know it at the time, I was learning to do that which these verses speak: lay aside the deeds of darkness, and clothe yourself with Jesus Christ.

Question 6. How will you specifically begin clothing yourself with Jesus Christ?

The above verse tells us to lay aside things done in darkness, and to clothe ourselves with the Light of Jesus Christ. Part of our clothing ourselves in Jesus is coming into the light, and exposing our sins.

We can't emphasize enough that, though it may be frightening to come into the light, the results will be immediate purity. A fungus exposed to the light is sapped of its strength and eventually withers away and dies. Sin exposed to the light loses all its power, and eventually is no more. So despite the initial difficulty of doing this, it is well worth the trouble. It will, indeed, provide freedom.

Let's read additional verses on this subject.

> When this became known to the Jews and Greeks living in Ephesus, they were all seized with fear, and the name of the Lord Jesus was held in high honor. [18] Many of those who believed now came and openly confessed their evil deeds. [19] A number who had practiced sorcery brought their scrolls together and burned them publicly. When they calculated the value of the scrolls, the total came to fifty thousand drachmas. [20] In this way the word of the Lord spread widely and grew in power (Acts 19:17-20).

The verses that precede this passage show the healing power of Jesus as He cast out unclean spirits. It is when this power of God was displayed that people were seized with fear and were in awe of Jesus' Name.

Question 7. Verses 18 and 19 show that those who were now reverencing the Name of Christ did two specific things. What two things did they do?

First, notice that they **"openly confessed their evil deeds."** They dragged their sin into the light, exposed and confessed it. Friends, let us be clear about this: there will be no true victory over pornography and sexual sin without an "open confession." I know it's scary; I've been there, remember? I had a good reputation and a good standing in the community, a lovely family, and a good job. I had much to lose. But I became so scared that my sins were dragging me into hell, I finally had to confess. First I confessed to my wife, then to my pastor, then a general apology to my children, then to my accountability partners at church and, finally, on this website. I'm in the light now, aren't I?

Question 8. As you know, and as we have been discussing for the past several weeks, the Bible does make confession of sin an imperative requirement to finding freedom. We truly desire to see you free from habitual sin and the trap of the devil and, because of this desire, we are requesting at this point that if there is yet any unconfessed sin, you deal with it immediately so that you might be free. Setting Captives Free has had thousands of people go through this course, and we do not know of a single person who has found genuine and lasting freedom from pornography and/or sexual impurity apart from full confession of sin to the people who were wronged. At this point, we strongly encourage you to confess all known sin before continuing on with the course. This is for your benefit, as we do not wish to see you have a fall in the future because of harboring unconfessed sin.

Second, notice that these people did not stop at public confession, they also **"radically amputated"** those things which had caused them to sin. They burned their scrolls publicly. Let me share with you that only confessing your sin will not be enough to keep you from sinning in the future. There must be a cutting off, a plucking out, a burning, and a total destruction of that which trips us up. This needs to be done with a vengeance, or "with attitude" as we are destroying that which would have destroyed us.

Question 9. Have you "burned" (or somehow destroyed) every trace of every ounce of sinful material that has caused you to sin in the past? If not, now is the time, and today is the day. Have you cut off all illicit relationships? Please write down here if you have radically amputated anything that causes you to sin.

Now let us get some additional "light" on this subject:

> This is the verdict: Light has come into the world, but men loved darkness instead of light because their deeds were evil. [20] Everyone who does evil hates the light, and will not come into the light for fear that his deeds will be exposed. [21] But whoever lives by the truth comes into the light, so that it may be seen plainly that what he has done has been done through God (John 3:19-21).

Friend, are you aware of the extreme importance of the teaching we are considering? The above verses tell us that all who do evil hate the light, and will not come into the light for fear that their deeds will be exposed, while those who live by the truth will come into the light. Which are you?

And finally, notice something else that exposing sin does: The visions of your prophets were false and worthless; they did not expose your sin to ward off your captivity. The oracles they gave you were false and misleading (Lamentations 2:14).

Question 10. What does the above verse state would have happened if these false prophets had exposed the sin of the people?

That's right! Exposing the sin would have warded off captivity. Let us be really clear on this: leaving sin covered by refusing to expose it leads to captivity. We become captives to the power of sin while it is hidden and kept secret. But if we expose it, we ward off captivity and live as free men and women!

I can't tell you the relief I feel now that I am no longer sneaking around, trying to hide my sin, always looking over my shoulder to see if I would be caught. Confession and amputation (with accountability) will produce complete and total freedom from pornography and sexual sin forever.

> For whatever is hidden is meant to be disclosed, and whatever is concealed is meant to be brought out into the open (Mark 4:22).

Friend, do you need help doing what you need to do? Speak to your mentor and pray together about your situation. They may offer suggestions and counsel as to how to proceed. But, please do not lose the value of the teaching in the Scriptures today, by continuing to hide and sin in the dark. Begin coming into the light. Confess openly, and amputate radically, and by God's grace you will be free!

The following testimony is from Keith:

I came to Setting Captives Free at the recommendation of the Christian counselor I had been seeing for depression.

I had been deeply oppressed by depression, to the point that I had started to slide into pornography as a way to "medicate" myself. The pornography began to escalate the depression, and cause even greater internal turmoil.

My emotions were stormier than ever before, my marriage and attitude towards life were suffering and I was beginning to be plagued by thoughts of suicide. I began to work through the Way of Purity course, as well as continuing with biblical counseling. God used the two together in a mighty way for me, not only helping me get free from pornography, but also in conquering the depression.

I worked with my counselor to uncover the lies and satanic strongholds that had infested my life. Meanwhile, I was getting a strong dose of truth and encouragement from the Way of Purity course.

I rediscovered the meaning of Gods grace, and the power that it has to transform lives. I rediscovered the amazing intensity of the love of Christ for me. I began to feel it again in a way that I had not experienced in several years. I began to believe again that God cared enough for me to take care of my emotional emptiness, and sustain me in the battle for my heart and mind. My experience of God's presence grew and intensified.

As I spent more time reading the Bible and pouring out my soul in prayer, God met me where I was; he forgave my sins and began to heal the wounds they had caused. He taught me how to fight back against the fear and anxiety that were the main weapons of the devil to keep me under the weight of depression.

And now, even in the middle of a very trying time in my life, I have greater peace than I have had in years. I have been free from sexual sin for over two months. The Way of Purity course was used by God to bring healing into my life. God brought it into my life at just the right time. I am grateful for the course, and for Setting Captives Free. And finally, I am grateful to God for pulling me back from the edge of destruction. I could have killed myself if it hadn't been for His grace reaching out to me to rescue me.

Course member John wrote, "I just wanted to tell you of some radical amputation. The other night I sat down with my wife and confessed my sin to her. She was incredibly gracious and she has promised to help me overcome my struggle with pornography. I have agreed with her that I will not look at the Internet unless she is around, and she is going to hold me accountable to that and to my continuing with the Setting Captives Free - The Way of Purity course. I have tried all these things before, but the difference is that I always tried to do them while hiding them from my wife. My sin was still in the darkness, at least in my own home where the rubber meets the road. Thank you for all your prayers and for encouraging me to bring my sin into the light."

Course member Tom wrote, "I am all done with hiding! I have pulled my sin out from the cellar of my life and am turning high-intensity aircraft lights on it. Yes, I can see that my addiction has lost its strength now, and purity and freedom are now mine. Praise God!"

Some people are downright scared when thinking of having to confess to a spouse or others. If you feel this way, I encourage you to read through the following testimony from Ryan:

"I grew up in a wonderful, God-fearing home, being taught about God by my parents and through the church. I can't imagine a better way to be raised.

"I can hardly remember the first time I was exposed to pornography. I was barely in my teens, and was at a friend's house whose dad had some magazines in the bathroom. I'm sure it was just a curiosity at first. It created an excitement yet, at the same time, I must have known it was wrong, because I felt like there was something to hide. I wasn't about to tell anyone what I had looked at.

"I can't remember how long it was before the next time I was exposed to pornography, but I do know that I eventually found myself seeking it out through my high school years and off and on for the next twenty-five years. There were times that it was totally consuming. It was a way to escape into a fantasyland that I had created, but it always ended the same way. Guilt! Even with the guilt, and crying out to God for help and strength, I found myself back in the same place. I would try to justify it, thinking that there must be a chemical or hormone released in my mind that makes it natural to react this way. Yet I knew it was wrong.

"I once heard a well-known Christian speaker address the issue and confirmed that the lusting was wrong, but that self-gratification wasn't. As long as you could control your thoughts you were fine. Who can do that?

"Over the years I found myself buying magazines, but only in areas where I didn't know anybody. With the Internet, I would find myself sitting at the computer for hours looking for something more exciting and pushing the limits even further. I thought by getting married I would be able to move beyond this struggle and finally be free. Yet I found myself in the same battle and, as always, covered with shame and guilt. I had read books and pamphlets about being free from this addiction, but I never succeeded.

"Out of desperation, I did a search on the web and found Setting Captives Free. Why not, I thought. It started out great for a few days, and then there was talk about confessing to your spouse and having someone hold you accountable. I had never done this. No one had ever known my secret, and it scared me to the point of almost not continuing the course. I decided that I would keep going with the course until I got to that day, and then reevaluate. But before that day came, I had an opportunity to share with my wife, and she was much more supportive than I had ever thought possible. There was new hope, and a feeling that God had just broken the chains that had bound me for so many years.

"The temptations continued, but by God's grace, victories continued also. By removing the vehicles of temptation, there are fewer battles to be fought. As time keeps passing, my mind keeps purging the imagery I had fed it for so many years. The temptations are few and far between now, but I still need to keep my guard up and flee from temptation. I will always need to fill my mind with the Living Water and enjoy my new freedom that Christ has given me."

Question 11. Have you accepted the challenge to bring your sins into the light? Use this space to record what happened.

Scripture to Consider

[17] So there is hope for your future," declares the LORD. "Your children will return to their own land (Jeremiah 31:17).

The visions of your prophets were false and worthless; they did not expose your sin to ward off your captivity. The oracles they gave you were false and misleading (Lamentations 2:14).

Were you free from pornography since you did the last lesson?

    Yes   No

Were you free from self-gratification since you did the last lesson?

    Yes   No

Were you free from sexual immorality since you did the last lesson?

    Yes   No

DAY 24–FLEEING TEMPTATION

Friend, today we will see a biblical story of victory! We will examine this story closely to see how the victory was won, and how we may apply these truths to our own lives. Are you starting to enjoy victory over this deadly spiritual disease called pornography and immorality? Me too! Please read the following story and answer the questions that follow.

> vs. 6—Now Joseph was well-built and handsome, vs. 7—and after awhile His master's wife took notice of Joseph and said, "Come to bed with me!" vs. 8—But he refused. "With me in charge," he told her, "my master does not concern himself with anything in the house; everything he owns he has entrusted to my care. vs. 9—No one is greater in this house than I am. My master has withheld nothing from me except you, because you are his wife. How then could I do such a wicked thing and sin against God?" vs.10—And though she spoke to Joseph day after day, he refused to go to bed with her or even be with her. vs. 11—One day he went into the house to attend to his duties, and none of the household servants was inside. vs. 12—She caught him by his cloak and said, "Come to bed with me!" But he left his cloak in her hand and ran out of the house (Genesis 39:6-12).

Question 1. What did Joseph say to his master's wife when she wanted to sleep with him?

A. "Well, nobody will see, so I guess so."

B. "No way"

C. "I'll think about it"

Question 2. Who Joseph was thinking when he said "No?" (Vs. 9)

A. Her husband catching them

B. Himself

C. God

Question 3. Please write your thoughts about this story. Why did Joseph "win?" How did he win? How will you apply this to your own situation?

Being tempted in this way is very difficult to handle (as you no doubt know)! But Joseph was focused. Did you notice his focus according to verse 9? It was God. To Joseph, God was very real, and he was "aware" of God always being with him. Keep in close contact with God; you will find strength against temptation, and saying "No" will be a lot easier. Next time you are tempted, act as if Jesus is right there with you. He really is! Focus on Him. Enjoy His presence, and you will run from sin!

Now, let us notice something important from this story: sin keeps coming after us. Notice that Joseph's master's wife kept after him. She kept pressing him, kept tempting him. She "spoke to Joseph day after day." Possibly you've experienced the same thing with pornography. The images come at you, and maybe you are able to pass them off once or twice. But they keep coming back, don't they? You may send them away, but soon like Potiphar's wife, they are begging and pleading with you and tempting you again. Or perhaps you have someone in your life who continues to tempt you to sin. Maybe it is a lust-filled relationship, or someone to whom you've become emotionally dependent. Perhaps you have even broken off the relationship, but they won't respect your wishes and keep coming after you as Potiphar's wife did Joseph.

To illustrate the truth that sin keeps pressing us, please read Samson's experience in Judges 16: 4-18:

> ⁴Some time later, he fell in love with a woman in the Valley of Sorek whose name was Delilah. ⁵ The rulers of the Philistines went to her and said, "See if you can lure him into showing you the secret of his great strength and how we can overpower him so we may tie him up and subdue him. Each one of us will give you eleven hundred shekels of silver."

> ⁶So Delilah said to Samson, "Tell me the secret of your great strength and how you can be tied up and subdued."

> ⁷Samson answered her, "If anyone ties me with seven fresh thongs that have not been dried, I'll become as weak as any other man."

> ⁸Then the rulers of the Philistines brought her seven fresh thongs that had not been dried, and she tied him with them. ⁹With men hidden in the room, she called to him, "Samson, the Philistines are upon you!" But he snapped the thongs as easily as a piece of string snaps when it comes close to a flame. So the secret of his strength was not discovered.

> ¹⁰Then Delilah said to Samson, "You have made a fool of me; you lied to me. Come now, tell me how you can be tied."

> ¹¹He said, "If anyone ties me securely with new ropes that have never been used, I'll become as weak as any other man."

> ¹²So Delilah took new ropes and tied him with them. Then, with men hidden in the room, she called to him, "Samson, the Philistines are upon you!" But he snapped the ropes off his arms as if they were threads.

> Delilah then said to Samson, "Until now, you have been making a fool of me and lying to me. Tell me how you can be tied."

He replied, "If you weave the seven braids of my head into the fabric on the loom and tighten it with the pin, I'll become as weak as any other man." So while he was sleeping, Delilah took the seven braids of his head, wove them into the fabric [14] and tightened it with the pin.

Again she called to him, "Samson, the Philistines are upon you!" He awoke from his sleep and pulled up the pin and the loom, with the fabric.

[15] Then she said to him, "How can you say, 'I love you,' when you won't confide in me? This is the third time you have made a fool of me and haven't told me the secret of your great strength." [16] With such nagging she prodded him day after day until he was tired to death.

[17] So he told her everything. "No razor has ever been used on my head," he said, "because I have been a Nazirite set apart to God since birth. If my head were shaved, my strength would leave me, and I would become as weak as any other man."

[18] When Delilah saw that he had told her everything, she sent word to the rulers of the Philistines, "Come back once more; he has told me everything." So the rulers of the Philistines returned with the silver in their hands.

Question 4. What did Delilah keep doing to Samson? How is that an illustration of the way sin presses us?

Course member Marc wrote, "She constantly tempted Sampson by saying, 'you don't really love me, you won't tell me your secret of strength, look at all I do for you, I love you, but you reject me. Oh, and by the way, ignore those guys who try to bind you every time you tell me something, they don't mean anything.' Sometimes you just have to wonder about God's chosen heroes. Sampson certainly was proud - because no one can be that stupid."

Question 5. Share an experience you've had where temptation kept after you.

If you study the temptation of Adam and Eve in the Garden of Eden, (Genesis 3) you will see this same truth illustrated again: The devil kept after Adam and Eve, kept tempting them, kept arguing with them and weakening them with each word. So, guess what? We'll never win an argument with the devil. And if we hang around long enough, we will develop enough excuses to just go ahead and sin. So, how in the world do we win against these pressing temptations?

RUN LIKE THE WIND!!

Flee the evil desires of youth... (2 Timothy 2:22).

But you, man of God, flee from all this... (1 Timothy 6:11).

Question 6. What did Joseph do when Potiphar's wife was tempting him?
A. He changed the subject, and began talking with her about the weather.
B. He decided to witness to her, so he sat down on the bed with her and explained the way of salvation.
C. He left his coat and ran!

Do you long to be able to look temptation squarely in the face and say, "NO!?" Chances are, we may never be able to do it. Temptation is more powerful than we are; it is more persistent than we are; and it is more persuasive than we are. Our only hope is to RUN, RUN, RUN. Flee away from it as if it is a burning house. Run from it no matter what the cost. Joseph would rather lose a good coat than a good conscience.

Question 7. What can we learn from the way Joseph handled this temptation?

Course member John wrote, "Yesterday I was at work praising God and having a great time, and all of a sudden images of women were running through my mind. Then the excuses started. I prayed to God and it seemed to get worse. Then, during supper I was getting gas and after I got done paying for it, like some kind of magnet I was at the magazine rack with my heart pumping. I did not take down a porn magazine, because God reminded me that he would always provide a way out of my temptation. At that second, I grabbed a Men's Health magazine, paid for it, and went to my car. As I got in the car, I felt relieved and let out a yell! I know about the battles in the mind, and I hate them and get very upset when it happens. Thank God he helped me!"

Dear friend, the above story and much of the content of this lesson came from a friend, named John, who is going through this course. Notice that he RAN from temptation. Maybe not physically, but he got himself away from it. This is no small thing. This is a huge victory! As he continues to develop the habit of running away, he is well on his way to lasting victory. Joseph was thinking of God and he ran. John was thinking of God and he ran. It's the only way to win.

Course member Dan wrote, "She kept prodding Samson for his secret. It said she 'prodded him day after day until he was tired to death.' Temptation can be like that - it keeps prodding and prodding until you almost feel compelled to give in. The pictures that get in my head from one sin prod me until they propagate another sin. It is an endless cycle that can only be broken by God.

Specifically, in regard to pornography, the hardest part is trying to clear the pictures out of my head. There have been times when I have fallen and immediately afterward vowed to never do it again. I would pray constantly for strength and I found that as I prayed there were the pictures prodding me again. I would pray to not give in to the temptation to look at pornography on the Internet, and as I did the pictures of the last time I did it would enter my mind. It made it so I almost didn't want to pray about it anymore..."

The following testimony is from Bill:

I was eleven years old when my older cousin first introduced me to the world of pornography. There was an immediate attraction to the visual images, and all through high school and into college I flirted with pornography.

After I married, I started using porn more frequently as a way of escaping the challenges marriage presented. The more I used it the more I wanted to go deeper into the porn world. Eventually I started taking every opportunity I could to view adult movies, and then about five years ago I was introduced to the Internet. From that point on, the Internet became my method for feeding my sinful desires.

I was able to hide my porn addiction, but people knew something was going on. My life was self-consumed. All I ever thought about was me - me - me. My wife and children paid dearly for my sinful habit. They paid because of our financial difficulties, and they paid because I just wasn't there for them.

About three months ago, hating what I had become, I typed in "addiction to pornography" on Google. The first website that appeared was The Way of Purity course from Setting Captives Free. I've not stopped praising God for leading me to and through this study. It has been used by Him to transform my heart and change my life forever. Only God in Christ Jesus changes lives - but He uses many different means and methods to work in people's lives. Setting Captives Free taught me to put God first in my life.

I had preached the truth in many sermons (yes, I'm a minister of 20+ years); but didn't have a clue as to how to implement it. What did it look like? How do I live by the Spirit and not satisfy the desires of my flesh? God used this course to teach me how to live for His glory and His glory alone.

Early in my marriage, my wife urged me to not worry about my sermons and classes - to just develop my relationship with God. I see now what a fool I'd been not to listen to her. Not only has my heart and life been changed in learning how to drink from the Living Water - but my ministry is stronger than it has ever been.

No longer is preaching and teaching all about me - it's about Him! Praise God, it's about Him! Only in coming to the point of seeing myself as completely helpless, undone, empty and unable to break the chains of bondage myself was I ready for Him to set me free. Through learning the art of radical amputation, true repentance, honest confession (to my mentor and my wife) and feasting on God, He has blessed me with a freedom I've never known in my life. The joy of His salvation has returned to my heart.

I've never been happier with my ministry than I am now. He has blessed me to enjoy my family in ways that I had not known before. Even as I write these words, tears are forming in my eyes. Not tears of sorrow, but of wonderful joy. "Jesus - thank You, thank You, thank You!" To all those at Setting Captives Free - thank you, thank you, thank you.

Scripture to Consider

"And it will be said: "Build up, build up, prepare the road! Remove the obstacles out of the way of my people (Isaiah 57:14).

May the God of hope fill you with all joy and peace as you trust in him, so that you may overflow with hope by the power of the Holy Spirit (Romans 15:13).

Were you free from pornography since you did the last lesson?

    Yes   No

Were you free from self-gratification since you did the last lesson?

    Yes   No

Were you free from sexual immorality since you did the last lesson?

    Yes   No

DAY 25 –
FLEE, ABSTAIN, RESIST

Today, we are going to study various passages of Scripture that relate to our battle against pornography, self-gratification, and all forms of sexual impurity. Our purpose is to gain understanding and practical assistance in how to win this battle, by God's grace. Please think through the following passages, specifically asking yourself how you will apply them in your own life, and then answer the questions below:

> "Flee the evil desires of youth, and pursue righteousness, faith, love and peace, along with those who call on the Lord out of a pure heart (2 Timothy 2:22).

Question 1. The above verse has two commands in it, what are they?

Question 2. Please think through how to apply these two commands in your own life. The first one is to "flee the evil desires of youth." In your specific situation, how might you do this? What desires do you have and how will you flee from them?

Question 3. We are not only to flee evil desires, but we are to pursue righteousness...etc. Again, in your situation, how might you do this? Please list some specific things you will do to pursue righteousness.

Now, will you please share these specific steps with your accountability partner and ask him or her to hold you accountable to these things?

Here are some things that I did to "pursue righteousness" during the first six months when coming out of pornography and sexual impurity:

1. My wife and I met with our pastor on a weekly basis for instruction in the Word and for accountability.
2. I arose early in the mornings and sought the face of God, asking Him to break the power of sin in my life.
3. My wife and I maintained daily accountability with regard to self-gratification. I knew I must report to her daily in this area until the power of sin was broken.
4. I studied many of the writings of the Puritans and sought to learn from their practical and godly wisdom.
5. I attended every service our church had, and sought the Lord during them.
6. My wife and I had daily devotionals where I washed her in the Word and we sought the Lord as a couple.

Question 4. We are to pursue righteousness "along with those who call on the Lord out of a pure heart." Are you calling to the Lord?

> I will lift up the cup of salvation and call on the name of the LORD (Psalm 116:13).

> Then will I purify the lips of the peoples, that all of them may call on the name of the LORD and serve him shoulder to shoulder. [10] From beyond the rivers of Cush my worshipers, my scattered people, will bring me offerings. [11] On that day you will not be put to shame for all the wrongs you have done to me (Zephaniah 3:9-11).

I remember when I first came out of pornography and immorality, I was pleading with the Lord to release me from the chains of sin. I was "calling on the Lord" in sincerity. I was calling out to Him often, begging for mercy, asking for Him to set me free, and pleading with Him to make me whole. Friends, don't hesitate to beg for God's help, to plead and cry to Him, and to latch onto Him as your only hope in life.

This type of crying out to God and begging Him for freedom is not a pleasant thing to watch, as people will plead with God out of desperation, and being nearly frantic for His help, they cry and wail and prostrate themselves before Him, seeking to be released from the trap they are in. Now I'm not suggesting that it is our tears or bodily contortions that help our prayers to be heard, but I am saying that a heart that is desperate for God will call on Him in reckless abandon, until He hears and answers.

> [12] For there is no difference between Jew and Gentile–the same Lord is Lord of all and richly blesses all who call on him, [13] for, "Everyone who calls on the name of the Lord will be saved (Romans 10:12-13).

> [11] Dear friends, I urge you, as aliens and strangers in the world, to abstain from sinful desires, which war against your soul. [12] Live such good lives among the pagans that, though they accuse you of doing wrong, they may see your good deeds and glorify God on the day he visits us (1 Peter 2:11,12).

Question 5. Verse 11 above tells us that we are in a war. Evil desires war against our soul, and we fight internal battles every day. The goal that the enemy has is to drag our soul into hell, and he uses "evil desires" to do it. According to verse 11 above, what are we to do with these evil desires?

Abstaining is the scriptural method to winning the battle against evil desires. We are not to give in, or to vent, or act out in other ways; we are to abstain from evil desires. In some ways, this is like the "just say no" philosophy the world promotes, but it is different, because the world only teaches half the truth. Yes, we are to "just say no" or rather, to "abstain", but according to the next verse, we are to "live such good lives among the pagans that, though they accuse us of doing wrong, they may see our good deeds…" We are not only to abstain, but we are also to live such godly lives that others see our good deeds. This is much like the first verse we studied (2 Timothy 2:22), which taught us not only to flee evil desires, but also to pursue righteousness, and both of these concepts must be embraced, not just one.

> ⁸ Be self-controlled and alert. Your enemy the devil prowls around like a roaring lion looking for someone to devour. ⁹ Resist him, standing firm in the faith, because you know that your brothers throughout the world are undergoing the same kind of sufferings (1 Peter 5:8-9).

You see many places in Scripture where the devil and sin are pictured as a lion seeking to devour us. This concept is important to understand, because it speaks of the strength of the enemy. He is a lion. Man is no match for a lion, as many martyrs in early church history show. The evil one and sin are as a lion. They are very strong, and their purpose is to "devour us." Note this passage in Genesis 4:7: "If you do what is right, will you not be accepted? But if you do not do what is right, sin is crouching at your door; it desires to have you, but you must master it." Sin here is "crouching" at Cain's door, desiring to "have" and devour him, as a lion kills its prey.

We have a strong enemy, and we have weak flesh. This combination works powerfully together, and can drag us into sin and maul us, chewing us up and leaving us half dead. I remember times of praying earnestly that I would not give in to temptation to do sex-chatting on the Internet in my hotel room, but as soon as I got there, the desire was overpowering, and I would immediately log on and give in. I might be up the entire night indulging the lusts of my flesh, and I would get changed and come downstairs the next day absolutely exhausted; mentally, emotionally and spiritually. Sin pounced on me and beat me up and, as this experience became more and more common in my life, the enemy nearly devoured me.

Question 6. According to verse 9 above, what are we to do with this lion?

Question 7. In your own situation, how can you resist? Think through specifics of your situation, and write out how you will resist the enemy.

When I was first coming out of pornography and impurity, my plan to resist was actually a radical amputation. I gave my notebook computer away to my pastor, so I resisted by not allowing any access to the temptation. The key to knowing whether you need to resist or to amputate is whether you are getting the victory or not.

According to verse 9 above, we are not only to resist the devil; but we are also to stand firm in the faith. Now, here is a key to doing this. The Bible says that "faith comes by hearing, and hearing by the Word of God" (Romans 10:17). Notice it does not say, "Faith comes by what you heard," but rather "Faith comes by hearing." There must be an ongoing "hearing" of God's Word in order for faith to remain active. So, how can we "stand firm in the faith?" One way is to involve ourselves in God's Word often.

Question 8. Finally, verse 9 above says that our brothers throughout the world are undergoing the same trials and temptations. Have you ever thought that you were the only one who was sinning in such a horrible manner? Have you ever felt isolated, thinking nobody else would understand?

> Not so! All our brothers and sisters get assaulted by the enemy; we are all under attack by evil desires. Our temptations, whatever they may be, no matter how severe or perverted they may be, are "common to man" (1 Corinthians 10:13).

So, today we learned to flee, abstain and resist. But we also learned to pursue righteousness, live good and godly lives, and stand firm in the faith. We have learned of the strength of our enemy, and we have thought through certain steps that we will take to ensure that we are pursuing righteousness. May our God enable us to do all these, by His grace.

Scripture to Consider

[20] I have been crucified with Christ and I no longer live, but Christ lives in me. The life I live in the body, I live by faith in the Son of God, who loved me and gave himself for me. [21] I do not set aside the grace of God, for if righteousness could be gained through the law, Christ died for nothing! (Galatians 2:20-21)

[21] A cry is heard on the barren heights, the weeping and pleading of the people of Israel, because they have perverted their ways and have forgotten the LORD their God. [22] "Return, faithless people; I will cure you of backsliding." "Yes, we will come to you, for you are the LORD our God. [23] Surely the idolatrous commotion on the hills and mountains is a deception; surely in the LORD our God is the salvation of Israel. [24] From our youth shameful gods have consumed the fruits of our fathers' labor – their flocks and herds, their sons and daughters. [25] Let us lie down in our shame, and let our disgrace cover us. We have sinned against the LORD our God, both we and our fathers; from our youth till this day we have not obeyed the LORD our God (Jeremiah 3:21-25).

Were you free from pornography since you did the last lesson?

    Yes   No

Were you free from self-gratification since you did the last lesson?

    Yes   No

Were you free from sexual immorality since you did the last lesson?

    Yes   No

The following testimony is from Mentor Ray:

I got caught up in pornography in my early teens, getting pornography magazines with allowance money and looking at them when I was alone. This happened to be quite often, as I was very responsible and could be trusted to be by myself. In college, I had a room to myself for most of the four years I was there. Again, this gave me much opportunity to dabble in porn and self-gratification.

After college I was married, but the pornography and self-gratification remained a significant part of my life. I would seek out whatever time I could have to get my sessions in, separating me from my family. As a child I went to church with my family, but in college I became somewhat "disassociated" and with my wife not being a believer I still lacked the spiritual walk I needed. Our marriage began to dissolve, pornography being one of the reasons, but there were others. I became disinterested in my wife, and she began looking outside the marriage herself. A few months before this, I did begin reading the Bible regularly. However, I still engaged in my porn sessions just as regularly. I can recall feeling as if I was being pulled from both sides.

After five years of marriage, it all collapsed and I was asked to leave the house. I took on a part-time job to help offset the costs of the counseling. It was only a couple of weeks later I was asked for a divorce. I was told it could not work anymore, and that it was better for the children. I dropped to my knees and wept before God. My life was crumbling around me. Not only was I losing my family, but I was also at the time working with her father. I was suddenly without a job too, aside from the part-time one.

But little by little, God began mending things back together. I found a place not far from my children so I could still be close to them. God provided a better job than I had before, one with a good group of believers that held an in-office Bible study! And I began going to a small church, and became a part of the worship team.

It was at my part-time job that I met a woman and began seeing her. As we got to know each other, she started going to my church and accepted the Lord into her life too! I promised God that everything would be different, that I wouldn't make the same mistakes again. Well, I made them again. After seeing each other for a few months, she "unexpectedly" became pregnant. Abortion was not an option; sin was not going to be covered with sin. I did the respectful thing and asked her to marry me.

The first year, especially the first several months, were absolutely rough and at times I doubted we were going to make it. Just coming out of a divorce, marrying again before we got to know one another because of a conception outside of marriage, financial difficulties, and other things barraged us constantly. But God saw us through it all. Our little daughter was born, and that perhaps was the one thing that held us together. Yet pornography still raised its ugly head, not to the same extent as in my first marriage, but it was still there and had its effects nonetheless. I was getting my fixes of pornography at work. Needless to say I was killing my productivity and running the risk of losing my job, the very one God provided in my time of need.

I knew all of this was bad and sinful, yet I could not pull away from it. I would go a week, maybe two or three, but then I would be right in the middle of it again. I was becoming irritable and defensive at home, taking every little comment personally. The attention I should have been giving my wife was not given because I was going to pornography instead. In a nutshell, I was walking down the same road I'd taken before.

Praise God that this time He woke me up and set me straight before I went down in flames again! We began seeing the leader of our congregation, and that is when I let it out that I was a porn addict. He quickly and lovingly shared the consequences of this addiction - spiritually, emotionally, physically, and mentally.

I quickly began seeking help on the Internet. God used the thing that once fueled my addiction to begin my freedom. I found Setting Captives Free and signed up for The Way of Purity course. I also found a discussion group for men addicted to pornography and became involved in that. I told a couple of deacons in our congregation about my fight with pornography, as well as a co-worker who is a believer.

Now as a mentor with Setting Captives Free, God is continuing to bless me as He uses me to help others be free.

DAY 26 – DON'T GO NEAR

In July of 1972, a McDonnell Douglas DC-9, loaded with 85 passengers and five crewmembers, was traveling from St. Louis, Missouri to Minneapolis, Minnesota. The time of departure was 2:30 p.m., and the aircraft had been airborne for approximately 25 minutes. It was a typically hot and humid summer afternoon in the Midwest, with numerous thunderstorms building along the route of flight.

The Air Traffic Control monitor noticed the aircraft approaching the vicinity of several heavy thunderstorm buildups, and radioed this information: "___ ____ (airline name) Flight 2164, weather radar indicates you are approaching an area of level 5 buildups with tops above flight level 410. Suggest an easterly deviation to heading 105 degrees within the next 10 miles."

The response from the pilots came back. "Uh, Roger, Kansas City Center, we see the thunderstorms. Onboard radar indicates a possible hole to penetrate through the buildups at our 12 o'clock position and 18 miles. Do you agree?"

Air traffic control replied, "Negative, Flight 2164, our radar does not confirm the existence of a hole in the storm, suggest an easterly deviation to the right immediately."

This is the last transmission recorded from this aircraft on air traffic control's tapes:

"Uh, Roger, Kansas City Center, we will proceed straight ahead. It may be a little close, but we, uh, do see a hole to penetrate."

The aircraft penetrated the severest part of the storm, a level 5 thunderstorm, and was sent plummeting to the earth, killing all 91 people aboard. What happened?

Aircraft radar is susceptible to what is known as "attenuation," which is the blocking of any weather returns that are behind severe storms. Because there is so much moisture in severe thunderstorms, the radar is unable to penetrate through the moisture to be able to accurately present any weather information immediately behind the severe storms. In the above situation, the radar, because of attenuation, falsely presented the appearance of a safe route of flight. Seasoned and well-trained pilots are aware of the problem of attenuation, and know to remain well clear of all thunderstorms. The key to safety is to not go anywhere near a storm.

For us, pornography is a thunderstorm. It can present the appearance of being harmless; a little fun, something that doesn't hurt anyone, a release for pent-up sexual energy, and/or a stimulus for better lovemaking with a spouse. And yet, pornography is a trap of the devil that has devastated the lives of countless people. How do we deal with this thunderstorm?

Answer: Don't go near!

Today, we will notice scriptural teaching on the subject "Don't go near." Please read the following passage and answer the questions at the bottom. Can you discover the approaching "thunderstorm?"

[6] At the window of my house I looked out through the lattice. [7] I saw among the simple, I noticed among the young men, a youth who lacked judgment. [8] He was going down the street near her corner, walking along in the direction of her house [9] at twilight, as the day was fading, as the dark of night set in. [10] Then out came a woman to meet him, dressed like a prostitute and with crafty intent. [11] (She is loud and defiant, her feet never stay at home; [12] now in the street, now in the squares, at every corner she lurks.) [13] She took hold of him and kissed him and with a brazen face she said: [14] I have fellowship offerings at home; today I fulfilled my vows. [15] So I came out to meet you; I looked for you and have found you! [16] I have covered my bed with colored linens from Egypt. [17] I have perfumed my bed with myrrh, aloes and cinnamon. [18] Come, let's drink deep of love till morning; let's enjoy ourselves with love! [19] My husband is not at home; he has gone on a long journey. [20] He took his purse filled with money and will not be home till full moon. [21] With persuasive words she led him astray; she seduced him with her smooth talk. [22] All at once he followed her like an ox going to the slaughter, like a deer stepping into a noose [23] till an arrow pierces his liver, like a bird darting into a snare, little knowing it will cost him his life. [24] Now then, my sons, listen to me; pay attention to what I say. [25] Do not let your heart turn to her ways or stray into her paths. [26] Many are the victims she has brought down; her slain are a mighty throng. [27] Her house is a highway to the grave, leading down to the chambers of death (Proverbs 7:6-27).

Questions

Question 1. In verse 8, above, the young man is doing something foolish. What is it?

Question 2. What words are used to describe this young man?
  A. Simple, lacking judgement
  B. Blond, well-muscled
  C. Able to go near temptation and say "No" to it

Question 3. Notice the personal nature of the temptation. How many times does the seductress use the word "you" in verse 15?

- A. 1
- B. 2
- C. 3

Question 4. To what is this "personal touch" designed to appeal in this young man?

Let me share a personal illustration: I remember going to my hotel room after a long day, turning on an adult channel, and immediately a seductress came on with a very personal message: "I've been waiting for **you**, I've taken a hot shower and I smell good just for **you**. Come on, tonight I'm all **yours**!" And, possibly, you have seen advertisements for 900 numbers: "I want to talk to **you**; I am sitting here waiting for **your** call. Come on, pick up the phone, I want to talk to **you**."

Question 5. Why is this personal, intimate form of communication so hard to resist? What are your thoughts?

Question 6. Verse 18 states, "Come, let us drink deep of love until morning..." Let's see how good your memory is. In the early days of this course, we studied through John 4 about "the woman at the well." How does verse 18 above compare with the story in John 4?

Course member Jeff wrote, "We must drink deep of the Living Waters of Jesus Christ. He is our fountain. I notice here the part of the verse, "...until morning..." This is very obviously not a fountain with any sustenance at all. It will go dry in the morning. There is nothing satisfying here. It has an end. Jesus' fountain has no end. And its drink gives us life."

Note: verse 22 states, "All at once he followed her." Here is the problem with going "near" the temptation: the choice to sin is often made all of a sudden and without rational thought. If this young man were reasonable and rational, he could have weighed out the benefits versus the disadvantages. He could have said, "I will think about it and let you know," or he could have asked a friend for advice before acting. But powerful temptation removes one's ability to be rational, and decisions are often made immediately. This is "impulse buying" at its worst. And the longer we stay involved in pornography, the more things we do simply by impulse.

Friend, after I had been involved in pornography for four or five years, my impulses were beginning to master me. I would find myself doing inappropriate things almost by reflex, without thinking about it, and later it left me wondering why. I now know that habitual giving in to sin leads to living by impulse. It still breaks my heart to think of this, and I am so thankful to be delivered from it now.

Question 7. Have you experienced this "all of a sudden" decision with porn? What happened?

Course member David wrote, "Once I had been to the porn shop and bought some magazines, I suddenly decided I just couldn't wait until I got home to look at one, I was so busy looking, that I ran into the car in front of me."

Question 8. Verses 22 and 23 use four analogies to describe what the end result of giving in to temptation is like. What are they? I will write the first one:

1. An Ox Going To The Slaughter
2.
3.
4.

It helps to keep in mind what the final outcome of any sin will be. Sin inevitably leads to death. It may lead to physical death, as in the case of Ted Bundy and numerous others, or it may lead to death of your marriage or death to your spiritual life, etc.

Question 9. The temptress promised an enjoyment of life. But, according to the last couple of verses, where did her paths actually lead?

- A. To the White House
- B. To the enjoyment of life
- C. To death and the grave

Question 10. There is only one admonition in this entire passage on how to escape the "slaughter," the "noose," the "arrow," and the "snare," meaning "death," and the "grave." It is found in verse 25. Please write out verse 25 here. It would be a good idea for us to memorize this verse.

Note: don't go near! Sometimes this is extremely difficult, as temptation is "now in the street, now in the squares, at every corner she lurks."

Here are some of the things I do to avoid temptation: I will not get in to an elevator alone with a woman; I will not meet alone with a woman; I will not counsel a woman - my wife must be present. I disassemble the TV in my hotel room, take it into a co-worker's room, or drop it off at the front desk. I do not go into newsstands because of the numerous inappropriate magazines. At the checkout stand in grocery stores, I "make a covenant with my eyes" to not look at the magazines.

I began the practice of self-gratification at age five. Unfortunately some older cousins taught me. I remember entering first grade when everyone had to walk to the front of the room and give their name. I couldn't look up because I was ashamed of myself. I clearly remember on that first day of school that people would hate me if they knew what I did. By then it was already a daily habit.

Unfortunately, as a boy growing up, I experimented with other boys, only reinforcing my habit.

When I was about 13 years old, I discovered my first Playboy magazine. That began my introduction into pornography. Pornography and self-gratification haunted me all through high school and into college. Three times a day was routine during those days. Along with this came an increasing awareness that I was attracted to both men and women. Clearly a homosexual "bent" was emerging.

Then in my third year of college I became a believer through the Navigator ministry. This had a significant impact on my practice of pornography and self-gratification. It diminished, but I was never able to completely conquer it. I struggled as I served several years in a campus ministry. Over time I entered seminary, even though I continued to struggle, and went into pastoral ministry. All through my nineteen years of pastoral ministry I struggled.

Five years ago I had a burnout and went for counseling. I opened up this whole area of struggle to the counselor. Although I had never acted out my homosexual desires, they existed and bothered me. Through counseling I dealt with some of the past sexual abuse and all the things I'd done as a younger boy. I had a significant release and victory. However, about that time I was connected to the Internet. In time curiosity took over and I was soon viewing pornography and practicing self-gratification. I knew it was wrong and kept trying to stop. I greatly feared being caught and devastating my family and ministry. However, nothing worked. No resolve was ever kept. I changed churches two years ago and hoped for better times, but this did not happen.

Finally, after forty-seven years of fighting self-gratification and after thirty-nine years of fighting pornography and after many years with conflictive desires, I anonymously sought out help from another pastor through the Internet. He eventually pointed me to Setting Captives Free. I began the course on Nov. 1, 2000. By then I'd already experienced 15 days of victory through self-effort. Right away I began to feel God's encouragement and help in staying pure. It as if God said, "Now you are ready." By coming out of the dark and letting others in on my struggle I was able to receive God's help, strength, and grace to overcome this life-long battle. Like everyone else who takes the course, the battle was strong. At times I felt like giving in, but it was only by God's grace that I have been able to complete the course without viewing any pornography or continuing on with self-gratification. That is totally God's power at work. I have NEVER had any such victory since I was five years old. Praise God!

Now that I'm ending the course I would like to "cut off" the giant's head by taking the mentor's course and become involved in helping others, particularly pastors who struggle in a deep, dark hole of secrecy. Church members can go to their pastor for help for sexual sin. Perhaps God can use me in this way.

Friends, a deadly air disaster could have been averted in 1972, had the pilots lived by the principle to "not go near." In flying, when I am faced with a radarscope showing thunderstorms, my one policy is avoidance. I do not look for holes or try to find a shortcut. When dealing with pornography, like deadly thunderstorms, the only safe approach is avoidance. "In the paths of the wicked lie thorns and snares, but he who guards his soul stays far from them" (Proverbs 22:5).

Question 11. What have been your areas of temptation in the past? Please give us your avoidance plan. How will you apply this principle now to "not go near?"

Scripture to Consider

[14] Do not set foot on the path of the wicked or walk in the way of evil men. [15] Avoid it, do not travel on it; turn from it and go on your way" (Proverbs 4:14-15).

Rather, clothe yourselves with the Lord Jesus Christ, and do not think about how to gratify the desires of the sinful nature (Romans 13:14).

You are to abstain from food sacrificed to idols, from blood, from the meat of strangled animals and from sexual immorality. You will do well to avoid these things (Acts 15:29).

Avoid every kind of evil. (1 Thessalonians 5:22).

For everything that was written in the past was written to teach us, so that through endurance and the encouragement of the Scriptures we might have hope (Romans 15:4).

Were you free from pornography since you did the last lesson?

    Yes   No

Were you free from self-gratification since you did the last lesson?

    Yes   No

Were you free from sexual immorality since you did the last lesson?

    Yes   No

DAY 27 - GROWING IN CHRIST

It is good to see from Scripture that there are different stages of growth in the Christian life. The teaching today will bring encouragement to those who stumble, strengthen the faith of those who are beginning to overcome, and confirm the faith of those walking in habitual victory.

Please read the following passage, and answer the questions below.

> 12 "I write to you, dear children, because your sins have been forgiven on account of his name. 13 I write to you, fathers, because you have known him who is from the beginning. I write to you, young men, because you have overcome the evil one. I write to you, dear children, because you have known the Father. 14 I write to you, fathers, because you have known him who is from the beginning. I write to you, young men, because you are strong, and the word of God lives in you, and you have overcome the evil one (1 John 2:12-14).

Notice the three different groups the Apostle John addresses above:

1. Children - verses 12, 13
2. Young men - verses 13, 14
3. Fathers - verses 12, 14

The Christian life is one of ongoing growth, development and maturity. We can learn much in our fight against pornography and sexual sin by studying what John wrote to each of the above groups.

Questions

Question 1. There are two things the Apostle John writes about "little children" above. What are those two things?
- A. They cried a lot and spilled their food
- B. They were forgiven, and knew the Father
- C. They often fell down and skinned their knees

The Apostle John writes to children - "Your sins have been forgiven on account of his name." And, "you have known the Father." We come into the Christian family by being born again and, through drinking the pure milk of God's Word, soon become little children. But little children fall a lot, so John writes to little children "your sins have been forgiven on account of his name."

Question 2. Have you come into God's family through the forgiveness of your sins?
- A. Yes, I am part of God's family because He has forgiven me.
- B. No, I do not need to be forgiven of any sins, because I'm not that bad.

Little children stumble as they are learning to walk; it is part of the growing process. And, initially, little children do more falling than walking. This is the reason that John speaks of little children as being forgiven. This should teach us caution when dealing with those who fall a lot; they may be unsaved and living in sin, or they might be saved, but are children who are just learning to walk. Be careful in judging those who fall often.

Question 3. Please provide your comments on the following Scripture:

> For though a righteous man falls seven times, he rises again, but the wicked are brought down by calamity (Proverbs 24:16).

Question 4. Please provide your comments on the following Scripture:

> 21 Then Peter came to Jesus and asked, "Lord, how many times shall I forgive my brother when he sins against me? Up to seven times?" 22 Jesus answered, "I tell you, not seven times, but seventy times seven (Matthew 18:21-22).

The passage we are studying in 1 John 2, "You have known the Father," tells us how one becomes born again - through a relationship with God. Jesus said, "And this is eternal life, that they may know You, the only true God, and Jesus Christ whom You have sent" (John 17:3). And, knowing God starts with receiving His forgiveness, "Your sins have been forgiven on account of His Name." So the little child in Christ has a relationship with God that is based on forgiveness. He may not have grown much beyond this initial relationship and, as a little child, stumbles as much as he walks. John emphasizes forgiveness for the little child. Some of us feel as if all we are doing is stumbling and falling, and are in constant need of forgiveness. If this is you, keep seeking the Lord for grace, because with growth comes strength.

The Apostle John writes to young men - "You have overcome the evil one" and "You are strong, and the word of God lives in you, and you have overcome the evil one."

How do we know we are progressing in the Christian life? We begin winning battles. The Word of God becomes our sword with which we defeat the evil one. The "young man" in the Lord is characterized as one who walks in victory over the enemy by the indwelling Word of God. Relating this to our subject, we are no longer living in the twin sins of pornography and self-gratification, but we have acquired the tools from Scripture to be strong in the Lord and overcome the evil one.

For many years of my life, I was, spiritually, a stumbling little child. I fell quite often and then repented, only to fall again, sometimes on the same day. This continued for way too long, as I had nobody who could assist me in growing spiritually. I am not blaming anyone, just stating the fact that there was no Setting Captives Free - The Way of Purity course back in the days when I was viewing pornography, and nobody I knew wanted to talk about it. I talked with several pastors, but they did not have the spiritual insight necessary to help me out, so I remained stunted in my growth, malnourished, and failed to thrive.

But then, through the assistance of my pastor, I learned the principles that make up this course, and experienced a growth spurt, spiritually. He helped me understand how to apply the principles of radical amputation, accountability, dragging sin into the light, feeding on the Word, etc., and now I am walking in perpetual victory over sin. I'm not sinless. No, sinless perfection does not happen in this life, but I am simply referring to living in victory over habitual sin, by God's grace.

What's more, is that God is using me to help others, and this has been a great delight as well.

So I can see that there has been growth in grace in my life. I have gone from an unsaved man who lived in sin continually, to a little child who stumbled often, to a young man who knows how to fight sin using the principles in God's Word, to a father who is helping others. I do praise God for growth in grace.

Question 5. According to the passage we are studying in 1 John 2, what is the evidence that one has grown from a "little child" to a "young man?" Write your thoughts here.

Question 6. Next, please provide your thoughts about the next two passages of Scripture. Include whether or not the author appears to be a "little child" or a "young man."

> ¹⁴ We know that the law is spiritual; but I am unspiritual, sold as a slave to sin. ¹⁵ I do not understand what I do. For what I want to do I do not do, but what I hate I do. ¹⁶ And if I do what I do not want to do, I agree that the law is good. ¹⁷ As it is, it is no longer I myself who do it, but it is sin living in me. ¹⁸ I know that nothing good lives in me, that is, in my sinful nature. For I have the desire to do what is good, but I cannot carry it out. ¹⁹ For what I do is not the good I want to do; no, the evil I do not want to do-this I keep on doing. ²⁰ Now if I do what I do not want to do, it is no longer I who do it, but it is sin living in me that does it. ²¹ So I find this law at work: When I want to do good, evil is right there with me. ²² For in my inner being I delight in God's law; ²³ but I see another law at work in the members of my body, waging war against the law of my mind and making me a prisoner of the law of sin at work within my members (Romans 7:14-23).

Now, please understand that many see this passage in Romans 7 in different ways. Some see Paul as an unsaved man here, for he seems to be enslaved to sin and somewhat hopeless. Others see this passage as the time in Paul's life when he was an immature Christian, before he grew to maturity. Still others see this as an

ongoing experience in Paul's life, as we always struggle with sin in this life. In any case, what is clear is that growth does come in the life of the Christian, where habitual sin does not have the power over us that it once did. Please write your own thoughts here.

The Apostle John writes to fathers, "You have known Him Who is from the beginning." The mature father in the Lord is again characterized by relationship. He still has his dependence on the Word of God, but His attention now is on the God of the Word, and he is characterized by His relationship to the Lord. He is a father, so he has children, and in our ministry, this mature man has not only overcome the evil one himself, but has to opportunity to assist others out of pornography, by the grace of God.

Question 7. Can you see the growth in the Lord that is taking place in this passage?

Question 8. Please compare the following passage of Scripture to our struggle with pornography and immorality:

> When I was a child, I talked like a child, I thought like a child, I reasoned like a child. When I became a man, I put childish ways behind me (1 Corinthians 13:11).

Question 9. Children, young men, and fathers - which are you? Explain how you know which one you are, currently.

Whatever your level of maturity, just know that there is growth ahead for all of us. The Way of Purity course is designed to assist in our growth, taking us from little children who fall much and are in need of forgiveness often (beginning the course), to young men who know how to fight and are characterized by winning battles (middle portions of the course), to fathers who are producing fruit of other "little children" (mentors).

Keep growing, dear children, and know that victory is around the next corner. Fight hard, young men for your adversary is angry at you. Enjoy your intimacy with the Father, fathers, and encourage your little ones to grow in the Lord.

Question 10. How is everything in your life? What are your struggles, temptations, and frustrations? What are the things in which you are doing well? Please record how you are doing now.

Scripture to Consider

[17] I will surely bless you and make your descendants as numerous as the stars in the sky and as the sand on the seashore. Your descendants will take possession of the cities of their enemies, [18] and through your offspring all nations on earth will be blessed, because you have obeyed me (Genesis 22:17-18).

And I tell you that you are Peter, and on this rock I will build my church, and the gates of Hades will not overcome it. 19 I will give you the keys of the kingdom of heaven; whatever you bind on earth will be bound in heaven, and whatever you loose on earth will be loosed in heaven (Matthew 16:18-19).

Were you free from pornography since you did the last lesson?

    Yes   No

Were you free from self-gratification since you did the last lesson?

    Yes   No

Were you free from sexual immorality since you did the last lesson?

    Yes   No

The following testimony is from Will:

I am an older man in my late fifties. I have been sexually addicted to one form of immorality or another for most of my life. My addictions to pornography and self-gratification began at an early age when I first discovered the stash of magazines, my dad kept hidden in his closet. As a teenager and a young man growing up in the 50's and the 60's, I tried to seduce as many girls as I could find into having sex with me. I joined the Navy at age seventeen and the availability of prostitutes back then only intensified my sexual addictions. I considered it normal to have intimate relations with as many women as I could find who were willing to indulge me in my sexual fantasies and pleasures. I had grown up with the "Playboy Philosophy" and firmly believed that this was what all men did.

After being discharged from the Navy, I entered college and got married. I thought that being married would end my preoccupation with sex, but it did not. Even though I had slept around with many women before marriage, I had no intentions of doing so after marriage. I started hanging out in strip bars and X-rated movie theaters because I did not want to be "unfaithful" to my wife. I wasted much time and money on my voyeurism during those years. My failed marriage ended three years later. I returned to my former practice of seducing women because I was now free from the constraints of marriage.

I met the woman who would later become my wife in 1969. We have now been married for thirty years. At first I hid my sexual addictions from her because I thought that she simply would not understand. I later discovered that secrecy is one of the devil's greatest devices to keep us in bondage to our sexual sins. Ten years after we were married, my wife and I became Christians in 1979. I was ashamed to be seen in strip bars and X-rated theaters after becoming a Christian so I concentrated my sexual addictions upon pornography alone. The 1980's brought a new form of technology to feed the sexual desires of men such as me. I soon became hooked on X-rated videos. With the advent of the "neighborhood video stores," it was no longer necessary for addicts such as me to go to the "seedier parts of town" to feed our lustful desires. My addiction to X-rated videos was one of the hardest things I have ever had to face. I even contemplated suicide several times because I could not find freedom from my bondage to those sexual sins.

I cried out to God for His help and He responded to my plea. The Lord led me to confess my sins to my wife and that confession finally broke the yoke of secrecy that had pervaded my life. I also found a man to whom I confessed my sexual addictions that later became my spiritual mentor. Together, we formed a group of men that met regularly to support each other and hold each other accountable. We met bi-monthly for several years before the group dissolved in 1998. Pornographic videos were no longer the problem for me that they once were and I thought that I no longer needed accountability.

Satan, however, had other plans to ensnare me into a final form of sexual addiction. The Worldwide Web became a reality in the mid 1990's and along with it came the pornography sites that proliferate the Internet today. I soon became hooked on this newest form of technology which brought pornography into the privacy of one's own home. I firmly believe that Internet porn is the scourge of many Christian men today. It is practiced in the secrecy of one's own home and most men will attempt to hide this sin from their wives, pastors and friends at church. I attempted to free myself from this sin by installing several different computer filters. I even subscribed to a filtered Christian ISP service once. None of these attempts to free myself from pornography on the Internet worked because I always found ways to circumvent them.

Once again I cried out to God and He led me to the Setting Captives Free website through a friend I had met online several years earlier. I enrolled in The Way of Purity Course and completed it without ever falling once back into my old habits of pornography and self-gratification. It was relatively easy for me to abstain from my sin while taking the course because I had been on the "road to recovery" already for several years prior to my enrollment in the course. The course gave me additional tools that I found useful in keeping me pure from all of my sexual sins.

I now truly believe that I have been set free from all forms of sexual addictions for the first time in my life. My only regret is that it has taken me so long to achieve sexual purity. It is therefore my desire to spend the remainder of my life helping other men achieve the sexual purity that God has so graciously granted to me. May the Lord Jesus Christ be eternally praised and glorified for what He has done in this redeemed sinner's life!

DAY 28 – SANCTIFICATION

Have you ever wondered about God's will for your life? Well, today we are going to explore this topic. We will be considering the following questions:

What is the will of God for our lives?
How do we find it?
How do we live it?
What does God's will have to do with sexual bondage?

> [1] Finally, brothers, we instructed you how to live in order to please God, as in fact you are living. Now we ask you and urge you in the Lord Jesus to do this more and more. [2] For you know what instructions we gave you by the authority of the Lord Jesus. [3] It is God's will that you should be sanctified: that you should avoid sexual immorality; [4] that each of you should learn to control his own body in a way that is holy and honorable, [5] not in passionate lust like the heathen, who do not know God; [6] and that in this matter no one should wrong his brother or take advantage of him. The Lord will punish men for all such sins, as we have already told you and warned you. [7] For God did not call us to be impure, but to live a holy life. [8] Therefore, he who rejects this instruction does not reject man but God, who gives you his Holy Spirit (1 Thessalonians 4:1-8).

Question 1. In this passage, Paul talks about avoiding sexual immorality, controlling our bodies, and living a holy life. But before he mentions all this, in verse one he provides a motive. What is this motive?

Question 2. In your own words, please tell why you believe Paul provides this motive for holy living.

There are many good reasons why we should avoid sexual immorality, and learn to control our bodies. However, if we are Christians, our primary motivation for pursuing purity should be so that we might please the Lord. Before we knew Jesus Christ, we lived to please ourselves in ever-increasing wickedness, but now God's grace has changed our hearts so that we now earnestly desire to please Him instead of ourselves. A sincere desire to please Him will drive us on to resist the devil, to die to our flesh daily, to continually forsake the pleasure of sin, to avoid sexual immorality, and to control our bodies in a way that is holy and honorable.

Question 3. Take a second and compare your past motives with your present motives. How do your present motives differ from those you had when involved in pornography and immorality?

When we offer ourselves to pornography or sexual impurity of any kind, we soon find that the enslavement process begins to increase. We want more pictures; we continually seek for something new and different; we go from soft core to hard core; or maybe from one sex partner to another, etc. We always want "more and more."

> ***Course member Paul wrote,*** "My lust pulled me deeper and deeper into more risqué and perverted activities. After awhile, the women were not as exciting as before, and I found myself drifting into homosexual erotica. This was something that would have repulsed me before I became entrapped in the cycle of 'more and more.'"

Question 4. When we present ourselves to the Lord and become slaves of Christ, we enter a path of increasing righteousness. What instruction does Paul give in verse one, above, to teach this truth? Write your thoughts here.

Note: The Christian life is one of ongoing improvement as we grow in purity, increase in holiness, and abound in the work of the Lord "more and more."

Question 5. Verse 3, above, tells us very clearly what God's will is. Please write out verse 3 here.

Question 6. As Christians, we must "learn something," according to verse 4. What is it?

  A. We must learn to talk the right way.

  B. We must learn how to get people to make a decision for Christ.

  C. We must learn how to control our bodies in an honorable way.

Question 7. Verse 5, above, describes those who live in "passionate lust" in two different ways. What are they?

  A. Oversexed and easily stimulated

  B. Heathen who do not know God

Note: Paul is instructing Christians not to live like their pagan neighbors, who did not know God. The pagans lived their lives in lust, giving in to the cravings of the flesh in sexual immorality, and the degrading of their bodies in sexual perversion.

History records that pornography played a major role in the culture of their day and that pornographic "art" abounded. All of this is descriptive of a culture alienated from God, a people who chose not to retain God in their knowledge, and who logically began to "worship" sex in all of its perversions. Paul's description of these people as those "who do not know God" is significant here. Knowing God, that is, having an intimate relationship with Him, is the key ingredient which will enable us to "escape the corruption in the world caused by evil desires" (2 Peter 1:4).

Question 8. According to verse 6, what will God do to people who live like this?

  A. In grace, He will overlook their sins.

  B. He will punish them.

  C. Nothing - He knows we are only human, and understands our weaknesses.

Question 9. How does Hebrews 13:4 reinforce this? "Marriage should be honored by all, and the marriage bed kept pure, for God will judge the adulterer and all the sexually immoral" (Hebrews 13:4).

Question 10. Verse 7 states what the "calling" of the Christian is. What is it?

  A. To convert others

  B. To hold up the Ten Commandments as the standard of God

  C. To live a holy life, and to be pure

Question 11. How are you doing with your calling?

As we seek to live a pure life in Christ, and do so "more and more," we will also be given opportunities to encourage others toward a holy life. Some may listen and heed our warnings and instructions, embrace Christ and forsake their sin. Others will cling to sin and attempt to justify themselves. Here, at Setting Captives Free, we have heard many different excuses from people who will not forsake their sin. Sadly, some of these people will use overtly spiritual language in their rejection of the truth.

Testimony

The following testimony is from Kurt:

For over thirty-five years I led a hidden and secret double life. There was a life I presented to everyone I knew, which was that of a righteous and upstanding man. Yet I also lived a life in secret and all alone. This second life placed me as the sole inhabitant of a world where the only neighbors, friends and relatives I had were in cyberspace through Internet pornography.

Like many of you reading this, I was a Christian choosing to play with the secret world of Internet pornography and self-gratification in an effort to gain something or reach something I thought I needed. I struggled for days, weeks and months to find what I was missing through pornography and self-gratification. I often found myself outside of my marriage bed, late at night, while my bride was sleeping, prowling the Internet for a secret and concealed conquest. These sexual pursuits were the other side of me and the double life I led before my bride and friends.

At home, at work and at church I showed everyone I knew what a good Christian I was and the life I wanted them to see. In my home I would assume the role of "Head of Household" and begin leading my bride and children as I interpreted God would have it. Yet, my bride and my children did not respect me and often were at odds with me. In my work life, I would flippantly throw Scripture around when I thought it was necessary, or try to use it to console someone when they confided in me. At the time, I could not understand why all my work to be an appealing Christian was coming up short with many people. In my men's group at my church there were many occasions I was called on to work alongside other men and, like the last kid picked for dodge ball, I was chosen last. I would often wonder, "Am I that repellant of a person?"

In the midst of these two lives I was leading, I built a computer for my family. For weeks after its installation my bride and I were at odds over installing Internet filters. We wanted to protect our children from the very Internet pornography to which my second life was accustomed. I showed her a method to track where our computer had been using cookies on our home PC and we tried it for a couple of weeks. Mind you, I also had a laptop computer in my office downstairs where I led my secret double life.

One day, I came home early to surprise my bride and children for lunch. I came in the front door, greeted my children, and proceeded downstairs to my office to check my email on my laptop. What I found in my office was a scene I will never forget. There sitting at my laptop, soaked in tears and trembling was my bride, broken before me. The only words she could mutter were, "How could you?" At that point my secret second life was exposed. Take my word for it, it's not worth it if the cost is destroying those people you love most. She was extremely wounded, and nothing I could say at that point could bring her healing.

Weeks of incredible pain between us went by. At a later point, she found Setting Captives Free while researching the Internet for godly weight assistance programs. She soon began The Lord's Table at Setting Captives Free. I was thrilled to watch her during her time with this course, and was drawn in like a moth to a flame. She was convicted and comforted by the Holy Spirit during her daily studies and that rubbed off on me. Her time with SCF lead me to visit the website on my own.

Initially I found The Lord's Table; however, the course titled The Way of Purity seemed more important to me, and without telling her, I enrolled. After several daily lessons and confession, I was compelled to tell my bride everything I had done in my secret life.

After confessing this secret second life and becoming a student and then a mentor with Setting Captives Free, I can safely say that I have become "One" with my bride. This is what we were meant to be from the beginning of our marriage (Ecclesiastes 4:12). My Lord, my bride and I have become fused and welded in unity through Jesus Christ, and the secret second sinful life I was once leading has melted away like slag falling to the floor of a steel foundry. As a result of my marriage and my relationship being forged like steel in Christ, I have accepted the call into ministry full time with the support of my bride and now my children.

Kurt's bride, Heidi, added this, "When Kurt first confessed this sin to me, I was completely devastated. I felt betrayed as a wife and felt that the most intimate part of our lives was invaded in a horrible way. I was so very hurt and was tempted to close myself off to him, physically, mentally and spiritually. Then God gently reminded me that true repentance leads to salvation and that I had been praying for the communication in our marriage to increase and for us to truly be each other's best friend. Kurt's confession and repentance revealed vulnerability in him that had not been there before. He really wanted to stop this sin and he said he needed my help. This opened a door of communication for us that had not been here before. If we could talk about this, we could talk about anything! I have seen Kurt change from being secretive and disconnected to being completely open, honest, transparent and completely engaged as a husband and father. He is transforming before my eyes into a man that brings glory to our Savior. Kurt's repentance is part of the reason that our marriage is better now after fifteen years that it has ever been and I give all the glory to Jesus Christ."

Notice the mixture of truth and error in the following message. Despite all his religious language, this gentleman is unable to forsake his sin, and is hostile to encouragement and warnings to do so.

Here is his email we received:

"When I was saved and regenerated by the Holy Ghost (as salvation precedes regeneration), God showed me that His grace, mercy and lovingkindness are there to forgive every sin I have ever committed and the sins I will continue to commit as a born-again, adopted, grace-bought child of God. He does not expect perfection from me; nor does He demand (under this dispensation of grace) that I forsake all sin in order for Him to love me. His grace increases with my sin, and is magnified every time I fall. No, I have not forsaken self-gratification and pornography, but yet remain convinced that I know God, am known by God, and loved unconditionally. I will remain His child, and do not need you to tell me to forsake sin. God knows I am a human being dwelling in flesh, and is sympathetic to the frailties of my flesh."

Question 12. According to verse 8, above, when people reject teaching about avoiding immorality, learning to control their bodies, and about future punishment of those who continue to live in sin, what are they really rejecting?

A. They may love God, but they are rejecting the person who brings the message.

A. While embracing God, they are rejecting the teaching of men.

B. They are rejecting God!

Question 13. What do the following verses have to do with the situation described above?

"19 But I will come to you very soon, if the Lord is willing, and then I will find out not only how these arrogant people are talking, but what power they have. 20 For the kingdom of God is not a matter of talk but of power." (1 Corinthians 4:19-20).

9 Do you not know that the wicked will not inherit the kingdom of God? Do not be deceived: Neither the sexually immoral nor idolaters nor adulterers nor male prostitutes nor homosexual offenders 10 nor thieves nor the greedy nor drunkards nor slanderers nor swindlers will inherit the kingdom of God. 11 And that is what some of you were. But you were washed, you were sanctified, you were justified in the name of the Lord Jesus Christ and by the Spirit of our God (1 Corinthians 6:9-11).

Those who belong to Christ Jesus have crucified the sinful nature with its passions and desires (Galatians 5:24).

Let us summarize the teaching of the above passage of Scripture:

What is God's will for our lives? That we should be sanctified, that we should avoid sexual immorality, and that we should learn how to control our bodies in a way that honors the Lord. Our motive for doing this is to live in such a way as to please the Lord. Viewing pornography and gratifying the flesh, like all sexual impurity, is a sin that, if not repented, will bring punishment from the Lord. If anyone rejects this teaching, they are rejecting God. If we were to continue in these sins, it would evidence that we do not know God, and no amount of "spiritual language" can fool God, who calls us to live a holy life and to be pure. God gives us His Holy Spirit to call us out of slavery to sin, to make us pure and to enable us to live holy lives.

Scripture warns us about presuming upon God's grace in any area of sexual immorality: "⁸We should not commit sexual immorality, as some of them did - and in one day twenty-three thousand of them died. ⁹We should not test the Lord, as some of them did - and were killed by snakes" 1 Corinthians 10:8-9).

Friend, those of us who are involved with The Way of Purity course have, in the past, lived in sexual immorality, in one form or another. For years, while in bondage to pornography, I rebelled against God and presumed upon His grace, by not forsaking my sins. God was, indeed, patient with me, and granted me repentance in His time. There is grace for all who will turn from their sin and turn to Christ; and grace will enable us to live a holy life now, regardless of where we have been. Grace is an amazing thing. It does not simply forgive the penalty of our sins, while leaving us under the power of sin. Instead, it forgives and enables; it pardons and empowers. And it does so "more and more" as we grow in grace.

Please heed the warnings in these words by L. Eiland.

Too Late

Too late, twill be for you to cry,
When mercy's day has passed you by!
When solemn night, of dark despair,
Shall come upon you halting there!
Too late, when death has barred the door,
Your wailings can be heard no more!
Rejected, there, thy soul will be
Shut out, through all eternity!
Will you not heed the voice today,
Inviting you to Christ obey?
And be prepared to enter there,
A pure and spotless robe to wear?
No longer, there in sin abide!
This all-important step decide!
Come out, where Christ can touch thy soul,
And at this moment be made whole!
Chorus:
Too late, too late, poor trembling soul!
O will this be your fate?
Too late, too late to be made whole!
Too late, too late, too late!

Question 14. Use this space to record your victories and/or challenges:

Scripture to Consider

"You have set our iniquities before you, our secret sins in the light of your presence" (Psalm 90:8).

"Whether you turn to the right or to the left, your ears will hear a voice behind you, saying, 'This is the way; walk in it.' Then you will defile your idols overlaid with silver and your images covered with gold; you will throw them away like a menstrual cloth and say to them, 'Away with you!'" (Isaiah 30:21, 22).

"...being confident of this, that he who began a good work in you will carry it on to completion until the day of Christ Jesus" (Phil. 1:6)

Were you free from pornography since you did the last lesson?

    Yes   No

Were you free from self-gratification since you did the last lesson?

    Yes   No

Were you free from sexual immorality since you did the last lesson?

    Yes   No

DAY 29 - OUR IDENTITY IN CHRIST

Thank you for continuing in The Way of Purity course. Today we are going to look at several verses in the book of Ephesians. We will consider:

Our Glorious Inheritance as God's Children
Our Identity in Christ

One of the lies that Satan wants us to believe is that our faith in Christ really has no effect on our lives, but that we are still the same old sinners we always were and haven't really changed a bit. This is a lie. In His Word, God tells us the truth about what really happens to people as they become His children and begin to escape the bondage they were in through Adam's sin.

The reason we need to understand our identity in Christ, is that knowing who we are will affect the way we respond to various events in our lives. When you are trying to overcome the sin of lust, for example, you need to know that you are not a lustful person in God's eyes, but that indeed, you have a new identity. If you believed that you were lustful, and you couldn't help yourself when tempted, you would very easily succumb to every temptation that comes your way. Knowing who we are in Christ will help us to be victorious over pornography and sexual sin. We do not go near the temptation because we are not the same people we were when we were "dead in sins and trespasses" (Ephesians 2:1). No, we are now "new creations in Christ" with new hearts and new desires and new motives. The Apostle Paul tells us in 2 Corinthians 5:17, "Therefore, if anyone is in Christ, he is a new creation; the old has gone, the new has come!" If we have repented of our sins, called out to Jesus to save us from them, and received Christ as Lord and Savior, then God tells us that we are "in Christ." What exactly does this mean? What is Paul saying when he states we are "in Christ?" My Bible happens to have study notes in it, and here's what it states about being "in Christ."

"In Christ. United with Christ through faith in Him and commitment to Him."

God is telling us that we have, as believers, a spiritual union with Jesus (and hence, with God Himself). The bond we have with the Lord is unseen, but it is nonetheless very real.

Jesus explains this truth in His prayer in John 14:20-21, "On that day you will realize that I am in my Father, and you are in me, and I am in you. Whoever has my commands and obeys them, he is the one who loves me. He who loves me will be loved by my Father, and I too will love him and show myself to him."

This describes our relationship with God very well. It is one of living in Him, and He living in us. He gives to us His life, and we give to Him our lives. He gives to us His love; we give to Him our love.

To enjoy our relationship with God to the fullest, we need to understand theologically how He has changed our lives, and then we need to experience that change, practically. Let's consider what God says about us, now that we are "in Christ."

Friend, let's look at Paul's letter to the Ephesians and contrast who we WERE, (¹ As for you, you were dead in your transgressions and sins, (Ephesians 2:1-10) with who we ARE now. First, we will examine who we USED to be. Next, we will see who we ARE.

Question 1. The rest of the questions for this day are all taken from Ephesians, chapter 2. According to verse 1, what were we?

   A.   Zombies
   B.   Living life to the fullest
   C.   Dead in sins and transgressions

Note: When we were born we were, in reality, dead! Obviously we are referring to being spiritually dead. And this "deadness" showed up in many ways in our lives, such as being in bondage to habitual sins of all kinds. And so to overcome this bondage to sin, we did not need education, behavior modification, or mere admonition to stop doing what we were doing. Instead, we needed life! We were born dead to God, dead to His Word, and dead to the church, etc.

> ² in which you used to live when you followed the ways of this world and of the ruler of the kingdom of the air, the spirit who is now at work in those who are disobedient.

Question 2. Who does verse 2 tell us we were?

   A.   Followers of Christ
   B.   Followers of the way to life
   C.   Followers of the world and Satan

Note: We were not only dead, but we were also devilish, as well; just following along after the "carrot" that Satan offered to lead us into his trap.

Question 3. What else does verse 2 tell us we were?

   A.   Satisfied by our enjoyment of pornography
   B.   Disobedient
   C.   Experiencing ever-increasing joy

> ³ All of us also lived among them at one time, gratifying the cravings of our sinful nature and following its desires and thoughts. Like the rest, we were by nature objects of wrath.

Question 4. What does verse 3 tell us we were?

   A.   Gratifiers of our sinful lusts
   B.   Gentle and loving people
   C.   Humble servants

Question 5. What else does verse 3 tell us we were?

   A.   Followers of every desire and thought
   B.   Able to resist temptation with ease

Note: Not only were we dead, devilish, and disobedient, but we were also depraved! This is the condition of all who follow their impulses and live to gratify their flesh. If we had an impulse to view porn and gratify the flesh, we did it. And slowly, over time, we began to be controlled by our impulses, which were becoming stronger and stronger.

Question 6. What does verse 3 tell us is the final description of who we used to be?
A. Objects of God's wrath
B. People who knew and loved God

Note: That's right, we were the destination of God's wrath! We were the bull's-eye for the arrows of God's hatred, the object of His anger. This ought to frighten us to the core of our very being, and if we have escaped the trap of pornography sexual impurity, we ought to be grateful for the grace of God!

Question 7. Please describe how your past life in pornography and/or immorality illustrates the above teaching. How were you dead, devilish, disobedient, depraved, etc.? Describe how your life verified the truth of Scripture.

We readily admit that a Christian who is, indeed, alive in Christ, may succumb to the temptation of pornography, adultery, or other sins. The believer is alive and, though he may be disobedient at the time, he is not dead, devilish, depraved, or under the wrath of God. The passage we have just studied is about unbelievers who live in sin. As it states in Ephesians 2, "¹ As for you, you were dead in your transgressions and sins, ² in which you used to live."

It is important that we understand that we were "objects of God's wrath" prior to our salvation. In that sense, the passage discussed today does not apply to those of us whose struggle(d) with immorality AFTER salvation.

Next, we will notice that a great transformation has taken place in those who receive Christ and become born again. We are not who we were! Our identity is different. Read the following passage, noticing who we are NOW.

⁴ But because of his great love for us, God, who is rich in mercy,

Question 8. According to verse 4, what are we?
A. Still hated by God
B. Loved by God
C. Somewhere in the middle

Note: It is God's love and grace that changes our identity.

The following testimony is from Kent:

Some may think that Satan wouldn't gain a foothold in a person's life when he appears to have had a good wholesome upbringing and all the tools to live a "good" life. But as we all learn, Satan is a roaring lion seeking anyone and everyone he may devour. And if we think we are strong enough to handle something or smart enough to not be sucked in by the wiles of the devil, then destruction looms at the door.

I grew up in a wonderful Christian home surrounded by love, peace, and security. In addition, God blessed me with a healthy body and a keen mind. With this kind of encouragement and foundation, I was able to accomplish many of the things I set out to do from my childhood into adulthood. Of course I thank God for the blessings of a loving family and would not trade my upbringing for something different; however, I was certainly in for a rude awakening when I realized I was in something that I could not overcome by my own strength or power.

I felt God's call at a young age of fourteen and turned my life over to Him. This also happened to be the time I was going through puberty and began to discover what sexuality was. Shortly after my conversion in the Lord, I discovered self-gratification, even though I didn't even know what the term meant. However, with my new relationship with God, I felt convicted that it wasn't right. As time went on, I confided my questions/guilt with my church leadership who encouraged me to abstain from this activity. However, I didn't seem to understand the true dangers of this problem or truly grasp what I needed to do to fully overcome. Over the course of the next fifteen years I continued to battle this addiction off and on.

I know now that the impurity of self-gratification opened the door to the sins of pornography. When I graduated from high school, I went away to college. Although I thought I was a responsible person, I began to realize that the devil was pounding away at this new independence from the structured and loving home in which I grew up. Although I was most likely viewed as an upstanding Christian, it was at this time in my life that I first saw and then looked at a pornographic magazine. Thankfully, I felt so guilty that I confessed to my parents and felt that it would never happen again. But unfortunately, I didn't learn how to apply the grace of God in battling this. Within the same year, I fell again.

So began a periodic falling to the sins of pornography and self-gratification. Sometimes, I was able to resist for months at a time. However, the time would eventually come when I would be lax in my vigilance and Satan would strike and I would fall. Each time, I would plead with God for forgiveness and promise to myself that this would never happen again. At times, I would seek out my parents or a church leader and confide my guilt, thinking each time that this would be the last time I would need to do this.

About five years ago, God led me to my marriage with a wonderful Christian woman. Our period of engagement was a true blessing, and I felt that this problem of pornography and sin was truly behind me. In the beginning months of our marriage, the temptations were minimal and I felt I was in the clear. However, the Internet was becoming more prevalent, and the ease of access became a new trap. I foolishly listened to the devil's persuasion that just looking to see what was out there would be good so I would know what to avoid. That of course was a lie, and I was foolish to listen.

So began the last chapter of my sin with pornography and self-gratification. My wife discovered my problem early on and she was deeply hurt and confused. I asked forgiveness and promised that it was not a problem and it would not happen again. You know that story; although I resisted for several months, I fell again. This happened several more times over the ensuing years. Each time I begged forgiveness and promised I could handle it. In actuality, that was the whole problem; I alone would never be able to handle it. For the first time in my life I began to feel trapped and in a position that I could not escape. Although I often consoled myself that I only viewed "free" pornography and wasn't involved in hardcore pornography or the purchasing of magazines or Internet subscriptions or Internet chatting, I finally came to the realization that I was bound by the chains of a habitual sin that was just as detestable to God as the vilest sin. I needed to humble myself, come in true repentance, and find the enabling grace of God to overcome this.

When I reached this low point, I began to see that I was putting my soul, my family, and my life in extreme jeopardy. My wife encouraged me to seek counseling, and I cried out to God for help. He opened the door to the Setting Captives Free website. Before truly committing to the course, I read the "95 Theses" document on the website and those truths convicted me and helped me realize that this course is what I needed. I began the course with a ray of hope wanting so badly to find real freedom, but wondering if God would truly forgive me for all those years of periodic but habitual sin. Through the course and the counsel of my mentor I found that, indeed, He would forgive me and set me free as a testimony of His love, mercy and grace.

Thanks be to God, I have repented and confessed my sin, found forgiveness through Jesus Christ, and by His grace have been walking in light and freedom for nearly four months. I now see how weak the flesh is, and that it is not by my strength but by God and God only can I live an overcoming life. There is true freedom through Jesus Christ, and I rejoice and thank God for His mercy, love, grace, and power. To Him be the power, glory, and honor. Amen!

Questions

Question 9. What else does verse 4 tell us we are?
A. Second-class Christians
B. Recipients of God's mercy
C. Step-children

⁵ made us alive with Christ even when we were dead in transgressions – it is by grace you have been saved.

Question 10. What does verse 5 tell us we are?
A. Mummies
B. Still dead in sin
C. Alive with Christ

Question 11. What do verses 5 and 8 tell us we are?
A. Trying to get saved
B. Saved by grace
C. Saved by our works

Note: Salvation is by grace alone. Not grace, plus what we do; it is all of grace. God chose us to be saved in eternity past (Ephesians 1, 2 Thessalonians 2:13), gave us grace to believe (Acts 18:27), and it is God who will keep us saved throughout eternity (Jude).

⁶ And God raised us up with Christ and seated us with him in the heavenly realms in Christ Jesus,

Question 12. What else are we in verse 6?
A. Seated on David's couch
B. Earthly people
C. Seated with Christ in heaven

Note: This very principle, of being alive and raised up from sin, is why man's methods of helping those with addictions will not work. Man can give advice, suggestions, and counsel, but man cannot impart life! Only God can raise the dead.

⁷ in order that in the coming ages he might show the incomparable riches of his grace, expressed in his kindness to us in Christ Jesus.

Question 13. According to verse 7 who are we?
A. Recipients of God's grace and kindness
B. Targets of wrath

⁸ For it is by grace you have been saved through faith–and this is not from yourselves, it is the gift of God–

⁹ not by works, so that no one can boast.

Question 14. According to verses 8 and 9, what are we?
A. Saved by faith in Christ
B. Saved by our own efforts to overcome sin

¹⁰ For we are God's workmanship, created in Christ Jesus to do good works, which God prepared in advance for us to do.

Question 15. What does verse 10 tell us we are?
A. Useless, broken vessels
B. God's workmanship

Note: The Greek word for "workmanship," in verse 10, is the word "poema," from where we get our word "poem." We are God's poem to the world, His art that displays His grace, His workmanship of love.

So, let us summarize who we used to be, versus who we are now:

WE WERE:

1. Dead in transgressions and sins (v. 1, 5)
2. Followers of the world and Satan (v. 2)
3. Disobedient to God (v. 2)
4. Gratifiers of our sinful lusts (v. 3)
5. Followers of our every desire and thought (v. 3)
6. Objects of God's wrath (v. 3)

WE ARE:

1. Loved by God (v. 4)
2. Recipients of God's mercy (v. 4)
3. Alive with Christ (v. 5)
4. Saved by grace (v. 5, 8)
5. Raised up with Christ (v. 6)
6. Seated with Christ in heaven (v. 6)
7. Recipients of God's grace and kindness in Christ (v. 7)
8. Saved through faith in Christ (not from ourselves, it is a gift of God, and not by our works) (v. 8, 9)
9. God's workmanship (v. 10)
10. Created (this means re-created) in Christ Jesus to do good works pre-prepared for us (v. 10)

Wow, isn't it awesome to consider all that God has done for us? Take time right now to praise God in prayer for all the wonderful things He's done in our lives. We are not the same anymore!

My challenge to you is to take the book of Ephesians and do this same kind of study. There are even more wonderful truths you will discover about who you are now in Christ Jesus! God's word has the power to literally transform us.

Paul said in 2 Corinthians 3:18, "And we, who with unveiled faces all reflect the Lord's glory, are being transformed into his likeness with ever-increasing glory, which comes from the Lord, who is the Spirit."

Question 16. Practically speaking, what are some differences in your life, now that you have left pornography and sexual impurity behind? Can you tell a difference? Does anyone else see the change?

There are two issues, however, which might lead Christians who struggled with impurity to apply this passage to our situation: (1) Obviously, if we continue to wallow in sin, we are creating doubt about our salvation (1 John 3:6-10; 1 Corinthians 6:9-11, etc.) So, if my sinful habits are a sign that I was never truly saved, then perhaps I am still an object of God's wrath! (2) Even if I am saved and no longer in danger of hell (that's the meaning of "object of God's wrath"), as a child of God, I am still setting myself up for God's CHASTENING if I persist in sinning. I can tell you, from personal experience, that sometimes God's chastening feels a lot like his wrath!

Scripture to Consider

I have been crucified with Christ and I no longer live, but Christ lives in me. The life I live in the body, I live by faith in the Son of God, who loved me and gave himself for me (Galatians 2:20).

Were you free from pornography since you did the last lesson?

Yes   No

Were you free from self-gratification since you did the last lesson?

Yes   No

Were you free from sexual immorality since you did the last lesson?

Yes   No

DAY 30 – NEW CREATIONS IN CHRIST (SALVATION ILLUSTRATED)

Today, we will study a passage that will encourage us toward a better understanding of how salvation works, and how it relates to our previous pornography and sexual impurity. It follows on the heels of yesterday's lesson, which taught us we are "new CREATIONS in Christ." (2 Corinthians 5:17) I truly can't wait to share this with you, so let's get started!

In the beginning God created the heavens and the earth. The earth was without form and void, and darkness was over the face of the deep, and the Spirit of God was hovering over the face of the waters. And God said, 'Let there be light,' and there was light (Genesis 1:1-2).

Therefore, if anyone is in Christ, he is a new creation; the old has passed away; behold, the new has come (2 Corinthians 5:17).

Friend, we are new "creations" in Jesus. I am not a "refurbished" Mike; I am totally new. God does not shave caterpillars, he makes butterflies! And so it is profitable for us to study the biblical account of the creation of the earth, for in it we see how God has saved us.

Notice there are three things said of the earth in the beginning. It was

1. Formless
2. Empty
3. In darkness

And, if we look at Genesis 1, verse 9, we see a fourth description of the earth:
   4. Submerged underneath water

Do you see how all of this relates to us as new creations in Christ? We, too, at one time were

Formless - this same word is translated "confusion" in Deuteronomy 32:10.
Empty - Why did we turn to pornography and immorality, anyway? Probably because we were trying to "fill the void." Emptiness in heart and life is the condition of all who are trapped in sexual sin. Instead of being "filled with all the fullness of God," and having an overflowing cup, as David did, we were inwardly empty, lonely, yearning people.

Course member Michael wrote, "I wanted to be filled with love and companionship, but by looking at porn, I alienated myself from any hope of ever finding a lasting love. My heart was empty, and I found the further into porn I went, the further I was from satisfaction and fullness."

In Darkness - Oh friend, can you remember the darkness that pervaded your life in pornography and impurity? The absence of light, wisdom, direction, and illumination all characterized my 15-year addiction to pornography and immorality.

Submerged underneath the water. We were dead and buried under the water of our sin. We were lost, sunk, submerged, and dead.

So, we have a perfect description of how we were when trapped in sin. We were "formless," confused, empty, in darkness and buried under the water of our sin.

Question 4. Referring to the word "submerged," above - Did you ever feel as if you were sunk down deep in it, and submerged? How so?

Question 5. Write out how the above verse applies to you and salvation.

> *Course member Tim wrote,* "When I was deep into it, it consumed me. A good portion of my time was spent in the pursuit of pornography."

Next, God "said" let there be light. Please don't miss this: It is the Word of God that brings light. Notice this verse: "The unfolding of your words gives light; it imparts understanding to the simple (Psalm 119:130).

Friend, if you are saved, there was a time in your life that you were in darkness. Possibly this was when you were in pornographic and sexual slavery. But then you began having an interest in Scripture, and you were drawn to Jesus Christ. He spoke light into your heart through His Word, dispelling your sin and darkness. And now you are becoming, for lack of a better word, "addicted" to God's Word and you are receiving illumination, understanding, and wisdom (light).

The Apostle Paul, under the inspiration of the Holy Spirit, applied Genesis 1:1-3 in this fashion. Paul says in 2 Corinthians 4:6 "For God, who said, 'Let light shine out of darkness,' has shone in our hearts to give the light of the knowledge of the glory of God in the face of Jesus Christ." It is the same God who spoke light into darkness in creation. He illuminates our hearts with Jesus Christ in salvation. Do you see it?

So we were indeed confused, empty, in darkness, and buried in sin. But the Holy Spirit was "hovering" over us and God said, "Let there be light," and the Word brought light into our hearts. Let us continue in our study.

> And God said, 'Let the waters under the heavens be gathered together into one place, and let the dry land appear.' And it was so (Genesis 1:9).

Now, this is where it begins to get truly exciting. Do you see what is happening here? The earth, which was submerged beneath the water, has now come bursting up through the water, sort of like a resurrection. What was once buried is now alive, and is about to begin producing fruit!

This is YOU, if you are in Christ. Once empty, in darkness, buried in sin, but now raised from the dead, full of the glory of God, enjoying the light of Jesus Christ. And watch this...

> And God said, 'Let the earth sprout vegetation, plants yielding seed, and fruit trees bearing fruit in which is their seed, according to its kind on the earth." And it was so (Genesis 1:11).

This gets better and better. Now, the earth is alive and producing fruit. Oh, how I wish you and I were sharing this Scripture together face-to-face right now, feeding on the truth of it. Do you see what is happening? Now, I am not going to comment on this verse. Instead, I'm going to ask you to do so.

> *Course member Troy wrote,* "In hindsight, I can see that NO part of my life was unaffected by my use of pornography and my submission to my lustful thoughts. There were parts of me, intellectual, spiritual, and physical that were wasted on pornography and lust. These parts of me have been released from the slavery of lust, just as my soul has been freed from the damnation of sin. These parts are now able to join the rest of me in celebrating life and the salvation Christ has freely offered to me."

The following testimony is from Dave:

I was a slave to lust and self-gratification for nineteen years. I came to this course disheartened and discouraged, believing that though I was "saved" and even deeply involved in ministry to His church, I would probably never be free from this bondage and the guilt and shame that accompanied it. When a friend told me about this course I was skeptical, but I went to check it out anyway. I signed up that night for the Way of Purity, began the daily lessons, began applying the biblical principles I found here, and have been free ever since. That was in January of 2003, and I have continued to walk in freedom and purity! I am now using my hard-fought and grace-given freedom to help others find their way back to obedience to our great God and Savior.

Question 6. John 15:5 states, "I am the Vine, you are the branches. Whoever abides in Me and I in him, he it is that bears much fruit, for apart from Me, you can do nothing." How does that verse apply to what we are studying?

Oh friend, it is truly quite wonderful to know God as Creator; not so much that He created the world (though that is important) but that He can create good out of bad, light out of darkness, and order out of chaos in our lives.

And now you can tell your testimony to others in a very short and simple manner: "I was empty, in darkness, and buried under the waters of sin; but God spoke light into my heart, raised me from the dead, filled me with His Son, and is making me fruitful." Amen!

Now one last point: Did you happen to notice that it was on the third day that the "resurrection" of the earth happened? This point is important. In creation, there was initial chaos, darkness, emptiness and death. And then on the third day, there was a resurrection unto life and fruitfulness! Do you understand? The Lord Jesus emptied Himself for us amidst the chaos of His crucifixion. Then He hung on the cross in darkness and died for our sins. But on the third day, He arose from the dead, victorious over sin, death, hell and the grave. And now you and I are the fruit of His suffering. We are the living souls He died to produce, and we carry precious seed to give life to others. Please do not miss this precious picture of our Lord Jesus Christ here in the first chapter of Genesis.

I'm now going to present to you a number of course member comments for your perusal and to show that our experiences while "submerged" in the darkness of pornography and sexual sin are common:

> *Course member Roy wrote,* "I hope the feelings I have do not constitute pride. But it seems as if I need to get to know myself all over again. This new person is one I definitely like better than the old - new, fresh, likeable. My wife and I kept our grandkids yesterday, and I actually felt like entering into their lives more than usual. Just being myself, and talking to each one of them was so neat. I actually wanted to just be with them. I've learned that self-gratification and porn certainly do dim the joy and light in one's heart, and bruise one's desire for living. Thanks for your ministry, and your loving concern."

> *Course member Joe wrote,* "This very much describes my past. I was submerged in the deep waters of pornography. I am now above those waters. The Lord has saved me from drowning, and from a horrible death/destruction, as in the case of Ted Bundy. I don't know where I would have ended up if I had gone further down, but I do know it would have been through the path to destruction. The Lord saved me and turned me to the opposite direction of this path."

> *Course member Micah wrote,* "I was drowning in life, without God's guidance. But now I feel as if I am walking on water."

Question 7. How are things in your life right now? Are you struggling with anything?

Scripture to Consider

[1] There is therefore now no condemnation for those who are in Christ Jesus. [2] For the law of the Spirit of life has set you free in Christ Jesus from the law of sin and death. [3] For God has done what the law, weakened by the flesh, could not do. By sending his own Son in the likeness of sinful flesh and for sin, he condemned sin in the flesh, [4] in order that the righteous requirement of the law might be fulfilled in us, who walk, not according to the flesh, but according to the Spirit (Romans 8:1-4).

Were you free from pornography since you did the last lesson?

    Yes   No

Were you free from self-gratification since you did the last lesson?

    Yes   No

Were you free from sexual immorality since you did the last lesson?

    Yes   No

DAY 31 – THE GREATNESS, MAJESTY, POWER AND GRACE OF GOD

This course is not just a "how to" guide for overcoming pornography and sexual impurity. The real purpose of this course is to assist us in viewing God as He really is, and to love Him supremely. For if the Holy Spirit opens our eyes to see the vastness, majesty and glory of God, and we are brought to see His power and grace, then our response will be one of worship and love of God. In other words, this course is not just about ceasing sinful behavior; it is about helping us to love God. It is not just about morality, it is about holiness.

Today, we will examine a passage of Scripture that shows the glory, majesty and power of God, as well as His grace and compassion. May Scripture expand our view of Who God is, and cause us to be in awe of Him; for surely we cannot view the greatness and glory of God, and still be involved in habitual sin. Please read the following verses, and answer the questions.

> See, the Sovereign LORD comes with power, and his arm rules for him. See, his reward is with him, and his recompense accompanies him (Isaiah 40:10).

The above verse describes God as the "Sovereign Lord" who comes with power and strength. This teaches us that God is God over all, the supreme Potentate, and the ruling King. "His arm rules for Him" is a metaphor for God being strong enough to rule, doing as He pleases, and being able to accomplish what He decrees.

> He tends his flock like a shepherd: He gathers the lambs in his arms and carries them close to his heart; he gently leads those that have young. (Isaiah 40:11).

Verse 10 described God as the Sovereign Lord displaying His power, but verse 11 describes Him as a loving Shepherd displaying His grace. This God is not only One Who is in control of the entire universe, but He is also the caring Shepherd who loves individual "sheep," carrying them closely and leading them gently.

This combination of Lord and Shepherd, of Divine Power and Divine Love, of Majesty and Grace, is what makes our God so amazing. "What makes Christ glorious is an admirable conjunction of diverse excellencies." (Jonathan Edwards, "The Excellency of Christ," in The Works of Jonathan Edwards, Vol. 1—Edinburgh: The Banner of Truth Trust, 1974—Page 680)

> Who has measured the waters in the hollow of his hand, or with the breadth of his hand marked off the heavens? Who has held the dust of the earth in a basket, or weighed the mountains on the scales and the hills in a balance? (Isaiah 40:12)

Scientists tell us that the entire existing universe is so vast and expansive that it cannot be measured, and yet God marks it off with His hand. The use of the word "hand," here, is not to teach us that God has body parts, for He is a Spirit, but to show the supreme greatness of God over His created universe. The vast universe, that baffles the scientific genius of man and leaves him speechless, is but a handbreadth to God. In verse 10, above, we saw the power of God; in verse 11, we saw His grace and now, in verse 12, we see His glory. Who is like unto our God?

> [13] Who has understood the mind of the LORD, or instructed him as his counselor? [14] Whom did the LORD consult to enlighten him, and who taught him the right way? Who was it that taught him knowledge or showed him the path of understanding? (Isaiah 40:13-14)

These questions, and the verses that follow, are designed to show the insignificance of man in light of the greatness of God. Is there anyone on earth who might suggest to God that He measure the universe differently, or that He should use a different basket in which to carry the entire dust of the earth, or that He weigh the mountains using different scales? Hollywood actress Shirley MacLaine may declare all she wants, "I Am God" but when has she measured the entire universe with her hand, or carried the dust of the earth in a basket or weighed mountains? **Those who do not see the greatness of God, become great in their own eyes.**

> [15] Surely the nations are like a drop in a bucket; they are regarded as dust on the scales; he weighs the islands as though they were fine dust. [16] Lebanon is not sufficient for altar fires, nor its animals enough for burnt offerings. [17] Before him all the nations are as nothing; they are regarded by him as worthless and less than nothing (Isaiah 40:15-17).

What type of God can look at teeming nations, such as China, whose population is 1,306,313,812 or Russia, whose population is 143,420,309, and call them "a drop in the bucket" and "dust on the scales?" What kind of a God is able to weigh an island? And in light of the greatness of God, these nations of man are considered by Him as "nothing," "worthless," and "less than nothing."

> To whom, then, will you compare God? What image will you compare him to? (Isaiah 40:18)

The Living God is the incomparably great God, unable to be reduced to words, inexplicable in human terminology, and unlike anything that has been or ever could be made.

Question 1. Please examine what these verses have to say about the greatness of God and compare it with your view of God, up to this point. Are you growing in comprehension of the greatness of God? What are your thoughts so far?

Question 2. According to the above verses, what will be the proper view of man, once we catch a glimpse of the greatness of God?

Question 3. If people think themselves to be great, what are they missing?

21 Do you not know? Have you not heard? Has it not been told you from the beginning? Have you not understood since the earth was founded? 22 He sits enthroned above the circle of the earth, and its people are like grasshoppers. He stretches out the heavens like a canopy, and spreads them out like a tent to live in. 23 He brings princes to naught and reduces the rulers of this world to nothing. 24 No sooner are they planted, no sooner are they sown, no sooner do they take root in the ground, than he blows on them and they wither, and a whirlwind sweeps them away like chaff (Isaiah 40:21-24).

The questions in verse 21 are almost a mimic of man's inability to perceive the greatness of God. What can't you understand? Can't you perceive that God is the God of the entire universe, the great King of all creation, who uses the entire heavens for His tent, who does as He pleases with all of mankind? Isn't this obvious to you? Paul says, 9 "Since what may be known about God is plain to them, because God has made it plain to them. 20 For since the creation of the world God's invisible qualities – his eternal power and divine nature – have been clearly seen, being understood from what has been made, so that men are without excuse (Romans 1:19-20).

25 "To whom will you compare me? Or who is my equal?" says the Holy One. 26 Lift your eyes and look to the heavens: Who created all these? He who brings out the starry host one by one, and calls them each by name. Because of his great power and mighty strength, not one of them is missing (Isaiah 40:25-26).

Though this passage compares mankind to "grasshoppers," yet God cannot be compared to anything, for He is too great. God is awesome in splendor, powerful in majesty, beautiful in grace, and He has no equal. Can the great gurus of other religions create the heavens? Can all the prophets of all the religions down through the ages bring out each star and give it a name?

Why do you say, O Jacob, and complain, O Israel, "My way is hidden from the LORD; my cause is disregarded by my God"? Do you not know? Have you not heard? The LORD is the everlasting God, the Creator of the ends of the earth. He will not grow tired or weary, and his understanding no one can fathom (Isaiah 40:27-28).

Since God is so great, and since He has created all things and is ruling over all things, can we hide from Him? When we rush to click onto the pornographic website, or we hurry to leave work so we can commit adultery, is our way hidden from God? Does God look the other way when we watch X-rated videos? "For a man's ways are in full view of the LORD, and he examines all his paths" (Proverbs 5:21). God sees everything we do, and though we may think we are sinning in secret, the things done in darkness will be exposed by the light one day. Our way is not hidden from the Lord, and we can never sin in secret. As Moses was about to kill the Egyptian, he "looked left and right," to see if anyone was watching. Having concluded that no one was watching, he killed the Egyptian. Although he looked left and right, he forgot to look up. God sees all we do, at all times (see Proverbs 5:21).

29 He gives strength to the weary and increases the power of the weak. 30 Even youths grow tired and weary, and young men stumble and fall; 31 but those who hope in the LORD will renew their strength. They will soar on wings like eagles; they will run and not grow weary, they will walk and not be faint (Isaiah 40:29-31).

Here is what today's teaching on the greatness and awesome power of the Lord comes down to: All of God's power is employed to strengthen the weary and to increase the power of the weak.

Question 4. Verse 31 is the "bridge" that enables us to cross over from stumbling and falling, to soaring and running. What is this bridge, and what does it mean?

Question 5. By way of review, please write down all the things that this passage teaches us about God. Please do not rush through this, but contemplate all that God is, and all that He can do.

Question 6. If God is showing you His own greatness, and your own insignificance, by comparison? How do you think this will affect your life?

Friend, when I was involved in the habitual sins of pornography, self-gratification, and adultery, I entertained great thoughts about myself. I thought I was more spiritual than others that I was an authority on Scripture and that people should look up to me. Sin hardens and deceives and that, combined with my biblical knowledge, led me into thinking I was somebody. All of these great thoughts about me were because my view of God was so small.

God gave me over to sin for a time, much like He gave King Nebuchadnezzar over to an insane mind for seven years (to live on the fields and eat grass like a cow.) He showed me that my will was only free to sin, that He was in control of all things, and that He held my life (both physical and spiritual) in His hands. Through my sin, the subsequent loss of my first marriage, and the labels placed on me by others, "Adulterer," "Fornicator," etc., God began bringing me low and reducing me to nothing. Finally, I had lost all self-respect, and thought God had thrown me away on the trash heap of sinful humanity. This is how I, as a young man, "stumbled and fell."

But then, God did an amazing thing. He began picking me back up, remaking me, giving me grace to forsake sin and embrace Christ, empowering me (when I was so weak) to "soar" and "run" and "walk", and now He is making me useful. This is causing me to say, "Wow, look at Who God is, and what He can do. He not only created the heavens and the earth, but He has also taken me out of the trap of the devil, is carrying me close to His heart, and giving me strength to overcome sin.

Finally, as a special treat for this lesson, I want to include a quote from John Piper's excellent book entitled, *Seeing and Savoring Jesus Christ*. This quote is from pages 36-38:

"'The Lion that is from the tribe of Judah, the Root of David, has overcome so as to open the book and its seven seals' (Revelation 5:5). Here is the triumphant lion-like Christ ready to unroll the scroll of history.

"But what do we see in the next verse? 'I saw between the throne (with the four living creatures) and the elders, a LAMB standing as if slain, having seven horns and seven eyes, which are the seven Spirits of God, sent out into all the earth' (verse 6). So the Lion is a Lamb—an animal that is weak and harmless and lowly and easily preyed upon, and sheared naked for clothes, and killed for our food. So Christ is a lamb-like Lion.

"The Lion of Judah conquered because he was willing to act the part of a lamb. He came into Jerusalem on Palm Sunday like a king on the way to a throne, and he went out of Jerusalem on Good Friday like a lamb on the way to a slaughter. He drove out the robbers from the Temple like a lion devouring its prey. And then at the end of the week He gave His majestic neck to the knife, and they slaughtered the Lion of Judah like a sacrificial lamb.

"But what sort of lamb? Revelation 5:6 says, the 'Lamb was standing, as if slain, having seven horns.' Notice two things. First, the Lamb is 'standing.' It is not slumped in a bloody heap on the ground as it once was. Yes, it had been slain. But now it is standing—standing in the innermost circle next to the throne.

"Second, the Lamb has seven horns. A horn is a symbol of strength and power throughout the book of Revelation (12:3; 13:1; 17:3,12), as well as in the Old Testament (Deuteronomy 33:17; Psalm 18:2; 112:9). And the number seven signifies fullness and completeness. So this is no ordinary lamb. He is alive from the dead, and He is completely mighty in His sevenfold strength. He is, in fact, a lion-like Lamb.

The following testimony is from John:

I grew up like any other kid in America. I played sports, football, wrestling, and track. I also went to church, sometimes against my will. I was on the honor roll. I was saved and baptized in my early teens. But I had this sin I always kept hiding. I could not get into R-rated movies at the theater when I was in high school, but I could rent soft porn at the family video store. This grew over the years as I began to buy porn magazines and rent R-rated movies. One day I decided I would go to a strip club and was hooked. Next came adult massage parlors and after the first time I vowed never to do it again. I bought a computer and got on to the Internet and saw the pictures at the porn sites. I was afraid I would get caught, so I made an appointment with the youth pastor at my church. He and I are close in age so I could trust him.

My youth pastor challenged me to confess my sins to an accountability partner. I confessed everything and held nothing back. When I was involved in this lifestyle I felt like dirt, like I was unclean. All the time I was involved in this lifestyle I knew I was doing wrong, that I was sinning against God. I rededicated my life to God and started living for Jesus. I started The Way of Purity course and fell once or twice, but quickly went to my pastor and confessed. Since I started that course, I try to picture myself walking with Jesus. It has been really cool.

So if you are struggling in any way, I encourage you to find someone you can trust and confess your sins. Believe me, it is worth it.

Scripture to Consider

But you are a chosen people, a royal priesthood, a holy nation, a people belonging to God, that you may declare the praises of him who called you out of darkness into his wonderful light. Once you were not a people, but now you are the people of God; once you had not received mercy, but now you have received mercy (1 Peter 2:9-10).

"...The gentleness and humility of the lamb-like Lion becomes brilliant alongside the limitless and everlasting authority of the lion-like Lamb. Only this fits our longing for greatness. Yes, we are weak and weary and heavy-laden. But there burns in every heart, at least from time to time, a dream that our lives will count for something great. To this dream Jesus said, 'All authority has been given to Me in heaven and on earth. Go therefore and make disciples of all the nations...and lo, I am with you always, even to the end of the age" (Matthew 28:18-20).

Were you free from pornography since you did the last lesson?

    Yes   No

Were you free from self-gratification since you did the last lesson?

    Yes   No

Were you free from sexual immorality since you did the last lesson?

    Yes   No

DAY 32 – BATTLE STRATEGIES

YOU ARE AT WAR, SOLDIER. IT'S TIME TO LEARN HOW TO FIGHT!

During the next several days, we will examine the tactics of the enemy of our souls, as well as develop some battle strategies of our own to combat them. Please read the following verses, paying close attention to exactly where the enemy wages war on us.

> For though we live in the world, we do not wage war as the world does. The weapons we fight with are not the weapons of the world. On the contrary, they have divine power to demolish strongholds. We demolish arguments and every pretension that sets itself up against the knowledge of God, and we take captive every thought to make it obedient to Christ (2 Corinthians 10:3-5).

Questions

Question 1. From the above verses, where does the devil attack us? In other words, where is the battle fought?
  A. In Battleground, Washington
  B. In political and cultural issues
  C. In the mind, in our thoughts

Question 2. What do the above verses call evil thoughts that can get lodged in our minds?
  A. Strongholds
  B. Brainteasers
  C. Common and ordinary thoughts

Soldiers, we are in a battle, and the battlefield is the mind. The enemy desires to set up "thought strongholds" in our minds. These are thoughts that won't go away, that eventually demand we act upon them. These "strongholds" are whatever is opposed to "the knowledge of God." Here is how one student put it on his enrollment form: "I want to leave behind all forms of sexual impurity that pervade my life. First, the endless and repetitive pornographic thoughts I have throughout the day which lead into viewing more pornography and then, of course, to self-gratification."

So here is what happens: Everything is going just fine, and all of a sudden a pornographic picture comes into our thoughts. Possibly it is of a pornographic movie we watched years ago, or it might be a more recent image we have seen over the Internet. Soldiers, THIS is the beginning of a thought-stronghold. This image that is lodging itself in the brain is in opposition to the knowledge of God. After all, the knowledge of God is whatever is true, noble, right, pure, lovely, and admirable (Philippians 4:8) and is what should constantly occupy our thoughts. We understand, then, that the evil one is setting that pornographic image up in our minds to turn us away from God. This image and the associated emotions that are conjured up in the heart, may well become a stronghold of the devil and lead us into self-gratification, adultery, and/or other sins.

If our particular downfall is Internet chatting, we could pray all day against going to the chat groups, but all of a sudden thoughts come into our heads, such as, "Everybody loves you there! Somebody is just waiting to see your name come on his or her screen. They need your gentle caring and loving concern, as well as your quick wit and romantic style. In fact, somebody there will no doubt want to have cyber-sex with you, and is probably waiting for you right now." Though we try to push these thoughts away, and may be successful the first or second time, eventually the thoughts get stuck in our minds, and we are soon involved in sin.

Questions

Question 3. What is your particular temptation scenario?

We need to make sure we understand that our minds are a battleground. And, more importantly, we need to possess "Divine weapons" and know how to fight using them. In today's study, it should become obvious that the enemy wages war on our minds. Notice the following verses:

> The mind of sinful man is death... (Romans 8:6).

The reason that the mind of sinful man is death is because the devil has numerous thought-strongholds there. Sinful man is fixated on sinful thoughts, and the wages of sin is death. In our case, pornographic images or impure memories may totally overwhelm and control our minds.

> The sinful mind is hostile to God. It does not submit to God's law nor can it do so (Romans 8:7).

The sinful mind is saturated in sinful thoughts. When God's law requires it to think pure, lovely, truthful thoughts, it is totally unable to do so. The sinful mind is filled with sinful images and is bent on fulfilling the desires of the flesh.

> Many live as the enemies of the cross of Christ. Their destiny is destruction, their god is their stomach, and their glory is in their shame. Their mind is on earthly things (Philippians 3:19).

Friend, our minds are the battleground. If the devil can just get our minds fixed on "earthly things," he knows that we will be "enemies of the cross" and, therefore, enemies of God.

> [28] Furthermore, since they did not think it worthwhile to retain the knowledge of God, he gave them over to a depraved mind, to do what ought not to be done. [29] They have become filled with every kind of wickedness, evil, greed and depravity. They are full of envy, murder, strife, deceit and malice" (Romans 1:28-29).

People who do not retain the knowledge of God are given over "to a depraved mind" to do what should not be done.

But I see another law at work in the members of my body, waging war against the law of my mind and making me a prisoner of the law of sin at work within my members (Romans 7:23).

In this verse, we see that the war is waged against the mind and, when the enemy is successful, we become prisoners of sin.

Question 4. Now it is time for personal reflection. What experiences have you had with pornography or other sexual memories that verify the truth that your mind is a battlefield? Have you felt, at times, that you were unable to control your mind? What "strongholds" have you experienced in the past?

Tomorrow, we will examine the resources we have to fight the battle. Meanwhile, we need to be aware of where the battlefield is –the thought life– and how the devil gets access to our hearts, through "thought strongholds." Friends, please be on guard. "Your enemy, the devil, prowls around like a roaring lion looking for someone to devour" (1 Peter 5:8). And one of the ways he "devours" is through these "thought strongholds."

Here are two things we might do to combat these thoughts that may get lodged in our minds:

1. We should refuse to have access to any further pornography, which will stop any incoming pornographic images that would drag us into sin. This point is key; by allowing ourselves zero access to inappropriate images, there really won't be any victory in this area. Please review Matthew 5:29-30, Romans 13:14 and Joshua 7:13.

2. We need to begin to immerse ourselves in Scripture, seeking God for grace to apply what we read. Taking in the Water of the Word has the effect of washing away the images that remain in the brain. Please review Joshua 1:8 and Psalm 1:3.

Over time, as we continue to put these two principles into practice, we will become free from all strongholds of the enemy, by the grace of God.

Question 5. Please record the two principles that will rid the brain of pornographic images:

1.

2.

Course member Dave wrote, "In the past, I sought pornography on the net and through the medium of print and video. I also frequented a strip club. This has left a sinful thought process imprinted on my mind. When meeting women, whether at work, on the street or even in church, I find myself invariably viewing them as an object of sexual desire. I know this is wrong, but it sometimes seems that I have no control over my thoughts, like an old TV I had when the tuner which was going bad and kept switching channels. It wouldn't stay on the selected channel for more than a few minutes, then it defaulted back to channel 2. My thought process is like that at present though, with God's help, it is changing."

The following testimony is from John:

My sin was in the area of lustful conversations and self-gratification. After stumbling across settingcaptivesfree.com, I decided to take a peak and see what the site was all about. My first impression was, "I don't really need this site, as I am not involved in pornography or anything like that." I moved on but bookmarked the site. About a month later after hitting frustration over these kinds of conversations, I decided that maybe I needed to go back to this site and see if I could find some help to stay pure in every area of my life.

I signed up for the 60-day Way of Purity course. I liked the idea of having an accountability partner, because I knew I would not want to give into sin as long as I had to confess to someone. I was surprised that when I repented of my sins and made the decision to begin the course the desire to do self-gratification or have anymore of these conversations totally left. I began the course with much anticipation of gaining true freedom once and for all. My relationship with the Lord really took off.

I had a hard time understanding intimacy with God because of past abuse but, during the course, God began to restore me in all of these areas and reveal what true intimacy with Jesus is - enjoying being in His presence and drinking from His life-giving waters of the Spirit of God. Where I once feared Him because of how I thought He viewed me, I love Him today. I know that I have been washed by the blood of the Lamb and am made clean. I can stand in His presence assured of my salvation and free from sin that once had me bound. His grace alone empowers me to walk away from my sin and remain free. I have found the source of true life. Living by the Spirit and drinking from the wells of Living Water will change you from the inside out, make you a new person, restore right relationships, give you new desires, and redeem your soul. PRAISE GOD!

Course member John wrote, "I have had many times that I would start to think about looking at pornography and, from the mental picture, would gratify my flesh."

Course member Hans wrote, "The images I have experienced pop up in my mind at the worst times for me, and the best times for the adversary. He and his henchmen have studied me, and know when to strike hard. I have not, by the grace of God, gone any farther than pornography and self-gratification, but this alone has given Satan a stronghold on my whole being. I have become limited or damned by this. I am slowly turning to God and asking him to fight the battle. I cannot win alone; I have tried for 15 years. The images and fantasies are the strongholds where Lucifer twists my logic and makes my addiction seem like a comfortable old friend. He is losing the fight, however, as day by day I feel more and more freedom."

Course member Jim wrote, "When we fight Satan, it is in our minds. We take down strongholds that he has put there. I have experienced this for a long time now, and even more since I started this course. Satan does not want me to be free from porn, and he is far from being done with me. I have fallen recently, and day 60 is a long way away. God will get me to that point, because it is His will; I am sure of this. However, Satan will continue to attack. I would be a fool to think that, after 60 days, Satan will just leave me alone. But he will be a lot weaker than he is now. God has been mighty in my life recently, and this is just the beginning. All of this has happened in my mind; in the spiritual realm. It is a war, and we are in the midst of it. I will not become a casualty of war. I will not become MIA or POW. I am going to pray that GOD will not let that happen. And because I know that that is HIS will, HE will do it. I have taken a few bullets, but no more. Best of all, we know who wins the war. GOD DOES!"

Dennis wrote, "The paragraph starting with "So, here is what happens. . ." is exactly describing the battlefield in my mind. I have pictures in my head of movies I watched as a teenager, and pictures I have seen on the Internet. Until I started this study and began to work on filling my mind with the things of God, when one of those images flashed into my head, it was all a downhill slide from there. Something would remind me of something I had seen and I would start "teasing" myself on the Internet - "Just a peek" is how I would convince myself it was okay. But of course that never worked. Even if I were satisfied temporarily with "just a peek," within a day or two I would give in completely. It's when Satan reminds me of the things I have done and seen that I feel the temptation the strongest to give in again."

Your comments:

Scripture to Consider

No one engaged in warfare entangles himself with the affairs of this life, that he may please him who enlisted him as a soldier (2 Timothy 2:4).

Were you free from pornography since you did the last lesson?

    Yes   No

Were you free from self-gratification since you did the last lesson?

    Yes   No

Were you free from sexual immorality since you did the last lesson?

    Yes   No

DAY 33 – DEMOLISHING STRONGHOLDS

Only Jesus Christ can give true and lasting victory.

Friend, there are many false saviors being offered today. If you were to do a search on the Internet for "help for addictions," you would discover 12-Step programs, psychological counseling programs, hypno-therapy, medication therapies, natural and alternative therapies, meditation, etc. I declare to you, on the authority of God's Word, that only Jesus Christ is able to deliver us out of true pornographic slavery and immorality.

> "Salvation is found in no one else, for there is no other name under heaven given to men by which we must be saved" (Acts 4:12).

> For though we live in the world, we do not wage war as the world does. The weapons we fight with are not the weapons of the world. On the contrary, they have divine power to demolish strongholds. We demolish arguments and every pretension that sets itself up against the knowledge of God, and we take captive every thought to make it obedient to Christ (2 Corinthians 10:3-5).

Question 1. We are continuing our study today in 2 Corinthians 10:3-5. Please fill in the blanks below:

"For though we live in the world, we do not _____ _____ as the world does."

"The weapons we _____ _____ are not the weapons of the world."

"On the contrary, they have divine power to _____ _____."

Why do the programs, mentioned above, not work? They do not work because only divine power and divine weapons are effective against the demonic strongholds that Satan has set up in our minds. And only Jesus Christ, as God, is "divine."

Question 2. According to the above verses, what does it take to be able to demolish thought-strongholds?
- A. A stick of dynamite
- B. Behavior modification therapy
- C. Divine power

My friend, no 12-step plan, no un-biblical counseling, no ____ Anonymous, no group therapy, no program of man (including this one) is able deliver us from the clutches of pornography and sexual sin. It takes divine power and divine weapons. This teaching leaves us dependent upon God, who alone is divine.

Demolishing thought strongholds - by God's power!

Jesus Christ, Himself, is God's "divine power" and His "divine weapon." Without Him, we have no way to permanently win the battle against porn and sexual impurity. So let us examine how to demolish strongholds, and how to demolish every argument that sets itself up against the knowledge of God. Read the following verses and answer the questions.

> We demolish arguments and every pretension that sets itself up against the knowledge of God (2 Corinthians 10:5).

Question 3. According to the above verse, what are we to do when we are bombarded with a pornographic thought or image that may become a stronghold?
- A. We are to entertain the thought and dwell on the image
- B. We are to demolish it

Question 4. If you have ever tried to "demolish" these thought strongholds in your own power, you've learned that it is impossible to do. It takes "divine power." Have you ever tried to just not dwell on pornographic images or lustful thoughts? What happened?

We are to "demolish" thought strongholds. We are to totally annihilate, exterminate, and eradicate sinful thoughts, so that our enemy does not gain a stronghold in our lives. Friends, if we begin to dwell on porn images, we are rolling out the red carpet for Satan. We are not talking about "mental warfare" here, but rather spiritual warfare. The difference is that in spiritual warfare we must possess Jesus Christ, and we must beg God for divine power in order to tear down the pornographic images. In spiritual warfare, we lose the battle when a thought is able to lodge in our minds; and we win the battle when we demolish the thought. Do you see how we must become dependent on God in this battle?

Please write out your thoughts on the following verses, and show how they teach us dependence on God.

Question 5. But thanks be to God Who gives us the victory through our Lord Jesus Christ (1 Corinthians 15:57).

Course member John wrote, "The victory over pornography, like salvation, is a gift. We don't earn it; we don't work for it, but we give the battle to Christ. He is great warrior who destroys the strongholds in my life."

Question 6. No, in all these things we are more than conquerors through Him who loved us (Romans 8:37).

Question 7. If the Son sets you free, you will be free indeed (John 8:36).

Course member John wrote, "I will no longer kneel at the altar of pornography, bound by chains of sin. He will break those chains, as only He can."

Question 8. For He has rescued us from the dominion of darkness and brought us into the kingdom of the Son He loves... (Colossians 1:13).

John wrote, "God has not only saved me, He has taken me to the stronghold of the Son. Here I am safe. Here there is rest and refreshment. There is no relaxation, for I am to be about His work. But here, He keeps me. Pornography cannot venture into this place. It is thrown back by the glorious light of God Almighty Himself."

Question 9. ¹¹ For the grace of God that brings salvation has appeared to all men. ¹² It teaches us to say No to ungodliness and worldly passions, and to live self-controlled, upright and godly lives in this present age (Titus 2:11,12).

Again we see, from the above verse, that we must depend upon "divine power" in order to "take every thought captive." This is not easy to do. War is difficult. And yet with Jesus Christ we will indeed win. We are to make our thoughts prisoners of war. We are to notice when a particular thought is attempting to become a stronghold, and we are to take it captive to Jesus.

This is what it may look like, practically. I'm cruising along in my day, doing just fine, when all of a sudden BAMMO; I'm hit with an 8 X 12 glossy image of something I viewed a year ago. WOW! It's appealing, too. And I start to look at it and...." Then I stop and cry out to God: "Oh, God, please Lord Jesus, rescue me. The devil is attempting to erect a stronghold in my mind to cause me to sin. Help! I see You there dying on the cross because You love me. I see You placed in the tomb so that my sins could be buried. I see You raised from the dead, and know that your resurrection power is at work in me right now. Thank You, Lord Jesus, for dying for me, and for always living to intercede for me. "

In the next lesson, we will look at some stories from the Bible that illustrate the truth we've been studying. But, perhaps right now, you are beginning to understand why you are not having success over pornographic images and sexual impurity. You might possibly be realizing for the first time that you do not have "divine power," and you simply are not able to "demolish strongholds." Maybe you realize that you need Jesus Christ. Please call to Him right now, won't you?

John wrote, "Yes! I am seeing my need of Jesus Christ to be my "divine power," so that I can "demolish strongholds." Lord helping me, I am going to begin earnestly seeking the Lord."

"I also went to a 12-step program for sexual addiction. After a year, I quit. I found it very difficult to deal with a group of individuals who would admit their problems, but who wouldn't admit that God had the power to change them. The only support was supposed to come from being able to unload within a safe group of people who had similar problems. They talked about a 'higher power', which could be anything, including a stuffed teddy bear. To this 'power' they gave the credit for their faithfulness, but then would have to admit failure again and again. It seemed to me they really had no hope and couldn't offer any. I know this system has benefits and works for some people but I was frustrated because I felt God was missing from the formula" Stone Cold in a Warm Bed by Kathryn Wilson with Paul Wilson, page 35,36.

John Bunyan, in Pilgrim's Progress described the battle that is fought with the enemy. In scene 4, he wrote, **"Apollyon, seeing an opportunity, came up close to Christian, and wrestled with him, giving him a dreadful fall; and with that Christian's sword flew out of his hand. Then Apollyon said, 'I have won now,' and nearly killed Christian. But, as God would have it, while Apollyon was about to strike the final blow, Christian nimbly reached out his hand for his sword, and grabbed a hold of it, saying,** Rejoice not against me, O mine enemy: when I fall, I shall arise," Micah 7:8**; and with that he thrust his sword into Apollyon, which made him fall back, as one that had received a deadly wound. Christian seeing the devil retreat, rushed at him again, saying,** No, in all these things we are more than conquerors, through Him Who loved us (Romans 8:37). And with that Apollyon spread forth his dragon wings, and hurried away, and Christian saw him no more (James 4:7).

"The devil does not sleep, nor is the flesh yet dead; therefore, you must never cease your preparation for battle, because on the right and on the left are enemies who never rest" (Thomas a Kempis).

"He gives thanks for victory. Truly we are more than conquerors through Him that loved us; for we can give thanks before the fight is done. Yes, even in the thickest of the battle we can look up to Jesus, and cry, Thanks to God. The moment a soul groaning under corruption rests the eye on Jesus, that moment his groans are changed into songs of praise. In Jesus you discover a fountain to wash away the guilt of all your sin. In Jesus you discover grace sufficient for you, grace to hold you up to the end, and a sure promise that sin shall soon be rooted out altogether" (Robert McCheyne).

Course member William wrote, "I subscribe to several newsletters about the PC industry. In one of them, mention was made of the fact that deleted files could be recovered, if one knew how, and had the right software. I already knew how, and I already had the software. I had just not even thought it. That night, in my sleep, it seems like just about every pic I used to have on a particular erased Zip disk, was played back into my brain. The temptation continued all throughout the next day. I knew I could recover those files. The following day, I took that Zip disk, two others like it, and every floppy disk that contained such material, smashed each of them. Although I'm not normally one to do such a thing, I threw them into a lake."

This guy is taking steps to knock down the strongholds of the enemy. Are you?

Course member Marc wrote, "The Lord has truly blessed me in bringing me to your ministry. Not only have I been able to conquer the temptations so far, but even the strongholds are weakening. It has been 25 days now and, with the help of Jesus, I will never fall back. Of course, as you know, this is probably a time when Satan is preparing to counterattack, but I'm prepared for it, because I've finally given my problem with porn and lust over to Christ for the first time in my Christian walk and I'm letting Him fight the war for me."

Question 10. Please write how you are doing now. Are you gaining the victory?

I want to share a poem that a Setting Captives Free student wrote as he completed this lesson. It is shared by permission from John Stroud:

Setting Captives Free

Great and simple men alike have known the horrid chains
Of sin's enslavement and defeat of struggle, without gain.

This battle common, though it be, takes daily casualties
And leaves the wounded living without hope of being free.

They walk in silent solitude behind their painted masks
And wallow in their private sins until somebody asks,

"Hey brother, how may I and these who know your desperate plight
Walk side by side with you in grace to end your pain and strife?"

We've known defeat and sorrow in this battle you now see,
But now we spend our lives instead in setting captives free.

Your battle scars and stories of entrapment and of blame,
we know them all, we've lived them all, we understand the shame.

Step up and walk beside us now, we're going the same way
We're seeking life in Jesus Christ and trusting more each day

That He will change our hearts and minds so we might come to be
Ones who pass the truth along by setting captives free.

The following testimony is from Steve:

I have been involved with pornography and self-gratification for the last twenty-six years. It started out small. I would buy a magazine and look at the pictures, and hide them in my car trunk. After high school I worked for a local company that supplied books to libraries. This included all types of books, even some that were pornographic in nature. Within a year, my addiction to pornography led to premarital relations.

Later I joined the military. I was stationed in various places during my military career. Pornography and self-gratification were the normal activity for military men. There was always easy access wherever I was stationed. I was also an alcoholic. One place where I was stationed was on the edge of a very rough town. The movie theater in town played XXX films twenty-four hours a day, and they did not cost much. If you had the money, anything could be bought.

I left the military service in 1983 and worked odd jobs till 1988 when I became a garbage man and a married man. My boss required the workers to save all the pornography for him. It was quite a collection. The most extreme hardcore is thrown out by the upper class.

I moved in 1995 to be a printer's helper. I acquired a computer in 1998, and started playing games and looking at pornography when my wife was not home or was sleeping. In 1999, I became a partner in a bagel shop, and my wife left me.

I finally realized that pictures were no longer enough, and while looking in a matchmaking site, I saw a banner for Setting Captives Free. I looked but did not start anything for a day or two. I finally began the course in December 2000.

Having accepted Jesus Christ as a child, the format appealed to me. Even though I no longer was indulging myself, I was still rebellious until January 2001. Since that day I have been attempting to live a life pleasing to God. It is easy only when I give God all my burdens. When I think I can handle a situation, it gets real hard. One of the things that gave me a challenge was my mentor stating that I would make a good mentor if I stayed pure. On December 31, 2000, I made the decision to stop fighting God.

Since that day there have been struggles, but by giving them to God, I am working through them. My only job is to give God the glory. As of this day, I am still married. Today is day fifty-nine of the course and I am fifty-nine days free from self-gratification and fifty-seven days free from pornography. I give God all the glory.

Scripture to Consider

For the LORD your God is the one who goes with you to fight for you against your enemies to give you victory (Deuteronomy 20:4).

He put garrisons throughout Edom, and all the Edomites became subject to David. The LORD gave David victory wherever he went (2 Samuel 8:14).

You give me your shield of victory; you stoop down to make me great (2 Samuel 22:36).

The horse is made ready for the day of battle, but victory rests with the LORD (Proverbs 21:31).

Were you free from pornography since you did the last lesson?

    Yes   No

Were you free from self-gratification since you did the last lesson?

    Yes   No

Were you free from sexual immorality since you did the last lesson?

    Yes   No

DAY 34 - DEMOLISHING STRONGHOLDS II

Okay, we have been studying about how to demolish strongholds and take every thought captive using God's divine power. Now, we will look at how God illustrates these truths in His Word.

In the book of Joshua, we read of the many battles the Israelites fought to conquer the land the Lord had given to them. Today, let us take note of one battle in particular in Joshua, chapter 11. It is the battle of the Israelites against the northern kings. These northern kings all bonded together to fight against the Israelites, and the Bible states that they made "a huge army, as numerous as the sand on the seashore." They were a formidable foe to be sure; but God told Joshua, "Do not be afraid...I will hand them over to you." So Joshua and the Israelites went out in battle against the huge army of the northern kings. And Joshua 11:12 states that, "Joshua took all these royal cities (where those kings had lived) and put them to the sword. He totally destroyed them as he had been commanded." That's right; Joshua and his people totally annihilated that huge army. And the Bible states they were victorious because the Lord fought for them!

Questions

Please answer the following questions.

Question 1. The army of the northern kings was:
- A. Very tiny
- B. As numerous as the sands on the seashore

Question 2. Joshua and the Israelites were to do what to the army of the northern kings?
- A. Make peace
- B. Leave them alone
- C. Destroy them

Question 3. Please write in your own words how this story applies to our situation with pornography and sexual sin. Find as many parallels as you can.

Fellow soldiers, pornographic images, as I'm sure you know by now, are a formidable foe. They may at times be like a huge army that is much stronger than we are. And yet, Scripture tells us that we are to demolish them, destroy them, annihilate them. Can you see how this does indeed take divine power?

And we take captive every thought to make it obedient to Christ (2 Corinthians 10:5).

Here is an illustration of taking our thoughts captive:

In the Old Testament, the nation of Israel was commanded to dislodge every nation that currently existed in the Promised Land. They had good success pulling down the strongholds of those nations, and dislodging most of them. However, a few nations were very powerful and very stubborn, and the Israelites were unable to demolish them. Notice what the Israelite nation did with those nations: "All the people left from the Amorites, Hittites, Perizzites, Hivites and Jebusites...all whom the Israelites could not exterminate - these Solomon conscripted for his slave labor force" (1 Kings 9:20-21).

Question 4. According to the above verses, what did King Solomon do with the nations the Israelites were unable to exterminate?

Friend, there might be some thoughts so powerful that we may not be able to keep them from infiltrating our minds, especially in the first couple of months after we have stopped viewing porn. But if we do not view any more porn, and we seek the Lord, eventually we will have no thoughts that overtake us as they previously did. The Israelites were told to completely demolish the enemy. They wiped out enough of the enemy to inhabit the land, but got tired of fighting and simply became accustomed to them. They apparently reasoned that, "Hey, we don't need to wipe these guys out; we will use them as our slaves." They justified their disobedience by keeping the enemy as slaves. However, it was disobedience because God had told them to wipe them all out. In the same way, the thoughts we don't demolish or have victory over, (and we think we are making them our slaves) are still there. Question: Did those slaves stay enslaved, or did they eventually rise up and cause problems? Wouldn't it have been better for the Israelites to completely wipe out the enemy? Total annihilation is the only answer!

Now, prepare yourself for this next power-packed verse: "If you do not drive out the inhabitants of the land from before you, then it shall come about that those whom you let remain of them will become as pricks in your eyes and as thorns in your sides and they shall trouble you in the land where you live" (Numbers 33:55). You know what this means? You know those thoughts we allow to remain? Those images we think aren't too bad? Those things we justify and say, "Hey, in comparison to where I was, this is nothing?" These are the areas where there is great potential for trouble in our lives. "...they shall trouble you in the land where you live." Annihilate!

Friend, before we move on, we should remind ourselves that we are in a very serious battle. We are instructed to use God's power to demolish demonic strongholds, and we are to take captive every thought to Christ. This is serious business, and cannot be taken lightly. If we truly want to win the battle, there must be a whole lot of crying out to God for victory, depending on God for power, and thanking God each time you win. If you have been winning battles for the past 34 days, then rejoice with Paul, who said, "I thank Christ Jesus our Lord, who has given me strength…" (1 Timothy 1:12). Jesus Christ gave the strength to Paul, and Jesus must give us strength, as well, in order for us to win the battle over sin. Will you pray right now and ask God to give you strength?

Dennis wrote, "I have been guilty of being soft on my enemy, and allowing him to gain a stronghold inside my defense perimeter. I have also sought to make peace with the enemy of my soul, rather than seek to totally destroy him. In addition, when the enemy promised to make peace, I found that he really had an innumerable army arrayed against me, ready to destroy me."

Steve wrote, "The army of the northern kings was huge. God told Joshua to destroy them. In order to move into the Promised Land (a porn-free life), the tenants (porn) have to move out, so I can get in. They do not want to leave (strongholds). They must be defeated (torn down). They have a huge army, and they will do anything to hold on to what they have. But God has promised that He will hand them over to me. In order to defeat them, I need to go into battle. Through God's power, I will be victorious, and the current tenants will be totally annihilated! No more porn! Solomon made the remaining tenants slaves. Although I cannot undo the fact that I have looked at porn, I can now use it to God's service. This story is teaching me to not be afraid of the battle because God will hand the enemy (porn) over to me. So I can go and fight, and not be afraid, because I sin will be annihilated."

Next, please read the following quote by Oswald Chambers and provide your thoughts on it below:

"Lift up your eyes on high, and behold who hath created these things (Isaiah 40:26). **The people of God in Isaiah's day had starved their imagination by looking on the face of idols, and Isaiah made them look up at the heavens; that is, he made them begin to use their imagination aright.**

"The test of spiritual concentration is bringing the imagination into captivity. Is your imagination looking on the face of an idol? Is the idol yourself? Your work? Your conception of what a worker should be? Your experience of salvation and sanctification? Then your imagination of God is starved, and when you are up against difficulties you have no power, you can only endure in darkness. If your imagination is starved, do not look back to your own experience; it is God Whom you need. Go right out of yourself, away from the face of your idols, away from everything that has been starving your imagination. Rouse yourself, take the gibe that Isaiah gave the people, and deliberately turn your imagination to God" (Oswald Chambers My Utmost for His Highest).

Question 5. Provide your thoughts about the quote from Oswald Chambers here.

The following testimony is from Larry:

I was once lost in sin. I chose to pursue pornography, but it eventually consumed me. Before I knew it, the images from these sites and movies began flooding into my mind, crowding out all that was good or wise. I defiled myself, and used others, seeing them only as objects of lust instead of people. To hide my growing dependence on pornographic images, I developed a "hidden life" surrounded by lies, secrecy, and distance from intimacy.

Each time I gave in to my lusts and the obsessive thoughts, I was filled with guilt, shame and self-loathing. The filth was corrupting me from the inside out. The longer the addiction went on, the more withdrawn I became from life around me. I drifted in and out of jobs and relationships. When I fell to the bottom of the pit, I began acting out some of the fantasies in my mind, and that scared me. I sought counseling and my own wisdom, but I fell again. Broken, I began frantically looking for help. I was about to lose everything.

I joined twelve-step programs, and had more counseling, but nothing helped. I was led to Setting Captives Free, and I enrolled in the 60-day program called The Way of Purity.

At first the religious message bothered me, but the accountability and daily training really helped. Eventually the message sank in that only Jesus Christ offers Living Water that refreshes. I quit drinking muddy water and accepted Jesus as my only Savior. When I put my burdens on His shoulders, the obsessive thoughts and images vanished! It was the beginning of freedom.

The course staff and mentors suggested going to a local Bible-believing church, and the next day a friend called to say he and his pastor had found one for me without even being asked! The next day I got a call from the pastor of the new church with an invitation to come to service. Going to church felt good. It felt clean.

I was baptized on the same day I finished the 60-day course. I am free from obsessive destructive thoughts, toxic guilt and shame, and free to live. For the first time in many years it feels good to be me. I cannot wait to start a ministry to help others find this wonderful course, and point some souls to God.

Next, read the following quote from Thomas a Kempis and comment on it below:

"Above all, we must be especially alert against the beginnings of temptation, for the enemy is more easily conquered if he is refused admittance to the mind and is met beyond the threshold when he knocks.

"Someone has said very aptly: Resist the beginnings; remedies come too late, when by long delay the evil has gained strength. First, a mere thought comes to mind, then strong imagination, followed by pleasure, evil delight, and consent. Thus, because he is not resisted in the beginning, Satan gains full entry. The longer a man delays in resisting, so much the weaker does he become each day, while the strength of the enemy grows against him." Thomas a Kempis, The Imitation of Christ

Question 6. Provide your comments about the quote:

John wrote, "Joshua's battle was just like my own. He faced insurmountable odds. There was no physical way that Israel could defeat the northern kings' armies. There is no way that I can defeat the sin of pornography in my life. But wait. Great words, aren't they? But wait. There is One, that One who holds the universe in the palm of His hand. He fights for me. His actions are the words of His mouth. He has said in His love, mercy, and grace that He would never forsake me. He, this One, fights for me. Just as He, this One, fought for Israel."

Question 7. Please write what you have learned today. How will you apply this teaching?

Scripture to Consider

When you go to war against your enemies, the Lord will help you defeat them so that you will take them captive (Deuteronomy 21:10).

[6] Now the men of Judah approached Joshua at Gilgal, and Caleb son of Jephunneh the Kenizzite said to him, "You know what the LORD said to Moses the man of God at Kadesh Barnea about you and me. [7] I was forty years old when Moses the servant of the LORD sent me from Kadesh Barnea to explore the land. And I brought him back a report according to my convictions, [8] but my brothers who went up with me made the hearts of the people melt with fear. I, however, followed the LORD my God wholeheartedly. [9] So on that day Moses swore to me, "The land on which your feet have walked will be your inheritance and that of your children forever, because you have followed the LORD my God wholeheartedly." [10] "Now then, just as the LORD promised, he has kept me alive for forty-five years since the time he said this to Moses, while Israel moved about in the desert. So here I am today, eighty-five years old! [11] I am still as strong today as the day Moses sent me out; I'm just as vigorous to go out to battle now as I was then (Joshua 14:6-11).

[45] David said to the Philistine, "You come against me with sword and spear and javelin, but I come against you in the name of the LORD Almighty, the God of the armies of Israel, whom you have defied. [46] This day the LORD will hand you over to me, and I'll strike you down and cut off your head. Today I will give the carcasses of the Philistine army to the birds of the air and the beasts of the earth, and the whole world will know that there is a God in Israel. [47] All those gathered here will know that it is not by sword or spear that the LORD saves; for the battle is the Lord's, and he will give all of you into our hands (1 Samuel 17:45-47).

Were you free from pornography since you did the last lesson?

    Yes   No

Were you free from self-gratification since you did the last lesson?

    Yes   No

Were you free from sexual immorality since you did the last lesson?

    Yes   No

DAY 35 - THE LOVE OF GOD AND TEMPTATION

Blessed is the man who perseveres under trial, because when he has stood the test, he will receive the crown of life that God has promised to those who love him. When tempted, no one should say, "God is tempting me." For God cannot be tempted by evil, nor does he tempt anyone; but each one is tempted when, by his own evil desire, he is dragged away and enticed. Then, after desire has conceived, it gives birth to sin; and sin, when it is full-grown, gives birth to death. Don't be deceived, my dear brothers (James 1:12-16).

Today, we will see very clearly what it is that will get us through every temptation and trial we face. Those who will embrace and apply the truths taught in this lesson will find that the teaching of God's Word in this area is powerful enough to release us from slavery to pornography and all habitual sin. Jesus said, "If you hold to my teaching, you are really my disciples. Then you will know the truth, and the truth will set you free." (John 8:31-32) The inevitable result of embracing Truth is pure freedom!

In James 1:12, above, we see a promise made to one who stands the test and "perseveres under trial," and we see the motive for persevering. The promise is "the crown of life," and the motive for standing and persevering is the love of God. The above verses make it clear that life will have its share of both trials and temptations, and this passage communicates God's way of victory through both. Let's see what we can learn, and may God help us to grasp His truth and enjoy the freedom that comes from it.

When I am faced with a severe trial or an intense temptation, I have a choice to either persevere in faith and stand up under the trial, or to fall down in sin and deception. The passage we are studying in James promises me the "crown of life" if I stand and persevere, and shows me that death will be the end result if I follow the path of temptation, desire, and sin. So, we are discussing life and death today. The critical question is this: What is the motive for choosing to stand and persevere?

Any methodology of man for bringing freedom to those trapped in sin is doomed to fail because it leaves out motive. For instance, worldly methodologies have taught those given over to excessive drinking that they need help outside of themselves, and they need to ask for help from a "higher power." But this model falls short of helping people have lasting heart change, because the program fails to address that man has a need to love, and is created with the desire to worship. There is no true freedom in the heart that does not love God. But once this love for God is planted in the heart, it will enable us to go through any trial, and to stand up under any temptation and not fall. If we are falling to sin, we do not have proper love for God. Notice how Paul's prayer for the Thessalonians reinforces the truth that it is the love of God that enables our perseverance: "May the Lord direct your hearts into God's love and Christ's perseverance" (2 Thessalonians 3:5).

This brings up the next question which is, "How, then, do I acquire love for God?" This is a difficult question, and does not come with a simple answer, but here are a few thoughts, along with some practical suggestions taken from my own experience in growing in love for God.

1. First, ask God to give you a heart that loves Him. "You may ask me for anything in my name, and I will do it" (John 14:14). "You do not have, because you do not ask God" (James 4:2b). If this teaching is new to you, you may want to pause here and acknowledge to the Lord that your love for Him needs to be increased, and ask Him to do it. Feel free to pause in prayer, or write out a request to God for Him to give you a heart that loves Him.

2. Dwell on the cross of Jesus Christ. "This is how we know what love is: Jesus Christ laid down his life for us" (1 John 3:16a). In all of human history, there has never been an act of love displayed to the world that demonstrates the love of God better than the cross of Christ. Meditate on this cross, asking God to give you love for the One who died in our place. Think often of the wounds in His hands and feet and side, which are really reminders of His love for us (Isaiah 49:15-16). Recall how He sweat drops of blood, how He offered His back to be smitten (Isaiah 50:6), and how He

Question 1. Please write out James 1:12 here.

Question 2. What motive do you see for persevering and standing under the trial?

Some may answer "the crown of life" to the question of motive. However, when we look a little deeper, we see that the real motive for persevering through the trial and standing up under temptation is the love of God. God promises the crown of life "to those who love Him."

was willingly beaten beyond recognition (Isaiah 52:14), all to pardon us from sin's penalty and free us from sin's power.

> But he was pierced for our transgressions, he was crushed for our iniquities; the punishment that brought us peace was upon him, and by his wounds we are healed. We all, like sheep, have gone astray, each of us has turned to his own way; and the LORD has laid on him the iniquity of us all" (Isaiah 53:5-6).

3. Obey God's Word. "But if anyone obeys his word, God's love is truly made complete in him" (1 John 2:5). Of course we know that it takes the grace of God in order for us to obey the Word of God. It is an amazing thing to begin walking in obedience to God, and to sense the love of God as we do. Do you want your heart flooded with the love of God? Walk in obedience, and you will have it.

4. "Keep yourselves in the love of God, looking for the mercy of our Lord Jesus Christ unto eternal life" (Jude 21). Again, God alone is able to keep us from falling (Jude 24), but we are exhorted to keep ourselves in the love of God. This is similar to John 15, where we are told to "abide in the Vine" and in 1 John, where we are told to "remain in Him" (1 John 2:27). This is a general statement that we are to do all we can to remain in God's love.

Question 3. Please write out the above four principles for walking in God's love, and indicate whether you are currently applying them.

Principle Number 1–

Principle Number 2–

Principle Number 3–

Principle Number 4–

Next, let us look at James 1:12-16 again:

> Blessed is the man who perseveres under trial, because when he has stood the test, he will receive the crown of life that God has promised to those who love him. When tempted, no one should say, "God is tempting me." For God cannot be tempted by evil, nor does he tempt anyone; but each one is tempted when, by his own evil desire, he is dragged away and enticed. Then, after desire has conceived, it gives birth to sin; and sin, when it is full-grown, gives birth to death. Don't be deceived, my dear brothers (James 1:12-16).

Verses 13 through 16 describe the nature of temptation by using two analogies. Let us look at each of them:

1 – Fishing. "But each one is tempted when, by his own evil desire, he is dragged away and enticed." The words "dragged away and enticed" have to do with bait. The bait is what the fisherman uses to lure the fish. When we are being enticed to sin, we only focus on the "bait," rather than the hook. In the Garden of Eden, Eve saw that the fruit was "pleasing to the eye," but she did not focus on the death that would result from her eating it. For years, I was enamored with the "perfect" images in pornography, never looking at the death of my marriage that would follow.

Question 4. What has been the "bait" to which you have been attracted in the past?

Question 5. In what ways has the "bait" hooked you?

> Then, after desire has conceived, it gives birth to sin; and sin, when it is full-grown, gives birth to death (James 1:15).

2 – Delivery: "Then, after desire has conceived, it gives birth to sin; and sin, when it is full-grown, gives birth to death." When desire and lust conceive, they give birth to sin and, when sin is full-grown, it gives birth to death. Again, when we are enticed to sin, all we see is the conception, rather than the birth. Temptation not only obscures the "hook" but the "birth of death," as well. But Scripture teaches us to have a different perspective, that is, to view the consequences of our actions all the way from taking the bait to becoming hooked, and then to death. The wages of sin is death (Romans 6:23).

Question 6. You've described your "bait" and how it has "hooked" you above. Now, determine how giving in to evil desires has given birth to death in your life. Some may describe how evil desires have taken them to such lengths that they have acquired a sexually transmitted disease, or even AIDS, and now they are awaiting their own physical death. For others, it will be that the mating of their evil desires with lust has conceived sin, and after sin grew up, their marriage died. Have you experienced a death from sin yet? If not, do you see how you were headed in that direction? What are your thoughts:

My friend, these verses end with a surprising remedy for this whole process of temptation and sin: "Don't be deceived, my dear brothers" (James 1:16). Sin is deception by its very nature. In displaying the bait, the fisherman is not offering the fish something which is good for it. Instead, the fisherman intends to kill the fish. Evil desire and lust do not ultimately relieve tension, provide excitement, and spice up our lives; they bring death. Do not be deceived. How do we overcome pornography and sexual sin? We see it for what it is. Pornography is the bait that is used to hook us and kill us, and the "excitement" of lust will bring about our death.

So, to summarize today's teaching: It is the love of God that enables us to endure trials and to stand up under temptation. It is the love of God that releases us from deception and frees us from sin's power. And it is the love of God that will bring us into glory as Christ's spotless bride. Oh, for more love of God!

Question 7. What are your final thoughts on today's teaching? Did you learn anything new, or will you do anything differently? How will you apply these Scriptures to the ongoing battle against pornography and all forms of impurity?

Scripture to Consider

Have nothing to do with the fruitless deeds of darkness, but rather expose them. For it is shameful even to mention what the disobedient do in secret. But everything exposed by the light becomes visible, for it is light that makes everything visible. This is why it is said: "Wake up, O sleeper, rise from the dead, and Christ will shine on you" (Ephesians 5:11-14).

Because of the LORD's great love we are not consumed, for his compassions never fail. They are new every morning; great is your faithfulness (Lamentations 3:22-23).

Were you free from pornography since you did the last lesson?

    Yes   No

Were you free from self-gratification since you did the last lesson?

    Yes   No

Were you free from sexual immorality since you did the last lesson?

    Yes   No

The following testimony is from Louis:

I come to you as one who was "hooked on pornography" at an early age. When I was nine or ten, I was walking in a field next to our house and found a very explicit Swedish porno magazine (the baited hook). I kept the magazine and more seemed to come my way.

As I grew up it seemed everywhere I turned there was pornography (hooks) of some sort in the strangest places. I was into sex and self-gratification like any "normal" teen, or so I thought. As I grew up I could not look at any female body without undressing her and having sex with her in my mind and turning to self-gratification.

I went to live with a brother in Tucson, AZ. I found a job at a factory there in Tucson. God used a woman there to invite me to church and I went there, and found myself at the altar. I gave my life to the Lord, and began a life of living for God, yet I had not given up my porn/sexual perversion addiction to God.

I met a wonderful woman whp was a believer and loved God with all her heart. We dated and then decided to get married. We were happily married but my addiction grew...

To make a horribly devastating story short, I lived with my addiction for a total of 34 years of my life. I could not get free by myself, and I was too ashamed to go to the church for help. There was no way I could ask for help. I did cry out to God for help, but I did not really mean it; I just wanted the guilt to be taken away.

Then the summer of the year 2000 I was surfing the net looking at porno, being convicted, and about to give up on ever being free, when I typed in at a search site the words "pornography addiction." I found the site SettingCaptivesFree and began to check it out. I went so far as to sign up for the course, completed one day of the course and did not come back for about two months.

Then early one morning, in my heart of hearts, a cry came up to God that I could not live like I was living anymore. I cried before God and He encouraged me in my spirit to start the course again. I came back to the "SettingCaptivesFree" website and restarted the course. I started drinking the Living Water and God began a powerful work of setting this captive free.

I will close here and say in all honesty were it not for the "SettingCaptivesFree" course and their ministry, I would of all people be most miserable, and might have found the guts to get out of this trap by killing myself.

Thanks be to God that I stand before you this day free from any desire for pornography, and have victory over the images of "having sex" in my mind. I can make love to my wife as it was meant to be, and not have a desire to fantasize about other women. I love the Lord my God with all my heart and desire to please only Him. Jesus Christ and His Word is the only way to be "set free."

DAY 36 – BREAK THE CHAIN

Misloaded Douglas DC-8 Pitches up Excessively on Takeoff, then Stalls and Strikes the Ground

The cargo was not loaded aboard the airplane according to the airlines instructions. As a result, the flight crew inadvertently used a horizontal-stabilizer-trim setting that was not correct for the airplane's aft center of gravity.

FSF Editorial Staff
"On Aug. 7, 1997, ——— ——- (airline name) Flight 101, a Douglas DC-8-61, stalled on takeoff and struck the ground approximately 3,000 feet (915 meters) from the end of Runway 27R at Miami (Florida, U.S.) International Airport. The three flight crewmembers, a security guard aboard the airplane and one person on the ground (a motorist) were killed. The U.S. National Transportation Safety Board (NTSB), in its final report, said, 'The accident resulted from the airplane being misloaded to produce a more aft center of gravity and a correspondingly incorrect stabilizer-trim setting that precipitated an extreme pitch-up at rotation.'

"NTSB said that the probable causes of the accident were: The failure of — — — — (airline name) to exercise operational control over the cargo-loading process; [and,] the failure of (—— ——-, a freight-forwarding company) to load the airplane as specified by ——- —— (airline name).

"Contributing to the accident was the failure of the (U.S.) Federal Aviation Administration (FAA) to adequately monitor (airline name) operational-control responsibilities for cargo loading and the failure of FAA to ensure that known cargo-related deficiencies were corrected at ——- ——- (airline name)," said NTSB.

"The captain, 42, was hired by ——- ——- (airline name) in October 1993. He had 12,154 hours of flight time, including 2,522 hours as a (airline name) DC-8 captain. NTSB said that in 1995 the FAA suspended the captain's airman certificate and medical certificate for 30 days because he had failed to report a revocation of his motor-vehicle driver's license. FAA records indicated that the captain was convicted for misdemeanor drunk driving in California in 1986 and convicted for driving under the influence in Arizona in 1994, said NTSB Flight Safety Foundation."

As an airline pilot, I often read up on the "how's and why's" of aircraft accidents. I do this to try to learn what happened, and how I might prevent something similar from happening to the crew and passengers I carry. As I read through the accident reports, one thing I have noticed is that there is usually an accident "chain" with many links that make up that chain. In the above accident, what "links" in the accident chain can you find? Here are some that I saw:

1. Improper loading of the aircraft by the company contracted to load.
2. Improper monitoring of the loading of the aircraft by the airline.
3. Failure of the FAA to properly monitor the loading operation of the airline.
4. Failure of the FAA to ensure previous known loading problems were corrected.
5. A possible 5th "link" in the accident chain could be the Captain's known drinking problem.

All the above links in the chain caused the accident of this Cargo Flight 101, killing a total of five people. What if just one link in the accident chain had been broken? For instance, what if the FAA, citing known loading problems with the airline, had decided to shut it down until its problems could be corrected? That one break in the chain would have saved the lives of five people.

My friend, you and I have had a problem with pornography and/or some form of sexual impurity. And if we examine our times of failure, we will always find a chain of events that lead up to the "crash." Here are some of mine:

1. I did not get up early to spend quiet time with the Lord.
2. I had a long day in the air and became tired.
3. My wife and I were at odds over something.
4. My last flight of the day was delayed because of weather.
5. I saw a partially clothed woman at the airport, and I couldn't get the image of her out of my head.
6. When I got to my hotel room, I turned the TV on and immediately saw an advertisement for a pornographic movie. Crash!

Now, I have learned to notice when links in an accident chain are developing, and to break at least one link in order to prevent a pornographic accident. Now, I rise early to spend time with the Lord, which puts me in a content and praying frame of mind throughout the day. I will communicate much with my wife and ensure we are acting in loving ways toward each other. If my day is long, I know I'm headed for trouble, so I begin watching and praying. And finally, I might take the TV out of my hotel room and drop it off at my co-pilot's room (this makes for an interesting discussion the next day).

Let's notice how these "accident links" are all present in a particular incident in Scripture.

In the life of Lot, the nephew of Abraham, there was a terrible tragedy. He came to live in a city that was ultimately destroyed by God for its wickedness. Lot lost all his possessions, his wife was killed and he barely escaped with his own life and the lives of his two daughters. Notice the following passage of Scripture, and see if you are able to spot the links in this developing "accident chain." Write in each "link" below.

> [8] So Abram said to Lot, Lets not have any quarreling between you and me, or between your herdsmen and mine, for we are brothers. [9] Is not the whole land before you? Let's part company. If you go to the left, I'll go to the right; if you go to the right, I'll go to the left. [10] Lot looked up and saw that the whole plain of the Jordan was well watered, like the garden of the LORD, like the land of Egypt, toward Zoar. (This was before the LORD destroyed Sodom and Gomorrah.) [11] So Lot chose for himself the whole plain of the Jordan and set out toward the east. The two men parted company: [12] Abram lived in the land of Canaan, while Lot lived among the cities of the plain and pitched his tents near Sodom. [13] Now the men of Sodom were wicked and were sinning greatly against the LORD. (Genesis 13:8-13).

> [8] Then the king of Sodom, the king of Gomorrah, the king of Admah, the king of Zeboiim and the king of Bela (that is, Zoar) marched out and drew up their battle lines in the Valley of Siddim [9] against Kedorlaomer king of Elam, Tidal king of Goiim, Amraphel king of Shinar and Arioch king of Ellasar-four kings against five. [11] The four kings seized all the goods of Sodom and Gomorrah and all their food; then they went away. [12] They also carried off Abram's nephew Lot and his possessions, since he was living in Sodom (Genesis 14:8-12).

Note: Eventually Sodom was destroyed by the fire of God's wrath.

Question 1. Did you spot the "links" that led to this disaster? Please write them here. I'll do the first one for you. (If you need help, keep reading.)

First link: Lot and Abraham separated because of a quarrel.

Second link:

Third link:

Fourth link:

Fifth link:

Break the Chain

My friend, to stop a pornographic accident, and possibly save our souls, it is important for us to break the link in the chain. If we remove one link, we won't crash. Had there been proper supervision in the loading of the cargo aircraft in Miami, five people would not have lost their lives. What if Lot had broken chain link number one, or even number two? These are the links I saw in the story of Lot:

1. Lot and Abraham quarrel and separate – (Genesis 13:8-11).
2. What if Lot and Abraham had worked out their differences, instead of separating? (Note: exercise caution in separating from fellow believers for any reason, even if the reason seems legitimate, as it did in Lot's case. There may come a time when separation is necessary, but weigh the option of separation carefully against the benefits derived from fellowship).
3. Lot "looked up and saw" the valley of Sodom – (Genesis 13:10). What if Lot had not focused on the valley, but on the hill country instead? (Note: be careful where you focus).
4. Lot "set out toward" Sodom – (Genesis 13:11). Would this "accident" have happened if Lot set out toward the great trees of Mamre, instead of Sodom? (Note: Be careful of the general direction of your life. We are always moving, either more toward righteousness, or more toward sin).
5. Lot "pitched his tent near" Sodom – (Genesis 13:12). Lot could have broken the "accident chain" even after he separated from Abraham, after he saw and set out toward Sodom, had he simply refused to pitch his tent so close to the filth and wretchedness of Sodom. (Note: To the extent possible, pitch your tent as far away from sinful traps as you can. We still must influence the world, but we have to watch ourselves, be discretionary, use wisdom and common sense as to how close we should get).
6. Lot "was living in" Sodom – (Genesis 14:12). Notice the progression: Lot separated from Abraham, saw Sodom, set out toward Sodom, pitched his tent near Sodom, and then lived in Sodom. Next we read he has been taken captive in battle. Friends, these may be our steps to destruction as well. We separate from fellowship, see something sinful and focus on it, set out toward it, pitch our tent near it, live in it, and are taken captive by it.

Question 2. Now please write out a quick summary of the above five points, just to reinforce the steps that lead to a fall.

Now, let us focus on your accident chain. What are the links? How can you remove one link (or more) and stop the accident? Please describe below your accident chain and your plan to "remove a link."

Question 3. What has been your accident chain in the past?

Question 4. Will you conscientiously remove some links in the chain? What links will you remove, and how will you do it?

Question 5. Will you share this plan with someone who can help you implement it, and hold you accountable for it?

The following testimony is from Adam:

I had been relatively free from porn while I was in college, having struggled with it as a teenager. God had used my former girlfriend's family to bring me back to the Lord after wandering away from Him. I gave up porn at that time, by God's grace. Somehow though, pride began to creep into my walk with God. Though I was very zealous for God during my college years, I did not have a very solid foundation for my faith. I was not accountable to anyone. I didn't know the principles of freedom in Christ. I was caught up in my works and what I could do for God.

Then God began to break me of my pride. I struggled with many sins of the heart: anger, jealousy, pride, fear. God showed me how much of a sinner I was. Yet I was still proud in my faith. I would not humble myself. I thought myself better than other believers. I didn't understand that I was saved by grace fully. I would say I understood it, but really I was not experiencing it. I was saved to be sure, but I certainly did not have a humble, thankful heart toward God.

On a mission trip to China, God humbled me. There was conflict with team members. I was not hearing God clearly and I was unsure of my direction. God had provided for my needs, but still I wasn't happy. I missed being back home. I lusted after my sisters in Christ in my heart. I was obsessive in my thoughts about sex. This had a stranglehold on my life. I am convinced that many Christian men live this way. They see their sisters in Christ as objects of desire. I was certainly one of them. Many people thought I was humble and kind, but so many times I was not.

When I returned from my trip, I stumbled onto Internet porn, and the hook of Satan was set. I started viewing a little bit, but then gradually more and more. I struggled with it for about 2 1/2 years before I found out about this online course, The Way of Purity. God led me to join and start going through it. By the grace of God I have found freedom from both pornography and self-gratification. God's grace has been working in my life greatly over the past year, especially the last few months.

The most life-changing things I have learned from this course are:

1. We must be satisfied with Jesus alone. Only He can fill us up and satisfy our hearts.

2. We must aggressively deal with sin, including confession, accountability, prayer, Bible study, cutting off the sources of sin, planning our day, avoiding temptation whenever possible.

3. We need to help others be free.

God is a good God. When I was in the sin I thought I would never get out. But by God's grace I can truly say that I am free from pornography and self-gratification. Now I have the responsibility to help others be free and to be diligent to stay free myself. I must be ever watchful and in prayer and accountable. I must not relax in the battle. The war still goes on. I must do all I can to continue to grow in grace and change other areas of my life that need changing, growing in the character of Christ.

Course member Dennis wrote, "The first link in the chain that bound me to porn was the excuse "Everyone is going to sleep, and now I have time to get online and 'check my email.' I would tell my wife that I would only be a moment, and after surfing the web for a couple of minutes, I knew that she would be asleep. The next link was to "accidentally" stumble upon some porn site and say to myself, 'Well, as long as I'm here...'

"From there, I would bring up deviant porn and the sex story sites, indulging in all manner of wicked fantasies. At a certain point, I would begin to gratify my flesh, and then there was no turning back. That was always the last link in the chain. The next day, my mind would still be racing with images, and I would again indulge in self-gratification. I repeatedly resolved to break the chain, but I was not strong enough. This was my nightly routine for seven long and frustrating years.

"To break the chain, I have moved the computer to the family room and do not access it after a certain hour. If I have not read my mail, checked the scores, or read the news by a certain time, it has to wait until tomorrow. Also, now that my wife is aware of my addiction, she is watchful of what is on the screen and holds me accountable. I no longer delete the history file or the temp file. She has full access to the computer. Additionally, when the temptation to "check my email" comes, I immediately turn off the computer and join the family. Already, I feel the strength of the Lord enabling me. I will be victorious by His grace."

Scripture to Consider

[8] Be sober, be vigilant; because your adversary the devil walks about like a roaring lion, seeking whom he may devour. [9] Resist him, steadfast in the faith, knowing that the same sufferings are experienced by your brotherhood in the world (1 Peter 5:8-9).

Were you free from pornography since you did the last lesson?

   Yes   No

Were you free from self-gratification since you did the last lesson?

   Yes   No

Were you free from sexual immorality since you did the last lesson?

   Yes   No

DAY 37 - SEEK THE LORD

"But what if I've done horrible things? What if I've made a real mess of my life, hurt other people, broken promises and vows, etc.? What if I've gone too far? Is it possible that what I've done is so bad, I'm unable to be forgiven?"

NO!

Read the following passage, and look for the words, "But if from there. . ."

> After you have had children and grandchildren and have lived in the land a long time–if you then become corrupt and make any kind of idol, doing evil in the eyes of the LORD your God and provoking him to anger, I call heaven and earth as witnesses against you this day that you will quickly perish from the land that you are crossing the Jordan to possess. You will not live there long but will certainly be destroyed. The LORD will scatter you among the peoples, and only a few of you will survive among the nations to which the LORD will drive you. There you will worship man-made gods of wood and stone, which cannot see or hear or eat or smell. But if from there you seek the LORD your God, you will find him if you look for him with all your heart and with all your soul (Deuteronomy 4: 25-29).

Question 5. How are we, as the Israelites, supposed to find God, and be forgiven?

   A. Seek the Lord your God

   B. Look for Him if you happen to have time

   C. Look for Him with all your heart and soul

   D. Option A and C, above

> And without faith it is impossible to please God, because anyone who comes to him must believe that he exists and that he rewards those who earnestly seek him (Hebrews 11:6).

Question 6. How does Hebrews 11:6 compare with what we are studying?

Question 1. Please list all the ways that the Israelites might do wrong, according to the above passage:

   A. They would become corrupt and make idols

   B. They would do evil and provoke God

   C. They would worship man-made gods of wood and stone

   D. All of the above

Question 2. What did God say would happen to them because of their sins:

   A. They would perish from the land.

   B. They would be destroyed.

   C. The Lord would scatter them among other nations.

   D. All of the above

Question 3. But, despite the horrendous sin in which these people were, was God willing to forgive them?

   A. Yes

   B. No

Question 4. How do we know God would still forgive them? What does He say? Write it here.

Course member Dennis wrote, "When we do seek Him, he earnestly rewards us. I was alienated from the blessing of God, because I refused to seek Him. I grew bitter because I wanted the rewards, but rejected a life of faith for a life of sin."

> [11] For I know the plans I have for you, declares the LORD, plans to prosper you and not to harm you, plans to give you hope and a future. [12] Then you will call upon me and come and pray to me, and I will listen to you. [13] You will seek me and find me when you seek me with all your heart" (Jeremiah 29:11-13).

Question 7. What are your comments on Jeremiah 29:11-13?

> In his pride the wicked does not seek him; in all his thoughts there is no room for God (Psalm 10:4).

Question 8. How does Psalm 10:4 compare?

Note: This passage teaches us some important things about the character of God: He forgives - any sin, at any time, for anyone who turns away from sin, and turns to the Lord! The truth taught today is "But if from there...you seek the Lord" and your "there" may be anywhere. From wherever you are, if you will turn to God, seek for Him, look for Him with all your heart and soul, you will find Him. He has promised!

Question 9. What are your thoughts on 2 Samuel 14:14?

But God does not take away life; instead, he devises ways so that a banished person may not remain estranged from him (2 Samuel 14:14).

Ask and it will be given to you; seek and you will find; knock and the door will be opened to you (Matthew 7:7).

Question 10. Comment on Matthew 7:7

Dennis wrote, "I was bitter that he would not bless me, but the truth was - I would not seek him. I refused to ask. What a miserable man I had become. I had no fruit to show for my years of salvation. My ground was all thorny and over-run with the weeds of lust and porn. I had become a disgrace. Only Jesus could save me from the sins that bound me. I asked, I sought, and I have found Him faithful. My great prayer is to overcome and help my children avoid the same sinkhole of sin."

My friend, there is no sin that God will not forgive, if we will seek Him wholeheartedly about it. This is serious business - no half-hearted seeking of the Lord will do. Eternity is at stake. Hell is real. Let us seek Him while He may be found, and we will rejoice in His forgiveness, love and acceptance.

⁴⁶ When they sin against you—for there is no one who does not sin—and you become angry with them and give them over to the enemy, who takes them captive to his own land, far away or near; ⁴⁷ and if they have a change of heart in the land where they are held captive, and repent and plead with you in the land of their conquerors and say, We have sinned, we have done wrong, we have acted wickedly; ⁴⁸ and if they turn back to you with all their heart and soul in the land of their enemies who took them captive, and pray to you toward the land you gave their fathers, toward the city you have chosen and the temple I have built for your Name; 49 then from heaven, your dwelling place, hear their prayer and their plea, and uphold their cause. 50 And forgive your people, who have sinned against you; forgive all the offenses they have committed against you, and cause their conquerors to show them mercy; 51 for they are your people and your inheritance, whom you brought out of Egypt, out of that iron-smelting furnace (1 Kings 8:46-51).

Question 11. Write out your comments on 1 Kings 8:46-51

Today, I want to again introduce you to some writings of the Puritans. The first is from a Puritan pastor, giving practical counsel to one in his congregation. My prayer is that his counsel will sink right in to your heart and soul as you read it. Once you get a taste of the medicinal value of these writings, you will want more and more. We've got to replace the hours spent on pornography and lust with something else; why not invaluable writings like these?

Memoirs of McCheyne: **"I DO NOT and cannot forget you; and though it is very late, I have to write you a few lines to say, 'Follow on to know Jesus.' I do not know if you can read my crooked writing, but I will make it as plain as I can. I was reading this morning, Luke 2:29, what old Simeon said when he got the child Jesus into his arms: 'Now lettest thou thy servant depart in peace, according to thy word: for mine eyes have seen thy salvation.' If you get a firm hold of the Lord Jesus, you will be able to say the same.**

"If you had died in your ignorance and sin, dear soul, where would you have been this night? Ah, how shall we sufficiently praise God if He really has brought you to the blood of the Lord Jesus Christ! If you all are really brought to Christ, it will be something like the case of the wise men of the East (Matthew 2). When they were in their own country, God attracted their attention by means of a star. They followed it, and came to Jerusalem, saying, 'Where is he that is born King of the Jews? . . . for we are come to worship him.' Herod and Jerusalem were troubled at the saying. No one was seeking Christ but the wise men. The world thought they were mad; but soon they saw the star again, and it led them to the house where the infant Saviour lay, His robe of state a swaddling band, His cradle the manger. Yet they kneeled down and called Him, 'my Lord and my God.' They got their own souls saved, and gave Him gifts, the best they had, and then departed into their own country with great joy in their hearts, and heaven in their eyes.

"So it may be with you. The most around you care not for Jesus. But you are asking, 'Where is He? We are come to be saved by Him.' None around you can tell. They think you are going out of your mind. But God is leading you to the very spot where the Redeemer is a lowly, despised, spit upon, crucified Savior. Can this be the Savior of the world? Yes, dear soul; kneel down and call Him your Redeemer. He died for such as you and me. And now you may go away into your own country again, but not as you came. You will carry with you joy unspeakable and full of glory."

Matthew Henry: **"Here observe, First, that whatever place we are in we may thence seek the Lord our God, though ever so remote from our own land or from his holy temple. There is no part of this earth that has a gulf fixed between it and heaven. Secondly, those, and those only, shall find God to their comfort, who seek him with all their heart, that is, who are entirely devoted to him, earnestly desirous of his favour and solicitous to obtain it. Thirdly, afflictions are sent to engage and quicken us to see God, and, by the grace of God working with them, many are thus reduced to their right mind, "When these things shall come upon thee, it is to be hoped that thou wilt turn to the Lord they God, for thou seest what comes of turning from him; see Daniel 9:11,12. Fourthly, God's faithfulness to his covenant encourages us to hope that he will not reject us, though we be driven to him by affliction. If we at length remember the covenant, we shall find that he has not forgotten it."**

Memoirs of McCheyne: **"Some of you may have seen how short life is in those around you. Your fathers, where are they? And the prophets, do they live forever? How many friends have you lying in the grave! Some of you have more friends in the grave than in this world. They were carried away as with a flood, and we are fast hastening after them. In a little while the church where you sit will be filled with new worshipers, a new voice will lead the psalm, a new man of God fill the pulpit. It is an absolute certainty that, in a few years, all of you who read this will be lying in the grave. Oh, what need, then, to fly to Christ without delay! How great a work you have to do! How short the time you have to do it in! You have to flee from wrath, to come to Christ, to be born again, to receive the Holy Spirit, to be made meet for glory. It is high time that you seek the Lord. The longest lifetime is short enough. Seek conviction of sin and an interest in Christ. Oh, satisfy me early with thy mercy, that I may rejoice and be glad all my days."**

Question 12. What are your thoughts on today's lesson?

Scripture to Consider

[3] Glory in His holy name; Let the hearts of those rejoice who seek the LORD! [4] Seek the LORD and His strength; Seek His face evermore! (Psalm 105:3-4).

Were you free from pornography since you did the last lesson?

    Yes   No

Were you free from self-gratification since you did the last lesson?

    Yes   No

Were you free from sexual immorality since you did the last lesson?

    Yes   No

The following testimony is from Doug:

My testimony of how I got here and, more importantly, where I am going starts a long time ago. I first looked at pornography when I was very young. I have brothers who are much older than I, and they always had pornography.

Because of this, I never felt like I was included in anything. I always felt different, like if they really knew me, people would not want to associate with me. I felt the same way about church. I went because it was expected, but I knew that what I did outside of church was not in harmony with what I learned inside. So I tried to tune out the church part. Eventually, I stopped going.

My addiction grew stronger but not much deeper. I went from innocent pictures to more hardcore pornography, and thankfully, it never went any farther. However, the amount of time I spent on it kept growing. I always thought that once I grew up and got married that everything would be fine.

I went from magazines, to movies, to Internet. I put my pleasure in my own desires. Last year, my wife and daughters took a trip to visit family I haven't seen in three years. I did not go, because I wanted to be able to do what I wanted.

It came to a head last November. My wife knew that there was a problem, but she just didn't know how bad it was. She checked the history on the computer one day, and found that I had surfed and found fifty-six sites in one day. She went ballistic, and then some. She was not happy at all. She told me yesterday, that the only reason she didn't throw me out, was because I had looked at Setting Captives Free, and had done day one lesson that day. I have a long way to go but with God's help everything is possible. I am much happier now.

Then something changed. My wife and I were not doing well, and I went into the bedroom to talk about it. I don't know what I was going to say but all I got out was "I'm sorry" over and over again as I bawled like a baby. After that we really talked. There were no new revelations, but now I felt we were at least on the same team again.

Since then, our marriage has changed. My daughter says I am not grumpy anymore. I am starting to have the feelings I felt for my wife before we got married. I want to do the little things to show her I love her. In some ways, it feels as if I am just waking up after being asleep for a long, long time.

I still have temptations; triggers that set me off when I get stressed. But she is helping me through that and we are deciding guidelines for how to deal with those things before they become an "I fell" instead of "I was tempted." I may struggle with this temptation for the rest of my life, but my plan is to immerse myself so fully in truth, that I won't pay them any attention.

When I started The Way of Purity course, I just wanted to get in, get "fixed" and get out. Now I am so grateful for all the help, love, support and freedom.

DAY 38 - RESTORATION AFTER LOSS

Viewing pornography is tremendously exciting, but only for awhile. It promises to give fulfillment, stimulation and satisfaction. But if you have been involved in it for any length of time, you know that the promises are really lies; pornography takes more than it ever gives! We will examine a story today of a young man who's heart was filled with the promise of excitement and satisfaction, and the gain of material wealth, lifelong friendships, ease and satisfaction. But he ended up losing everything. Let's read:

> [11] There was a man who had two sons. [12] The younger one said to his father, "Father, give me my share of the estate." So he divided his property between them. [13] Not long after that, the younger son got together all he had, set off for a distant country and there squandered his wealth in wild living. [14] After he had spent everything, there was a severe famine in that whole country, and he began to be in need. [15] So he went and hired himself out to a citizen of that country, who sent him to his fields to feed pigs. [16] He longed to fill his stomach with the pods that the pigs were eating, but no one gave him anything (Luke 15:11-16).

This young man was not content with his life, so he asked his father to give him his inheritance. Then he went to a "distant country" and began living a "wild life" where he "spent everything."

Pornography and virtual sex plant seeds of discontentment in a very powerful way. Internet sex may plant the seed of physical discontentment by its display of the seemingly flawless appearances of the actors and actresses. It may plant the seeds of emotional discontentment through the endless exhibitions of physical "love" repeatedly demonstrated in the scenes. And following discontentment comes covetousness, or wanting what we do not have. In the above passage, this problem is stated in the words, "Give me my share." Pornography is an extremely powerful tool in the hands of the devil to make us discontented and covetous.

If we were to follow the lives of people who have been involved in pornography for any length of time, we would discover lives of loss, of need, and of emptiness. Here is the way one man stated it: "I have been involved in pornographic movies, pornographic Internet surfing, night clubs, strip shows, prostitution, and self-gratification. I am a former pastor, and could no longer remain in the ministry and keep up my involvement in this." Unfortunately, this is a common scenario.

Questions

Please answer the following questions:

Question 1. From verse 14 above, there are two things that caused this young man to "be in need." What are those two things?

Note: Regarding the famine, it may be that Providence is against us when we are sinning. And yet in some cases, God is disciplining in order to restore. This famine in the above story, was of Divine Providence, designed to increase the "need" of the young man, and its purpose was his restoration.

Questions

Question 2. There is a word in verse 16 that describes all who are not being satisfied in Jesus Christ. Fill in the blank. "He longed to fill his stomach."

So, the young man initially longed to have his inheritance and longed to live the wild life; now he was longing for food. "Longing" is the characteristic of those who are not drinking the Living Water of Jesus Christ. Remember the woman at the well and her six relationships?

Question 3. When we were viewing pornography, we were longing for something. For what were you longing?

Question 4. Write down everything you can think of from the above story that this young man lost by going to the far country.

Question 5. Have you lost anything through involvement with pornography or immorality?

> And the God of all grace...will himself restore you and make you strong, firm and steadfast (1 Peter 5:10).

Our God is a restoring God. The devil prowls around like a roaring lion seeking for someone to devour. But God is able to forgive, save, heal, deliver, and restore us when we fall. And, He is able to keep us from falling again. Notice the rest of the passage in Luke 15:

> [17] When he came to his senses, he said, "How many of my father's hired men have food to spare, and here I am starving to death! [18] I will set out and go back to my father and say to him: 'Father, I have sinned against heaven and against you. [19] I am no longer worthy to be

123

called your son; make me like one of your hired men.'" [20] So he got up and went to his father. But while he was still a long way off, his father saw him and was filled with compassion for him; he ran to his son, threw his arms around him and kissed him. [21] The son said to him, "Father, I have sinned against heaven and against you. I am no longer worthy to be called your son." [22] But the father said to his servants, "Quick! Bring the best robe and put it on him. Put a ring on his finger and sandals on his feet. [23] Bring the fattened calf and kill it. Let's have a feast and celebrate. [24] For this son of mine was dead and is alive again; he was lost and is found." So they began to celebrate (Luke 15:17-24).

Question 6. Verse 17 says that the young man "came to his senses." So what was this man's condition while in the far country?

A. Stable

B. Out of his right mind

C. Fully satisfied and happy

Note: viewing pornography is insanity! It puts us out of our right minds.

Question 7. What two words does the father use in verse 24, above, to describe his son when he was in the far country?

_____ and _____

Question 8. When he "came to his senses," where did he want to go?

A. To the Far Country Bar N Grill

B. To the Superbowl

C. Back to his father

The first indicator of true repentance is a desire for God. We know we are beginning to think correctly, after a time in the far country, when we want to go to our Heavenly Father.

Let's review the picture we have been given of this young man: According to Jesus, this man was, for a time, not in his right mind, but he did come back to his senses. According to his father, he was dead and lost. According to his own words, he had sinned and was unworthy.

Question 9. Do you see yourself and your involvement with pornography and impurity in the life of this prodigal? Write your thoughts here.

Like the prodigal, I was once discontent with what I had, and pornography stirred up lust in my heart. I was longing for intimacy, and I attempted to satisfy it in the wrong way - a way that is far away from God. When involved with pornography and sexual sin, we are out of our minds; dead and lost spiritually, sinful and unworthy, and we may lose much while in this condition. But, when we "come to our senses," and return to our Heavenly Father, He will accept, embrace, love and restore us.

But while he was still a long way off, his father saw him and was filled with compassion for him; he ran to his son, threw his arms around him and kissed him (Luke 15:20).

Are there any sweeter words in all of Scripture? This verse reveals the heart of God the Father toward those who are leaving sin and coming to Him. If you are leaving pornography and sexual impurity and coming back to God, you will be received warmly, no matter how far away you went, how long you have been gone, or how much you lost. Our God loves those who leave their sin and come to Him.

Notice that the father was "filled with compassion." If you are returning from pornography and immorality, our God has a heart wide open for you. His heart beats with love for those who are returning, and just the sight of us when we return fills our Father's heart with compassion. As a father has compassion on his children, so the Lord has compassion on those who fear him (Psalm 103:13).

[22] But the father said to his servants, "Quick! Bring the best robe and put it on him. Put a ring on his finger and sandals on his feet. [23] Bring the fattened calf and kill it. Let's have a feast and celebrate. [24] For this son of mine was dead and is alive again; he was lost and is found." So they began to celebrate (Luke 15:22-24).

The end of this story is all about loving and joyous restoration. He who had sinned, squandered the wealth, and had been living with pigs, was now reconciled to his father, given a robe, ring and sandals, and was feasting on the fatted calf.

How instructive this is for us, who through pornography and impurity, squandered away our spiritual inheritance, and possibly much more. But now we are reconciled to God, graced with the robe of righteousness, granted the ring of authority, and wearing the sandals of readiness to tell the gospel. And most importantly, we are feasting on the Lord Jesus by reading and meditating on His Word, the Scriptures! Oh, friend, we were saved to celebrate! Reconciled to God to delight in His Son! Rescued from sexual sin to feast on Jesus!

Today's study is all about restoration after loss. Are you one who has lost a great deal through involvement with pornography and immorality? Oh my friend, if you come to God, or come back to God, you will see His heart of compassion for you. You will see your life restored, and made a blessing to others. You will look good in your new robe, and will enjoy a feast that will satisfy your longings. God will restore to you the years the locust has eaten (Joel 2:25).

Question 10. What progression do you perceive in the young man's 180-degree turn-about?

Question 11. The young man wanted to come back and be a "servant." What did the father call him in verse 24?

Question 12. If you have "squandered your life," does this story give you hope of restoration? How so?

Question 13. Does this story move you to believe in the possibility of new or fresh changes in your relationship with God and/or others?

How do the following verses reinforce the truth we have been studying today? Please write your thoughts after each one:

The following testimony is from Darryn:

I remember the first time I discovered self-gratification, though I did not know that is what it was back then. I must have been about ten years old. It was not long after that my friends and I found some pages from a magazine that were just lying around on someone's yard.

My addiction went on for many years, through two years of the army, and through the start of college.

It must have been about nine years ago that God really grabbed hold of me. I had a really great youth pastor that held me accountable and inspired me to get straightened out, even though he did not know about all these things. By the grace of God and some literal fights with myself, I overcame the sexual sins in my life, and was free from those sins for over eight months. Then I met the one who would ultimately become my wife.

We did not do anything until after we were engaged, but we did have sex before we were married. That was bad and sinful, but I still did not fall back into pornography and self-gratification. That came later.

We had been married about a year and a half, and things were not going well. Our first daughter was born seriously handicapped, and it tore us apart. I turned back to pornography and self-gratification mainly because I did not want to "bother my wife so much about sex." That was a terrible mistake. With the Internet around now, I had tons of "free" pornography to look at. Then, because of all the things that had happened, I turned my back on God. I basically told Him that He had hurt me, now I was going to get even.

That led to a five-year addiction and self-gratification at least once a day if not more. Finally, as my marriage dissolved around me, God got my attention and brought me back to church. But there was still this issue with sex. It had become such a part of me that I defined myself by it.

Ultimately, we got a new pastor at church and he asked me to lead worship on Wednesday nights. I knew that I needed to tell him about this problem before he could let me do that, and that has helped me so much to get through this. Then I found the Setting Captives Free site, and a month or two later started it.

God has proven Himself to me in many ways. He has shown that He knows my needs, he understands my pain, He cares about me, and He hates my sin. God's grace alone has brought me to this point. The addiction is broken, but the desire is not fully broken. There are still days, in the pit of my loneliness that my flesh craves the sin I left behind, and I am not perfect. I have overcome only by the blood of Jesus Christ working in me. I need to always be on guard for my soul, be diligent and mindful, watching for the signs of weakness so that I can run to my Savior.

God has delivered me from the pit of sin. There are still parts that need to be cleaned up in me, and the race will only be over when I reach heaven, but I know who holds my hand all the way.

Question 14. What are your thoughts on Joel 2:25-26 "I will repay you for the years the locusts have eaten - the great locust and the young locust, the other locusts and the locust swarm my great army that I sent among you. ²⁶ You will have plenty to eat, until you are full, and you will praise the name of the LORD your God, who has worked wonders for you; never again will my people be shamed."

Note: This passage seems to be a promise of God that He would restore what the disobedience of the Israelites destroyed. The "locusts" here are used to picture sin, which devours and destroys everything in its path.

Question 15. What are your thoughts on Hosea 6:1-2 "Come, let us return to the LORD. He has torn us to pieces but he will heal us; he has injured us but he will bind up our wounds. ² After two days he will revive us; on the third day he will restore us, that we may live in his presence."

Question 16. What are your thoughts on Isaiah 61:1-4 "The Spirit of the Sovereign LORD is on me, because the LORD has anointed me to preach good news to the poor. He has sent me to bind up the brokenhearted, to proclaim freedom for the captives and release from darkness for the prisoners, ² to proclaim the year of the LORD's favor and the day of vengeance of our God, to comfort all who mourn, ³ and provide for those who grieve in Zion to bestow on them a crown of beauty instead of ashes, the oil of gladness instead of mourning, and a garment of praise instead of a spirit of despair. They will be called oaks of righteousness, a planting of the LORD for the display of his splendor. ⁴ They will rebuild the ancient ruins and restore the places long devastated; they will renew the ruined cities that have been devastated for generations."

Scripture to Consider

¹⁸ Thus says the LORD: "Behold, I will bring back the captivity of Jacob's tents, And have mercy on his dwelling places; The city shall be built upon its own mound, And the palace shall remain according to its own plan. ¹⁹ Then out of them shall proceed thanksgiving And the voice of those who make merry; I will multiply them, and they shall not diminish; I will also glorify them, and they shall not be small" (Jeremiah 30:18-19).

Were you free from pornography since you did the last lesson?

    Yes   No

Were you free from self-gratification since you did the last lesson?

    Yes   No

Were you free from sexual immorality since you did the last lesson?

    Yes   No

DAY 39 – SPECIFIC BIBLICAL PRINCIPLES OF FREEDOM FROM SIN

Submit yourselves, then, to God. Resist the devil, and he will flee from you. Come near to God and he will come near to you. Wash your hands, you sinners, and purify your hearts, you double-minded. Grieve, mourn and wail. Change your laughter to mourning and your joy to gloom. Humble yourselves before the Lord, and he will lift you up (James 4:7-10).

Today we will see from Scripture that we are to take specific action to be free from sin. But first, let us notice from the above passage some characteristics of those who are in sin. We'll list them here:

1. They do not submit to God (verse 7)
2. They do not resist the devil (verse 7)
3. They remain at a distance from God (verse 8)
4. They have dirty hands and a defiled heart (verse 8)
5. They are double-minded (verse 8)
6. They are light and joking, and laugh much (verse 9)
7. They are prideful (verse 10)

I can think back on my time of habitual viewing of pornography and of sexual impurity, and see every one of these characteristics in my life:

1. My spirit was domineering and dictatorial, not submissive toward God or others

2. I freely embraced pornography on many occasions, not realizing that, in so doing, I was worshiping at a demonic shrine (1 Corinthians 10:20-21).

3. I was far from God during this time, even though I claimed to be a servant of His. My life illustrated Proverbs 28:9 "If anyone turns a deaf ear to the law, even his prayers are detestable."

4. My hands were dirty from all my sin activity, and my heart was defiled all the time. Oh, what a horrible condition in which to live! Now I understand why Scripture compares sin to leprosy, for leprosy is a disease that defiles one entirely, and makes a person unclean. Just as lepers had to remain isolated or in colonies of other lepers, so I came to feel that I should be banished from society because my guilt and shame were so great. Oh, how I thank God that He still cleanses lepers!

5. I was double minded and unstable because, while I attempted to pray and meditate on Scripture, my thoughts often slid into pornographic images. This hindered time with my family, as I was always entertaining some sinful image. It made me unstable, for I could not keep my thoughts together on any one subject. James says, "That man (who doubts God) should not think he will receive anything from the Lord; he is a double-minded man, unstable in all he does" (James 1:7-8).

6. I was never very serious, but was light and airy, joking all the time and laughing quite frequently. This was a cover up for my sinful ways, as I tried to hide all my pain with laughter.

7. I was very prideful and often put others down, hoping to lift myself up

Course member Mike wrote "I, too, can see each one of these characteristics in my life as a result of my past involvement with pornography, especially the pride part. Nobody could tell me anything; I knew it all. And when it came to spiritual things, I was a self-proclaimed expert, always using Scripture to justify myself, while condemning others. I can see how these verses in James point me to the way out of my bondage in pornography; Lord, help me to apply them!"

Question 1. Thinking through the above seven characteristics, which one (or more) describe your life when you were in pornography or sexual sin? Please give some instances where these characteristics showed themselves most clearly.

These verses also show us the remedy for our sin-sickness, and we are about to study specific principles on how to be free from habitual sin. But let us be careful to note that doing what Scripture commands requires the grace of God. This would be a good point to stop today's lesson and beseech God for grace to enable you to actually take the necessary action. I often pray, "God help me to apply what I learn today. I need your grace to actually do what your Word says to do, so please keep me from just gaining knowledge, but help me to obey You." Feel free to write out a prayer to God.

Truth 1

"Submit yourselves, then, to God." (verse 7) Submission, in Scripture, means humbling ourselves and obeying God, whereas sin is obeying the evil one. Job 22:21-27 contain much truth on how to be free from sin, and the first principle is listed in verse 21: "Submit to God and be at peace with him;"

Question 2. Please write out in what areas you have failed to submit to God in the past, and then explain how you will submit to Him from now on.

Truth 2

"Resist the devil, and he will flee from you" (verse 7). To resist means to set yourself against someone or something, or to stand in opposition to them. For me, this meant developing a "battle plan" of how to set myself against the evil one. Among other things, this meant taking the TV out of my hotel room at night, and giving away my notebook computer.

Question 3. How will you set yourself against the devil and stand in opposition to him? Please be specific.

Truth 3

"Come near to God and He will come near to you" (verse 8). Friend, let me speak a truth to your heart right now. There will be no real freedom, or any lasting victory in a life that is not seeking closeness and union with Christ. Sure, we may be able to "white-knuckle" it, grit our teeth, and use sheer "will power" for a short time, but we will not have freedom, because that comes only through intimacy with Christ. We must not only resist the devil, but we must also draw near to God, and experience His presence, in order to overcome sin. For me, that meant spending much time in prayer and Bible study, attending church whenever possible, and counseling with my pastor, etc.

Question 4. What will it look like for you to draw near to God? Again, please be specific.

Truth 4

"Wash your hands, you sinners, and purify your hearts, you double-minded" (verse 8). There must be a cleansing of what we do (our hands), what we love (our hearts), and what we think (our minds). Scripture admonishes us to "wash" and "purify," and this requires diligence and effort, as well as the proper cleansing tools.

Question 5. Please list how you are planning to cleanse your hands, your heart and your mind.

Truth 5

Become single-minded (verse 8). Yes, it is entirely possible to rid our brains of those pornographic images. It requires no longer allowing ourselves access to any additional images and cleansing our minds of the images that remain from the past. It also requires the ceasing of self-gratification, because self-gratification solidifies those images in our brains. This cleansing took me a few months, once I began the process of coming out of pornography and impurity, but I can tell you that I have not had a pornographic image lodge in my brain for several years now.

Question 6. Are you "double-minded" now? Or do you remember what it was like in the past?

Truth 6

"Grieve, mourn and wail. Change your laughter to mourning and your joy to gloom." (verse 9) The basic instruction in this verse is to get serious, rid your life of flippancy, and begin to mourn over your sin. Now, some will say that this is a life of morbid despair and gloom, and is contradictory to all the passages that refer to unspeakable joy (1 Peter 1:8), and being content in life (Hebrews 13:5). But this is not so. This passage in James refers to a person who is in need of repentance, whereas the other passages refer to the effects of repenting. Genuine repentance includes submitting to God, resisting the devil, gaining intimacy with Christ, purifying ourselves, changing our joy to gloom, and mourning over our sins.

Question 7. Have you sincerely mourned over your sin? Are you seeking to exchange light-hearted laughter for seriousness and sadness, at least for a time? Please explain…

Truth 7

"Humble yourselves" (verse 10). During my years of pornography and immorality, I thought myself to be the final say on Scripture. I considered myself to be an authority, because of my frequent study, and I did not like to be challenged by those whom I considered to be inferior, such as my pastor, my seminary teachers, and obviously, everybody else. Oh, how deceived I was, and how ignorant to the ways of God! When I went to my pastor in January of 1999 and asked for help, I determined not to argue with him, nor to teach, or to "prove my point," but only to ask for help and listen to his counsel. THIS is what is required to get out of habitual sin, my friend. It requires us to humble ourselves.

We can tell when God is working in the heart of a course member here, because they do not want to argue or point out all the wrongs of the course, but desire simply to learn, and will ask for assistance. They recognize their need, and so they humble themselves and ask God and us for help. We have noticed that the people who are serious about humbling themselves always find victory. Indeed, the last half of the verse that tells us to humble ourselves says, "and He will lift you up" (verse 10). Victory and freedom are the results of those who humble themselves!

Question 8. Finally, please share what you have learned today, or what you will put into practice. Have you seen yourself in this passage, and are you now aware of some things that will need to change in order to be truly free from habitual sin?

Scripture to Consider

Flee from sexual immorality. All other sins a man commits are outside his body, but he who sins sexually sins against his own body. Do you not know that your body is a temple of the Holy Spirit, who is in you, whom you have received from God? You are not your own; you were bought at a price. Therefore honor God with your body (1 Corinthians 6:18-20).

But among you there must not be even a hint of sexual immorality, or of any kind of impurity, or of greed, because these are improper for God's holy people (Ephesians 5:3).

[21] Submit to God and be at peace with him; in this way prosperity will come to you. [22]Accept instruction from his mouth and lay up his words in your heart. [23] If you return to the Almighty, you will be restored: If you remove wickedness far from your tent [24] and assign your nuggets to the dust, your gold of Ophir to the rocks in the ravines, [25] then the Almighty will be your gold, the choicest silver for you. [26] Surely then you will find delight in the Almighty and will lift up your face to God. [27] You will pray to him, and he will hear you, and you will fulfill your vows. [28] What you decide on will be done, and light will shine on your way (Job 22:21-28).

There I will give her back her vineyards, and will make the Valley of Achor [valley of Trouble] a door of hope. There she will sing as in the days of her youth, as in the day she came up out of Egypt (Hosea 2:15).

Were you free from pornography since you did the last lesson?

    Yes   No

Were you free from self-gratification since you did the last lesson?

    Yes   No

Were you free from sexual immorality since you did the last lesson?

    Yes   No

The following testimony is from Ronnie:

I became involved in pornography and self-gratification when I was a teenager. One day I got my hands on a pornographic magazine. When I first practiced self-gratification and had a release, I thought something was wrong with me. I didn't know what was happening to me, but I knew that it felt pretty good and began to do it more and more. I got dirty magazines by stealing them off a rack outside at a store. I would never buy them, but as I became more involved in pornography, I needed to feed this sinful hunger with something.

As I got older, I started dating the girl that is now my wife. Until this time I never had intercourse with a girl. When we got married, I figured that the sin would stop. It did for a little while, but came back again. One night, my wife found out that I had an addiction. From there my life started to go downhill. We had two children, but our intimate life began to suffer. She would be tired all of the time, and put me off until the next day, which did not usually come. I stopped asking to have intimate relations, as I would be turned down again, so I continued on in pornography and self-gratification, and I could satisfy myself whenever I wanted. My life continued to be destroyed, and I looked for a self-help book on the subject. I read some books but it never did any good. It was hopeless, and I thought I would live this way the rest of my life.

One Saturday night while looking on the web, I came across the Setting Captives Free web site. I started to check it out, but was unsure of what this was all about. I did not sign up that night, but the next morning at church, I became excited as I knew that the course is what I wanted. I signed up that day, and began the course.

The Lord has truly led me to freedom from sexual sin through this Spirit-filled course. God led me to this ministry and He began to show me how much I had drifted from Him. I never thought I could go sixty days without practicing self-gratification. I thought that there was no way I could last that long, but I am lasting that long, and will last from this course on. Freedom from sexual immorality is so sweet and I never want to return to what I came from.

I now have a closer relationship with my Lord, as I never knew I would have. The Lord is opening doors for me, and my life has become a blessing. I will continue to live free from sexual sin, and I know that my Lord loves me and I love Him. I will live in Him eternally. Praise The Lord, for His grace to free me from sin, and to the Setting Captives Free course, for showing me the wonderful teachings of my Lord. I am totally free from sexual sin, and I will stay free. Oh, how sweet it is to be free!

DAY 40 - THE HEART, THE MIND, AND THE ACTIONS

Since, then, you have been raised with Christ, set your hearts on things above, where Christ is seated at the right hand of God. Set your minds on things above, not on earthly things. For you died, and your life is now hidden with Christ in God. When Christ, who is your life, appears, then you also will appear with him in glory. Put to death, therefore, whatever belongs to your earthly nature: sexual immorality, impurity, lust, evil desires and greed, which is idolatry. Because of these, the wrath of God is coming. You used to walk in these ways, in the life you once lived. But now you must rid yourselves of all such things as these: anger, rage, malice, slander, and filthy language from your lips. Do not lie to each other, since you have taken off your old self with its practices and have put on the new self, which is being renewed in knowledge in the image of its Creator (Colossians 3:1-10).

When I was involved in pornography and immorality, my heart was set on impure things. I would walk around during the day with my heart racing, my hands sweating, my mind dwelling on pornographic images, just waiting to get to the hotel where I could indulge my flesh and appease my sinful appetite. That is how many of my days were spent.

Today, we want to study how the heart and mind affect the actions, and we want to learn how to live in freedom from habitual sin.

The above passage of Scripture talks about the "heart" (verse 1), the "mind" (verse 2), and the actions (verses 5-10), and shows how they affect each other. The heart affects the mind, which in turn affects the actions. Let us look at each one of these in today's lesson.

The Heart: The heart loves and feels excitement. The heart longs, yearns, and lusts. The heart of one in bondage, loves to sin and feels excitement while sinning. It longs, yearns, and lusts after sin, and is kept in bondage to its cravings. In contrast, the heart of one who is being set free loves God and feels excitement over growing in righteousness. That heart longs, yearns and earnestly desires the holiness of God and purity.

In the above passage, we are instructed to "set our hearts on things above, where Christ is seated at the right hand of God." In other words, we are to set our hearts on loving Christ. Oh dear friend, here is freedom from pornography and impurity! Involve your heart with Jesus Christ. Become excited about Christ. Long to be with Him, yearn for intimacy with Him, lust after a closer walk with Him. Let the cry of the beloved be yours: "Take me away with you - let us hurry! Let the king bring me into his chambers" (Song of Solomon 1:4).

The heart that is set on Christ, is the heart that is free from sin. The heart that is apprehended by Christ refuses to let Him go but, instead, embraces Him and clings to Him. "Scarcely had I passed them when I found the one my heart loves. I held him and would not let him go till I had brought him to my mother's house, to the room of the one who conceived me" (Song of Solomon 3:4). This is our goal in The Way of Purity course! We desire for your heart to be affected with Christ. Colossians 3:1 tells us to "set our hearts on things above, where Christ is seated..."

Question 1. What does your heart love right now?

Question 2. List some practical ways that you will begin to set your heart on things above.

The Mind: The mind obviously refers to our thoughts. The mind that is in sin is continually thinking sinful thoughts. Pornographic images previously consumed my mind while awake, and my dreams while sleeping. Those thoughts and images interrupted my work, my recreation, my family time, and all other areas of life. Romans 1:28 describes my previous condition: "Furthermore, since they did not think it worthwhile to retain the knowledge of God, he gave them over to a depraved mind, to do what ought not to be done."

Colossians 3:2 tells us "set your minds on things above, not on earthly things." When I was involved in sexual sin, I was so earthly minded, I was no heavenly good. But now we are told to set our minds on Christ, which will inevitably bring about a real battle since we have immersed ourselves in sinful images for so long. Now we are to think heavenly thoughts; thoughts about Christ and God, thoughts about eternity and about heaven. We are to discern whatever is true, noble, right, pure, lovely, admirable, excellent or praiseworthy (in other words, Christ!) and we are to think on these things. (Philippians 4:8)

The reason we are to do this is found in Colossians 3:3: "For you died, and your life is now hidden with Christ in God." On the cross, Jesus died for us, but we also died in Him. Our old sinful nature hung on that tree with Christ. My old heart that loved sin died 2,000 years ago. My mind that was consumed with sinful images was killed at the hands of Roman soldiers, and then my old sinful self was buried in a tomb.

Question 3. Notice that verse 2 does not tell us "Stop thinking about sinful things" but rather "set your minds on things above." Why is this so?

The Actions: What we do is tied in with what we love and what we think about. As Christians, we are not about behavior modification without a heart change. We are about loving God passionately, about having our thoughts consumed in Christ, and then about walking in freedom from sin.

Colossians 3:5 tells us that we are to put to death whatever belongs to our flesh, and lists "sexual immorality" as the first thing to crucify. Friends, here is where the Christian life turns violent, and where murder of our pet sins is encouraged. We are to put to death sexual immorality and to crucify our lusts. This requires spiritual acts of violence. It requires a battle plan, it uses spiritual weapons, and requires a complete annihilation of the sin. When I first started coming out of pornography and impurity, I took the TV out of my hotel room, gave away my notebook computer, got rid of the TV in my home, and took many other "radical" actions to be free from the power of sin.

So, set out to chop up the cable that has been seducing you; burn all the magazines the devil has used as bait; take the TV out of your hotel room and deposit it at the front desk. Cut off your Internet access; rip up your video store card, and refuse to take any cash or credit cards with you in case you are tempted by a favorite strip joint. Next, set up fences for yourself that will not allow you to go back to these sins. This may be embarrassing to you, but unless we are willing to be embarrassed, we will never be free.

We are to not only crucify sexual immorality, but also all "impurity, lust, evil desires and greed, which is idolatry." Everything must go. Just as the children of Israel were told to stone Achan, his family, his sheep and cattle, and everything connected with him (Joshua 7), so we are to do violence to the entire realm of everything sinful. We are not only to destroy sexual immorality, impurity, evil desires, etc., but we are to also rid our lives of anger, rage, malice, slander, and filthy language from your lips (Colossians 3:8). We will consider this concept further in upcoming lessons, as we study how to employ offensive, aggressive, violence in wiping out our sins.

Question 4. Read verse 5 in the introduction. What does it call sexual immorality, impurity, lust, and evil desires, etc.?

My friend, sexual immorality, lust and all other forms of self-pleasing are idolatry. Idolatry is the worship of false gods. Did you know you were worshiping false gods when you were giving in to evil desires? When I was viewing pornography, I was kneeling down to a demonic god (1 Corinthians 10:19-20), and worshiping at the shrine of the devil. When I was gratifying the flesh, I adored myself and was living to please myself, which is self-idolatry. I did not know this at the time, but the devil was deriving worship from me through pornography and self-gratification. No wonder the next sentence in Colossians 3 says, "Because of these, the wrath of God is coming." God will destroy all idolaters and, as you read these words, this may be your last chance to repent of your idolatry before the wrath of God destroys you. We must destroy sin in our lives before we are destroyed.

Question 5. How does Exodus 20:4-5 go with today's teaching?

"You shall not make for yourself an idol in the form of anything in heaven above or on the earth beneath or in the waters below. You shall not bow down to them or worship them; for I, the LORD your God, am a jealous God..."

Today we have seen how the heart, the mind, and the actions are all tied together, and we were given specific instructions about each one. We are to set our hearts on things above; we are to set our minds on things above; and we are to put to death all sinful actions. This teaching really is a summary of the Christian life. We are to set our hearts toward loving God, we are to dwell on thoughts of Christ, and we are to destroy all sin in our lives.

Friend, I know people who are off-balance in these three areas. One person wants to focus only on his heart, as he believes love for God is the only thing required to walk in victory. He may be very much into emotionalism, praise songs, and worshiping with his eyes closed, etc., while practically ignoring the teaching about the mind being engaged to dwell on Christ, and not concentrating spiritual energy on putting to death the lusts of his flesh. There are others who are intellectuals, who have much

The following testimony is from Jason:

I am twenty-three years old and I have been completely free from pornography and self-gratification for fifty-nine days. I had been a slave to these sins for years, and before I started the Way of Purity cuorse, I believed that I could never get out of the pit I had dug for myself.

By the way, I am single. I used to think that because of my body chemistry, there was no way I could expect to stop self-gratification. I half-believed that my anatomy would shrivel up and stop working. Well, that is a LIE from the devil! I have learned that all sexual impurity is linked. There are certainly not some kinds of impurity that are all right just for "maintenance purposes."

I led a fairly sheltered young life. As my teenage years began, I began to look for every opportunity to satisfy my sexual curiosity. I am grateful to my family and friends that I had few opportunities to do so.

In my third year of college, I moved into a single room and got a high-speed Internet connection. If there was ever a time that I made a conscious decision to give myself over to sin, this was it. I used to be a pretty sociable guy, but after this I found myself avoiding my friends more and more so I could stay in my room and act out.

I remember about the lowest I ever felt was when I seriously began to question my sanity. I was home from school this last Christmas, and determined to keep myself pure while I was in my parent's home. But about a week into my vacation, I succumbed. As I sat there in the middle of the night, in the old house I grew up in, with my loving parents and my brother sleeping in the adjoining rooms, I looked at the most depraved images anyone has ever seen. After I had done it, I did not know who I was anymore. This sweet boy everybody knew and liked was some kind of monster. I imagined the police showing up at my door after I had left and telling my parents what I had done.

Around this time, I also began to feel God's calling on my life. I became certain that Jesus Christ wanted me to be a real disciple and a campus evangelist, not just a "Sunday morning" Christian.

On Saturday, February 3rd, 2001 I got up, sat around in my room for two hours doing nothing, then finally acted out. I was so disgusted with myself. I felt like I had ruined yet another day of my life. That was the day I started The Way of Purity course for the third and, by the grace of God, the final time. This time, I actually registered for the course so I could receive mentoring. That was fifty-nine days ago, and I have not practiced self-gratification or looked at pornography since.

It has not always been easy. I think if there were any possible way this could be easy, I would have been walking in purity long before now. Many days I actually had to pull my body away from the computer and go for a walk until I came back to my senses. I found that I had to do things that seemed overly harsh just to stop a small bit of desire. It does get easier, but the thing is, it does not get easier until much later than you think it should. But after a few tough victories, I began to genuinely believe that God would give me strength to not look at pornography. I think that was the turning point. In other words, faith was the key.

This is the most amazing thing that God has ever done for me. Sometimes I just get ecstatic at the thought that God has given this gift of freedom to me. I feel like a kid at Christmas. Whenever I feel down, all I have to do is remember how God freed me from pornography and self-gratification, and I am reassured that He will watch over me no matter what.

information and learning, who know all the correct doctrine, but have no passion for Christ, or for the destroying of sin in their lives. Still others focus all their efforts on stopping sinful behavior, of crucifying their flesh, of doing spiritual damage to their lusts, but where is their love for God?

Question 6. Think for a moment about what would happen if any one of these three things were missing in your life. Think through how these three spiritual truths all work together, and write out your thoughts on how all three must be present to have victory.

Question 7. What have you learned today, or have been reminded of, that will make a difference in your fight against sin? Please share your final thoughts here.

Scripture to Consider

No one whose hope is in you will ever be put to shame, but they will be put to shame who are treacherous without excuse (Psalm 25:3).

But you, man of God, flee from all this, and pursue righteousness, godliness, faith, love, endurance and gentleness. Fight the good fight of the faith. Take hold of the eternal life to which you were called when you made your good confession in the presence of many witnesses. In the sight of God, who gives life to everything, and of Christ Jesus, who while testifying before Pontius Pilate made the good confession, I charge you to keep this command without spot or blame until the appearing of our Lord Jesus Christ, which God will bring about in his own time - God, the blessed and only Ruler, the King of kings and Lord of lords, who alone is immortal and who lives in unapproachable light, whom no one has seen or can see. To him be honor and might forever. Amen (1 Timothy 6:11-16).

Were you free from pornography since you did the last lesson?

    Yes   No

Were you free from self-gratification since you did the last lesson?

    Yes   No

Were you free from sexual immorality since you did the last lesson?

    Yes   No

DAY 41 - BATTLE STRATEGIES

In His Word, God tells us how to defeat the devil and overcome sin in our lives. Today's teaching will be a clear presentation of the truths of Scripture on how to eradicate bondage to pornography and sexual sin.

There is a primary principle expressed throughout Scripture which teaches us how to leave sin behind, and it is this: We are to deal harshly with it, to be merciless in eradicating it, to annihilate every speck of it from our lives, and to seek God for grace to accomplish it. Notice the following Scripture, and its practical application to ridding our lives of pornography and sexual impurity:

> I pursued my enemies and overtook them; I did not turn back till they were destroyed. I crushed them so that they could not rise; they fell beneath my feet (Psalm 18:37-38).

We notice that the writer of this Psalm took the offensive, in that he pursued and overtook his enemies. He was aggressive in his attack; he destroyed his enemies. We note, also, that he was violent in the war; he crushed his enemies so they could not rise again. Let us apply these principles to fighting against our enemies of pornography and self-gratification in today's lesson.

Questions

We must take the offensive in our fight. For many years, I walked around in a defensive mode, just hoping to be able to dodge the next incoming fiery dart of the devil. I lived in fear that I would succumb to the lust of my flesh, and I lived in defeat, week after week, month after month and year after year. But now I see that type of a battle plan as all wrong, and instead, I pursue the enemy for the purpose of annihilation. How do I do this?

I take the TV out of my hotel room at night and deposit it with a co-worker. I bring home the receipts from my trips and ask my wife to verify that no pornographic movies were purchased. I put a filter on my notebook computer, which would send an email to my wife if I were to try to visit a pornographic website. We removed the TV from our home. I refuse to go anywhere near the magazine rack at the grocery store or in airport terminals. I try to get involved in ministry to other people who want out of pornography and immorality whenever possible. This is our way to "get even" with the enemy for his devastation in our lives, as we use the grace of God to drag others from the jaws of the lion.

Some people say that the above suggestions are too "radical," and that it is not a "normal" life. My response is, "So? That's OK. God is enabling me to be free from the trap of the devil in pornography, self-gratification and immorality, and it does not bother us to be thought a little strange. Walking in purity, enjoying fellowship with Christ, and having effectiveness in ministry are more important.

Question 1. In what ways are you taking the offensive in your battle against the deception of pornography and sexual sin? Could you do more? Have fun thinking of new offensive moves against the enemy. My wife and I like to be creative as we plot our next offensive move against the devil.

Questions

We must pursue this enemy with a healthy dose of spiritual aggression. I drag every little temptation into the "light." This means, if I am tempted in some way, I tell my wife right away or I'll email a friend to expose it. Sexual sin is like a fungus; it grows best in the dark. Learn to drag the temptation into the light to sap it of its strength. Become accustomed to emailing a friend (or one of us in The Way of Purity course) to say "I am tempted to view pornography on the Internet just now, can you help?" One of the great joys for us is when people write in to ask for help and prayer in order to prevent a fall. This is exposing the temptation to the light.

I often run to the Word of God for help. "You, Oh Lord, are a Strong Tower, a sure defense against my foe."

I seek to destroy the enemy when he first peeks his head around the corner. BAM! I immediately hit him hard. By this I mean, as soon as I sense an uprising of temptation, I open my Bible, begin singing a hymn, or I contact my wife or a friend. Be aggressive in the initial stages of temptation.

We must be spiritually violent with our "pet" sins:

> From the days of John the Baptist until now, the kingdom of heaven has been forcefully advancing, and forceful men lay hold of it (Matthew 11:12).

> [43] If your hand causes you to sin, cut it off. It is better for you to enter life maimed than with two hands to go into hell, where the fire never goes out. [45] And if your foot causes you to sin, cut it off. It is better for you to enter life crippled than to have two feet and be thrown into hell. [47] And if your eye causes you to sin, pluck it out. It is better for you to enter the kingdom of God with one eye than to have two eyes and be thrown into hell..." (Mark 9:43,45,47).

Treat pornography as if it were your worst enemy trying to drag your soul into hell, and "hack," "chop," and "pluck out" your way to freedom from it.

Look for ways you may expose the deeds done in darkness. Crush pornography and grind it to powder, or it will rise again and you will be defeated in a weak moment.

Finally, we must pray for God's grace to accomplish this aggressive battle plan against the enemy. We make our plans but the Lord directs our steps (Proverbs 16:9), so we must seek Him for grace to carry out the plans. Notice David's understanding of grace in Psalm 18:

You armed me with strength for battle; you made my adversaries bow at my feet. You made my enemies turn their backs in flight, and I destroyed my foes (Psalm 18:39-40). Jesus said, ". . . apart from me you can do nothing" (John 15:5), so we must be dependant on, and united with Him.

My friend, in order to overcome pornography and sexual impurity in our lives, we must have a grace-empowered battle plan. One man I know plans his victory strategy for the entire next day before he goes to bed at night, and then prays to accomplish his plan. He knows that things don't always go according to schedule, so He also asks God for grace to deal with the unexpected. He is wise, and enjoys lasting victory.

Our desire is that this teaching would inspire you to stop treating your enemy as your friend, to begin to take the offensive in the war, to use healthy aggression toward eradicating the bondage to pornography and immorality, and to be spiritually violent in the destruction and annihilation of all sexual sin. It can be done, by the grace of God!

Please read through the following Scriptures and provide your comments on how they apply to the teaching today on using offensive, aggressive violence in this battle. We have given you a "starter thought" before each passage.

Be merciless against all sin:

When the LORD your God brings you into the land you are entering to possess and drives out before you many nations – the Hittites, Girgashites, Amorites, Canaanites, Perizzites, Hivites and Jebusites, seven nations larger and stronger than you – and when the LORD your God has delivered them over to you and you have defeated them, then you must destroy them totally. Make no treaty with them, and show them no mercy. Do not intermarry with them. Do not give your daughters to their sons or take their daughters for your sons, for they will turn your sons away from following me to serve other gods, and the LORD's anger will burn against you and will quickly destroy you. This is what you are to do to them: Break down their altars, smash their sacred stones, cut down their Asherah poles and burn their idols in the fire. For you are a people holy to the LORD your God. The LORD your God has chosen you out of all the peoples on the face of the earth to be his people, his treasured possession (Deuteronomy 7:1-6).

Question 2. Please record your thoughts about the above passage here.

No matter what it may be worth, destroy it:

When Moses approached the camp and saw the calf and the dancing, his anger burned and he threw the tablets out of his hands, breaking them to pieces at the foot of the mountain. And he took the calf they had made and burned it in the fire; then he ground it to powder, scattered it on the water and made the Israelites drink it (Exodus 32:19-20).

Question 3. Record your thoughts about the above passage here.

Course member Jeff wrote, "These verses are awesome. Moses just went wild. That moment is what we are working toward here - an indignant fire against that which causes sin. By this time, Moses had just had enough and made them drink the water, which must have been bitter to the Israelites. It must have been disgusting, and there is Moses forcing it down their throats. I can imagine chards of it lodging in their mouths and throats, making them cry out in pain. Then, once in their stomachs, it would have made them ill, causing great pain. What a day that was. They swallowed their vulgarity."

The Lord will drive them out little by little:

You may say to yourselves, "These nations are stronger than we are. How can we drive them out?" Do not be terrified by them, for the LORD your God, who is among you, is a great and awesome God. The LORD your God will drive out those nations before you, little by little. You will not be allowed to eliminate them all at once, or the wild animals will multiply around you" (Deuteronomy 7:17,21-22).

Question 4. Record your thoughts on the above passage here.

Weary, yet pursuing:

Gideon and his three hundred men, exhausted yet keeping up the pursuit, came to the Jordan and crossed it (Judges 8:4).

Question 5. Record your thoughts on the above passage here.

Expose them:

Have nothing to do with the fruitless deeds of darkness, but rather expose them. For it is shameful even to mention what the disobedient do in secret. But everything exposed by the light becomes visible, for it is light that makes everything visible. This is why it is said: "Wake up, O sleeper, rise from the dead, and Christ will shine on you (Ephesians 5:11-13).

Question 6. Record your thoughts on the above passage here:

Jeff wrote, "Yes. We cannot live dark lives and also live in the light; it is impossible! It is physically impossible, and it is spiritually impossible! Part of my battle plan has been to keep the lights on. To some it sounds odd, but every time I fell to pornography and self-gratification, it was in the dark. I'd close all the shades and turn off the lights. How evil. It is like preparing a temple for worship. My physical temple and my spiritual temple were dark, with no light. Now that I have the lights on all the time, it is a physical reminder of the spiritual reality. The light is such a simple thing, but it does extreme violence to the darkness. There is no place for the darkness to hide."

So, we see there must be an offensive, aggressive, violent battle plan in order to eradicate our enemies of pornography, self-gratification, and immorality. Do you have such a battle plan? What have you learned from the Scriptures today?

Question 7. If you have not developed a battle plan in the past, will you do so now? Write your thoughts here.

Scripture to Consider

He has delivered us from such a deadly peril, and he will deliver us. On him we have set our hope that he will continue to deliver us (2 Corinthians 1:10).

Were you free from pornography since you did the last lesson?

    Yes   No

Were you free from self-gratification since you did the last lesson?

    Yes   No

Were you free from sexual immorality since you did the last lesson?

    Yes   No

The following testimony is from Carl:

I came across pornography when I was about twelve years old. I found some magazines that my father had hidden, and started viewing them after school before my parents came home from work. I was hooked. Even though I always felt guilty, I kept going back for more and eventually started practicing self-gratification. Then I found the videos, and watched them every chance I got. When I got older I started to buy my own magazines and videos so I didn't have to sneak around with my dad's "stash." I could not stop my addiction to pornography, and I would start to look forward my next fantasizing session.

When I got to college, I found that other people were doing the same thing. I still hid it because I had a reputation of being a "good" boy. I had too much pride and let the deception go on. Eventually, I tried to justify my sin as socially acceptable. But if that were true, why was I still hiding it?

Then I discovered Internet pornography. That made things very accessible and very private. I started getting bored with it, or maybe it was a feeling of guilt that caused me to start going cycles. I would resist for weeks; then I would fall for weeks at a time, even after I became a Christian a couple years ago.

As my relationship with the Lord grew, I started feeling tremendously guilty. I found later that I was being convicted. I tried to stop my addiction, but eventually always fell. My conviction started to affect my relationships at work, at home, at church, and everywhere. I was moody and negative all of the time. I finally asked God to help me. That was the best thing I ever did in my fight against pornography and self-gratification. God lead me to Psalm 51, and I prayed that Psalm everyday, sometimes a few times a day. Then He led me to The Way of Purity course.

From the first day, I felt like I was free. The passage about the Living Water vs. well-water hit me like a ton of bricks. I felt the desire for my sin disappear and I've been free for over two months. It has led me to a closer and stronger relationship with the Lord. I feel His spiritual protection over me, and I am growing more spiritually mature since I've eradicated my hidden sin from between God and me.

I praise God everyday for His grace and His faithfulness.

DAY 42 - FOCUS!

They traveled from Mount Hor along the route to the Red Sea, to go around Edom. But the people grew impatient on the way; they spoke against God and against Moses, and said, "Why have you brought us up out of Egypt to die in the desert? There is no bread! There is no water! And we detest this miserable food!" Then the LORD sent venomous snakes among them; they bit the people and many Israelites died. The people came to Moses and said, "We sinned when we spoke against the LORD and against you. Pray that the LORD will take the snakes away from us." So Moses prayed for the people. The LORD said to Moses, "Make a snake and put it up on a pole; anyone who is bitten can look at it and live." So Moses made a bronze snake and put it up on a pole. Then when anyone was bitten by a snake and looked at the bronze snake, he lived (Numbers 21:4-10).

Truth to memorize: ***The cure for sin is to focus on Jesus Christ!***

Questions

Please review the passage above and answer the following questions:

Question 1. The people were complaining against God. What did He do to them to make them stop?
- A. Sent snakes among them
- B. Sent fire from heaven

Question 2. When the people died from snakebite, how did God tell Moses to fix the problem?
- A. Make a cut and suck out the venom
- B. Rush them to Sinai Medical Center
- C. Put a bronze snake up on a pole

Question 3. What were the people to do with the bronze snake upon the pole?
- A. Charm it
- B. Kill it
- C. Look at it

Please write out the "Truth to memorize" from above:

Question 4. What happened as the people looked at the snake on the pole?
- A. They died of snakebite
- B. They were cured of snakebite

OK, I'm not getting this - people get bit by snakes, Moses puts up a pole with a snake on it, people look at the snake and they're cured. So, what does that have to do with me, pornography, sin, overcoming, etc.?

Let's examine this story a little closer. Think of it this way:

The serpent of sin has bitten you and me! It's a deadly bite, the venom of sin is running through our veins, and we will die from the fatal wound. But God erected a cross-like pole, and on that pole He hung a Savior. If we look at the Savior, we will live. We will be cured from the snakebite of sin, and we will not perish, but have everlasting life!

> ***Course member Jim wrote,*** "GOD sent snakes to the Israelites to make them stop complaining. Then He told Moses to put a bronze snake on a pole. All the people had to do was look on it. In much the same way, 'The cure for sin is focusing on Jesus Christ.' When the people focused on the snake, they were cured. I often forget that pornography is deadly, just like the snakebites. Isaiah also said to just look on Him, and you will be saved. Again in Hebrews, it says we are to look to Jesus."

Questions

But wait a minute! Is this the correct way to interpret and understand this story? How can a snake represent Jesus Christ? Actually, it is not that the snake represents Christ, but rather that it points forward to our sin that was nailed to the cross with Christ. "Just as Moses lifted up the snake in the desert, so the Son of Man must be lifted up, that everyone who believes in him may have eternal life" (John 3:14).

Observe: The people who were bitten by snakes were simply to look! That is what would cure them. Jesus Christ was lifted up on a cross, where He died for our sins. LOOK! Do you see Him there? He is wounded in His hands for the wrong we've done with our hands. His feet are pierced because of the wrong places our feet have taken us. He is wearing a crown of thorns because of the wrong thoughts we've cherished, His heart is broken because of the wrong loves we've had. LOOK! There He is! Do you see Jesus there on the cross? He's our cure! Look, believe and live!

There are many "cures" being offered by society today. But if we examine most of them, we will see some consistent themes. For instance, we are told the "cure" is to examine the snakebite. Focus on your pain, your past and your parents. Dear friends, these other "cures" are not of much value in helping us overcome bondage to pornography and sexual sin. The cure for the snake-bitten Israelites was simple, yet profound: LOOK! The cure for habitual viewing of pornography, or impurity of any kind, is to have the focus of our lives be on Jesus Christ.

Question 5. Why do you think God chose a serpent to be uplifted on the pole? What did the serpent represent? What are your thoughts?

A snake is used in Scripture as a symbol of evil. Satan embodied a serpent when he tempted Adam and Eve.

Notice 2 Corinthians 5:21: "God made him who had no sin to be sin for us, so that in him we might become the righteousness of God."

"God made Him...to be sin for us." On the cross, Jesus Christ took our sins upon Himself. This passage, 2 Corinthians 5:21, refers back to the Mosaic law (specifically Leviticus. 4-5), where the priest laid his hands on the animal that was to be the sin offering, symbolically placing the sins of the people on the animal. Jesus Christ bore our sins in His own body on the tree of the cross, and by looking at Him, our Sin-Bearer, we will discover that sexual sin loses its appeal, and we are cured.

Guilt and bondage to sin go hand in hand. In the physical realm, when a criminal is declared guilty by the judge, incarceration soon follows. But in the spiritual realm, if we look on the cross of Jesus Christ, we see the penalty for our sin being paid, and our guilt removed. Freedom from guilt and freedom from the power of sin go hand in hand. Look on that cross and see guilt and sin, that which has "bitten us," being crucified with Christ! Look at the cross and be healed!

Question 6. Write out how the following three verses go with the teaching in this lesson:

Look to Me, all the ends of the earth, and be saved! (Isaiah 45:22).

Let us fix our eyes on Jesus, who for the joy set before Him, endured the cross. . . (Hebrews 12:2).

For we have no power to face this vast army that is attacking us. We do not know what to do, but our eyes are upon you (2 Chronicles 20:12).

My friend, one of the verses above is 2 Chronicles 20:12. This verse contains everything we need to know to defeat the "vast army" of pornographic images that attack us. There are three specific truths listed in that verse. Note them with me:

1. **They admitted their powerlessness.** They said, "For we have no power."

2. **They admitted their ignorance.** They said, "We do not know what to do." In order to truly defeat our enemy, we must admit that we are without resources to fight it. We have neither the power to fight nor the knowledge of how to win.

3. **They focused on God.** Having admitted their own lack of power and ability, knowledge and resources, they did not stop there. They looked to God for help, and "focused" on Him as their Resource. If you read the rest of this story in 2 Chronicles 20, you will see that God totally defeats the "vast army." Here is the key, "But our eyes are upon You." Focus!

My eyes are ever on the LORD, for only he will release my feet from the snare (Psalm 25:15).

Notice the connection between focusing on the Lord and escaping from the trap!

⁴When your children sinned against him, he gave them over to the penalty of their sin. ⁵But if you will look to God and plead with the Almighty, ⁶...even now he will rouse himself on your behalf and restore you to your rightful place (Job 8:4-6).

The gracious hand of our God is on everyone who looks to him, but his great anger is against all who forsake him (Ezra 8:22-23).

During the fourth watch of the night Jesus went out to them, walking on the lake. When the disciples saw him walking on the lake, they were terrified. "It's a ghost," they said, and cried out in fear.

But Jesus immediately said to them: "Take courage! It is I. Don't be afraid."

"Lord, if it's you," Peter replied, "tell me to come to you on the water."

"Come," he said.

Then Peter got down out of the boat, walked on the water and came toward Jesus. But when he saw the wind, he was afraid and, beginning to sink, cried out, "Lord, save me!"

Immediately Jesus reached out his hand and caught him. "You of little faith," he said, "why did you doubt?" (Matthew 14:25-31).

As long as he was looking at Jesus, Peter walked on water, but when he "saw the winds and the waves" he began to sink. Please note how this passage applies to our teaching today, and draw comparisons between this story and our own victory over pornography and impurity:

Note what "looking at Jesus" means in each of the eight passages of Scripture above, so we may begin to apply this teaching to our lives today:

- In Numbers 21, looking at the serpent meant that they were in need of a cure for their snakebite. In just this way, we look to Jesus Christ to eradicate sin from our lives.
- In Isaiah 45:22, we are instructed to look to Jesus for salvation.
- In Hebrews 12:2, the context of the passage calls us to focus on Christ as a preventative to weariness and discouragement, and to give us strength to finish the race.
- In 2 Chronicles 20:12, we are instructed to look to Jesus to defeat the vast army of sin, and to give us victory over the world, the flesh and the devil.
- In Psalm 25:15, we are instructed to focus on Jesus in order to be released from the trap of sin.
- In Job 8:4-6, we are instructed to look to Jesus to restore us.
- In Ezra 8:22-23, we are invited to look to Jesus to receive grace.
- In Matthew 14:25-31, we are shown that looking to Jesus enables us to live supernaturally, walking on the water of our sin.

To summarize these passages, we are to look to Jesus to save us, to eradicate sin in our lives, to strengthen us for the race, to defeat all our enemies, to release us from the trap of sin, to restore us and give us grace, and to enable us to be victorious.

Do you see why focusing on Christ is so important?

Course member, Pastor Joe, wrote, "Focusing on Jesus Christ means to put Him first. To look at, study, and concentrate so strongly that you see the details and characteristics of Christ and NOT to focus on something else (like porn and such). More practically, we can focus on Him by praise & worship, prayer and Bible study. Focus on Jesus, also, by asking Him to be Lord of our lives (EVERY area) and following Him, by being like Him in character, morality and deed."

Testimony

The following testimony is from Jim:

I grew up in a home where pornography was not available. It was through my fifth-grade peers that I was first exposed to it, but it was not something which created a craving within me. My best friend in high school had a huge stash of the magazines which we would look at, but again, no cravings were really developed. I was introduced to self-gratification along the way, and this was the beginning of an addiction. I did this quite frequently into my early 20's at which time I was introduced to adult videos.

In 1985, I met the girl that would become my wife, and my cravings went into submission. It was also during this time when I accepted Jesus as my personal Savior. The next two years were actually quite normal. I began to secretly view adult movies every now and then. This is truly when the hook was set. I began to take any and every opportunity to "secretly" rent these videos and practice self-gratification to them. In 1992, it became crystal clear to me I had a problem because I rented a pornographic movie and when the tape got all messed up in the VCR, I had to literally destroy the VCR in order to save the tape. When my wife came home I told her that our two-year-old son had jammed something into it and that is what ruined the VCR. I would continue on in this deceptive lifestyle for the next five years.

In 1997, God began letting me know it was time to reckon with Him for my sins. I searched out a brother at church whom I really did not even know, but felt safe to tell him my struggles. It turned out he had the same struggles. In the same year I went to a men's conference, which has forever changed my life as I wholly gave my devotion to God. Unfortunately, it also marked my seemingly unbeatable war with this addiction as I added illicit telephone calls to my resume. I never spent any money on these two ventures, but I spent an incredible amount of time with the phone. Then along came the Internet. I was capsized, thinking there was no way that I would ever get myself out of this pit. My wife has virtually no trust in me any more and has only stuck around by the grace of God.

On January 14 of 2000, my beloved Minnesota Vikings got trounced in a playoff game so I started drowning myself in pornography on the Internet. It was at this time that I found Setting Captives Free. I "chatted" with Mike Cleveland, and he taught me about purity before power before I even enrolled. It has totally changed my life. I have only had one fall during this course.

I now know that there is freedom available to me. I am thankful for the encouragement my mentor has given me, and I look forward to being able to be used of God in the same way.

Oh how I wish I could sit down with you, and explain to you the joy in my heart as my life is now focused on Jesus Christ. Those years involved in pornography and immorality were detrimental to my family and me, as my focus was taken off Christ and put onto all forms of impurity. But now, God has opened the eyes of this blind man and granted me the ability to turn from my idolatry and to focus on the living God. And, focusing on Him brings all other areas of my life into perspective too. I now see how to be a good husband and father, how to bless my employer by doing a good job, how to interact with others, so as to bless them, and how to build up the body of Christ, instead of tearing it down, etc. Focusing on Jesus Christ has brought amazing clarity and focus in all other areas of my life. Amen to God's grace, and His ability to refocus us!

Question 7. For the final question of the day, please write out what it would look like, practically, to have your life "focused" on Jesus Christ. Be specific. What will you do differently because of this teaching?

Scripture to Consider

If then you have been raised with Christ, seek the things that are above, where Christ is, seated at the right hand of God (Colossians 3:1 ESV).

Were you free from pornography since you did the last lesson?

Yes   No

Were you free from self-gratification since you did the last lesson?

Yes   No

Were you free from sexual immorality since you did the last lesson?

Yes   No

DAY 43 - ROMANS 6

Today we will do something a little bit different. We will do a Bible study, basically using one chapter of the Bible, and it will be a little more interactive than some of the other lessons. We are about to drink from the Living Water!

What shall we say, then? Shall we go on sinning so that grace may increase? By no means! We died to sin; how can we live in it any longer? (Romans 6:1,2)

If we have been united with him like this in his death, we will certainly also be united with him in his resurrection (Romans 6:5).

Question 5. This verse gives us hope! But it is a hope that is conditional (if we have...). According to this verse, upon what should we base our assurance of eternal life?

Question 1. What is the central truth taught in the above verse? Write your answer here.

Friend, right about here some people are quick to point out that we are to trust in the righteousness of Christ alone for salvation, not in our own overcoming of sin (or lack thereof). But the one who is righteous by the imputation of Christ's righteousness will have imparted righteousness daily at work in their life. It can be no other way, as the Holy Spirit, sent to dwell in us, will not allow ongoing sin in our life without rebuke and chastisement. Here is the important matter. He who is righteous by imputation is saved. BUT, if he is not striving with imparted righteousness, he has NO assurance of his imputed righteousness. Assurance of imputed righteousness can only come through imparted righteousness. One (imputed) is actual birth and the other (imparted) is actual proof. We will have both imputed righteousness and imparted righteousness. Let us examine these two thoughts further:

Question 2. Romans 6:6 states, "For we know that our old self was crucified with him so that the body of sin might be done away with, that we should no longer be slaves to sin." If we are, indeed, "dead to sin," when did we die to it? Write your thoughts here.

Imputed righteousness is that which Christ gives me as a free gift (Romans 5:12-18). It is an immediate gift to me, happening at once, and is not progressive. It is done to me, or imputed. That is, His righteousness is credited to my account, similar to someone depositing money into my bank account (Romans 4:23-25).

Or don't you know that all of us who were baptized into Christ Jesus were baptized into his death? We were therefore buried with him through baptism into death in order that, just as Christ was raised from the dead through the glory of the father, we too may live a new life (Romans 6:3-4).

Question 3. There is a reason why we died to sin, why those of us were buried with Christ, and why we have risen from the dead with him. That reason is stated at the end of verse 4. That we too may...

Imparted righteousness is that righteousness that is progressively changing my heart and life by the power of the Holy Spirit (Philippians 2:13). Whereas imputed righteousness is an instant and immediate gift, imparted righteousness is a progressive and ongoing gift. My heart continually becomes more broken before the Lord. My self-will is continually crushed, my rebellion is progressively broken, and my pride is being overcome, all by God's grace. I am openly and overtly changed to detest the sin I once loved, and to love the Savior with whom I was once at odds.

Question 4. What application does this have for we who were previously involved in pornography and sexual sin?

Course member Walter wrote, "It shows that the old man (the old sinner, Walter) was crucified with Jesus, and therefore as a new creation, is resurrected with Christ and joined with him by the indwelling of the Holy Spirit. I am free from the bondage of sin and its power, and can now live a life of purity and holiness in him."

Those who are in bondage to sin, but profess salvation, often cling to imputed righteousness, saying, "We must not look to ourselves for any assurance of salvation, but only to Christ." This is dangerous, for there are those who live as unbelievers, gratifying their lust, in depravity and rebellion, but who presume that Christ has given them imputed righteousness. They do not understand that imputed and imparted righteousness always go together. As we read Scripture, we need to use careful discernment to know whether a particular passage is referring to imputed righteousness or imparted righteousness.

> For we know that our old self was crucified with him so that the body of sin might be done away with, that we should no longer be slaves to sin — because anyone who has died has been freed from sin (Romans 6:6-7).

Question 6. What was crucified with Christ? And what was the purpose for our crucifixion in him?

Walter wrote, "My old man, the old me, the self/flesh was crucified with Christ, that we would no longer be slaves to sin.

> Now if we died with Christ, we believe that we will also live with Him (Romans 6:8).

Question 7. What hope is Paul expressing here?

Question 8. According to the above verses, if we continue in slavery to pornography, or any other sin, should we have assurance of eternal life in Christ?

Question 9. Do you have the hope of living with Jesus Christ throughout eternity? If you do, upon what is your hope based?

> For we know that since Christ was raised from the dead, he cannot die again; death no longer has mastery over him. The death he died, he died to sin once for all; but the life he lives, he lives to God. In the same way, count yourselves dead to sin but alive to God in Christ Jesus (Romans 6:10,11).

Question 10. Verse 10 above states that death no longer has mastery over Christ. Since we are united with Christ, what does this mean for us?

Question 11. What does it mean to count ourselves dead to sin, but alive to God in Christ Jesus?

Question 12. Can a dead person sin? How will this teaching help us in times of temptation?

> Therefore do not let sin reign in your mortal body so that you obey its evil desires (Romans 6:12).

Question 13. The above verse contains imagery. We are not to let sin reign in our bodies. How is sin pictured?
    A. A general in an army
    B. A king on the throne
    C. A teacher at school

Question 14. How does Colossians 1:13 relate to our study today? "For He has rescued us from the dominion of darkness and brought us into the kingdom of the Son He loves, in whom we have redemption, the forgiveness of sins." Please write your thoughts here.

Do not offer the parts of your body to sin, as instruments of wickedness, but rather offer yourselves to God, as those who have been brought from death to life; and offer the parts of your body to him as instruments of righteousness (Romans 6:13).

Question 15. The above verse states that our body "parts" are to be offered to the Lord. Describe how you can offer each "part" to the Lord - your head, heart, hands, etc.

For sin shall not be your master, because you are not under law, but under grace (Romans 6:14).

Question 16. How is being "under grace" different than being "under law?" What does it mean to be "under grace," and how are we free from sin's mastery by being under grace?

Question 17. How are you progressing in the grace of God? What is going on in your life today, this week, this month?

The following testimony is from Lars:

When I was about six years old, I remember climbing the steps to the attic at my grandfather's home, and seeing a stash of pornography that must have been worth thousands of dollars.

Then, as a teenager, I watched my father plummet downward into pornography, which caused the divorce of my parents and the loss of my father's engineering job, which he had for thirty years.

I became involved with pornography at the same time, and went spiraling downward so fast that, before I knew it, I was watching stuff that would have made me sick less than a year earlier.

I stayed in this helpless and hopeless condition for ten years, until I came to Setting Captives Free and enrolled in The Way of Purity course. By God's grace, I have now been free for three months, which is a record for me, and I have no desire to go back!

Scripture to Consider

[19] I put this in human terms because you are weak in your natural selves. Just as you used to offer the parts of your body in slavery to impurity and to ever-increasing wickedness, so now offer them in slavery to righteousness leading to holiness. [20] When you were slaves to sin, you were free from the control of righteousness. [21] What benefit did you reap at that time from the things you are now ashamed of? Those things result in death! [22] But now that you have been set free from sin and have become slaves to God, the benefit you reap leads to holiness, and the result is eternal life. [23] For the wages of sin is death, but the gift of God is eternal life in Christ Jesus our Lord (Romans 6:19-23).

Were you free from pornography since you did the last lesson?

> Yes   No

Were you free from self-gratification since you did the last lesson?

> Yes   No

Were you free from sexual immorality since you did the last lesson?

> Yes   No

DAY 44 - DARK NIGHT OF THE SOUL (ROMANS 7)

We know that the law is spiritual; but I am unspiritual, sold as a slave to sin (Romans 7:14).

My friend, have you ever fought pornography or immorality so hard, and lost so much, that you felt there would be no way to gain the victory? Have you felt like the apostle Paul - that you are sold as a slave to sin?

Believe it or not, this is a common experience in the lives of Christians. As we will see later in Romans 7, Paul struggled with sin to the point of despair (verse 24). Have you struggled greatly? Are you currently falling so often that you feel like a slave to sin? By this time in the course, many people are walking in habitual victory over pornography and sexual sin, but some continue to fall. Of course, if you have followed the earlier lessons about "radical amputation," there is no opportunity for you to fall, and yet some still struggle with lust, and fall often.

I went through this dark night of the soul, where sin seemed to have dominion over me, and where I felt I was sold as a slave to sin. Does that mean I was not a Christian? It might. Or it may have meant that I was being tried in the furnace, or that I was going through a desert experience; a dark night of the soul. We must be careful not to be too quick to judge those who fall often, and then repent.

How did Paul describe this experience?

I do not understand what I do. For what I want to do I do not do, but what I hate I do (Romans 7:15).

Question 1. Have you had this experience? Describe it here.

Course member Raul wrote, My sin left me totally confused. I knew what was right, agreed that the law was good, and even preached the glory of it. Yet, I did not have the power to do what I preached, which left me in a state of confusion and despair.

¹⁶ And if I do what I do not want to do, I agree that the law is good. ¹⁷ As it is, it is no longer I myself who do it, but it is sin living in me (Romans 7:16-17). ²⁰ Now if I do what I do not want to do, it is no longer I who do it, but it is sin living in me that does it (Romans 7:20).

Here is one of the greatest truths we can learn, and that is the teaching of "identity." Paul's identity, as a Christian, was in his "new man," not his old, sinful self. When he sinned he said, "It is no longer I myself who do it," because he knew that his old man was crucified with Christ, as we saw in yesterday's lesson. Christians are those who are redeemed, who are new creations in Christ (2 Corinthians 5:17), and whose inner man is created in true holiness and righteousness (Ephesians 4:24). BUT, Christians do still have flesh, which is the residue of the old nature, the remnants of the old, dead man. Christians are indeed, new creations, but we live in fallen flesh and therefore still sin.

Question 2. This is honesty time. How do you see yourself right now? Do you see your identity as a sinner, or as a saint who sins sometimes? Write your thoughts here.

I know that nothing good lives in me, that is, in my flesh. For I have the desire to do what is good, but I cannot carry it out (Romans 7:18).

Paul, as a Christian, had the desire to do good, but he lacked the power to carry it out. This was me for many years. I desired to do good and to be free from pornography and sexual impurity, but did not have the power to accomplish it.

Question 3. Has this been your experience as well? Describe what it was like.

For what I do is not the good I want to do; no, the evil I do not want to do - this I keep on doing (Romans 7:19).

Paul did not want to sin. Everything within him opposed it, and yet he "kept on" sinning. Friends, this is a horribly dark night to experience. You want to do what is right, you want to cease habitual sin, but somehow you just can't. You don't have the power. Oh, the pain of this is still fresh in my memory. I think back on the years spent sinning against my family, which I did not want to do. Yet I did it anyway, and kept on doing it.

Question 4. Have you been mastered by sin as Paul describes here? Share your thoughts.

> So I find this law at work: When I want to do good, evil is right there with me (Romans 7:21).

Are you tracking with Paul, as I am? I recall longing to be free from pornography and adultery, committing to not indulge on a particular layover, resolving all day long to stay free from it. But in all my desires to do good, evil was right there with me. Oh, what a dark night of the soul this is. If you are going through this right now, please know that the dark of night precedes the light of day. Morning is coming and with it, grace and mercy to enable you to be free from this plaguing sin.

Question 5. What are your thoughts on Romans 7:21?

> [22] For in my inner being I delight in God's law; [23] but I see another law at work in the members of my body, waging war against the law of my mind and making me a prisoner of the law of sin at work within my members (Romans 7:22-23).

Oh, how the long, dark night drags on at times. I remember praying for years, weeping out tears to God to be free from pornography and immorality. I was becoming a broken man, as I felt God had left me to die in my sins. Paul describes himself above as a "slave" and a "prisoner." I felt exactly the same way.

Question 6. Have you felt this war going on inside you?

> What a wretched man I am! Who will rescue me from this body of death? (Romans 7:24).

> **Raul wrote,** "Oh how wretched I am! How wretched I have been. My pornography addiction led me to say and do things I would never have imagined. My night was so dark, I could not see my hand in front of my face. I thank God for having mercy on my soul!"

The dark night may lead to overwhelming despair. It might be so dark in sin, that you see no way out. All your friends tell you to read your Bible and pray, and you hear some people talk about overcoming sin, as if it were a small thing for them. And you wonder if God has forsaken you forever, because their experience is not yours.

Friend, if this is you, take heart. God is at work even still. For God must break a man before He remakes him (Hosea 6:1-3); He must "hand all men over to sin" so that He may have mercy on them (Romans 11:32). This does not make God the author of our sin; rather, it shows that He works through the sin to bring forth a good outcome.

Is your night dark? Are you frustrated, disappointed, discouraged or near suicidal? If so, you are right there with the Apostle Paul. I've been there, too. I thank God that Paul did not stay in Romans 7, but moved on to Romans 8, which is what we will study tomorrow.

If your darkness is thick, you feel yourself being sold as a slave to sin, and are in the prison of sin and can't get out, please have hope that God, by His grace, will make a way for you, as He has me.

Again, it is possible that you are entirely beyond this Romans 7 experience by this time in the course. If you are walking in victory, please never forget your struggle. It will help you deal in grace with your brothers and sisters who are falling.

Paul's horrible struggle with sin ended in praise of Jesus Christ. "But thanks be to God, through Jesus Christ our Lord." Here is where we need to run when the night is dark. If you are feeling the power of sin, run to Jesus. Give thanks to God for giving you His Son.

Now, please read the following commentary on Romans 7:24-25 by Matthew Henry and provide your thoughts below:

His great comfort lay in Jesus Christ (v. 25): "I thank God, through Jesus Christ our Lord." In the midst of his complaints he breaks out into praises. It is a special remedy against fears and sorrows to be much in praise: many a poor drooping soul hath found it so. And, in all our praises, this should be the burden of the son, "Blessed be God for Jesus Christ." Who shall deliver me? says he (v. 24), as one at a loss for help. At length he finds an all-sufficient friend, even Jesus Christ. When we are under the sense of the remaining power of sin and corruption, we shall see reason to bless God through Christ (for, as he is the mediator of all our prayers, so he is of all our praises)-to bless God for Christ; it is he that stands between us and the wrath due to us for this sin. If it were not for Christ, this iniquity that dwells in us would certainly be our ruin. He is our advocate with the Father, and through him God pities, and spares, and pardons, and lays not our iniquities to our charge. It is Christ that has purchased deliverance for us in due time. Christ's death will put an end to all these complaints, and waft us to an eternity which we shall spend without sin or sigh. Blessed be God that giveth us this victory through our Lord Jesus Christ!

Question 7. Please provide your comments on the above quote here.

Question 8. Where are you in your spiritual life right now? Is your night pitch black? Do you see some rays of dawn approaching? Or are you walking in the light of day and enjoying it? Please share your thoughts here.

The following testimony is from Greg:

My whole life has been one dark night of the soul. I've lived in sin so much I hardly know where to start. I was the youngest of six children, and have been drawn to pornography ever since I can remember. I was addicted by the age of ten, and it grew worse and worse. By the time I was old enough to drive, I was completely bound up in sin. In fact, the first place I drove was to a strip joint, and after that I went and found a prostitute.

After I came to Jesus Christ, I thought I would get the victory over this horrible sin, but I didn't; it persisted. Both my first and second marriages broke up. It was the same story, but different day — sin, sin, and more sin.

Then one day as I was surfing to sin, I ran across a banner ad that said, "The Way of Purity, Want it?" and I did. I wanted it desperately. I clicked on the banner and enrolled in The Way of Purity course, only to drop out a week later to return to my sin. But that site was in the back of my mind, and, one day after I had completed my sinning again, I went back to the site. I asked Mike if I could come back and his answer surprised me. He said, "I have been waiting for you, and am running to meet you with open arms." Never had I felt such love. I took the course, employed the principles, found freedom from sin, and am a living testimony of the grace of God now. I am free for eighteen months and counting!

Scripture to Consider

For though a righteous man falls seven times, he rises again, but the wicked are brought down by calamity (Proverbs 24:16).

[21] Then Peter came to him and asked, "Lord, how often should I forgive someone who sins against me? Seven times?" [22] "No!" Jesus replied, 'seventy times seven!'" (Matthew 18:21-22).

Then Christian fell down at his feet as dead, crying, Woe is me, for I am undone! At the sight of which Evangelist caught him by the right hand, saying, "All manner of sin and blasphemies shall be forgiven unto men" (Matthew 12:31). "Be not faithless, but believing" (John 20:27). Then did Christian again a little revive, and stood up trembling, as at first, before Evangelist. (Pilgrim's Progress)

This also shall not be, any more than that. It is the glory of God that he multiplies to pardon, that he spares, and forgives, to more than seventy times seven times. (Pilgrim's Progress)

Were you free from pornography since you did the last lesson?

    Yes   No

Were you free from self-gratification since you did the last lesson?

    Yes   No

Were you free from sexual immorality since you did the last lesson?

    Yes   No

DAY 45 - NO CONDEMNATION! (ROMANS 8)

Oh, dear friends, the dark night of the soul is temporary! The intense struggle against sin does not last forever! If we are in Christ, we will be victorious! Let us see this truth from Romans 8:

> Therefore, there is now no condemnation for those who are in Christ Jesus (Romans 8:1).

How wonderful to know that this shining sentence, declaring "no condemnation," follows Romans 7, where the intense war with sin is pictured. What do those who battle sin, and lose often, dread the most? Condemnation! And here Paul declares, under the inspiration of the Holy Spirit, that there is no condemnation for those who are in Christ.

> because through Christ Jesus the law of the Spirit of life set me free from the law of sin and death (Romans 8:2).

Talk about "setting captives free!" Paul is a released captive. He has been set free from the law of sin and death. Not only is he not condemned, but he is also not enslaved. Freedom has come through the Spirit of life. The Holy Spirit came to Paul, set him free from habitual sin, and enabled him to triumph over the law of sin and death. Friend, with God life always triumphs over death. In Scripture, whenever Jesus attended a funeral he raised the dead to life.

Question 1. Do you sense the joy in this particular verse? Write your thoughts here.

Question 2. Where are you, currently? Are you under "the law of sin and death," or are you a freed captive, where life and victory are triumphing? Write your answer here.

> For what the law was powerless to do in that it was weakened by the sinful nature, God did by sending his own Son in the likeness of sinful man to be a sin offering. And so he condemned sin in sinful man (Romans 8:3).

Let's understand this one well! The law was powerless. It could command me to cease viewing pornography, but could not enable me to do so. It was powerless to change my heart, give me new desires, or release me from the trap of the devil in pornography and self-gratification. But what the law could not do, God did! And how did He do it?

Question 3. God did what the law could not do, free us from sin's power. How did God do this?

- A. He gave us the law which frees us
- B. He commanded us to stop
- C. He sent Jesus Christ to be a sin offering

Oh, friend, the death of Jesus Christ has everything to do with our being free from pornography and sexual sin! Don't miss the connection here between Jesus becoming our sin offering, and our becoming free from sin. Jesus took our sin upon Himself; therefore, we are neither condemned nor enslaved! He breaks the power of canceled sin! He sets the captive free.

> in order that the righteous requirements of the law might be fully met in us, who do not live according to the flesh but according to the Spirit (Romans 8:4).

Again, we see that Jesus' death has done something magnificent. It not only frees us from sin's penalty and sin's power, but it also fulfills the law in us. You see, the law said, "Do this or die." The law, requiring death for sin, was fulfilled when Jesus died. He died in order that the righteous requirements of the law might be fully met in us! And now we who are in Christ are counted as lawkeepers.

Question 4. Verse 4, above, describes we who are in Christ as living a certain way. What way is it?

- A. We are those who do not live according to the flesh, but according to the Spirit
- B. Those who have never sinned
- C. Those who keep the law perfectly

> [5] Those who live according to the flesh have their minds set on what the flesh desires; but those who live in accordance with the Spirit have their minds set on what the Spirit desires. [6] The mind of sinful man is death, but the mind controlled by the Spirit is life and peace; [7] the sinful mind is hostile to God. It does not submit to God's law, nor can it do so. [8] Those controlled by the sinful nature cannot please God (Romans 8:5-8).

Question 5. Please write out everything from verses 5-8, state about those who live according to the flesh. I'll write the first one:

1. They have their minds set on what the flesh desires

2. They _____

3. They _____

4. They _____

5. They _____

Question 6. What do verses 5-8 say about those who live according to the Spirit? Write your answer here.

> You, however, are controlled not by the flesh but by the Spirit, if the Spirit of God lives in you. And if anyone does not have the Spirit of Christ, he does not belong to Christ (Romans 8:9).

The above verse makes it clear that if God's Spirit is living in us, He will control us. While I was viewing pornography and involved in sexual sin, my flesh controlled me. That is what characterized me. But now, God's Spirit is living in me and controlling me.

Question 7. Overall, would you say you are controlled by the Spirit of God, or by your flesh?

> [10] But if Christ is in you, your body is dead because of sin, yet your spirit is alive because of righteousness. [11] And if the Spirit of him who raised Jesus from the dead is living in you, he who raised Christ from the dead will also give life to your mortal bodies through his Spirit, who lives in you (Romans 8:10-11).

According to verse 10, above, Christians are characterized by "dead flesh." Their bodies are dead because of sin. In other words, they are not characterized by giving in to the flesh and sinning, but by being controlled by the Spirit of God.

Now see how interesting it is that Paul connects our "dead flesh" with our assurance of eternal life. Our bodies are dead because of sin, but will live forever through the Spirit of Christ who lives in us. Those who know their flesh is crucified also know that they will live forever with Christ.

> [12] Therefore, brothers, we have an obligation - but it is not to the flesh, to live according to it. [13] For if you live according to the flesh, you will die; but if by the Spirit you put to death the misdeeds of the body, you will live, [14] because those who are led by the Spirit of God are sons of God (Romans 8:12-14).

This chapter started out with "no condemnation" (verse 1) and ends with "no separation" (verses 35-39), but right in the middle we are told that we have "no obligation" to live according to the flesh. Catch this truth, friend. When our flesh cries out to be satisfied, we have no obligation to gratify it.

Question 8. If we do live to gratify our flesh, according to verse 13 above, what will happen?

Question 9. What are we to do with the misdeeds of the body?
A. Be gracious with the sins of the body, and don't be too harsh
B. Gratify these misdeeds
C. Put them to death

Paul started this discourse by sharing his freedom from sin with us, and here he instructs us to put to death the misdeeds of the body. Freedom from habitual sin includes the crucifying of our flesh. Paul said "I die daily," and he was referring to putting his flesh to death each day. This shows that our flesh is to be crucified, not gratified.

Question 10. Is God giving you grace to crucify your flesh, or are you gratifying it?

Friend, let me share with you that there is much discomfort and pain involved in crucifying our flesh. For us, denying ourselves self-gratification when we are burning with desire is most uncomfortable, and even painful. Read how one student describes this pain:

> ***Course member Mike wrote,*** "Wow, I did not know that there would be so much pain associated with denying myself. I have literally ached with pain from the denial. And yet, God is granting me much grace to endure. This is my 45th day free from self-gratification. I believe I am now free from the law of sin, and that I am in a constant habit pattern of denying and crucifying my flesh. This also makes love-making with my wife so much more enjoyable. It's good to know that I am no longer satisfying myself by sinful means, but rather, I am being satisfied in Christ and in my wife. Oh, this is so much better. The pain is worth the gain!"

Please know that the pain is indeed worth the gain. Our bodies adjust, our habits change, and soon we are no longer even thinking of self-gratification. And please don't let the false notion that we MUST gratify the flesh in order to relieve tension or, worse yet, to prevent some physical problem from occurring. God did not make our bodies in such a way so as to require us to sin in order to stay healthy.

Question 11. Please summarize today's teaching.

We must rest ourselves upon his power; we must be confident of this, that Christ can make us clean. No guilt is so great but that there is a sufficiency in his righteousness to atone for it; no corruption so strong, but there is a sufficiency in his grace to subdue it.

Question 12. What is going on in your life right now?

Scripture to Consider

But now he has reconciled you by Christ's physical body through death to present you holy in his sight, without blemish and free from accusation 23 if you continue in your faith, established and firm, not moved from the hope held out in the gospel. This is the gospel that you heard and that has been proclaimed to every creature under heaven, and of which I, Paul, have become a servant (Colossians 1:22-23).

[19] But I will bring the people of Israel back to their own pasture. They will eat on Mount Carmel and in Bashan. They will eat and be full on the hills of Ephraim and Gilead. [20] The LORD says, "At that time people will try to find Israel's guilt, but there will be no guilt. People will try to find Judah's sins, but no sins will be found, because I will leave a few people alive from Israel and Judah, and I will forgive their sins (Jeremiah 50:19-20).

And can it be that I should gain an interest in the Savior's blood? Died He for me, who caused His pain? For me, who Him to death pursued? He left His Father's throne above, so free, so infinite His grace! Emptied Himself of all but love, and bled for Adam's helpless race. No condemnation now I dread; I am my Lord's and He is mine: Alive in Him, my living Head, and clothed in righteousness divine.

Refrain: Amazing love! How can it be that Thou, my God, shouldst die for me?

(Written by Charles Wesley © 1951 by Singspiration).

Were you free from pornography since you did the last lesson?

    Yes   No

Were you free from self-gratification since you did the last lesson?

    Yes   No

Were you free from sexual immorality since you did the last lesson?

    Yes   No

DAY 46 - IMMORALITY CAN'T HOLD WATER

In this lesson, we will examine two things:

1. What God is like
2. What immorality is like

Please read the following scripture in preparation for today's study. You may want to memorize this verse, as there will be several questions on it today.

> My people have committed two sins: they have forsaken me, the spring of living water, and have dug their own cisterns, broken cisterns that cannot hold water (Jeremiah 2:13).

My people have committed two sins: They have forsaken me, the spring of living water, and have dug their own cisterns, broken cisterns that cannot hold water (Jeremiah 2:13).

Question 5. Write your thoughts on Jeremiah 2:13 here.

Question 1. In the above verse, how does God describe himself?
   A. An angry judge
   B. The spring of living water

Question 2. What does living water provide?
   A. Life
   B. Refreshment
   C. Satisfaction
   D. Joy
   E. Health
   F. All of the above

Note: God describes himself as the spring of living water. He alone is the source of life, refreshment, joy, and nourishment for us. He is ever fresh and new, as a spring and, to drink of God, is to receive life and satisfaction!

Please read and comment on the following Scriptures:

> There is a river whose streams make glad the city of God, the holy place where the Most High dwells (Psalm 46:4).

Question 3. Write your thoughts on Psalm 46:4 here.

> ¹ Then the angel showed me the river of the water of life, as clear as crystal, flowing from the throne of God and of the Lamb ² down the middle of the great street of the city. On each side of the river stood the tree of life, bearing twelve crops of fruit, yielding its fruit every month. And the leaves of the tree are for the healing of the nations. ³ No longer will there be any curse (Revelation 22:1-3).

Question 4. Write your thoughts on Revelation 22:1-3 here.

Course member Andre wrote, "The first sin we have committed is that we have rejected God and the satisfying water that He provides. We have laid down our beautiful, holy cisterns, and picked up dirty, broken cisterns that cannot hold water, leaving us thirsty. The only way to find satisfaction again is to repent, to go back to our true cisterns, and start drinking of the Living Water again."

Course member Tony wrote, "This verse brings to mind Dante's Inferno. In his description of hell, the inhabitants of one particular circle are sentenced to eternally fill and re-fill leaky jars. When I find myself constantly refilling my leaky "jar" of pornography, it's a reminder that I'm not looking to the Lord to fulfill my needs."

Question 6. According to Jeremiah 2:13, above, when people forsake God, they turn to something else. According to the above verse, to what do they turn?
   A. Something better
   B. Something enjoyable
   C. Something broken, that can't hold water or satisfy

Question 7. Early in this course we learned two important truths:
   1. Pornography and impurity will not ultimately satisfy,
   2. Only Jesus can satisfy.

How does Jeremiah 2:13 teach these two truths? Please write your answer here.

Course member Andre wrote, "We are trying to find satisfaction in pornography with these broken cisterns. We try again and again, but it continues to leave us thirsty, because we are using broken cisterns. We need to return to our Spring and drink of the water that Jesus provides. That is the only way we can truly be satisfied."

Question 8. Please read this quote from the famous preacher, Charles Spurgeon, and record your comments about it,

Men are in a restless pursuit after satisfaction in earthly things. They will exhaust themselves in the deceitful delights of sin, and finding them all to be vanity and emptiness, they will become very perplexed and disappointed. But they will still continue their fruitless search.

Though wearied, they still stagger forward under the influence of spiritual madness, and though there is no result to be reached except that of everlasting disappointment, yet they press forward. They have no forethought for their eternal state; the present hour absorbs them. They turn to another and another of earth's broken cisterns, hoping to find water where not a drop was ever discovered yet.

Course member Paul wrote, "Madness! What a perfect description of my relentless pursuit of the next sexual image that will be the one that will satisfy. As the hours slip away and my eyes grow heavy with sleep, I cannot stop. Yet, moments after I have "satisfied" myself, it starts again. What madness, indeed!"

Question 9. From Jeremiah 2:13, please complete these sentences:

God is like... _____

Pornography is like... _____

Question 10. How does Ephesians 4:19 apply to what we are studying? "Having lost all sensitivity, they have given themselves over to sensuality so as to indulge in every kind of impurity, with a continual lust for more." Write your answer here.

Question 11. Please comment on the following quote:

For what is the sum and substance of these simple words? It is this: Christ is that Fountain of Living Water, which God has graciously provided for thirsting souls. From Him, as out of the rock smitten by Moses, there flows an abundant stream for all who travel through the wilderness of this world. In Him, as our Redeemer and Substitute, crucified for our sins and raised again for our justification, there is an endless supply of all that men can need: pardon, absolution, mercy, grace, peace, rest, relief, comfort and hope (J. C. Ryle).

Sometimes it is difficult to read the Puritan writers, because of their style. But we can hardly find writing that matches theirs for practical godliness. This is Matthew Henry's commentary on Jeremiah 2:13. I believe you will profit from reading it:

There is in Him an all-sufficiency of grace and strength; all our springs are in Him and our streams from him; to forsake Him is, in effect, to deny this. He has been to us a bountiful benefactor, a fountain of living waters, overflowing, ever flowing, in the gifts of his favor; to forsake Him is to refuse to acknowledge His kindness and to withhold that tribute of love and praise which His kindness calls for.

Those who forsake Him cheat themselves, they forsook their own mercies, but it was for lying vanities. They took a great deal of pains to hew themselves out cisterns, to dig pits or pools in the earth or rock which they would carry water to, or which should receive the rain; but they proved broken cisterns, false at the bottom, so that they could hold no water. When they came to quench their thirst there they found nothing but mud and mire, and the filthy sediments of a standing lake. Such idols were to their worshippers, and such a change did those experience who turned from God to them.

If we make an idol of any creature - wealth, or pleasure, or honor, if we place our happiness in it, and promise ourselves the comfort and satisfaction in it which are to be had in God only, if we make it our joy and love, our hope and confidence, we shall find it a cistern, which we take a great deal of pains to hew out and fill, and at the best it will hold but a little water, and that dead and flat, and soon corrupting and becoming nauseous. No, it is a broken cistern, which cracks and cleaves in hot weather, so that the water is lost when we have most need of it. Let us therefore with purpose of heart cleave to the Lord only, for where else shall we go? He has the words of eternal life.

Question 12. Have you gained any insights, or been reminded of any truths in this lesson?

The following testimony is from John:

I was born in poverty and was determined to make something of myself. I began studying the stock market at a young age and became quite knowledgeable about trading and investing. In my early twenties, I learned how to "Day Trade" and became hooked as I started doing very well at it.

Unfortunately, the market started to take a nosedive after I had many stocks bought on margin and, after four years of extremely successful trading activity, I found my net worth dwindling away to nothing. Surely riches have wings, and they take off and fly away.

I continued trading, but my life became seriously stressful. At night, when I would go home, I began viewing pornography as a stress releaser. Some stress releaser; I soon discovered that I could not quit, and the intensity of my passions were becoming too much for me.

My wife caught me one night, and that started a search for help. I went to see two psychiatrists, and went to Sexaholics Anonymous (SA) for several months. Neither one of these helped, and my bondage to this sin became worse. I finally found The Way of Purity course on the Internet, and God used it to break the power of sin. Soon after we started going through the course we were counseled to find a local church, which we did. I gave my life to Jesus Christ, and our pastor now is involved with accountability with me, and I am growing more and more in Jesus Christ.

By the way, stocks and trading are still eating my lunch. But pornography is nowhere in sight, and I would rather have it that way than vice-versa.

Scripture to Consider

For with You is the fountain of life... (Psalm 36:9a).

[14] A despairing man should have the devotion of his friends, even though he forsakes the fear of the Almighty. [15] But my brothers are as undependable as intermittent streams, as the streams that overflow [16] when darkened by thawing ice and swollen with melting snow, [17] but that cease to flow in the dry season, and in the heat vanish from their channels. [18] Caravans turn aside from their routes; they go up into the wasteland and perish. [19] The caravans of Tema look for water, the traveling merchants of Sheba look in hope. [20] They are distressed, because they had been confident; they arrive there, only to be disappointed. [21] Now you too have proved to be of no help; you see something dreadful and are afraid (Job 6:14-21).

[1] As a deer thirsts for streams of water, so I thirst for you, God. I thirst for the living God. [2] When can I go to meet with him? (Psalm 42:1-2)

Were you free from pornography since you did the last lesson?

    Yes   No

Were you free from self-gratification since you did the last lesson?

    Yes   No

Were you free from sexual immorality since you did the last lesson?

    Yes   No

DAY 47 - BROKENNESS: KEY TO VICTORY

This lesson comes from my own experience and that of others, of discovering exactly what it takes to truly be done with habitual sin. Today, we will study a truth that absolutely must be experienced in the soul, if there is to be real, lasting victory over pornography and sexual impurity. The truth is, my friend, that God must break us! "Well, that is not very encouraging or hope-inspiring," you may say. However, it actually is. Read what several authors have said on this subject:

"The kingdom of God is a kingdom of paradox, where through the ugly defeat of a cross, a holy God is utterly glorified. Victory comes through defeat; healing through brokenness; finding self through losing self."
Charles Colson

"God will never plant the seed of his life upon the soil of a hard, unbroken spirit. He will only plant that seed where the conviction of His spirit has brought brokenness, where the soil has been watered with the tears of repentance as well as the tears of joy." **Alan Redpath**

"Deliverance can come to us only by the defeat of our old life. Safety and peace come only after we have been forced to our knees. God rescues us by breaking us, by shattering our strength and wiping out our resistance." **A. W. Tozer**

"True prayer is born out of brokenness." **Francis J. Roberts**

(Quotations taken from Edith Draper's *Book of Quotations for the Christian World* - Wheaton: Tyndale House publishers, Inc. 1992)

So why are we devoting an entire lesson to the subject of brokenness? Because as the authors state above, brokenness brings healing, life, revival, rescue, and true prayer. So, we see that becoming broken before the Lord is indispensable.

Please read the following passage and answer the questions below:

[1] (A psalm of David. When the prophet Nathan came to him after David had committed adultery with Bathsheba). Have mercy on me, O God, according to your unfailing love; according to your great compassion blot out my transgressions. [2] Wash away all my iniquity and cleanse me from my sin. [3] For I know my transgressions, and my sin is always before me. [4] Against you, you only, have I sinned and done what is evil in your sight, so that you are proved right when you speak and justified when you judge. [5] Surely I was sinful at birth, sinful from the time my mother conceived me. [6] Surely you desire truth in the inner parts; you teach me wisdom in the inmost place. [7] Cleanse me with hyssop, and I will be clean; wash me, and I will be whiter than snow. 8 Let me hear joy and gladness; let the bones you have crushed rejoice. [9] Hide your face from my sins and blot out all my iniquity. [10] Create in me a pure heart, O God, and renew a steadfast spirit within me. [11] Do not cast me from your presence or take your Holy Spirit from me. [12] Restore to me the joy of your salvation and grant me a willing spirit, to sustain me. [13] Then I will teach transgressors your ways, and sinners will turn back to you. [14] Save me from bloodguilt, O God, the God who saves me, and my tongue will sing of your righteousness. [15] O Lord, open my lips, and my mouth will declare your praise. [16] You do not delight in sacrifice, or I would bring it; you do not take pleasure in burnt offerings. [17] The sacrifices of God are a broken spirit; a broken and contrite heart, O God, you will not despise (Psalm 51).

Note: This is a prayer of David, for forgiveness and cleansing. The prophet Nathan had confronted him about his sin with Bathsheba, and he was now brokenhearted over it.

Question 1. Write the words David uses in Psalm 51 which ask God to do something. The first ones are "cleanse me," and "wash me." What are the others?

Question 2. What sacrifices does God accept?
   A. Lambs, catle and oxen
   B. Ten percent tithe, and giving to the building fund
   C. A depressed person with no hope
   D. A broken spirit; a broken and contrite heart

Note: David said that God receives brokenness as the only acceptable sacrifice. The previous verse states that God does not take pleasure in burnt offerings. The reason for this is obvious: someone could give burnt offerings (or tithes, or church-work, etc.) without the heart being involved.

Question 3. Hebrews 3:13 states, "But encourage one another daily, as long as it is called Today, so that none of you may be hardened by sin's deceitfulness." What does sin do to our hearts?
   A. Sin hardens and deceives us
   B. Sin softens us, and makes us open to the needs of others

Those of us who have spent many years in bondage to pornography and immorality have become hardened by sin's deceitfulness. Hearts turn cold, brittle, unfeeling and desensitized by sexual sin. Since God disciplines those he loves, he will break our hard hearts, cold and unyielding spirits, and harsh attitudes. God breaks us so that he can remake us (Jeremiah 18). Friend, if you are experiencing genuine brokenness over your sin before God, know that God is working. If you are not broken before the Lord, will you pray that God would do this miraculous work in your heart, lest you die in a hard-hearted condition?

Question 4. Honestly assess the condition of your heart and life right now. Where are you in the process of offering the acceptable sacrifice of brokenness before the Lord? Ask the Lord to reveal your heart's condition to you. Write it here.

Today we will read some very instructive writings on this important subject. Please give your thoughts after each writing.

Matthew Henry writes about the Passover lamb: **"It was to be eaten with bitter herbs in remembrance of the bitterness of their bondage in Egypt. We must feed upon Christ with sorrow and brokenness of heart, in remembrance of sin; this will give an admirable relish to the lamb. Christ will be sweet to us if sin be bitter."**

Question 5. Provide your comments about Matthew Henry's quote, above.

Course member Mary wrote, "Jesus, you brought me out of Egypt. Thank you. You were the sinless Lamb, and you suffered on the cross for me. Help me to see what you did for me that I will not want to sin against you, the one who loves me so much. You are so beautiful to me, and I don't want to have secret sexual sin that hurts you. Break my heart over my sin. Help me to leave all and follow you."

Charles Spurgeon hits the nail on the head as usual. Read this carefully: **"True repentance has a distinct and constant reference to the Lord Jesus Christ. If you repent of sin without looking to Christ, away with your repentance. If you are so lamenting your sin as to forget the Savior, you have a need to begin all this work over again. Whenever we repent of sin, we must have one eye upon sin and another upon the cross; or, better still, let us have both eyes upon Christ, seeing our sin punished in him, and by no means let us look at sin except as we look at Jesus. A man may hate sin just as a murderer hates the gallows but this does not prove repentance. If I hate sin because of the punishment, I have not repented of sin; I merely regret that God is just.**

But if I can see sin as an offense against Jesus Christ, and loathe myself because I have wounded him, then I have a true brokenness of heart. If I see the Savior and believe that those thorns upon his head were put there by my sinful words; if I believe that those wounds in his heart were pierced by my heart-sins; if I believe that those wounds in his feet were made by my wandering steps, and that the wounds in his hands were made by my sinful deeds, then I repent after a right fashion. Only under the cross can you repent. Repentance elsewhere is remorse, which clings to the sin and only dreads the punishment. Let us then seek, under God, to have a hatred of sin caused by a site of Christ's love."

Question 6: Please comment on Spurgeon's quote, above.

Charles Spurgeon tells us what "normal" should be: **"When I sat on this platform on Monday night, and marked your sobs, in tears, and heard the suppressed sighs and groans of the great multitude then assembled, I could not but say, 'Behold!' And yet it ought not to be a wonder, it ought not to be a strange thing for God's people to be in earnest, or for sinners to feel brokenness of heart."**

Question 7. Please write your comments on Spurgeon's quote, above.

"John Bradford said that, when he was in prayer, he never liked to rise from his knees till he began to feel something of brokenness of heart. Get up to your chamber, then, poor sinner, if you would have a broken and contrite spirit, and come not out until you have it. Remember, you will never feel so broken in heart as when you can see Jesus bearing all your sins; faith and repentance are born together, and aid the health of each other."

> Law and terrors do but harden,
> All the while they work alone;
> But a sense of blood bought pardon,
> Will dissolve a heart of stone.

Spurgeon wrote, **"Go as you are to Christ, and ask him to give that tenderness of heart which shall be to you the indication that pardon has come; for pardon cannot and will not come unattended by a melting of soul and a hatred of sin. Wrestle with the Lord! Say, 'I will not let you go except you bless me.' Get a fast hold upon the savior by a vigorous faith in his great atonement. Oh! May his spirit enable you to do this! Say in your soul, here I will abide, at the horns of the altar; if I perish I will perish at the foot of the cross. From my hope in Jesus I will not depart; but I will look up and still say, 'Savior, your heart was broken for me, break my heart! You were wounded, wound me! Your blood was freely poured forth, for me, Lord let me pour forth my tears that I should have nailed you to the tree. Oh Lord, dissolve my soul; melt it in tenderness, and you will be forever praised for making your enemy your friend.'**

"May God bless you, and give you repentance, if you have not repented; and if you have, may he enable you to continue in it all your days, for Jesus Christ's sake. Amen."

Question 8. Please write your comments on the above quote here.

"Psalm 51 is the photograph of a contrite spirit. Oh, let us seek after the like brokenness of heart, for however excellent our words may be, yet if the heart is not conscious of the blackness and hell-deservingness of sin, we cannot expect to find mercy with the Judge of all the earth. If the Lord will break your heart, consent to have it broken; asking that he may sanctify that brokenness of spirit to bring you in earnest to a savior, that you may yet be numbered with the righteous ones."
Charles Spurgeon

Question 9. Please provide your comments here.

Scripture to Consider

For this is what the high and lofty One says - he who lives forever, whose name is holy: "I live in a high and holy place, but also with him who is contrite and lowly in spirit, to revive the spirit of the lowly and to revive the heart of the contrite (Isaiah 57:15).

Were you free from pornography since you did the last lesson?

     Yes   No

Were you free from self-gratification since you did the last lesson?

     Yes   No

Were you free from sexual immorality since you did the last lesson?

     Yes   No

The following testimony is from David:

I was raised in a fairly moral and religious home. That is, we were average citizens. My parents did not really condone drunkenness, but didn't tell us never to do it, either; the only rule was "Don't drive." You could have girls sleep over, but don't be overly obvious about it. Basically, the rules were lax and we only had to go to church on Christmas and Easter. Church was a chore and a duty.

I lived in this state for nearly twenty years. For some odd reason, while going for the God and Country merit badge in Boy Scouts, I learned about praying to God and decided to start doing it. I would pray every night and wanted to do what was right and good. This meant that I would help people and be a hero. I didn't know that serving God WAS the highest good. I really didn't know anything, and my life didn't change much. My knowledge of Scripture was so low, that I really didn't think it was TOO bad to go to strip clubs, watch pornographic movies, or lust after girls. But inside, which I told no one about, I actually believed that sex before marriage was wrong.

I joined the Air Force, went to the Academy, and "fell" into a Bible study that actually taught the Bible. I can see God's sovereign hand in it all. As I started hearing the Word of God preached by those who actually believed it and lived it, I began to be convicted of my sinful life. I dedicated my life to the Lord and began to live purposefully for Him. That was in the spring of 1996, my sophomore year. Since that time, I stopped getting drunk, going to bars, chasing women, and even stopped swearing, to a large degree, even though I confess that things do slip out - to my shame. I started to plan my life in view of what I learned in the Bible and wanted to live for God wherever His will put me.

The one sin that would not leave was lust. I had already built in my mind a good library of pornography, and practiced self-gratification frequently. I kept these two parts of my life separate. I had a Christian girlfriend by my senior year and tried harder than ever to kick the pornography habit but it got worse. By the time we broke-up in April of 1998, I had started to call phone sex lines and rent porn movies anywhere I could.

Still, I went to the Bible studies every Friday and Saturday night, which kept me out of trouble. This went on for two-and-one-half years. I studied the Bible more and more, even learning so much on my own, but still the pornography addiction kept getting worse.

After graduation, I was sent to Delaware but, no matter where I was stationed in the Air Force, my lust followed me. I started to get into chat rooms where you could see the girl and call her. It was like visiting a prostitute. Soon, that would start to lose its appeal as it became mundane. During this time I read many books and listened to tapes on how to break free, but nothing worked.

One night after a major session of pornography over the Internet and in despair looking for something, ANYTHING, to help me I saw Porn Struggler's Help as I searched for "PORN" over some search engine. I found Setting Captives Free and joined the group.

Since that time, I fell many times up until about day twelve of The Way of Purity course when all the teaching I had been getting finally clicked. I did not have to anymore — I could choose purity. I had to radically amputate my access to this filth (no TV or unfiltered Internet) to help me choose purity. I learned about accountability a long time ago and had a partner that I called every so often, but not one that would really ask me the hard questions. I now have that many times over.

By the grace of God, He has washed me and set me free from this sin. I am still tempted mightily and do not feel that I am ready to shepherd a wife yet. I don't even date. I think that it will take some time of real habitual holiness and purity to really be sure that I have the character necessary to help others. I want to be the man of high moral character and godly self-discipline that my future wife is praying for. That is not yet the case. I have lived in purity for over two months now. That is wonderful, but God is still working in my life. God's grace is real and powerful. He can pull down any stronghold, but sometimes it takes a little more time to complete the work than in others.

That is my testimony in a nutshell - from the depths of sin to purity. You can see how the Lord has changed me. For that I am thankful to God.

All my love in Christ to all of you at Setting Captives Free. The Lord is using you to help me when I had just about given up hope. Thank you, Lord, for this ministry.

DAY 48 - SUCH WERE SOME OF YOU

One of the greatest benefits of being a Christian is that God makes us different than we used to be. As God rescues as from impurity and makes us slaves of righteousness, we become totally different people. This truth is so good to know, because I used to be a pornographer and an adulterer; but that is not who I am now. Some of you may have had an extreme addiction to pornography, you may have been sleeping with prostitutes, or become a homosexual or a pedophile; you may have had extramarital affairs or contracted an incurable sexually transmitted disease. The truth of Scripture is that, no matter what you were, that is not what you are now, if you are in Christ.

This truth is important, because how we see ourselves affects our behavior. I am no longer a pornographer so I do not act like one. I am not addicted to anything impure, so I do not stare at women walking toward me in the airport, nor do I even glance a second time at magazines with women on them. I am not who I used to be, nor do I act as I previously did. Do you see it?

Today we will see this truth in Scripture, and we will read a phenomenal testimony of how the grace of God has changed a friend of ours into a totally new person.

Please read the following passage and answer the questions below:

> ⁹Do you not know that the wicked will not inherit the kingdom of God? Do not be deceived: Neither the sexually immoral nor idolaters nor adulterers nor male prostitutes nor homosexual offenders ¹⁰nor thieves nor the greedy nor drunkards nor slanderers nor swindlers will inherit the kingdom of God. ¹¹And that is what some of you were. But you were washed, you were sanctified, you were justified in the name of the Lord Jesus Christ and by the Spirit of our God" (1 Corinthians 6:9-11).

Course member Dan wrote, "I think it is part of human nature to really hope that everyone can get to heaven. It's easy to fool ourselves into thinking that God will 'let you in' no matter what you say or do or believe. Paul is making it clear here that people whose lives are controlled by sin and not by God are not going to make it into God's kingdom."

Question 3. Were the people Paul was writing to still practicing these sins? Before you answer, carefully review verse 11 above.

- A. No, they were no longer involved in these habitual sins, but were washed, and changed
- B. Yes, they were still living in these sins

Question 4. What verses tell us these people were no longer the same?

Question 5. According to the above passage, what changed them? How were they changed?

Question 1. What kind of people made up the church at Corinth during Paul's day?
- A. Homosexuals
- B. Wicked
- C. Sexually immoral
- D. Adulterers
- E. Male prostitutes
- F. Thieves
- G. Drunkards
- H. All of the above

Question 2. In verses 9-10, Paul mentions the types of people who will not inherit the kingdom of God. Why do you think he warns against being deceived about this (verse 9)? Write your thoughts here.

The New Testament church has inspired both exciting and disastrous experiments down through history. Hoping to create the perfect New Testament community, some have tried to design groups where all the gifts are expressed, worship is spontaneous and fellowship is deep. But they forget the common element of all New Testament churches — problems!

In chapters one through four of First Corinthians, Paul dealt with divisions in the church. Now he focuses on serious moral problems in Corinth. Incest and drunkenness (chapter 5) during communion are hardly what we hope to find in church. But we must remember that growing churches are not usually filled with well-scrubbed Christians but, rather, with a motley collection of sinners being saved.

Paul warns against being deceived, because deception regarding this concept is common. After all, salvation is by grace, not by works, and Jesus came to save sinners. What does it matter, we think, if sinners keep on sinning? But such thinking overlooks the fact that a new life in Christ results in a new lifestyle (verse11). Genuine salvation results in actually being saved from ongoing, habitual sin.

The sins listed referred to a continuous lifestyle or practice, and not to a onetime involvement. Paul's list is similar to the works of the flesh in Galatians 5:19-21 (See also Ephesians 5:5). In both cases, a persisting in fleshly living is implied.

Likewise, Paul's mention of both male prostitutes and homosexual offenders does not mean that a person with homosexual tendencies, who is living chastely, is excluded from the kingdom. The two words Paul uses here, "malakoi" (men or boys who allow themselves to be misused homosexually) and "arsenokoitai" (a male homosexual, pederast, sodomite) both have an active meaning.

The teaching today is that Christians are no longer who we used to be. Please state how the following passages confirm this truth:

Question 6. Please provide your thoughts on this verse: "I have been crucified with Christ and I no longer live, but Christ lives in me. The life I live in the body, I live by faith in the Son of God, who loved me and gave himself for me" (Galatians 2:20).

Question 7. Please provide your thoughts on this verse: "For you died, and your life is now hidden with Christ in God. When Christ, who is your life, appears, then you also will appear with him in glory" (Colossians 3:3,4).

First, let me show you how this teaching may be practically applied. We act according to our nature. If we are sinners who are trying to be good, we will inevitably fall. But, if we are saints who occasionally sin, our nature is such that we hate sin, and our habitual pattern of life will be to walk in righteousness. Do you see it?

Now let me share with you some writings that will confirm this truth, and ask you comment on them:

The previous character of those who seem to have been converted was various. I could name many who have been turned from the paths of open sin and profligacy, and have found pardon and purity in the blood of the Lamb, and by the Spirit of our God; so that we can say to them, as Paul said to the Corinthians, "Such were some of you; but you were washed, but you are sanctified, but you are justified." I often think, when conversing with some of these, that the change they have undergone might be enough to convince an atheist that there is a God, or an infidel that there is a Savior. Memoirs of McCheyne

Question 8. Please write your comments here on the quote by McCheyne.

He puts them in mind what a change the gospel and grace of God had made in them: Such were some of you (verse 11), such notorious sinners as he had been reckoning up. The Greek word for "such things were some of you" is tauta: very monsters rather than men. Note: some that are eminently good after their conversion have been as remarkably wicked before. How glorious a change does grace make! It changes the vilest of men into saints and children of God. Such were some of you, but you are not what you were. You are washed, you are sanctified, and you are justified in the name of Christ by the Spirit of our God.

Note, the wickedness of men before conversion is no bar to their regeneration and reconciliation to God. The blood of Christ, and the washing of regeneration, can purge away all guilt and defilement. Note, none are cleansed from the guilt of sin, and reconciled to God through Christ, but those who are also sanctified by His Spirit. All who are made righteous in the sight of God are made holy by the grace of God. - Matthew Henry Commentary

Question 9. Please comment on the above quote by Matthew Henry here:

Course member Brian wrote, "I was reading today's lesson when I had an 'Aha' moment. I never thought about Scripture from Paul's letter to the Corinthians quite the way you put it. I am no longer to think of myself as an ex-alcoholic, ex-smoker, and an ex-pornography addict. Those sins are behind and I need to go forth as a new man, a Christian. I believe the statement, 'You are what you think you are or if you think you can, or you think you can't, you are right' is relevant here. I can now see the freedom Jesus gave us when He paid the price for our sin. I have nothing against 12-Step programs, but they seem to lock some people into a mindset that they will be addicts forever. If I am, indeed, free because of Jesus, then I am no longer a recovering addict, I am free indeed. God bless you."

Course member Roy wrote, "I thank God for your lesson today. Satan has been planting the old thoughts back into my mind in the past few days. 'Don't you want the old stuff you use to love,' he tauntingly asks? After reading this morning's lesson, a new strength has welled up inside of me; a satisfaction, and a consolation that I'm not what I used to be! Christ has washed me clean and has sanctified me and I don't have to buckle under to the strongholds that once bound me. It has now been 48 days of being free from pornography and self-gratification. That blows me away and lifts my soul."

My friend, if we are in Christ, we are not who or what we were. The story is told of Augustine who passed a familiar prostitute without turning a second glance at her. She turned and said, "Augustine, it is I." To which he replied, "Yes, but it is not I." He knew the truth that he was not who he used to be. Do you? One of our course members always signs his posts to the discussion group, "Not I, not ever!"

Question 10. How are you doing today?

The following testimony is from Tony:

I have just completed Day 5 on the mentorship course. It reminded me of the times I came so close to watching something on TV. I can honestly only claim grace and circumstance as the reasons I did not fall. I doubt those things would hold the same draw now, but then they did.

I'm continuing to enjoy my freedom, and God is constantly drawing people to me, not just for problems with pornography, but many believers who seem to be struggling. It's as though they can tell that I have something, and they want it, too. My heart has become passionate to rescue believers who are going through this lack of life. I find myself angry that the devil has robbed and blinded so many people. Having had my eyes opened again, I see the possibility for all those around me. Truly I am in a war here, but truly I am filled with such joy to be in it.

Scripture to Consider

For you have heard of my previous way of life in Judaism, how intensely I persecuted the church of God and tried to destroy it. [14] I was advancing in Judaism beyond many Jews of my own age and was extremely zealous for the traditions of my fathers. [15] But when God, who set me apart from birth and called me by his grace, was pleased [16] to reveal his Son in me so that I might preach him among the Gentiles, I did not consult any man, [17] nor did I go up to Jerusalem to see those who were apostles before I was, but I went immediately into Arabia and later returned to Damascus.

[18] Then after three years, I went up to Jerusalem to get acquainted with Peter and stayed with him fifteen days. [19] I saw none of the other apostles-only James, the Lord's brother. [20] I assure you before God that what I am writing you is no lie. [21] Later I went to Syria and Cilicia. [22] I was personally unknown to the churches of Judea that are in Christ. [23] They only heard the report: "The man who formerly persecuted us is now preaching the faith he once tried to destroy." [24] And they praised God because of me (Galatians 1:13-24).

Were you free from pornography since you did the last lesson?

    Yes   No

Were you free from self-gratification since you did the last lesson?

    Yes   No

Were you free from sexual immorality since you did the last lesson?

    Yes   No

DAY 49 - WALKING IN THE SPIRIT

So I say, live by the Spirit, and you will not gratify the desires of the flesh (Galatians 5:16).

Scripture describes for us how to live in a way that honors the Lord. This way involves a continual drinking of the Living Water, continuous and unbroken fellowship with Christ, and a refusal to gratify the desires of the flesh. This type of life is extremely rewarding; as Scripture states, "Happy is he whose God is the Lord" (Psalm 144:15b).

As believers, most of us would acknowledge this truth, yet we find within us competing desires and inner conflict. "For the flesh desires what is contrary to the Spirit, and the Spirit what is contrary to the flesh. They are in conflict with each other, so that you do not do what you want" (Galatians 5:17).

So, are we to live the rest of our lives with this inner struggle going on all the time? Should we just give up, thinking we will always have these intense temptations, these fiery darts from the enemy? Will we at times, have victory over them, and at other times simply give in to them? Many people do just that. They are tired of fighting, tired of resolving to stop sinning, only to fall again, and worn out by the vicious cycle. But friend, this sin cycle does not need to continue. Scripture makes a declarative statement: "So I say, live by the Spirit and you will not gratify the desires of the sinful nature." We may still have the desires, but we are enabled to live above them, as we live by the Spirit.

What does it mean to live by the Spirit? Please read this quote from Matthew Henry and be ready to answer the question below:

Note, the best antidote against the poison of sin is to walk in the Spirit, to be much conversing with spiritual things, to mind the things of the soul, which is the spiritual part of man, more than those of the body, which is his carnal part, to commit ourselves to the guidance of the word, wherein the Holy Spirit makes known the will of God concerning us, and in the way of our duty to act in a dependence on his aids and influences. And, as this would be the best means of preserving them from fulfilling the lusts of the flesh, so it would be a good evidence that they were Christians indeed; for, says the apostle 'if you would be led by the Spirit, you are not under law.' As if he had said, 'You must expect a struggle between flesh and spirit as long as you are in the world, that the flesh will be lusting against the spirit as well as the spirit against the flesh; but if, in the prevailing bent and tenor of your lives, you be led by the Spirit, if you act under the guidance and government of the Holy Spirit and of that spiritual nature and disposition he has wrought in you, if you make the word of God your rule and the grace of God your principle, it will hence appear that you are not under the law, not under the condemning... (Comments on Galatians 5:16-18).

Question 1. Write down everything you find that defines what living by the Spirit means, according to this quote.

Question 2. Obviously we have come to a crucial portion of Scripture for overcoming slavery to sexual sin when we read, "So I say, live by the Spirit, and you will not gratify the desires of the flesh." Please explain, in your own words, what you think it means to "live by the Spirit." Write your answer here.

Please read the passage we are studying in context, and answer the questions below:

¹⁶ So I say, live by the Spirit, and you will not gratify the desires of the flesh. ¹⁷ For the flesh desires what is contrary to the Spirit, and the Spirit what is contrary to the flesh. They are in conflict with each other, so that you do not do what you want. ¹⁸ But if you are led by the Spirit, you are not under law.

¹⁹ The acts of the flesh are obvious: sexual immorality, impurity and debauchery; ²⁰ idolatry and witchcraft; hatred, discord, jealousy, fits of rage, selfish ambition, dissensions, factions ²¹ and envy; drunkenness, orgies, and the like. I warn you, as I did before, that those who live like this will not inherit the kingdom of God.

²² But the fruit of the Spirit is love, joy, peace, patience, kindness, goodness, faithfulness, ²³ gentleness and self-control. Against such things there is no law. ²⁴ Those who belong to Christ Jesus have crucified the sinful nature with its passions and desires. ²⁵ Since we live by the Spirit, let us keep in step with the Spirit. ²⁶ Let us not become conceited, provoking and envying each other (Galatians 5:16-26).

Question 3. Please list the acts of the flesh as listed in verse 19.

Question 8. What does it mean to "keep in step with the Spirit?"

The first act listed here is "sexual immorality," and the second is "impurity." These two get top billing as to the acts of the flesh, and if our lives are characterized by these acts, we are not living by the Spirit.

Note: There is a real possibility of being deceived when involved in acts like these. So Paul warns in verse 21, "I warn you, as I did before, that those who live like this will not inherit the kingdom of God." Oh, how we need to heed the warning. Friends, please understand Paul's words, and don't try to explain them away. He is issuing a warning to those who live in the acts of the flesh, that they will not inherit the kingdom of God. In other words, hell is the destination of all who live by these acts, regardless of how much knowledge they have, how articulate they are, or what position they have in the church. This is serious. Do not be deceived.

Question 4. According to verse 24, what evidence must be in our lives to show that we belong to Christ?

A. We must say that we are believers

B. We must have bumpers sticker that read, "Honk if you love Jesus"

C. We must have crucified the flesh with its passions and desires

Question 5. What does the above passage teach about our relationship to the Spirit? What are we to do in relationship to Him?

Question 6. Please list the fruit of the Spirit from verse 22.

Question 7. In the context of this passage, what does it mean to be led by the Spirit?

Note: The Christian life may be described as a walk with God. Just as "Enoch walked with God, and was no more," so we are to be in a daily relationship with Him. And it is this daily relationship, or this walking with God, that keeps us away from sin. Compare Psalm 56:13: "Because you have saved me from death. You have kept me from being defeated. So I will walk with God in light among the living. (NCV)

The Christian life begins with a step of faith for salvation. Then it continues, step by step toward spiritual maturity as we develop a growing closeness to God.

It is a painful business to get through into the stride of God, it means getting your 'second wind' spiritually. In learning to walk with God, there is always the difficulty of getting into His stride; but when we have got into it, the only characteristic that manifests itself is the life of God. The individual man is lost sight of in his personal union with God, and the stride and the power of God alone are manifested.

It is difficult to get into stride with God, because when we start walking with Him we find He has outstripped us before we have taken three steps. He has different ways of doing things, and we have to be trained and disciplined into His ways.

Question 9. How does 1 John 1:7 add perspective on the above teaching? "If we walk in the light, as He is in the light, we have fellowship with one another and the blood of Jesus, His Son, purifies us from all sin." Write your answers here.

Question 10. In Galatians 5, Paul talks about the battle between the flesh and the Spirit. He states, "so that you do not do what you want." Does this refer to believers or unbelievers?

A. Believers

B. Unbelievers

John Calvin adds some clarity here: **"So that you do not do what you want. This refers, unquestionably, to the regenerate (believers). Carnal men have no battle with depraved lusts, no proper desire to attain to the righteousness of God. Paul is addressing believers. The things that you want must mean, not our natural inclinations, but the holy affections which God bestows upon us by grace. Paul therefore declares, that believers, so long as they are in this life, whatever may be the earnestness of their endeavors, do not obtain such a measure of success as to serve God in a perfect manner. The highest result does not correspond to their wishes and desires"** (John Calvin, commentary on Galatians 5).

Note: Because of the war in the soul of every believer (the flesh against the Spirit and the Spirit against the flesh) we are unable to perfectly do what we would like to do. We desire to seek God wholeheartedly, but the flesh wars against that desire. We desire ongoing intimacy and unbroken fellowship with Jesus Christ, but the flesh vehemently resists this. We want to show others only a sweet aroma of Christ, letting our gentleness be evident to all; we want to be gracious at all times, completely humble, submitting to one another always and forgiving each other as we have been forgiven. The flesh resists and fights against all of this so that we cannot perfectly, and at all times, do what we want to do. Should we then despair and give up?

The Galatians passage states there is a way to keep from fulfilling the lusts of the flesh. It is to live by the Spirit. It is to be led by the Spirit. It is to walk with the Spirit. Our "fight" is not so much with avoiding pornography or greed, being selfish or divisive, it is with maintaining our walk with the Lord. For if we live by the Spirit, are led by the Spirit, and walk with the Spirit, the promise of Scripture is that we will not gratify our flesh. We will not view pornography; we will not be sexually immoral, etc. This is our answer!

I have been learning, over the past several years, what it means to walk with God. It is an experience to be sure, and it is not like anything we learn in school. It is exercising the spiritual disciplines of being in the Word daily, of being in prayer continually, and of recognizing the leading and prompting of God in our daily activities. This is all foreign to our natural state. But I tell you, I would not trade it for anything. I love walking in and living by the Spirit of God (though my flesh hates it), and I don't ever want to return to the acts of the flesh. My wife, also, is thankful that I am walking in the Spirit, as she and I are much closer than when I was living in sin. I hope you are finding the same thing. Or if you are single, remember that the goal in your search for freedom is not to be married: it is to walk closely with the Lord and to learn how to be satisfied in Christ. The one who finds freedom from habitual sin will find that Christ will satisfy and complete him, and also make his relationship with others more satisfying and godly.

Question 11. How are you doing right now? Are you learning to live by the Spirit? Record your thoughts here:

The following testimony is from Carlos:

Oh, how desperately wicked I have been, and how deep the roots of my sin went. For twenty-nine years I walked with sin, lived in sin, gratifying my flesh and pleasing my sinful nature. I have done all the sinful acts of the flesh listed on today's teaching: sexual immorality, impurity, greed, rage, hatred, etc. I have slept with prostitutes and with other men.

I was like King Nebuchadnezzar, who was insane until he acknowledged the sovereignty of God. I, too, was out of my right mind, and it wasn't until I came to The Way of Purity course that I was granted repentance and my sanity was restored. This began when I enrolled in the course, but the root system of the weeds of sexual immorality were very deep, and I could not continue. I went back "out to pasture" and lived in my insanity for another two months.

I don't know what clicked when I returned this time, but God simply granted me repentance, and I was able to radically amputate the causes of my sin, and learn how to walk with God. I have been doing this now for six months - free and clear!

Scripture to Consider

He has shown you, O man, what is good; And what does the LORD require of you But to do justly, To love mercy, And to walk humbly with your God? (Micah 6:8).

Were you free from pornography since you did the last lesson?

    Yes   No

Were you free from self-gratification since you did the last lesson?

    Yes   No

Were you free from sexual immorality since you did the last lesson?

    Yes   No

DAY 50 - FREEDOM THROUGH FELLOWSHIP

The final weekend before Christmas is not a great time to visit a shopping mall. If you are fortunate enough to find a parking spot, the press of people inside makes shopping almost impossible. I heard one mother giving final instructions to her young son before plunging into the crowd, "Stay close to me and hold my hand all the time. We won't get separated if we hold on to each other."

As Jesus prepared his disciples to face life without his visible presence, he impressed on them the importance of staying close to him, spiritually. He said, "Remain in Me." If you have ever longed to understand the secret of spiritual growth, you will find it in Jesus' words to us in John 15.

Here is a truth to memorize:

To truly stop the habits of pornography, self-gratification, and immorality requires ongoing intimacy with God.

Or, stated another way, enjoying true intimacy with Jesus Christ breaks the attraction of the false intimacy offered by pornography and sex outside of marriage. This is the reason why all psychologically based programs to "change behavior" will not produce genuine and lasting freedom. Enjoying Jesus Christ Himself must replace the love of pornography and impurity.

Please read the following Scripture:

> [4] Remain in me, and I will remain in you. No branch can bear fruit by itself; it must remain in the vine. Neither can you bear fruit unless you remain in me.
>
> [5] "I am the vine; you are the branches. If a man remains in me and I in him, he will bear much fruit; apart from me you can do nothing. 6 If anyone does not remain in me, he is like a branch that is thrown away and withers; such branches are picked up, thrown into the fire and burned. [7] If you remain in me and my words remain in you, ask whatever you wish, and it will be given you. [8] This is to my Father's glory, that you bear much fruit, showing yourselves to be my disciples.
>
> [9] "As the Father has loved me, so have I loved you. Now remain in my love. [10] If you obey my commands, you will remain in my love, just as I have obeyed my Father's commands and remain in his love. [11] I have told you this so that my joy may be in you and that your joy may be complete (John 15:4-11).

Questions

Spend a little time thinking through the above passage to the delight of your soul. When you're ready, please answer these questions:

Question 1. Jesus' instructions to his disciples in this passage revolve around three symbols - the vine, the gardener, and the branches. What is Jesus communicating by calling Himself the Vine?

A. He is the Source of Life
B. He nourishes and sustains us
C. He lives in us
D. All of the above

Question 2. What is the significance of calling His disciples "branches?"

A. They were dependent on Jesus for life and fruitfulness
B. The could do nothing on their own
C. They were dead without Jesus
D. All of the above

Questions

Note: We see here the necessity of actually being a "branch." Nobody shares in the life of Christ unless there is an actual faith relationship with Christ.

Question 3. Please select how many times the word "remain" is used in the verses above:

A. 3
B. 7
C. 11

Question 4. Instead of commanding us to bear fruit, why is Jesus' only command "Remain in Me" (vs. 4)?

Now let us summarize: Remain in the love of Jesus, and your joy will be complete. And if your joy in Jesus is complete, you will not need to look for it anywhere else. Your slavery to sin is broken when your love and joy are complete.

Question 5. What do you think it means to remain in Christ?

Question 6. The fruit produced by the remaining branch is often viewed as a reference to new converts. But branches produce grapes, not other branches. What other possible meanings are there for fruit?

Question 7. Read Galatians 5:22-23: "But the fruit of the Spirit is love, joy, peace, patience, kindness, goodness, faithfulness, gentleness and self-control." How do these verses fit into what we are studying?

Note: We can do "nothing" on our own, certainly not overcome pornography, self-gratification, adultery, or any type of sexual impurity. But if we remain in Jesus, He will produce fruit through us; one particular fruit being that of "self-control." So we do not focus as much on overcoming sexual sin as we do on abiding, or dwelling in Jesus Christ. This is the "secret" to growing in Christ, to leaving pornography and immorality behind, and to experiencing genuine love and real joy!

Please read the following story:

> ⁵⁴ Then seizing him, they led him away and took him into the house of the high priest. Peter followed at a distance. ⁵⁵ But when they had kindled a fire in the middle of the courtyard and had sat down together, Peter sat down with them. ⁵⁶ A servant girl saw him seated there in the firelight. She looked closely at him and said, "This man was with him."
>
> ⁵⁷ But he denied it. "Woman, I don't know him," he said.
>
> ⁵⁸ A little later someone else saw him and said, "You also are one of them."
>
> "Man, I am not!" Peter replied.
>
> ⁵⁹ About an hour later another asserted, "Certainly this fellow was with him, for he is a Galilean."
>
> ⁶⁰ Peter replied, "Man, I don't know what you're talking about!" Just as he was speaking, the rooster crowed. ⁶¹ The Lord turned and looked straight at Peter. Then Peter remembered the word the Lord had spoken to him: "Before the rooster crows today, you will disown me three times." ⁶² And he went outside and wept bitterly (Luke 22:54-62).

In this story, we find that Peter denied Christ, began cursing, and stated that he did not know Jesus. He fell three times in a row, one right after the other. Why? What happened?

Question 8. Please write out the second sentence of verse 54 above:

"And Peter followed at a distance." Friend, this is a warning for us: anytime we begin distancing ourselves from Christ, we will fall. We must remain intimate with Him, enjoying fellowship with our Savior moment by moment. This is the key to ongoing victory and fruitfulness.

Next, please read the following quote from Robert Murray McCheyne, and write your thoughts on it below.

Not all that seem to be branches are branches of the true Vine. Many branches fall off the trees when the high winds begin to blow - all that are rotten branches. So in times of temptation, or trial, or persecution, many false professors drop away. Many that seemed to be believers went back, and walked no more with Jesus. They followed Jesus, they prayed with Him, they praised Him; but they went back, and walked no more with Him. So it is still. Many among us doubtless seem to be converted; they begin well and promise fair, who will fall off when winter comes. Some have fallen off, I fear, already; some more may be expected to follow. These will not be blessed in dying. Oh, of

all deathbeds may I be kept from beholding the deathbed of the false professor! I have seen it before now, and I trust I may never see it again. They are not blessed after death. The rotten branches will burn more fiercely in the flames.

Oh, think what torment it will be, to think that you spent your life in pretending to be a Christian, and lost your opportunity of becoming one indeed! Your hell will be all the deeper, blacker, hotter, that you knew so much of Christ, and were so near Him, and found Him not.

Question 9. Write your thoughts on the above quotation here:

Question 10. How does 1 John 2:27 compare with what we are studying today? "As for you, the anointing you received from him remains in you, and you do not need anyone to teach you. But as his anointing teaches you about all things and as that anointing is real, not counterfeit-just as it has taught you, remain in him."

Course member Tom wrote, "Just as the vine cannot bear fruit, neither can we, without Christ. We cannot free ourselves from sin. We need Him in every step of this battle. Through Christ, I will be freed from pornography. That is a promise in the Bible. I have asked that He would free me, and I am sure it is in God's will for it to be, so it is going to be done! Truly stopping a pornographic addiction requires an ongoing intimacy with God."

Question 11. And finally, please provide your thoughts on this quote from Charles Spurgeon:

We are plainly taught in the Word of God that as many as have believed are one with Christ: they are married to him, there is a conjugal union based upon mutual affection. The union is closer still, for there is a vital union between Christ and his saints. They are in him as the branches are in the vine; they are members of the body of which he is the head. They are one with Jesus in such a true and real sense that with him they died, with him they have been buried, with him they are raised; with him they are raised up together and made to sit together in heavenly places. There is an indissoluble union between Christ and all his people: I in them and they in me.

Thus the union may be described: "Christ is in his people the hope of glory, and they are dead and their life is hid with Christ in God. This is a union of the most wonderful kind, which figures may faintly set forth, but which it is impossible for language completely to explain.

Oneness to Jesus is one of the fat things full of marrow. For if it be so, indeed, that we are one with Christ, then because he lives we must live also; because he was justified by his resurrection, we also are justified in him; because he is rewarded and forever sits down at his Father's right hand, we also have obtained the inheritance in him and by faith grasp it now and enjoy its earnest.

Question 12. Philippians 4:13 states, "I can do all things through Christ, who gives me strength." Can you break free from an addiction to pornography and immorality through Jesus Christ?

A. Yes

B. No

C. Through Him? You bet – I'm doing it!

The following testimony is from Don:

I was caught in slavery to pornography, chained to something I did not want to do and yet could not stop doing in my own power. I sinned against my God, against my wife, against my family and against my church family. I deceived myself and was deceived that I truly wasn't committing adultery because I was not gratifying my flesh with self-pleasure - what deception.

As I sank deeper and deeper into this bondage, my ability to minister was obviously hampered and, even worse, the Lord allowed my heart to harden. This was the scariest part of all. I knew I was sinning, I didn't want to sin and I couldn't stop - or at least I did not know how. Sometimes through shear willpower I could stop for days, weeks, even months, but I would always go back like a dog to its own vomit.

Finally the Lord placed an article about Setting Captives Free in front of me. I went to the website but didn't do anything right away - I guess I was counting the cost. That Sunday, the Lord softened my heart and that night I started this journey. It has been a total blessing. Except for two stumbles early in the course I have been totally free of pornography. I am in the Word every day and what was once drudgery has become an integral part of my day.

The Bible is truly a manifestation of Christ as the Living Water in our lives, and I can't get through the day without it. I have repented, confessed, renounced my sin, and I am now living in freedom. I have learned to be vigilant, broken, and humble and I won't take any of this for granted.

I thank Setting Captives Free and, of course, God, for the weapons I have gained for this battle and my conviction that I never need to be chained to this monster again. I'M FREE, BABY!

Scripture to Consider

[20] "My prayer is not for them alone. I pray also for those who will believe in me through their message, [21] that all of them may be one, Father, just as you are in me and I am in you. May they also be in us so that the world may believe that you have sent me. [22] I have given them the glory that you gave me, that they may be one as we are one: [23] I in them and you in me. May they be brought to complete unity to let the world know that you sent me and have loved them even as you have loved me" (John 17:20-23).

Were you free from pornography since you did the last lesson?

    Yes   No

Were you free from self-gratification since you did the last lesson?

    Yes   No

Were you free from sexual immorality since you did the last lesson?

    Yes   No

DAY 51 - LIVE FOR PLEASURE!

My friend, did you know that it is biblical to live for pleasure? In fact, it is commanded of us to live for pleasure. We are to be "Christian hedonists," as John Piper stated in his book, *Desiring God*. It seems some people in the Christian world are not happy until they are miserable. However, we are not doomed to this type of existence. The biblical principles in this lesson have the power to change your entire outlook on life, as they have mine.

I conducted a search for "Sexual Addiction" on the Internet, to see what solutions are given by the "experts." Most of it is a joyless list of things to do in order to change your behavior. For instance: when hit with temptation, visualize a policeman running up to you with a big red stop sign and handcuffs. You might picture an emotionally charged moment, as the death of a parent or the birth of a child, to create an emotional pull away from the temptation. Or place a rubber band on your wrist and snap it hard every time you are tempted. This associates temptation with pain, supposedly causing you to avoid the temptation in the future.

Oh friend, how sad and lifeless; how ineffective are the cures of the world! What about the heart? Jesus said lust is a heart problem (Matthew 15:18). No snap of the wrist or thoughts of a policeman will change my heart. Instead, what will so motivate my heart with love and joy that I can't possibly think of going back to pornography or adultery? Oh friend, we have a Savior who has come to us in passion, and promises to baptize us with the fire of the Holy Spirit (Matthew 3:11)! He has come, not only to suffer and die to remove the penalty of our sins, but also to live in our hearts and shower us with love. Oh, how He delights the soul and stirs the affections. How pleasurable to live life, in love with Him. Would I prefer a cop with a red stop sign and handcuffs, or a Savior who captivates the heart? Hmmm....let me think.

The key is to live for *pleasure* in God!

It is a bad world, an incredibly bad world. But I have discovered in the midst of it a quiet and holy people who have learned a great secret. They have found a joy that is a thousand times better than any pleasure of our sinful life. They are despised and persecuted, but they care not. They are masters of their souls. They have overcome the world. These people are the Christians - and I am one of them. Saint Cyprian (200-258)

Dear friend, this is our calling: to find joy in Christ, which is a *thousand times better* than any sinful pleasure. Sometimes I find it hard to believe I spent 15 long years following the "pleasures of sin" in sexual immorality, when there was Someone "a thousand times better" waiting for me. And, it is the ongoing experience of a relationship with Jesus Christ which keeps me from having a desire to go back to my life of sin. I can't get enough of this Man, this God-Man who longs to pour His life into me, and to fill me with all the fullness of God. In this lesson, we will examine the sheer pleasure available in God. Oh friend, open your heart to this God, for if you do, you will live in pleasure for the rest of your life and throughout all eternity.

> Live while you live, the Epicure would say,
> And seize the pleasures of the present day;
> Live while you live, the sacred preacher cries,
> And give to God each moment as it flies;
> Lord, in my view let both united be;
> I live in pleasure when I live to thee.
> Philip Doddridge (1702-1751)

Please study through the following passages and provide your comments:

> You have made known to me the path of life; you will fill me with joy in your presence, with eternal pleasures at your right hand (Psalm 16:11).

Question 1. According to this verse, what is at the right hand of God?

A. Eternal pleasures

B. Many hard-to-follow rules and regulations

C. A strong bodyguard

> The Son is the radiance of God's glory and the exact representation of his being, sustaining all things by his powerful word. After he had provided purification for sins, he sat down at the right hand of the Majesty in heaven (Hebrews 1:3).

Question 2. According to this verse, who is at the right hand of God?

A. A strong bodyguard

B. Jesus Christ

The above verses tell us there are eternal pleasures at the right hand of God, and also that Jesus Christ is at the right hand of God. Do you see it? The message is clear: eternal pleasure is in Jesus Christ! Sin's pleasures are only "for a season", but with Jesus Christ, the pleasure never ends!

> A fool finds pleasure in evil conduct, but a man of understanding delights in wisdom (Proverbs 10:23).

Question 3. What type of person finds pleasure in sexual sin or other evil conduct?

A. A good-time, fun-loving person

B. A wise and godly man

C. A fool

Pleasure is our greatest evil or our greatest good (Alexander Pope 1688-1744).

Question 4. According to Proverbs 10:23, how does a man of understanding approach wisdom?

A. He delights in it

B. He looks for it

C. He gains it

D. He endures it

> To whom can I speak and give warning? Who will listen to me? Their ears are closed so they cannot hear. The word of the LORD is offensive to them; they find no pleasure in it (Jeremiah 6:10).

Question 5. According to Jeremiah 6:10, what is the attitude of these people toward the Word of God?

A. They find no pleasure in it

B. It brings them great delight

C. They love it

Question 6. If the unrighteous are characterized as people who find no pleasure in the Word of God, how are we, who love God, to approach Scripture?

A. We are to read it every Sunday at church

B. We find pleasure in it; it is a delight to our hearts

C. We have to read it to be saved

Then Hannah prayed and said: "My heart rejoices in the LORD; in the LORD my horn is lifted high. My mouth boasts over my enemies, for I delight in your deliverance (1 Samuel 2:1).

Question 7. This verse is the record of Hannah praying to the Lord. What is her attitude toward the Lord and His deliverance?

A. She endures it quietly

B. She rejoices and delights in the Lord and in His salvation

There is no pleasure comparable to not being captivated by any external thing whatever (Thomas Wilson, 1663-1735).

Delight yourself in the LORD and he will give you the desires of your heart (Psalm 37:4).

Question 8. According to Psalm 37:4, what are we to do with the Lord?

A. Accept Him

B. Delight in Him

C. Obey Him

Question 9. What is the reward for delighting in the Lord?

A. It's... a new car!

B. If we make the Lord our delight, we receive the desires of our hearts.

Praise the LORD. Blessed is the man who fears the LORD, who finds great delight in his commands (Psalm 112:1).

Question 10. In what does the man who fears the Lord delight?

A. Going to movies, plays, and fine art museums

B. The commands of God, the Word of God

C. Pornography

¹ Come, all you who are thirsty, come to the waters; and you who have no money, come, buy and eat! Come, buy wine and milk without money and without cost. ² Why spend money on what is not bread, and your labor on what does not satisfy? Listen, listen to me, and eat what is good, and your soul will delight in the richest of fare. ³ Give ear and come to me; hear me, that your soul may live. I will make an everlasting covenant with you, my faithful love promised to David (Isaiah 55:1-4).

Question 11. These verses make it clear there is a "delight of soul" awaiting all who will eat what is good. Are you eating what is good (God's Word)? Are you learning to delight in the Lord? Please write your answer here.

I delight greatly in the LORD; my soul rejoices in my God. For he has clothed me with garments of salvation and arrayed me in a robe of righteousness, as a bridegroom adorns his head like a priest, and as a bride adorns herself with her jewels (Isaiah 61:10).

Question 12. In whom or what is the author finding pleasure?

A. The pleasures of sin

B. Being wealthy

C. The Lord

Question 13. Why is he rejoicing?

A. Because he is not naked in sin, but clothed with the garments of salvation

B. Because he won the lottery

C. Because sin is fun!

Remember Adam and Eve, who after their sin were naked and ashamed? God came and clothed them with a sacrifice. God provides all of His children with the garments of salvation; that is, with the sacrifice of Jesus Christ. This brings us pleasure, and causes us to rejoice.

To stand by the shadows of a friendly tree with the wind tugging at your coattail and the heavens hailing your heart, to gaze and glory and to give oneself again to God, what more could a man ask? Oh the fullness, pleasure, sheer excitement of knowing God on earth." (Jim Elliot in The Journals of Jim Elliot. Christianity Today, Vol. 31, no. 12.)

When we look at the Song of Songs, we see the joy we're supposed to find in Jesus Christ. That's the model we have to go by - not one of drudgery, but pleasure, joy and anticipation. (Mary Ann Mayo, Marriage Partnership, Vol. 7, no. 3.)

Nothing will supply the needs, and satisfy the desires of a soul, but water out of this rock (Jesus Christ), this fountain opened. The pleasures of sense are puddle-water; spiritual delights are rock-water, so pure, so clear, so refreshing-rivers of pleasure. (Matthew Henry)

Now, please read through the following passage and give your thoughts below. This passage is a prescription for finding delight in God.

²¹ Submit to God and be at peace with him; in this way prosperity will come to you. ²² Accept instruction from his mouth and lay up his words in your heart. ²³ If you return to the Almighty, you will be restored: If you remove wickedness far from your tent ²⁴ and assign your nuggets to the dust, your gold of Ophir to the rocks in the ravines, ²⁵ then the Almighty will be your gold, the choicest silver for you. ²⁶ Surely then you will find delight in the Almighty and will lift up your face to God (Job 22:21-26).

Question 14. There are four requirements which must be met in order to delight in God. What are they? I'll write the first one:

Verse 21: **Submit to God**

Verse 22:

Verse 23:

Verse 23,24:

Question 15. What this mean? "Then the Almighty will be your gold, the choicest silver for you."

Question 16. According to the passage above, what needs to be done in order to truly delight in God? Please restate it in your own words.

Friend, there is exquisite joy and pleasure to be found in Jesus Christ. This must be experienced to be understood, because words fall far short of the reality. How wonderful to trade the temporary "pleasures of sin" for an eternity of pleasure with Christ! With Him is fullness of joy, overflowing pleasure, ongoing delight. Will you commit to seeking your pleasure in Jesus Christ? Once you taste the joy found in Him, you won't want to go back to the temporary pleasures of pornography and impurity.

The following testimony is from Jerry:

It wasn't but six months ago that I was desperately seeking pleasure in everything the world has to offer. Like the teacher, I sought for pleasure in pleasing the flesh, in business, in social clubs, in sports, in drinking, and much more. But like the wind, I could never catch it. True pleasure always eluded me. But when I was convicted of my sin, in July of 2000 and began seeking Christ, I found in Him an endless stream of delights. Oh, how He encourages the heart, and soul.

If you are seeking pleasure in pornography and sexual impurity, you are drinking water from the wrong source. If you are seeking it in any other source than Jesus, you are dooming yourself to an eternity of thirsting, and never being quenched.

Oh friend, do as I did and give up! Submit to God, listen to Him, remove wickedness far from your tent, and assign your golden nuggets of earthly pleasure to the dust to be trampled on. Then watch how your heart begins to delight in the Almighty God.

I am glad I discovered how to delight in the Lord. And I am glad I am finding joy in Him. I will not trade this birthright of joy in Jesus Christ for all the worldly delights there are; they are but a mess of pottage in comparison.

Scripture to Consider

[4]For the LORD takes pleasure in His people; He will beautify the humble with salvation. [5]Let the saints be joyful in glory; Let them sing aloud on their bed. (Psalm 149:4-5).

Were you free from pornography since you did the last lesson?

    Yes   No

Were you free from self-gratification since you did the last lesson?

    Yes   No

Were you free from sexual immorality since you did the last lesson?

    Yes   No

DAY 52 - HAPPY ARE THE HELPLESS

When Christ began this Sermon on the Mount, He began at the narrow gate of the basic need of man before God. Man needs what only God can give him, and that is life. Without God, man is hopelessly lost and eternally condemned.

I am amazed at the published material (sometimes Christian) that caresses the pride of man. Titles such as, "Choosing Your Own Greatness," "You're Nature's Greatest Miracle," "You've Got What It Takes," and "Unlocking Your Potential" are indicative of our man-focused society.

You've heard it said, "God helps those who help themselves," but this is not true. According to Scripture, God helps the helpless!

In this lesson, we will study an important subject which will help us overcome pornography, self-gratification, and all sexual immorality. We will learn that "Blessed are the poor in spirit." Or in other words, "Happy are the helpless!"

So, let us seek to understand what the term "poor in spirit" means. Here are some definitions:

> Bankrupt in myself (I am totally without resources)
> I am nothing without God
> All I am, have, and do is worthless apart from God
> I understand my **total inability** before God

This word "poor" has to do with "one who crouches or cowers," and refers to one who is beggarly.

Question 1. Have you approached God as a beggar, or have you come with something to give? In other words have you approached God as "poor in spirit?"

Let us note the importance of recognizing our spiritual bankruptcy in coming to God.

This spiritual poverty is, in reality, the foundation of all graces. God gives grace to the humble, not to the proud. The humble, or those who recognize their own impoverished condition, are given grace.

Emptiness precedes fullness. We cannot receive anything from God until we have empty hands. He who recognizes he has nothing to offer God will receive everything from God.

Self must be denied in order for Christ to be wanted. If our goal is to honor ourselves, Christ will be far from us. But, he who honors God will, himself, be honored.

A starving heart will give all to have the Bread of Life. It is only the hungry who senses his need of Jesus, not the full.

Question 2. Do you see the benefits of being poor in spirit? From the above thoughts, please list the blessings which come to a spiritually poor person.

Friend, in order to overcome life-dominating sins, such as pornography and immorality, one must be poor in spirit. Overcoming sexual sin requires the presence of God and the power of God, and these are only given to the destitute ones, the broken and empty ones, and the poor in spirit. God blesses those who are poor in spirit. Let us notice four ways in which He blesses them by examining the following verses:

1. God is near to the poor in spirit: "The LORD is close to the brokenhearted and saves those who are crushed in spirit" (Psalm 34:18).

2. God will not despise the poor in spirit: "The sacrifices of God are a broken spirit; a broken and contrite heart, O God, you will not despise" (Psalm 51:17).

3. God dwells with the poor in spirit: "For this is what the high and lofty One says- he who lives forever, whose name is holy: "I live in a high and holy place, but also with him who is contrite and lowly in spirit, to revive the spirit of the lowly and to revive the heart of the contrite" (Isaiah 57:15).

4. God esteems the poor in spirit: "This is the one I esteem: he who is humble and contrite in spirit, and trembles at my word" (Isaiah 66:2).

Question 3. In your own words, write out the blessings received by the poor in spirit. As you are writing, ask God to work poverty of spirit deep within you, that He might bless you in these ways.

Number 1 blessing to the poor in spirit:

Number 2 blessing to the poor in spirit:

_____

Number 3 blessing to the poor in spirit:

_____

Number 4 blessing to the poor in spirit:

_____

Please read the following quote:

A castle that has been long besieged and is ready to be taken will deliver up on any terms to save their lives. He whose heart has been a garrison for the devil and has held out long in opposition against Christ, when once God has brought him to poverty of spirit and he sees himself damned without Christ, let God propound what articles He may, he will readily subscribe to them. "Lord, what will you have me to do?" Thomas Watson

Question 4. Please write your thoughts on the above quote from Thomas Watson:

Watson connected the attitude "Lord, what will you have me to do?" with one who is poor in spirit. We have also noticed that those who come to The Way of Purity course in humility, with a desire to learn, asking questions for the purpose of implementing the answers, will always become free from sexual sin. On the other hand, those who think they have something to give and contribute, who come to the course teaching and instructing, will usually fall often. It is the "poor in spirit" who are blessed with freedom from habitual sin.

Please read the following passage, paying particular attention to which of the praying men received the blessing from God:

> [9] To some who were confident of their own righteousness and looked down on everybody else, Jesus told this parable: [10] "Two men went up to the temple to pray, one a Pharisee and the other a tax collector. [11] The Pharisee stood up and prayed about himself: 'God, I thank you that I am not like other men - robbers, evildoers, adulterers - or even like this tax collector. [12] I fast twice a week and give a tenth of all I get.'
>
> [13] But the tax collector stood at a distance. He would not even look up to heaven, but beat his breast and said, 'God, have mercy on me, a sinner.'
>
> [14] I tell you that this man, rather than the other, went home justified before God. For everyone who exalts himself will be humbled, and he who humbles himself will be exalted" (Luke 18:9-14).

Question 5. It is obvious that the tax collector was the one who was poor in spirit. Please write out the evidences of his poverty of spirit. What did he do and say that show us he was spiritually impoverished?

Question 6. From Luke 18:9-14, what blessing was received by the man who was poor in spirit?

Next, let us notice additional rewards and blessings to those who are poor in spirit.

1. God thinks on and delivers the poor in spirit: "Yet I am poor and needy; may the Lord think of me. You are my help and my deliverer; O my God, do not delay" (Psalm 40:17).

2. God hears and does not despise the poor in spirit: "The LORD hears the needy and does not despise his captive people" (Psalm 69:33).

3. God spares and saves the poor in spirit: "He will take pity on the weak and the needy and save the needy from death" (Psalm 72:13).

4. God gives success to the poor in spirit: "But he lifted the needy out of their affliction and increased their families like flocks" (Psalm 107:41).

Question 7. Again, we find the poor in spirit are blessed. From these verses, please write down the four ways God blesses them and add any personal comments you may have.

Number 1 blessing to the poor in spirit:

_____

Number 2 blessing to the poor in spirit:

_____

Number 3 blessing to the poor in spirit:

_____

Number 4 blessing to the poor in spirit:

_____

Question 8. Psalm 107:41 states, "But He lifts the needy out of their affliction..." Please describe how this verse shows that the poor in spirit will be rescued from pornography, self-gratification, and sexual immorality, etc.

Friend, throughout this course I have shared with you that it was not until I became poor in spirit that I received the blessing of God in being lifted out of my affliction. I was teaching and preaching on a regular basis, even while involved in habitual sin.

But when I talked with my pastor that day in January of 1999, I went as a beggar. I went as a dying man who needed life. I was willing to do anything to be free. I listened to his advice because I trusted him, and I determined to follow his instructions. It was very embarrassing to take the TV out of my hotel room and deposit it with my co-pilot, or leave it outside in the hall. But I was willing to do anything, and that is the key to overcoming sexual sin. Are you willing to do anything to be free, and do you listen and obey instructions?

Finally, please note the evidences and applications of the poor in spirit.

Poverty of spirit brings about a:

Weaning from self - Galatians 2:20; Philippians 1:21

Delighting in God's glory - 2 Corinthians 3:18

Seeking God's fingerprints - Romans 8:17, 18, 28

Seeing the best in others and the worst in yourself

Praying like a beggar and praising like a son

Serving like a slave

Question 9. Do you see any or all of the above evidences of spiritual poverty in your life? If so, which ones?

Course member Mike wrote, "Yes, I see this weaning from self happening now. I look at myself while I was enslaved to pornography, and I see one who was thoroughly selfish, and who lived to please himself in all things. Since I have been walking in freedom from this habitual sin, I am becoming less and Jesus is becoming more. I praise God for this change that He is working in my heart and in my life. My wife commented to me the other day that I am living a life that is non-selfish. Wow, I never thought I would hear that from her."

Question 10. Please write your thoughts on this lesson and what is going on in your life at present.

The following testimony is from Larry:

I have been in love with myself from as early as I can remember. I have always thought I was an extremely good-looking man, and have always thought women would think that about me as well. I had myself convinced that most women I came in contact with wanted me, lusted after me, and would do anything to have me.

That was in the days of my selfish life. One of the things that God did to break me of my love affair with myself was to convince me of sin, and to show me the solid death-grip it had on my life. I could not overcome pornography and self-gratification for the life of me. That is, until I came to The Way of Purity course. I remember learning one truth that sank home to my heart, somewhere around day 50, and that was that it was the poor in spirit who were blessed by God. You could have knocked me over with a feather, as God turned the search light of His Word on my heart right then and there. I began to see how grossly disgusting my love affair with me was. I began seeing how spiritually "rich" I thought I was, and how I felt I had so much to offer God and everyone else. This sight of myself made me sick of myself, and I repented to God for my disgusting "wealth" that I thought I had in myself. I came to God as a beggar; desperate and needy, without resources and helpless. Oh, I can't begin to describe to you the joy that has come from my own crucifixion in Christ.

Since Jesus has eradicated the sins of pornography and self-gratification from my life, I want to praise God all day long. I am crucified with Christ, and I no longer live. Oh how good it is to be dead to sin and alive to God! Blessed are the poor in spirit! Happy are the helpless!

Scripture to Consider

[1] Guard your steps when you go to the house of God. Go near to listen rather than to offer the sacrifice of fools, who do not know that they do wrong. [2] Do not be quick with your mouth; do not be hasty in your heart to utter anything before God. God is in heaven and you are on earth, so let your words be few" (Ecclesiastes 5:1,2).

[24] The God who made the world and all things in it, since He is Lord of heaven and earth, does not dwell in temples made with hands; [25] nor is He served by human hands, as though He needed anything, since He Himself gives to all people life and breath and all things (Acts 17:24-25).

Were you free from pornography since you did the last lesson?

Yes   No

Were you free from self-gratification since you did the last lesson?

Yes   No

Were you free from sexual immorality since you did the last lesson?

Yes   No

DAY 53 - THE POWER OF THE WORD

There is a continual need to profit from Scripture and to utilize the power of God's Word in our lives. The antidote to self-deception is to listen to God through His Word, and to mistrust one's own capacity to reason (Proverbs 3:5-6, 13:14, 14:15, 14:27). The propensity of the human heart to rationalize and justify sin is an active force in the tangled lives of those enslaved to sin. Only by fearing the Lord (yielding oneself to the Word of God), may one find life and freedom. Today's lesson is written by Pastor Dave Wagner from Windsor Ontario, Canada. Please read this excellent article and answer the imbedded questions.

Power of the Word
Learning to Enjoy Freedom in Christ

The biblical principles in The Way of Purity course have the ability to help shape the hearts, minds, souls and spirits of the students who come seeking freedom from addiction. The majority of those who come to the course are Christians, or at least have a church background. In spite of the "availability of Scripture and Truth," many come to the site hopelessly enslaved to pornography, self-gratification and/or other sexual sin.

Many students have been reading the Bible for years, yet the truth has escaped them! They find no spiritual profit from their study of it. The evidence of "bad fruit" in their lives brings us rapidly to the conclusion that, although their store of knowledge has increased, so also has their pride. As a chemist, engaged in making interesting experiments, the intellectual searcher of the Word is quite elated when he makes some discovery in it. However, the joy he has holds no spiritual meaning for him. His success and sense of self-importance only increase and cause him to look with distain upon others more "ignorant" than himself.

The intellectual searcher often makes frequent references to scripture and yet consistently selects "No" to the accountability questions at the end of each lesson. In this case, it is apparent there is no correlation between the individual's knowledge of Scripture and the application of it.

Question 1. How should we read Scripture?
  A. To convince others of our spirituality
  B. To apply it directly to life's circumstances
  C. To correct other's unscriptural views

Some may read the Word of God for the wrong reasons, such as curiosity or pride (to tell others how often they read it). Others may read to accumulate knowledge as a weapon of war, but not against Satan. Instead, they use it for the purpose of arguing with those who have an opposing point of view. As a result of their wrongful reading, there is no thought of God, no yearning for spiritual edification, no benefit to the soul, and most important, there is no power in their lives to overcome the addictive lifestyle in which they find themselves.

Our goal for you is to help you profit from the Word. 2 Timothy 3:16-17 gives us clear guidance as to how the Word should influence our lives.

All Scripture is inspired by God and profitable for teaching, for reproof, for correction, for training in righteousness; so that the man of God may be adequate, equipped for every good work (2 Timothy 3:16-17).

Question 2. Please write down what things Scripture is profitable for:

The Word of God will accomplish many things!
A. First, the Word of God will convict of sin and reveal our depravity, expose our vileness, and make known our wickedness. One of the ways you will know you are profiting from the Word, and not merely gaining knowledge, is when you begin to see your sin and the depravity of your heart.

Question 3. Friend, is this happening in your life? If so, please give an example.

B. The Word of God will make the captive Christian sorrow over sin. Many students come to the course with a stony heart. As the Holy Spirit applies the Word, the student is able to see and feel his inward corruption and discover the strongholds Satan has set up in his life. This discovery produces a broken heart, and leads him to humble himself before God.

Question 4. Has God been revealing your sinfulness and causing you to sorrow over it?

You will know you are on the right track when you see this humbling of spirit begin to take place, which will be evident in the words you write. If God is at work in your heart in this way, you will be brought to a daily repentance before Him. You will also experience the liberation from guilt and shame, and you will be enabled, with joy, to answer "Yes" to the daily accountability questions at the end of each lesson. This "sorrow over sin" goes through a pre-defined process. God had a process for the Pascal lamb - it was to be eaten with "bitter herbs" (Exodus 12:8). As the Word does the work on your heart, the Holy Spirit makes it "bitter," before it becomes sweet to your taste. So, we see there must be mourning before comfort (Matthew 5:4), and humbling before exalting (1 Peter 5:6).

The reading of the Word of God causes us to remember our sinful life, which was a bitter experience for us. As God changes our hearts and lives, that bitterness is changed to sweetness. The cross of Jesus Christ brings us to a place of forgiveness, and the bitterness of our former sins is changed to sweetness of new life in Christ.

C. The Word of God leads to confession of sin. The Scriptures are profitable for reproof (2 Timothy 3:16). When you come to God with an honest heart and soul, you begin to confess sin and acknowledge your faults.

For every one that doeth evil hateth the light, neither cometh to the light, least his deed should be reproved (John 3:20).

Bringing sin into the light is often difficult for students enrolling in The Way of Purity course. They are often like people who gather on the fringe of darkness around the campfire in a dark forest. They know they will need to choose to either step forward and drag their sins out into the light, where the sin will die, or stay in the comfort of the shadows, slipping in and out of the light and never fully committing to the light. By its very nature, sexual sin is often a secret sin.

He that covereth his sins shall not prosper: but whosoever confesseth and forsaketh them shall have mercy (Proverbs 28:13).

There can be no spiritual prosperity or fruitfulness while we conceal within our breasts our guilty secrets. (Psalm 1:3) There is no real peace for the conscience or rest for the heart while there the burden of unconfessed sin remains.

Question 6. Is there any unconfessed or secret sin in your life?

D. The Word of God will produce within you a deeper hatred of sin. When you reach the place where you really hate the sin and hate the addiction it brings, you will begin to find freedom.

ye that love the Lord, hate evil (Psalm 97:10a).

We cannot love God without hating that which he hates. "Through Thy precepts I get understanding: therefore I hate every false way (Psalm 119:104). It is not merely "I abstain from," but "I hate;" not "some" or "many," but "every" false way.

Question 7. Is God producing this hatred of sin in your life? If so, how is He accomplishing it?

E. The Word of God should produce a forsaking of sin. It is very simple. Satan's job is to keep us from reading the Word or, failing that, to prevent us from applying it. Like the parable of the sower with the seed, some will read it and it will take root, causing a forsaking of sin. Others will read it, but there is no forsaking of sin.

Let every one that nameth the name of Christ depart from iniquity (2 Timothy 2:19).

The study of God's Word should produce a purging of our sinful ways. If it is not doing this, we need to ask - "Why Not?" When the Word is personally applied to the life, the end results are dynamic. It causes mentors and students alike to "cleanse our ways." It causes us to "take heed," and it exhorts us to "flee fornication." Sin needs to be not only confessed, but also forsaken. (Proverbs 28:13)

F. The Word of God produces a fortification against sin.

Thy Word have I hid in my heart that I might not sin against thee (Psalm 119:11).

The more Christ's Word dwells in us richly (Colossians 3:16), the less room there will be for the exercise of sin in the heart and life as the Word of God fortifies us. Nothing protects us from the infections of this world, delivers us from the temptations of Satan, and is so effective a preservative against sin as the Word of God. As long as we love the truth and it is active within us, stirring the conscience, we will be kept from falling. We must be prepared for Satan's attacks; we must have a "plan of action." Storing up the Word in our hearts prepares us for the attacks of Satan.

Question 8. In your own words, please state what six things the Word of God is designed to do, and provide any additional comments you may have.

Question 9. Are you beginning to live in victory and closer fellowship with God? Explain:

Scripture to Consider

[12] For the word of God is living and active. Sharper than any double-edged sword, it penetrates even to dividing soul and spirit, joints and marrow; it judges the thoughts and attitudes of the heart. [13] Nothing in all creation is hidden from God's sight. Everything is uncovered and laid bare before the eyes of him to whom we must give account (Hebrews 4:12-13).

[14] I write to you, fathers, because you have known him who is from the beginning. I write to you, young men, because you are strong, and the word of God lives in you, and you have overcome the evil one (1 John 2:14).

Were you free from pornography since you did the last lesson?

    Yes   No

Were you free from self-gratification since you did the last lesson?

    Yes   No

Were you free from sexual immorality since you did the last lesson?

    Yes   No

The following testimony is from Régis:

When I was a teen, I became enslaved to pornography and self-gratification. For years I was addicted to the stuff. All efforts to break free were useless. I often shed tears because of this sin to which I was enslaved thirty-seven years. In 1975, I became a Christian through the ministry of the Groupes Bibliques Universitaires, the French branch of Inter-Varsity Christian Fellowship. The year that followed my conversion, I had no problems with pornography and self-gratification. I was free; it was like I never had any problem with it. But after a year I went back to my former sin. So I spent the next few decades confused and serving the Lord with no power. I was a miserable Christian.

Then in 2001, the Lord heard my cries and began to move in my life. A man who had problems with homosexuality came and asked me if I would translate the chapter dealing with his problem in a Christian book. I agreed to help him, but the book was dealing with all types of sexual problems, not only homosexuality. I asked him to lend me the book so I could read it all. I was not set free by reading the book, but the author said that having fellowship with God should be more important than having victory over sin. A few months later, I read another Christian book. It had a chapter on perfectionism and the Lord spoke to me. He showed me I was a perfectionist, and that I wanted the admiration and the approval of people more than His approval. I would not exhort people when I should have for fear of losing their friendship. I wasn't loving my neighbor, and God wanted me to do so. I was a nice guy with no real friends because I wasn't a real friend.

So I asked God to show me who could help me, and He did. I opened up to a Christian counselor. Then later on, a man from my church asked me if I would be his accountability partner because he was enrolled in The Way of Purity course. I agreed to be his partner, but I was not open to the idea of an online ministry. But since I had agreed to be his accountability partner, I thought I should check the course. I did, and I enrolled in it. From then on, there were showers of blessings. Each daily lesson became a time of face to face with God, and He revealed Himself and His grace to me. As I completed day 42, the Spirit spoke to my heart, and I knew I was free.

The Lord found me a job with a Christian ministry. After four years, I still rejoice in my freedom. Fellowship with God is restored, and I enjoy reading the Puritan writers.

DAY 54 - DO EVERYTHING TO STAND

Therefore put on the full armor of God, so that when the day of evil comes, you may be able to stand your ground, after you have done everything to stand (Ephesians 6:13).

By this time in The Way of Purity course, most students are enjoying consistent freedom from pornography, self-gratification and immorality. However, on occasion, we encounter some students who continue to stumble. Over the course of time, we have discovered that all who continue to be defeated have at least two things in common:

1. They have not done all they can to rid their lives of the source of sexual sin.

2. They are not following the advice of godly mentors who see what needs to be done to extract them from the grip of lust.

Let us examine these two problems in some depth.

First, if we have any access to pornography or illicit relationships, we are sure to fall. Please provide your comments on the following verses:

Question 1. What are your thoughts on Romans 13:14: But put ye on the Lord Jesus Christ, and make no provision for the flesh, to fulfill the lusts thereof. Write your answer here:

By leaving ourselves any access to pornography, we are making provision for the flesh, and in a weak moment we will fall. We simply must remove all access to anything or anyone which might trip us up.

Question 2. What are your thoughts on Matthew 5:29-30: "²⁹ If your right eye causes you to sin, gouge it out and throw it away. It is better for you to lose one part of your body than for your whole body to be thrown into hell. ³⁰ And if your right hand causes you to sin, cut it off and throw it away. It is better for you to lose one part of your body than for your whole body to go into hell."

Question 3. What are your thoughts on Joshua 7:13: "Go, consecrate the people. Tell them, 'Consecrate yourselves in preparation for tomorrow; for this is what the LORD, the God of Israel, says: That which is devoted is among you, O Israel. *You cannot stand against your enemies until you remove it.*"

In this lesson, we will talk very practically about the subject of "doing everything to stand." Let us review Ephesians 6:13 again: "Therefore put on the full armor of God, so that when the day of evil comes, you may be able to stand your ground, after you have done everything to stand" (Ephesians 6:13). When it comes to fighting sexual sin, Ephesians 6:13 tells us we not only need to be wearing armor, but we must also "do all we can to stand." Since this course began in July, 2000, we have watched many people take this verse to heart, and do all they can to stand. Here are some practical ideas our course members have shared with us:

- Removed cable TV from home or cut the cable
- Moved the computer from the "dungeon of privacy" to the open living room
- Removed TV from home and/or hotel room
- Refused to take cash or credit cards with them when driving in the neighborhood of a strip club or movie house
- Spent all night in prayer, begging God for grace to overcome
- Locked up the VCR and gave the key to a family member
- Drove a different route to work to avoid areas of temptation
- Refused to go out of town except with spouse
- Cut off all Internet access
- Changed jobs
- Started going to church
- Started working with an accountability partner
- Began counseling with pastor
- Burned all pornographic magazines
- Reformatted hard drives

171

- Installed Safe Eyes software: www.settingcaptivesfree.com/home/reportingsw.php
- Slept with curtains open in bunkroom to avoid privacy
- Stopped counseling with worldly counselors
- Refused to go where temptation has been strong
- Cut off relationships that promoted sin
- Confessed to spouse, asked for assistance
- Changed stores to shop only where pornography was not available
- Moved out of current residence where pornography was in use
- Moved to a different city
- Cut up video store rental cards
- Slept with clothes on to avoid self-gratification
- Called spouse from hotel to ensure avoidance of sin
- Threw pornographic disks in lake
- Called accountability partner every time he had to go somewhere tempting and called again afterward

Question 4. Please list here everything you have done to stand:

By now we all should recognize that being free from sexual impurity is an act of God and is only by His grace: "⁸ For it is by grace you have been saved, through faith - and this not from yourselves, it is the gift of God- ⁹ not by works, so that no one can boast" (Ephesians 2:8-9). "¹¹ For the grace of God that brings salvation has appeared to all men. ¹² It teaches us to say "No" to ungodliness and worldly passions, and to live self-controlled, upright and godly lives in this present age" (Titus 2:11-12). Had it not been for God's grace, we would still be serving sin, self, and Satan. Sin is powerful and our wills are so enslaved to it by nature that we could not, on our own, extricate ourselves from its grip.

And yet, there is nothing contradictory to the above truth that we must "do all we can do to stand." In fact, the two work together. We do all we can do because of the grace God has given us. "I worked harder than all of them - yet not I, but the grace of God that was with me" (1 Corinthians 15:10). "For we are God's workmanship, created in Christ Jesus to do good works, which God prepared in advance for us to do" (Ephesians 2:10).

Question 5. How does Philippians 2:12-13 compare with what we have studied in this lesson? "¹² Therefore, my dear friends, as you have always obeyed - not only in my presence, but now much more in my absence - continue to work out your salvation with fear and trembling, ¹³ for it is God who works in you to will and to act according to his good purpose."

Friend, we indeed must "do all we can do" to stand. We must "work harder than all the rest," by God's grace. We must work out the salvation that God is working in us for, if we don't, we will continue to fall. And continuing to fall weakens us every time. Those who continue to fall may find themselves back in the death-grip of pornography and impurity again. This is serious business.

Again, the passage we studied in this lesson states that we must put on the full armor of God, and that after we "do all we can do" to stand, that we do indeed stand by grace. It is by grace that we do not fall into sin. If we fail to do all we can do to stand, we should not be surprised when we fall.

Question 6. Has God brought to mind anything else that you could do to stand?

The following testimony is from Bart:

I have practiced self-gratification ever since I can remember, even before I knew what it was called, I remember the feelings it gave me and became addicted. This behavior became thoroughly enslaving in my teen years when I was lusting so often after women that this practice happened many times a day. I was controlled by my sinful nature, and had no hope of ever breaking the habit.

Then I came to Setting Captives Free and to this course, The Way of Purity, and within two weeks I had ceased self-gratification entirely, and have not done it now for approximately sixty days. I am elated. God's grace has enabled me to be severe in my dealing with lust and the power of it is completely broken in my life! Thank you Jesus!

Some people believe (or in some cases are taught falsely by their church) that they cannot overcome self-gratification, but that gratifying the flesh is good and healthy, when used in the right circumstances. Many of us who were previously captives to self-gratification, know this is a lie from the pit of hell. We know that self-gratification gives the devil a stronghold in our minds, with which he may make us his slaves again. Every time we gratify the flesh we become spiritually weaker, because we have indulged the flesh, rather than denied and crucified it, as we are taught in God's Word (Galatians 5:24).

Question 7. How are you doing with ceasing the habit of self-gratification?

Those who continue gratifying their flesh after leaving pornography other sexual sin behind, must realize what is going on: they are yet captive to lust and a slave to carnal desires. Why? Because they are not "doing all they can do" to stand in grace. Instead, there is a chink in the armor which allows the evil one to shoot flaming darts to seduce and deceive them, and goes right along with his schemes to overthrow their souls. Their flesh is their master, and they gratify themselves rather than deny the pleasures of sin. This will continue until they "do all they can do." In other words, we must declare war on our own lusts, make a battle plan to defeat them, and beg God for grace to carry it through to completion.

My friend, the story of Achan (which we studied in lesson 19) teaches us there must be a total eradication of not only the cause of sin, but also of everything associated with that sin. When we are dealing with sexual sin, we must declare an all-out war on evil desires leading to self-gratification, and do all we can do to cease this insidious habit.

Here are some things I have personally done to break the power of sin, by God's grace:

  Slept with clothes on

  Walked around the block in a blizzard

  Called a godly friend when severely tempted

  Read Scripture

  Wrote a Scripture diary

  Sang songs

  Slept outside my hotel room sitting up

These things may seem too radical to some, but they are not too extreme to a dying man, who needs to be free from sin in order to live. We need to "do all we can do," until the habit of refusing self-gratification is deeply ingrained into our very being. Once the new habit of denial is developed, we may slowly begin to go back to a less war-oriented lifestyle; always being watchful that we are not sucked back in to the trap from which we barely escaped.

This lesson was developed because of observing heart-breaking falls from some course members who were well along in this course. Each and every time someone falls to lust and gives in to self-gratification, it is evident they have not done all they can do to rid their lives of the sin, and to stand in grace.

Oh friend, purity in Christ and freedom from sin are worth the battle. As we give up all sexual impurity, we gain far more than we lose. We gain mastery over ourselves, enjoyment of the presence of God, freedom from enslaving habits, and power in witnessing, etc. It is well worth "doing all we can do" to stand by grace.

Question 8. Please make an honest assessment of where you are, spiritually. Are you truly becoming free from habits that would master you? Specifically, have you done all you can do to stand?

Scripture to Consider

Jesus looked at them and said, "With man this is impossible, but not with God; all things are possible with God" (Mark 10:27).

Were you free from pornography since you did the last lesson?

  Yes   No

Were you free from self-gratification since you did the last lesson?

  Yes   No

Were you free from sexual immorality since you did the last lesson?

  Yes   No

DAY 55 – DON'T LOOK BACK!

There is a wide variety of worldly teaching in the area of sexual "addiction recovery". If you do a search on the Internet for "sexual addiction," you will find teaching about returning to your past, digging up repressed memories, reliving past hurts, etc., to aid in escaping your current trap. Here is one example from a book advertisement: "Buried memories of sexual abuse can have a devastating impact on relationships, work and health. Uses case histories to stress the importance of recovering these memories as a crucial step in healing and explains various therapeutic processes used in memory retrieval."

Here is another example of the world's teaching: "I take a history of the man's exposure to pornography and masturbation to it (or masturbation with no pornography) and sexual acting out. I do this in the wife's presence, which helps her understand more clearly that in some ways her husband was a victim usually starting at an early age. I next inquire about possible sexual abuse or early seduction of the husband as a child or as an adolescent, which have eroticized him prematurely. In taking this history, I start with his first memory of exposure to pornography—what its form was (magazine, video, phone sex, etc.) and if he masturbated to it—and continue with the history up to the day of interview."

As Christians, we do not treat sexual abuse lightly. We do not pass it off as insignificant, or tell people to "just get over it." The compassion that a Christian has in dealing with a case of real sexual abuse must exceed that of the unbelieving world; for Christ, in us, has compassion for the hurting. And it is helpful for us to know a person's background in order to show compassion as we interact with them.

However, the Bible nowhere instructs us to return to our past to understand how to get out of sexual sins in the present. In fact, it is quite the opposite. We are instructed, "Brothers, I do not consider myself yet to have taken hold of it. But one thing I do: forgetting what is behind and straining toward what is ahead, ¹⁴ I press on toward the goal to win the prize for which God has called me heavenward in Christ Jesus" (Philippians 3:13-14).

Questions

Question 1. In Philippians 3:13-14, what did Paul say he did with his past?
A. He forgot it
B. He delved into it to discover why he acted in certain ways

In the highly therapized world in which we live, this teaching may come as quite a shock to some. Many have been taught that the past is key to the present, and that reliving the pain of the past will remove the pain in the present. This is not biblical truth, but rather man's theory. Personally, I was never "eroticized prematurely" but, rather, chose to view pornography when older. We work with many students here who were never abused during childhood, but are just as thoroughly addicted as others who were abused.

Question 2. Where are you, currently, with understanding the past and the present? If you believe the past is key to the present, please state where you learned it. Write your thoughts here:

Questions

Christians are not focused backward and downward, but rather forward and upward. If we are in a burning building, we aren't so much interested in how the fire started; we just want to get out!

Please read the following story and provide your comments below.

"So Joseph went after his brothers and found them near Dothan. ¹⁸ But they saw him in the distance, and before he reached them, they plotted to kill him.

¹⁹ "Here comes that dreamer!" they said to each other. ²⁰ "Come now, let's kill him and throw him into one of these cisterns and say that a ferocious animal devoured him. Then we'll see what comes of his dreams."

²¹ When Reuben heard this, he tried to rescue him from their hands. "Let's not take his life," he said. ²² "Don't shed any blood. Throw him into this cistern here in the desert, but don't lay a hand on him." Reuben said this to rescue him from them and take him back to his father.

²³ So when Joseph came to his brothers, they stripped him of his robe-the richly ornamented robe he was wearing- 24 and they took him and threw him into the cistern. Now the cistern was empty; there was no water in it.

²⁵ As they sat down to eat their meal, they looked up and saw a caravan of Ishmaelites coming from Gilead. Their camels were loaded with spices, balm and myrrh, and they were on their way to take them down to Egypt.

²⁶ Judah said to his brothers, "What will we gain if we kill our brother and cover up his blood? ²⁷ Come, let's sell him to the Ishmaelites and not lay our hands on him; after all, he is our brother, our own flesh and blood." His brothers agreed. So when the Midianite merchants came by, his brothers pulled Joseph up out of the cistern and sold him for twenty shekels of silver to the Ishmaelites, who took him to Egypt" (Genesis 37:17-27).

Joseph's brothers plotted his death, cruelly mistreated him by throwing him into a pit, and left him there. Then they sold him into the hands of slave traders, where he became a slave in a foreign land. Eventually he thrown in the dungeon because of the lies of another. These were horrible injustices done to one who was innocent of any crime. Can you imagine the temptation toward bitterness that Joseph must have had? He could have felt terribly angry in his heart towards his brothers, and even toward God.

Question 3. Please take a moment and write down any injustices that were done to you in your past. We are not asking for a book here, but rather a few simple statements of any mistreatment you have endured.

If we follow the story of Joseph in the remaining chapters of Genesis, we read how he became exalted to the position of prime minister of all Egypt, and how he was second in command of the entire nation, second only to Pharaoh himself. And, because of a famine, his brothers had to travel to Egypt to buy food. Through the providence of God, they needed to ask Joseph for food. When they discovered it was him, -the brother they had mistreated so badly, they were scared to death. Would Joseph now get even with them? Would he have them killed? Oh no, because Joseph walked with His God, he was not bitter or angry; nor did he seek revenge. Notice his answer to his brothers as they came trembling before him:

But Joseph said to them, "Don't be afraid. Am I in the place of God? ²⁰ You intended to harm me, but God intended it for good to accomplish what is now being done, the saving of many lives. ²¹ So then, don't be afraid. I will provide for you and your children." And he reassured them and spoke kindly to them" (Genesis 50:19-21).

How did Joseph deal with the abuse of his past? He recognized God was in control of all things, and that God had a purpose in everything that happened to him. Oh friend, if you have been abused, here is real and lasting help. Know that God was in control even during the bad times, and acknowledge that He had a purpose in it. Joseph said that "God intended it for good..." and you can say the same thing. No, this does not make God the author of sin, but it does say that God is working out His plan at all times (please see Daniel 4:35, Ephesians 1:11 and Job 42:2).

Next, notice what Joseph named one of his children, and the reason he named him the way he did. "Before the years of famine came, two sons were born to Joseph by Asenath, daughter of Potiphera, priest of On. ⁵¹ Joseph named his firstborn, Manasseh, and said, "It is because God has made me forget all my trouble and all my father's household" (Genesis 41:50-51). Manasseh sounds like the Hebrew word for "forget," and Joseph named his son Manasseh, based on the work of God in his life. God enabled him to forget all his trouble. The psychologist and psychiatrist can't do this; only God can enable us to know that He is in control of all things, and make us forget all our troubles. Praise Him!

Question 4. How does the name of Joseph's son correspond with this teaching in this lesson?

Again, as stated earlier, we are not teaching people to simply "forget about the past." No, we are teaching that God is in control, that God has a purpose and a plan for all things, and that He is able to bring good out of bad. One lady I know personally, who was abused as a little girl and again as a teenager, is now being used greatly in ministry to others, as God is bringing good out of her past. Her constant theme is that God is sovereign, He is in charge, He is carrying out His plan in all things and at all times, and that He can and does turn bad things of the past into good.

Nowhere is this thought of God using sin for His own purposes more clearly shown than in the cross of Jesus Christ. It was the Jews who demanded His death, though He had done nothing wrong. And it was the Romans who crucified Him, though there were no legitimate charges. And both were sinning as they did so. But ultimately it was God Who gave His Son, and He used the sin of the people involved to bring about the salvation of all who will believe. Notice how these two thoughts, of men doing the sinning, but of God being in control, are woven together in this passage: "This man was handed over to you by God's set purpose and foreknowledge; and you, with the help of wicked men, put him to death by nailing him to the cross" (Acts 2:23).

Not only does the world teach us to "go back" if we have been abused, but if we are the abuser, we will be tempted to remain in the past as well. Guilt is like the undertow that will drag us back out into the sea of sin again. Likewise, consequences of our sin may last a lifetime in some cases, and may be very discouraging at times. And finally, the devil is called "the accuser of the brothers," and he works in that capacity very well.

But the Christian has the unique ability to run to Jesus when plagued with guilt, discouraged by consequences, or accused by the enemy. We can pour out our hearts to our Father and ask for help in time of need. Christians have the ability to turn to Scripture in these times.

If we are feeling guilty, we may read Hebrews 9:14.

If we are sad about the lasting consequences, we may read Revelation 21:3-4.

If we are being accused by the evil one, we may read Colossians 1:22-23.

Question 5. Of the three things listed above (guilt, consequences, and the devil), which one bothers you the most? Write your answer here:

So, whether abuser or abused, we do not focus on the past to help us. We go to Christ, for He is sufficient for every problem. We have worked with those who were horribly abused in childhood, and have seen them restored to wholeness. And we have worked with those who have abused others and caused them much pain, and have seen them restored, as well. The method is by listening to the stories of abuse, having compassion on the ones involved, and then seeking to gently point to Christ as the answer.

Question 6. How are you doing now? What are your thoughts on today's lesson?

Course member Fred wrote: "Until this course, I was afraid to talk about what was holding me in bondage, which was just plain sin. With the problem recognized as sin, I have now received God's remedy, the blood of His cross for forgiveness, and His death for mine, His life for mine. While I thought it was a 'sickness,' or 'psychological weakness,' I saw myself as the victim, rather than the perpetrator, and could never find healing, for no one knew the cure."

Scripture to Consider

"Let us look only to Jesus, the One who began our faith and who makes it perfect. He suffered death on the cross. But he accepted the shame as if it were nothing because of the joy that God put before him. And now he is sitting at the right side of God's throne. ³Think about Jesus' example. He held on while wicked people were doing evil things to him. So do not get tired and stop trying" (Hebrews 12:2-3).

Were you free from pornography since you did the last lesson?

 Yes No

Were you free from self-gratification since you did the last lesson?

 Yes No

Were you free from sexual immorality since you did the last lesson?

 Yes No

The following testimony is from Howard:

My sinful life of sex and drugs cost me much. I lost everything (profession, wife, house, family) and in 1998 I was in a suicide unit in Atlanta, Georgia. I went to a treatment center in Florida for help, but I wasn't done with my habitually sinful life.

In 2000, after my third treatment center, a good friend asked me if I wanted to go with him to church. I was raised Jewish and I remember my parents telling me never to believe in Jesus, so to go with him to church was difficult for me - but I was literally dying inside and out. At church all I could do was cry, and for the first time I had some relief. It was now decision time, with feelings of betraying my heritage - should I keep going to church or should I stay where I was.

Three months later, I was saved and six months later I was baptized. I stopped drugs and met a beautiful woman who is now my wife. But the lust was still there, and I could not get rid of it. I wanted to stop and I knew without a doubt that I was blocking the Spirit from doing any work in me.

I came to the Setting Captives Free course by the recommendation of another friend. I tried to do it by just using the workbook but I could not. I tried it again and this time I heeded all the suggestions and took the course with a mentor online. I still face temptation, mostly with my eyes, but I am free.

I'm free and my relationship with God and living for His glory is so beautiful. The Spirit has poured out His sweet power and grace, and today I can call sexual sin the lie that it is, and focus on Christ. Before I was scared to tell my wife anything, today we pray for each other and read a daily devotion together. I am free! I am free and God gets all the glory. I did not do it. There is just no way I did this by myself. I am free!

DAY 56 - NORMAL SEXUAL RELATIONS

¹ Now for the matters you wrote about: It is good for a man not to marry. ² But since there is so much immorality, each man should have his own wife, and each woman her own husband. 3 The husband should fulfill his marital duty to his wife, and likewise the wife to her husband. ⁴ The wife's body does not belong to her alone but also to her husband. In the same way, the husband's body does not belong to him alone but also to his wife. 5 Do not deprive each other except by mutual consent and for a time, so that you may devote your-selves to prayer. Then come together again so that Satan will not tempt you because of your lack of self-control (1 Corinthians 7:1-5).

My friend, today's lesson deals with some very intimate issues; we have attempted to treat them delicately, yet forthrightly. We have waited until nearly the end of the course to address this issue, so as to avoid tripping people up, if at all possible. However, these issues need to be discussed, as many who come out of pornography and other sexual sin wonder if they are able to have a "normal sex life." Today's discussion is geared toward married people, but if you are single, please study through it as well.

Please read the following two emails we received here at Setting Captives Free:

"I am so angry! I don't know what to do, and I am writing you because I really do not want to view pornography and gratify my flesh as I used to, but my insides are all in turmoil. You see, my wife is having her period and, during these times, she wants nothing to do with intimacy. Yet I am "burning inside," and long to be with her. Please don't misunderstand, I am not blaming her and I do understand what her monthly cycle does to her physically, so I never pressure her. It's just that I very much want to be intimate. What do I do during these times?"

And here is the second one:

"I'm writing you in hope that you can help me understand if there is something wrong with me, and how I can change. You see, my husband has been involved with pornography for much of our 18 years of marriage and, in the last few years, has begun to slowly pull away from me. We have not made love in nearly a year. I feel like I'm going crazy, thinking I can never match those "glamour girls" and be what he needs me to be, but yet I long to be with him. Why is he not interested in me?"

Let us examine what God says on this subject, and then we will apply the truth to the above situations.

² But since there is so much immorality, each man should have his own wife, and each woman her own husband. ³ The husband should fulfill his marital duty to his wife, and likewise the wife to her husband (1 Corinthians 7:2-3).

Marriage may be a deterrent to sexual immorality. This is not to say that if a person is in bondage to pornography, getting married will break the sinful habit. But it is to say that each of us is built with longings for intimacy which culminates in sexual union. And while some singles have the gift of being single, the majority of us are built for relational intimacy. If this desire goes unmet, temptation often comes in, and people may turn to pornography and self-gratification or sexual immorality in an attempt to satisfy the yearning

within to be "one flesh" with some-one. This is the reason Paul says, "Since there is so much immorality, each man should have his own wife, and each woman her own husband." The sexual intimacy that is provided in marital union is designed to satisfy the need and longing God placed within the hearts of men and women to enjoy physical togetherness and closeness.

Do not deprive each other except by mutual consent and for a time, so that you may devote yourselves to prayer. Then come together again so that Satan will not tempt you because of your lack of self-control (1 Corinthians 7:5).

Having exhorted single people to marry, he next exhorts married people to not deprive each other of sexual intimacy, unless certain conditions are met. These conditions are:

1. Mutual consent
2. For a time
3. To seek the Lord together

Questions

Question 1. Please re-write the acceptable conditions for withholding intimacy in marriage. Explain them in your own words:

According to Scripture, the frustrated and burning friend who wrote the email referenced above should have been able to turn to his wife to have his desire quenched, but he could not. And we see that his wife's denial may open the door to the evil one to cause strife in the marriage.

Now it is important to state at this point that the verses from 1 Corinthians 7 are not to be used as a weapon against a spouse to demand sex. 1 Peter 3 tells us that the man is to live with his wife in an understanding and considerate way; so if she is feeling tired or sick or in need of emotional support, then he should be sensitive to her needs and put them ahead of his own! Yet the wife is not to deprive the husband just because she is tired or sick. These are not biblical reasons to deprive; if full sexual intercourse is not possible or desirable, the wife should seek to find other ways to quench the burning of her husband.

On the other hand, if a man has been intoxicating himself at the devil's bar of pornography and self-gratification, his wife might be deprived of having her sexual needs met by her sinning husband, as was the case in the second email, referenced above. As men view pornography, they begin to buy into the deception that only "perfect" models can satisfy them, and they may begin to lose interest in their less-than-perfect (read "real-life" and not "air-brushed") wives. They often begin to withdraw from their wives, as they meet their own sexual needs through self-gratification. In addition, with pornography there is no need for building a relationship or being vulnerable, which is necessary for true intimacy in marriage.

Another common hindrance we see is the belief promoted by some counselors that normal sexual relations are not always possible if one spouse has been sexually abused in the past. Some have been told that their spouse's deep issues must be resolved before sexual intimacy may resume. This belief system states that the sexual abuse has produced emotional trauma and scars which, if not dealt with properly, cause the abused victim to withdraw from marital relations and "shut down" to avoid dealing with the pain of the past. It is said that sexual intimacy in this situation is like reopening a previous wound.

While we do not pass off any kind of past abuse as unimportant, we also do not believe that two wrongs make a right. It is a sin to deprive a spouse of sexual relations. To cling to a wound from the past, as reason to deny a spouse in the present, is not right. The abuse suffered in the past needs to be forgiven, by God's grace, and not used as a reason to deny the spouse. Scripture tells us the regular delight in sexual enjoyment between spouses is a deterrent to the work of the devil in our lives. And in fact, sexual relations in a loving marriage bed may even be very healing and comforting, according to the biblical examples of Rebekah and Isaac (Genesis 24:67) and David and Bathsheba (2 Samuel 12:24).

Question 2. Where are you with understanding the passage above; what are your thoughts?

So how are couples, who have denied each other for long periods of time, and who can hardly think of being intimate with each other, to begin the process of regular intimacy?

Begin by setting goals and then start slowly toward them. Set a goal to be intimate once a week for the first month, then twice a week for the second, working toward daily intimacy. This intimacy does not necessarily need to be full sexual intercourse every day, but the goal should be daily intimacy in some form. Start with gentle touching and soft kissing and work toward the joining of the bodies in sexual unity.

But what if you agree to this and see the truth from Scripture, as well as the practical value in daily intimacy, but your spouse is unwilling to be intimate?

First begin by asking questions. Why does your spouse not desire intimacy? Be sure you are doing all you can to be in a right relationship with your spouse. If you remember that you have sinned against your spouse, go to him or her, confess it, and ask for forgiveness.

If the denial of intimacy is based on a lack of forgiveness for past wrongs which have been confessed and repented of, or if it is based on anything other than a biblical foundation, see if your spouse would be willing to read 1 Corinthians 7:1-5, and talk through it with you. Your desire is to show them the importance of not allowing the evil one to have a foothold in your relationship. Do not threaten to sin if he or she does not meet your desires, but seek to show evidence of a desire to be united in all ways against the enemy.

If your spouse continues to deprive you for unbiblical reasons, you may need to implement the principle of Matthew 18:15-17. You might talk with your pastor about the matter and seek his counsel, or possibly meet with an older couple in your church with the intention for your spouse to hear the need for sexual intimacy in marriage. For a more detailed description of the biblical response to a sinning spouse, please read Martha Peace's book titled "The Excellent Wife" or Stuart Scott's "The Exemplary Husband." (www.focuspublishing.com)

So to recap, a normal couple who enjoys biblical truth will strive for intimacy often. Scripture does not say how often, but it does say that the lack of it will bring on temptation from the evil one.

Finally, let us examine some select passages from the Song of Solomon that will again show what normal sexual intimacy between a man and wife is:

> Let him kiss me with the kisses of his mouth, for your love is more delightful than wine (Song of Solomon 1:2).

Here the woman is speaking of her great desire to be intimate with her lover, and compares the delight of his love with wine. It is normal for the woman to desire her husband, even as the church desires intimacy with Christ. The woman should long to be with her husband and earnestly desire his intimacy (the kisses of his mouth).

Question 3. If you are a wife, do you show your husband that you long to be with him?

A. Yes

B. No

C. Single (doesn't apply)

> Take me away with you–let us hurry! Let the king bring me into his chambers (Song of Solomon 1:4).

Again the woman shows desire for her husband, and yearns to be in his bedchambers. One of the greatest thing wives can do for their husbands is to desire to "rush" into intimacy, saying, "let us hurry." Other times of intimacy may be prolonged, and still others can be a mixture of "hurry" and "wait."

> Like a lily among thorns is my darling among the maidens (Song of Solomon 2:2).

Here the man is speaking and favorably comparing his beloved to others. One of the greatest things a husband can do is to be in awe of his wife, and often compare her in a favorable light to other women. Statements such as "My darling, you were the most beautiful woman at the party tonight." or "There is nobody who can hold a candle to you, you are more beautiful than them all" go a long way. Of course, the husband's life needs to reflect that he really feels this way, and he needs to refrain from the viewing of pornography and looking lustfully at other women.

Question 4. If you are a husband, are you seeing the beauty in your wife, and telling her?

- A. Yes
- B. No
- C. Single (doesn't apply)

³ Like an apple tree among the trees of the forest is my lover among the young men. I delight to sit in his shade, and his fruit is sweet to my taste. ⁴ He has taken me to the banquet hall, and his banner over me is love. ⁵ Strengthen me with raisins, refresh me with apples, for I am faint with love (Song of Solomon 2:3-5).

Awake, north wind, and come, south wind! Blow on my garden, that its fragrance may spread abroad. Let my lover come into his garden and taste its choice fruits (Song of Solomon 4:16).

These verses reinforce the delightful, nourishing value of sexual relations in a pure marriage.

One of the books we highly recommend is entitled *The Excellent Wife* by Martha Peace. In her book, Mrs. Peace states, "Pleasure resulting from physical intimacy between husband and wife is assumed by Scripture. It should be fun. There will, of course, be times when, for various reasons, the sex act may not be at the same level of intensity as other times. However, it should still be pleasurable and a sweet time between each married couple. ... Generally both husband and wife should come to a climax, but if one or the other is too tired or is providentially hindered in some way (such as the wife's period or pregnancy) they can still express love to the other, if not through vaginal intercourse, through manual stimulation."

My friend, the devil hates intimacy between Christ and the church. He would rather we would be lukewarm toward our First Love (Jesus), than to be zealous, and on fire for Him. He tries to ruin our devotion (2 Corinthians 11:3) and closeness with Christ. Likewise, sexual intimacy in marriage is a picture of that intimacy the church has with Christ (Ephesians 5:32). Let us not neglect either one, but enjoy them fully. What is normal sex between married people? It is the exquisite enjoyment and celebration of intimacy, as a reflection of the oneness that the church has with Jesus Christ.

Question 5. What have you learned today? If you are married, please state how you will put the above truths into practice.

The following testimony is from Ben:

I was born with an intense desire and drive for pleasure, and I am talking true pleasure. I can remember at a very young age wanting to have things my way, and being frustrated when the joy fizzled in my possessions. This spark was truly ignited by the lighter fluid of pornography.

I was introduced to it at a very young age, and it became the type of thing that I sought for pleasure. I saw nothing wrong with it, even after I committed my life to God in the seventh grade. I was just being a normal kid, in my eyes. Gradually, I started to notice and be frustrated by the same phenomenon, that is, the joy was fizzling out after every time. I would look at pornography, practice self-gratification, and instead of feeling fulfilled, I would feel empty. So I began to look even deeper into it.

The advent of the Internet was a big step in this, and I got very deep into sexual chatting, as well as hardcore pornography. I was still unhappy. That year God started to show me that if I am really serious about my relationship with Him, this stuff has got to go. I went on a Campus Crusade for Christ summer project this past summer, and I was almost completely free from pornography and self-gratification for three months, due to a large amount of accountability, and complete lack of access to pornography. It was awesome, and I grew immensely. I thought that I had built up enough to resist it forever. But the very day that project ended, I was back into slavery. I fell harder than ever.

That's when God brought me to Setting Captives Free and to The Way of Purity course. It is through this site that I recognized those things that helped me this past summer, the radical accountability, the radical amputation, and the radical appropriation. I realized that in order to be free forever, I just had to incorporate those things in my life. It has been immensely freeing. God has allowed me to stumble in each area, as far as amputation, accountability, and appropriation go, and it has given me a healthy respect for his word, and for his strength. I look forward to many years of basking in the light of His glory!

Finally, here are some thoughts worth reading from a friend of ours: "The wooing and romancing of Christ toward us is our role model. Jesus Christ never worried about whether His own needs would be met, because He knew all of His needs were supplied by Father God. When scripture says, *'And my God will meet all of your needs through Christ Jesus (Philippians 4:19),'* we can believe that when we release one another from the responsibility to meet our needs, and abide in the Lord, there will be no deficit. Instead, when we as Christian spouses are able to see the unconditional love of Christ in one another's eyes, we become more than willing to do our human best to meet each other's needs. But we will always fall short. In every human life the invitation to receive satisfaction for our heart's deepest longings comes from Jesus Christ, through the love of Father God, by the power of the Holy Spirit. Jesus says, 'Come unto Me...' In Him there is no deficit." Amen!

Scripture to Consider

For this is the will of God, your sanctification: that you should abstain from sexual immorality; ⁴ that each of you should know how to possess his own vessel in sanctification and honor, ⁵ not in passion of lust, like the Gentiles who do not know God (1 Thessalonians 4:3-6).

Were you free from pornography since you did the last lesson?

　　　Yes　　No

Were you free from self-gratification since you did the last lesson?

　　　Yes　　No

Were you free from sexual immorality since you did the last lesson?

　　　Yes　　No

DAY 57 –
CUT HIS HEAD OFF

There is a giant in the land, and he is wreaking havoc among God's people. He is more powerful than all of God's army, by themselves, and he is out to kill and destroy us. His hatred is against God Himself, and there is not a man (or woman) among us who can stand against him. His name is Satan. He is filthy and vile, armed with cruel hate, and he rides forth taking captive numerous slaves for his kingdom. He is never satisfied, always wanting to have more pawns to serve him, and he sets his sights specifically on the church of Jesus Christ. He despises us!

What are we to do? Is there a David among us, one who can't stand to hear the mocking of the giant, and who knows that the battle belongs to the Lord? Who will take him on? Who has an arsenal of five stones of grace with which to knock the giant down and is able use the Sword of the Spirit, which is the Word of God, to take his head off? Who wants to take the offensive, vindicate the name of God, and bring victory for the people of God? I hope you will respond, "I do!" In this day and age, the church of Jesus Christ needs a David: one who takes no confidence in the armor of kings, or in his own ability, but one who relies on the sovereign grace of God and the power of the gospel to defeat sin's giant.

Are you the one who wants a piece of the giant? Are you sick and tired of seeing the devil gain more and more captives for his kingdom? Do you want to do something about it? You can!

Please read the following passage and answer the questions below:

> [41] Meanwhile, the Philistine, with his shield bearer in front of him, kept coming closer to David. [42] He looked David over and saw that he was only a boy, ruddy and handsome, and he despised him. [43] He said to David, "Am I a dog, that you come at me with sticks?" And the Philistine cursed David by his gods. [44] "Come here," he said, "and I'll give your flesh to the birds of the air and the beasts of the field!"
>
> [45] David said to the Philistine, "You come against me with sword and spear and javelin, but I come against you in the name of the LORD Almighty, the God of the armies of Israel, whom you have defied. [46] This day the LORD will hand you over to me, and I'll strike you down and cut off your head. Today I will give the carcasses of the Philistine army to the birds of the air and the beasts of the earth, and the whole world will know that there is a God in Israel. [47] All those gathered here will know that it is not by sword or spear that the LORD saves; for the battle is the LORD's, and he will give all of you into our hands."
>
> [48] As the Philistine moved closer to attack him, David ran quickly toward the battle line to meet him. 49 Reaching into his bag and taking out a stone, he slung it and struck the Philistine on the forehead. The stone sank into his forehead, and he fell face down on the ground.
>
> [50] So David triumphed over the Philistine with a sling and a stone; without a sword in his hand he struck down the Philistine and killed him.
>
> [51] David ran and stood over him. He took hold of the Philistine's sword and drew it from the scabbard. After he killed him, he cut off his head with the sword.
>
> When the Philistines saw that their hero was dead, they turned and ran. [52] Then the men of Israel and Judah surged forward with a shout and pursued the Philistines to the entrance of Gath and to the gates of Ekron. Their dead were strewn along the Shaaraim road to Gath and Ekron. [53] When the Israelites returned from chasing the Philistines, they plundered their camp. [54] David took the Philistine's head and brought it to Jerusalem, and he put the Philistine's weapons in his own tent (1 Samuel 17:41-54).

180

Question 1. Verse 44 speaks of the intent of the Philistine toward David, and it is also the intent of the devil toward us. What is that intent?

  A. He intends to be friends with us and give us everything we want

  B. He intends to totally destroy us

My friend, make no mistake: this is a fight to the death! Goliath wanted to kill and destroy not only David, but also the entire Israelite army. This is the intention of Satan against us, as well. Either we will triumph over this giant, or we will die by his hands.

Question 2. According to verse 45, Goliath came against David with "sword, and spear and javelin." With what did David come against Goliath?

  A. An Uzzi

  B. The Lord Almighty

  C. A cannon

Question 3. Consider 2 Corinthians 10:3-4 and write your thoughts: "For though we live in the world, we do not wage war as the world does. The weapons we fight with are not the weapons of the world."

Note: If we want to do battle with the devil and help rescue others from sexual sin, we better make sure that (1) we are free, ourselves, and (2) God is fighting for us.

Question 4. What are your thoughts on verse 48? Apply it to yourself and your life right now. Write your thoughts here:

Friend, as soldiers in the Lord's army, we need to have an eagerness to kill the enemy, through the power of God. There must be a "running quickly" toward the battle line to meet him. The Bible states that the gates of hell will not prevail against us (Matthew 16:18), which implies that we are to take the offensive and storm the fortified city of the devil. And we may fully expect to have success, since the gates of hell will not be able to keep us out.

This type of eagerness to take on the enemy comes from experiencing many previous victories over the power of the devil. In the same chapter we are studying today, David recalls previous victories, which gives him the present conviction of the power of God to destroy the giant. He states, "34 Your servant has been keeping his father's sheep. When a lion or a bear came and carried off a sheep from the flock, 35 I went after it, struck it and rescued the sheep from its mouth. When it turned on me, I seized it by its hair, struck it and killed it. 36 Your servant has killed both the lion and the bear; this uncircumcised Philistine will be like one of them, because he has defied the armies of the living God" (1 Samuel 17:34-36).

If you have experienced several victories over sin, you may be ready to take on the giant.

Question 5. According to verse 51, what did David do to strike terror into the hearts of the enemy?

   A. A hand grenade

   B. He took Goliath's sword and beheaded him

   C. David prayed and thanked God for the victory

Verse 51 tells us that David used Goliath's own weapon to behead the giant, and by so doing he freed all Israel from their fear of the giant. This is an amazing foreshadow of the work of Jesus Christ as He took death, the devils own weapon, and used it to destroy the devil. Notice how Hebrews 2:14 compares: "...He too shared in their humanity so that by His death he might destroy him who holds the power of death - that is, the devil - and free those who all their lives were held in slavery by their fear of death." See it? Jesus took the devil's own weapon, death, and used it to destroy the devil!

> *Pastor Joe wrote,* "Just living and hoping the attacks of Satan will go away will never give us victory. I have found that I must be on the offensive in every area of spiritual life and warfare. Most of my life, I have just tried to dodge Satan's bullets. Now I seek not only to stay undefeated by his power, but to defeat him in the name of the Lord Jesus and for His glory."

Question 6. According to verses 51-54, what did David do to the giant?

   A. Cut off his head

   B. Buried him

   C. Left him for dead

According to verse 55, David not only killed the giant but he also cut off his head. Isn't this a bit much? Isn't this overkill, so to speak? Here is an important lesson for us: when dealing with our sins, we need to take such drastic action against them that we prevent them from ever rearing their ugly heads in our lives again. Do not merely kill the giant, but cut his head off!

Question 7. What did the Israelite army do when they discovered that Goliath was dead?

   A. They retreated in fear of the rest of the Philistines

   B. They rushed forward and pursued their enemies

   C. They did nothing

Friend, your own pursuit of purity, of defeating the giant in your life, will have an effect on others and encourage them toward

victory also. As the months of victory over the power of the devil roll on, you soon discover that God's power is stronger and you have killed the enemy. But helping others to enjoy victory as well is like cutting the enemy's head off.

You are nearing the end of The Way of Purity course, and if you are free from sexual sin, it is a great victory. But now it may be time for you to start thinking and praying about a ministry to help others out of the fire from which God rescued you. Don't merely relish your own victory over the giant, but cut his head off and inspire numerous others also to pursue victory as David did.

But be cautious! Please do not become involved in ministry, if you are still viewing pornography or involved in any sexual sin. The reason for this is that your soul is still in deception. You are intoxicating yourself at the devil's bar, and you will not be able to truly help others to sexual sobriety. Knowledge is not enough; power in your life is essential. "Who can bring what is pure from the impure? No one!" (Job 14:4).

Some people have asked how long they need to be pure before they begin a ministry. We don't know, because the answer varies. God will make it known at the right time, and you simply need to know in your heart that you are completely and fully finished with all sexual sin for good and have an eagerness to help others out of the trap also.

There are many different types of ministries to help those enslaved to pornography, and we cannot list them all here. Here are some examples, however. With some thought, you may be able to add to this list.

   Be a mentor with us to assist others to purity

   Build your own Internet ministry

   Start an email list specifically for reaching people trapped in pornography.

   Share your freedom with your pastor, and ask for his help in starting a ministry at your church. You may use our curriculum and other available tools, if you wish.

   Begin a Bible study in your home for pornographers and sex addicts. Advertise it in churches, on the Internet, in newspapers, etc. The way the cancer of pornography is spreading, you may have a huge group.

   Open a chat room with discussions about overcoming pornography

   Share your testimony with your church, and see what God does with it

   Write out your testimony and post it all over the Internet; invite people to email you

   Begin a prison ministry to help inmates find freedom from pornography

   Write periodicals about the way to be free from pornography and submit them to Christian sites such as Crosswalk.com and others

   Begin a newsletter to circulate through churches and on the Internet

Question 8. Are you ready to begin taking the offensive in the battle with the giant, to help your fellow brothers and sisters to victory?

   A. Yes, I am more than ready! I want to run into battle!

   B. I am free, but need more time before I jump into the battle

   C. No, I am still falling into the trap of the devil, and will need to wait

Once you finish this course, you may also want to consider taking the follow-up course called "The Cross, Finding Life in Jesus' Death," which may be found at the Setting Captives Free homepage under "Online Courses."

Question 9. What ministries can you think of that would fit you, and how might you go about initiating them? Write your answer here.

Scripture to Consider

But thanks be to God! He gives us the victory through our Lord Jesus Christ (1 Corinthians 15:57).

Were you free from pornography since you did the last lesson?

    Yes   No

Were you free from self-gratification since you did the last lesson?

    Yes   No

Were you free from sexual immorality since you did the last lesson?

    Yes   No

The following testimony is from Gordon:

I was exposed to pornography in my teens. My father thought nothing about it and even said, "Some guys like this stuff. Just don't let your mother catch you with it." He also told me it was all right to practice self-gratification, "Just to let your frustrations out," so I did. I bought a few magazines here and there and saw a few movies, but after a while grew tired of this. After all, it cost a great deal of money to really get into this stuff in the 70s.

I went through one marriage not knowing the Lord and not knowing how to love a woman, due to these twisted ideas. I married my present wife in 1990 and became a Christian in 1995. We had our three boys in two years time. Everything was going well, and pornography seemed to be out of my mind.

Then one day my wife brought in a magazine called "Dimensions," which features large women. My wife is a large woman and very attractive to me. The women in this magazine were in various states of dress and undress and attractively photographed. During this time I began steadily moving up the ladder in church, serving on committees and teaching Sunday school. I thought I was living a righteous Christian life. Then everything exploded.

In December, 1999, we bought a new computer with unlimited Internet. One of the first things I did when I set it up was to go surfing for pornography sites featuring large women. My wife even encouraged me, at times, "to spice up our love life." I suddenly found myself surfing for hours on end for this material. After all, one could look at this stuff for free. I discovered that I had unlimited, unmonitored access at work as well. I was wasting many hours of the day and neglecting my work, family and Sunday School teaching. My lessons suffered. I was exhausted from the nights I spent surfing and was also afraid of being caught, and confronted by any church people.

Then one day when I was on "Crosswalk" seeking relief, I found a link to Setting Captives Free. The first thing I was confronted with was the Ted Bundy Story. Seeing a picture of his body literally scared the hell out of me. I knew that my problem was serious and would result in losing my wife, boys, job, and eventually end up in death. I would then probably hear the Lord's words "Away from me you worker of iniquity, I never knew you." That was about six months ago.

I fell twice during the early days of the course but, since then, the Lord has clothed me in His armor and built defenses in my life that have set me free. I use the sword of the Spirit each day to ward off attacks. The site has helped me greatly. In fact, I plan to use the "Never Thirst" emails to keep me straight. Please feel free to use my testimony if you wish. I hope it would help someone else. In fact, I suspect that there are many men in our churches who have this problem, but are too ashamed and prideful to admit it!!

Thanks for this ministry. It is truly a lifesaver.

DAY 58 - FINAL REVIEW

This lesson material is a review of the material covered in the 60-day course. Feel free to look back over the days of the course to answer the questions. Primarily, we are interested in how the scriptural truths and testimonies have affected your heart and changed your life. We are approaching the end of the 60 lessons, and the question we have is "Are you actually becoming free from pornography, self-gratification and sexual impurity?" Please keep this question in mind as you answer the following questions.

Question 3. Radical Amputation! This truth is prevalent throughout the course. Basically, this truth teaches us that we must do whatever it takes to rid our lives of any access to impurity. Please state here what you specifically have "cut off" and "plucked out" and whether or not there is anything left with which to indulge your flesh in a moment of weakness.

Question 1. Early in The Way of Purity course, we teach through John chapter 4, the story of the woman at the well. We remember that Jesus taught her that the "well" from which she had been drinking would leave her thirsty, and that He had water to give to her that would eternally quench her thirst. Please summarize the teaching of this chapter, state what you have learned from it, and how you have personally applied it in your life.

Question 4. In this course, we taught the necessity of accountability. What role has accountability played in your escaping from the trap of impurity and coming to freedom in Jesus Christ? Has your accountability partner been important to you, and helped you in any way?

Question 2. One of the most important teachings in the course is on the subject of repentance. We showed from Scripture how repentance is a gift of God (2 Timothy 2:21-26), and that genuine repentance includes both godly sorrow and turning from sin to God. Please think through this issue of repentance, and write out your understanding of it, noting specifically whether or not you have repented of the sin of pornography, self-gratification, and all sexual impurity.

Question 5. In lesson 31, we discussed the majesty, greatness, power and grace of God. This is one of the more important teachings in the course, for to see and savor the supremacy of Christ is to see lust become weak and powerless, whereas those who view Christ as small and powerless find that lust is big and powerful. Are you learning to treasure the supremacy of Jesus Christ in all things? How has your view of Christ changed since coming into purity?

Of course, there is also the need to confess all sin (it is helpful to confess to your pastor and/or elder, and especially your spouse) and have the understanding that God set you free for HIS glory and HIS name's sake, and that you are sharing your testimony of freedom with those whom God would bring across your path. But the above six truths are the main teachings of this course, so please take a moment and review the questions above and your responses. If we ensure that these truths are implemented in our lives, we may realistically expect to remain free from sin's trap for the rest of our lives, and to honor God in doing so. To summarize, we can quench our thirst in Jesus Christ if we repent of sin and turn to Him, removing that which trips us up, being accountable to others, discovering the greatness and majesty of our Lord Jesus Christ, and continually walking in the Spirit.

Question 6. Toward the latter part of the course, we encouraged you to "walk in the Spirit." We described this "walking in the Spirit" as immersing ourselves in God's Word and prayer, worshiping the Lord always, walking with Him in constant fellowship, etc. Do you remember what the Bible says is the result of walking in the Spirit (Galatians 5:16)? Please describe how you "walk in the Spirit," and if you are indeed experiencing the biblical result of this "walking."

DAY 59 - YOUR TESTIMONY

Today we want to give you a place to record your testimony. Feel free to write as the Lord leads you, but keep in mind that the most effective testimonies are brief (usually one page in length), and should include three aspects. Job 33 tells us the formula for sharing a testimony: "Then he comes to men and says, I sinned, and perverted what was right, but I did not get what I deserved. He redeemed my soul from going down to the pit, and I will live to enjoy the light" (Job 33:27-28). Notice the three aspects to this testimony: "I sinned...God redeemed...I will live."

A biblical testimony touches on:

"My sin," and the areas in which I was involved, and what that brought about in my life (be cautious about sharing any details, so as to not stir up sin in others).

Redemption. This explains how I was bought out of the slave market of sin. How did God reach me, give me repentance, and bring me into the Light. What means did He use?

How I am living to enjoy the Light (Christ).

Please try to include the above three aspects in your testimony. In the days and months ahead, you may return to this workbook many times for reference or to refresh your mind. Reading your final testimony of victory will be of great encouragement to you.

Write your testimony here:

Scripture to Consider

Pray that God would make your testimony useful to others who need hope, who need to be free from sexual sin, by the grace of God!

But in your hearts set apart Christ as Lord. Always be prepared to give an answer to everyone who asks you to give the reason for the hope that you have (1 Peter 3:15).

Were you free from pornography since you did the last lesson?

Yes   No

Were you free from self-gratification since you did the last lesson?

Yes   No

Were you free from sexual immorality since you did the last lesson?

Yes   No

DAY 60 - FEEDBACK

Dear friend,

This is the final lesson in The Way of Purity course, and we would like to solicit your input regarding your experience here. Please answer the questions below. We value any and all feedback for this study. If you are willing, please make a copy of this form and mail it to: Setting Captives Free
PO Box 1527
Medina, OH 44258-1527

Question 1. Overall, what was the best part of the course?
A. The Bible Studies
B. The accountability
C. The testimonies
D. The feedback from the mentor
E. Other (please explain):

Question 2. On a scale of 1 to 10, how helpful was this course to you in overcoming sexual sin - 1 being of little help and 10 being of great help.
A. 1-2
B. 3-4
C. 5-7
D. 8-9
E. 10

Question 3. Friend, please describe what changes have taken place in your heart and life since starting this course.

Question 4. Have you started any kind of a ministry of your own to help others break free from sexual sin?
A. Yes, I'm currently in a ministry to help people find freedom from sexual sin
B. No, not yet

Question 5. If you answered "Yes" to the above question, please describe your ministry, and state whether or not you would like Setting Captives Free to assist you in any way.

Question 6. How might we improve the course? What are your suggestions?

Question 7. Have you told anyone else about this course and, if so, have they taken it?

Question 8. Here is a place for your final comments. Write anything you would like to convey to us.

Additional Resources

1. Trench, Richard Chevenix, *Notes on the Parables of Our Lord*. New York, NY, D. Appleton & Co., 1895.

2. Spurgeon, Charles Haddon, *The New Park Street Pulpit, Volume 6: 1860*, London, Banner of Truth Trust, 1964.

3. Pink, Arthur W., *The Gospel of John*, Grand Rapids, MI, Zondervan, 1945.

4. Chambers, Oswald, *My Utmost for His Highest*, December 7th Devotional, Ulrichsville,OH, Barbour Publishing, 1963.

5. Henry, Matthew, *Matthew Henry's Commentary on the Whole Bible, Complete and Unabridged*, Peabody, MA, Hendrickson Publishers, 1991.

6. Daniels, Robert, *The War Within: Experiencing Victory in the Battle for Sexual Purity*, Wheaton, IL, Crossway, 1997.

7. *Logos Lesson Builder*, Oak Harbor, WA, (CD-Rom) Logos Research Systems, Inc., 1997.

8. Reinicke, Melinda, "The Dragon" is one of 19 stories by Dr. Melinda Reinicke from the book *Parables for Personal Growth*, dealing with life issues for adults through parables, journaling and experiential exercises. Available for $17.95 (includes US postage and state tax) from Reinicke Counseling Associates (619) 298-8722x110 or www.christiancounseling.cc

9. Salzman, Timothy, *Sixty Days to Freedom: A Biblical Guide to Freedom from Sexual Addictions*, Colorado Springs, CO, Legacy Press, 1996.

10. Spurgeon, Charles H. "The Chief of Sinners," a sermon on 1 Timothy 1:15, #530, *The Metropolitan Tabernacle Pulpit*, Volume 9. 1863.

11. Spurgeon, Charles H. "Christ's Plea for Ignorant Sinners," a sermon on Luke 23:34, #2263, *The Metropolitan Tabernacle Pulpit*, Volume 38, 1892.

12. Bunyan, John, *Pilgrim's Progress*, Ulrichville, OH, Barbour & Co, 1985.

13. Wilson, Kathryn with Paul Wilson, *Stone Cold in a Warm Bed*, pp 35.6, Christian Publications, Camp Hill, PA,1998.

14. A. Kempis, Thomas, The *Imitation of Christ, Chicago*, Moody Press, 1984.

15. Bonar, Andrew A., *Memoir and Remains of Robert Murray McCheyne*, Grand Rapids, MI, Baker Publishers, 1978.

16. Peterson, John, Ed., *Great Hymns of the Faith*, "O For a Thousand Tongues to Sing." Wesley, Charles, Grand Rapids, MI, Zondervan Publishing House, 1968.

17. Peterson, John, Ed., Great Hymns of the Faith, "And Can It Be That I Should Gain?" Wesley, Charles, Grand Rapids, MI, Zondervan, 1968.

18. Ryle, J.C., *J.C. Ryles Tracts: "If Any Man-!"*, Scotland, Drummond's Tract Depot.

19. Spurgeon, Charles H., "The Pierced One Pierces the Heart" A sermon on Zechariah 12:10, #575, *The Metropolitan Tabernacle Pulpit*, Volume 10, 1864.

20. Spurgeon, Charles H., quoting Bradford, "Confession of Sin Illustrated by the Cases of Dr. Pritchard and Constance Kent," a sermon on Psalm 32:5, #641, *The Metropolitan Tabernacle Pulpit*, Volume 11, 1865.

21. Spurgeon, Charles H., *Morning and Evening*, April 7th Evening Devotional, Christian Focus Publications, Portmahomack, United Kingdom, 1994.

22. Bonar, Andrew, *A Memoir and Remains of Robert Murray McCheyne*.

23. Calvin, John, *Calvin's New Testament Commentaries*, Volume 11 (Galatians-Colossians) Grand Rapids, MI, Erdmans Publishing Co, 1965.

24. Spurgeon, Charles H., "Good Cheer for Christmas" a sermon on Isaiah 25:6, #846, *The Metropolitan Tabernacle Pulpit*, Volume 14, 1868.

25. Coleman, Robery E., *Songs of Heaven*, Old Tappan, NJ, Revell, 1980.

26. Elliot, Jim, Editor: Elisabeth Elliot, *The Journals of Jim Elliot*, Old Tappan, NJ, Revell, 1983.

27. Mayo, Mary Ann, *Marriage Partnership Magazine*, Volume 7, #3, 1990

28. Watson, Thomas, *The Beatitudes: Puritan Vision of the Christian Life*, Carlisle, PA, Banner of Truth, 1971.

29. Wagner, David, *The Power of the Word: Learning to Enjoy Freedom in Christ*, Windsor, Ontario, Canada, 2000, www.settingcaptivesfree.com.

30. Scott, Stuart, *The Exemplary Husband: A Biblical Perspective*, Bemidji, MN, Focus Publishing, 2000.

31. Peace, Martha, *The Excellent Wife: A Biblical Perspective*, Bemidji, MN, Focus Publishing, 1996.

Notes

Notes

Notes

Notes